ChemCom
Chemistry in the Community

A Project of the American Chemical Society

Second Edition

KENDALL/HUNT PUBLISHING COMPANY
4050 Westmark Drive   Dubuque, Iowa 52002

ChemCom
Second-Edition Revision Team

Project Manager:
Keith Michael Shea

Chief Editor:
Henry Heikkinen

Assistant to Chief Editor:
Wilbur Bergquist

Editor of Teacher's Guide:
Jon Malmin

Second Edition Editorial Advisory Board:
Diane Bunce, Henry Heikkinen (ex officio), S. Allen Heininger, Donald Jones (chair), Jon Malmin, Paul Mazzocchi, Bradley Moore, Carolyn Morse, Keith Michael Shea (ex officio), Sylvia Ware (ex officio)

Teacher Reviewers of First Edition:
Vincent Bono, New Dorp High School, New York; Charles Butterfield, Brattle Union High School, Vermont; Regis Goode, Spring Valley High School, South Carolina; George Gross, Union High School, New Jersey; C. Leonard Himes, Edgewater High School, Florida; Gary Hurst, Standley Lake High School, Colorado; Jon Malmin, Peninsula High School, Washington; Maureen Murphy, Essex Junction Educational Center, Vermont; Keith Michael Shea, Hinsdale Central High School, Illinois; Betsy Ross Uhing, Grand Island Senior High School, Nebraska; Jane Voth-Palisi, Concord High School, New Hampshire; Terri Wahlberg, Golden High School, Colorado.

Safety Consultant:
Stanley Pine

Editorial:
The Stone Cottage

Design:
Bonnie Baumann

Art:
Additional art for this edition by
Seda Sookias Maurer

This material is based upon work supported by the National Science Foundation under Grant No. SED-88115424 and Grant No. MDR-8470104. Any opinions, findings, and conclusions or recommendations expressed in this publication are those of the authors and do not necessarily reflect the views of the National Science Foundation. Any mention of trade names does not imply endorsement by the National Science Foundation.

Thanks to the faculty, administration, and students of Hinsdale Central High School (Illinois) for use of their chemistry laboratory facilities in photographs depicting laboratory set-ups and procedures in this textbook.

CONTENTS

Important Notice   x
Preface   xi
Credits   xiii
A Special Note to Students   xv
Safety in the Laboratory   xvi

SUPPLYING OUR WATER NEEDS   1

A. The Quality of Our Water   2
  1. Measurement and the Metric System   5
  2. Laboratory Activity: Foul Water   8
  3. *You Decide:* Information Gathering   10
  4. Water and Health   11
  5. Water Uses   11
  6. Back through the Water Pipes   15
  7. Where Is the Earth's Water?   17
  8. *You Decide:* Water Use Analysis   17
  9. *You Decide:* Riverwood Water Use   18

B. A Look at Water and Its Contaminants   20
  1. Physical Properties of Water   21
  2. Mixtures and Solutions   23
  3. Laboratory Activity: Mixtures   25
  4. Molecular View of Water   26
  5. Symbols, Formulas, and Equations   28
  6. The Electrical Nature of Matter   29
  7. Pure and Impure Water   31
  8. Laboratory Activity: Water Testing   32
  9. *You Decide:* The Riverwood Mystery   36
 10. What Are the Possibilities?   37

C. Investigating the Cause of the Fish Kill   39
  1. Solubility   39
  2. Solution Concentration   42
  3. Oxygen Supply and Demand   44
  4. Temperature and Gas Solubility   46
  5. *You Decide:* Too Much, Too Little?   47
  6. Acid Contamination   51
  7. Ions and Ionic Compounds   52
  8. Dissolving Ionic Compounds   55
  9. Heavy Metal Ion Contamination   56
 10. *You Decide:* Heavy Metal Ions   58
 11. Molecular Substances in the River   59
 12. Laboratory Activity: Solvents   60

D. Water Purification and Treatment   **63**
  1. Natural Water Purification   64
  2. Laboratory Activity: Water Softening   65
  3. Hard Water and Water Softening   67
  4. Municipal Water Purification   69
  5. Chlorine in Our Water   74
  6. *You Decide:* Chlorination and THMs   74

E. Putting It All Together: Fish Kill—Who Pays?   **76**
  1. Directions for Town Council Meeting   78
  2. Looking Back and Looking Ahead   82

CONSERVING CHEMICAL RESOURCES   84

Introduction   **86**

A. Use of Resources   **88**
  1. Laboratory Activity: Striking It Rich   89
  2. Using Things Up   91
  3. Tracking Atoms   91
  4. Laboratory Activity: Using Up a Metal   94
  5. Resources and Waste   95
  6. Disposing of Things   97
  7. *You Decide:* Consuming Resources   99

B. Why We Use What We Do   **102**
  1. Properties Make the Difference   102
  2. The Chemical Elements   104
  3. Laboratory Activity: Metal, Nonmetal?   105
  4. The Periodic Table   107
  5. *You Decide:* Grouping the Elements   108
  6. The Pattern of Atomic Numbers   108
  7. Chemical Reactivity   112
  8. Laboratory Activity: Metal Reactivities   113
  9. What Determines Properties?   115
  10. Modifying Properties   115
  11. *You Decide:* Restoring Ms. Liberty   116

C. Conservation in Nature and the Community   **120**
  1. Sources of Resources   120
  2. Conservation Is Nature's Way   122
  3. Atom, Molecule, and Ion Inventory   124
  4. Conservation Must Be Our Way   127
  5. *You Decide:* Recycling Drive   128

D. Metals: Sources and Replacements   **131**
  1. Copper: Sources and Uses   131
  2. Evaluating an Ore   133
  3. Metal Reactivity Revisited   135
  4. Metals from Ores   136

5. Laboratory Activity: Producing Copper 138
6. Future Materials 139

E. Putting It All Together: How Long Will the Supply Last? 144
1. Metal Reserves: Three Projections 144
2. Options and Opportunities 145
3. Looking Back and Looking Ahead 146

PETROLEUM: TO BUILD? TO BURN? 150

Introduction 152

A. Petroleum in Our Lives 154
1. *You Decide:* It's a Petroleum World 154
2. Petroleum in Our Future? 155
3. *You Decide:* Who's Got the Oil? 156

B. Petroleum: What Is It? What Do We Do with It? 158
1. Working with Black Gold 158
2. Petroleum Refining 159
3. Laboratory Activity: Viscosity 160
4. *You Decide:* Crude Oil to Products 164
5. A Look at Petroleum Molecules 166
6. Chemical Bonding 167
7. Laboratory Activity: Modeling Alkanes 169
8. Laboratory Activity: Alkanes Revisited 172

C. Petroleum as an Energy Source 176
1. *You Decide:* The Good Old Days? 177
2. Energy: Past, Present, and Future 178
3. Energy and Fossil Fuels 181
4. The Chemistry of Burning 186
5. Laboratory Activity: Combustion 186
6. Using Heats of Combustion 189
7. Altering Fuels 192

D. Useful Materials from Petroleum 196
1. Beyond Alkanes 196
2. Laboratory Activity: The Builders 197
3. More Builder Molecules 198
4. Builder Molecules Containing Oxygen 199
5. Creating New Options: Petrochemicals 200
6. Laboratory Activity: Petrochemicals 204

E. Alternatives to Petroleum 207
1. Alternative Energy Sources 207
2. Builder Molecule Sources 211

F. Putting It All Together: Choosing Petroleum Futures 213
1. Confronting the Issues 213
2. Looking Back and Looking Ahead 215

UNDERSTANDING FOOD 216

Introduction **218**
You Decide: Keeping a Food Diary 219

A. Foods: To Build or to Burn? **220**
   1. Nutritional Imbalances 220
   2. *You Decide:* Dimensions of Hunger 221
   3. Why Hunger? 222

B. Food as Energy **224**
   1. Food for Thought—and for Energy 224
   2. *You Decide:* Energy In—Energy Out 226
   3. Carbohydrates: The Energizers 228
   4. Fats: Stored Energy with a Bad Name 230

C. Foods: The Builder Molecules **236**
   1. Foods as Chemical Reactants 236
   2. Limiting Reactants 237
   3. Proteins 241
   4. Laboratory Activity: Milk Analysis 246

D. Other Substances in Foods **251**
   1. Vitamins 251
   2. Laboratory Activity: Vitamin C 254
   3. Minerals: Part of Our Diet 256
   4. Laboratory Activity: Iron in Foods 259
   5. Food Additives 260
   6. *You Decide:* Food Additive Survey 265

E. Putting It All Together: Nutrition Around the World **267**
   1. *You Decide:* Diet Analysis 267
   2. *You Decide:* Meals Around the World 268
   3. Looking Back and Looking Ahead 269

NUCLEAR CHEMISTRY IN OUR WORLD 270

Introduction **272**
You Decide: Public Understanding 272

A. Energy and Atoms **275**
   1. Laboratory Activity: Radioactivity 275
   2. Different Kinds of Radiation 275
   3. The Great Discovery 278
   4. Nuclear Radiation 280
   5. Laboratory Activity: The Black Box 281
   6. Gold Foil Experiment 282
   7. Architecture of Atoms 283
   8. Laboratory Activity: Isotopic Pennies 285
   9. Isotopes in Nature 286

B. Radioactive Decay 291

1. Laboratory Activity: α, β, and γ Rays   291
2. Natural Radioactive Decay   295
3. Half-Life: A Radioactive Clock   299
4. Laboratory Activity: Half-Life   299
5. Radiation Detectors   302
6. Laboratory Activity: Cloud Chambers   303
7. Artificial Radioactivity   304

C. Nuclear Energy: Powering the Universe 308

1. Splitting the Atom   308
2. The Strong Force   309
3. Chain Reactions   309
4. *You Decide:* The Domino Effect   310
5. Nuclear Power Plants   311
6. Nuclear Fusion   314

D. Living with Benefits and Risks 316

1. *You Decide:* The Safest Journey   317
2. Benefits of Radioisotopes   318
3. *You Decide:* Putting Atoms to Work   322
4. Measuring Ionizing Radiation   322
5. Radiation Damage: Now and Later   323
6. Exposure to Radiation   324
7. Radon in Homes   326
8. Nuclear Waste: Pandora's Box   328
9. Catastrophic Risk: A Plant Accident   331

E. Putting It All Together: Separating Fact from Fiction 335

1. Processing the Survey Information   335
2. Looking Back   337

CHEMISTRY, AIR, AND CLIMATE 338

Introduction 340

A. Living in a Sea of Air 341

1. *You Decide:* The Fluid We Live In   341
2. Lab Demonstration: Gases   342
3. Air: The Breath of Life   343

B. Investigating the Atmosphere 346

1. Laboratory Activity: The Atmosphere   346
2. A Closer Look at the Atmosphere   351
3. *You Decide:* Atmospheric Altitude   354
4. Air Pressure   356
5. Boyle's Law: Putting on the Squeeze   359
6. Laboratory Activity: T-V Relationships   362
7. *You Decide:* A New Temperature Scale   364
8. Ideally, Gases Behave Simply   366

C. Atmosphere and Climate   370

  1. The Sunshine Story   371
  2. Earth's Energy Balance   372
  3. At the Earth's Surface   374
  4. Changes on the Earth's Surface   375
  5. *You Decide:* Trends in CO_2 Levels   379
  6. Laboratory Activity: CO_2 Levels   380
  7. *You Decide:* Reversing the Trend   381
  8. Off in the Ozone   382

D. Human Impact on Air We Breathe   385

  1. To Exist Is to Pollute   385
  2. *You Decide:* What Is Air Pollution?   387
  3. *You Decide:* Major Pollutants   387
  4. Smog: Hazardous to Your Health   388
  5. Pollution Control   390
  6. Industrial Emission of Particulates   390
  7. Lab Demonstration: Cleansing Air   392
  8. Photochemical Smog   392
  9. *You Decide:* Autos and Smog   393
  10. Controlling Automobile Emissions   394
  11. Acid Rain   398
  12. Laboratory Activity: Acid Rain   399
  13. pH   400

E. Putting It All Together: Is Air a Free Resource?   403

  1. Air Pollution Control: A Success?   403
  2. *You Decide:* Just Another Resource?   404
  3. Paying the Price   405
  4. Looking Back   407

HEALTH: YOUR RISKS AND CHOICES   408

Introduction   410

A. Risk and Personal Decision-Making   411

  1. Making Judgments about Risk   411
  2. Studying Human Disease   414

B. Your Body's Internal Chemistry   415

  1. Balance and Order: Keys to Life   415
  2. Elements in the Human Body   416
  3. Cellular Chemistry   418
  4. Lab Demonstration: Enzymes   418
  5. How Enzymes Work   419
  6. How Energy Is Released and Stored   420
  7. Laboratory Activity: Enzymes   423

C. Acids, Bases, and Body Chemistry   426

  1. Structure Determines Function   426
  2. Strengths of Acids and Bases   427

3. Acids, Bases, and Buffers in the Body 429
4. Laboratory Activity: Buffers 430
5. pH in Balance 432

D. Chemistry at the Body's Surface 434

1. Keeping Clean with Chemistry 434
2. Skin: It's Got You Covered 438
3. Protecting Your Skin from the Sun 439
4. Laboratory Activity: Sunscreens 441
5. Getting a ''D'' in Photochemistry 442
6. Our Crowning Glory 443
7. Laboratory Activity: Chemistry of Hair 444
8. Hair Styling and Chemical Bonding 447

E. Chemical Control: Drugs and Toxins in the Human Body 450

1. A Glimpse of Drug Function 450
2. *You Decide:* Pros and Cons of Aspirin 452
3. *You Decide:* Effects of Alcohol 453
4. Notes on Some Other Drugs 454
5. Foreign Substances in the Body 455
6. Drugs in Combination 457
7. Cigarette Use 459
8. Laboratory Activity: Cigarette Use 460
9. *You Decide:* Smoking? 461

F. Putting It All Together: Assessing Risks 463

1. Risks from Alcohol and Other Drugs 463
2. Personal Control of Risk 464
3. Looking Back 465

THE CHEMICAL INDUSTRY: PROMISE AND CHALLENGE 466

Introduction 468

A. A New Industry for Riverwood? 470

1. Basic Needs Met by Chemistry 470
2. Industry as a Social Partner 473
3. Class Activity: Perspectives 474
4. *You Decide:* Products of Industry 475
5. *You Decide:* Asset or Liability? 476

B. An Overview of the Chemical Industry 478

1. From Raw Materials to Products 479
2. From Test Tubes to Tank Cars 483
3. Close-up: The EKS Company 484

C. The Chemistry of Some Nitrogen-Based Products 487

1. Laboratory Activity: Fertilizer 487
2. Fertilizer's Chemical Roles 491
3. Laboratory Activity: Phosphates 493

4. Fixing Nitrogen   495
5. Nitrogen Fixation at Riverwood   498
6. Nitrogen's Other Face   500
7. *You Decide:* Food or Arms   504

D. Chemical Energy ↔ Electrical Energy   506
1. Laboratory Activity: Voltaic Cells   506
2. Electrochemistry   509
3. Laboratory Activity: Electroplating   512
4. Industrial Electrochemistry   515
5. *You Decide:* Planning for an Industry   517

**E. Putting It All Together: Chemical Industry Past,
Present, and Future   519**
1. Future Developments   519
2. Looking Back and Looking Ahead   521

Appendix: Composition of Foods   523
Objectives   538
Glossary   546
Index   556
Visual Credits   568
Chemical Matrix   571

IMPORTANT NOTICE

ChemCom is intended for use by high school students in the classroom laboratory under the direct supervision of a qualified chemistry teacher. The experiments described in this book involve substances that may be harmful if they are misused or if the procedures described are not followed. Read cautions carefully and follow all directions. Do not use or combine any substances or materials not specifically called for in carrying out experiments. Other substances are mentioned for educational purposes only and should not be used by students unless the instructions specifically so indicate.

The materials, safety information, and procedures contained in this book are believed to be reliable. This information and these procedures should serve only as a starting point for laboratory practices, and they do not purport to specify minimal legal standards or to represent the policy of the American Chemical Society. No warranty, guarantee, or representation is made by the American Chemical Society as to the accuracy or specificity of the information contained herein, and the American Chemical Society assumes no responsibility in connection therewith. The added safety information is intended to provide basic guidelines for safe practices. It cannot be assumed that all necessary warnings and precautionary measures are contained in this document and that other additional information and measures may not be required.

PREFACE

The United States is a world leader in science, technology, and the education of scientists and engineers. Yet, overall, U.S. citizens are barely literate in science. In responding to this situation, our government and many professional groups have assigned high priority to improving the nation's science literacy.

Chemistry in the Community (ChemCom) represents a major effort to enhance science literacy through a high school chemistry course that emphasizes chemistry's impact on society. Developed by the American Chemical Society (ACS) with financial support from the National Science Foundation and several ACS funding sources, *ChemCom* was written by teams of high school, college, and university teachers, assisted by chemists from industry and government.

Briefly, *ChemCom* is designed to help students

- realize the important role that chemistry will play in their personal and professional lives.
- use chemistry knowledge to think through and make informed decisions about issues involving science and technology.
- develop a lifelong awareness of both the potential and limitations of science and technology.

Following six years of development, testing and revision, the first edition of *ChemCom* was released in 1988. Since then, *ChemCom* has been successfully implemented by chemistry teachers in thousands of classrooms. Many teachers report that the program offers a motivational, engaging approach to the study of chemistry for a remarkably wide range of students.

This new edition of *ChemCom*, while maintaining the overall structure and approach of the first edition, provides updated information on many *ChemCom* topics as well as detailed improvements based on suggestions from classroom experience. A new feature describes how individuals in widely diverse careers find uses for chemistry in their daily work. All second-edition changes are intended to make *ChemCom* even more "user-friendly" for both teachers and their students.

Each of *ChemCom*'s eight units centers on a chemistry-related technological issue currently confronting our society and the world. The topic serves as a basis for introducing the chemistry needed to understand and analyze it. The setting for each unit is a community. This may be the school community, the town or region in which the students live, or the world community—Spaceship Earth.

The major *ChemCom* topics are: "Supplying Our Water Needs"; "Conserving Chemical Resources"; "Petroleum: To Build? To Burn?"; "Understanding Food"; "Nuclear Chemistry in Our World"; "Chemistry, Air, and Climate"; "Health: Your Risks and Choices"; and "The Chemical Industry: Promise and Challenge."

The eight units support the major concepts, vocabulary, thinking skills, and laboratory techniques expected in any introductory chemistry course. However, the program contains a greater number and variety of student-oriented activities than is customary. In addition to numerous laboratory exercises including many developed especially for *ChemCom* each unit contains three levels of decision-making activities, and several types of problem-solving exercises.

Dozens of professionals from all segments of the chemistry community contributed their talents and energies to create *ChemCom*. Their hope is that its impact will be substantial and lasting, and that those who study *ChemCom* will find chemistry interesting, captivating, and useful.

CREDITS

ChemCom is the product of teamwork among individuals from all regions of the United States over the past decade. The American Chemical Society is pleased to recognize all who contributed to *ChemCom*.

The team responsible for this new edition of *ChemCom* is listed on the copyright page. Those individuals who contributed to the initial development of *ChemCom*, and to the release of the program's first edition in 1988, are listed below.

Principal Investigator:
W. T. Lippincott

Project Manager:
Sylvia Ware

Chief Editor:
Henry Heikkinen

Contributing Editor:
Mary Castellion

Assistant to Contributing Editor:
Arnold Diamond

Editor of Teacher's Guide:
Thomas O'Brien

Revision Team:
Diane Bunce, Gregory Crosby, David Holzman, Thomas O'Brien, Joan Senyk, Thomas Wysocki

Editorial Advisory Board:
Glenn Crosby, James DeRose, Dwaine Eubanks, W. T. Lippincott (ex officio), Lucy McCorkle, Jeanne Vaughn, Sylvia Ware (ex officio)

Writing Team:
Rosa Balaco, James Banks, Joan Beardsley, William Bleam, Kenneth Brody, Ronald Brown, Diane Bunce, Becky Chambers, Alan DeGennaro, Patricia Eckfeldt, Dwaine Eubanks (dir.), Henry Heikkinen (dir.), Bruce Jarvis (dir.), Dan Kallus, Jerry Kent, Grace McGuffie, David Newton (dir.), Thomas O'Brien, Andrew Pogan, David Robson, Amado Sandoval, Joseph Schmuckler (dir.), Richard Shelly, Patricia Smith, Tamar Susskind, Joseph Tarello, Thomas Warren, Robert Wistort, Thomas Wysocki

Steering Committee:
Alan Cairncross, William Cook, Derek Davenport, James DeRose, Anna Harrison (ch.), W. T. Lippincott (ex officio), Lucy McCorkle, Donald McCurdy, William Mooney, Moses Passer, Martha Sager, Glenn Seaborg, John Truxall, Jeanne Vaughn

Consultants:
Alan Cairncross, Michael Doyle, Donald Fenton, Conard Fernelius, Victor Fratalli, Peter Girardot, Glen Gordon, Dudley Herron, John Hill, Chester Holmlund, John Holman, Kenneth Kolb, E. N. Kresge, David Lavallee, Charles Lewis, Wayne Marchant, Joseph Moore, Richard Millis, Kenneth Mossman, Herschel Porter, Glenn Seaborg, Victor Viola, William West, John Whitaker

Synthesis Committee:
Diane Bunce, Dwaine Eubanks, Anna Harrison, Henry Heikkinen, John Hill, Stanley Kirschner, W. T. Lippincott (ex officio), Lucy McCorkle, Thomas O'Brien, Ronald Perkins, Sylvia Ware (ex officio), Thomas Wysocki

Evaluation Team:
Ronald Anderson, Matthew Bruce, Frank Sutman (dir.)

Field Test Coordinator:
Sylvia Ware

Field Test Workshops:
Dwaine Eubanks

Field Test Directors:
Keith Berry, Fitzgerald Bramwell, Mamie Moy, William Nevill, Michael Pavelich, Lucy Pryde, Conrad Stanitski

Pilot Test Teachers:
Howard Baldwin, Donald Belanger, Navarro Bharat, Ellen Byrne, Eugene Cashour, Karen Cotter, Joseph Deangelis, Virginia Denney, Diane Doepken, Donald Fritz, Andrew Gettes, Mary Gromko, Robert Haigler, Anna Helms, Allen Hummel, Charlotte Hutton, Elaine Kilbourne, Joseph Linker, Larry Lipton, Grace McGuffie, Nancy Miller, Gloria Mumford, Beverly Nelson, Kathy Nirei, Elliott Nires, Polly Parent, Mary Parker, Dicie Petree, Ellen Pitts, Ruth Rand, Kathy Ravano, Steven Rischling, Charles Ross, Jr., David Roudebush, Joseph Rozaik, Susan Rutherland, George Smeller, Cheryl Snyder, Jade Snyder, Samuel Taylor, Ronald Tempest, Thomas Van Egeren, Gabrielle Vereecke, Howard White, Thomas Wysocki, Joseph Zisk

Field Test Teachers:
Vincent Bono, Allison Booth, Naomi Brodsky, Mary D. Brower, Lydia Brown, George Bulovsky, Kay Burrough, Gene Cashour, Frank Cox, Bobbie Craven, Pat Criswell, Jim Davis, Nancy Dickman, Dave W. Gammon, Frank Gibson, Grace Giglio, Theodis Gorre, Margaret Guess, Yvette Hayes, Lu Hensen, Kenn Heydrick, Gary Hurst, Don Holderread, Michael Ironsmith, Lucy Jache, Larry Jerdal, Ed Johnson, Grant Johnson, Robert Kennedy, Anne Kenney, Joyce Knox, Leanne Kogler, Dave Kolquist, Sherman Kopelson, Jon Malmin, Douglas Mandt, Jay Maness, Patricia Martin, Mary Monroe, Mike Morris, Phyllis Murray, Silas Nelsen, Larry Nelson, Bill Rademaker, Willie Reed, Jay Rubin, Bill Rudd, David Ruscus, Richard Scheele, Paul Shank, Dawn Smith, John Southworth, Mitzi Swift, Steve Ufer, Bob Van Zant, Daniel Vandercar, Bob Volzer, Terri Wahlberg, Tammy Weatherly, Lee Weaver, Joyce Willis, Belinda Wolfe

Field Test Schools:
California: Chula Vista High, Chula Vista; Gompers Secondary School, San Diego; Montgomery High, San Diego; Point Loma High, San Diego; Serra Junior-Senior High, San Diego; Southwest High, San Diego; Colorado: Bear Creek Senior High, Lakewood; Evergreen Senior High, Evergreen; Green Mountain Senior High, Lakewood; Golden Senior High, Golden; Lakewood Senior High, Lakewood; Wheat Ridge Senior High, Wheat Ridge; Hawaii: University of Hawaii Laboratory School, Honolulu; Illinois: Project Individual Education High, Oak Lawn; Iowa: Linn-Mar High, Marion; Louisiana: Booker T. Washington High, Shreveport; Byrd High, Shreveport; Caddo Magnet High, Shreveport; Captain Shreve High, Shreveport; Fair Park High, Shreveport; Green Oaks High, Shreveport; Huntington High, Shreveport; North Caddo High, Vivian; Northwood High, Shreveport; Maryland: Charles Smith Jewish Day School, Rockville; Owings Mills Junior-Senior High, Owings Mills; Parkville High, Baltimore; Sparrows Point Middle-Senior High, Baltimore; Woodlawn High, Baltimore; New Jersey: School No. 10, Patterson; New York: New Dorp High, Staten Island; Texas: Clements High, Sugar Land; Cy-Fair High, Houston; Virginia: Armstrong High, Richmond; Freeman High, Richmond; Henrico High, Richmond; Highland Springs High, Highland Springs; Marymount School, Richmond; Midlothian High, Midlothian; St. Gertrude's High, Richmond; Thomas Dale High, Chester; Thomas Jefferson High, Richmond; Tucker High, Richmond; Varina High, Richmond; Wisconsin: James Madison High, Madison; Thomas More High, Milwaukee; Washington: Bethel High, Spanaway; Chief Sealth High, Seattle; Clover Park High, Tacoma; Foss Senior High, Tacoma; Hazen High, Renton; Lakes High, Tacoma; Peninsula High, Gig Harbor; Rogers High, Puyallup; Sumner Senior High, Sumner; Washington High, Tacoma; Wilson High, Tacoma

Social Science Consultants:
Ross Eshelman, Judith Gillespie

Art:
Rabina Fisher, Pat Hoetmer, Alan Kahan (dir.), Kelly Richard, Sharon Wolfgang

Copy Editor:
Martha Polkey

Administrative Assistant:
Carolyn Avery

Student Aides:
Paul Drago, Stephanie French, Patricia Teleska

ACS also offers thanks to the National Science Foundation for its support of the initial development of *ChemCom*, and to NSF project officers Mary Ann Ryan and John Thorpe for their comments, suggestions, and unfailing support.

A SPECIAL NOTE
TO STUDENTS

Chemistry is a part of everyone's life. As we increase our use and dependence on technology (the application of science), more decisions of individuals, communities, and countries will involve scientific concepts and consequences. Everyone—not just scientists and science educators—should know about scientific concepts and the vital contributions of science to society. As a future voter, you will help make decisions on issues involving chemical knowledge.

Chemistry is the study of the substances in our world—from sugar and baking soda to propane and water. What are substances made of? How do they act and interact with each other and in the presence of various forms of energy, such as heat or electricity? What are their roles in living things? Chemistry focuses on food, photographic film, moon rocks, fabrics, medicines, life processes—in fact, chemistry is concerned with all materials.

In response to a growing need for scientific awareness and good decision-making skills, the Education Division of the American Chemical Society has developed this high school chemistry course. *Chemistry in the Community (ChemCom)* uses chemical concepts to help you understand the chemistry behind some important societal issues.

ChemCom is composed of eight units. Within each you will find issues and concerns affecting your life and community. You will become involved in activities exploring how chemistry relates to these topics. At the close of each unit you will be invited to apply your chemical knowledge to a specific problem; to describe or propose solutions; and to evaluate the consequences of your solutions.

We hope *ChemCom* will help you view the world with greater understanding and appreciation. You may even decide to study more chemistry. However, whether you do or not, we hope you will experience some of the challenge and excitement felt by those of us involved in chemistry and chemical education. Water is our first major topic. You will enter the fictional town of Riverwood as a student at Riverwood High School. We will begin with a newspaper article about a water-related emergency in Riverwood. The story surrounding this problem will serve as the theme of the first unit. Welcome to Riverwood and to *ChemCom*!

SAFETY IN THE LABORATORY

In *ChemCom* you will frequently perform laboratory activities. While no human activity is completely risk free, if you use common sense and a bit of chemical sense, you will encounter no problems. Chemical sense is an extension of common sense. Sensible laboratory conduct won't happen by memorizing a list of rules, any more than a perfect score on a written driver's test ensures an excellent driving record. The true "driver's test" of chemical sense is your actual conduct in the laboratory.

The following safety pointers apply to all laboratory activities. For your personal safety and that of your classmates, make following these guidelines second nature in the laboratory. Your teacher will point out any special safety guidelines that apply to each activity.

If you understand the reasons behind them, these safety rules will be easy to remember and to follow. So, for each listed safety guideline:

- Identify a similar rule or precaution that applies in everyday life—for example in cooking, repairing or driving a car, or playing a sport.
- Briefly describe possible harmful results if the rule is not followed.

Rules of Laboratory Conduct.

1. Perform laboratory work only when your teacher is present. Unauthorized or unsupervised laboratory experimenting is not allowed.
2. Your concern for safety should begin even before the first activity. Always read and think about each laboratory assignment before starting.
3. Know the location and use of all safety equipment in your laboratory. These should include the safety shower, eye wash, first-aid kit, fire extinguisher, and blanket.
4. Wear a laboratory coat or apron and protective glasses or goggles for all laboratory work. Wear shoes (rather than sandals) and tie back loose hair.
5. Clear your benchtop of all unnecessary material such as books and clothing before starting your work.
6. Check chemical labels twice to make sure you have the correct substance. Some chemical formulas and names may differ by only a letter or a number.
7. You may be asked to transfer some laboratory chemicals from a common bottle or jar to your own test tube or beaker. Do not return any excess material to its original container unless authorized by your teacher.
8. Avoid unnecessary movement and talk in the laboratory.
9. Never taste laboratory materials. Gum, food, or drinks should not be brought into the laboratory.

10. If you are instructed to smell something, do so by fanning some of the vapor toward your nose. Do not place your nose near the opening of the container. Your teacher will show you the correct technique.

11. Never look directly down into a test tube; view the contents from the side. Never point the open end of a test tube toward yourself or your neighbor.

12. Any laboratory accident, however small, should be reported immediately to your teacher.

13. In case of a chemical spill on your skin or clothing rinse the affected area with plenty of water. If the eyes are affected, water-washing must begin immediately and continue for 10 to 15 minutes or until professional assistance is obtained.

14. Minor skin burns should be placed under cold, running water.

15. When discarding used materials, carefully follow the instructions provided.

16. Return equipment, chemicals, aprons, and protective glasses to their designated locations.

17. Before leaving the laboratory, make sure that gas lines and water faucets are shut off.

18. If in doubt, ask!

SUPPLYING OUR WATER NEEDS

- Can we continue to obtain *enough* water to supply our needs?

- Can we get sufficiently *pure* water?

- How do everyday decisions affect the quality and quantity of our water supplies?

- How can chemistry help explain water's personal and societal importance?

THE QUALITY OF OUR WATER

Fish Kill Causes Water Emergency in Riverwood
Severe Water Rationing in Effect

By Lori Katz
Staff writer of Riverwood News

Mayor Edward Cisko, citing possible health hazards, today announced that he would stop withdrawal of water from the Snake River and shut down the Riverwood water treatment plant. He also announced cancellation of the community's "Fall Fish-In" that was to begin Friday. River water will not be pumped into the water treatment plant for at least three days, starting at 6 P.M. tonight. No plans were announced for rescheduling the annual fishing tournament.

During the pumping station shutdown, water engineers and chemists from the County Sanitation Commission and Environmental Protection Agency (EPA) will search for the cause of a fish kill discovered yesterday at the base of Snake River Dam, five miles upstream from Riverwood's water pumping station.

"There's no cause for alarm, since preliminary tests show no present danger to townspeople.

However, consensus at last night's emergency Town Council meeting was to start a thorough investigation of the situation immediately," said Mayor Cisko.

The alarm was sounded when Jane Abelson, 15, and Rob Steiner, 16, both students at Riverwood High School, found many dead pike floating in a favorite fishing spot. "We thought maybe

someone had poured poison in the reservoir or dam," explained Rob.

Mary Steiner, biology teacher at Riverwood High School, accompanied the students back to the river. "We hiked downstream for almost a mile. Dead fish of all kinds were washed up on the banks and caught in the rocks as

See Page 3

From Page 2

far as we could see," Abelson reported.

Mrs. Steiner contacted the County Sanitation Commission, which made preliminary tests for substances that might have killed the fish. Chief Engineer Hal Cooper reported at last night's emergency meeting that the water samples looked completely clear and that no toxic substances were found. However, he indicated some concern. "We can't say for sure that our present water supply is safe until the reason for the fish kill is known. It's far better that we take no chances until we know the water is safe," Cooper advised.

Arrangements are being made for drinking water to be trucked from Mapleton, with the first shipments due to arrive in Riverwood at 10 A.M. tomorrow. Distribution points are listed on page 8, along with guidelines on saving water in a bathtub for uses other than drinking or cooking during the water emergency.

Mayor Cisco gave assurances that essential municipal services would not be affected by the water crisis. Specifically, he stated that the fire department would have access to adequate supplies of water to meet any fire-fighting needs.

Riverwood schools will be closed Monday, Tuesday, and Wednesday. No other closings or cancellations are known at this time. Local TV and radio stations will announce any as they occur.

The Town Council reached agreement to stop drawing water from the Snake River after five hours of heated debate. Councilman Henry McLatchen, also a member of the Chamber of Commerce, described the decision as a highly emotional and unnecessary reaction. He cited the great financial loss that Riverwood's motel and restaurant owners will suffer from the fish-in cancellation, as well as the potential loss of future tourism dollars as the result of adverse publicity. He and others sharing his view were outvoted by the majority, who expressed concern that the fish kill might have public health implications.

A public meeting will be held at 8 P.M. tonight at the Town Hall. Dr. Margaret Brooke, expert on water systems at State University, will answer questions concerning water safety and use. Dr. Brooke has agreed to aid the County Sanitation Commission in explaining the situation to the town.

Asked how long the water emergency would last, Dr. Brooke refused to speculate until she had talked to chemists conducting the investigation. EPA scientists, in addition to collecting and analyzing water samples, will examine dead fish to determine if a disease caused their deaths.

RIVERWOOD U.S.A.

Townspeople React to Fish Kill and Water Crisis

By Juan Hernandez
Staff contributor to Riverwood News

In a series of person-on-the-street interviews, Riverwood citizens expressed their feelings about the crisis. "It doesn't bother me," said nine-year-old Jimmy Hendricks. "I'm just going to drink milk and canned fruit juice."

"I knew it was just a matter of time before they killed the fish," complained Harmon Lewis, a lifelong resident of the Fieldstone Acres area. Lewis, who traces his ancestry back to original county settlers, still gets his water from a well and will be unaffected by the water crisis. Lewis drew his well water by hand until 1967. He installed his present system after area development brought electricity to his property. "I wouldn't have even done that except for the arthritis in my shoulders," said Lewis. He plans to pump enough well water to supply the children's ward at Community Hospital if the emergency continues more than a few days.

Bob and Ruth Hardy of Hardy's Ice Cream Parlor expressed annoyance at the inconvenience but felt relieved about Council actions. They were anxious to know the reason for the fish kill and its possible effects on future water supplies.

The Hardys' daughter Toni, who loves to fish, expressed concern that the late summer fishing season would be ruined. Toni and her father won first prize last year in the Chamber of Commerce's angling competition.

Don Harris, owner of the Uptown Motel, expressed concern regarding the health of town residents, as well as the loss of business due to the tournament cancellation. "I always earn a reasonable amount of money from this event and will most likely have to get a loan to pay my bills in the spring."

The unexpected school vacation was "great" according to twelve-year-old David Price. Asked why he thought schools needed to be closed because of a water shortage, Price said all he could think of was that "the drinking fountains won't work."

Elmo Turner, whose yard and flower beds have won Garden Club recognition for the last five years, felt reassured on one point. Since this past summer was so wet, grass-watering is unnecessary, and lawns are not in danger of drying out due to water rationing.

Riverwood will be without adequate water for three days. As these newspaper articles indicate, the water emergency has created understandable concern among Riverwood citizens, town officials, and business owners. What caused the fish kill? Does the fish kill mean that the community's water supply poses hazards to humans? We will follow the town's progress in answering these questions as we learn about water's properties.

Even though Riverwood is imaginary, its problems have already been faced by residents of real communities. In fact, two water-related challenges confront all of us. Can we continue to obtain *enough* water to supply our needs? Can we get sufficiently *pure* water? These two questions are the major themes of this unit. Such challenges require us to understand water's chemistry, uses, and importance.

Water has many important properties (characteristics). Some of its properties, such as color and taste, can be observed by the unaided senses. Others must be observed indirectly, by measurement and calculation.

Measurements and calculations are useful only when everyone uses the same units. So, to be consistent, scientists in all countries report their measurements and calculations in units of the metric system.

A.1 MEASUREMENT AND THE METRIC SYSTEM

Metric units were first introduced in France more than 100 years ago. A modernized form of the metric system was internationally adopted in 1960. It is called "SI," which is an abbreviation of the French name, *Le Système International d'Unités*. SI units are used by scientists in all nations, including the United States. You are already familiar with some SI units, such as the gram, degree Celsius, and second. Other SI units you will encounter in your study of chemistry (such as the pascal, joule, and mole) may be new to you. We will explain each unit when it is first used.

In the following laboratory activity, you will make measurements of length and volume. The SI unit of length is the **meter** (symbolized by m). Most doorways are about two meters high. Many lengths we may wish to measure are either much larger or smaller than a meter. SI prefixes have been defined to indicate different fractions and multiples of all SI units, including the meter. Important prefixes for our present use are **deci-,** meaning one-tenth (1/10); **centi-,** meaning one one-hundredth (1/100) (recall that a cent is one one-hundredth of a dollar); and **milli-,** meaning one one-thousandth (1/1000).

An audiocassette cartridge has a width of one decimeter (dm); its thickness is about one centimeter (cm). A millimeter (mm) is approximately the diameter of the wire in a paper clip.

The derived SI unit for volume is the cubic meter (m^3). You can visualize one cubic meter as the space occupied by a box one meter on each edge. (The volume of a cube is calculated as length $\times$ width $\times$ height.) This 1-m^3 box would be big enough to hold a very large dog comfortably. This is too large a volume unit for convenient use in chemistry!

$1\,dm = 0.1\,m$
$1\,cm = 0.01\,m$
$1\,mm = 0.001\,m$

$1\,mL = 1\,cm^3$

$1000\,cm^3 = 1\,dm^3$
$1000\,mL = 1\,L$

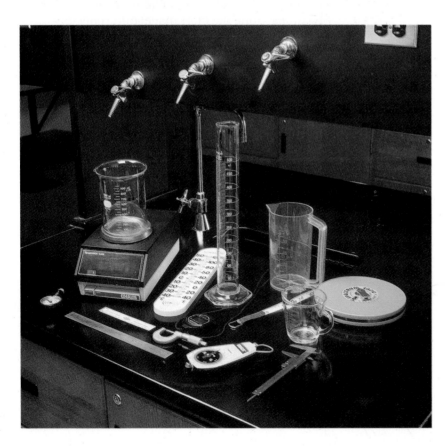

Can you think of a use for each measuring device?

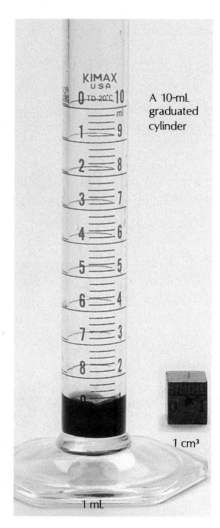

A 10-mL graduated cylinder

1 cm³

1 mL

Figure 1 One cubic centimeter (cm³) equals one milliliter (mL).

Include units; multiply and divide them like numbers. This is helpful in solving problems of many kinds.

Consider a smaller cube, one decimeter (dm) on each edge. The volume of this cube is one cubic decimeter (dm³). Although a cubic decimeter may not be familiar to you, you probably know it by another name—a **liter** (L). For example, the volume of a large bottle of cola can be given as 2 L or 2 dm³. One cubic decimeter (or one liter) of volume is exactly equal to 1000 cm³ (cubic centimeters). A full-scale photo of one cubic centimeter is shown in Figure 1. You may know the cubic centimeter by another name—the **milliliter** (mL). Because the liter and the milliliter are more familiar, we will use these units for volume.

Let's summarize the metric units for volume by considering a can of soft drink labeled 12 fluid ounces. If we ''think metric,'' this is 355 cm³ or 355 mL of beverage. Using larger units, we have 0.355 dm³ or 0.355 L of drink. Notice that this change in metric units involved just a shift in decimal point location. This illustrates one advantage of metric units over U.S customary units.

The following exercises will help you become more familiar with common metric length and volume units.

YOUR TURN

Meters and Liters

Examine a ruler graduated in millimeters. Note the 10 markings between each centimeter (cm) mark. These smaller markings represent millimeter (mm) divisions, where 10 mm = 1 cm, or 1 mm = 0.1 cm.

A small paper clip is 8 mm wide. What is this width in centimeters? Since 10 mm equals 1 cm, there's a ''10 times'' (one decimal place) difference between units of millimeters and centimeters. Thus the answer must be either 80 cm or 0.8 cm, depending on which direction the decimal point moves. Since it would take *10* mm to equal 1 cm, the *8*-mm paper clip must be slightly *less* than 1 cm. The answer must be 0.8 cm. Thus to convert the answer from millimeters to centimeters we just move the decimal point one place to the left.

The conversion of 8 mm to centimeters can also be written like this:

$$8 \text{ mm} \times \frac{1 \text{ cm}}{10 \text{ mm}} = 0.8 \text{ cm}$$

The same paper clip is 3.2 cm long. What is this length in millimeters? This answer can be reasoned out just as we did for the first question, or written out:

$$3.2 \text{ cm} \times \frac{10 \text{ mm}}{1 \text{ cm}} = 32 \text{ mm}$$

1. Measure the diameter of a penny, a nickel, a dime, and a quarter. Report each diameter
   a. in millimeters
   b. in centimeters.
2. Sketch a 10 cm-by-10 cm square. Now imagine a three-dimensional box or cube that is made up

of six of these 10 cm-square sides. The volume of a cube can be found by multiplying its length $\times$ width $\times$ height. What would be the total volume of this cube expressed

    a. in cubic centimeters (cm^3)?

    b. in milliliters (mL)?

    c. in liters (L)?

    d. Grocery-store sugar cubes each have a volume of about 1 cm^3. How many of these cubes could you pack into the cube with 10-cm sides?

3. Read the labels on some common beverage containers, such as a carton of milk, fruit juice can, or a soft drink, to see how volume is indicated.

    a. Can you find any beverage containers that list *only* U.S. customary volume units such as the quart, pint, or fluid ounce? If so, describe them.

    b. Describe at least three beverage containers that specify their volumes in *both* U.S. customary units and SI units. Include each container's volume expressed in both types of units.

4. a. State at least one advantage of SI units over U.S. customary units. (*Hint*: How are units—such as length—subdivided in each system? How are units of volume related to units of length?)

    b. Can you think of any disadvantages to using SI units?

Even such an apparently simple idea as "water use" can present some fascinating puzzles, particularly when data on the volumes of water involved are included. For example, consider the following *ChemQuandary*.

CHEMQUANDARY

Water, Water Everywhere

It requires 120 L of water to produce a 1.3-L can of juice   and   it takes about 450 L of water to place a single egg on your breakfast plate.

What explanation can you give for these two statements?

A.2 LABORATORY ACTIVITY: FOUL WATER

Getting Ready

If you haven't already done so, read carefully *Safety in the Laboratory,* found on page xvi.

The purpose of this activity is to purify a sample of "foul" water, producing as much "clean" water as possible. *Do not test the purity of the water by drinking it.*

Three water purification procedures will be used: (1) oil-water separation, (2) sand filtration, and (3) charcoal adsorption/filtration. (**Filtration** is a general term for separating solid particles from a liquid by passing the mixture through a material that retains the solid particles. The liquid collected after filtration is called the *filtrate.*)

Prepare a table similar to the one below in your laboratory notebook (provide more space for your entries).

Data Table

	Color	Clarity	Odor	Presence of Oil	Presence of Solids	Volume
Before treatment						
After oil-water separation						
After sand filtration						
After charcoal adsorption/filtration						

Procedure

1. Obtain approximately 100 mL of foul water, provided by your teacher. Measure its volume precisely with a graduated cylinder; record the value (with units) in your data table.
2. Examine the properties of your sample: color, odor, clarity, presence of solids or oily regions. Record your observations in the "Before treatment" section of your data table.

Oil-Water Separation

Oil and water do not noticeably dissolve in each other. If oil and water are mixed and left undisturbed, two layers form—the oil floats on top of the water.

1. Place a funnel in a clay triangle supported by a ring clamp and ring stand. Attach a rubber hose to the funnel tip as shown in Figure 2.
2. Close the rubber tube by nipping it with your fingers (or by using a pinch clamp). Shake or stir the foul-water sample. Then pour about half the sample into the funnel and let it stand for a few seconds until the liquid layers separate. (Gentle tapping may encourage oil droplets to float free.)
3. Carefully open the tube to release the lower layer into a 150-mL beaker. When the lower layer has drained out, quickly close the rubber tube.
4. Drain the remaining layer into a second 150-mL beaker.

Figure 2 Funnel in clay triangle.

5. Repeat Steps 2–4 using the remainder of your sample, adding each liquid to the correct beaker.

6. Dispose of the top, oily layer as instructed by your teacher. Observe the properties of the remaining layer and measure its volume. Record your observations and data. Save the water sample for the next procedure.

7. Wash the funnel with soap and water.

Sand Filtration

A sand filter traps solid impurities that are too large to fit between sand grains.

1. Using a straightened paper clip, poke small holes in the bottom of a paper cup (Figure 3).

2. Add pre-moistened gravel and sand layers to the cup as shown in Figure 4. (The bottom gravel prevents the sand from washing through the holes. The top gravel keeps the sand from churning up when the sample is poured in.)

3. *Gently* pour the sample to be filtered into the cup. Catch the filtrate (filtered water) in a beaker as it drains through.

4. Dispose of the used sand and gravel according to your teacher's instructions. Do *not* pour sand or gravel into the sink!

5. Observe the properties and measure the volume of the water. Record your results. Save the water sample for the next procedure.

Charcoal Adsorption/Filtration

Charcoal **adsorbs** (attracts and holds on its surface) many substances that could give water a bad taste, odor, or cloudy appearance. Fish tanks include charcoal filters for the same purpose.

1. Fold a piece of filter paper as shown in Figure 5.

2. Place the folded filter paper in a funnel. Wet the paper slightly so it adheres to the funnel cone.

3. Place the funnel in a clay triangle supported by a ring clamp (see Figure 2). Lower the ring clamp so the funnel stem extends 2–3 cm inside a 150-mL beaker.

4. Place one teaspoon of charcoal in a 125- or 250-mL Erlenmeyer flask.

5. Pour the water sample into the flask. Shake vigorously. Then gently pour the liquid through the filter paper. Keep the liquid level below the top of the filter paper—no liquid should flow between the filter paper and the funnel.

6. If the filtrate is darkened by small charcoal particles, refilter the liquid. Use a clean piece of moistened filter paper.

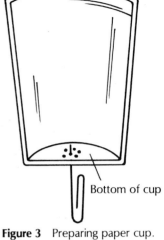

Figure 3 Preparing paper cup.

Bottom of cup

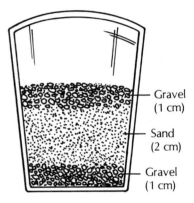

Gravel (1 cm)

Sand (2 cm)

Gravel (1 cm)

Figure 4 Sand filtration.

Figure 5 Folding filter paper.

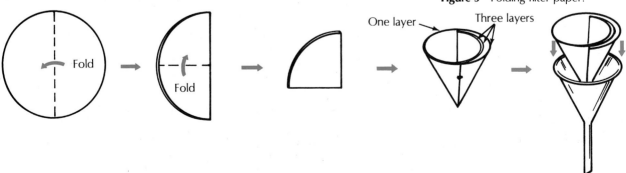

Fold

Fold

One layer

Three layers

7. When you are satisfied with the appearance and odor of your purified water sample, pour it into a graduated cylinder. Observe and record the properties and the final volume of the sample.
8. Wash your hands thoroughly before leaving the laboratory.

Calculations

Complete the following calculations. Record your work and answers in your notebook.

1. What percent of the original foul-water sample did you recover as ''pure'' water?

$$\text{Percent of water purified} = \frac{\text{Vol. of water purified}}{\text{Vol. of foul-water sample}} \times 100\%$$

2. What volume of liquid did you lose during purification?
3. What percent of your original foul-water sample was lost during purification?

Post-Lab Activities

1. Your teacher will demonstrate another water purification technique, called **distillation.**
   a. Write a complete description of the steps in distillation.
   b. Why did your teacher discard the first portion of recovered liquid?
   c. Why was some liquid left in the distilling flask at the end of the demonstration?
2. Your teacher will test the **electrical conductivity** of the purified water samples obtained by your class. This test checks for the presence of dissolved, electrically-charged particles in the water (discussed on page 31). Your teacher will also check the electrical conductivity of samples of distilled water and tap water. What do these tests suggest about the purity of your water sample?

Questions

1. Compare your water purification experiences and data with those of other lab teams. How should the success of various teams be judged?
2. Distillation is not used by municipal water treatment plants. Why?

A.3 YOU DECIDE: INFORMATION GATHERING

Keep a diary of water use in your home for three days. Using a chart similar to the one on page 11, record the number of times various water-use activities occur. Ask each family member to help you.

Check the activities listed on the chart. If family members use water in other ways during the three days, add these to your diary. Estimate the quantities of water used by those activities.

The data you gather will help you see how much water you and your family use every day, and for what purposes. You may be surprised at the amount you use, which will lead you to think about the next important question, Why is water such an important substance?

Data Table

	Day		
	1	2	3
Number of persons in family			
Number of baths			
Number of showers			
Length of each in minutes			
Number of washing machine loads			
Low setting			
High setting			
Dish washing			
Number of times by hand			
Number of times by dishwasher			
Number of toilet flushes			
Watering lawn			
Time in hours			
Number of car washes			
Cooking and drinking			
Number of cups			
Running water in sink			
Number of minutes			
Other uses and number of each			

A.4 WATER AND HEALTH

Living organisms require a continual supply of water. A human must drink about two liters (roughly two quarts) of water-containing liquids daily to replace water losses through bodily excretions and evaporation from skin and lungs. You can live 50 to 60 days without food but only 5 to 10 days without water.

Early humans simply drank water from the nearest river or stream with few harmful effects. However, as cities were built, this practice became risky. Wastes were dumped, or washed by rain, into the same streams from which people drank.

As the number of people increased, there was less time for natural processes to purify dirty water before someone drank it. Eventually, mysterious outbreaks of fatal diseases occurred, such as in London in the 1850s, when the Thames River became contaminated with cholera bacteria from sewage.

Today, water quality has become everyone's concern. We can no longer rely on obtaining pure water from streams and lakes; most often we must purify the water ourselves. Because we use large quantities, we must be sure not only that we have enough water, but also that it is pure enough for our needs. How can this be accomplished? We will begin to answer that question by examining our nation's overall use of water and some typical ways our communities and industries use this resource.

A.5 WATER USES

Do we use so much water that we are in danger of running out? The answer is both no and yes. The total water available to us is far more than enough. Each day, some 15 trillion liters (4 trillion gallons) of rain or snow fall in the United States. Only 10% is used by humans. The rest flows back into large bodies of water, evaporates, and falls again as part of a perpetual **water cycle.** However, the distribution of rain and snowfall does not necessarily correspond to the locations of high water use.

There are also regional differences in the way we affect the water cycle. In the eastern half of the nation, 88% of used water is returned to natural waterways. However, only 48% is returned to waterways in the western half of the country, with the rest returning directly to the air. Why should there be such a great difference?

In eastern states, rainwater soaking into the ground provides much of the moisture needed by crops. However, in many other parts of the country much less rain falls, and so irrigation water must be obtained from streams or wells, many of which are far from the croplands. Most irrigation water evaporates from the leaves of growing plants. The rest evaporates directly from spray irrigation or from the moist soil, before plants can use it. This evaporated moisture is blown by prevailing winds to fall, days later, on eastern crops.

YOUR TURN

U.S. Water Use

Refer to Figure 6 in answering these questions.

1. In the United States, what is the greatest single water use in

    a. the East?   d. the West?

    b. the South?   e. Alaska?

    c. the Midwest?   f. Hawaii?

2. Suggest reasons for differences in water use among these six U.S. regions.

3. Explain the differences in how water is used in the East and the West. Think about where most people live and where most of the nation's factories and farms are. What other regional differences help explain patterns of water use?

According to authorities, an average U.S. family of four uses about 1360 liters (360 gallons) of water *daily.* This value represents direct, measurable use, but beyond that are many hidden or indirect uses you probably have never considered. Each time you eat bread, a hamburger, or an egg, you are "using" water! Why? Because water was needed to grow and process the food.

Let's reconsider *ChemQuandary: Water, Water Everywhere* (page 7). At first glance the volumes of water mentioned in this *ChemQuandary* probably seemed absurd. How could so much water be required for providing you with one egg or one can of fruit juice?

These examples illustrate two typical hidden (indirect) uses of water. The chicken that laid the egg needed drinking water. Water was used to grow the chicken's feed. Even the small quantities of water used for other purposes in processing add up, when billions of eggs are consumed.

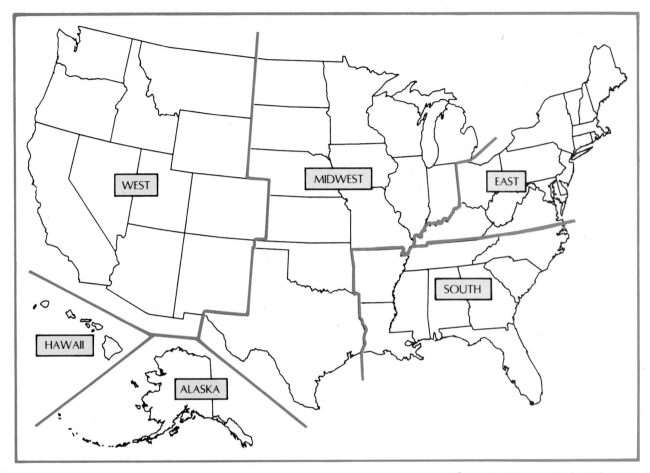

Figure 6 Water use in the U.S.

PERCENT OF WATER USED

Purpose	Area					
	East	South	Midwest	West	Alaska	Hawaii
Irrigation	6%	53%	75%	90%	1%	79%
Other agricultural	2%	3%	4%	1%	—	—
Homes, offices	32%	14%	6%	5%	13%	11%
Manufacturing	40%	17%	8%	2%	19%	10%
Steam-electric generating	13%	10%	4%	1%	1%	—
Mining	7%	3%	3%	1%	66%	—

In one Riverwood newspaper article you read earlier, one youth said he'd just drink milk and canned fruit juice until the water was turned back on. However, drinking a glass of water consumes much less water than does drinking the same amount of canned fruit juice. Why should that be so? Because the liquid *in* the can is insignificant when compared to the water used to make the metal can itself. That's where the mysterious 120 L of water mentioned in the *ChemQuandary* arises!

Though we depend on large quantities of water, we are scarcely aware of it because, in normal times, when faucet taps are turned on—in Riverwood or in your own community—water flows freely. How does this happen? What is the source of this plentiful supply? Let's review and extend what you already know by taking an imaginary "upstream" journey through water pipes back to the water's origin.

Keeping Florida Fresh

By Jack Sampson
Neptune Beach Tribune *Staff Writer*

Diseases like cholera and typhus take many lives daily in other parts of the world. In the United States this doesn't happen because of the work of dedicated professionals like Patrick Karney. For nearly a decade Patrick has been Division Chief for the Waste Water Division of Jacksonville, Florida. As Division Chief, he is responsible for protecting public health and ensuring the quality of the water supply. This is a multi-faceted job with many challenges and many opportunities for problem-solving.

The city of Jacksonville and adjacent Duval County have a combined area of approximately 840 square miles, which is served by one of the larger waste water treatment operations in the United States. Patrick is responsible for the total operation of the waste water facilities. He manages a multi-million dollar budget and coordinates the operations of 430 pumping stations, five regional treatment plants (staffed 24 hours a day for 365 days a year by 440 employees), and six smaller treatment plants. His talents lie in the effective utilization of the resources available, including employees, equipment, and finances. He uses all of these resources to protect the local Florida environment and the people within it.

Patrick's most recent special project has been the initiation of a water pre-treatment program. By Federal law, waste water departments are required to monitor industrial users and establish pre-treatment programs. This means that waste water from industrial sites must be

Photo by Patrick Karney

treated by the user company before it leaves the site and combines with the waste water in the main system. Companies are required to restore the proper pH levels, remove heavy metal precipitates, and separate oils from the water. In Jacksonville, a local ordinance led to beginning a pre-treatment program for 130 significant industrial users. Patrick retrained staff from his existing operation as industrial waste technicians who could develop and oversee the new program. The technicians schedule site inspections, issue permits, take samples, and perform chemical analyses.

Patrick has a strong engineering background. His chem-istry knowledge is particularly important since it helps him to understand the legal and chemical language used in his work. He also has management training. As a good manager he must be open-minded to new ideas and be able to compromise, as well as delegate responsibility to his subordinates.

For a job like Patrick's, a person needs a degree in mechanical engineering, engineering management, or civil engineering, with special courses in waste water operations. Special courses in law are also helpful in interpreting the Clean Water and Clean Air Acts that relate to waste water.

A water treatment plant.

A.6 BACK THROUGH THE WATER PIPES

If you live in a city or town, your home's water pipes are linked to underground water pipes. These pipes carry water from a reservoir or a water tower, which is usually located at the highest point in town. From there water flows downhill to all faucets. Before water is pumped into the water tower, it is cleaned and purified at a water treatment plant.

Water may enter the water treatment plant from a reservoir, a lake, a river, a stream, or a well. If your community gets its water from a river or stream, it uses **surface water,** which flows on top of the ground. If the water comes from a well, it is **groundwater,** which collects underground and must be pumped to the surface. About 20% of the water supply in the U.S. is groundwater.

Immense supplies of groundwater are under your feet. The world's supply of groundwater is many times greater than all the water held in the world's rivers and lakes. Even when surface soil appears dry and dusty, millions of liters of fresh water are stored below in regions called **aquifers.** These porous rock structures act like sponges, holding water sometimes for thousands of years.

Neither groundwater nor surface water is completely pure. As water flows over the ground to join a stream, or seeps far into the soil to become groundwater, it dissolves small amounts of soil and rock. These dissolved substances are usually not removed at the water treatment plant; they are harmless in the amounts normally found. In fact, some (such as iron, zinc, and calcium ions) are essential to human health in small quantities.

If you live in a rural area, your home probably has its own water supply system. A well driven deep into an aquifer brings water to the surface by an electric pump. A small pressurized tank holds the water before it enters the pipes in your home.

Let's continue tracing water to its origins. Most water falls to the earth as rain (and, if it's cold enough, as snow). Most of the rain that falls on flat ground soaks directly into the soil, seeping downward to join the groundwater. When it falls on sloping terrain, much of it runs downhill before it soaks into the soil.

Water that does not become groundwater runs off into waterways. It collects into brooks, which flow into streams, rivers, and lakes. A substantial quantity of this water eventually finds its way to the ocean.

Where does rainwater come from? Rain falls as tiny water droplets from clouds formed when heat energy from the sun causes surface water to evaporate. Upon cooling at higher elevations, the evaporated water forms droplets that gather in large quantities to become clouds. This endless sequence of events is called the water cycle. Another name for it is the **hydrologic cycle** (Figure 7).

We can go back even further—to where water *originally* came from. Most scientists believe our modern world's supply of liquid water originally was formed by the condensation of water vapor. That vapor had been released from volcanoes on the young Earth's surface; and within the volcanoes, the vapor had been formed by the combination of hydrogen and oxygen gases. Geologists believe the total amount of water in the world has remained constant for billions of years, and has continued cycling through the environment.

Figure 7 The hydrologic cycle.

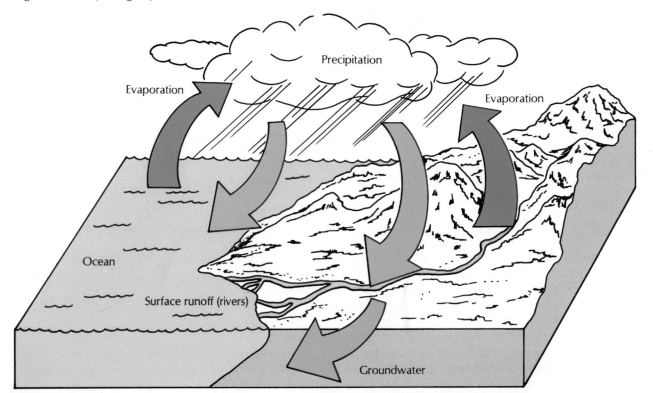

A.7 WHERE IS THE EARTH'S WATER?

According to scientists, about 97% of the Earth's total water is stored in the oceans. The next largest storage place is not as obvious. A common incorrect guess is in rivers and lakes. Actually, the second largest quantity of water is stored in Earth's ice caps and glaciers! Figure 8 shows how the world's supply of water is distributed.

Water may be found not only in different places, but also in three different **states** (forms), as it goes through its cycle. Water vapor in the air is in the **gaseous state.** In some regions of the United States, water in the gaseous state is the high humidity that contributes to human discomfort during the summer. Water is most obvious in the **liquid state,** found in lakes, rivers, oceans, clouds, and rain. Water in the **solid state** may occur as ice, snowflakes, frost, and even hail.

Water vapor will fill any size container because, as a gas, it has no fixed volume. It also has no fixed shape, since it takes the shape of the container in which it is held. On the other hand, a sample of liquid water has a definite volume. But liquid water has no shape of its own; it takes on the shape of the container into which it is poured. In the solid state, a water (ice) sample has both a fixed volume and a shape of its own. (Though we are discussing water here, the characteristics of other gases, liquids, and solids are similar to these.)

We are very fortunate in most of the United States to have an abundant water supply at present. We turn on the tap, use what we need and go on about our business, not thinking about how much water we use. When the water supply is shut off, as in Riverwood, it's usually for a short time.

But, suppose there were a drought lasting several years. Or suppose the shortage were a perpetual problem, as it is in many countries. Priority would go to "survival" uses of available water. Some non-essential water uses would probably stop entirely.

What water uses would you give up first? Refer to your completed water-use diary. How much water did *you* use in your home during the three-day period? For what purposes? Let's examine your water-use data.

A.8 YOU DECIDE: WATER USE ANALYSIS

Table 1 (page 18) lists typical quantities of water used in the home. Use the table to answer the following questions.

Questions
1. Estimate the total water volume (in liters) used by your household during the three days.
2. What was the average amount of water (in liters) used by *each* family member over the *three* days? *Note:* To find the average, divide the total volume of water used in three days by the number of family members. This answer will be in units of liters per person per three days.
3. On average, how much water (in liters) did *each* family member use in *one* day?
4. Compare the average water volume used daily by each person in your household (Answer 3) with the reported average water volume used daily by each person in the United States, 340 L.

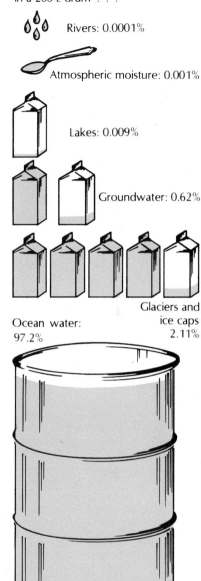

If the world's total water supply were in a 200-L drum . . .

Rivers: 0.0001%

Atmospheric moisture: 0.001%

Lakes: 0.009%

Groundwater: 0.62%

Glaciers and ice caps 2.11%

Ocean water: 97.2%

Figure 8 Distribution of the world's water supply.

Table 1 indicates that a regular showerhead delivers 19 L each minute—in English units, that's five gallons per minute, or 25 gallons for a five-minute shower!

Table 1   **WATER REQUIRED FOR TYPICAL ACTIVITIES**

Bathing (per bath)	130 L
Showering (per min.)	
Regular showerhead	19 L
Water-efficient showerhead	9 L
Cooking and drinking	
Per 10 cups of water	2 L
Flushing toilet (per flush)	
Conventional toilet	19 L
"Water-saver" toilet	13 L
"Low-flow" toilet	6 L
Watering lawn (per hour)	1130 L
Washing clothes (per load)	
Low setting	72 L
High setting	170 L
Washing dishes (per load)	
By hand (with water running)	114 L
By hand (washing and rinsing in dishpans)	19 L
By machine (full cycle)	61 L
By machine (short cycle)	26 L
Washing car (running hose)	680 L
Running water in sink (per min.)	
Conventional faucet	19 L
Water-saving faucet	9 L

What reasons can you give to explain any differences between your average and the national average?

You are now quite aware of the average amount of water you use daily. Suppose you had to live with much less. How would you ration your allowance for survival and comfort? This is exactly the question Riverwood residents had to answer.

A.9   YOU DECIDE: RIVERWOOD WATER USE

Riverwood authorities have severely rationed your home water supply for three days while possible causes of the fish kill are investigated. The County Sanitation Commission recommends cleaning your bathtub and filling it with water. That water must be used for everything except drinking and cooking during the three-day period. (Water for drinking and cooking will be trucked in from Mapleton.)

Assuming that your family has one tub of water, 375 L (100 gal), to use during these three days, consider this list of typical water uses:

- washing car, floors, windows, pets
- bathing, showering, washing hair, washing hands
- washing clothes, dishes
- cooking and preparing food
- drinking
- watering indoor plants, outdoor plants, lawn
- flushing toilet

1. a. Which water uses could you completely avoid?
   b. What would be the consequences?

2. a. For which tasks could you reduce your water use?
   b. How?
3. Impurities added by some water uses may not interfere with reusing the same water for other purposes. For example, you might decide to save hand-washing water, using it later to wash the pet dog.
   a. For which activities could you use such impure water ("gray water")?
   b. From which prior uses could this water be taken?

   Clearly, pure water is a valuable resource no one should take for granted. Unfortunately, water is easily contaminated. In the next part of this unit we will examine why.

PART A: SUMMARY QUESTIONS

1. For each item, select the better answer:
   a. Is the thickness of a dime closer to 1 mm or to 1 cm?
   b. Is the volume of a glass of water closer to 250 dm^3 or to 250 cm^3?
   c. Is the diameter of a pencil closer to 7 mm or to 7 cm?
   d. Is one gallon of gasoline closer to 38 mL or to 3.8 L?
2. Complete these conversions:
   a. 735 cm^3 = ? mL = ? L
   b. 10.7 mm = ? cm
3. Describe some implications if there were a lack of water
   a. within your family
   b. in your town
   c. in your region of the country
   d. in the entire United States.

4. a. What does "indirect water use" mean?
   b. List at least two indirect uses of water needed to put a loaf of bread on your table.
5. The total supply of water in the world has been the same for billions of years. Explain why.
6. Name a serious epidemic that can be caused by drinking polluted water.
7. Consider Earth's large ocean water volume and also your laboratory experience in purifying a water sample.
   a. Why is there worldwide concern about water's availability and purity?
   b. What could be done to use more of Earth's water?
   c. How could more ocean water be used?

EXTENDING YOUR KNOWLEDGE (OPTIONAL)

- One of water's unique characteristics is that it occurs in all three states (solid, liquid, and gas) at normal temperatures found on our planet. How would the hydrologic cycle be different if this were not true?
- Using an encyclopedia or other reference, compare the maximum and minimum temperatures naturally found on the surfaces of Earth, the moon, and Venus. The large amount of water on Earth serves to limit the natural temperature range found on this planet. Suggest ways that water does this. As a start, find out what the terms *heat of*

fusion, heat capacity, and *heat of vaporization* mean.
- Look up the normal freezing point, boiling point, heat of fusion, and heat of vaporization of ammonia (NH$_3$). If a planet's life forms were made up mostly of ammonia rather than of water, what special survival problems might they face? What temperature range might be reasonable for this planet to support "life"?
- Write a report on the development and spread of SI metrics and its precursor, the metric system.

A LOOK AT WATER AND ITS CONTAMINANTS

Meeting Raises Fish Kill Concerns

By Carol Simmons
Staff writer of Riverwood News

An Environmental Protection Agency (EPA) scientist, Dr. Harold Schmidt, reported last night that evidence so far indicates no danger, past or future, to Riverwood water users. Dr. Schmidt presented his report at a Riverwood Town Hall public meeting attended by over 300 concerned citizens.

Dr. Margaret Brooke, a State University water-systems specialist, helped interpret information and answer questions regarding the still-mysterious Snake River fish kill. Local physician Dr. Jason Martingdale and Riverwood High School home economics teacher Alicia Green joined the speakers during the question-and-answer session following the reports.

Dr. Brooke confirmed that preliminary water-sample analyses have shown no likely cause for the fish kill. She reported that EPA chemists will collect water samples at hourly intervals today to look for any unusual fluctuations in dissolved oxygen levels. Although fish don't breathe as we do, Brooke explained, they must take in an adequate amount of the oxygen dissolved in water

through their gills.

Dr. Schmidt expressed regret that the fishing tournament had to be cancelled but strongly supported the Town Council's action, saying that it was the safest course in the long run. He reported that "nothing has yet been found to determine the cause of the fish kill," but that "all fish examined, including ones found since the initial discovery of the kill, show unexpected and puzzling signs of biological trauma. These signs include hemorrhaging and small bubbles under the skin along the lateral line." His laboratory is presently looking into the implications of these findings. In response to questions, Dr. Schmidt advised against rescheduling the fishing tournament yet.

Concerning possible causes of the fish kill, Dr. Brooke reported that "it must be something dissolved in the water, since suspended materials filtered from the water show nothing unusual." She emphasized that water's unique properties make the question of the fish kill quite complicated. Important factors to consider include the relative amounts of various substances that water can dissolve and the effect water temperature has on

solubility. She expressed confidence, however, that further studies would shed light on the situation.

Dr. Martingdale reassured citizens that "thus far, no illness reported either by private physicians or the hospital can be linked to drinking water." Green offered water-conservation tips for housekeeping and cooking that could make life easier for inconvenienced citizens. She distributed an information sheet that will also be available at the Town Hall office.

Mayor Edward Cisko confirmed that water supplies will again be trucked in from Mapleton today and expressed hope that the crisis will last no longer than three days.

Those attending the meeting appeared to be dealing with the emergency in good spirits. Citizens leaving Town Hall expressed a variety of opinions.

"I'll never take my tap water for granted again," said Trudy Anderson, a resident of southern Riverwood. "I thought scientists had all the answers," puzzled Robert Morgan of Morgan Enterprises. "They don't know either! What's going on here? There's certainly more involved in all of this than I ever imagined."

B.1 PHYSICAL PROPERTIES OF WATER

Water is a familiar substance. We drink it, wash with it, swim in it, and sometimes grumble when it falls from the sky. We are so accustomed to water that most of us are unaware it is one of the rarest and most unusual substances in the universe. As space probes have explored our solar system and collected data as pictures, we have learned that water is almost totally absent on Mars, Jupiter and other planets and moons. Earth, on the other hand, is half-covered by water-laden clouds. More than 70% of the Earth's surface is covered by oceans having an average depth of more than three kilometers (two miles).

Kilo is the prefix meaning 1000. 1 km = 1000 m

To understand the issues involved in the fish kill, we need to know more about water itself. First, you will take a look at water's **physical properties**—those distinctive characteristics shared by all water samples. (Later, you will see some of the chemical properties of water. Those properties can be studied only by changing water into something else.)

Water is the only ordinary liquid found naturally in our environment. That is partly because so many things dissolve easily in water; many other liquids are actually water solutions. Even water that seems pure never is entirely so. Surface water contains dissolved minerals as well as other substances. Even the distilled water used in steam irons and car batteries contains dissolved gases from the atmosphere. So does rainwater.

Pure water is clear, colorless, odorless, and tasteless. Some tap water samples have a characteristic taste and even a slight odor, caused by other substances in the water. (You can confirm this by boiling, then refrigerating some distilled water. When you compare its taste with the taste of chilled tap water, you may notice that "pure" distilled water tastes flat.)

Density is an important physical property that can help identify a substance. To determine it, you need two measurements of a sample of matter—volume and mass. The *mass* of material present in one unit of *volume* of the material is its **density.** The SI unit of mass used most often in chemistry is the **gram** (g). A nickel coin has a mass of about 5 g. You have

How many states of water are shown in this photograph?

Table 2	DENSITIES (g/mL)
Solids	
Cork	0.24
Ice	0.92
Aluminum	2.70
Iron	7.86
Liquids	
Gasoline	0.67
Water	1.00
Glycerin	1.27
Gases	
(at 25° C, 1 atm pressure)	
Hydrogen	0.00008
Oxygen	0.0013
Carbon dioxide	0.0018

already been introduced to a commonly-used unit of volume, the milliliter (mL).

At 4° C, the mass of 1.0 mL of liquid water is 1.0 g. Thus the density of water is about one gram per milliliter (1.0 g/mL).

How does the density of water compare with that of other familiar liquids? Corn oil has a density of 0.92 g/mL. That means one milliliter of corn oil has a mass of 0.92 g. Thus a given volume of corn oil has less mass than the same volume of water. That's why corn oil is able to float on the surface of water.

Some other liquids are denser than water. Permanent antifreeze for a car has a density of 1.11 g/mL. Therefore, a given volume of antifreeze has more mass than the same volume of water. Liquid mercury, at a density of 13.6 g/mL, is one of the densest common substances. Table 2 shows some densities of other materials.

Gases are much less dense than liquids, and the solid form of a substance is usually denser than its liquid form. However, ice is an important exception. As a water sample freezes, it expands to occupy a larger volume, and so one milliliter of ice has a density of 0.92 g/mL. That is slightly less than the density of liquid water (1.0 g/mL). As a result, ice floats on water. If ice had a greater density than liquid water and sank to the bottom as it froze, aquatic life in rivers and lakes could not survive.

This special property of water is responsible for much erosion. Rainwater seeps into tiny cracks in rocks, freezes, then expands and cracks them further. After many seasons, with other factors contributing, rocks become soil. In a similar fashion, highway pavement is broken up. This type of erosion is particularly rapid because of the effect of traffic on the cracked pavement. You will notice that potholes are particularly bad following a winter of many freezes and thaws.

Among the other important physical properties of water are its **boiling point** and ***freezing point.*** The Celsius temperature scale, used in most of the world, divides the interval between the freezing point of water and its boiling point into 100 parts. Water's freezing point is defined as 0° C, and its normal boiling point as 100° C.

A series of freezes and thaws have broken up the pavement of this highway.

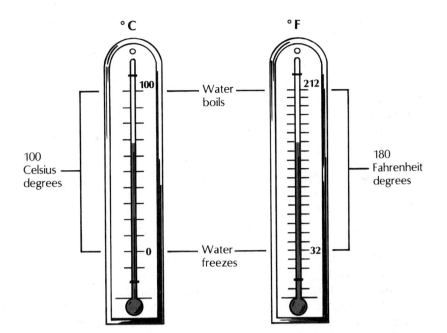

Figure 9 Celsius and Fahrenheit temperature scales. Reference temperatures for water are based on one atmosphere of pressure.

The Fahrenheit temperature scale is still used in the United States. Water boils at 212° F and freezes at 32° F on this scale; there are 180 divisions between these freezing and boiling temperatures (Figure 9).

Evaporation and boiling are related physical properties of liquids. In both processes, liquid changes to gas. However, evaporation occurs at all temperatures—but only at the surface of the liquid. At higher temperatures, evaporation occurs more rapidly. During boiling, by contrast, gaseous water (water vapor) forms *under the surface* of the liquid. Because the vapor is less dense than the liquid, it rises to the surface and escapes as steam. We cannot see steam, but it condenses into visible clouds of tiny droplets as it contacts cooler air.

Water has an unusually high boiling point. The life-supporting form of water is its liquid state; water's high boiling point is responsible for its being a liquid at normal temperatures.

Another very important and unusual physical property of water is its high **surface tension.** This property causes water to form spherical drops and to form a curved surface in a small container. Surface tension enables a water bug to dart across the surface of a quiet pool and makes it possible to float a dry needle on the surface of a dish of water (Figure 10).

Figure 10 Water has a high surface tension, allowing a needle to float on its surface, and causing it to form beads on a newly polished car surface.

B.2 MIXTURES AND SOLUTIONS

Samples of water collected from waterways for testing are often cloudy. Or, they may look clear but contain invisible substances. The samples of Riverwood's water, for example, contained things other than pure water. But were they dissolved in the water, or temporarily mixed in it? The difference could be important to Riverwood's future.

If two or more substances combine and retain their individual properties, a **mixture** has been produced. A mixture of salt and pepper is described as **heterogeneous** because it is not completely uniform throughout. A pepper and water mixture is also heterogeneous.

Solutions in which water is the solvent are called aqueous solutions.

suspension
(largest solute particles)
↓
colloid
(intermediate-sized solute particles)
↓
solution
(smallest solute particles)

Mixing salt and water has a very different result—a **solution** is formed. A solution is a mixture that is completely uniform throughout. In water, the salt crystals dissolve by separating into particles so small that they cannot be seen even at high magnification. These particles become uniformly mingled with the particles of water, producing a **homogeneous** mixture, one that is uniform throughout. All solutions are homogeneous mixtures. In the salt solution, the salt is the **solute** (the dissolved substance) and the water is the **solvent** (the dissolving agent).

Water mixtures are classified according to the size of particles dispersed in the water. **Suspensions** are mixtures containing relatively large, easily-seen particles. The particles remain suspended for a while after stirring, but then settle out or form layers within the liquid. Suspensions are classified as heterogeneous mixtures because they are not uniform throughout.

Muddy water includes suspended particles of soil and other matter. A solid layer forms when muddy water is left undisturbed. Even after several days without stirring, the liquid still appears slightly cloudy. Some very small particles remain distributed throughout the water. These tiny particles, still large enough to produce the cloudy appearance, are called colloidal particles. This type of mixture is called a **colloid.**

Milk is a colloid with small butterfat particles dispersed in water. These colloidal butterfat particles are not visible to the unaided eye. Thus milk can be classified as homogeneous, leading to the familiar term *homogenized milk.* Under high magnification, however, individual butterfat globules can be seen floating in the water. Milk no longer appears homogeneous (Figure 11).

There's a simple way to decide whether the particles in a mixture are large enough to consider the liquid a colloid rather than a solution. *When a light beam shines through a colloidal liquid, the beam's path can be clearly seen in the liquid.* The particles are too small to see, but are large enough to reflect light off their surfaces. This reflection is called the **Tyndall effect,** named after the Irish physicist who first explained the phenomenon. *Solutions do not show a Tyndall effect.* The particles in a solution are so small that they do not settle out and cannot be seen even at high magnification.

The foul-water sample you purified earlier illustrates all three types of mixtures. The sample certainly contained some

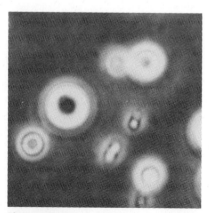
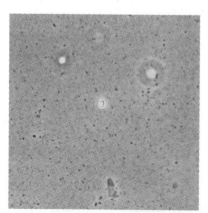
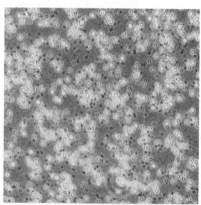

Figure 11 Fat globules appear under magnification, so that milk no longer looks homogeneous. *Left:* Whole milk under 100× magnification. *Center:* Skimmed milk under 10× magnification. *Right:* Whole milk under 10× magnification.

The Tyndall effect is apparent in the colloidal suspension on the left. The solution on the right is not colloidal, and so the light beam cannot be seen.

particles large enough to form a suspension. The sample's persistent cloudiness suggests that suspended colloidal particles were also present. Even the final clear, purified sample had atmospheric gases and electrically-charged particles dissolved in it. Thus your "purified" water was actually a solution.

Now, you can put your knowledge of water mixtures to work. The following laboratory activity will give you some firsthand experience in distinguishing among these types of mixtures.

B.3 LABORATORY ACTIVITY: MIXTURES

Getting Ready

In this laboratory activity, you will examine four different water-containing mixtures and classify each as a suspension, a colloid, a solution, or a combination of these. You will filter each sample and look for the Tyndall effect in both the filtered and unfiltered samples. Particles in a suspension can be separated by filtration, while those in a colloid or a solution are too small to be retained by the filter paper. The Tyndall effect will reveal the presence of colloidal particles.

In your laboratory notebook, prepare data tables for entering your observations on the original samples and filtrates, and your conclusions about each mixture.

Data Table   ORIGINAL SAMPLE

Beaker	Color	Clarity (Clear or Cloudy?)	Settle Out?	Tyndall Effect	Mixture Classification		
					Suspension	Colloid	Solution
1.							
2.							
3.							
4.							

Data Table

Beaker	Color	Clarity	Settle Out?	Tyndall Effect	Filter Paper?	Mixture Classification		
						FILTRATE Suspension	Colloid	Solution
1.								
2.								
3.								
4.								

Procedure

1. Obtain two 100- or 150-mL beakers. Fill one beaker half-full of one of the unknown mixtures.
2. Carefully examine the unknown mixture. Record observations on its appearance.
   a. Is the sample colored?
   b. Is the sample clear or cloudy?
   c. Do any particles settle out after you stir the mixture?
3. Perform a Tyndall effect test on the mixture as demonstrated by your teacher. If the liquid is relatively clear, shine a light beam through the side of the beaker and observe the liquid from the top. (Suggestion: If you are uncertain how to interpret a "faint" test result, compare the results to a Tyndall effect test on a reference beaker half-filled with pure water.) If the liquid is very cloudy, shine the beam across the liquid surface and observe the beaker from the side. Can you see the light beam as it passes through the sample? Record your observations.
4. Filter the unknown sample, using the apparatus shown in Figure 12. (If you have forgotten how to fold a filter paper, look back at Figure 5 on page 9.) Use a fresh filter paper for each sample. Collect enough filtrate in a clean, numbered beaker to repeat Steps 2 and 3.
5. Examine the filter paper. Were any particles removed from the liquid? Record your observations.
6. Repeat Step 2 with the filtrate; record your observations. Compare properties of the filtrate with those of the original liquid sample. Note and record any differences.
7. Repeat Step 3 with the filtrate; record your observations.
8. Based on your observations, decide whether the unknown mixture was a solution, a colloid, a suspension, or some combination. Record your classifications.
9. Clean and rinse your two beakers.
10. Repeat Steps 1 through 9 with another unknown. Continue until four unknown mixtures have been tested.
11. Compare your observations and conclusions with those of other laboratory teams.
12. Wash your hands thoroughly before leaving the laboratory.

Figure 12 Filtration setup: filter paper, funnel, clay triangle, ring clamp, ring stand, beaker.

B.4 MOLECULAR VIEW OF WATER

So far in our investigation of water, we have focused on observing its properties with our unaided senses. To understand

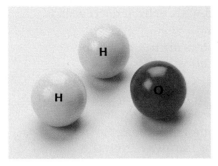

Atoms of hydrogen and oxygen.

A molecule of water.

why water has such special properties, however, we must examine it at the level of its **atoms.**

All samples of matter are composed of atoms. Oxygen is considered an **element** because it is composed of only oxygen atoms. Likewise, the element hydrogen contains only hydrogen atoms. Approximately 90 elements are found in nature, each with its own type of atom and having unique identifying properties.

Water is not classified as an element because its atoms are of two types—oxygen and hydrogen. Nor is it classified as a mixture, since its properties are different from those of either oxygen or hydrogen. Also, water cannot be separated into oxygen and hydrogen by simple physical means.

Instead, water is an example of a substance called a **compound.** To date, chemists have identified over 10 million compounds. Every compound is composed of atoms of two or more different elements linked together by **chemical bonds.** Two hydrogen atoms and one oxygen atom bond together to form a unit called a water **molecule.** A molecule is the smallest unit of a substance that retains the properties of that substance. Even one drop of water contains an unimaginably large number of water molecules.

The following *Your Turn* will give you a chance to apply an atomic and molecular view to explain a variety of common observations.

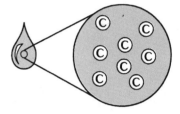

Figure 13 Schematic view of a drop of food coloring. Each food coloring molecule is represented by Ⓒ.

Figure 14 Food coloring molecules, Ⓒ, begin spreading among water molecules, Ⓦ.

YOUR TURN

Matter at the Microlevel

If you add a few drops of food coloring to an undisturbed glass of water, you can see the color slowly spread out. If you stir this mixture, the color will become lighter and evenly distributed. How can this be explained in terms of molecules?

The food coloring contains molecules that appear colored. (See Figure 13 in the margin.) After the drop of food coloring enters the water, these molecules begin to spread among the colorless water molecules (Figure 14). Eventually a solution forms with uniform distribution of color (Figure 15).

Now decide how each of the following observations can be explained in terms of molecules. Feel free to draw sketches to clarify your explanations.

Figure 15 Uniform solution of food coloring and water.

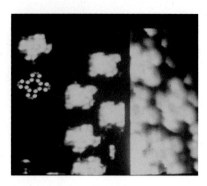

A scanning tunneling microscope image of copper-phthalocyanine. The image reveals individual atoms in the distinctive four-leaf-clover-shaped molecule.

1. a. A regular balloon filled with helium decreases in volume as time passes.
   b. Metal-foil (Mylar) balloons shrink much more slowly than do plastic ones.
2. The solid form of a substance is usually denser than the liquid form, which is, in turn, much denser than the gaseous form.
3. A bottle of perfume is opened in a room. Soon the perfume's odor is apparent far away from the bottle.

B.5 SYMBOLS, FORMULAS, AND EQUATIONS

To represent atoms, elements, and compounds on paper, a useful international chemical language has developed. The "letters" in this language are **chemical symbols.** Each element is assigned a chemical symbol of one or two letters. Only the first letter of the symbol is capitalized. For example, C is the symbol for the element carbon and Ca is the symbol for the element calcium. Symbols for some common elements are listed in Table 3.

The "words" or **chemical formulas** of this chemical language each represent a different chemical substance. In the chemical formula of any substance, symbols represent each element present.

Subscripts (numbers that are written below the normal line of letters) indicate how many atoms of each element are in one molecule or unit of the substance. For example, as you no doubt already know, the chemical formula for water is H_2O. The subscript 2 indicates that each water molecule contains two hydrogen atoms. Each water molecule also contains one oxygen atom. However, chemists do not include the subscript 1 in chemical formulas.

"Sentences," in the special language of chemistry, are **chemical equations.** Each chemical equation summarizes the details of a particular chemical reaction. **Chemical reactions** involve the breaking and forming of chemical bonds, causing atoms to become rearranged into new substances. These new substances have different properties than the original material. Not only are their physical properties different, but the chemical reactions in which they participate are also different. In other words, the new substances formed in a chemical reaction have different **chemical properties** than those of the reactants. The chemical equation for the formation of water

$$2\,H_2 \quad + \quad O_2 \quad \rightarrow \quad 2\,H_2O$$
$$\text{Hydrogen} \quad \text{Oxygen} \quad \text{Water}$$
$$\underbrace{\phantom{\text{Hydrogen} \quad \text{Oxygen}}}_{\text{reactants}} \quad \underbrace{\phantom{\text{Water}}}_{\text{product}}$$

shows that two hydrogen molecules ($2\,H_2$) and one oxygen molecule (O_2) react to produce ($\rightarrow$) two molecules of water ($2\,H_2O$). The original substances in a chemical reaction are called the **reactants;** their formulas are always written on the left. The new substance or substances formed from the rearrangement of the reactant atoms are called **products;** their formulas are always written on the right. Note that this equation, like all chemical equations, is balanced—the total number of atoms (four H atoms and two O atoms) is the same for both reactants and products.

Table 3 COMMON ELEMENTS

Element Name	Symbol
Aluminum	Al
Bromine	Br
Calcium	Ca
Carbon	C
Chlorine	Cl
Cobalt	Co
Gold	Au
Hydrogen	H
Iodine	I
Iron	Fe
Lead	Pb
Magnesium	Mg
Mercury	Hg
Nickel	Ni
Nitrogen	N
Oxygen	O
Phosphorus	P
Potassium	K
Silver	Ag
Sodium	Na
Sulfur	S
Tin	Sn

Symbols, Formulas, and Equations

Let's look at the kind of information available from a simple chemical equation and the formulas included in it:

$$N_2 \quad + \quad 3\,H_2 \quad \rightarrow \quad 2\,NH_3$$
Nitrogen   Hydrogen   Ammonia

First, we can complete an "atom inventory" based on this chemical equation:

$$N_2 \quad + \quad 3\,H_2 \quad \rightarrow \quad 2\,NH_3$$
2 N atoms + 6 H atoms = 2 N atoms and 6 H atoms

Note that the total atoms of N (the element nitrogen) and H (the element hydrogen) remain unchanged during this chemical reaction.

We can also interpret the equation in terms of molecules: One molecule of N_2 reacts with three molecules of H_2 to produce two molecules of the compound NH_3, called ammonia. We also note that molecules of nitrogen (N_2) and hydrogen (H_2) are each made up of two atoms, while ammonia molecules are each composed of four atoms—one nitrogen atom and three hydrogen atoms.

1. Name the element represented by each symbol:

   a. P   c. N   e. Br   g. Na

   b. Ni   d. Co   f. K   h. Fe

2. For each formula, name the elements present and give the number of atoms of each element shown in the formula.

   a. H_2O_2 Hydrogen peroxide (antiseptic)

   b. $CaCl_2$ Calcium chloride (de-icing salt for roads)

   c. $NaHCO_3$ Sodium hydrogen carbonate (baking soda)

   d. H_2SO_4 Sulfuric acid (battery acid)

3. The following chemical equation shows the formation of the air pollutant nitric oxide, NO:

   $$N_2 + O_2 \rightarrow 2\,NO$$

   a. Interpret this equation in terms of molecules.

   b. Complete an atom inventory for this equation.

Household ammonia is made by dissolving ammonia (a gas) in water.

We must consider another question before we return to our discussion of "foul water" and the problems in Riverwood: Why is the water molecule in Figure 16 (page 30) shown in that particular shape, rather than in some other shape? That is, does the arrangement of atoms in a molecule (called **molecular structure**) affect the substance's observed properties?

B.6 THE ELECTRICAL NATURE OF MATTER

You have already had direct experience with matter's electrical nature, most probably without realizing it. Clothes often display "static cling" when they exit the dryer. Pieces of apparel stick firmly together, and can be separated only with effort. The shock you sometimes receive after walking across a rug and touching a metal doorknob is another reminder of matter's electrical nature. If two inflated balloons are rubbed against your hair, both will attract your hair, but will repel each other. (This experiment is best conducted in air with low humidity.)

The electrical properties of matter can be summarized as follows:

Like charges repel. ←(+) (+)→ **or** ←(−) (−)→

Unlike charges attract. (+)→ ←(−)

What are these positive and negative charges? How do they relate to the idea of atoms and molecules? For now, you need to know only a few key points:

- Neutral (uncharged) atoms contain equal numbers of positively charged particles (called **protons**) and negatively charged particles (called **electrons**). In addition, most atoms contain one or more neutral particles (called **neutrons**).

- Positive-negative attractions between the protons of one atom and the electrons of another atom provide the "glue" that holds different atoms together. This "glue" helps explain **chemical bonding.**

A variety of observations suggest that a hydrogen atom can bond to only one other atom at a time. By contrast, an oxygen atom can form two bonds, and thus be joined to two hydrogen atoms. The result: H_2O!

Experiments suggest that water molecules are electrically **polar.** A polar molecule has an uneven distribution of electrical

Hydrogen molecule, H_2

Oxygen molecule, O_2

Water molecule, H_2O

Figure 16 Two representations of hydrogen, oxygen, and water molecules. Atoms in molecules are held together by chemical bonds, shown by the springs and sticks on the right.

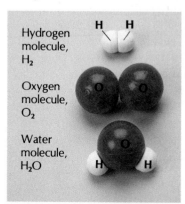

Hydrogen molecule, H_2

Oxygen molecule, O_2

Water molecule, H_2O

charge. This means that each molecule has a positive region on one end and a negative region on the other end. Evidence also suggests that the water molecule has a bent or V-shape (see Figures 16 and 17), rather than a linear, stick-like shape as in H—O—H. The "oxygen end" is an electrically-negative region (having a *greater* concentration of electrons, shown as δ⁻), compared to the two "hydrogen ends" which are electrically positive (shown as δ⁺). The entire water molecule is still electrically neutral, even though the electrons are not evenly distributed in its structure.

The combined effects of water's molecular shape and electrical polarity help explain many properties of water described earlier. For example, since unlike charges attract, the oppositely charged "ends" of neighboring water molecules attract each other, causing them to stick to one another. This gives water its high boiling point. (It takes a large quantity of thermal energy to separate the "sticky" liquid water molecules to form water vapor.)

Water's high surface tension and reduced density when it crystallizes as ice can also be explained by its molecular shape and electrical polarity. Polar water molecules are attracted to other polar substances and to substances composed of electrically charged particles. These attractions make it possible for water to dissolve a great variety of substances.

In certain substances, such as common table salt, the smallest particles are neither uncharged atoms nor molecules. Atoms can gain or lose electrons to form negatively or positively charged particles called **ions.** Compounds that are called **ionic compounds** or ionic substances are composed of ions. There are always enough positively and negatively charged ions so that the total positive charge equals the total negative charge.

In solid ionic compounds, such as table salt, the ions are held together in clusters by attraction between negative and positive charges. The resulting compound has no overall electric charge. When an ionic compound dissolves in water, individual ions become separated from each other and disperse in the water. The designation (aq) following the symbol for an ion, as in Na⁺(aq), means that the ion is present in water (aqueous) solution.

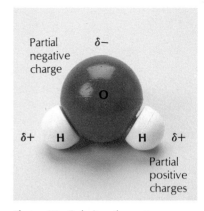

Figure 17 Polarity of a water molecule. The δ+ and δ− indicate partial charges. Because they balance, the molecule as a whole is neutral.

Na	*sodium atom*
Na⁺	*sodium ion*
Cl	*chlorine atom*
Cl⁻	*chloride ion*
Na⁺Cl⁻	*sodium chloride (table salt)*

B.7 PURE AND IMPURE WATER

We are now ready to return to the problem of Riverwood's fish kill. Recall that various Riverwood residents had different ideas about the cause of the problem. For example, longtime resident Harmon Lewis was sure the cause was pollution of the river water. Let's examine water pollution in greater detail.

Families in most U.S. cities and towns receive clean, but not pure, water at an extremely low cost. If you use municipal water, check your family's water bill to find the current cost per gallon. Divide that number by 3.8 (the number of liters in one gallon) to find your cost for one liter of water.

It's useless to insist on *pure* water. The cost of processing water to make it completely pure would be prohibitively high. Even if costs were not a problem it would still be impossible to have pure water. Atmospheric gases nitrogen (N_2), oxygen (O_2), and carbon dioxide (CO_2) will always dissolve in the water to some extent.

In fact, it's unnecessary and even undesirable to remove all substances from the water we use. Some dissolved gases and minerals give water a pleasing taste. Fish and other water-dwelling creatures depend on the oxygen gas dissolved in the water for survival. Some dissolved substances also promote human health. For example, adding a small amount of certain chlorine-containing compounds ensures that harmful bacteria are not present.

Unfortunately, not all substances that become suspended or dissolved in water are desirable there. High concentrations of substances containing iron (Fe) give water a bad taste and cause unwanted deposits in pipes and fixtures. Some compounds containing sulfur (S) give water a bad odor. Compounds containing elements such as mercury (Hg), lead (Pb), cadmium (Cd), and arsenic (As) can dissolve in water. Even at low concentrations all can be harmful to human health.

Manufactured substances such as pesticides, and commercial and industrial waste products, particularly solvents, can also find their way into drinking water, with harmful effects. Even sunlight can produce potentially harmful substances in chlorinated water containing certain types of contaminants.

Our real challenge is to ensure that our water supplies do not become polluted with unwanted substances. This is accomplished by preventing such substances from entering our water supplies and removing those already present.

B.8 LABORATORY ACTIVITY: WATER TESTING

Getting Ready

Chemists can detect and identify ions in water solution in several different ways. In this activity you will use some chemical tests to check for the presence of certain ions in aqueous solution. Positively charged ions have a deficiency of electrons and are called **cations;** negatively charged ions have an excess of electrons and are called **anions.** You will investigate two cations and two anions.

The tests you will perform are **confirming tests.** That is, if the test is positive it confirms that the ion in question is present. In each confirming test you will look for a change in solution color, or the appearance of an insoluble material called a **precipitate.** A negative test (no color or precipitate) doesn't necessarily mean the ion in question is not present. The ion may simply be present in such a small amount that the color or precipitate cannot be seen.

You will test for the presence of the cations iron(III), Fe^{3+}, and calcium, Ca^{2+}, as well as the anions chloride, Cl^-, and sulfate, SO_4^{2-}. (Notice that when the positive or negative charge of an ion is more than one, the amount of the charge is shown with the plus or minus sign for the ion.) You'll perform each confirming test on three different samples:

- a **reference solution** (known to contain the ion of interest)
- **tap water** (which may or may not contain the ion)
- a **control** (distilled water, known *not* to contain the ion).

There are two types of iron ions: Fe^{2+} is called iron(II); Fe^{3+} is called iron(III).

Data Table

Solutions	Color	Precipitate	Is Ion Present?
Fe^{3+} reference			
Tap water			
Control			
Ca^{2+} reference			
Tap water			
Control			
Cl^- reference			
Tap water			
Control			
SO_4^{2-} reference			
Tap water			
Control			

Prepare a data table similar to the one shown above in your laboratory notebook.

Here are some suggestions to guide your ion analysis:

1. If the ion is in tap water, it will probably be present in a lower amount than in the same volume of reference solution. Thus the color or quantity of precipitate produced in the tap water sample will be less than in the reference solution.

2. When completing an ion test, mix the test tube contents thoroughly, unless the instructions give other directions. Follow the mixing procedure illustrated in Figure 18.

3. In a confirming test based on color change, so few color-producing ions may be present that you remain doubtful the reaction actually occurred. Here are several ways to decide whether the expected color is actually present:

   • Look through the side of the tube (Figure 19). Placing a sheet of white paper behind or below the test tube may make any color more visible (Figure 20).

   • Compare the color of the control (distilled water) test to that of tap water. Distilled water doesn't contain any of the ions

Figure 18 Tapping a forefinger against a test tube mixes its contents.

Figure 19 Look through the side of the test tube to check for color.

Figure 20 Hold the test tube over white paper to check for color.

tested. Thus even a faint color in the tap water confirms that the ion is present.

4. In a confirming test involving a precipitate, you may remain uncertain whether a precipitate is present even after thoroughly mixing the solutions. In this case shine a light beam through the tube to see whether the beam's path can be clearly seen in the liquid (the Tyndall effect test; see page 25). Such light scattering confirms the presence of a precipitate in the form of colloidal particles.

Procedure

1. Wash three test tubes thoroughly with tap water and rinse with distilled water.

2. Measure 2 mL of tap water in a graduated cylinder; pour the water into one test tube. Use a grease pencil to mark the 2-mL level on the outside of the tube. Mark the other two tubes with a line at the same level. Label the three test tubes Reference (R), Tap Water (TW), and Control (C).

3. Complete each of the following four tests on the respective reference solution provided by your teacher, on tap water, and on a control sample of distilled water.

Iron(III) Ion Test (Fe³⁺)

1. Pour 2 mL of iron(III) reference solution into the clean Reference test tube.

2. Add three drops of potassium thiocyanate (KSCN) solution.

3. Mix the test tube contents thoroughly. Record your observations. The confirming test you observed for Fe^{3+} can be represented as follows:

Only ions that take part in the reaction are included in this type of chemical equation.

Iron(III) ion (reference solution)		Thiocyanate ion (test solution)		Iron(III) thiocyanate ion (red color)
$Fe^{3+}(aq)$	$+$	$SCN^-(aq)$	$\rightarrow$	$Fe(SCN)^{2+}(aq)$

4. Repeat the iron(III) ion test on a 2-mL sample of tap water and on a 2-mL sample of distilled water, placing each sample in its properly labeled test tube. Record your observations and conclusions.

5. Discard the test tube contents as instructed by your teacher. Wash the tubes thoroughly with tap water and rinse with distilled water before continuing with the next test.

Calcium Ion Test (Ca²⁺)

1. Pour 2 mL of calcium ion reference solution into the clean Reference test tube.

2. Add three drops of dilute acetic acid ($HC_2H_3O_2$).

3. Add three drops of sodium oxalate ($Na_2C_2O_4$) solution to the tube.

4. Mix the test tube contents thoroughly. Record your observations. The confirming test you observed for Ca^{2+} can be represented as follows:

Calcium ion (reference solution)		Oxalate ion (test solution)		Calcium oxalate (precipitate)
$Ca^{2+}(aq)$	$+$	$C_2O_4^{2-}(aq)$	$\rightarrow$	$CaC_2O_4(s)$

5. Repeat the calcium ion test on a 2-mL sample of tap water and on a 2-mL sample of distilled water, placing each sample

in its properly labeled test tube. Record your observations and conclusions.

6. Discard the test tube contents as instructed by your teacher. Wash the tubes thoroughly with tap water and rinse with distilled water before continuing with the next test.

Chloride Ion Test (Cl⁻)

1. Pour 2 mL of chloride ion reference solution into the clean Reference test tube.
2. Add three drops of silver nitrate ($AgNO_3$) test solution. Avoid contact with skin.
3. Mix the test tube contents thoroughly. Record your observations. The confirming test you observed for Cl^- can be represented as follows:

Silver ion		Chloride ion		Silver chloride
(test solution)		(reference solution)		(precipitate)
$Ag^+(aq)$	$+$	$Cl^-(aq)$	$\rightarrow$	$AgCl(s)$

4. Repeat the chloride ion test on a 2-mL sample of tap water and on a 2-mL sample of distilled water, placing each sample in its properly labeled test tube. Record your observations and conclusions.
5. Discard the test tube contents as instructed by your teacher. Wash the tubes thoroughly with tap water and rinse with distilled water before continuing with the next test.

Sulfate Ion Test (SO₄²⁻)

1. Pour 2 mL of sulfate ion reference solution into the clean Reference test tube.
2. Add three drops of barium chloride ($BaCl_2$) test solution.
3. Mix the test tube contents thoroughly. Record your observations. The confirming test you observed for SO_4^{2-} can be represented as follows:

Barium ion		Sulfate ion		Barium sulfate
(test solution)		(reference solution)		(precipitate)
$Ba^{2+}(aq)$	$+$	$SO_4^{2-}(aq)$	$\rightarrow$	$BaSO_4(s)$

4. Repeat the sulfate ion test on a 2-mL sample of tap water and on a 2-mL sample of distilled water, placing each in its properly labeled test tube. Record your observations and conclusions.
5. Discard the test tube contents as instructed by your teacher. Wash the tubes thoroughly with tap water and rinse with distilled water.
6. Wash your hands thoroughly before leaving the laboratory.

Questions

1. a. Why was a control used in each test?
   b. Why was distilled water chosen as the control?
2. Describe some difficulties associated with the use of qualitative tests.
3. These tests cannot absolutely confirm the absence of an ion. Why?
4. How might your observations have changed if you hadn't cleaned your test tubes thoroughly between each test?

B.9 YOU DECIDE: THE RIVERWOOD MYSTERY

Your teacher will divide the class into groups composed of four or five students. Each group will complete this decision-making activity. When all groups have finished, the entire class will compare and discuss the answers obtained by each group.

At the beginning of this unit, you read newspaper articles describing the Riverwood fish kill and several citizens' reactions to it. Among those interviewed were Harmon Lewis, a longtime resident of Riverwood, and Dr. Margaret Brooke, a water-systems scientist. These two individuals had very different reactions to the fish kill. Harmon Lewis was angry, certain that human activity had caused the fish kill—probably some sort of pollution. Dr. Brooke refused even to speculate about the cause of the fish kill until she had run some tests. Which position comes closer to your own reaction?

Let's investigate this issue further.

1. Reread the fish kill newspaper reports located at the beginning of Parts A and B. List all *facts* (not opinions) concerning the fish kill found in these articles. Scientists often refer to facts as **data.** Data are objective pieces of information. They do not include interpretation.

2. List at least five factual questions you would want answered before you could decide on possible causes of the fish kill. Some typical questions: Do barges or commercial boats travel on the Snake River? Were any shipping accidents on the river reported recently?

3. Look over your two lists—one of facts and the other of questions.

   a. At this point, can you rule out any possible fish-kill causes as unlikely?

b. Can you suggest any probable cause? Be as specific as possible.

Later in this unit you will have an opportunity to test the reasoning you used in answering these questions.

B.10 WHAT ARE THE POSSIBILITIES?

The activities you just completed (gathering data, seeking patterns or regularities among the data, suggesting possible reasons to account for the data) are typical of scientists' approaches in attempting to solve problems. Such scientific methods are a combination of systematic, step-by-step procedures and logic, as well as occasional hunches and guesses.

A fundamental and difficult part of scientists' work is knowing what questions to ask. You have listed some questions that might be asked concerning the cause of the fish kill. Such questions help focus a scientist's thinking. Often a large problem can be reduced to several smaller problems or questions, each of which is more easily managed and solved.

The number of possible causes for the fish kill is large. Scientists investigating this problem must find ways to eliminate some causes and zero in on more promising ones. They either try to disprove all but one cause or to produce conclusive proof in support of a specific cause.

Water-systems analyst Brooke reported that suspended materials had already been eliminated as possible causes of the fish kill. She concluded that if the actual cause were water-related, it must be due to something dissolved in the water.

In the next part of this unit we will examine several major categories of water-soluble substances and consider how they might be involved in the fish kill. The mystery of the Riverwood fish kill will be confronted at last!

PART B: SUMMARY QUESTIONS

1. a. List three unusual properties of water. Indicate to which state(s) of water—solid, liquid, or gas—each property applies.
   b. Briefly describe the importance of each property to life on this planet.
2. When gasoline and water are mixed, they form two distinct layers. Which liquid—gasoline or water—will be found in the top layer? (*Hint:* Refer to Table 2, page 22.)
3. Decide which material in each pair has the higher density:
   a. Ice or liquid water
   b. Lead or aluminum
   c. Silver chloride (AgCl) precipitate or liquid water (*Hint:* Check your Chloride Ion Test observations in the *Water Testing* activity.)
   d. Hot air or cold air

4. Identify each of the following as either a solution, suspension, or colloid.
   a. A medicine that says "shake before using"
   b. Rubbing alcohol
   c. Italian salad dressing
   d. Mayonnaise
   e. A cola soft drink
   f. An oil-based paint
   g. Milk
5. Using what you know about chemical notation, which of the following is an element, and which is a compound?
   a. CO   b. Co
6. a. Is 100% pure, chemical-free water possible?
   b. What do we actually want when we ask for "pure" water?

7. Name the elements in each substance. List the number of atoms of each element shown in the substance's formula.

   a. Phosphoric acid, H_3PO_4 (used in some soft drinks and to produce some types of fertilizer)

   b. Sodium hydroxide, NaOH (found in some drain cleaners)

   c. Sulfur dioxide, SO_2 (a by-product of burning some types of coal)

8. The following chemical equation represents the burning of methane, CH_4.

$$CH_4 + 2\ O_2 \rightarrow CO_2 + 2\ H_2O$$

   a. Interpret this equation in terms of molecules.

   b. Complete an atom inventory.

EXTENDING YOUR KNOWLEDGE (OPTIONAL)

• The Celsius temperature scale is used in scientific work worldwide, and is used in normal activities by most of the world's citizens. However, Fahrenheit temperatures are still used in weather reports in the United States. From the normal freezing and boiling points of water expressed in these two scales, try to develop an equation that converts a Celsius temperature to its Fahrenheit equivalent. (*Hint:* To start, recall that there are 180 Fahrenheit degrees but only 100 Celsius degrees between the freezing point and boiling point of water.)

• The density of petroleum-based oil is approximately 0.9 g/mL. By contrast, the density of water is 1.0 g/mL. What implications does this density difference have for an "oil spill" in a body of water? Consider the implications for aquatic life, oil spill cleanup operations, and the possibility of an oil fire.

• Some elements in Table 3 (page 28) have symbols that are not based on their modern names (such as K for potassium). Look up their historic names and explain the origin of their symbols.

This land in Nevada is desert except in the irrigated area.

C INVESTIGATING THE CAUSE OF THE FISH KILL

The immediate challenge facing investigators of the Riverwood fish kill is to decide whether some dissolved substance was responsible for the crisis.

C.1 SOLUBILITY

Solubility of Solids

How much of a substance will dissolve in a given amount of water? Imagine preparing a water solution of potassium nitrate, KNO_3. You pour water into a beaker and then add a scoopful of solid, white potassium nitrate crystals. As you stir the water, the solid crystals disappear. The liquid remains colorless and clear. In the resulting solution, water is the solvent, and potassium nitrate is the solute.

You add a second scoopful of potassium nitrate crystals to the beaker and stir. These crystals also dissolve. But as you continue adding more solid, eventually some potassium nitrate crystals remain on the bottom of the beaker, no matter how long you stir. There is a maximum quantity of potassium nitrate that will dissolve in a beaker of water at room temperature.

The **solubility** of a substance in water refers to the maximum quantity of the substance, expressed in grams, for example, that will dissolve in a certain quantity of water (e.g. 100 g) at a specified temperature. The solubility of potassium nitrate, for example, might be expressed in units of "grams per 100 g water" at a certain temperature.

The term "soluble" is actually a relative term, since everything is soluble in water to some extent. The term "insoluble," therefore, really refers to substances that are only very, very slightly soluble in water. Chalk, for example, is insoluble in water.

The size of the solute crystals and the vigor and duration of stirring help determine the time needed for a solute to dissolve at a given temperature. However, these factors do not affect *how much* substance will eventually dissolve.

When a solvent holds as much of a solute as it normally can at a given temperature, we say the solution is **saturated.** Any lesser amount of dissolved solute at that temperature produces an **unsaturated** solution.

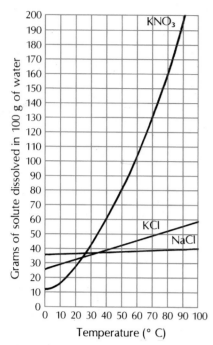

Figure 21 Relationship between solubility in water and temperature.

Figure 21 shows the maximum mass (in grams) of three ionic compounds that will dissolve in 100 g of water at temperatures from 0° C to 100° C. The plotted line for each solute is called a **solubility curve.**

Let's look first at the curve for potassium nitrate (KNO_3) in Figure 21. The graph indicates that, at 80° C, 160 g of potassium nitrate will dissolve in 100 g of water, forming a saturated solution. Thus the *solubility* of potassium nitrate in 80° C water is 160 g per 100 g water. By contrast, potassium nitrate's solubility in 20° C water is about 30 g per 100 g water. (Check your ability to "read" this value on the graph.)

Note that the solubility curve for sodium chloride (NaCl) is nearly a horizontal line. This means that the solubility of sodium chloride is affected very little by changes in water temperature. In contrast, the curve for potassium nitrate (KNO_3) rises steeply as temperature increases, showing that its solubility in water is greatly influenced by water temperature.

Each point on a solubility curve represents a saturated solution. For example, the graph shows that about 39 g of sodium chloride dissolved in 100 g of water at 100° C produces a saturated solution.

Any point on a graph *below* a solubility curve represents an unsaturated solution. For example, a solution containing 80 g of potassium nitrate and 100 g of water at 60° C is an unsaturated solution. (Locate this point on the graph; note that it falls below the potassium nitrate solubility curve.)

If you could cool this solution to 40° C (moving to the left on the graph) without forming any solid crystals, you would have a **supersaturated** solution of potassium nitrate at this lower temperature. (Note that this new point lies *above* the solubility curve for potassium nitrate.) A supersaturated solution contains more dissolved solute than a saturated solution. Any jarring, however, would cause 18 g of solid potassium nitrate crystals to appear and settle to the bottom of the beaker. The remaining liquid would then contain 62 g (80 g − 18 g) of solute per 100 g water—a stable, saturated solution at 40° C. Table 4 gives the quantities of potassium nitrate in saturated, unsaturated, and supersaturated solutions at 20° C.

Table 4 SOLUTIONS OF KNO_3

Solution Description	Quantity of Solute/Solvent
Unsaturated KNO_3 solution (at 20° C)	Less than 30 g/100 g water
Saturated KNO_3 solution (at 20° C)	30 g/100 g water
Supersaturated KNO_3 solution (at 20° C)	More than 30 g/100 g water

Solubility of Gases

We have seen that the solubility of a solid in water often decreases when the water temperature is lowered. The solubility behavior of gases in water is quite different. As water temperature decreases, a gas becomes *more* soluble! Because of its importance to aquatic life, let's see what happens to the solubility of oxygen gas when water temperature changes.

Figure 22 shows the solubility curve for oxygen gas, plotted as milligrams of oxygen dissolved per 1000 g of water. Note that the solubility of oxygen at 0° C is about twice its solubility at 30° C. The values for oxygen solubility are much smaller than the values shown in Figure 21 for solid solutes. For example, at 20° C, about 37 g of sodium chloride will dissolve in 100 g of water. By contrast, about 9 mg (0.009 g) of oxygen gas will dissolve in *ten* times more water—1000 g of water—at this temperature. It's clear that gases are *far* less soluble in water than many ionic solids are.

The solubility of a gas depends not only on water temperature, but also on gas pressure. Gas solubility is directly proportional to the pressure of the gas on the liquid. That is, if the pressure of the gas were doubled, the amount of gas that dissolves would also double. You see one effect of this every time you open a can or bottle of carbonated soft drink. Dissolved carbon dioxide gas (CO_2) escapes from the liquid in a rush of bubbles. Carbon dioxide gas was originally forced into the container at high pressure just before it was sealed, to increase the amount of carbon dioxide dissolved in the beverage. When the can is opened, gas pressure on the liquid drops back to atmospheric pressure. Dissolved carbon dioxide gas escapes from the liquid until it reaches its lower solubility at this lower pressure. (When the fizzing stops, an individual might remark that the beverage has "gone flat." Actually, the excess carbon dioxide gas has simply escaped into the air; the resulting solution is merely saturated.

The following exercise will help you become more familiar with the information found in the solubility graphs in Figures 21 and 22. Refer to the appropriate graph to answer each question.

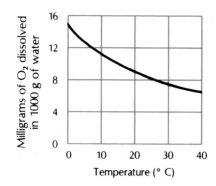

Figure 22 Solubility curve for O_2 gas in water in contact with air.

Be sure to note differences in axis labels when you compare graphs.

YOUR TURN

Solubility and Solubility Curves

What is the solubility of potassium nitrate at 80° C? The answer is found by locating, in Figure 21, the intersection of the potassium nitrate curve with the vertical line representing 80° C. The solubility is found by following the horizontal line to the left. Thus, the solubility of potassium nitrate in water at 80° C is 160 g per 100 g of water.

At what temperature will the solubility of dissolved oxygen be 10 mg per 1000 g of water? See Figure 22. Think of the space between 8 and 12 mg/1000 mg on the axis in Figure 18 as divided into two equal parts; follow an imaginary horizontal line at "10 mg/1000 g" to its intersection with the curve. Follow a vertical line down to the *x* axis. As the line falls half-way between 10° C and 20° C, the desired temperature must be about 15° C.

It's possible to calculate the solubility of a substance in various amounts of water. The solubility curve indicated that 160 g of potassium nitrate will dissolve in 100 g of water at 80° C. How much potassium nitrate will dissolve in 200 g of water at this temperature? We can "reason" the answer as follows: The amount of solvent (water) has doubled from 100 g to 200 g. That means that twice as much solute can be dissolved. Thus: 2×160 g $= 320$ g KNO_3. Done! The calculation can also be written out as a simple proportion, giving the same answer:

$$\left(\frac{160 \text{ g } KNO_3}{100 \text{ g } H_2O}\right) = \left(\frac{x \text{ g } KNO_3}{200 \text{ g } H_2O}\right)$$

$$x = \left(\frac{160 \text{ g } KNO_3}{100 \text{ g } H_2O}\right) \times (200 \text{ g } H_2O) = 320 \text{ g } KNO_3$$

1. Refer to Figure 21 in answering these:
   a. What mass (in grams) of potassium nitrate (KNO_3) will dissolve in 100 g of water at 50° C?
   b. What mass of potassium chloride (KCl) will dissolve in 100 g of water at this temperature?

2. Refer to Figure 21 in answering these:
   a. We dissolve 25 g of potassium nitrate in 100 g of water at 30° C, thus producing an unsaturated solution. How much *more* potassium nitrate (in grams) must be added to form a saturated solution at 30° C?
   b. What is the minimum mass (in grams) of 30° C water needed to dissolve 25 g of potassium nitrate?

3. Refer to Figure 22 in answering these: What mass of oxygen gas can be dissolved in 1000 g of water
   a. at 30° C?   b. at 20°C?

4. What mass of oxygen gas can be dissolved in 100 g of water at 20° C?

C.2 SOLUTION CONCENTRATION

Some substances dissolved at very low concentrations in water may pose no problems to our using water, and may even be beneficial. However, these same substances dissolved in larger quantities may be harmful. For example, the level of chlorination in a swimming pool and the amount of fluoridation in a municipal water system must be carefully measured and controlled. For these applications and countless others, we need to specify exact, numerical concentrations of solutions.

Solution concentration refers to the quantity of solute dissolved in a specific quantity of solvent or solution. You have already worked with one type of concentration expression. The water solubility graphs reported solution concentrations as a mass of a substance dissolved in a given mass of water.

Another way to express concentration is with percentages. For example, dissolving 5 g of table salt in 95 g of water produces 100 g of solution, or a 5% salt solution (by mass).

$$\left(\frac{5 \text{ g salt}}{100 \text{ g solution}}\right) \times 100\% = 5\%$$

"Percent" means parts per hundred parts. Thus a 5% salt solution *could* also be reported as five parts per hundred of salt

(5 pph salt), even though percent is much more commonly used.

To prepare 10 times as much salt solution of the same concentration, you would need to dissolve 10 times more salt (50 g) in 10 times more water (950 g) to make 1000 g of solution.

$$\left(\frac{50 \text{ g salt}}{1000 \text{ g solution}}\right) \times 100\% = 5\%$$

This solution can be described as containing 50 parts per thousand of salt (50 ppt salt), or, since it has the same concentration as the original solution, as 5% (5 pph) salt.

For solutions involving much smaller quantities of solute (such as dissolved gases in water), concentration units of parts per million, ppm, are useful. What's the concentration of the 5% salt solution expressed in ppm? Since 5% of 1 million is 50,000, a 5% salt solution is 50,000 parts per million.

The notion of concentration is part of our daily lives. Interpreting recipes, adding antifreeze to an automobile, or mixing a cleaning solution all require using solution concentrations. The following exercises will help you review solution concentration terminology and ideas. You will also gain experience with the chemist's view of this concept.

$$\frac{5}{100} = \frac{50}{1000} = \frac{50,000}{1,000,000}$$

$5\% \ (5pph) = 50 \ ppt =$
$50,000 \ ppm$

YOUR TURN

Describing Solution Concentrations

Solution concentrations can be used in calculations, just as we used solubilities in *Your Turn: Solubility and Solubility Curves*. For example, 25 g of fertilizer is dissolved in 75 g of water. What is the concentration of this solution, expressed as grams of fertilizer per 100 g of solution? The arithmetic is as follows:

$$\frac{25 \text{ g fertilizer}}{25 \text{ g fertilizer} + 75 \text{ g water}} = \frac{25 \text{ g fertilizer}}{100 \text{ g solution}}$$
$$\text{or 25 pph fertilizer}$$

The concentration of this solution can be expressed as 25 g of fertilizer/100 g of solution. The concentration of this solution in mass percent is found as follows, using the total mass of the solution, which is 100 g (25 g of fertilizer + 75 g of water):

$$\left(\frac{25 \text{ g fertilizer}}{100 \text{ g solution}}\right) \times 100\% = 25\%$$

The solution is 25% by mass—or it could be expressed as 25 pph, 250 ppt, or 250,000 ppm.

Consider this second example: One teaspoon of sucrose, which has a mass of 10 g, is dissolved in 240 g of water.

    a. What is the concentration of the solution, expressed as grams of sucrose per 100 g of solution (percent sucrose by mass, or pph)?

    b. What is the concentration in ppt?

These two questions can be answered as follows:

    a. Since we have 10 g of sucrose and 240 g of water, the solution has a total mass of 250 g.

$$\left(\frac{10 \text{ g sucrose}}{250 \text{ g solution}}\right) \times 100\% = 4\% \text{ sucrose by mass}$$
(4 pph sucrose)

b. Since 4/100 = 40/1000, this solution has a concentration of 40 parts per thousand (ppt) sucrose. Or, reasoning another way, 4% of 1000 (0.04 x 1000) is 40—so the concentration is 40 ppt.

1. One level teaspoon of table sugar (sucrose) is dissolved in a cup of water. Identify
   a. the solute.
   b. the solvent.
2. What is the percent concentration sucrose (or pph sucrose) in each solution?
   a. 17 g sucrose is dissolved in 183 g water.
   b. 34 g sucrose is dissolved in 366 g water.
3. What does the term "saturated solution" mean?
4. A water sample at 25° C contains 8.4 ppm dissolved oxygen. The water is heated in an open pan to a higher temperature.
   a. Would the dissolved oxygen concentration in the warmer water be greater or less than that in the original water?
   b. Why? (*Hint:* Refer to Figure 22.)

C.3 OXYGEN SUPPLY AND DEMAND

All animals need oxygen gas (O_2) to survive. Although an oxygen atom is present in every water molecule (the O in H_2O), animals cannot extract this oxygen—the atoms are strongly bonded to hydrogen atoms. Aquatic organisms such as fish, frogs, insect larvae, and bacteria must have a continuous supply of oxygen gas *dissolved* in the water they inhabit.

Was a shortage of dissolved oxygen gas in the Snake River responsible for the Riverwood fish kill? To explore this possibility, we must consider several factors. How much oxygen gas

"Frothy" water is a mixture of air and water. This is one way that oxygen gas becomes dissolved in water.

Dissolved oxygen in water is not accessible to humans.

(or other substances) will dissolve in water? How does water temperature affect the amount of dissolved oxygen? How much oxygen do various aquatic creatures actually consume?

Some oxygen used by fish and other creatures living in water comes from oxygen gas that dissolves directly from the air above the calm water surface.

Additional oxygen gas mixes into the water by **aeration,** which occurs when water plunges over a dam, flows across boulders in a stream, or breaks as waves on a beach, forming water-air "froth." Oxygen gas is also added to natural waters through **photosynthesis,** the process by which green plants and ocean plankton make sugars from carbon dioxide and water in the presence of sunlight. During daylight hours, aquatic green plants constantly produce the sugar glucose. Oxygen gas, also a product of photosynthesis, is released from aquatic green plants to the surrounding water. The overall chemical equation for the formation of glucose ($C_6H_{12}O_6$) and oxygen gas through photosynthesis is

Energy (from sunlight) $+\ 6\ CO_2\ +\ 6\ H_2O \rightarrow C_6H_{12}O_6\ +\ 6\ O_2$

The organisms living in a water environment continuously compete for the available oxygen. Oxygen-consuming bacteria

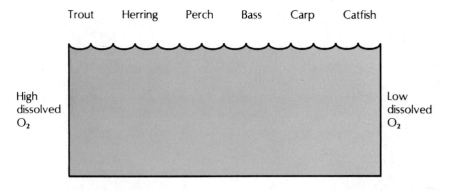

Figure 23 Dissolved oxygen required for various species of fish.

Trout   Herring   Perch   Bass   Carp   Catfish

High dissolved O₂

Low dissolved O₂

(***aerobic bacteria***) feed on solid wastes of larger animals and on their remains after they die.

Aerobic bacteria also feed on certain industry-produced substances found in the water. Such ***biodegradable*** substances are broken down to simpler substances by these aerobic bacteria.

If the water contains large quantities of biodegradable materials, bacteria thrive and multiply. The resulting bacterial "population explosion" places greater demands on the available dissolved oxygen. Aquatic creatures needing the largest amounts of dissolved oxygen are at greatest risk if the bacterial population gets too large. Their survival is then in question.

The minimum concentration of dissolved oxygen (abbreviated ***DO***) needed to support aquatic life depends on the type of animal being considered. Fish cannot live in water with a dissolved oxygen level less than 0.004 grams per 1000 g of solution. This concentration equals 0.004 parts per thousand (ppt), but is more conveniently expressed as four parts per million, 4 ppm (0.004/1000 = 4/1,000,000).

A concentration as small as four parts per million is difficult to visualize, but we'll try. Assume that a water sample is represented by a million pennies, stacked one on top of another. This stack would rise 1.6 kilometers (one mile) high! Just four pennies in this stack would represent the minimum level of dissolved oxygen needed for fish to survive. It's a very small, but absolutely essential quantity!

If water's dissolved oxygen concentration decreases, species of fish requiring more oxygen will migrate to other water regions or die. Unfortunately, such species include desirable sport fish, such as pike and trout. Figure 23 summarizes the relative dissolved oxygen requirements of several fish species.

When studying systems in nature, we must consider many factors. This is particularly true in exploring possible reasons for a community problem such as the fish kill in Riverwood. We've considered several factors that would influence the dissolved oxygen concentration. Can you think of any others?

C.4 TEMPERATURE AND GAS SOLUBILITY

In Section C.1 we noted that water temperature helps determine the maximum amount of oxygen gas that water can dissolve. This dissolved oxygen concentration, in turn, helps determine water's ability to support oxygen-consuming creatures. Water temperature also affects the amount of oxygen actually needed by aquatic organisms.

A biodegradable material can be broken down by organisms in the environment.

Fish are "cold-blooded" animals. That is, their body temperatures rise and fall with the surrounding water temperature. Body temperature affects the fish's metabolism—the complex series of interrelated chemical reactions that keep the fish alive. A 10° C temperature rise roughly doubles the rates or speeds of many chemical reactions. Cooling a system by 10° C slows down the rates of such reactions by a similar factor. (Thus, for example, food spoilage—involving complex chemical reactions—is significantly slowed down when foods are stored in a refrigerator rather than left at room temperature.)

If water temperature increases, fish body temperatures will also increase. Chemical reactions inside the fish then speed up; they become more active. Fish eat more and swim faster. As a result, they use up more dissolved oxygen. Bodily processes of aerobic bacteria also speed up in warmer water, thus increasing their oxygen consumption.

During warm summer months, competition among water inhabitants for dissolved oxygen can become quite severe. With rising temperatures, bacteria and fish require more oxygen. But warmer water is unable to dissolve as much oxygen gas. After a long stretch of hot summer days, some streams experience large fish kills, in which hundreds of fish suffocate. Table 5 summarizes the maximum water temperatures at which selected fish species can survive.

High lake or river water temperatures can sometimes be traced to human activity. Many industries depend on natural water bodies to cool heat-producing processes. Cool water is drawn into the plant. Devices called heat exchangers transfer thermal energy (heat energy) from the processing area to the cooling water. The heated water is then released back into lakes or streams—either directly, or after the water has partially cooled. Industrialists and environmentalists share the concern that released cooling water not upset the balance of life in rivers and lakes.

Did thermal pollution lower the Snake River's dissolved oxygen level, thus leading to the fish kill? Let's examine dissolved oxygen data obtained prior to the Riverwood fish kill.

Table 5	SURVIVAL	
	Maximum Temperature	
Fish	°C	°F
Trout	15	59
Perch and pike	24	75
Carp	32	90
Catfish	34	93

C.5 YOU DECIDE: TOO MUCH, TOO LITTLE?

Your teacher will divide the class into groups of four or five students each. All groups will read the following passage and use the information supplied to complete the exercises. After groups have finished their work, the class will compare their conclusions.

Joseph Fisker of the County Sanitation Commission has measured dissolved oxygen levels in the Snake River for 18 months. These data help the Sanitation Commission monitor the river's water quality. Fisker takes daily measurements at 9 A.M. under the bridge near Riverwood Hospital, at a water depth of one-half meter.

In addition, Fisker records the water temperature and consults a table to find the DO that would produce a saturated water solution at that temperature.

Let's examine Snake River data for last year and also for this summer (Tables 6 and 7).

Graphing Hints

A graph of experimental data often highlights regularities or patterns among the values. Here are some suggestions on preparing and interpreting such graphs.

- Choose your scale so the graph becomes large enough to fill most of the available graph paper space.
- Each regularly-spaced division on the graph paper should equal some convenient, constant value. In general, each interval between graph paper lines should have a value easily "divided by eye," such as 1, 2, 5, or 10, rather than a value such as 6, 7, 9, or 14.
- An axis scale does *not* need to start at "zero", particularly if the plotted values cluster in a narrow range not near zero. For example, if all values to be plotted on the *x* axis are between 0.50 and 0.60, the *x*-axis scale can be drawn as shown in Figure 24.
- Label each axis with the quantity and unit being graphed. For example, a scale might be labeled "Temperature (°C)." Plot each point. Then draw a small circle around each point, like this: ⊙ If you plot more than one curve on the same graph, distinguish each set of points by using a different color or geometric shape, such as △, ▽ , or ☐.
- After you have plotted all the points, draw the best possible "smooth line" (a line passing through as many points as possible). Give your graph a suitable title.

1. Prepare a graph of the Snake River's monthly dissolved oxygen levels during last year (Table 6). Label the *y* axis as dissolved oxygen level in ppm, and the *x* axis as water temperature in °C. How is the dissolved oxygen level related to the water temperature?

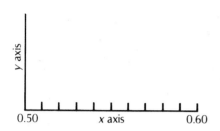

Figure 24 A possible *x*-axis scale (see text).

Table 6   **LAST YEAR'S DOs**

Month	Average Water Temperature (°C)	Average Dissolved Oxygen (ppm)
January	2	12.7
February	3	12.5
March	7	11.0
April	8	10.6
May	9	10.4
June	11	9.8
July	19	9.2
August	20	9.2
September	19	9.2
October	11	10.6
November	7	11.0
December	7	11.0

Table 7   **THIS SUMMER'S DOs**

Month	Average Water Temperature (°C)	Average Dissolved Oxygen (ppm)
June	14	10.2
July	16	9.6
August	18	9.6

2. On the same graph, plot the dissolved oxygen levels and river temperatures collected during this year's summer months (Table 7). Use a different plotting symbol for this set of points.

3. a. Compare the dissolved oxygen concentrations measured in December and June. How do you explain this difference?

   b. How do you account for the similar concentrations in March and November?

4. Compare the average dissolved oxygen concentration in August of this year with that of August last year. What reasons might explain the difference?

Questions

In September, soon after the Riverwood fish kill, the County Sanitation Commission invited the Environmental Protection Agency to help with the river water analysis. The EPA sent Marilyn Crocker to measure dissolved oxygen in the Snake River hourly for one day. The goal was to detect any short-term changes in either the temperature or the dissolved oxygen concentration. Crocker decided to measure dissolved oxygen at the same location used by Fisker. Her data are listed in Table 8 and graphed in Figures 25 and 26 (page 50).

1. a. Compare the two graphs. Is any pattern apparent in either graph?

   b. Can you explain any pattern that you detect?

   c. Compare the DO levels during daylight and nighttime hours. How do you account for this difference?

2. Calculate the average water temperature and the average concentration of DO for this one-day period.

3. No daily water temperatures or DO levels were reported during September this year. Thus the only possible comparison is between the average for one day in September this year and the monthly average for all of September last year. Is this a valid comparison? Why or why not?

4. Now consider the one-day Snake River measurements. Which do you think provides more useful information—the average temperature and DO values, or the maximum and minimum values? Give reasons to support your answer.

5. The DO concentrations needed for saturated water solutions at various temperatures are provided in Table 9. Use this table to decide whether the DO is below, at, or above the saturation level for each measurement in Table 8. You'll also need the following formula:

$$\text{Percent of saturation} = \left(\frac{\text{ppm DO measured}}{\text{ppm DO for saturation}}\right) \times 100\%$$

For example, at 8 A.M. during the one-day measurements (Table 8), the water temperature was 21° C and the dissolved oxygen concentration was 9.1 ppm. According to Table 9, 9.0 ppm dissolved oxygen is a saturated solution at 21° C.

$$\text{Percent of saturation} = \left(\frac{9.1 \text{ ppm}}{9.0 \text{ ppm}}\right) \times 100\% = 101\%$$

So at 8 A.M., the saturation level of dissolved oxygen was 101%—slightly supersaturated.

Table 8	HOURLY DOs	
Time	Water Temperature (°C)	Dissolved Oxygen (ppm)
8 A.M.	21	9.1
9	21	9.1
10	21	9.1
11	21	9.1
12	22	9.2
1 P.M.	23	9.3
2	23	9.3
3	23	9.2
4	23	9.2
5	23	9.2
6	23	9.2
7	23	9.2
8	22	9.2
9	22	9.2
10	22	9.2
11	21	9.1
12	21	9.1
1 A.M.	21	9.1
2	19	9.0
3	19	9.0
4	19	9.0
5	19	9.0
6	19	9.0
7	19	9.0

Table 9	DO NEEDED
Water (°C)	100% Oxygen Saturation (ppm)
0	14.6
1	14.2
2	13.9
3	13.5
4	13.2
5	12.8
6	12.5
7	12.2
8	11.9
9	11.6
10	11.3
11	11.1
12	10.8
13	10.6
14	10.4
15	10.2
16	9.9
17	9.7
18	9.5
19	9.3
20	9.2
21	9.0
22	8.8
23	8.7
24	8.5
25	8.4

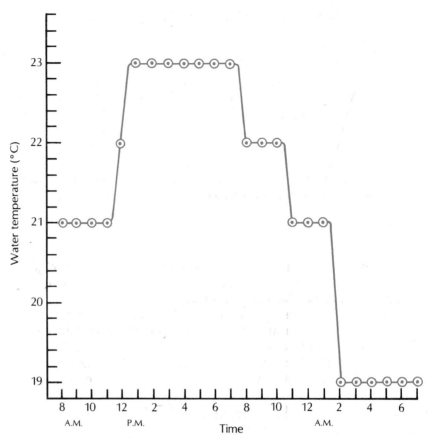

Figure 25   Changes in Snake River water temperature during one day.

Figure 26   Changes in Snake River dissolved oxygen during one day.

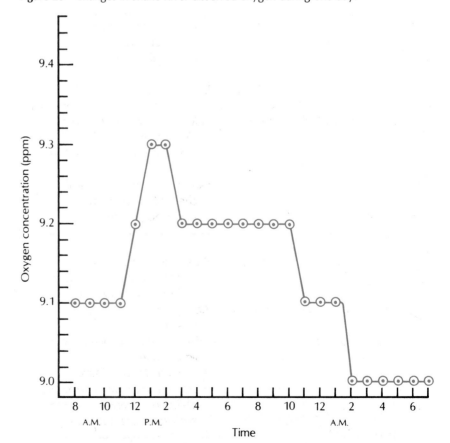

6. Acceptable and unacceptable dissolved oxygen levels in river water for fish life are given below:

125% or more
of saturation: Too high for survival of some fish species
80–124%:   Excellent for survival of most fish species
60–79%:   Adequate for survival of most fish species
Below 60%:   Too low; most fish species die

Based on this information, do the collected data suggest that Snake River's dissolved oxygen level range is acceptable for supporting fish life?

7. Is the amount of dissolved oxygen in the Snake River a likely cause of the Riverwood fish kill? Explain your answer.

C.6 ACID CONTAMINATION

We will now turn to a classification scheme that plays a major role in water quality and the life of aquatic organisms—the acidity or basicity of a water sample.

Acids and *bases* can be identified in the laboratory by certain characteristic properties. For example, the vegetable dye litmus turns blue in a basic solution, and red in an acidic solution. Other vegetable dyes, including red cabbage juice, also have distinctively different colors in acid and base solutions.

Basic solutions are sometimes also called "alkaline" solutions.

Table 10   **SOME COMMON ACIDS AND BASES**

Name	Formula	Use
Acids		
Acetic acid	$HC_2H_3O_2$	In vinegar (typically a 5% solution of acetic acid)
Carbonic acid	H_2CO_3	In carbonated soft drinks
Hydrochloric acid	HCl	Used in removing scale buildup from boilers and for cleaning materials
Nitric acid	HNO_3	Used in the manufacture of fertilizers, dyes, and explosives
Phosphoric acid	H_3PO_4	Added to some soft drinks to give a tart flavor; also used in the manufacture of fertilizers and detergents
Sulfuric acid	H_2SO_4	Largest volume industrial chemical; present in automobile battery fluid
Bases		
Calcium hydroxide	$Ca(OH)_2$	Present in mortar, plaster, and cement; used in paper pulping and dehairing animal hides
Magnesium hydroxide	$Mg(OH)_2$	Active ingredient in milk of magnesia
Potassium hydroxide	KOH	Used in the manufacture of some liquid soaps
Sodium hydroxide	$NaOH$	A major industrial chemical; active ingredient in some drain and oven cleaners; used to convert animal fats into soap

Many acids are molecular substances. Most have one or more hydrogen atoms that can be detached rather easily. These hydrogen atoms are usually written at the left end of the formula for an acid (see Table 10). Some compounds lacking the characteristic acid formula still dissolve in water to produce an acidic solution. One of these substances is ammonium chloride, NH_4Cl.

Many bases are ionic substances that include the hydroxide ion (OH^-) in their structures. Other bases, such as ammonia (NH_3) and baking soda ($NaHCO_3$, sodium bicarbonate) contain no OH^- ions but still produce basic water solutions. Such substances act like bases because they react with water to generate OH^- ions. Human blood has enough sodium bicarbonate and similar substances dissolved in it to be slightly basic.

Some substances display neither acidic nor basic characteristics. Chemists classify them as **neutral** substances. Water, sodium chloride (NaCl), and table sugar (sucrose, $C_{12}H_{22}O_{11}$) are all examples of neutral compounds.

When an acid and a base react with each other the characteristic properties of both substances are destroyed. Such a reaction is called **neutralization.**

The acidic, basic, or neutral character of a solution can be measured and reported using the **pH scale.** Nearly all pH values range from 0 to 14, although some very basic or acidic solutions may be outside this range. At 25° C, a pH of 7 indicates a neutral solution. pH values less than 7 indicate acids; the lower the pH the more acidic the solution. Solutions with pH values greater than 7 are basic; the higher the pH the more basic the solution. The pH values of some common materials are shown in Figure 27. EPA standards specify that the pH of drinking water supplies should be within 6.5 to 8.5.

Rainwater is naturally slightly acidic. This is because the atmosphere includes substances—carbon dioxide (CO_2) for one—that produce an acidic solution when dissolved in water. When acidic or basic contamination causes problems in a body of water, it is usually due to substances or wastes from human activities such as coal mining or industrial processing.

Most fish can tolerate a pH range from 5 to 9 in lake or river water. Serious fishermen look for freshwater sport fish in water between pH 6.5 and pH 8.2. Snake River measurements near Riverwood revealed that the stream pH during the fish kill ranged from 6.7 to 6.9, well within acceptable limits. Thus, we can dismiss an abnormal pH as the cause of the fish kill.

Our next major candidate for investigation as a Snake River contaminant will be so-called heavy metal ions. The following overview provides some useful background.

C.7 IONS AND IONIC COMPOUNDS

We noted earlier that ions are electrically charged particles, some positively charged and others negatively charged. Positive ions are called cations and negative ions are called anions. An ion might be a charged individual atom, such as Na^+ or Cl^-, or a group of bonded atoms, such as NO_3^-, which also possesses an electrical charge.

Solid sodium chloride, NaCl, consists of equal numbers of positive sodium ions (Na^+) and negative chloride ions (Cl^-) arranged in three-dimensional networks that form crystals (Figure

"Household ammonia" is actually a water solution of NH_3.

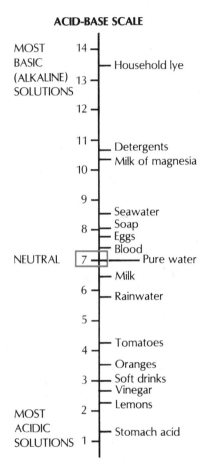

ACID-BASE SCALE

MOST BASIC (ALKALINE) SOLUTIONS	14	
	13	Household lye
	12	
	11	Detergents
	10	Milk of magnesia
	9	
	8	Seawater / Soap / Eggs
NEUTRAL	7	Blood / Pure water
	6	Milk / Rainwater
	5	
	4	Tomatoes
	3	Oranges / Soft drinks / Vinegar
	2	Lemons
MOST ACIDIC SOLUTIONS	1	Stomach acid

Figure 27 The pH of some common materials.

Micrograph of sodium chloride crystals (NaCl) at 70× magnification. Note the characteristic cubic geometry.

Table 11 **COMMON IONS**

Cations					
+1 Charge		**+2 Charge**		**+3 Charge**	
Formula	**Name**	**Formula**	**Name**	**Formula**	**Name**
Na^+	Sodium	Mg^{2+}	Magnesium	Al^{3+}	Aluminum
K^+	Potassium	Ca^{2+}	Calcium	Fe^{3+}	Iron(III)*
NH_4^+	Ammonium	Ba^{2+}	Barium		
		Zn^{2+}	Zinc		
		Cd^{2+}	Cadmium		
		Hg^{2+}	Mercury(II)*		
		Cu^{2+}	Copper(II)*		
		Pb^{2+}	Lead(II)*		
		Fe^{2+}	Iron(II)*		

Anions					
−1 Charge		**−2 Charge**		**−3 Charge**	
Formula	**Name**	**Formula**	**Name**	**Formula**	**Name**
F^-	Fluoride	O^{2-}	Oxide	PO_4^{3-}	Phosphate
Cl^-	Chloride	S^{2-}	Sulfide		
Br^-	Bromide	SO_4^{2-}	Sulfate		
I^-	Iodide	SO_3^{2-}	Sulfite		
NO_3^-	Nitrate	SeO_4^{2-}	Selenate		
NO_2^-	Nitrite	CO_3^{2-}	Carbonate		
OH^-	Hydroxide				
HCO_3^-	Hydrogen carbonate (bicarbonate)				

*Some metals form ions with one charge under certain conditions and a different charge under different conditions. To specify the charge for these metal ions, Roman numerals are used in parentheses after the metal's name.

28). An ionic compound such as calcium chloride, $CaCl_2$ (road de-icing salt), presents a similar picture. However, unlike sodium ions, calcium ions (Ca^{2+}) each contain a charge of $2+$. Table 11 lists the formulas and names of common cations and anions.

The name of an ionic compound is composed of two parts. First the cation is named, then the anion. As the table suggests, many cations have the same name as their original elements. Anions composed of a single atom, however, have the last few letters of the element names changed to the suffix *-ide*. For example, the negative ion formed from fluorine (F) is fluor*ide* (F^-). Thus KF is named potassium fluoride.

Formulas for ionic compounds can be easily written, if a simple rule is followed. *The correct formula contains the fewest positive and negative ions needed to make the total electrical charge zero.* In sodium chloride the ion charges are $1+$ and $1-$. Since one ion of each type results in a total charge of zero, the formula for sodium chloride must be NaCl.

When the two ion charges do not add up to zero, add ions of either type until the charges fully cancel. In calcium chloride, one Ca^{2+} ion has a charge of $2+$. Each chloride ion has a charge of $1-$; two of these are needed to equal $2-$. Thus *two* chloride ions ($2\ Cl^-$) are needed for each calcium ion (Ca^{2+}). The subscript 2 written after chlorine's symbol indicates this—thus the formula for calcium chloride is $CaCl_2$.

This explains why the relative numbers of chloride ions in sodium chloride and calcium chloride are different, as we will soon see.

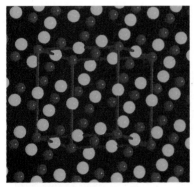

Figure 28 Sodium chloride crystal (NaCl) shown in space-filling molecular modeling. Sodium ions are shown in pink; chloride ions, in green.

Formulas for compounds containing **polyatomic** (many atom) ions follow this same basic rule. However, if more than one polyatomic ion is needed to bring the total charge to zero, the polyatomic ion formula is enclosed in parentheses before the needed subscript is added. Ammonium sulfate is composed of the ammonium cation (NH_4^+) and the sulfate anion (SO_4^{2-}). Two ammonium ions with a total charge of $2+$ are needed to match the $2-$ charge of sulfate. Thus the formula for ammonium sulfate is written $(NH_4)_2SO_4$.

The following exercises will help you recognize ionic compounds and practice naming and writing formulas for them.

YOUR TURN

Ionic Compounds

In writing the formula for an ionic compound, first decide how many of each type of ion are needed to make their total electric charge add to zero. Then write the formula for the cation followed by the formula for the anion. Add any needed subscripts and parentheses.

Prepare a chart describing the composition of each ionic compound described below. Your chart should have four columns, as shown in the sample. Refer to Table 11 as needed to complete this exercise.

Data Table

	Cation	Anion	Formula	Name
1.	K^+	Cl^-	KCl	Potassium chloride
(Complete this chart for substances 2 through 10.)				

1. Potassium chloride is the primary ingredient in "lite salt," designed for people on low-sodium diets. (Answers for this item are already provided in the sample data table; follow the same pattern for the other ionic compounds below.)
2. $CaSO_4$ is a component of plaster.
3. A substance composed of Ca^{2+} and PO_4^{3-} ions is found in some brands of phosphorus-containing fertilizer. This substance is also a major component of bones and teeth.
4. Ammonium nitrate, a rich source of nitrogen, is often used in fertilizer mixtures.
5. Iron(III) chloride is used in water purification.
6. $Al_2(SO_4)_3$ is another substance used to purify water in some municipalities.
7. Baking soda is an ionic compound composed of sodium ions and hydrogen carbonate ions.
8. Magnesium hydroxide is called milk of magnesia.
9. A compound composed of Fe^{3+} and O^{2-} is a principal component of rust.
10. Limestone and marble are two common forms of the compound calcium carbonate.

C.8   DISSOLVING IONIC COMPOUNDS

The dissolving of a substance in water—either from the Snake River or from the tap in your kitchen—is like a tug of war. A solid substance will dissolve if its particles are attracted strongly enough to water molecules to release them from the crystal. To dissolve, attractive forces between particles at the solid crystal surface must be overcome for the ions to separate from the crystal and move into the solvent.

Water molecules are attracted to the ions located on the surface of an ionic solid. As we have noted earlier, water molecules have both an electrically negative region (the oxygen end) and an electrically positive region (the hydrogen end). The water molecule's negative (oxygen) end is attracted to the crystal's positive ions. The positive (hydrogen) ends of other water molecules are attracted to the negative ions. When an ionic crystal dissolves in water, the ions leave the crystal and become surrounded by water molecules. That is, they dissolve in the water. Figure 29

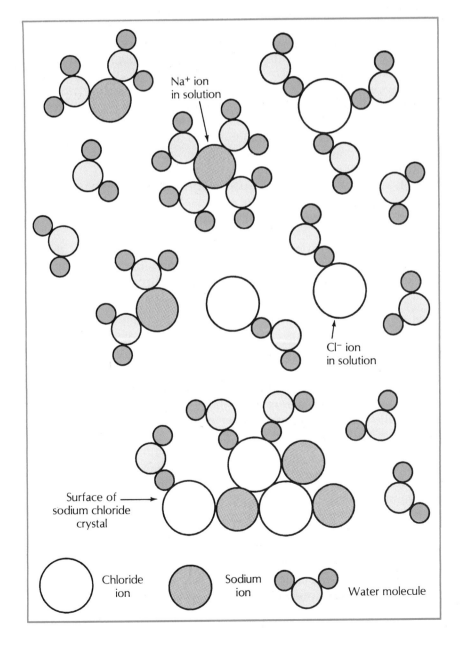

Figure 29 Sodium chloride dissolving in water.

illustrates such a dissolving process. If positive-negative attractions among ions in the crystal are sufficiently strong, an ionic compound may be only slightly soluble in water.

With this background on ions in solution, you are now prepared to consider whether certain dissolved metal ions were responsible for the Riverwood fish kill.

C.9 HEAVY METAL ION CONTAMINATION

Many ions of metallic elements, including iron (Fe), potassium (K), calcium (Ca), and magnesium (Mg) are essential to human health. As much as 10% of our requirements for these elements is obtained from minerals dissolved in drinking water.

Other metallic elements, termed **heavy metals** because their atoms are generally more massive than those of essential metallic elements, can also dissolve in water as ions. The heavy metal ions causing greatest concern in water are cations of lead (Pb), mercury (Hg), and cadmium (Cd). These elements are toxic, even in small amounts. Their ions can attach to proteins in our bodies, prohibiting the proteins from functioning properly. Effects of heavy metal poisoning are severe. They include damage to the nervous system, kidneys, and liver, probable mental retardation, and even death.

Heavy metal ions are not removed as wastes as they move through the food chain. Even when the original level is as low as two to four parts per billion, these ions can become concentrated within bodies of fish and shellfish. Such aquatic animals then become hazardous for humans and other animals to eat.

Lead, mercury, and cadmium are particularly likely to cause harm because they are widely used. These metal ions enter streams and rivers primarily in wastewater released by industry and (in the case of lead) from leaded gasoline automobile exhaust.

In low concentrations, heavy metal ions are difficult to detect in water. Removing them from water is very difficult and thus very expensive. It is easier and less costly to prevent the heavy metal ions from entering waterways in the first place.

Lead (Pb)

Lead is probably the heavy metal most familiar to you. Its chemical symbol, Pb, is based on the element's original Latin name *plumbum*, also the source of the word "plumber."

Most of the lead in our environment comes from human activities. Lead and lead compounds have been used in pottery, automobile electrical storage batteries, solder, cooking vessels, pesticides, and household paints. One compound of lead and oxygen, red lead (Pb_3O_4), is the primary ingredient of paint that protects bridges and other steel structures from corrosion.

Romans constructed lead water pipes more than 2000 years ago; some are still in working condition. Lead water pipes were used in the United States in the early 1800s, but were replaced by iron pipes after it was discovered that water transported through lead pipes could cause lead poisoning. Some medical historians suspect that lead poisoning even contributed to the fall of the Roman Empire. Copper or plastic water pipes are used in modern homes, although some older homes may have lead water pipes and shower pans.

Until recently, a molecular compound of lead, tetraethyl lead, $(C_2H_5)_4Pb$, was added to automobile gasoline to produce a better burning fuel. Unfortunately, such lead enters the atmosphere through auto exhaust. The phaseout of most leaded gasoline since the 1970s has reduced lead emissions to date by about 90%. Even so, some studies suggest that most urban children's primary exposure to lead is through soil and dust originally contaminated by use of leaded gasoline. In homes built before 1978, the flaking of paint is another source.

Most drinking water in the United States contains dissolved lead ions at about half the U.S. Environmental Protection Agency allowable limit of 0.05 ppm. However, water supplies in about 9% of U.S. rural households had lead levels above this in 1984.

Most of the lead we take in is excreted in the urine. Nevertheless, in the U.S. about one out of nine children under the age of six has a dangerously high blood level of lead.

Mercury (Hg)

Mercury is the only metallic element that is a liquid at room temperature. In fact, its symbol comes from the Latin *hydrargyrum*, meaning quick silver or liquid silver.

Mercury has several important uses, some due specifically to its liquid state. Mercury, an excellent electrical conductor, is used in "silent" light switches. It is also found in fever and weather thermometers, thermostats, mercury-vapor street lamps, fluorescent light bulbs, and in some paints. As a pure liquid element, mercury is not particularly dangerous. However, liquid mercury slowly evaporates and its vapor is quite hazardous to health. Thus you should always avoid direct exposure to mercury.

Some mercury compounds are useful as antiseptics, fungicides, and pesticides. You may have used mercurochrome on a wound to kill bacteria. The toxicity of mercury compounds to bacteria extends also to humans. In the eighteenth and nineteenth centuries, mercury(II) nitrate, $Hg(NO_3)_2$, was used in making felt hats. After absorbing this compound for many years, hatmakers often suffered from mercury poisoning. Symptoms included numbness, staggered walk, tunnel vision, and brain damage, giving rise to the expression "mad as a hatter."

Organic compounds containing the methylmercury ion (CH_3Hg^+) are highly poisonous. (Organic compounds are composed of carbon atoms attached to other atoms, predominantly hydrogen.) A danger to humans can arise if mercury-containing industrial wastes in acidic river-bottom sediments are converted to these highly toxic compounds. The methylmercury is converted from mercury by **anaerobic bacteria** (bacteria that do not require oxygen). In the late 1950s, villagers near Minamata Bay, Japan, suffered serious brain and nerve damage, and many died from eating fish contaminated with methylmercury formed from discharges from a nearby chemical plant.

Fortunately, the concentration of mercury ion in U.S. water supplies is usually quite low. The danger of mercury poisoning from aqueous sources is an occasional local problem where mercury-containing waste is discharged into acidic waters.

Cadmium (Cd)

Cadmium's properties are similar to those of zinc (Zn); the two are usually found together. Galvanized steel is electrically plated

Mercury was eliminted from all indoor U.S. latex paints in 1990. Mercury-based biocides had been previously added to 20–25% of indoor latex paints.

Collecting water samples.

with zinc; it normally contains about 1% cadmium. Cadmium is used in photography and in paint manufacturing; it is also a component of nickel-cadmium (NiCad) batteries and certain special solders.

Cadmium is a very toxic element. Some cases of cadmium poisoning have been traced to cadmium-plated food utensils. In low doses it produces headaches, coughing, and vomiting. With extended exposure, cadmium ions (Cd^{2+}) can accumulate in the liver and kidneys, causing irreversible damage. Cadmium ions may also replace some calcium ions (Ca^{2+}) in bones, resulting in painful bone disorders. Such cadmium poisoning struck several hundred people in northern Japan in the 1960s; zinc mine drainage had caused cadmium ions to enter a local river.

In this country, most drinking water contains very little cadmium. Drinking water concentrations of cadmium in the U.S. have been estimated to be less than or about equal to 1 ppb, considerably less than the Environmental Protection Agency limit of 10 ppb. However, cadmium ions can leach into groundwater supplies or home water systems from galvanized water pipes and solder (found in older homes), particularly if the water is slightly acidic.

Low cadmium ion concentrations found in most drinking water supplies do not seem to cause harm, although some evidence connects such concentrations to high blood pressure. Caution is certainly justified, however, since cadmium taken into the body remains there. Thus bodily cadmium levels increase slowly year by year.

Cadmium creates greater human health problems when it is inhaled than when it is ingested. Tobacco smoke is a major source of inhaled cadmium.

C.10   YOU DECIDE: HEAVY METAL IONS

Following the Riverwood fish kill, County Sanitation Commission members, working with the EPA and other water-quality scientists, gathered concentration data on certain ions in Snake River water. Table 12 lists ions EPA officials decided to measure in the Snake River as possible fish-kill causes. The table also includes levels of these ions measured six months ago, their present levels, and EPA limits for freshwater aquatic and human life.

Table 12   ION CONCENTRATIONS IN THE SNAKE RIVER

Ion	Concentration Six Months Ago (ppm)	Present Concentration (ppm)	EPA Limit for Freshwater Aquatic Life (ppm)	EPA Limit for Humans (ppm)
Arsenic	0.0002	0.0002	0.44	0.05
Cadmium	0.0001	0.001	0.0015	0.01
Lead	0.01	0.02	0.074	0.05
Mercury	0.0004	0.0001	0.0041	0.05
Selenium	0.004	0.008	0.26	0.01
Chloride	52.4	51.6	No limit	250.0
Nitrate (as N)	2.1	1.9	No limit	10.0
Sulfate	34.0	35.1	No limit	250.0

1. Which ions decreased in concentration in the Snake River over the past six months?
2. Which ions have increased in concentration over the past six months?
3. Calculate an aquatic life **risk factor** for Snake River ions that have increased in concentration. Use this equation:

$$\text{Risk factor} = \frac{\text{Present concentration of ion}}{\text{EPA concentration limit}}$$

Any ion that exceeds the EPA limit for freshwater aquatic life will have a risk factor larger than 1. Ions below the EPA limit will have risk factors smaller than 1.

4. Which ion has the largest risk factor for freshwater aquatic life?
5. Calculate the risk factor for human life for ions that have increased in concentration.
6. Do you think Riverwood residents should be concerned about possible health effects of ions that have increased in concentration? Why or why not?

Analysis of more extensive Snake River ion concentration data convinced County Sanitation Commission and EPA representatives that the fish kill was not caused by excessively high concentrations of any hazardous ions. So the Riverwood mystery continues!

In addition to dissolved ionic substances, another class of solutes could serve as the source of Riverwood's water problem. The presence of certain molecular substances in Snake River water might provide the answer to the fish kill. These are the next focus of our investigation.

C.11 MOLECULAR SUBSTANCES IN THE RIVER

Most molecules contain atoms of nonmetallic elements. These atoms are held together by the attraction of one atom's nucleus for another atom's electrons. However, the difference in electron attraction between the two atoms is too small for electrons to transfer from one atom to another. Thus ions are not formed, as often happens when metallic and nonmetallic atoms interact.

Unlike ionic substances, which are solid crystals at normal conditions, a substance composed of molecules may be a solid, liquid, or a gas. Molecular substances like oxygen (O_2) and carbon dioxide (CO_2) have little attraction among their molecules; these substances are gases at normal conditions. Molecular substances like alcohol (C_2H_5OH) and water (H_2O) have larger between-molecule attractions; these are liquids at normal conditions. Other molecular substances such as table sugar (sucrose, $C_{12}H_{22}O_{11}$) are solids at normal conditions; these substances have even greater between-molecule attractions.

The attraction of a substance's molecules for each other compared to their attraction for water molecules helps determine how soluble the substance will be in water. But what causes these attractions? The distribution of electrical charge within the molecules has a great deal to do with it.

As you know, the "oxygen end" of a water molecule is electrically negative compared to its positive "hydrogen end." That is, water molecules are polar. Such charge separation is found in many molecules whose atoms have differing attraction for electrons.

Polar molecules tend to dissolve readily in water, which is a polar solvent. For example, water is a good solvent for sugar and alcohol, which are both composed of polar molecules. Similarly, **nonpolar** substances are good solvents for other nonpolar molecules. For example, nonpolar cleaning fluids are used to "dry clean" clothes. They readily dissolve away nonpolar body oils found in the fabric. By contrast, nonpolar molecules (such as those of oil and gasoline) do not dissolve well in polar solvents (such as water and alcohol).

These general patterns of solubility behavior—polar dissolving in polar, nonpolar dissolving in nonpolar—are often summarized in the statement "like dissolves like." The rule can be applied to explain why nonpolar molecules are ineffective solvents for ionic or polar molecular substances.

Were dissolved molecular contaminants present in Snake River water when the fish died? Most likely yes—at least in some small amounts. Were they responsible for the fish kill? That depends on which molecular contaminants were present and at what concentrations. That, in turn, depends on how each molecular solute interacts with the polar solvent water.

In the following laboratory activity you will compare the solubilities of typical molecular and ionic substances.

C.12 LABORATORY ACTIVITY: SOLVENTS

Getting Ready

In this laboratory activity you will investigate the solubilities of seven solutes in two different solvents—water (H_2O), a polar solvent, and hexane (C_6H_{14}), a nonpolar solvent. You will interpret your observations in terms of "like dissolves like" (see above).

Avoid direct contact of chemicals with your skin. Mix test tube contents as illustrated earlier (Figure 18 on page 33). Transfer solid solute samples with the tip of a spatula or wooden splint. Iodine can irritate the skin and eyes; handle it with particular caution.

Prepare a data table, as illustrated below, in your laboratory notebook. This table provides names and chemical formulas of the seven solutes you will investigate.

A nonpolar molecule has an even distribution of electric charge.

The familiar saying "oil and water don't mix" finds support from chemistry!

Hexane is a highly flammable solvent. Do not use near a flame.

Data Table

Solute	Solubility in	
	Water (H_2O)	Hexane (C_6H_{14})
Urea [$CO(NH_2)_2$]		
Iodine (I_2)		
Ammonium chloride (NH_4Cl)		
Naphthalene ($C_{10}H_8$)		
Copper(II) sulfate ($CuSO_4$)		
Ethanol (C_2H_5OH)		
Sodium chloride ($NaCl$)		

Procedure

1. Using a graduated cylinder, measure and pour 5 mL of water into a test tube. Mark the height of this volume on the test tube with a marking pencil. Place the same height mark on six other test tubes. These marks will allow you to estimate 5-mL volumes without using a graduated cylinder.
2. Add 5 mL of water to each test tube.
3. Test the water solubility of each of the seven solutes by adding a different solute to each test tube. For liquid solutes, add 1 mL (about 20 drops). Transfer a matchhead-size sample of each solid solute, using a metal spatula or wood splint. You must use a wood splint for iodine; discard the splint after use.
4. Gently mix each test tube's contents by firmly "tapping" the tube (see Figure 18).
5. Judge how well each solute dissolved in the polar solvent water. Record your observations, using this key: S = soluble; SS = slightly soluble; IN = insoluble.
6. Discard all test tube contents, following your teacher's directions.
7. Wash and thoroughly dry the test tubes.
8. Repeat Steps 3 through 7, using nonpolar hexane as the solvent, rather than water.
9. Wash your hands thoroughly before leaving the laboratory.

Marking 5-mL heights on test tubes.

Questions

1. Which solutes were more soluble in water than in hexane?
2. Which were more soluble in hexane than in water?
3. Explain the observations summarized by your answers to Questions 1 and 2.
4. Did any solutes produce unexpected results? If so, briefly describe them. Can you suggest reasons for this behavior?

PART C: SUMMARY QUESTIONS

1. Explain why a bottle of warm soda produces more "fizz" when opened than a bottle of cold soda does.
2. Explain the phrase "like dissolves like."
3. Why does table salt (NaCl) dissolve in water but not in cooking oil?
4. From each pair below, select the water source more likely to contain the greater amount of dissolved oxygen. Give a reason for each choice.
   a. A river with rapids or a quiet lake
   b. A lake in spring or the same lake in summer
   c. A lake containing only catfish or a lake containing trout
5. Refer to Figure 21 to answer the following questions.

   a. What mass of potassium nitrate, KNO_3, must be dissolved in 100 mL of water at 50° C to make a saturated solution?
   b. We dissolve 50 g potassium nitrate in 100 mL of water at 30° C. Is this solution saturated, unsaturated, or supersaturated? How would you describe the same solution if it were heated to 60° C?
6. A water sample has a dissolved oxygen concentration of 9 ppm. What does "ppm" mean?
7. Seawater has a pH of about 8.6. Is seawater acidic, basic, or neutral?
8. Name these compounds:
   a. $NaNO_3$ (used in meat processing)
   b. $MgSO_4$ (Epsom salt)

c. Al_2O_3 (aluminum "rust" which adheres to an aluminum surface, protecting the underlying metal)

d. $BaSO_4$ (used when taking X rays of the gastrointestinal system)

9. A 35-g sample of ethanol is dissolved in 115 g of water. What is the concentration of the ethanol, expressed as grams ethanol per 100 g solution?

10. What are heavy metals? Why are they such an environmental problem? List some general effects of heavy-metal poisoning.

EXTENDING YOUR KNOWLEDGE (OPTIONAL)

• Organic pesticides such as DDT can become concentrated in fatty tissues of animals. Explain this effect using the "like dissolves like" rule. Why don't water-soluble substances become concentrated in fatty tissues in a similar way?

• Prepare a report on the biological magnification (or concentration) of DDT in food chains, and the banning of DDT from use in this country.

As part of its water quality monitoring program, the U.S. Environmental Protection Agency (EPA) employs a specially-modified Huey helicopter to obtain samples along ocean beaches.

WATER PURIFICATION AND TREATMENT

By now you probably share an interest in resolving the Snake River fish kill mystery with Riverwood residents. However, you have a bigger stake in the quality of your *own* community's water supply. We will temporarily leave Riverwood to discuss how natural and community purification systems can jointly ensure the safety of community water supplies, including those in your community.

Until the late 1800s, Americans obtained water from local ponds, wells, and rainwater holding tanks. Wastewater was discarded in dry wells or leaching cesspools (pits lined with broken stone), or was just dumped on the ground. Human wastes were usually thrown into holes or receptacles lined with brick or stone. These were either replaced or emptied periodically.

By 1880, about one-quarter of U.S. urban households had flush toilets; municipal sewer systems were soon constructed. However, as recently as 1909, nearly all sewer wastes were released without treatment into streams and lakes from which others drew their water supplies. Many community leaders believed that natural waters would purify themselves indefinitely.

As you might expect, water-borne diseases increased along with the concentration of intestinal bacteria in the drinking water. As a result, water filtering and chlorinating of water supplies soon began. However, municipal sewage—the combined waterborne wastes of a community—remained generally untreated. Today, with large quantities of generated sewage and extensive recreational use of natural waters, sewage treatment has become essential.

To act intelligently about water use—whether in Riverwood or in our own community—we need to know how clean our water is, how it can be brought up to the quality we require, and how waterborne community wastes can be treated. An emergency or crisis shouldn't be necessary to focus our attention on these issues. Let's look first at ways that water is naturally purified.

Fish Kill Remains a Mystery

In a brief communication to the *Riverwood News*, Dr. Harold Schmidt, an EPA consultant investigating the recent Snake River fish kill, reported more negative results. Extensive chemical tests apparently failed to reveal any unusual levels of organic compounds in the river water. Thus, pesticides, fertilizers, and industrial wastes have been ruled out as culprits in the mysterious death of the fish. More details will be reported as they become available.

D.1 NATURAL WATER PURIFICATION

We noted that many early community leaders believed natural waters would, if left alone, purify themselves. Under some conditions they do!

Nature's water cycle, the hydrologic cycle, was briefly described on page 16. Recall that thermal energy from the sun causes water to evaporate from oceans and other water sources, leaving behind dissolved minerals and other substances carried by the water. Water vapor rises, condenses to tiny droplets in clouds, and, depending on the temperature, eventually falls as rain or snow. It then joins surface water or seeps into the ground to become groundwater. Eventually groundwater may become surface water and evaporate again, continuing the cycle.

Raindrops and snowflakes are nature's purest form of water, containing only dissolved atmospheric gases. Unfortunately, human activities release a number of gases into the air, making present-day rain less pure than it was in earlier times.

When raindrops strike soil, water quickly loses its relative purity. Organic substances deposited by living creatures become suspended or dissolved in the rainwater. A few centimeters below the soil surface, bacteria feed on these substances, converting organic materials to carbon dioxide, water, and other simple compounds. Such bacteria thus help re-purify the water.

As water seeps farther into the ground, it usually passes through gravel, sand, and even rock. Your first laboratory activity in this unit (page 8) demonstrated that gravel and sand can act as a water filter. In the ground, waterborne bacteria and suspended matter are removed by such filtration.

In summary, three basic processes make up nature's water purification system:

- **Evaporation,** followed by **condensation,** removes nearly all dissolved substances.
- **Bacterial action** converts dissolved organic contaminants to a few simple compounds.
- **Filtration** through sand and gravel removes nearly all suspended matter from the water.

Given appropriate conditions, we could depend solely on nature to purify our water. "Pure" rainwater is our best natural supply of clean water. If water seeping through the ground encounters enough bacteria for a long enough time, all natural organic contaminants can be removed. Flowing through sufficient sand and gravel will remove suspended matter. However, nature's system cannot be overloaded if it is to work well.

If groundwater is slightly acidic (pH less than 7) and passes through rocks containing slightly soluble magnesium and calcium minerals, a problem arises. Chemical reactions with these minerals may *add* substances to the water rather than *remove* them. In this case the water may contain too high a concentration of dissolved minerals.

Water containing an excess of calcium (Ca^{2+}), magnesium (Mg^{2+}), or iron(III) (Fe^{3+}) ions does not form a soapy lather easily and is therefore called **hard water.** Because hard water can cause a variety of problems (described later), it is important to remove these ions from solution. The process of removing Ca^{2+}, Mg^{2+}, or Fe^{3+} from water, known as **water softening,** results in water that readily forms a lather with soap.

Water cleaned by nature is not always safe to drink.

D.2 LABORATORY ACTIVITY: WATER SOFTENING

Getting Ready

In this laboratory activity you will explore several ways of softening water. You will compare the effectiveness of three water treatments for removing calcium ions from a hard-water sample: sand filtration, treatment with Calgon, and treatment with an ion-exchange resin.

Calgon (which contains sodium hexametaphosphate, $Na_6P_6O_{18}$) and similar commercial products "remove" hard-water cations by causing them to become part of larger soluble anions, for example:

$$2\ Ca^{2+}\ (aq)\quad +\quad P_6O_{18}{}^{6-}\ (aq)\quad \rightarrow\quad Ca_2(P_6O_{18})^{2-}\ (aq)$$

| Calcium ion from hard water | Hexametaphosphate ion from Calgon | Calcium hexametaphosphate ion |

Calgon also contains sodium carbonate, Na_2CO_3, which softens water by removing hard water cations as precipitates such as calcium carbonate, $CaCO_3$ (see below). Calcium carbonate solid particles are washed away with the rinse water.

Another water-softening method involves **ion exchange.** Hard water is passed through an ion-exchange resin like those found in home water-softening units. The resin consists of millions of tiny, insoluble, porous beads capable of attracting positive ions (cations). Cations causing water hardness are retained on the ion exchange resin; cations that do not cause hardness (usually Na^+) are released from the resin into the water to take their place. We will consider such water-softening procedures in greater detail following this laboratory activity.

Two laboratory tests will help you decide whether the water has been softened. The first involves the reaction between calcium cation and carbonate anion (added as sodium carbonate, Na_2CO_3, solution), forming a calcium carbonate precipitate:

$$Ca^{2+}\ (aq)\quad +\quad CO_3{}^{2-}\ (aq)\quad \rightarrow\quad CaCO_3(s)$$

| Calcium ion in hard water | Carbonate ion from sodium carbonate | Calcium carbonate precipitate |

The second laboratory test is to note the effect of adding soap to the water to form a lather.

In your laboratory notebook, prepare a data table as illustrated below:

Data Table

	Filter Paper	Filter Paper and Sand	Filter Paper and Calgon	Filter Paper and Ion-Exchange Resin
Reaction with sodium carbonate (Na_2CO_3)				
Degree of cloudiness (turbidity) with Ivory soap				
Height of suds				

Figure 30 Filtration apparatus.

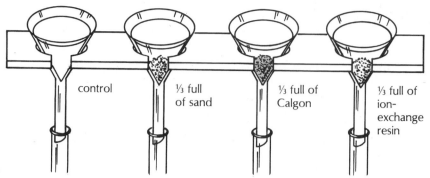

control | ⅓ full of sand | ⅓ full of Calgon | ⅓ full of ion-exchange resin

Procedure

1. Prepare the equipment as shown in Figure 30. Lower each funnel stem tip into a test tube supported in a test tube rack.

2. Fold four pieces of filter paper; insert one in each funnel. Number the funnels 1 to 4.

3. Funnel 1 should contain only the filter paper; it serves as the control (Hard water ions in solution cannot be removed by filter paper.) Fill Funnel 2 one-third full of sand. Fill Funnel 3 one-third full of Calgon. Fill Funnel 4 one-third full of ion-exchange resin.

4. Pour about 5 mL of hard water into each funnel. Do not pour any water over the top of the filter paper or between the filter paper and the funnel wall.

5. Collect the filtrates in the test tubes. *Note:* The Calgon filtrate may appear blue due to other additives in the softener. This will cause no problem. However, if the filtrate appears cloudy, some Calgon powder may have passed through the filter paper. In this case, use a new piece of filter paper and re-filter the test tube liquid.

6. Add 10 drops of sodium carbonate (Na_2CO_3) solution to each filtrate. Does a precipitate form? Record your observations. A cloudy precipitate indicates that the Ca^{2+} ion (a hard-water cation) was not removed.

7. Discard the test tube solutions. Clean the test tubes thoroughly with tap water and rinse with distilled water. Do *not* empty or clean the funnels; they're used in the next step.

8. Pour another 5-mL hard water sample through each funnel, collecting the filtrates in clean test tubes. Each filtrate should be the same volume.

9. Add one drop of Ivory brand liquid hand soap (not liquid detergent) to each test tube.

10. Stir each tube gently. Wipe the stirring rod before inserting it into another test tube.

11. Compare the cloudiness (***turbidity***) of the four soap solutions. Record your observations. The greater the turbidity, the greater the quantity of soap that dispersed. The quantity of dispersed soap determines the cleaning effectiveness of the solution.

12. Shake each test tube vigorously, as shown by your teacher. The more suds that form, the softer the water. Measure the height of suds in each tube and record your observations.

13. Wash your hands thoroughly before leaving the laboratory.

Questions

1. Which was the most effective water-softening method? Suggest why this worked best.
2. What relationship can you describe between the amount of hard-water ion (Ca^{2+}) remaining in the filtrate and the solubility of Ivory brand liquid soap?
3. What effect does this relationship have on the cleansing action of the soap?
4. Explain the advertising claim that Calgon prevents "bathtub ring." Base your answer on observations made in this laboratory activity.

D.3 HARD WATER AND WATER SOFTENING

You have now investigated several ways to soften hard water, using the calcium ion (Ca^{2+}) as a typical hard-water ion. River water usually contains low concentrations of three hard-water ions—iron(III) (Fe^{3+}), calcium (Ca^{2+}), and magnesium (Mg^{2+}). Groundwater, flowing over limestone, chalk, and other calcium-, magnesium-, and iron-containing minerals, often has much higher concentrations of these hard-water ions (see Figure 31 and Table 13).

Table 13   SOME MINERALS CONTRIBUTING TO WATER HARDNESS

Mineral	Chemical Composition	Chemical Formula
Limestone or chalk	Calcium carbonate	$CaCO_3$
Magnesite	Magnesium carbonate	$MgCO_3$
Gypsum	Calcium sulfate	$CaSO_4 \cdot 2H_2O$
Dolomite	Calcium carbonate and magnesium carbonate combination	$CaCO_3 \cdot MgCO_3$

Figure 31 U.S. groundwater hardness.

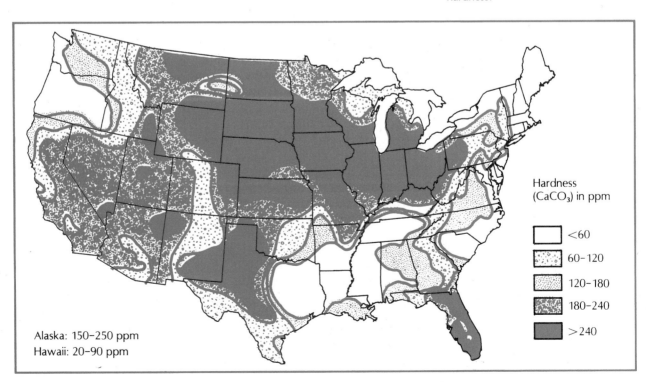

Hardness
($CaCO_3$) in ppm

☐ <60
▨ 60–120
▨ 120–180
▨ 180–240
■ >240

Alaska: 150–250 ppm
Hawaii: 20–90 ppm

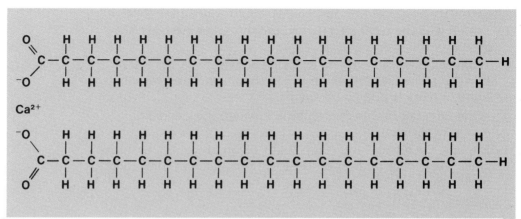

Figure 32 Structure of a typical soap scum. This substance is calcium stearate.

Water samples can be classified as follows:

< 120 ppm $CaCO_3$ Soft
120–350 ppm $CaCO_3$ Moderately hard
> 350 ppm $CaCO_3$ Very hard

The brown stains in this swimming pool are mineral deposits from the water.

Laboratory activity Questions 2 and 3 highlighted some household problems caused by hard water. First, hard water interferes with soap's cleaning action. When soap mixes with soft water, it disperses to form a cloudy solution with a sudsy layer on top. In hard water, however, soap reacts with hard-water ions, forming insoluble compounds (precipitates). These insoluble compounds appear as solid flakes or a sticky scum—the source of a "bathtub ring!" This precipitated soap is not available for cleaning. Worse yet, soap curd can deposit on clothes, skin, and hair. The structure of this objectionable substance, formed through reaction of soap with calcium ions, is shown in Figure 32.

If hydrogen carbonate (bicarbonate, HCO_3^-) ions are present in hard water, boiling the water causes solid calcium carbonate ($CaCO_3$) to form. This removes undesirable calcium ions and thus softens the water. The solid calcium carbonate, however, produces rock-like scale inside tea kettles and household hot water heaters. This scale (the same compound found in marble and limestone) acts as thermal insulation. Heat flow to the water is partially blocked. More time and energy are required to heat the water. Such deposits can also form in home water pipes. In older homes with this problem, water flow can be greatly reduced.

Fortunately, as the laboratory activity demonstrated, it's possible to soften hard water by removing some calcium, magnesium, and iron(III) ions. Adding sodium carbonate to hard water, (as in the laboratory activity) was an early method to soften water. Sodium carbonate (Na_2CO_3), known as washing soda, was added to laundry water along with the clothes and soap. Hard-water ions, precipitated as calcium carbonate ($CaCO_3$) and magnesium carbonate ($MgCO_3$), were washed away with the rinse water. Other water softeners in common use are borax, trisodium phosphate, and sodium hexametaphosphate (Calgon). As you learned in the laboratory activity, Calgon does not tie up hard-water ions as a precipitate, but rather as an ion that doesn't react with soap.

Synthetic detergents act like soap, but do not form insoluble compounds with hard-water ions. Most cleaning products sold today contain such detergents. Unfortunately, many early detergents were not easily decomposed by bacteria in the environment—that is, they were not biodegradable. At times, mountains of foamy suds were observed in natural waterways. These early detergents also contained phosphate ions (PO_4^{3-}), which encouraged extensive algae growth, choking lakes and streams. Many

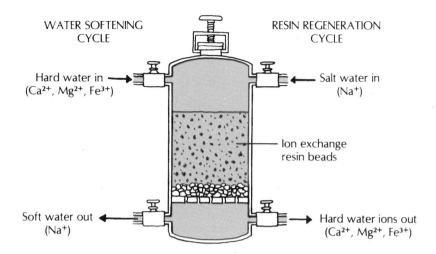

WATER SOFTENING CYCLE

RESIN REGENERATION CYCLE

Hard water in (Ca²⁺, Mg²⁺, Fe³⁺)

Salt water in (Na⁺)

Ion exchange resin beads

Soft water out (Na⁺)

Hard water ions out (Ca²⁺, Mg²⁺, Fe³⁺)

Figure 33 Ion exchange water softener cycles.

of today's detergents are biodegradable and phosphate-free; they do not cause these problems.

If you live in a hard-water region, your home plumbing may include a **water softener.** Hard water flows through a large tank filled with an ion-exchange resin similar to the resin you used in the water-softening activity. Initially, the resin is filled with sodium cations. Calcium and magnesium cations in the hard water are attracted to the resin and become attached to it. At the same time, sodium cations leave the resin to dissolve in the water. Thus undesirable hard-water ions are *exchanged* for sodium ions (Figure 33), which do not react to form soap curd or water pipe scale.

Eventually, of course, the resin fills with hard-water ions and must be **regenerated.** Concentrated salt water (containing sodium ions and chloride ions) flows through the resin. This process replaces hard-water ions held on the resin with sodium ions. The released hard-water ions are washed down the drain with excess salt water. Since this process takes several hours, it is usually completed at night. After the resin is regenerated and water softener valves reset, the softener is again ready to exchange ions with incoming water.

Water softeners are most often installed in individual homes. Other water treatment occurs at a municipal level, both in Riverwood and other cities. How are community water supplies made drinkable? How is wastewater treated before it is returned to the environment? Such questions are our next concern.

Biodegradable materials were discussed on page 46.

It may not be economical to soften water unless the hardness is over about 200 ppm $CaCO_3$.

A typical water-softening unit uses 5–6 pounds of sodium chloride (salt) for one regeneration.

D.4 MUNICIPAL WATER PURIFICATION

Today, many rivers are both a source of municipal water and a place to dump wastewater (sewage). So water must be cleaned twice—once before we use it, and again after we use it. Pre-use cleaning, called **water treatment,** takes place at a municipal filtration and treatment plant. Figure 34 (on page 70) diagrams typical water treatment steps. Each step in the figure is briefly described below:

- *Screening.* Metal screens prevent fish, sticks, soda cans, and other large objects from entering the water treatment plant.
- *Pre-chlorination.* Chlorine, a powerful disinfecting agent, is added to kill disease-causing organisms.

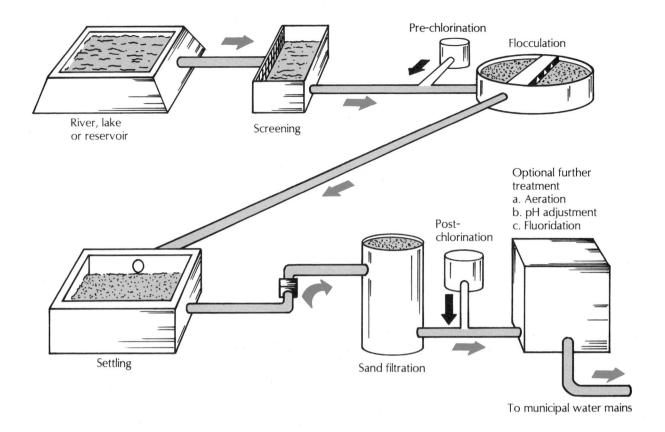

Pre-chlorination

Flocculation

River, lake
or reservoir

Screening

Optional further
treatment
a. Aeration
b. pH adjustment
c. Fluoridation

Post-
chlorination

Settling

Sand filtration

To municipal water mains

Figure 34   Diagram of a municipal
water purification plant.

- *Flocculation.* Crystals of alum—aluminum sulfate,
  $Al_2(SO_4)_3$—and slaked lime—calcium hydroxide, $Ca(OH)_2$—
  are added to remove suspended particles such as colloidal
  clay from the water. Such suspended particles give water an
  unpleasant, murky appearance. The added substances react to
  form aluminum hydroxide, $Al(OH)_3$, a sticky, jellylike material
  which traps the colloidal particles.
- *Settling.* The aluminum hydroxide (with trapped colloidal
  particles) and other solids remaining in the water are allowed
  to settle to the tank bottom.
- *Sand filtration.* Any remaining suspended materials that did
  not settle out are removed here. (This process should remind
  you of a procedure used to purify your foul-water sample.)
- *Post-chlorination.* The water's chlorine concentration is
  adjusted so residual chlorine remains in the water, protecting
  it from bacterial infestation.
- *Optional further treatment.* Depending on community
  decisions, one or more additional steps might also occur
  before water leaves the treatment plant.

  Aeration. Sometimes water is sprayed into the air to remove
  odors and improve its taste.

  pH adjustment. Well water may be acidic enough to dissolve
  metallic water pipes slowly. This not only shortens pipe life,
  but may also cause cadmium (Cd^{2+}) and other undesirable ions
  to enter the water supply. Calcium oxide (CaO), a basic
  substance, may be added to neutralize such acidic water, thus
  raising its pH.

Fluoridation. Up to about 1 ppm of fluoride ion (F^-) may be added to the treated water. At this low concentration, fluoride ion can reduce tooth decay, and also reduce cases of osteoporosis (bone-calcium loss among older adults) and hardening of the arteries.

Post-use cleaning of municipal water occurs at a **sewage treatment plant.** The major goal of wastewater treatment is to prevent bacteria and viruses in human waste from infecting the public. However, sewage also contains other undesirable materials, including garbage-disposal scraps, used wash water, slaughterhouse and food-packing plant scraps, as well as organic solvents and waste chemicals from homes, businesses, and industry. Ideally, these should all be removed before "used" water is returned to rivers and streams.

Figure 35 (page 72) summarizes the main steps in sewage treatment. Each step is described below.

- *Screening and grit removal.* Sand and gravel are allowed to settle out; other large objects are removed. Smaller debris is ground up. Solid residues are hauled to an incinerator or landfill for burial.

- *Primary settling.* Floating grease and scum are skimmed off and solids are allowed to settle out as sludge.

- *Aeration.* In one method, sewage filters through sludge held on baseball-sized rocks (or plastic baffles) in an aeration tank. Air circulates between the rocks; there large numbers of aerobic bacteria digest complex organic substances.

- *Final settling.* More sludge settles out. Most of the sludge is aerated, chlorinated, dried, and sent to an incinerator or landfill. Some sludge may be sent back to the aeration tank.

- *Disinfection.* Chlorine or other substances are added to kill germs.

- *Optional further treatment.* The pH of the water may be lowered with carbon dioxide, CO_2. When this gas dissolves in water, carbonic acid (H_2CO_3) is formed, which neutralizes basic compounds in the cleaned-up sewage. In some systems, phosphate ions ($PO_4{}^{3-}$) are also removed by precipitation. Heavy-metal ions may be also be removed.

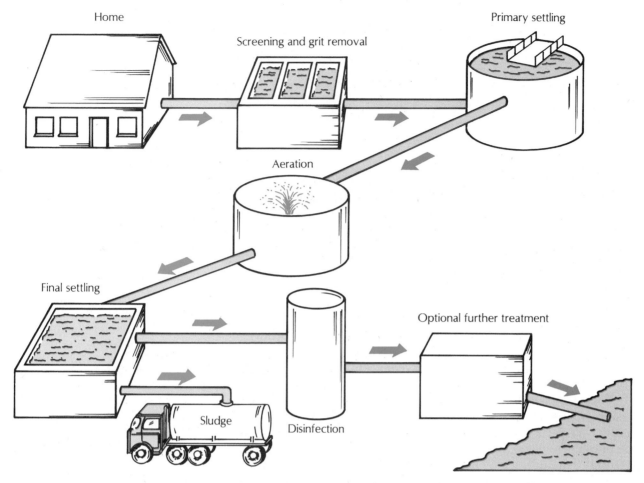

Figure 35 Diagram of a municipal sewage treatment plant.

Gas is produced during sludge aeration and digestion. This **sludge gas** usually contains about 65% methane (CH_4) and 25% carbon dioxide (CO_2). Methane is a good fuel—it's probably the major component in your community's natural gas supply. In some water-treatment systems the collected methane is burned to heat and dry the sludge residue.

Chlorine is probably the best known and most common water-treatment substance. It is found not only in community water supplies, but also in swimming pools. Let's examine its use in greater detail.

Aerial view of a sewage treatment plant in Jacksonville, Florida.

Taking the Risk Out of Swimming

By Nancy Hunter
Rock Creek Journal *Staff Writer*

Lorn Hill's motto is "I take the water you drink and make it better!" Why does he do this? As the Director of the Aquatics Division of the District of Columbia (DC) Department of Recreation and Parks, Lorn is responsible for the operation of 45 swimming pools. In this capacity, Lorn uses chemistry to serve the public.

Lorn uses water-related chemistry in his position every day. Currently, he is testing methods of disinfecting water that can provide alternates for chlorination. Lorn is studying disinfectant options ranging from solid chemicals to ozone. Each of the pools (ten of which are indoors and operate year round) may be disinfected by a variety of methods. Unfortunately, the chemical packages used to disinfect the water are destroying the pools themselves and must be replaced.

The system that Lorn is searching for is one that is: (1) reliable, (2) easy to maintain by the operator, (3) designed to decrease operator error, and (4) safe for public use. The ideal system should have an automatic chemical feeder that monitors and controls the flow of chemicals into the pool. One such feeder is a brominator. Bromine and carbon dioxide are added to the water "slow and low" because it is considered safer to add the chemicals at a slow rate and in low quantities.

Lorn must also consider a system that is safe for the handler and cost-effective. The risks to personal health for those who come in contact with the disinfectant must be weighed with the costs involved. Such a system

Photo by Shutter Priority

could involve ozone. Disinfection of water with ozone differs from other methods in that the micro-explosions of combining oxygen atoms kill the bacteria. The difficulty with this system is that equipment failure is common.

Lorn is responsible for instructing his staff in water chemistry: how to test water, what to look for, why they are testing, and what to conclude from what they are testing. The water testing regimen at the D.C. pools is rigorous and goes beyond what is normally expected. In addition to the tests of standard pH and chloride levels, Lorn's operators perform total alkalinity and calcium hardness tests on the water. It is important to monitor the water conditions continually, not only for the safety of the swimmers but also for the safety of the pool itself.

Lorn has instituted safety training programs for his employees. One life-threatening incident can change the entire direction of the programs available through the division. Lorn's personal safety record is impressive: 14 persons are still alive through his efforts. The D.C. pools' safety record is equally impressive. In the twelve years of operation under Lorn's supervision, no water-related fatalities have been recorded with one million people walking through the doors of his facilities annually.

Lorn enjoys the variety of his job. He shifts gears many times during the day: from people to paper to hardware. He works with senior citizens and children, and is responsible for creating new programs. He developed the first summer aquatics day camp in the United States and the Black History Invitational Swim Meet in the District of Columbia. He finds designing a program from start to finish to be one of his most challenging responsibilities. Lorn oversees the budget, performs field visits and walk-throughs, makes maintenance recommendations, organizes community outreaches, and recruits students from local colleges and schools to fill the 400 employment slots.

Lorn has a bachelor's degree in Urban Planning and Sociology from the University of Baltimore. He took many courses in industrial management, psychology, urban planning, and chemistry. Lorn learned his trade while in school and applies his textbook learning to the field through his practical experience.

D.5 CHLORINE IN OUR WATER

Only about half the world population in developing nations have access to safe drinking water.

Chlorine has served as a water disinfectant for decades. When added to water, it kills disease-producing microorganisms. As the most common cause of illness throughout the world is unhealthy water supplies, the chlorine in public water supplies has doubtlessly saved countless lives by controlling waterborne diseases.

In most municipal water treatment systems, chlorine addition (**chlorination**) takes place in one of three ways:

- *Chlorine gas (Cl_2) is bubbled into the water.* Chlorine gas, a nonpolar substance, is not very soluble in water. It does react with water, however, producing a water-soluble, chlorine-containing compound.
- *A water solution of sodium hypochlorite (NaOCl) is added to the water.* (Laundry bleach is also a sodium hypochlorite solution.)
- *Calcium hypochlorite, $Ca(OCl)_2$, is dissolved in the water.* Available both as a powder and small pellets, it is often used in swimming pools.

Regardless of how chlorination occurs, chemists believe that chlorine's active form in water is hypochlorous acid, HOCl. This substance forms whenever chlorine, sodium hypochlorite, or calcium hypochlorite dissolves in water.

One potential problem is associated with adding chlorine to municipal water. The following *You Decide* provides the background.

Chlorinating tablets are added to swimming pools to rid the water of bacteria and algae.

D.6 YOU DECIDE: CHLORINATION AND THMs

Under some conditions, chlorine in water can react with organic compounds produced by decomposing plant and animal matter, forming substances harmful to human health. One group of these substances is known as the trihalomethanes (THMs). One common THM is chloroform ($CHCl_3$), which is carcinogenic. Due to concern over the possible health risks of THMs, the Environmental Protection Agency has placed a limit of 100 ppb (parts per billion) on total THM concentration in municipal water-supply systems. Possible risks associated with THMs must be balanced, of course, against disease-prevention benefits of chlorinated water.

Operators of municipal water-treatment plants can avoid possible THM health risks several ways, but each method has disadvantages:

I. Treatment plant water can be passed through an activated charcoal filter. Activated charcoal can remove most organic compounds from water, including THMs. *Disadvantage:* Charcoal filters are expensive to install and operate.

II. Chlorine could be eliminated altogether. Ozone (O_3) or ultraviolet light could be used to disinfect the water. *Disadvantage:* These methods do not protect the water once it leaves the treatment plant. Treated water can be infected by later addition of bacteria—for example, through faulty water pipes. Also, ozone can pose toxic hazards if not handled and used properly.

III. Pre-chlorination can be eliminated. Chlorine would be added only once, after the water has been filtered and much of the

This form of charcoal is also known as granular activated carbon, GAC.

organic material removed. *Disadvantage:* The chlorine added in post-chlorination can still promote the formation of THMs, but to a lesser extent than with pre-chlorination. A decrease in chlorine concentration might also allow bacterial growth in the water.

Your teacher will divide the class into working groups. Your group will be responsible for one of the three alternatives outlined above. Answer these questions:

1. Consider the alternative assigned to your group. Is this choice preferable to standard chlorination procedures? Explain your reasoning.

2. Can you suggest other alternatives beyond the three given above?

Something in the Snake River water was responsible for the fish kill and possible danger to Riverwood residents. Yet, tests for the most common causes of water contamination have not revealed the source of the problem. In fact, the tests have shown that the water is totally safe for human use and contains enough oxygen to support aquatic life. However, the fish kill remains unexplained. Perhaps tomorrow's Riverwood newspaper will finally bring an answer to the mystery!

PART D: SUMMARY QUESTIONS

1. List and explain the basic steps involved in nature's water purification system, the hydrologic (water) cycle.

2. a. How do municipal water purification and sewage treatment resemble nature's "purification system"?

   b. How are they different from it?

3. a. What advantages does chlorinated drinking water have over untreated water?

   b. What are some disadvantages of using chlorinated water?

EXTENDING YOUR KNOWLEDGE (OPTIONAL)

- During the past century, water-quality standards have become increasingly strict. Discuss several reasons for this trend.

- In recent years many communities have invested in tertiary sewage treatment. Investigate the purpose, design features, advantages, and disadvantages of tertiary treatment. Prepare a written statement that either supports or opposes such water treatment within a community.

- High concentrations of iron(III) ions are undesirable in drinking water. Write a balanced equation showing how these ions might be removed by a sodium ion-exchange resin.

- Prepare a report on the growing controversy over the use and abuse of groundwater supplies within the United States.

PUTTING IT ALL TOGETHER: FISH KILL— WHO PAYS?

Fish Kill Cause Found; Meeting Tonight

By Karen O'Brien
Staff contributor to Riverwood News

The massive fish kill in the Snake River was caused by "gas bubble disease," Mayor Edward Cisko announced at a news conference early today. Since gas bubble disease is noninfectious, humans are at no risk from the water.

Accompanying Mayor Cisko at the conference was Dr. Harold Schmidt of the Environmental Protection Agency. Dr. Schmidt explained that the disease is caused by an excess of air dissolved in the river water. "The excess dissolved air, mostly oxygen and nitrogen, passes through the fish's gills, where it forms gas bubbles. Consequently, less oxygen circulates through the fish's bloodstream. The fish usually die within a few days if the situation is not corrected."

Dr. Schmidt dissected sample fish within a short time after death and found evidence of such gas bubbles, providing positive identification of the disease.

Dr. Schmidt gave assurances that river water containing excess air is not harmful to human health, and that the town's water supply is "fully safe to drink."

Mayor Cisko refused comment on reasons for the water condition, saying, "The cause is still under investigation." But an informed source close to the mayor's office stated that "the most likely cause is the power company's release of water from the dam upstream of Riverwood." The mayor's secretary confirmed that power company officials will meet with the mayor and his staff later today.

Mayor Cisko also invited the public to a special Town Council meeting scheduled for 8 P.M. tonight in Town Hall. The council will discuss who is responsible for the fish kill, and who should pay the costs associated with the three-day water shutoff. Several area groups plan to make presentations at tonight's meeting.

Editorial:
Attend the Special Council Meeting

Tonight's special Town Council meeting could result in important decisions affecting all Riverwood citizens. The meeting will address two primary questions: Who is responsible for the fish kill? Who should pay the expenses involved in trucking water to Riverwood during the three-day water shutoff? These questions have financial consequences for all town taxpayers.

Those testifying at tonight's public meeting include power company officials, scientists involved in the river water analyses, and engineers from an independent consulting firm familiar with power plant design. Chamber of Commerce members representing Riverwood store owners, representatives from the County Sanitation Commission, and the Riverwood Taxpayers Association will also make presentations.

We urge you to attend this meeting. Many unanswered questions remain. Was the fish kill an "act of nature" or was some human error involved? Was there negligence? Should the town's business community be compensated, at least in part, for financial losses resulting from the fish kill? If so, how should they be compensated, and by whom? Who should pay for the drinking water brought to Riverwood? Can this situation be prevented in the future? If so, at what expense? Who will pay for it?

This newspaper will devote a large portion of its "Letters to the Editor" column in coming days to your comments on these and other issues related to our community's recent water crisis.

Community council meeting, Austin, Texas.

You will be assigned to one of six "special interest" groups who will testify at the special meeting of the Riverwood Town Council. You will receive some suggestions on information to include in your group's presentation. Consider these suggestions only as a starting point. Identify other points you intend to stress.

Use your planning time to select a group spokesperson and to organize the presentation. Consider preparing written notes. Each group will have two minutes to present its position and one minute for rebuttal. Failure to stay within presentation time limits will result in loss of rebuttal time. Students assigned to the Town Council group will serve as official timekeepers.

Following the meeting, each group (or, alternatively, each student) will write a letter to the editor of the Riverwood newspaper suggesting answers to questions posed in the editorial reprinted in this section.

Rather than preparing a letter to the editor, your teacher may ask each group to prepare for a simulated television interview. In this case, a television interview team will question one spokesperson from each group. Questions will be based, at least in part, on those raised in the newspaper editorial.

After preparing the letters to the editor or holding the television interviews, viewpoints expressed in the letters or interviews will be compared and discussed by the entire class.

E.1   DIRECTIONS FOR TOWN COUNCIL MEETING

Town Council Members (Two Students)

Your group is responsible for conducting the meeting in an orderly manner. Be prepared to:

1. Decide and announce the order of presentations at the meeting. Groups presenting factual information should be heard before groups voicing opinions.
2. Explain the meeting rules and the penalties for violating those rules (see below).
3. Recognize each special interest group at its assigned presentation time.
4. Enforce the two-minute presentation time limit. One suggestion: Prepare time cards with "one minute," "30 seconds," and "time is up," written on them. These cards, placed in the speaker's line of sight, can serve as useful warnings.

Meeting Rules and Penalties for Rule Violations

1. The order of presentations is decided by council members and announced at the start of the meeting.
2. Each group will have two minutes for its presentation. Time cards will notify the speaker of time remaining.
3. If a member of another group interrupts a presentation, the offending group will be penalized 30 seconds for each interruption, to a maximum of one minute. If the group has already made its presentation, it will forfeit its rebuttal time.

Power Company Officials

The following will help with your presentation:

Normally, only small volumes of water are released from the dam at any particular time. However, releasing large quantities of water from the dam is a standard way to prevent flooding. The potential for flooding was increased due to unusually heavy rains in the area this past summer. The last time such a large volume of water was released from the dam was 30 years ago. A fish kill was reported then but the cause remained unknown. On that occasion, Riverwood and surrounding areas also had experienced an unusually wet summer.

The dam was constructed in the 1930s and had the most current design of that time. Its basic design has not been altered since it was constructed.

Scientists

The following will help with your presentation:

Gas bubble disease is a noninfectious disease caused by excessive gas dissolved in water. When the quantity of dissolved gases—primarily oxygen and nitrogen—reach a *combined* total of 110–124% of saturation (see page 51), gas bubble disease symptoms can occur in fish. However, such water causes no known harm to humans.

The most dangerous component to fish is excess nitrogen gas dissolved in the water. Fish metabolism can partially reduce the effect of excess oxygen, but there is no way to handle excess nitrogen in blood.

Fish die because the supersaturated gases in the water produce gas bubbles in fish blood and tissues. These bubbles often form in blood vessels of the gills and heart. Blood is unable to circulate throughout the fish's bodies, and death results. Some fish varieties also develop distended (bloated) air bladders. Death can occur from a few hours to several days after gas bubble formation.

A definitive indicator of gas bubble disease is the presence of gas bubbles in the gills of dead fish. However, because some gas bubbles disappear rapidly after fish die, prompt dissection and analysis are required.

Supersaturation of water with oxygen and nitrogen gas may occur near dams and hydroelectric projects as released water forms "froth," trapping large quantities of air. Water at the dam's base may contain oxygen and nitrogen dissolved up to 139% of saturation. Even 90 km (50–60 miles) downstream, gas supersaturation may be as high as 111% of saturation. The Environmental Protection Agency limit for combined oxygen and nitrogen supersaturation in rivers is 110%. Specially designed spillways, providing gradual water release from dams, may substantially lessen or even prevent such gas supersaturation in river water.

Engineers

The following will help with your presentation:

Engineers can predict whether large quantities of air will be trapped in water released from a dam spillway. This involves knowledge of the spillway's physical structure and the water volume that will be released.

The U.S. Corps of Engineers has investigated whether operational or structural changes in dams might reduce the chance of gas supersaturation in released water. Their main goal has been to find ways to reduce the water volume released from spillways and to prevent released water from plunging deeply beneath the river's surface. When water plunges to great depths the increased pressure can force greater amounts of air to dissolve in the water (see page 41).

Laguna Dam, Arizona. Sluice gates and retaining rocks on the Colorado River.

Three specific suggestions might help Riverwood. The first is to enlarge the reservoir located upstream from the dam. This would provide greater water storage capacity during times of heavy rain and runoff. Water could thus be released from the spillway in smaller quantities, decreasing formation of high levels of gas supersaturation.

The second suggestion is to start a major fish-collecting operation upstream from the dam. Collected fish would be trucked

Figure 36 Spillway and deflector.

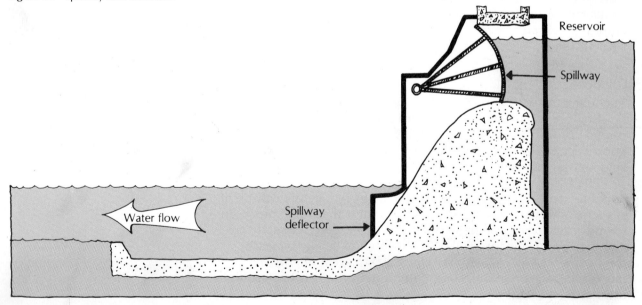

around the dam and released at downstream locations where supersaturation levels are low enough to ensure fish survival.

The third suggestion is to install deflectors on the spillway's downstream side. Spillway deflectors prevent released water from plunging to great depths (see Figure 36). Deflectors release the water at the river surface where the chance of large quantities of air dissolving is reduced.

Chamber of Commerce

The following will help with your presentation:

Canceling the annual fishing tournament cost Riverwood merchants a substantial sum. Nearly a thousand out-of-town tournament participants were expected. Many would have rented rooms for at least two nights and eaten at local restaurants and diners. In anticipation of this business, extra help and food supplies were arranged. Fishing and sporting goods stores stockpiled extra fishing supplies. Some businesses have applied for short-term loans to help pay for their extra, unsold inventories.

Local churches and the high school planned family social activities as revenue-makers during the tournament. The school band, for instance, planned a benefit concert for the tournament weekend. The concert would have raised money to send band members to the spring state band competition.

People are likely to remember the fish kill for many years. Tournament organizers predict that fishing competition revenues in Riverwood will be substantially reduced in the future because of this year's adverse publicity. Thus *total* financial losses resulting from the water emergency may be much higher than most current estimates.

County Sanitation Commission

The following will help with your presentation:

Analyses of Snake River water after the fish kill (see page 58, Table 12) confirmed the safety of Riverwood drinking water according to Environmental Protection Agency guidelines. However, one water contaminant, selenium, significantly increased in concentration since earlier river tests. Despite this increase, selenium's 0.008-ppm level is still below the EPA's 0.01-ppm limit.

The main source of selenium in water is soil runoff. Selenium's soil concentration depends on the soil's geologic origin. Selenium-containing soil near Riverwood came from the debris of prehistoric volcanic eruptions which carried selenium from deep within the Earth's crust to its surface.

Selenium, in trace amounts, is essential to human and animal health. However, if ingested in excessive amounts, its toxic effects are similar to those of arsenic poisoning.

The estimated safe and adequate daily human dose of selenium is 0.05 mg to 0.20 mg. It is contained in foods such as wheat, asparagus, and seafood. The body needs selenium to assist enzymes in protecting and repairing cell membranes. Some authorities think that selenium may—at least in trace amounts—help protect cells against cancer.

Riverwood Taxpayer Association

The following will help with your presentation:

Who will pay for the water brought into Riverwood during the water shutoff?

Will taxes be increased to compensate local business people for the financial losses they experienced? (Keep in mind that local merchants themselves are likely to be Riverwood taxpayers!)

If the power company redesigns the dam's spillway, will construction costs be passed on to taxpayers? If so, how?

To what extent (if at all) should information presented by other groups influence your group's opinion regarding who pays? You may find it useful, if possible, to obtain written briefs from the other groups prior to the council meeting. What other sources of information might be useful?

E.2 LOOKING BACK AND LOOKING AHEAD

The Riverwood water mystery is finally solved. It's ironic that the water "contaminants" responsible for the fish kill and for the town's understandable concern are excessive amounts of oxygen and nitrogen gas dissolved in the water. Neither substance qualifies as toxic or dangerous—after all, we live immersed in an atmosphere of these gases.

However, deep sea divers have long feared and respected the hazard known as the "bends"—the formation of nitrogen gas bubbles in a diver's blood if bodily pressure drops too quickly in moving back to the water surface. Thus, even for humans, a substance as seemingly harmless as nitrogen gas can pose life-threatening risks under certain conditions.

Although the analogy is not perfect, the gas bubble disease that killed the fish can be considered a form of the bends. In fact, the same principle that explains "fizzing" in a freshly-opened carbonated beverage accounts for both hazardous situations.

The fishing season can resume at Riverwood.

Were the analyses of the Snake River water a waste of time or money? Of course not. Even though the tests failed to locate a probable cause for the fish kill, they eliminated several major possibilities, and thus narrowed the field of investigation. In scientific research negative results are often as important and useful as positive ones.

In the case of the Riverwood investigation, one unexpected finding has given chemists an "early warning" of a possible future water-quality problem. The selenium concentration in the Snake River, although not responsible for the fish kill, has increased enough over the past months to merit serious attention and action by authorities. If the fish kill had not happened, would this potential problem have been identified this soon? Possibly. But it's not unusual for a search for a solution to one scientific or technological problem to uncover one or more new problems. In fact, this helps explain why scientific work is considered so challenging and interesting by those who work as scientists and technicians.

Of course, Riverwood and its citizens only exist on the pages of this book. Their water-quality crisis, however, could be real. And the chemical facts, principles, and procedures that clarified their problem and its solution also apply to many experiences in your own home and community.

Although we are now prepared to leave Riverwood, our exploration of chemistry has only just begun. Many issues involving chemistry in the community remain, and water and its chemistry are only one part of a larger story.

CONSERVING
CHEMICAL
RESOURCES

- Do we have enough resources to meet future human needs?

- How can chemistry help create new alternatives for scarce materials?

- What is being done about the growing problem of waste disposal?

- How does chemistry explain the similarities and differences among substances?

INTRODUCTION

Within his or her lifetime, a typical U.S. citizen uses an estimated 26 million gallons of water, 52 tons of iron and steel, 6.5 tons of paper, 1200 barrels of petroleum, 21,000 gallons of gasoline, 50 tons of food, 5 tons of fertilizer, plus a wide variety of other chemical resources. By contrast, ancient societies used only tiny fractions of natural resources such as forests, metal ores and minerals, and animals and plants. The chemical resources removed from the earth were miniscule compared to the amounts remaining.

As humans have gained knowledge and skills in farming, metallurgy, crude manufacturing, and medicine, longevity has increased and human populations have grown. Gradually, people began organizing their discoveries about the natural world, and applied this organized knowledge to invent devices and techniques to make life easier. Early metalworkers, for example, learned the properties of metals and used them wisely, combining them in proportions that gave the best results. Their work helped give rise to **science,** the gathering, analyzing, and organizing of knowledge about the natural world. Science, in turn, aided **technology,** applications of science in converting natural resources into goods and services to satisfy human needs.

Science and technology have advanced together rapidly. Today, scientific knowledge doubles each nine or ten years. Technology seems to change even more rapidly. Scientific and technological advances have given us stainless steel and polyester fiber, video games and laptop computers, Space Shuttles and brain scanners, automobile air bags and compact disk players, fast food and diet soft drinks.

Industries that make these products have grown rapidly. In the United States, 5% of the world's population uses more than half of the world's processed resources. In fact, during the last 40 years, the United States consumed more fossil fuels (petroleum, natural gas, and coal) and metal ores than were used by all of the world's inhabitants up to that time.

Resources are used in producing many different goods.

These advances in science and technology can be put into perspective by focusing on energy, an essential part of processing Earth's resources. Egyptian pharaohs used the energy of 100,000 laborers to build the Pyramids. In building the Great Wall, Chinese emperors used the energy of two million workers. To keep you warm and clothed, grow and process your food, transport you and your necessities, and to entertain you during leisure hours, you have at your personal service enough energy to equal the labor of 200 full-time workers.

These services are costly. We have taken vast amounts of resources from Earth—and, in the process, have greatly altered it. We have also generated large quantities of waste materials. The combined effects of mining, processing, using, and discarding materials have caused environmental damage.

We must become more aware of the consequences of using resources. We must learn to balance our withdrawals by returning materials to the environment in useful—or at least not harmful—forms. Then the world's resources can continue to support its inhabitants.

In this unit, you will explore some issues surrounding our use of resources. You will also become more familiar with some materials that add either richness or discomfort to your life, and you will learn how to help conserve valuable materials.

Human power can be an energy source today as well.

Many of the goods sold here are provided by the work of chemists and chemical engineers.

USE OF RESOURCES

How much is a penny worth? "One cent" is certainly correct. But then again, maybe it's not. It depends! Confused? Read on.

CHEMQUANDARY

A Penny for Your Thoughts

Consider this article:

Zinc Made More Cents

By Karen Chapman
Staff writer for The Alexandria Post

After remaining largely un-changed since the first re-lease in 1909, the Lincoln Head penny's mass lost a full 20% in 1982. The change (no pun intended) was a money-saving mea-sure. Less expensive and lower density zinc was sub-stituted for some of the original copper. Copper prices had risen so much that the copper in a penny was worth more than one cent. The pre-1982 pen-nies were 95% copper and 5% zinc. Current pennies are 97.6% zinc, coated with a thin copper layer.

When a coin's material value becomes greater than its face value, two unde-sirable things can happen. First, the U.S. Treasury loses money in manufac-turing the coin. When the content of the penny was changed in 1982, it was es-timated that the United States would save $25–50 million annually. Second, individuals may remove the coins from circulation, selling them—at a profit—for their metal content.

In light of this information, how much *is* a penny of today really worth?

Chemists are often asked to find ways to substitute less costly, more plentiful resources for scarce and expensive ones, without sacrificing key advantages of the original materials. The new pennies are almost as durable as the old pennies, since the strong copper plating protects the zinc—which is more chemically reactive than copper—from the wear and tear of daily use.

As the ChemQuandary suggested, "worth" of coins has at least two meanings. If the values of the metals in a coin are considered, a penny may be—depending on the current market value for the metals—worth more or less than one cent. As money, of course, a penny is still just a penny.

The U.S. Mint is able to make what is essentially a zinc coin look like a "copper penny." Let's see if you can use some chemistry to alter the appearance of a metallic coin.

To some hobbyists, U.S. pennies (and coins in general) have a third kind of "worth." What is it?

A.1 LABORATORY ACTIVITY: STRIKING IT RICH

Getting Ready

Seeing is believing—or so it is said. In this activity the properties of a metal will appear to change. You will change the properties of the metal in pennies by heating it with zinc (Zn) metal in a solution of sodium hydroxide (NaOH).

In your laboratory notebook prepare a table like that below, leaving plenty of room for your observations.

Data Table

	Appearance
Untreated penny	
Penny treated with Zn + NaOH	
Penny treated with Zn + NaOH and heated in flame	

You will use a Bunsen burner to heat the copper. Before starting the laboratory procedure, examine your burner and identify the parts shown in Figure 1.

Then practice lighting and adjusting the burner as follows:

1. Attach the burner hose to the gas outlet (which should be closed).
2. Close the air valve and the gas valve on the burner.
3. Open the gas outlet valve.
4. Light a match or have your striker ready.
5. Open the burner's gas valve; light the burner by bringing the lighted match to the top of the barrel or sparking the striker.
6. Adjust the burner flame height, using the gas valve.
7. Adjust the flame temperature by rotating the air valve. The hottest part of the flame is just above the inner (blue) cone, which is about 2–3 cm high with a relatively high air setting. Cooler flames (lower air settings) have a smaller or undefined inner cone and often include orange-colored regions.
8. Close the gas outlet to extinguish the flame.

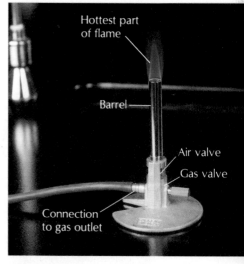

Figure 1 A Bunsen burner.

Be sure to keep your head back away from the burner.

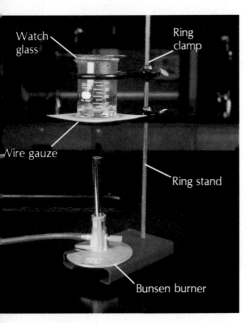

Watch glass

Ring clamp

Wire gauze

Ring stand

Bunsen burner

Figure 2 Setup for reaction between zinc and sodium hydroxide. The beaker rests on the wire gauze and is encircled by a ring clamp to prevent tipping. A watch glass tops the beaker, keeping the solution from splashing out.

Procedure

1. Obtain three pennies.
2. Assemble a ring stand with a ring clamp and wire gauze. As shown in Figure 2, place a 150-mL beaker on the wire gauze and surround the beaker with a second ring clamp so that the beaker cannot tip over.
3. Weigh a 0.5-g sample of mossy zinc (Zn) or zinc foil. Place it in the beaker.
4. Carefully pour 15 mL of sodium hydroxide (NaOH) solution into the beaker and place a watch glass on it. Sodium hydroxide solution is very caustic—it damages skin. If any of it gets on your skin, immediately wash the affected area with cold tap water. Notify your teacher.
5. Heat the beaker gently with the Bunsen burner until the solution just begins to bubble. Then lower the burner flame to continue gentle bubbling. *Caution:* Avoid inhaling the vapor rising from the beaker. Do not allow the solution to boil vigorously or heat it to dryness.
6. Using forceps or tongs, carefully add two pennies to the hot sodium hydroxide solution. Do not drop the coins into the solution; avoid causing a splash. Set the third penny aside as a **control**—an untreated sample that can be compared with the treated coins.
7. Observe and record any changes in the appearance of the coins. Continue until you note no further changes.
8. Fill two 250-mL beakers with distilled water.
9. With forceps or tongs, remove the two pennies from the solution. Place them both in one beaker of distilled water. Remove heat from the beaker of sodium hydroxide, but do not discard the solution.
10. Using forceps or tongs, remove the coins from the beaker of water. Rinse them under running tap water, then dry gently with a paper towel. Set one treated coin aside for later comparisons.
11. Briefly heat the other treated, dried coin in the outer cone of the burner flame, holding it vertically with forceps or tongs as shown in Figure 3. Heat the coin only until you observe a change—this will take only a few seconds. Do not overheat.
12. Immediately immerse the coin in the second beaker of distilled water. Record your observations.
13. Remove the coin from the beaker of water. Gently dry it with a paper towel.
14. Observe the appearance of the three pennies. Record your observations.
15. When finished, discard the sodium hydroxide solution and the used zinc, as directed by your teacher.
16. Wash your hands thoroughly before leaving the laboratory.

Questions

1. a. Compare the colors of the three coins (untreated, heated in sodium hydroxide solution only, heated in sodium hydroxide solution and in burner flame).
   b. Do the appearances of the treated coins remind you of other metals? If so, explain.

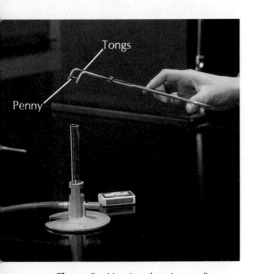

Tongs

Penny

Figure 3 Heating the zinc-sodium hydroxide treated coin. Using tongs, hold the coin in the outer cone of the burner flame.

2. If someone says that gold was made in this activity, how can you decide whether it was?

3. Can you think of any practical uses for the metallic changes you observed in this activity?

4. a. What happened to the copper atoms originally present in the treated pennies?

   b. Do you think we could convert the treated pennies back to normal coins?

A.2 USING THINGS UP

In the laboratory activity you just completed, copper seemed to "disappear." Many things we use daily also seem to disappear. Fuel in the gasoline tank is depleted as a car speeds along the highway. The ice cream we eat vanishes—often too quickly. Steel in automobile bodies rusts away.

Even though the original forms of such materials do disappear when they are used, the atoms composing them remain:

- In the laboratory activity, copper became coated (plated) with zinc. When heated, copper atoms mixed with zinc atoms to form the mixture we call brass. The original atoms of copper and zinc were unchanged, though.

- Gasoline burns (reacts with oxygen gas from air) in a car's cylinders, producing energy to propel the vehicle. During burning, carbon and hydrogen atoms from gasoline react with oxygen atoms from air, forming carbon monoxide (CO), carbon dioxide (CO_2), and water (H_2O). These products exit through the car's exhaust system. The original atoms of carbon, hydrogen, and oxygen have become rearranged in new molecules, but not destroyed.

- As ice cream is digested, atoms from sugars and fats in the ice cream combine with other substances, providing both energy and new compounds needed by the body.

- Even though a steel automobile frame may become pitted by corrosion, the iron atoms can still be found in the rust.

In short, "using things up" means *changing* materials rather than *destroying* them. Nothing is ever really lost in chemical changes if atoms are counted. Sometimes resources can be reclaimed, as in the recovery of aluminum from recycled cans. Other times, the atoms and molecules are so scattered they cannot be efficiently collected again. The products of burned gasoline, for example, become dispersed in air.

The **law of conservation of matter,** like all scientific laws, summarizes what has been learned by careful observation of nature: *In a chemical reaction, matter is neither created nor destroyed.* Matter at the level of individual atoms is always fully accounted for. Nature is an exacting bookkeeper. This is why chemical equations must always be balanced. Balanced equations help us represent on paper how nature accounts for all atoms in chemical reactions.

A.3 TRACKING ATOMS

Coal is mostly carbon (C). If carbon completely burns, it combines with oxygen gas (O_2) producing carbon dioxide (CO_2). Here is how this carbon-burning reaction is written chemically:

$$C(s) \quad + \quad O_2(g) \quad \rightarrow \quad CO_2(g)$$

Carbon and Oxygen React to Carbon
(coal)   gas   produce dioxide

In equations, (s), (l), or (g) indicate the state —solid, liquid, or gas— of each substance at the conditions of the reaction.

Formulas for the two reactants (C and O_2) are placed to the left of the arrow ($\rightarrow$); the formula for the product (CO_2) appears on the right. The state of each substance is often added, as well.

Besides indicating which substances react and are formed, a chemical equation is a ''bookkeeping'' statement. All atoms appearing in the product originally came from the reactants: Producing one molecule of carbon dioxide, CO_2, requires one carbon atom and two oxygen atoms. The carbon atom is furnished by the coal; the two oxygen atoms come from one **diatomic** (two-atom) oxygen molecule, O_2.

If copper (Cu) metal is exposed to the atmosphere, it can take part in several chemical reactions. One is the formation of copper(I) oxide, Cu_2O. This substance contains no molecules—it is an ionic compound composed of Cu^+ and O^{2-} ions. Since the combination of ions shown as Cu_2O cannot be called a molecule, a new name is needed. Chemists refer to Cu_2O as a **formula unit** of copper(I) oxide.

The chemical statement

$$Cu(s) \quad + \quad O_2(g) \quad \rightarrow \quad Cu_2O(s)$$

Copper   Oxygen   Copper(I)
metal   gas   oxide

A chemist's ''bookkeeping standards'' are set by the fact that in a chemical reaction atoms are neither created nor destroyed.

is not an equation. It correctly identifies reactants and products, but does not meet ''bookkeeping'' standards. For each molecule of $O_2(g)$ that reacts, two oxygen atoms must appear on the product side. That means that two formula units of Cu_2O (each containing one atom of oxygen) must form:

$$Cu(s) + O_2(g) \rightarrow 2\ Cu_2O(s)$$

How many copper atoms are needed to produce these two units of Cu_2O? Each Cu_2O unit contains two copper atoms. Thus four copper atoms are needed to form two units of Cu_2O:

$$4\ Cu(s) + O_2(g) \rightarrow 2\ Cu_2O(s)$$

This is the completed equation for the chemical reaction of copper metal with oxygen gas, producing copper(I) oxide. The numbers placed in front of chemical symbols or formulas (in this case, the 4 and 2) are called **coefficients.**

coefficient
$\downarrow$
2 Cu_2O
$\uparrow$
subscript

An atom inventory can help confirm that a chemical equation is balanced. Just count the atoms of each element on both sides of the equation:

Reactant (left) side	Product (right) side
4 atoms Cu	2 formula units Cu_2O
1 molecule O_2	(containing 4 atoms Cu
(containing 2 atoms O)	and 2 atoms O)

The following *Your Turn* will help you practice recognizing and writing chemical equations. Then you will observe a chemical reaction in the laboratory in which copper seems (once again!) to disappear. Carefully observing the reaction products, however, will help you decide the fate of reactant atoms.

Balanced Equations

For each chemical statement written below,

- a. interpret the statement in words
- b. complete an atom inventory of the reactants and products
- c. decide whether the statement—as written—is a chemical equation.

To help guide your work, the first item is worked out.

1. The reaction between propane, C_3H_8, and oxygen gas, O_2, is a common **thermal energy** (heat) source for campers, recreational vehicle users, and others using liquid propane fuel (LPG). The reaction can be represented by

$$C_3H_8(g) + O_2(g) \rightarrow CO_2(g) + H_2O(g) + \text{thermal energy}$$

- a. Interpreting this statement in words, we can write: "Propane gas reacts with oxygen gas to give carbon dioxide gas, water vapor, and energy."
- b. Listing all reactant and product atoms, we find

Reactant side	Product side
3 carbon atoms	1 carbon atom
8 hydrogen atoms	2 hydrogen atoms
2 oxygen atoms	3 oxygen atoms

- c. Since the numbers of carbon, hydrogen and oxygen atoms are different in reactants and products, the original statement is not a chemical equation.

To balance the original statement, first note that each reactant carbon atom appears on the product side in a CO_2 molecule. As a CO_2 molecule can have only one C atom, the original three carbon atoms must appear in *three* CO_2 molecules (3 CO_2). Next consider the fate of hydrogen atoms. The reactant hydrogen atoms appear—on the product side—as parts of water molecules. Since two hydrogen atoms are needed in each water molecule, eight hydrogen atoms must appear in *four* H_2O molecules (4 H_2O).

As we have added two coefficients to the original chemical statement, the carbon and hydrogen atoms are now balanced:

$$C_3H_8(g) + O_2(g) \rightarrow 3\ CO_2(g) + 4\ H_2O(g) + \text{thermal energy}$$

Now consider oxygen. We find *ten* oxygen atoms on the product side—six oxygens in 3 CO_2 ($3 \times 2 = 6$) and four oxygens in 4 H_2O ($4 \times 1 = 4$). Five pairs of oxygen atoms (5 O_2) will be needed to furnish these ten oxygen atoms. The completed chemical equation must be:

$$C_3H_8(g) + 5\ O_2(g) \rightarrow 3\ CO_2(g) + 4\ H_2O(g) + \text{thermal energy}$$

To check this result, we can complete a new atom inventory:

Reactant side	Product side
3 carbon atoms (in C_3H_8)	3 carbon atoms (in 3 CO_2)
8 hydrogen atoms (in C_3H_8)	8 hydrogen atoms (in 4 H_2O)
10 oxygen atoms (in 5 O_2)	10 oxygen atoms (in 3 CO_2 and 4 H_2O)

This confirms that a chemical equation has been written. The final equation and atom inventory both suggest that matter has neither been created nor destroyed—a scientific principle that is called the law of conservation of matter.

Now try these on your own:

2. The burning of wood or paper:

$$C_6H_{10}O_5(s) + 6\ O_2(g) \rightarrow 6\ CO_2(g) + 5\ H_2O(g) + \text{thermal energy}$$

3. The decomposition of nitroglycerine when dynamite explodes:

$$4\ C_3H_5(NO_3)_3(l) \rightarrow 6\ N_2(g) + O_2(g) + 12\ CO_2(g) + 10\ H_2O(g)$$

4. Combining metallic silver with hydrogen sulfide and oxygen gases in air, forming silver tarnish (silver sulfide is black):

$$4\ Ag(s) + 4\ H_2S(g) + O_2(g) \rightarrow 2\ Ag_2S(s) + 4\ H_2O(l)$$

A.4 LABORATORY ACTIVITY: USING UP A METAL

Getting Ready

In this activity you will observe the chemical reaction between nitric acid, HNO_3, and copper metal, Cu. Many metals are chemically attacked by acids. As you will see, such a reaction causes the metal material to deteriorate or be worn away. *Caution:* Acids also chemically attack skin!

Be careful not to splash the acid solution on yourself.

Procedure

1. Obtain a piece of copper wire from the container at your table.
2. Place the wire in the test tube.
3. Carefully add just enough nitric acid (HNO_3) to the tube to cover the copper wire. *Caution:* Nitric acid is corrosive to skin. If any acid accidentally spills on you, wash the affected area with tap water for several minutes. Notify your teacher.
4. Observe the reaction. Record observations of changes in the wire, the solution, and the test tube. (Placing a sheet of white paper behind the test tube will make the changes easier to observe.)
5. Discard the test tube contents according to your teacher's directions.
6. Wash your hands thoroughly before leaving the laboratory.

Questions

1. How do you explain the color that forms in the test tube?
2. What happened to the copper wire during the reaction?
3. Here is a chemical equation for the reaction you just observed:

$$Cu(s) + 4\ HNO_3(aq) \rightarrow Cu(NO_3)_2(aq) + 2\ NO_2(g) + 2\ H_2O(l)$$

Copper + Nitric acid → Copper(II) + Nitrogen + Water
　　　　　　　　　　　　 nitrate　　　 dioxide

The expression (aq)—short for aqueous—indicates that the substance is dissolved in water.

Use this equation and your original observations to answer these questions.

a. You observed several color changes during the reaction. Identify the color of each substance in the chemical equation.
b. Where did the copper atoms from the wire go?
c. What elements were in the colored gas molecules released by the reaction?
d. Where did these atoms come from?
e. Where did the atoms in the water come from?

A.5 RESOURCES AND WASTE

Resources are simply materials—such as plants, animals, minerals, rocks, or gases—that can be withdrawn from the natural environment to satisfy human needs.

Earth is, in many ways, like a spaceship. The resources "on board" are all we can count on for our lifelong "trip." Some resources—such as fresh water, air, fertile soil, plants, and animals—can eventually be replenished by natural processes. These are **renewable resources.** If we are careful, nature will help us maintain supplies of these materials. That means neither using renewable resources faster than they can be replenished, nor creating environmental damage by using renewable resources carelessly.

Other materials—such as metals, natural gas, coal, and petroleum—are considered **nonrenewable resources,** since they

Waste and resources share a common fate at a landfill.

Coal contains sulfur. The corrosive gases sulfur dioxide (SO_2) and sulfur trioxide (SO_3) are formed in burning.

cannot be replenished. Nonrenewable resources can be "used up," or become so widely dispersed that it is virtually impossible to gather them back together again.

As scientific and technological knowledge increase, our society uses resources at ever-increasing rates. To satisfy the needs of an average U.S. citizen, some 23,000 kg (25 tons) of various resources must be withdrawn from Earth each year.

Using or obtaining a resource often results in producing new, unwanted material. Burning coal generates corrosive gases that enter the atmosphere. Extracting a metal from an ore often leaves behind solid wastes that must be discarded.

We also produce waste when we use many common consumer products. Foil wrappers become waste when we use chewing gum. Some products—such as yesterday's newspaper—become waste after they fulfill their initial purpose. Others, such as electric coffee makers, become waste when we discover it is cheaper to buy a new one than to repair an old one.

When we throw such materials away, we do not really get rid of them. At the atomic level, there is no "away." The chemical elements found in trash may not be useful to us in that form, but they are still there—and must be dealt with.

Our society faces increasing problems associated with **waste**—things we no longer want or need. Each person in this country throws "away," on average, nearly 2 kg (4 lbs) of unwanted materials daily. About half of this is paper and other combustibles. Combined, the materials directly discarded by U.S. citizens would fill the New Orleans Superdome from floor to ceiling twice each day! And this does not include the far larger amounts of discards generated in producing the original consumer items.

Waste has earned several names depending on where we deposit it. Materials we gather and throw into cans or garbage disposal units are called "trash" or "garbage." "Pollution" is often caused by unwanted, sometimes harmful materials, discarded carelessly.

In Europe and Japan most glass bottles are refillable.

Many potential discards are actually "resources out of place." For example, used glass bottles can often be sterilized,

U.S. citizens discard a Superdome of trash every 12 hours.

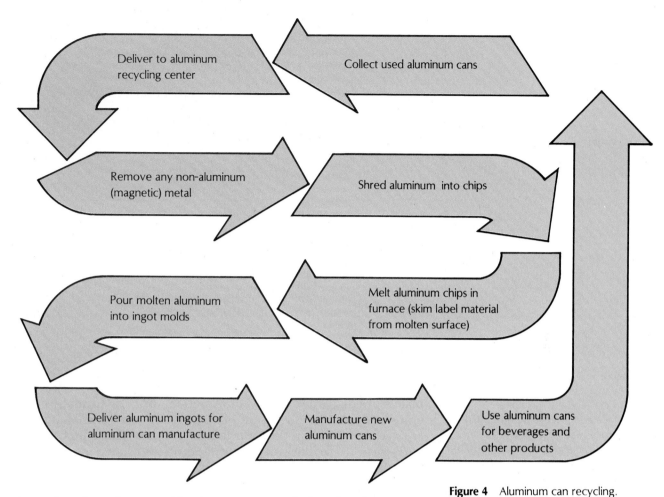

Figure 4 Aluminum can recycling.

Text within flowchart arrows:
Deliver to aluminum recycling center
Collect used aluminum cans
Remove any non-aluminum (magnetic) metal
Shred aluminum into chips
Pour molten aluminum into ingot molds
Melt aluminum chips in furnace (skim label material from molten surface)
Deliver aluminum ingots for aluminum can manufacture
Manufacture new aluminum cans
Use aluminum cans for beverages and other products

cleaned and used again. Aluminum cans and glass bottles can also be reprocessed—or recycled—at a lower cost than making containers from new materials. **_Recycling_** means reprocessing the materials from manufactured items to make new manufactured items (e.g., using glass from old bottles to make new ones). Figure 4 illustrates the general steps involved in a typical recycling process—the recycling of aluminum cans.

What do you do with wastes generated by your daily activities? You probably throw many of them into wastebaskets or trash containers. But where do they go from there?

A.6   DISPOSING OF THINGS

The graph in Figure 5 (page 98) shows what happens to discards after they leave our trash cans. The top line represents the total tons of solid waste handled by U.S. municipalities each year. The quantities recovered for recycling, or burned to produce useful energy, are also shown. The rest—net discards—are deposited in landfills and dumps. The graphs have been extended to the year 2000.

Increased attention to waste disposal is vital for us as individuals, communities, nations, and planetary inhabitants. Figure 6 (page 98) shows the composition of solid waste. You may be surprised to learn that the largest single category of discarded material is paper and paperboard (36%), followed closely by yard wastes (20%). Newspapers alone compose 14% of landfill volume.

At the present time, the most optimistic estimates indicate that about 13% of U.S. municipal waste is recycled, 14% incinerated to produce electrical energy. The remainder —73% —is in landfills.

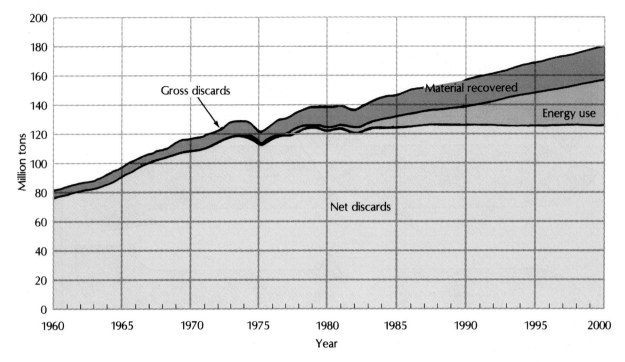

Figure 5 Municipal solid waste. The total quantity discarded (gross discards) and the quantities recovered for recycling or burned to produce useful energy are shown. The remainder (net discards) must be disposed of by landfill, dumping, or incineration.

In this throw away society, some two billion razors and blades are discarded each year. American drivers annually generate nearly 250 million scrap tires. Our nation's wastes have created a $20-billion-per-year industry that collects, processes, and stores these discarded materials. Waste-related issues are becoming urgent—some 80% of our currently-used landfills will become filled and close down within the next 20 years. The "away"—as used in the phrase "throwing away"—will become less clear in coming years!

What are the prospects for addressing these problems? Changing our habits might, of course, alter what happens in the future. Research into new uses of waste is under way. Compacted waste can be coated with asphalt to produce building materials. A process developed by the U.S. Bureau of Mines can convert 1000 kg of organic waste materials (those with high amounts of carbon and hydrogen) into 250 kg of oil. Crushed

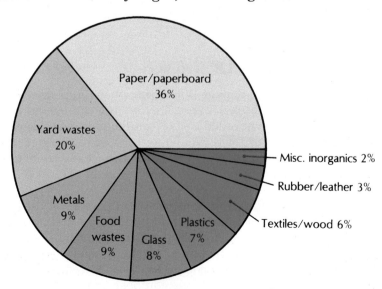

Figure 6 Estimated portions of materials in municipal solid waste, by mass.

glass can replace as much as 30% of the stone and sand used in asphalt for road construction. Since the nation produces about a billion tons of asphalt each year, this could be a significant use for waste glass.

Over 130 waste-to-energy plants currently operate in this country. Each ton of garbage that serves as "fuel" in these plants produces about a third of the energy released by a similar quantity of coal. Also, some of the residue of burning can be used as deposits for future resource "mining."

However, there are some problems with these plants. Although many organic wastes—composed primarily of carbon, hydrogen, and oxygen (such as paper, fabric, and some polymers)—can be burned essentially to carbon dioxide gas and water vapor, metallic and mineral-based materials are not combustible. And materials that do burn create ash and other solid residues that cause air pollution or require disposal.

CHEMQUANDARY

Wondering about Resources and Waste

A common consumer choice is involved in the question posed by grocery store clerks, "Paper or plastic bags?" What decision would you recommend? What information would you use to support your choice?

In fact, we rarely think about the variety of natural and manufactured things we use, or about resources involved in making them. What materials do we use daily? What chemical resources are involved in supporting our daily activities? What items do we throw away? What happens to them?

It's time to take stock!

A.7 YOU DECIDE: CONSUMING RESOURCES

In this activity you will identify several items you use daily and analyze the resources involved in their use or manufacture.

Assume you use a wooden pencil today. It is probably composed of wood, graphite (a form of carbon produced from wood or other natural materials), and paint. The paint contains natural or synthetic (manufactured) pigments (coloring materials), originally dispersed in a solvent (possibly from petroleum). The pencil's eraser is made of rubber (either extracted from a plant or synthetic), held in place by a metal collar. Of these materials, wood, graphite, natural rubber, and plant pigments come from renewable resources, while synthetic pigments, solvents, and metal come from nonrenewable resources.

You will also be asked to identify waste materials involved in using each item. For example, if you used the pencil eraser, you probably just brushed the eraser crumbs aside, which eventually merged with dust on the floor. Once the wooden pencil becomes too short to hold, you would probably throw the pencil stub into a waste basket.

We can never have more aluminum than was in the earth at its formation. Unlike aluminum, wood is a renewable resource.

1. List five things you used or used up since yesterday. (Focus on *simple* things, such as toiletries or packaged foods—you may have used an automobile or portable TV, but these would involve nearly every type of natural resource.)

2. For each listed item, answer two questions:
   a. What resources were used in its manufacture?
   b. How did (or will) you dispose of unwanted materials involved in its use?

3. Classify each resource in Question 2a as renewable or nonrenewable.

   Your class will divide into small groups to discuss the remaining questions. A full-class discussion will then highlight major points developed by the groups.

4. Prepare a summary list of all items identified by each group member.

5. a. How many items listed by your group were made from renewable resources?
   b. What percent of all items listed were made from renewable resources?

6. a. Identify four items from your group's summary list that are made mainly of nonrenewable resources.
   b. Try to think of a substitute for each item that would involve mainly renewable resources.

7. a. List all the waste disposal methods identified by group members in Question 2b.
   b. If everyone in the U.S. used these same disposal methods, what benefits or problems might arise?

   We use resources in many ways. But how do we decide which resource to select for a particular use? Clearly, we must know the requirements of the intended use, key properties of available materials, and their cost. Two of these concerns involve important applications of chemical knowledge, as we will soon discover.

1. a. State the law of conservation of matter.
   b. How is such a scientific law different from a law created by the government?

2. Complete atom inventories to decide whether each of these equations is balanced:
   a. The preparation of tin(II) fluoride (an ingredient of some toothpastes; called "stannous fluoride" on some labels):

$$Sn(s) \; + \quad HF(aq) \quad \rightarrow SnF_2(aq) + \quad H_2(g)$$

   Tin   Hydrofluoric   Tin(II)   Hydrogen
   metal   acid   fluoride   gas

   b. The synthesis of carborundum for sandpaper:

$$SiO_2(s) \; + \; 3\,C(s) \; \rightarrow \; SiC(s) \; + \; 2\,CO(g)$$

   Silicon   Carbon   Silicon   Carbon
   dioxide   carbide   monoxide
   (sand)   (carborundum)

   c. The reaction of an antacid with stomach acid:

$$Al(OH)_3(s) \; + \; 3\,HCl(aq) \; \rightarrow \; AlCl_3(aq) \; + 3\,H_2O(l)$$

   Aluminum   Hydrochloric   Aluminum   Water
   hydroxide   acid   chloride

3. Why are the phrases "using up" and "throwing away" inaccurate from a chemical viewpoint?

4. It has been suggested that Earth is similar to a spaceship (Spaceship Earth).
   a. In what ways is this analogy useful?
   b. In what ways is it misleading?

5. Describe at least two benefits of discarding less and recycling more waste material. Consider the law of conservation of matter and resources available on Spaceship Earth in forming your answer.

6. What advantages does reuse have over recycling?

7. List
   a. four renewable resources, and
   b. four nonrenewable resources.

Recycling takes a lot of space and time, but the savings make it profitable.

B

WHY WE USE WHAT WE DO

Every human-produced object, old or new, is made of materials selected for their suitable characteristics or properties. What makes a specific material best for each use? We can begin to answer this question by looking at some properties of materials.

B.1 PROPERTIES MAKE THE DIFFERENCE

The Statue of Liberty, built in the late 1860s, had to be strong yet flexible to withstand the winds of New York Harbor. It had to be made of material that could be shaped and would maintain a pleasing appearance. The materials had to be readily available at reasonable cost. The artist and the architect needed to know the characteristics of available materials, and to select those used to build the Statue and its base.

The unique properties of materials make them suitable for specific purposes. These often include **physical properties** such as color, density, or odor—properties that can be determined without altering the chemical makeup of the material. A **physical change,** such as melting or boiling at certain temperatures, may also be important. In a physical change, the identity of the substance is not changed.

The **chemical properties** of a material may also play important roles in its usefulness. Such properties involve transforming the substance into new materials. A chemical property might be, for example, the reactivity of a substance with oxygen or with acids, such as iron's rusting when exposed to moist air. In a

A knowledge of chemistry was essential for the renovation of the Statue of Liberty.

Rescuers free a victim of an auto wreck, an example of a physical change. Firefighters control a fire, an example of a chemical change.

chemical change (a chemical reaction), the identity of one or more substances changes, and one or more new substances are formed. A chemical change can often be detected by observing the formation of a new gas or solid, a color change, a change in the surface of a solid material, or a temperature change (indicating that heat has been absorbed or given off).

Let's classify some common properties of materials as physical or chemical properties.

YOUR TURN

Properties: Physical or Chemical?

Consider this statement: *Copper compounds are often blue or green in color.* Does that statement describe a physical or a chemical property? To answer, first consider whether a change in the *identity* of a substance is involved. Has it been chemically changed? If the answer is "no," then it is a physical property; if "yes" it involves a chemical property.

Color is a characteristic property of individual chemical compounds. A green copper compound in a jar on the shelf is not undergoing any change in its identity. Color is, therefore, a physical property. (Note, however, that a *change* in color often indicates a change in identity and therefore may represent a chemical property.)

Consider this statement: *Oxygen gas supports the combustion of a fuel.* Does this refer to a physical or chemical property of oxygen? We apply the same key question: Is a change in the identity of a substance involved? Fuel combustion—or burning—involves a chemical reaction between the fuel and oxygen gas, changing the identities of both reactants. Thus, the statement refers to a chemical property of oxygen gas.

Now, classify each of these statements as describing a physical or a chemical property:

1. Metals, when pure, have a high luster (are shiny and reflect light).
2. Some metals may become dull when exposed to air.
3. Mercury's high density and liquid state at room temperature make it useful in barometers.
4. Milk turns sour if left too long at room temperature.
5. The hardness of diamonds enables them to be used on drill bits.
6. Metals are typically ductile (can be drawn into wires).
7. Bread dough increases in volume if it is allowed to "rise" before baking.
8. Tungsten's high melting point makes it useful for light bulb filaments.
9. Metals are typically much better conductors of heat and electricity than are nonmetals.

A blacksmith modifies properties of a metal sample through a variety of treatments.

For background, see the opening pages of Part A.

Densities: Cu = 8.94 g/mL;
Zn = 7.14 g/mL

It is possible that a substance needed for a certain use may either not be available or may be too expensive. Or perhaps the substance has an undesirable chemical or physical property that overshadows its desirable properties. What can be done in such situations? Often, a substitute material with most of the important properties of the original substance can be found and used.

That is what happened in the early 1980s when copper became too expensive to be used as the primary metal in pennies. Zinc is about as hard as copper. Zinc's density, although somewhat less, is still near that of copper. It is also readily available and less expensive than copper. For these reasons, zinc was chosen to replace most of the copper in all post-1982 pennies. However, zinc is chemically more reactive than copper. Zinc-plated pennies made during World War II—known to coin collectors as "white cents" or "steel cents"—had no protective coating and quickly corroded. Post-1982 pennies are plated with copper to increase their durability and also to maintain the coin's familiar appearance.

Whether it's copper or zinc in a penny, or tungsten in a light bulb, each substance has its own specific chemical and physical properties. With millions of substances available, how can we sift through the options to identify the "best" substance for a given need?

Luckily, nature has simplified things. All substances are made of a relatively small number of building blocks—atoms of the different chemical elements. Knowledge of similarities and differences among common elements can greatly simplify the challenge of matching substances to uses. We will learn more about elements in the next section.

B.2 THE CHEMICAL ELEMENTS

Earlier (page 27) we noted that all matter is composed of atoms. One element differs from another because its atoms have different properties. More than 100 chemical elements are known. However, only about one-third are important to us on a daily basis. Table 1 lists some common elements and their symbols.

The next activity will help you become more familiar with the common elements listed in Table 1.

Table 1 COMMON ELEMENTS

<table>
Aluminum	Al
Antimony	Sb
Argon	Ar
Barium	Ba
Beryllium	Be
Bismuth	Bi
Boron	B
Bromine	Br
Cadmium	Cd
Calcium	Ca
Carbon	C
Cesium	Cs
Chlorine	Cl
Chromium	Cr
Cobalt	Co
Copper	Cu
Fluorine	F
Gold	Au
Helium	He
Hydrogen	H
Iodine	I
Iron	Fe
Krypton	Kr
Lead	Pb
Lithium	Li
Magnesium	Mg
Manganese	Mn
Mercury	Hg
Neon	Ne
Nickel	Ni
Nitrogen	N
Oxygen	O
Phosphorus	P
Platinum	Pt
Potassium	K
Silicon	Si
Silver	Ag
Sodium	Na
Sulfur	S
Tin	Sn
Tungsten	W
Uranium	U
Zinc	Zn
</table>

YOUR TURN

Chemical Elements Crossword Puzzle

Your teacher will distribute a crossword puzzle for you to complete. Puzzle clues, appearing at the close of this Unit (page 147), are descriptions of properties and uses of all elements listed in Table 1. Use this table as a guide in completing the puzzle.

Properties of elements, as shown by Table 2, vary over wide ranges. Some elements, such as magnesium and aluminum, are very similar, while others, such as iodine and gold, are quite different. Chemical compounds composed of similar elements often share similar properties.

Table 2   SOME PROPERTIES OF THE ELEMENTS

Property	From	To
Density		
Metallic elements	0.53 g/mL (Li)	22.6 g/mL (Os)
Nonmetallic elements	0.0008 g/mL (H_2)	4.93 g/mL (I_2)
Melting point		
Metallic elements	−33° C (Hg)	3410° C (W)
Nonmetallic elements	−249° C (Ne)	3727° C (C)
Chemical Reactivity		
Metallic elements	Low (Au)	High (Cs)
Nonmetallic elements	None (He)	High (F_2)

Elements can be grouped or classified in several ways according to similarities and differences in their properties. Two major classes are **metals** and **nonmetals.** Everyday experience has given you some knowledge of the properties of metals. In the next laboratory activity you will have a chance to explore further the properties of metals and nonmetals.

Several elements are not clearly metals or nonmetals; they have properties that are intermediate. These elements are called **metalloids.** In some properties metalloids are like metals and in others they are like nonmetals.

Every element can be classified as a metal, a nonmetal, or a metalloid. What properties of matter are involved in this classification? The next activity will help you find out.

B.3 LABORATORY ACTIVITY: METAL, NONMETAL?

Getting Ready

In this activity you will investigate properties of seven elements in order to classify them as metals, nonmetals, or metalloids. You will examine each for its physical properties of color, luster, and form (for example, is it crystalline, like table salt?). By attempting to crush each sample with a hammer, you will decide whether each element is malleable or brittle. You may also test for the physical property of electrical conductivity. (As an alternative, your teacher may demonstrate this test.)

Next, you will observe differences among these elements' chemical properties. You will find out whether each element reacts with hydrochloric acid, HCl(aq), and with a copper(II) chloride (CuCl$_2$) solution.

Prepare a data table in your notebook, leaving plenty of space to record the properties of the seven element samples, which have been coded with letters a to g.

Data Table

Element	Appearance	Result of Crushing	Conductivity (Optional)	Reaction with Acid	Reaction with CuCl$_2$(aq)
a.					
b.					
c.					
d.					
e.					
f.					
g.					

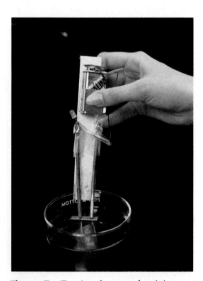

Figure 7 Testing for conductivity.

Procedure

Physical Properties

1. *Appearance:* Observe and record the appearance of each element. Include physical properties such as color, luster, and also the form.
2. *Crushing:* A material is **malleable** if it flattens without shattering when struck. A sample is **brittle** if it shatters into pieces. Gently rap each element sample with a hammer. Decide whether the samples are malleable or brittle.
3. *Conductivity (optional):* If a conductivity apparatus is available, use it to test each sample. *Caution:* Avoid touching the electrodes with your hands; you can get an electric shock. Touch both electrodes to the element sample. If the bulb lights, the sample has allowed electricity to flow through it. Such a material is called a **conductor.** If the bulb fails to light, the material is a **nonconductor** (see Figure 7).

Chemical Properties

1. Test each sample for reactivity with acid as described below. The formation of gas bubbles indicates that a chemical reaction has taken place.
   a. Prepare seven test tubes labeled a to g. Place 5 mL of water in one tube. Draw a grease pencil line on each test tube wall to indicate a 5-mL height. Pour out the water.
   b. Place a sample of each element in its appropriately-labeled tube. The sample should be a 2-cm length of wire or ribbon, or 0.5–1.0 g of solid.

Be careful not to splash the acid solution on yourself.

   c. Add 5 mL of hydrochloric acid (HCl) to each tube.
   d. Observe and record each result.
   e. Discard the test tube contents as instructed by your teacher.

2. Test each element sample for reactivity with copper(II) chloride ($CuCl_2$) solution as described below. Changes in the appearance of any element sample indicate a chemical reaction has taken place.

   a. Repeat Steps 1a and 1b.

   b. Add approximately 5 mL of $CuCl_2$ solution to each tube.

   c. Observe the test tubes for five minutes—changes may be slow.

   d. Discard the test tube contents as instructed by your teacher.

3. Wash your hands thoroughly before leaving the laboratory.

Questions

1. Sort the seven coded elements into two groups, based on similarities in their physical and chemical properties.

2. Which elements could fit into either group, based on certain properties?

3. Consider the following information. Then reclassify each element as a metal, a nonmetal, or a metalloid.

   - Metals are elements that have a luster, are malleable, and conduct electricity (physical properties).

   - Many metals react with acids and with copper(II) chloride solution (chemical properties).

   - Nonmetals are usually dull in appearance, brittle, and do not conduct electricity (physical properties).

   - Most nonmetals do not react with acids or with copper(II) chloride solution (chemical properties).

   - Elements that have some properties of both metals and nonmetals are metalloids.

Metalloids are often used as "semiconductors" in the manufacture of electronic chips.

Even though we have narrowed our view from all known substances to slightly more than 100 chemical elements, the quantity of information known about all these elements is still great. How can we manage and conveniently organize our knowledge about these fundamental building blocks of the world's resources? Nature again comes to our rescue with an answer.

B.4   THE PERIODIC TABLE

Scientists search for patterns and regularities in nature. If an underlying pattern can be found, information can be organized to increase its usefulness, clarity, and applicability. The ability of chemists to predict properties of newly-developed or even imagined substances has been greatly enhanced by the discovery of a pattern among the elements. That discovery has guided the development of new and useful materials.

By the mid-1800s, about 60 elements were known. The five nonmetals known at that time—hydrogen (H), oxygen (O), nitrogen (N), fluorine (F), and chlorine (Cl)—are gases at room temperature. Two other elements are liquids—the metal mercury (Hg) and the nonmetal bromine (Br). The rest are solids, with widely differing properties.

The gaseous elements discovered first were all diatomic—H_2, O_2, N_2, F_2, and Cl_2.

Several scientists of that era tried to devise a classification system that placed elements with similar properties near each other on a chart. Such an arrangement is called a ***periodic***

Dimitri Mendeleev (1834–1907) published the first useful periodic table.

table. Dimitri Mendeleev, a Russian chemist, published a periodic table in 1869. We still use a very similar table today. The periodic table has a pattern similar in some respects to a monthly calendar.

The properties of elements determined the designs of early periodic tables. The tables were arranged according to the masses of the atoms and their ability to combine with atoms of other elements. It was known that atoms of different elements have different masses. For example, hydrogen atoms have the lowest mass of all, oxygen atoms are about 16 times more massive than hydrogen atoms, and sulfur atoms are about twice as massive as oxygen atoms (making them about 32 times more massive than hydrogen atoms). Based on such comparisons, an **atomic mass** can be assigned to each element.

Atoms of various elements also differ in how many atoms of other elements they combine with. For example, one atom of potassium (K) or cesium (Cs) combines with only one atom of chlorine (Cl), producing the compounds KCl and CsCl. We can represent such one-to-one compounds as ECl (E stands for the Element combining with chlorine). Atoms of other elements may combine with two, or three, or four chlorine atoms, giving sets of compounds with the general formulas ECl_2, ECl_3, and ECl_4. Many elements can be organized in patterns based on their "combining capacity" with oxygen and with chlorine.

In the first periodic tables, elements with similar properties were placed in vertical groups (columns). However, rather than just telling one of the great scientific detective stories, we invite you to follow a similar path.

B.5   YOU DECIDE: GROUPING THE ELEMENTS

You will be given a set of 20 element data cards. Each card lists some properties of one of the first 20 elements.

1. Arrange the cards in order of increasing atomic mass.
2. Next, place the cards in a number of different groups. Each group should include elements with similar properties. For example, you might put all elements with boiling points below 0° C in one group, and in another all elements with boiling points above 0° C. Or you might examine the formulas of chlorine-containing compounds, and group the elements by the number of chlorine atoms in these formulas.
3. Examine the cards within each group for any patterns. Arrange cards within each group in some logical sequence.
4. Observe how particular properties vary from group to group.
5. Arrange all the card groups into some logical sequence.
6. Decide on the most reasonable and useful patterns within and among card groups. Then tape the cards onto a sheet of paper to preserve your pattern for classroom discussion.

B.6   THE PATTERN OF ATOMIC NUMBERS

Early periodic tables offered no explanation for similarities found among element properties. The reason for these similarities was discovered about 50 years later. It serves as the basis for the modern periodic table.

Recall that all atoms are composed of smaller particles, including equal numbers of positively-charged protons and negatively-charged electrons (page 30). One essential difference discovered later among atoms of different elements is their number of protons—a value called the **atomic number.** Every sodium atom contains 11 protons; the atomic number of sodium is 11. Each carbon atom contains 6 protons. If the number of protons in an atom is 9, it is a fluorine atom; if 12, it is a magnesium atom. In short, knowing the atomic number or the number of protons allows us to identify which element it represents.

All elements are in sequence according to their atomic numbers in the modern periodic table. This table also reflects the arrangement of electrons in atoms. As we shall see, electron arrangement is closely related to the properties of atoms.

In the next exercise you will draw graphs to explore the relationship between atomic numbers and the groupings of elements having similar properties in the periodic table.

YOUR TURN

Periodic Variation in Properties

Your teacher will give you the atomic numbers of the 20 elements you arranged in Section B.5. Use these atomic numbers and information on the element cards to prepare the two graphs described below. It will be helpful to label each plotted point with the symbol of the element involved.

Graph 1. Trends in a chemical property.

1. Label the x axis with atomic numbers from 1 to 20.
2. Select either the formulas for oxide or chloride compounds. Label the y axis for the number of chlorine or oxygen atoms as follows:
   a. To prepare to plot chloride data, label the y axis 0 for formation of no chloride, 1 for ECl compounds (1 chlorine atom for each E atom), 2 for ECl_2, 3 for ECl_3, and 4 for ECl_4.
   b. To prepare to plot oxide data, label the y axis 0 for formation of no oxide, 0.5 for E_2O (0.5 oxygen atom for each E atom), 1 for EO, 1.5 for E_2O_3 (do you see why?), 2 for EO_2, and 2.5 for E_2O_5.
3. Plot the oxide or chloride data from the element cards.

Graph 2. Trends in a physical property.

4. Label the x axis with the atomic numbers from 1 to 20.
5. Select either melting point or boiling point data; label the y axis as shown in the accompanying figure. Use as much of the space on your graph paper as possible.
6. Plot the data from the element cards. Do not include data for the element with atomic number 8 (carbon)—the y axis value for this element will be quite far off the graph.
7. Connect adjacent points on both graphs with straight lines.

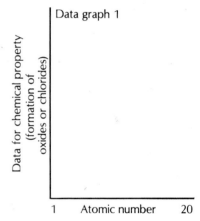

Graph 1 Trends in a chemical property.

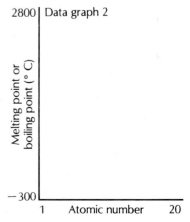

Graph 2 Trends in a physical property.

Questions

1. a. Does either graph reveal a repeating or cyclic pattern? (*Hint:* Focus on elements in the peaks or valleys.)
   b. Are these graphs consistent with your earlier grouping of the elements? Why or why not?
2. Based on these graphs, why is the chemist's organization of elements called a *periodic* table?

*The repetition of similar properties at regular intervals when elements are arranged by increasing atomic number is known as the **periodic law.***

When elements are listed in order by their atomic numbers, and grouped according to similar properties, they form seven horizontal rows, called **periods.** This periodic relationship among elements is summarized in the modern periodic table, shown in Figure 8 and also inside the back cover. To become more familiar with the periodic table, locate the 20 elements you classified earlier (page 108). How do their relative positions compare with those shown on your chart?

Helium-family elements are known as noble gases.

Each vertical column in the table contains elements with similar properties. These are called **groups** or **families** of elements. The lithium (Li) family, for example, consists of the six elements in the first column at the left side of the table. These elements are all highly reactive metals, which form ECl chlorides and E_2O oxides. Like sodium chloride (NaCl), all chlorides and oxides of lithium family elements are ionic compounds. By contrast, the helium family, at the right side of the table, consists of very unreactive elements (only xenon and krypton are known to form any compounds at all).

Based on his table, Mendeleev correctly predicted the properties of several elements that had not been discovered yet.

The arrangement of elements in the periodic table provides an orderly summary of the key characteristics of elements. If we know the major properties of a certain chemical family, we can predict some of the behavior of any element in that family.

YOUR TURN

Periodic Table

Some properties of an element can be estimated by averaging the properties of the elements located just above and just below the element in question. This is how Mendeleev predicted the properties of elements unknown in his time. He was so certain about his conclusions that he left gaps in his periodic table for missing elements, with predictions of their properties. When these elements were eventually discovered, they fit in exactly as expected. Mendeleev's fame rests largely on the correctness of these predictions.

As an example, suppose that krypton (Kr) is an unknown element. Estimate the boiling point of krypton, given that the boiling point (under similar conditions) for argon (Ar) is −186° C, for xenon (Xe), −112° C.

In its periodic table group, krypton is preceded by argon and followed by xenon. Taking the average of the boiling points of these elements gives

$$\frac{(-186° \text{ C}) + (-112° \text{ C})}{2} = -149° \text{ C}$$

Periodic Table of the Elements

1 **H** 1.008																	2 **He** 4.003
3 **Li** 6.941	4 **Be** 9.012											5 **B** 10.81	6 **C** 12.01	7 **N** 14.01	8 **O** 16.00	9 **F** 19.00	10 **Ne** 20.18
11 **Na** 22.99	12 **Mg** 24.31											13 **Al** 26.98	14 **Si** 28.09	15 **P** 30.97	16 **S** 32.07	17 **Cl** 35.45	18 **Ar** 39.95
19 **K** 39.10	20 **Ca** 40.08	21 **Sc** 44.96	22 **Ti** 47.88	23 **V** 50.94	24 **Cr** 52.00	25 **Mn** 54.94	26 **Fe** 55.85	27 **Co** 58.93	28 **Ni** 58.69	29 **Cu** 63.55	30 **Zn** 65.39	31 **Ga** 69.72	32 **Ge** 72.59	33 **As** 74.92	34 **Se** 78.96	35 **Br** 79.90	36 **Kr** 83.80
37 **Rb** 85.47	38 **Sr** 87.62	39 **Y** 88.91	40 **Zr** 91.22	41 **Nb** 92.21	42 **Mo** 95.94	43 **Tc** 98.91	44 **Ru** 101.1	45 **Rh** 102.9	46 **Pd** 106.4	47 **Ag** 107.9	48 **Cd** 112.4	49 **In** 114.8	50 **Sn** 118.7	51 **Sb** 121.8	52 **Te** 127.6	53 **I** 126.9	54 **Xe** 131.3
55 **Cs** 132.9	56 **Ba** 137.3	57 **La★** 138.9	72 **Hf** 178.5	73 **Ta** 180.9	74 **W** 183.9	75 **Re** 186.2	76 **Os** 190.2	77 **Ir** 192.2	78 **Pt** 195.1	79 **Au** 197.0	80 **Hg** 200.6	81 **Tl** 204.4	82 **Pb** 207.2	83 **Bi** 209.0	84 **Po** (210.0)	85 **At** (210.0)	86 **Rn** (222.0)
87 **Fr** (223.0)	88 **Ra** 226.0	89 **Ac•** 227.0	104 (261)	105 (262)	106 (263)	107 (262)											

★Lanthanoid series	58 **Ce** 140.1	59 **Pr** 140.9	60 **Nd** 144.2	61 **Pm** 144.9	62 **Sm** 150.4	63 **Eu** 152.0	64 **Gd** 157.3	65 **Tb** 158.9	66 **Dy** 162 5	67 **Ho** 164.9	68 **Er** 167.3	69 **Tm** 168.9	70 **Yb** 173.0	71 **Lu** 175.0
•Actinoid series	90 **Th** 232.0	91 **Pa** 231.0	92 **U** 238.0	93 **Np** 237.0	94 **Pu** 239.1	95 **Am** 243.1	96 **Cm** 247.1	97 **Bk** 247.1	98 **Cf** 252.1	99 **Es** 252.1	100 **Fm** 257.1	101 **Md** 256.1	102 **No** 259.1	103 **Lr** 260.1

Figure 8 Periodic table of the elements.

The estimated boiling point for krypton, $-149°$ C, is within 5% of krypton's known boiling point, $-157°$ C. The periodic table has helped guide us to a useful prediction.

Here is an example of how formulas for chemical compounds can be predicted from periodic table relationships:

Carbon and oxygen form carbon dioxide (CO_2). What formula would you predict for a compound of carbon and sulfur?

The periodic table indicates that sulfur (S) and oxygen (O) are in the same family. Knowing that carbon and oxygen form CO_2, the best guess for carbon and sulfur would be CS_2 (carbon disulfide)—a correct prediction!

1. One element undiscovered in Mendeleev's time was germanium (Ge). Given the information that the melting points of silicon (Si) and tin (Sn) are 1410° C and 232° C respectively, estimate the melting point of germanium.

2. a. Estimate the melting point of rubidium (Rb). The melting points of potassium (K) and cesium (Cs) are 64° C and 29° C respectively.

   b. Would you expect the melting point of sodium (Na) to be higher or lower than that of rubidium (Rb)?

3. Here are formulas for several known compounds: NaI, $MgCl_2$, CaO, Al_2O_3, and CCl_4. Using that information, predict the formula of a compound formed from:

   a. C and F.   d. Ca and Br.

   b. Al and S.   e. Ba and O.

   c. K and Cl.

4. Which family of elements is so lacking in chemical reactivity that its elements were originally regarded as "inert"?

B.7 CHEMICAL REACTIVITY

Magnesium reacts with oxygen. In fact, it reacts so quickly that we place small samples of magnesium in some types of fireworks. When magnesium is heated it ignites, producing a brief, blinding flash. The equation for the reaction of magnesium with oxygen is written below.

$$2\ Mg(s)\quad +\quad O_2(g)\quad \rightarrow\quad 2\ MgO(s)$$

Magnesium   Oxygen gas   Magnesium oxide

Iron reacts with oxygen also, but it does so much more slowly. Rusting is the chemical combination of these two elements. Rusting (a form of corrosion) includes a complex series of reactions involving water as well as oxygen gas. It is commonly known, for example, that dry iron utensils do not rust. Also, automobiles rust faster near an ocean than they do in a desert.

The reaction between oxygen and iron is destroying this truck.

To a chemist, "rust" is a combination of several iron-containing compounds including iron(III) oxide:

$$2 \text{ Fe(s)} + 3 \text{ O}_2\text{(g)} \rightarrow 2 \text{ Fe}_2\text{O}_3\text{(s)}$$

Iron   Oxygen gas   Iron(III) oxide

By contrast, gold (Au) does not react with oxygen gas. This is one reason gold is prized as a material for long-lasting, highly decorative objects (such as the Statue of Liberty's torch). Gold-plated electrical contacts are dependable since nonconducting gold oxides do not form on their surfaces.

By observing how readily certain metals react with oxygen, we learn something about their reactivities. In the following laboratory activity you will investigate another way to compare the relative chemical reactivities of metals and their ions.

B.8 LABORATORY ACTIVITY: METAL REACTIVITIES

Getting Ready

In this activity you will observe and compare some chemical reactions of several metallic elements. These reactions involve a metal and a solution containing ions of a different metal. You will investigate reactions of three metals (copper, magnesium, and zinc) with solutions of ionic compounds that contain metal ions (copper(II) nitrate, magnesium nitrate, zinc nitrate, and silver nitrate).

In your laboratory notebook, prepare a data table like the one below.

Data Table   **RELATIVE REACTIVITIES OF METALS**

Metal	Solutions			
	Cu(NO₃)₂	Mg(NO₃)₂	Zn(NO₃)₂	AgNO₃
Cu	—			
Mg		—		
Zn			—	
Ag	NR	NR	NR	—

We have filled in results for reactions of silver metal, Ag (too expensive for this use). NR stands for "no visible reaction." The dashes indicate reaction combinations that are not needed.

Procedure

1. Obtain four strips (approx. 3 cm $\times$ 0.5 cm) of each of the three metals to be tested.
2. Clean the surface on each metal strip by rubbing it with sandpaper or emery paper. Record observations on the metals' appearance.
3. Label four test tubes for each of the four solutions to be used. Pour 2 mL of water in one tube. Mark all tubes with a grease pencil to show this 2-mL level. Discard the water from the tube.
4. Place 2 mL of test solutions in appropriately-labelled tubes. *Caution:* Avoid touching skin or clothing with the $AgNO_3$ solution; it causes dark, non-washable stains.
5. Add a copper strip to each solution to be tested (see Figure 9). Observe the results for three to five minutes. If no reaction is observed, write NR in your data table. If you observe a reaction, record the observed changes.
6. Remove the copper strips from the tubes. Dry the strips with a paper towel and clean them with sandpaper so they will be ready for the next group of students.
7. Discard the used solutions as directed by your teacher. Wash these test tubes.
8. Repeat Steps 4 through 7 with each of the other two metals. Complete all entries in the data table.
9. Wash your hands thoroughly before leaving the laboratory.

Questions

1. Which metal reacted with the most solutions?
2. Which metal reacted with the fewest solutions?
3. List the four metals in order, placing the most reactive metal first (the one that reacted with the most solutions) and proceeding in order to the least reactive metal (the one that reacted with the fewest solutions). Such a ranking of elements in order of their chemical reactivity is called an ***activity series.***

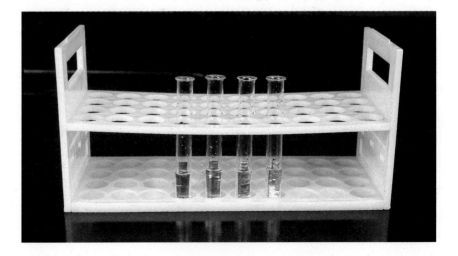

Figure 9 Testing copper's reactivity. The test tubes each contain 2 mL of a test solution. Place a copper strip in each test tube and observe the results.

4. Refer to your activity series list in Question 3. Can you tell why the Statue of Liberty was made with copper instead of zinc?

5. a. Which material that you observed in this activity might have been a better choice for the Statue than copper?

   b. Why wasn't it chosen?

6. Given your knowledge of relative chemical activity among these four metals,

   a. which metal is most likely to be found in an uncombined or "free" state in nature?

   b. which metal would be least likely to be found uncombined with other elements?

B.9 WHAT DETERMINES PROPERTIES?

What causes differences in the reactivities of the metals—or in other properties that vary from element to element? Recall that atoms of different elements have different numbers of protons (atomic numbers). Therefore, these atoms also have different numbers of electrons. Many properties of elements are determined largely by the number of electrons in their atoms and how these electrons are arranged.

We will look more closely at electron arrangements in the Petroleum unit.

A major difference between metals and nonmetals is that metal atoms lose their outer electrons much more easily than do nonmetal atoms. Under suitable conditions, one or more of these outer electrons may transfer to other atoms or ions.

For example, in Laboratory Activity B.8, magnesium atoms each transferred two electrons to zinc cations:

$$Mg(s) \quad + Zn^{2+}(aq) \rightarrow \quad Mg^{2+}(aq) \quad + Zn(s)$$

| Magnesium metal | Zinc ion | Magnesium ion | Zinc metal |

The nitrate anions, NO_3^-, remain unchanged in this reaction.

Active metals can give up one or more of their electrons to ions of less-active metals. You observed similar reactions between other pairs of metals and cations.

Some physical properties of metals depend on attractions among atoms. For example, stronger attractions among atoms of a metal result in higher melting points. Magnesium's melting point is 651° C, while sodium's is 98° C. Thus we can infer that the attractions between the atoms in magnesium metal are stronger than in sodium metal.

Chemical and physical properties for other kinds of substances are also explained by the make-up of their atoms, ions, or molecules and by attractions among these particles. As we pointed out earlier, water's unusually high melting and boiling points are due to the strong attraction between water molecules.

Understanding properties of atoms is the key to predicting and correlating the behavior of materials. This information, often combined with a bit of imagination, allows chemists to find new uses for materials and to create new chemical compounds to meet specific needs.

B.10 MODIFYING PROPERTIES

Throughout history—first by chance and more recently guided by science—we have greatly extended the array of materials

When first discovered, graphite was mistakenly identified as a form of lead; the name has stuck.

available for human use. Chemists have learned to modify the properties of matter by physically blending or chemically combining two or more substances. Sometimes only slight changes in a material's properties are desired. At other times chemists may create new materials with dramatically different properties.

The black "lead" in a pencil is mainly graphite, a natural form of the element carbon. Pencil lead is available in various levels of hardness. Hard pencil lead, No. 4, produces very light lines on paper. Softer writing lead (such as No. 1) makes very black, easily-smudged lines. Pencil lead hardness is controlled by the amount of clay mixed with the graphite. Increasing the quantity of clay produces harder pencil lead (less graphite can be rubbed off onto paper).

The laboratory activity Striking It Rich (page 89) demonstrated how metallic properties can be modified by creating **alloys,** solid mixtures of atoms of different metals. Brass was formed when you heated the zinc-coated penny. Brass is an alloy of copper with from 10 to 40% zinc. It is harder than copper and has an attractive gold color, unlike either copper or zinc.

Examples of materials designed to meet specific needs are easily found. The properties of certain plastics can be made to order—in some cases even without changing the material's chemical composition. For example, polyethene can be tailored to display relatively soft and pliable properties (as in a squeeze bottle for catsup), or can be crafted to be hard and brittle—almost glass-like in its behavior.

Penicillin is an antibiotic produced in nature by a mold. The penicillin molecule has been modified by chemists, resulting in a family of "semisynthetic" penicillins with improved or more specific effectiveness.

Such custom-tailoring at the atomic and molecular level is possible because of chemical knowledge—knowledge of how the atomic composition of materials affects their observable properties and behavior.

CHEMQUANDARY

Frozen Smoke?

A newly-produced solid substance, Aerogel, has such a low density that it looks like and has some properties of chemically inert, solid smoke. However, since it is a solid, it can be cut and patterned into various sizes and shapes. What uses can you propose for this material? Why do Aerogel's properties make it suitable for these uses?

B.11 YOU DECIDE: RESTORING MS. LIBERTY

Corrosion—the chemically-produced deterioration of metals—extracts a costly toll on the U.S. economy. The rusting, weakening, and degradation of metals within such diverse settings as automobiles, bridges, ship hulls, gardening utensils, and porch railings costs our economy an estimated $70 billion each year. A portion of the world's resources are used simply to replace or rebuild structures that have experienced serious corrosion. Not even the Statue of Liberty—that unique and instantly-recognized national symbol—is immune.

By the early 1980s it was apparent that serious corrosion within the Statue of Liberty demanded major attention. Several questions faced restoration experts, including what caused the Statue to deteriorate, how damage could be repaired, and how further deterioration could be avoided.

The Statue's body is composed of 300 individual copper plates. Each plate was originally connected by riveted copper straps to an iron-bar framework, as shown in Figure 10a. When different metals contact each other in the presence of moisture and dissolved ions, the metals react, causing corrosion.

The original Statue designers attempted to prevent copper from contacting the iron framework; they knew such contact would cause corrosion. The builders in the 1870s used shellac-soaked asbestos to separate copper from the iron wherever the two materials met. Over the years, condensed water vapor and rain collected at the junctions. The humid interior of the Statue, which was far from waterproof, also hastened corrosion of the iron. The iron bars rusted and swelled; some lost a large portion of their mass. As a result of the swelling, more than 40% of the 450,000 rivets pulled loose. This left holes in the copper and allowed the plates to sag (Figure 10b and c).

In addition to internal structural damage, the Statue's copper exterior had suffered the effects of air pollution. Copper metal normally reacts with substances in the air to form a stable, attractive, green coating or **patina,** on the exposed copper surface. This protects the underlying copper.

However, acidic pollutants can convert copper patina into a related substance that is more soluble in water. As rainwater dissolves this new substance, more copper metal is exposed and can undergo further corrosion.

In short, three major sources of Statue deterioration required attention:

- Corrosion of the iron framework at contact points between iron and copper.
- The humid atmosphere inside the Statue, which hastened iron corrosion.
- Removal of the protective patina coating on the copper exterior caused by airborne pollution.

A further problem was created by the multiple coats of paint and tar applied to the Statue's interior over the years. The damage due to corrosion could not be fully assessed—nor repairs made—until the paint and tar were removed.

How would you have tried to solve these restoration problems?

1. Using common experience and your chemistry knowledge, propose one or more solutions to each of the three problems identified above.

2. If substituting materials is part of your proposal, consider factors such as the chemical and physical properties of materials you propose using, their cost, and the need to preserve the Statue's design and appearance.

You will share your ideas with the class and compare them to the actual solutions chosen by the restoration committee.

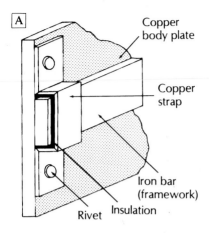

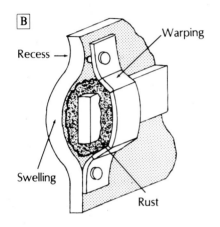

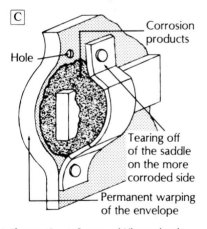

Figure 10 A Statue of Liberty body plate-iron framework connection, as originally constructed (A). Corrosion of the framework (B and C).

Preserving the Past

By Thomas Simon
West Hollywood Gazette *Staff Writer*

A museum curator is interested in buying a 2,000-year-old gold coin from a coin dealer. How does the curator know that the coin really is 2,000 years old? Mary Striegel can answer this question. She is a conservation scientist, but sometimes thinks of herself as a detective. To solve the puzzle, she looks at the coin through a microscope. She sees no evidence that the gold was struck by the tools of an ancient goldsmith, but does see tiny pieces of plastic embedded in the coin. Mary knows that plastic is left behind in coins made from molds; if the gold coin had been struck by a goldsmith, she would have seen stress fractures instead. From these observations, Mary concludes that the coin is a fraud, and advises the curator not to buy it, saving the museum money and embarrassment.

Mary Striegel works for the Getty Conservation Institute in Marina del Rey, California where teams of conservation scientists work on a variety of projects. One group is preparing to travel to China to study the effects of wind, rain, and temperature on ancient Buddhist sculptures, to help protect them from further erosion. Another group is designing display cases to preserve royal Egyptian mummies from future decay. A third group is investigating the deterioration of the Great Sphinx at Gaza in the desert environment. Mary's work involves analyzing museum environments and their effects on displayed artifacts such as Greek pottery containers, Roman lead letter seals, small Greek or Roman marble sculptures, or Chinese porcelain vases.

In developing a procedure to conserve irreplaceable ancient

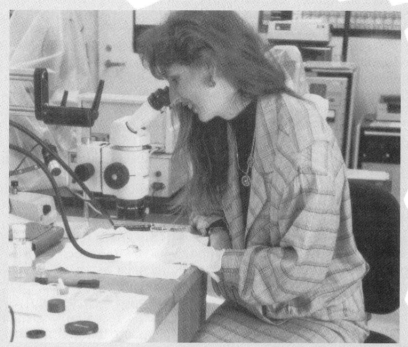

Photo by David Scott, The Getty Conservation Institute

artifacts, Mary must first determine the condition of the artifacts. She needs to know how the artifacts have changed over time, what caused these changes, how the artifacts could be repaired, and what can be done to preserve them for the future.

With help from her colleagues, she is currently studying the effects of trace amounts of pollutants in the museum environment on inorganic materials like glass, ceramics and glazes, metals, and sea shells. This involves doing library research to gather information about the materials and techniques used in making ancient sculptures. Mary also collects data on the environmental conditions of the museum to gain a thorough understanding of the chemical and physical conditions that might be affecting the collection.

With this information, Mary selects appropriate experimental techniques to investigate causes of the damage, and the best ways to preserve a specific artifact. Mary tests her proposed conservation methods on samples of similar modern metals to ensure that there is no damage to price-

less artifacts. For example, she determines the effects of formaldehyde production (which may come from display case materials), temperature, and relative humidity on the test metal.

Mary publishes her research in scientific journals, or presents it to her colleagues at professional meetings. Mary informs art conservators (who are responsible for the repair of artifacts) of the damaging effects of formaldehyde on metals, and suggests ways in which they can identify the damage on other artifacts. She also suggests ways of removing corrosion from metal sculptures and new ways to store and display them so that further damage is avoided.

While Mary has specialized in the protection of metal objects from formaldehyde damage, conservation scientists examine a variety of artifacts which might need protecting from a range of environmental insults. Thus, the background of a conservation scientist must be extremely diverse, encompassing a knowledge of several sciences including chemistry, as well as a knowledge of art history or studio art.

1. Describe how a chemical or physical property could be used to distinguish
   a. brass from gold.
   b. hydrogen from helium.
   c. tungsten from iron.
   d. a lithium-family metal from silver.

2. What two properties make nonmetals unsuitable for electric wiring?

3. Given the correct formulas Al_2O_3 and $BeCl_2$, predict formulas for compounds containing
   a. Mg and F.
   b. B and S.

4. For medical reasons, people with high blood pressure are advised to limit the amount of sodium ions in their diet. Normal table salt (NaCl) is sometimes replaced by a commercially-available substitute, potassium chloride.
   a. Write the formula for potassium chloride.
   b. Why are its properties similar to those of sodium chloride?

5. Decide whether each group of elements belongs to the same chemical family. If not, identify the element that does not belong with the other two:
   a. Sodium, potassium, magnesium
   b. Helium, neon, argon
   c. Oxygen, arsenic, sulfur
   d. Carbon, nitrogen, phosphorus

6. Why is it incorrect to consider any particular metal as chemically "perfect" or "best"?

7. If two different metals are used in construction, why is it desirable to separate them with a nonconducting material?

This gold-plated jewelry will not corrode. This property plus its pleasing appearance, malleability, and ductility make gold an ideal ornamental metal.

CONSERVATION IN NATURE AND THE COMMUNITY

You are now prepared to explore the chemical "supplies" aboard Spaceship Earth. Let's consider how nature conserves resources and examine the need for appropriate conservation practices within our society.

C.1 SOURCES OF RESOURCES

Despite advances in space travel, human needs for resources must continue to be met by chemical supplies currently present on Earth. These supplies or resources are often cataloged by where they are found. Table 3 indicates the composition of our planet.

Table 3   **EARTH'S COMPOSITION**

Layer of Planet	Thickness (Average)	Composition (Decreasing Order of Abundance)
Atmosphere	100 km	N_2 (78%), O_2 (21%), Ar (0.9%), He + Ne (<0.01%), variable amounts of H_2O, CO_2, etc.
Hydrosphere	5 km	H_2O, and in the oceans that cover some 71% of Earth's surface, approximately 3.5% NaCl and smaller amounts of Mg, S, Ca, and other elements as ions
Lithosphere: Crust	6400 km Top 40 km	Silicates (compounds formed of metals, Si, and O atoms). Metals include Al, Na, Fe, Ca, Mg, K, and others Coal, oil, and natural gas Carbonates such as $CaCO_3$ Oxides such as Fe_2O_3 Sulfides such as PbS
Mantle	40–2900 km	Silicates of Mg and Fe
Core	2900 km to the earth's center	Fe and Ni

The atmosphere, hydrosphere, and outer portion of the lithosphere are sources of *all* resources for *all* human activities. We use nitrogen, oxygen, neon, argon, and a few other gases from the atmosphere. We take water and some dissolved minerals from the hydrosphere. However, we mainly rely on the lithosphere, the solid part of Earth, for chemical resources. For example, that is where we find petroleum and metal-bearing ores. Our deepest mines barely scratch the surface of Earth's crust.

If Earth were the size of an apple, all the lithosphere's resources would be concentrated in the apple skin. From this thin band of soil and rock we obtain almost all the raw materials needed to build homes, automobiles, appliances, computers, cassette tapes, CDs, and tennis rackets—in fact, all manufactured objects.

*An **ore** is a naturally occurring rock or mineral from which it is profitable to recover a metal or other material.*

These chemical supplies are well suited to support a variety of life forms. However, many important resources are not uniformly distributed. There is no connection between the abundance of these resources and either land area or population. For example, the Republic of South Africa has only 0.7% of the world's population. However, as shown in Table 4, extraordinary amounts of many important resources are located there—particularly when compared to those in other major nations.

Table 4   **SOUTH AFRICA'S RESOURCES**

Resource	Percent of World's Known Reserve of Resource
Land area	0.8
Population	0.7
Platinum group metals (Pt, Pd, Ir, Rh, Ru, Os)	75
Chromium	68
Gold	51
Gemstones (diamonds, etc.)	34
Titanium	25

Many nations have a surplus of one or more chemical resources but deficiencies in others. Throughout history, unequal resource distribution has motivated great achievements and brutal wars. The development of the United States as a major industrial nation has been largely because of the quantity and diversity of our chemical resources. Yet, in recent years the United States has imported increasing amounts of certain chemical resources. For example, about 75% of the nation's requirements for the metal tin (Sn) are currently met by imported supplies.

In addition to land, which provides most of our chemical resources, ocean waters contain significant dissolved amounts of compounds of nearly 20 metals. Also, solid nodules on the ocean floor contain as much as 24% manganese (Mn), 14% iron (Fe), and trace amounts of copper (Cu), nickel (Ni), and cobalt (Co).

Even if the oceans were to become a major new source of minerals, the total supply of nonrenewable resources "aboard" Earth would remain unchanged. We may be able to postpone, but cannot avoid, the possibility of running out of some nonrenewable resources. The central question still remains: How can we deal wisely with the world's resources? Conservation is the best answer.

C.2 CONSERVATION IS NATURE'S WAY

The law of conservation of matter is based on the notion that Earth's basic "stuff"—its atoms—are indestructible. All changes we observe in matter can be interpreted as rearrangements among atoms.

It is often important to know how much of a desired element or a compound we can obtain from a natural resource. The answer to such a question usually begins with a chemical equation. Earlier (page 93) you practiced how to recognize properly-written chemical equations. Now you will learn how to write such balanced equations for yourself.

This reaction can occur with explosive violence, or can be controlled to power some types of rockets—or, in the case of fuel cells, to generate electricity.

As an example, consider the reaction of hydrogen gas with oxygen gas, producing gaseous water. First, write the reactant formula(s) to the left of the arrow and the product formula(s) to the right.

$$H_2(g) + O_2(g) \rightarrow H_2O(g)$$

Check this expression by completing an atom inventory: Two hydrogen atoms appear on the left and two on the right. So, the hydrogen atoms are balanced. However, there are two oxygen atoms on the left and only one on the right. Since oxygen is not balanced, the expression requires additional work.

Here is an *incorrect* way to complete the balanced equation:

$$H_2(g) + O_2(g) \rightarrow H_2O_2(g)$$
Incorrect!

In dilute water solution, H_2O_2 can be used as an antiseptic.

Even though this chemical statement satisfies atom-inventory standards (two hydrogen and oxygen atoms on both sides), the expression is wrong. The answer changes the product's identity from water, H_2O, to hydrogen peroxide, H_2O_2. Hydrogen peroxide is *not* produced in this reaction. The statement is incorrect, since it does not identify the correct substances.

The *correct* way to balance an equation is to place appropriate coefficients *before* chemical formulas. Select coefficients so the atoms of each element become balanced. Here is one way to proceed:

To balance oxygen atoms, write the coefficient 2 in front of water's formula:

$$H_2(g) + O_2(g) \rightarrow 2\ H_2O(g)$$

Now two oxygen atoms appear on each side. But, unfortunately, there are two hydrogen atoms on the left and four on the right—hydrogen is no longer balanced.

We can correct this by placing the coefficient 2 in front of the formula for hydrogen gas:

$$2\ H_2(g) + O_2(g) \rightarrow 2\ H_2O(g)$$

Two pairs of hydrogen atoms contain four hydrogen atoms. The equation is now balanced. When two molecules of hydrogen gas react with one molecule of oxygen gas, two molecules of gaseous water are formed. This is a correct symbolic summary of the reaction. It is based on nature's conservation of atoms.

The coefficient 1 is understood and not normally written.

Here are some additional rules of thumb to help you balance equations:

- Treat polyatomic ions, such as NO_3^- and CO_3^{2-}, as units rather than balancing their atoms individually.
- If water is present in a chemical equation, balance hydrogen and oxygen atoms last.

- Re-count all atoms when you believe an equation is balanced—just to be sure!

YOUR TURN

Balancing Equations

For another example of how a chemical statement can be converted to a chemical equation, consider this:

The reaction of methane (CH_4) with chlorine (Cl_2) occurs in sewage water plants and often in chlorinated water supplies. A common product is chloroform ($CHCl_3$). Chloroform is also made by the chemical industry for use in certain pharmaceutical preparations. A chemical statement describing this reaction is

$$CH_4(g) \quad + \quad Cl_2(g) \quad \rightarrow \quad CHCl_3(l) \quad + \quad HCl(g)$$

Methane   Chlorine   Chloroform   Hydrogen
gas   chloride

To change this expression to an equation, we can be guided by this line of reasoning: One carbon atom appears on both sides of the arrow, so carbon atoms balance. The coefficients for the two compounds containing carbon—CH_4 and $CHCl_3$—can be left as 1's. We will write these coefficients into the expression to help keep track of our work; they can be removed later:

$$1\ CH_4(g) + Cl_2(g) \rightarrow 1\ CHCl_3(l) + HCl(g)$$

Four hydrogen atoms are on the left, but only two on the right. To increase the number of hydrogen atoms on the right side, the coefficient for HCl can be adjusted. Since two more hydrogens are needed on the right side, the number of HCl molecules must increase by two, giving a total of three:

$$1\ CH_4(g) + Cl_2(g) \rightarrow 1\ CHCl_3(l) + 3\ HCl(g)$$

Now both carbon and hydrogen atoms are in balance. How about chlorine? We note there are two chlorine atoms on the left and six on the right side. These six chlorine atoms must have come from three chlorine (Cl_2) molecules. Thus we add this coefficient and—in keeping with common chemical practice—remove the two "1" coefficients:

$$CH_4(g) + 3\ Cl_2(g) \rightarrow CHCl_3(l) + 3\ HCl(g)$$

Here is an atom inventory for the completed equation:

Reactant side	Product side
1 atom C	1 atom C
4 atoms H	4 atoms H
6 atoms Cl	6 atoms Cl
(in 3 molecules Cl_2)	(3 in each product)

Copy each chemical expression onto your own paper and—if needed—balance it:

1. Two blast furnace reactions used to obtain iron from its ore:

   a. $C(s) + O_2(g) \rightarrow 2\ CO(g)$

   b. $Fe_2O_3(s) + CO(g) \rightarrow Fe(l) + 3\ CO_2(g)$

Chloroform is one of the THMs mentioned in the Water unit, page 74.

Blast furnace at one of the Inland Steel Company facilities.

2. Two reactions in the refining of a copper ore:
   a. $Cu_2S(s) + O_2(g) \rightarrow CuO(s) + SO_2(g)$
   b. $CuO(s) + C(s) \rightarrow Cu(s) + CO_2(g)$
3. Ammonia (NH_3) in the soil reacts continuously with oxygen gas (O_2):
$$NH_3(g) + O_2(g) \rightarrow NO_2(g) + H_2O(l)$$
4. Ozone, O_3, can decompose to form oxygen gas, O_2:
$$O_3(g) \rightarrow O_2(g)$$
5. Copper metal reacts with silver nitrate solution to form copper(II) nitrate solution and silver metal:
$$Cu(s) + AgNO_3(aq) \rightarrow Cu(NO_3)_2(aq) + Ag(s)$$
6. Combustion of gasoline in an automobile engine can be represented by:
$$C_8H_{18}(l) + O_2(g) \rightarrow CO_2(g) + H_2O(g)$$

C.3 ATOM, MOLECULE, AND ION INVENTORY

As part of your answer to Question 2 above, you obtained the balanced equation

$$2\ CuO(s) + C(s) \rightarrow 2\ Cu(s) + CO_2(g).$$

Here is one interpretation of this equation: *Two formula units of copper(II) oxide and one atom of carbon react to produce two atoms of copper and one molecule of carbon dioxide.* This interpretation—although correct—involves such small quantities of material that such a reaction would be completely unnoticed. Such information would not be not very useful, for example, to a metal refiner who wants to know how much carbon would be needed to react with a certain amount of copper(II) oxide.

Chemists have devised a counting unit called the **mole** (symbolized mol) that helps solve the refiner's problem. You are familiar with other counting units such as "pair" or "dozen." A pair of water molecules would be two water molecules. One dozen water molecules refers to 12 water molecules. Likewise, one mole of water molecules is 602,000,000,000,000,000,000,000 water molecules. This number—the number of particles (or "things") in one mole—is more conveniently written as 6.02×10^{23}. In either case, this is a very large number!

Suppose you could string a mole of paperclips (6.02×10^{23} paperclips) together and wrap the string around the world. It would circle the world about 400 trillion (4×10^{14}) times.

However, as large as one mole of molecules is, drinking that amount of water would leave you quite thirsty on a hot day. One mole of water is less than one-tenth of a cup of water—only 18 g (or 18 mL) of water. But that is why the mole is so useful in chemistry. It represents a number of atoms, molecules, or formula units large enough to be conveniently weighed or measured in the laboratory. Furthermore, the atomic masses of elements can be used to find the mass of one mole of any substance—a value known as the substance's **molar mass.**

This notion can be developed through some specific examples. Suppose we want to find the molar masses of carbon (C)

There are about 2×10^{25} (20,000,000,000,000,000,000,000,000) molecules of water in this beaker.

Don't even think of trying this experiment! Even if you connected a million paperclips together each second, it would take 190 million centuries to finish stringing the entire mole of paperclips.

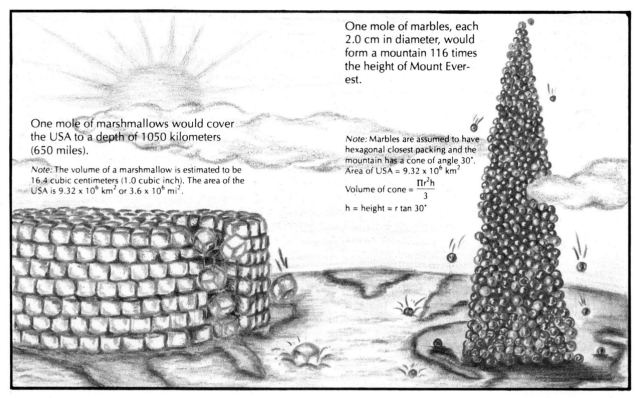

One mole of marshmallows would cover the USA to a depth of 1050 kilometers (650 miles).

Note: The volume of a marshmallow is estimated to be 16.4 cubic centimeters (1.0 cubic inch). The area of the USA is 9.32×10^6 km^2 or 3.6×10^6 mi^2.

One mole of marbles, each 2.0 cm in diameter, would form a mountain 116 times the height of Mount Everest.

Note: Marbles are assumed to have hexagonal closest packing and the mountain has a cone of angle 30°.
Area of USA = 9.32×10^6 km^2

Volume of cone = $\dfrac{\Pi r^2 h}{3}$

h = height = r tan 30°

The mole concept.

and copper (Cu). Or, putting it another way, we want to know the mass of one mole of carbon atoms and one mole of copper atoms (6.02×10^{23} atoms in either case).

Rather than counting these atoms onto a laboratory balance (good luck!), we can quickly get the answers from the elements' atomic masses. Here is how:

First find the atomic masses of these elements on the periodic table (located inside the back cover). Carbon's atomic mass is 12.01; copper's is 63.55. If we simply add units of "grams" to these values, we have their molar masses:

$$1 \text{ mol C} = 12.01 \text{ g} \qquad 1 \text{ mol Cu} = 63.55 \text{ g}$$

Recall that mol *is the symbol for the unit* mole.

In brief, the mass (in grams) of one mole of an element's atoms equals the numerical value of the element's atomic mass. As you have seen, this is much more easily done than said!

The molar mass of a compound is the sum of the molar masses of its component atoms. To illustrate this idea, consider two compounds of interest to the copper metal refiner—copper(II) oxide (CuO) and carbon dioxide (CO_2).

In a sense, this is just an application of the idea that the whole equals the sum of its parts.

One dozen units of CuO contains one dozen Cu atoms and one dozen O atoms. Likewise—using the chemist's counting unit—one mole of CO_2 contains one mole of C atoms and two moles of O atoms.

Using the molar mass of copper and that of oxygen atoms gives

$$1 \text{ mol Cu} \times \frac{63.55 \text{ g Cu}}{1 \text{ mol Cu}} = 63.55 \text{ g Cu}$$

$$1 \text{ mol O} \times \frac{16.00 \text{ g O}}{1 \text{ mol O}} = \underline{16.00 \text{ g O}}$$

Molar mass of CuO = 79.55 g CuO

The molar mass of carbon dioxide—or any other compound—is found similarly.

$$1 \; \cancel{mol \; C} \times \frac{12.01 \; g \; C}{1 \; \cancel{mol \; C}} = 12.01 \; g \; C$$

$$2 \; \cancel{mol \; O} \times \frac{16.00 \; g \; O}{1 \; \cancel{mol \; O}} = 32.00 \; g \; O$$

Molar mass of CO_2 = 44.01 g CO_2

In brief, the molar mass of a compound is found by first multiplying the moles of each element present in the formula by the molar mass of the element. Then the total element molar masses are added to give the compound's molar mass.

YOUR TURN

Molar Masses

Find the molar mass of each substance:
1. The element nitrogen, N
2. Nitrogen gas: N_2
3. Sodium chloride (table salt): NaCl
4. Sucrose (table sugar): $C_{12}H_{22}O_{11}$
5. Chalcopyrite: $CuFeS_2$
6. Malachite: $Cu_2CO_3(OH)_2$ (*Hint:* This formula shows 5 mol of oxygen atoms)

The expression "one mole of nitrogen" can be confusing. It might refer to a mole of N atoms (as in Question 1) or a mole of N_2 molecules (as in Question 2). That is why it is important to specify the exact identities of substances involved.

Now we can return to metal refining. The mole "counting unit" makes it easy to find the mass, for example, of sulfur dioxide released during refining. The coefficients in a chemical equation show both the numbers of molecules (or formula units) of reactants and products *and* the numbers of moles of these substances:

$$2 \; CuO(s) \; + \quad C(s) \quad \rightarrow \quad 2 \; Cu(s) \; + \quad CO_2(g).$$

2 units of CuO	1 atom of C	2 atoms of Cu	1 molecule of CO_2
2 moles of CuO	1 mole of C	2 moles of Cu	1 mole of CO_2

Thus, for every two moles of CuO that react, one mole of CO_2 will be formed. We already know the molar masses of all four substances in the equation:

$$2 \; CuO(s) \; + \quad C(s) \quad \rightarrow \quad 2 \; Cu(s) \; + \; CO_2(g).$$

2 moles of CuO	1 mole of C	2 moles of Cu	1 mole of CO_2
159.10 g of CuO	12.01 g of C	127.10 g of Cu	44.01 g of CO_2

The table indicates that the mass of 2 moles of CuO is 159.10 g. This value is found by recognizing that 2 moles of CuO contains 2 moles of Cu atoms and 2 moles of O atoms. Thus: (2 × 63.55 g) + (2 × 16.00 g) = 159.10 g of CuO.

Our metal refiner now knows that if 159.10 g of CuO is processed by this reaction, 127.10 g of Cu will be produced, along with 44.10 g of CO_2.

Check the table again. Note that the total mass of reactants (159.10 g + 12.01 g = 171.11 g) equals the total mass of products (127.10 g + 44.01 g = 171.11 g). This is a good illustration of the law of conservation of matter—in a chemical reaction matter is neither created nor destroyed.

Thanks to the mole concept, chemical equations allow chemists to account for the masses of all substances involved in chemical reactions. However, monitoring and accounting for resources used in the manufacture of materials and goods is more difficult.

C.4 CONSERVATION MUST BE OUR WAY

If nature always conserves, why do we read at times that a resource is "running out"? In what sense can we "run out" of a resource?

First, remember that nature conserves *atoms,* but not necessarily *molecules.* For example, nature's current production of molecules found in petroleum is far less than the rate at which society extracts and burns them, changing petroleum's molecules to carbon dioxide and other molecules. We cannot easily put the smaller molecules together to make petroleum again.

We can deplete a resource—particularly metals—another way. For profitable mining, an ore must contain some minimum percent of metal. (This limit depends on the metal ore—from as low as 1% for copper or 0.001% for gold to as high as 30% for aluminum.) As ores with high metal concentrations are depleted, lower-concentration ores are processed. Meanwhile, through use, we disperse the originally-concentrated resource. Atoms of the metal, once located in rich deposits in limited parts of the world, become "spread out" over the entire globe. Our economy may eventually become unable to support further extraction of such a metal for general use. For practical purposes, our supply of this resource will be depleted.

Can we avoid this situation? We know that nature conserves automatically at the atomic level. How can we conserve our resources? That is, how can we slow down the rate at which we use them?

The "four Rs" of resource conservation and management are rethink, replace, reuse, recycle. As an overall strategy, we should continually *rethink* our personal and societal habits and practices involving resource use. For example, when you respond to the grocery clerk's question "Paper or plastic?" what consequences—if any—does your answer have? Such rethinking can help us to re-examine old assumptions, identify resource-saving strategies, and—at times—uncover new solutions to old problems.

To *replace* a resource means finding substitute materials with similar properties—preferably materials from renewable resources.

Some manufactured items can be refurbished or repaired for *reuse* rather than sent to a landfill. Unwanted or outgrown clothing can be redistributed to others. Broken equipment can be repaired.

To *recycle* means to gather and collect certain items for reprocessing, allowing the resources present in them to be used again. Many communities realize the wisdom of this aspect of resource management. How is a recycling program planned and organized? Let's consider such an activity in detail.

Which 2 of the "4 Rs" are represented here?

C.5 YOU DECIDE: RECYCLING DRIVE

Our nation has been called a "throwaway" society. We discard about 1.1 million tons of disposable plates and cups each year. That represents enough to offer six picnics annually to the entire world's population! In a more general sense, about 30% of U.S. production of major materials is eventually discarded.

Some critics say that our society overpackages food and consumer items. Packaging materials constitute about a half of all solid wastes in the U.S. by volume, and nearly a third by mass.

Think about the single-use packaging involved in a fast-food meal. The throwaway inventory would include a hamburger container, disposable cup, plastic lid, plastic straw, paper french fry bag, plastic catsup pouch, paper packages for salt and pepper, paper napkin, and—if it is a take-out order—a paper bag to hold the meal!

Some packaging is necessary. Packaging protects ingredients, keeps small items together, and in many instances promotes cleanliness and safety. But even a simple ballpoint pen is often packaged in plastic and cardboard, and is placed in a bag by the cashier for you to take home. (And finally—like some other consumer items—the pen itself might be designed to be discarded rather than refilled or reused.)

What are the alternatives? One is to use less. Another is to buy in bulk to use less packaging material. Other alternatives are to use items for longer times or to reuse or recycle them.

Recycling requires considerable commitment and effort. What are its benefits? To find answers, let's examine three materials: paper, aluminum, and glass.

Paper. This is an important renewable resource. Since paper is made from tree pulp, new seedlings can be planted to replace trees cut down. However, it takes about 25 years for seedlings to grow to trees large enough to be economically useful. "Renewing" of this resource takes time! About 17 trees are needed to produce a ton of paper. That is just enough to supply two citizens with the paper they will use in one year!

Energy is required to make paper from a tree. Less than half as much energy is needed to process recycled paper as is used in making new paper. Unfortunately, only about 20% of the paper we use is currently recycled.

Consumers can exchange used cans and plastic and glass containers for money at these automatic recycling units.

Recycling Limits

This textbook is not printed on recycled paper, despite the efforts of the publisher to find suitable material. Why do you think this is so?

Aluminum (Al). This is a nonrenewable chemical resource—the total number of aluminum atoms in the world is, for all practical purposes, fixed and unchanging. Once we have consumed this resource, there will be no more.

Aluminum is the most abundant metal in the earth's crust (8%). However, much of this aluminum is locked in silicates, from which it cannot be easily extracted. U.S. demand for aluminum is so great that domestic supplies of the ore (bauxite) do not meet national needs.

We import about 85% of aluminum resources used in this country. Producing aluminum from bauxite ore requires considerable energy. Recycling used aluminum consumes only 5–10% of the energy needed to produce aluminum from its ore. Thanks to organized national efforts, we now recycle over half of our used aluminum cans.

Glass. A simple form of glass is made by melting together, at high temperatures, sand (silicon dioxide, SiO_2), soda ash (sodium carbonate, Na_2CO_3) and limestone (calcium carbonate, $CaCO_3$). All three materials are nonrenewable but plentiful. It is estimated that about 20 to 25% of each new glass container currently made in the U.S. is produced from waste glass or recycled glass.

According to recent analyses, glass recycling helps reduce a portion of the energy involved in glass manufacture. If 100% waste glass and recycled glass were used in new containers, energy savings in processing would be about 15%, with an additional 16% savings due to the lack of mining and transportation costs for new materials.

Working in small groups, discuss possible answers to the following questions. Your group's answers will be discussed later by the entire class.

1. Which of the three materials—paper, aluminum, or glass—is most important to recycle
   a. for economic reasons?
   b. for environmental reasons?
      Explain your answers.

2. a. If recycling is important, should the federal government require that certain materials be recycled?
   b. If so, identify some materials that should be recycled under such a law.
   c. How could such a law be enforced?

3. As individuals, we can replace, reuse, or recycle materials in various ways. For example, we can use both sides of paper for writing, or—when given a choice—purchase beverages in returnable bottles and return them. Identify at least five other ways we, as individuals, can replace, reuse, or recycle certain materials.

4. We plant forests to supply our paper needs. Assume that all printed and typewritten communication is replaced in the future by computer-based electronic networks.
   a. What current uses of paper would cease?
   b. What occupations or jobs would be eliminated?
   c. What occupations or jobs would be created?
   d. What would you be reading instead of this paper chemistry textbook?
   e. How else would your daily routine change due to this technological advancement?

PART C: SUMMARY QUESTIONS

1. a. List and briefly describe the three major regions of Earth.
   b. Which region serves as the main "storehouse" of chemical resources used in manufacturing consumer products?

2. Write balanced chemical equations for each of these:
   a. Preparing phosphoric acid (used in making soft drinks, detergents, and other products) from phosphate rock and sulfuric acid:

$$Ca_3(PO_4)_2(s) + H_2SO_4(aq) \rightarrow H_3PO_4(aq) + CaSO_4(s)$$

   b. Preparing tungsten from its ore:

$$WO_3(s) + H_2(g) \rightarrow W(s) + H_2O(l)$$

   c. Heating lead sulfide ore in air:

$$PbS(s) + O_2(g) \rightarrow PbO(s) + SO_2(g)$$

3. Describe an everyday routine you would be willing to change to reduce problems of solid waste disposal.

4. Find the molar mass of each substance:
   a. Oxygen atom, O
   b. Oxygen gas, O_2
   c. Ozone, O_3
   d. Epsom salt, $MgSO_4$
   e. Lye drain cleaner, NaOH
   f. Aspirin, $C_9H_8O_4$

5. One method to produce chromium metal includes, as the final step, the reaction of chromium(III) oxide with silicon at high temperature:

$$2\ Cr_2O_3(s) + 3\ Si(s) \rightarrow 4\ Cr(s) + 3\ SiO_2(s)$$

   a. How many moles of each reactant and product are shown in this chemical equation?
   b. What mass (in grams) of each reactant and product is specified by this equation?
   c. Show how this equation illustrates the law of conservation of matter.

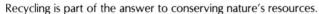

Recycling is part of the answer to conserving nature's resources.

METALS: SOURCES AND REPLACEMENTS

Technological advances and life-style changes can rapidly alter our resource needs. Even though such changes are difficult to predict, we must be prepared to deal with them.

Copper serves as a useful case study regarding present and projected uses of a vital chemical resource. We will consider sources of our copper supply and how these materials are converted to pure copper. You will produce a sample of metallic copper. Finally, we will look at some possible replacements for this resource.

D.1 COPPER: SOURCES AND USES

Copper is among the most familiar and widely-used metals in modern society. Among the elements, it has the second-highest electrical conductivity (silver is first). This property, together with its low cost, corrosion resistance, and ability to be drawn easily into thin wires, has made copper the world's most common "electrical wiring" and "electrical transmission" option. It is also used in the manufacture of brass, bronze, and other copper alloys, a variety of important copper-based compounds, and works of art.

Copper resources are widely (but unevenly) distributed throughout the world. The United States has been a major world supplier of copper ore. Canada, Chile, Peru, and Zambia also have significant supplies of copper ore.

Can adequate profit can be earned from mining a particular metallic ore at a certain site? The answer depends on several factors:

- the metal's supply-demand status
- type of mining and processing needed to obtain the metal
- amount of useful ore at the site
- percent of metal in the ore.

The first rich copper ores mined contained 35–88% copper. Such ores are no longer available. In fact, it is now possible economically to mine ores with less than 1% copper. Copper ore is chemically processed to produce metallic copper, which is then formed into a variety of useful materials. Figure 11 (page 132) summarizes the copper cycle from sources to uses to waste products.

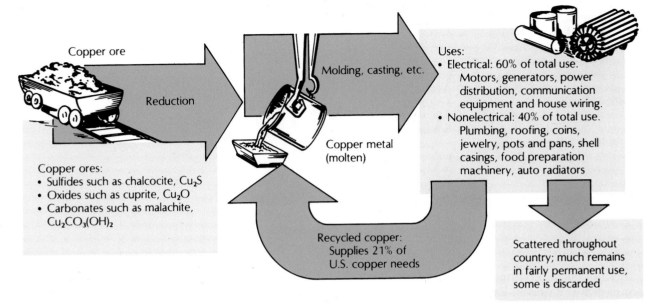

Figure 11 The copper cycle.

Will future developments increase or decrease our need for copper? Are we doomed to deplete the rich deposits of this valuable resource? What copper substitutes are available? This activity will help you answer these questions.

A malleable material can be flattened without shattering. Ductile materials can be drawn out into wire.

YOUR TURN

Uses of Copper

Some copper properties are listed in Table 5. Let's consider how these properties make copper suitable for uses listed in Figure 11.

Table 5	PROPERTIES OF COPPER
Malleability and ductility	High
Electrical conductivity	High
Thermal conductivity	High
Chemical reactivity	Relatively low
Resistance to corrosion	High
Useful alloys formed	Bronze, brass, etc.
Color and luster	Reddish, shiny

Here is an example: What properties make copper suitable for use in electrical power generators? Certainly copper's high electrical conductivity is essential to this application. Copper's malleability and ductility are also important, so it can form wires and be looped in a generator armature. Corrosion resistance is also a benefit in such large, expensive equipment.

1. Consider the remaining copper uses that are listed in Figure 11. For each, identify particular properties that explain copper's appropriateness.
2. a. How would increased recycling of scrap copper affect future availability of this metal?
   b. Is there a limit to the role recycling can play?
   c. Why?

3. For each copper use listed below, describe a technological change that could decrease the demand for copper:

   a. Communications

   b. Coins

   c. Power generation

   d. Wiring inside appliances

D.2   EVALUATING AN ORE

How do geologists know how much copper or other metal is present in a particular ore? Some fundamental chemical ideas apply.

A compound's formula indicates the relative number of atoms of each element in the substance. For example, one common commercial source of copper is the mineral chalcocite—copper(I) sulfide, Cu_2S. Its formula tells us that copper(I) sulfide contains two copper atoms for each sulfur atom. The formula can also help us find out how much of the mineral's mass can be converted to pure copper—an important factor if copper mining and production are under consideration.

In short, the percent of metal in an ore helps determine whether a particular deposit is worth mining. Apply your knowledge of chemical composition in completing this exercise.

Chalcocite.

Mine at Bingham Canyon, Utah—largest human-made hole on Earth.

Percent Composition

A mineral is a chemical compound—it has a definite formula and chemical composition. An ore is usually a mixture of minerals—some useful, some not.

Some copper-containing minerals are listed in Table 6. Let's find the percent copper in chalcocite, Cu_2S, and in an ore containing 5.0% chalcocite.

Table 6   COPPER-CONTAINING MINERALS

Common Name	Formula
Chalcocite	Cu_2S
Chalcopyrite	$CuFeS_2$
Malachite	$Cu_2CO_3(OH)_2$
Azurite	$Cu_3(CO_3)_2(OH)_2$

From the formula Cu_2S we know that one mole of Cu_2S contains two moles of Cu, or (as shown in the margin) 127.1 g Cu. We also know that the molar mass of Cu_2S is 159.2 g. Therefore,

To find the mass of two moles of Cu:

$$2 \, \text{mol Cu} \times \frac{63.55 \text{ g Cu}}{1 \text{ mol Cu}} = 127.1 \text{ g Cu}$$

$$\% \text{ Cu} = \frac{\text{Mass of Cu}}{\text{Mass of } Cu_2S} \times 100 =$$

$$\frac{127.1 \text{ g Cu}}{159.2 \text{ g } Cu_2S} \times 100 = 79.84\% \text{ Cu}$$

A similar calculation (try it yourself) indicates that Cu_2S contains 20.16% sulfur. Note that the sum of percent copper and percent sulfur equals 100.00%. (Why?)

To find the percent copper in the ore, assume we have a 100-g sample of the ore. Since the ore is 5.0% chalcocite, 100 g of ore will contain 5.0 g chalcocite $(0.050 \times 100 \text{ g} = 5.0 \text{ g})$. From our first calculation, we know that 79.84% of this mass is copper. Thus

$$5.0 \text{ g } Cu_2S \times 0.7985 = 4.0 \text{ g Cu}$$

If 4.0 g of copper is present in 100 g of ore, the ore contains 4.0% copper, $(4.0 \text{ g}/100 \text{ g}) \times 100 = 4.0\%$.

1. a. Calculate the percent copper in each of the last three copper minerals listed in Table 6.
   b. Assume that each mineral was present at the same concentration in an ore. Also assume that copper could be extracted from each ore at the same cost. Which of the four could be mined most profitably?

2. Two common iron-containing minerals are hematite (Fe_2O_3) and magnetite (Fe_3O_4). If you had an equal mass (such as 1 kg) of each, which sample would contain the greater amount of iron? Support your answer with calculations.

3. Assume that a 100-g sample of iron ore from Site A contains 20 g of Fe_2O_3, while a 100-g sample from Site B contains 15 g of Fe_3O_4.
   a. What is the mass of iron in each sample?
   b. Which ore contains the larger percent of iron?

D.3 METAL REACTIVITY REVISITED

Humans have been described as "tool-making animals." Readily-available stone, wood, and natural fibers became the earliest tool materials. A variety of useful implements could be made from such naturally-occurring materials. However, the discovery that fire could transform certain rocks into strong, malleable materials (metals) triggered a dramatic leap in civilization's growth.

Gold and silver, found as uncombined elements, were probably the first metals used by humans. These metals were formed into decorative objects. It is estimated that copper has been used for 10,000 years for tools, weapons, utensils, and decorations. Bronze, an alloy of copper and tin, was invented about 3800 B.C. Thus humans moved from the Stone Age into the Bronze Age.

Eventually iron metallurgy was developed, leading to the start of the Iron Age more than 3000 years ago. In time, as humans learned more about chemistry and fire, a variety of metallic ores were transformed into increasingly useful materials.

CHEMQUANDARY

Discovery of Metals

Copper, gold, and silver are not Earth's most abundant metals. Aluminum, iron, and calcium, for example, are all much more plentiful. Then why were copper, gold, and silver among the first metallic elements discovered?

You explored some chemistry of metals in the laboratory activity Metal Reactivities (page 113). You found, for example, that copper is more reactive than silver, but less reactive than magnesium. A more complete activity series is given in Table 7, which includes brief descriptions of common methods for retrieving these metals from their ores.

Table 7   **METAL ACTIVITY SERIES**

Element	Metal Ion(s) Found in Ore	Metal Obtained	Reduction Process Used to Obtain the Metal
Lithium	Li^+	$Li(s)$	Pass electric current through the molten salt (electrolysis)
Potassium	K^+	$K(s)$	
Calcium	Ca^{2+}	$Ca(s)$	
Sodium	Na^+	$Na(s)$	
Magnesium	Mg^{2+}	$Mg(s)$	
Aluminum	Al^{3+}	$Al(s)$	
Manganese	Mn^{2+}	$Mn(s)$	Heat with coke (carbon) or carbon monoxide (CO)
Zinc	Zn^{2+}	$Zn(s)$	
Chromium	Cr^{3+}, Cr^{2+}	$Cr(s)$	
Iron	Fe^{3+}, Fe^{2+}	$Fe(s)$	
Lead	Pb^{2+}	$Pb(s)$	Element occurs free or is obtained by heating in air (roasting)
Copper	Cu^{2+}, Cu^+	$Cu(s)$	
Mercury	Hg^{2+}	$Hg(l)$	
Silver	Ag^+	$Ag(s)$	
Platinum	Pt^{2+}	$Pt(s)$	
Gold	Au^{3+}, Au^+	$Au(s)$	

The most reactive metals are listed first; less reactive metals are closer to the bottom. Reactive metals are more difficult to retrieve from their ores than are less-active metals.

An activity list can be used to predict whether certain reactions can be expected. For example, you found in the laboratory that zinc metal, which is more reactive than copper, will react with copper ions in solution. However, zinc metal will not react with magnesium ions in solution, since zinc is less reactive than magnesium. In general, *a more reactive metal will release a less reactive metal from its compounds.*

Use Table 7 and the periodic table to complete the following exercise.

YOUR TURN

Metal Reactivity

1. What trend in metallic reactivity is found from left to right across a horizontal row (period) of the periodic table? (*Hint:* Compare the reactivities of sodium, magnesium, and aluminum. In which part of the periodic table are the most reactive metals found? Which side of the periodic table contains the least reactive metals?)

2. a. Will iron (Fe) metal react with a solution of lead nitrate, $Pb(NO_3)_2$?

   b. Will platinum (Pt) react with a lead nitrate solution?

   c. Explain your answers.

3. Compare the three reduction processes described in the activity table.

   a. Which would you expect to require the greatest quantity of energy? Why?

   b. Which is likely to be least expensive? Why?

4. The least reactive metals are easiest to obtain from their ores. Use specific examples from the activity series in your answers to these questions:

   a. Would least-reactive metals necessarily be the cheapest metals?

   b. If not, what other factor(s) influence the market value of a given metal?

D.4 METALS FROM ORES

The process of converting a combined metal (usually a metal ion) in a mineral into a free metal is called **reduction.** This term has a specific chemical meaning. To convert metal ions to metal atoms, the ions must gain electrons. *Any* process in which electrons are gained by a species is called "reduction." Reduction of one copper(II) ion, for example, requires two electrons:

$$Cu^{2+} \quad + \quad 2\,e^- \quad \rightarrow \quad Cu \quad \text{(Reduction)}$$

| Copper(II) ion | two electrons | Copper metal |

The reverse process, in which an ion or other species loses electrons, is called **oxidation.** Under the right conditions copper *atoms* can be oxidized:

$$Cu \rightarrow Cu^{2+} + 2\,e^- \quad \text{(Oxidation)}$$

Copper   Copper(II)   two
metal   ion   electrons

We live in an electrically-neutral world. Whenever one species loses electrons another must gain them. That is, oxidation and reduction never occur separately. They occur together in what chemists call **oxidation-reduction reactions** or **redox reactions.**

You have already observed redox reactions in the laboratory. For example, in the laboratory activity Metal Reactivities (page 113), some metals were oxidized. Here is one oxidation-reduction reaction you observed:

$$Cu(s) + 2\,Ag^+(aq) \rightarrow 2\,Ag(s) + Cu^{2+}(aq)$$

Copper   Silver   Silver   Copper(II)
metal   ion   metal   ion

Copper atoms were oxidized (converted to Cu^{2+} ions) and silver ions (Ag^+) from $AgNO_3$ solution were reduced (converted to Ag atoms).

In the same activity you found that copper ions could be recovered from solution by reaction with magnesium, a more active metal than copper. Magnesium atoms were oxidized, copper ions reduced:

$$Mg(s) + Cu^{2+}(aq) \rightarrow Cu(s) + Mg^{2+}(aq)$$

Magnesium   Copper(II)   Copper   Magnesium
metal   ion   metal   ion

In some circumstances this might be a useful way to obtain copper metal. However, as is always the case, to obtain a desired product, something else is used up—in this case another desirable metal, magnesium.

How do redox reactions occur? Many metallic elements are found in nature as ions (components of minerals) because they

*A good way to keep this straight is to remember that "**LEO** the lion goes **GER**": **L**oss of **E**lectrons is **O**xidation, **G**ain of **E**lectrons is **R**eduction.*

Molten aluminum metal from electrolytic cells.

combine readily with other elements to form ionic compounds. Obtaining a metal from its mineral requires not only energy, but also a source of electrons, known as a ***reducing agent.*** As Table 7 shows, a variety of techniques are used, depending on the metal's reactivity, and the availability of inexpensive reducing agents and energy sources. We will consider the methods used.

Pyrometallurgy is the treatment of metals and their ores by heat, as in a blast furnace. Two of the three reduction processes shown in Table 7 are based on pyrometallurgy—heating an ore in air (roasting) and heating it with an added reducing agent. Carbon (coke) and carbon monoxide are commonly used. A more active metal can be used if neither of these will do the job. Pyrometallurgy is the most important and oldest ore-processing method.

Electrometallurgy involves using an electric current to supply electrons to metal ions, thus reducing them. Electrometallurgy includes electroplating, electrorefining, and use of an electric arc furnace to make steel. This process is used when no adequate reducing agents are available or when very high metal purity is needed.

Hydrometallurgy is the treatment of ores and other metal-containing materials by reactants in water solution. You used such a procedure when you compared the reactivity of four metals as directed on page 114. Hydrometallurgy is not commonly used industrially due to the high cost of the more active metal. However, as ore supplies become less concentrated in the desired metal, it will become economically feasible to use hydrometallurgy and other "wet processes" with minerals that can be dissolved in water.

In the following laboratory activity you will try your hand at electrometallurgy.

D.5   LABORATORY ACTIVITY: PRODUCING COPPER

Getting Ready

In this activity you will produce copper metal from a solution of copper(II) chloride ($CuCl_2$) by electrolysis. A 9-V battery will provide the electric current.

Industrial-scale electrolysis uses large quantities of electrical energy, making it an expensive—although effective—way to obtain or purify metals.

In the industrial refining of copper, pure copper is obtained by electrometallurgy from less-pure copper produced by pyrometallurgy.

Procedure

1. Obtain two graphite (carbon) rods in the form of pencil lead. (Depending on the size of the electrolysis apparatus you will use, the graphite rods may still be encased inside two wooden pencils. If so, just be sure graphite protrudes from both ends so electrical contact can be made.) These rods will serve as the terminals or ***electrodes*** for the electrolysis process.

2. Set up the apparatus shown in Figure 12. Attach the 9-V battery connector to the battery, but *do not* connect the wire leads to the electrodes or allow the two wires to touch each other.

3. Pour enough copper(II) chloride ($CuCl_2$) solution into the U-tube so the graphite electrodes can be partially immersed in the solution.

4. Have your teacher approve the set up.

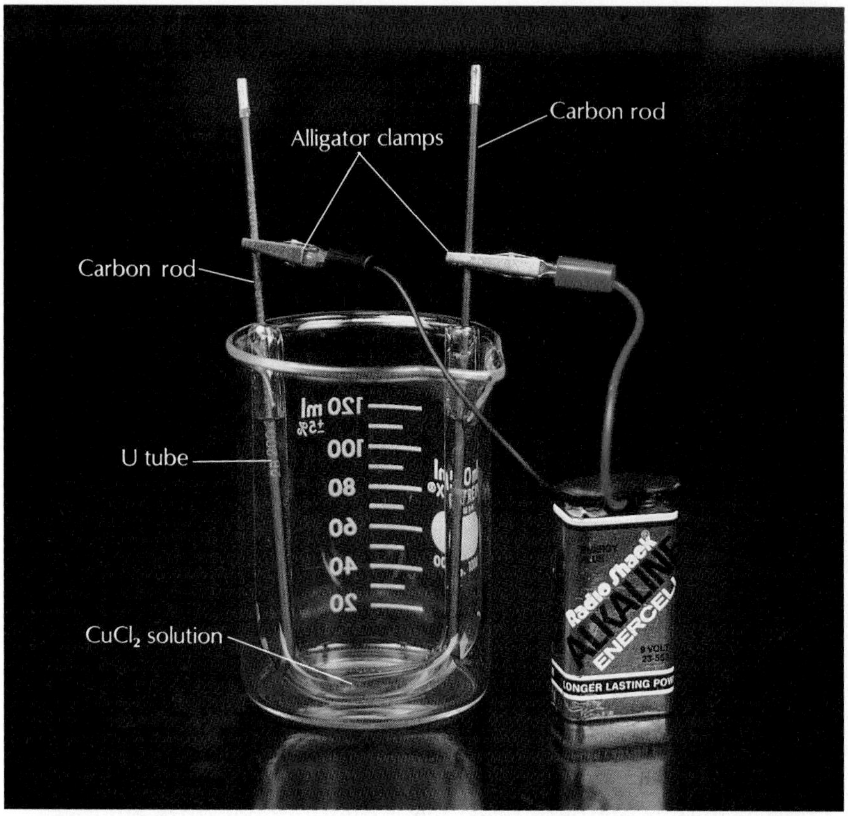

Figure 12 Apparatus for electrolysis of copper(II) chloride solution.

5. Attach wires to the two graphite terminals.
6. Observe the reaction for approximately five minutes. Record your observations in your notebook.
7. *Cautiously* sniff each electrode.
8. Reverse the wire connections to the electrodes and repeat Step 6.
9. Wash your hands thoroughly before leaving the laboratory.

Questions

1. Describe changes observed during the electrolysis.
2. The **cathode** is the terminal (electrode) at which reduction occurs.
   a. Which electrode was the cathode in the electrolysis?
   b. What change did you observe at the cathode?
3. The other electrode, the **anode,** is where oxidation occurs.
   a. Which electrode was the anode in the electrolysis?
   b. What change did you observe at the anode?
4. Write a balanced equation for the overall chemical change in this electrolysis reaction. The oxidation product is chlorine gas, $Cl_2(g)$.

D.6 FUTURE MATERIALS

As we continue extracting and using chemical resources from Spaceship Earth, we are sometimes forced to consider alternatives. One option is to find new materials that can substitute for less-available resources. An ideal substitute satisfies three requirements: Its properties should match or exceed those of the original material; it should be plentiful; and, of course, it should be inexpensive. Substitute materials seldom meet these conditions completely. Thus, we must consider the benefits and burdens involved in such substitutions. We will consider the promises and challenges of several representative new materials in this section.

Clay is one of the most plentiful materials on this planet. It is mainly composed of silicon, oxygen, and aluminum, along with magnesium, sodium, and potassium ions and water molecules. Early humans found that clay mixed with water, then molded and heated, formed useful ceramic products such as pottery and bricks.

In more recent times, researchers found that when other common rock materials are heated to high temperatures, useful "fired" compounds, also called *ceramics*, can form. Figure 13 compares the sources, processing, and products of conventional ceramics with newer, stronger engineering ceramics.

What properties of conventional ceramics made them useful in pottery and bricks? Characteristics such as hardness, rigidity, low chemical reactivity, and resistance to wear were certainly important. The main attractions of ceramics for future use, however, are their high melting points and their strength at high temperatures. They might become, in fact, attractive substitutes in some steel applications. For example, scientists believe that diesel or turbine engines made of ceramics might be able to operate at higher temperatures. Such high-temperature engines would run with increased efficiency, reducing fuel use.

The major problem still facing researchers, however, is that ceramics are brittle. They can fracture if exposed to rapid temperature changes, such as during hot-engine cool-down. Great hope remains, however, for the future of ceramics. They have become vitally important materials.

Plastics have already replaced metals for many uses. These synthetic substances are composed of complex carbon-atom chains and rings with hydrogen and other atoms attached. Plastics weigh less and can be designed to be "springy" or resilient in situations where metals might become dented. Plastic bumpers on automobiles are one example.

Plastics can be designed with a wide range of properties, from soft and flexible to hard, rigid, and brittle. Unfortunately, plastics are made from petroleum, an important nonrenewable resource already in great demand as a fuel.

Optical fibers have already revolutionized communications. Voice or electronic messages can be sent through these thin, specially-designed glass tubes as pulses of laser light. As many as 50,000 phone conversations or data transmissions can take place simultaneously in one glass fiber the thickness of a human hair. A typical 72-strand optical fiber ribbon can carry well over a million messages.

Optical fibers are on their way toward replacing conventional copper wires in phone and data transmission lines. The fiber's larger carrying capacity and noise-free characteristics outweigh their higher initial cost. Some forecasters predict that at least half of all U.S. homes will have optical fiber installed by 2015. A fundamentally new way to send signals has been created.

Advanced polymer composites find use already in a variety of important applications, ranging from "Stealth" aircraft and

Optical fibers. Single optical fiber filaments such as these can be as long as 100 km.

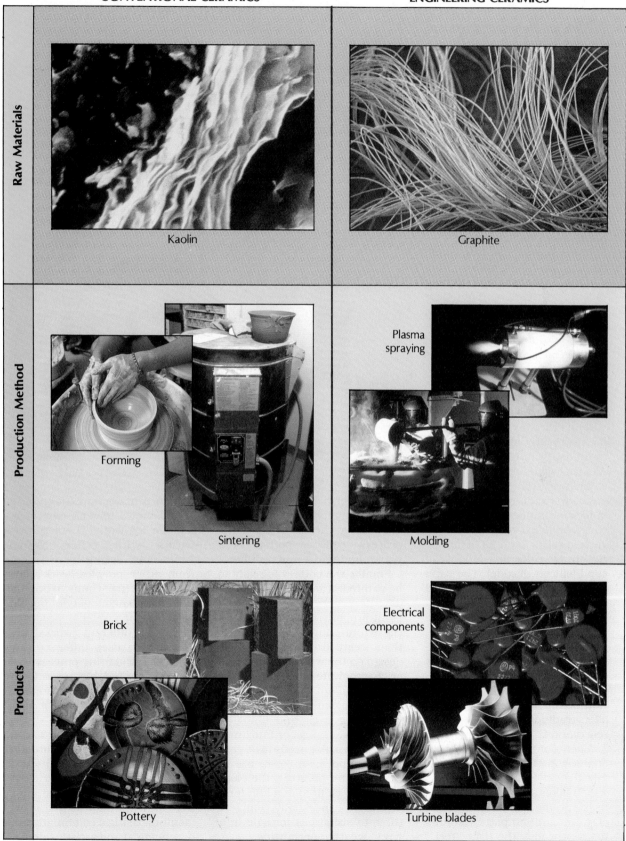

Figure 13 Conventional ceramic products such as bricks and pottery are produced from clay. Engineering ceramics, which may be higher melting, stronger, or less brittle than conventional ceramics, are produced from various natural and synthetic minerals.

Beautiful Chemistry

By Shannon Ware
Gallup Post *Staff Writer*

A piece of Acoma pottery is displayed for sale in a Dallas art gallery. This piece of art is very intricately designed and finely crafted. How does a potter, such as John Aragon from the Acoma reservation in New Mexico, create an exquisite piece of work using Native American methods?

John collects the raw materials for producing pottery from various areas on the Acoma Indian reservation. The older part of this pueblo community, Sky City, is situated on a mesa where John and his family find the special clay needed for his designs. In addition to the clay, John finds inspiration for his work at the traditional ceremonies held in Sky City.

John searches the reservation for raw materials to make the traditional paints and pigments. A black color is created by boiling edible wild spinach to a pulp to produce a gummy residue as a binder for minerals and metallic compounds extracted from pulverized rocks such as hematite. An orange color is a product of sand (silicon dioxide). The sand is placed in water, soaked, and then the water is then strained to produce a fine suspension. The white pottery slip (primer) is a by-product of sandstone. The sandstone goes through a process similar to that of the orange sand. Generally, all of the raw materials John uses are found in specific traditional spots on the reservation.

When John is ready to begin creating pottery, he must first mix the clay properly, a process which takes about half a day. He uses specific amounts of water, clay, and ground pottery shards to give the clay the right "feel." During the rest of the day, he shapes a piece until it is in an ac-

Photo courtesy of the Don Drees Collection

ceptable form for drying, first in the cooler air of the workshop and then in the desert sun. This process produces pottery of a particular texture and resilience.

Finally, the pottery is ready to be painted. It takes two or three days for John to build up the paint properly. First, he puts on the white slip (whitewash). He then freely draws a geometric design on the white slip in pencil or charcoal. He puts down black or orange paint by first outlining the design with the paint and then going back and filling in with black, orange, or fine lines. An Acoma artist needs to be very patient and have a sense of design. After painting, the piece is ready to be fired in a kiln for a day. John can usually complete three to six pieces for sale in a week, weather permitting.

Some pieces fill special orders; others are sold retail or whole-

sale in Albuquerque. John goes to art shows to seek new markets for his work. There he networks with other Native Americans, seeing how potters from other pueblos work clay, and showing them what is unique to Acoma-style pueblo pottery. Each pueblo produces distinctly different works because each uses different raw materials and firing processes.

John learned his trade from practical experience. As a child, he was encouraged by his grandmother to play with and shape clay. In high school, he began working small pieces, eventually picking up the traditional methods of making pottery. His grandmother, mother, and aunt were his inspiration as well as his mentors. Using a combination of his chemical and artistic talents, John produces exceptional native crafts.

race cars to rocket motor cases and tennis rackets. These fiber-reinforced resins have a variety of attractive features, including their low densities, ability to withstand high temperatures, and strength and dimensional stability. Such composites have replaced metals in many applications. Current advanced polymer composite prices can be as high as hundreds of dollars per pound, but such composites deliver unique and highly desirable properties.

By now it should be apparent that chemists, chemical engineers, and materials scientists continue to find new and better alternatives to traditional materials for a variety of applications.

Now it's time to try your hand regarding possible uses of some alternative materials.

Reinforcing fibers in composites are usually made of glass, carbon, or organic polymers.

In 1986 the experimental aircraft Voyager completed the first non-stop flight around the world without refueling. Voyager was made of lightweight composite materials.

YOUR TURN

Alternatives to Metals

1. Select four copper uses from the list found in Figure 11 (page 132). For each, suggest an alternative material that could serve the same purpose. Consider both conventional materials and possible new materials.
2. Suggest some common metallic items that might be replaced by ceramic or plastic versions.
3. Suppose silver became as common and inexpensive as copper. In what uses would silver most likely replace copper? Explain.

PART D: SUMMARY QUESTIONS

1. Give at least two reasons why estimates of future resource supplies might be highly uncertain.
2. a. Why is metal recycling important?
   b. Does such recycling guarantee we will always have sufficient supplies of a given metal? Why?
3. In selecting a metal to meet a particular need, chemists and engineers consider the properties desired to meet the need.
   a. List three uses of copper metal.
   b. For each, list the property or properties that explain copper's use for that particular application.
4. Give the chemical name and find the percent metal (by mass) in each compound:
   a. Ag_2S
   b. Al_2O_3
   c. $CaCO_3$
5. A 100-g sample of ore contains 10 g of lead(II) sulfate, $PbSO_4$.

   a. What is the percent $PbSO_4$ in this ore?
   b. What is the percent Pb in $PbSO_4$?
   c. Finally, what is the percent Pb in the original ore sample?
6. Consider these two equations. Which reaction is more likely to occur? Why?
   a. $Zn^{2+}(aq) + 2\ Ag(s) \rightarrow 2\ Ag^+(aq) + Zn(s)$
   b. $2\ Ag^+(aq) + Zn(s) \rightarrow Zn^{2+}(aq) + 2\ Ag(s)$
7. a. Would it be a good idea to stir a solution of lead nitrate with an iron spoon? Explain.
   b. Write a chemical equation to support your answer.
8. Which two families of elements contain the most active metals?
9. Three different types of reduction processes are used to process metallic ores (Table 7, page 135). What *similarities* do these different processes share?

E

PUTTING IT ALL TOGETHER: HOW LONG WILL THE SUPPLY LAST?

E.1 METAL RESERVES: THREE PROJECTIONS

The change from an agricultural to an industrial society puts great demands on a country's chemical resources. Industrial nations often need to supplement their own chemical resources with imports from other countries. As technology spreads worldwide, additional nations compete for the world's limited supply of minerals. Technology is partly responsible for this competition. But technology can also assist in better use or reuse of already-secured resources.

In Figure 14 the known world reserves of metal ore are plotted versus time. All lines begin at the same point on the left side of the graph. This point represents the total reserves known now.

Reserves refer to ores from which metals can be extracted at economically favorable cost with known technology.

Each curve represents a possible way in which we might consume ore reserves as time passes. Plot I is a straight line. In this case, we would continue to use ore reserves at the same rate they are used today. Reserves still available would decrease steadily each year.

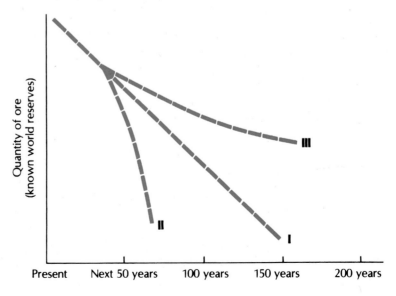

Figure 14 Possible depletion scenarios for metal resources.

Plot II would apply if we use reserves increasingly faster over the years. Each year the quantity of ore used would be greater than the year before.

By contrast, if we use less and less ore reserves each year, then Plot III would apply. The reserves would last longer than they would under Plot I and Plot II.

What control do we have over which plot will apply to a given resource in the future? In the next section you will examine some facts concerning aluminum use. You will consider how aluminum conservation plans might affect how much aluminum ore is used. Finally, you will select from among the possibilities those that seem most likely to succeed in conserving aluminum.

The Newtsuit, a deep-water diving system, is made of composite materials.

E.2 OPTIONS AND OPPORTUNITIES

Some properties that make aluminum so useful are listed in Table 8. Except for iron, aluminum is the most-used metal in the United States. Automobile and airplane industries use aluminum as a structural component due to its strength and low density. Weight savings due to aluminum in cars and planes have reduced U.S. fuel consumption.

Table 8	PROPERTIES OF ALUMINUM
Malleability and ductility	High
Electrical conductivity	High
Thermal conductivity	High
Resistance to corrosion	High
Useful alloys formed	Aluminum bronze, Alnico, etc.
Color and luster	Silvery white, shiny

Aluminum is also an excellent conductor of electricity. A given mass of aluminum is more than twice as conductive as the same mass of copper. Most overhead power transmission lines are made of aluminum. Figure 15 summarizes the most common uses of aluminum in the United States.

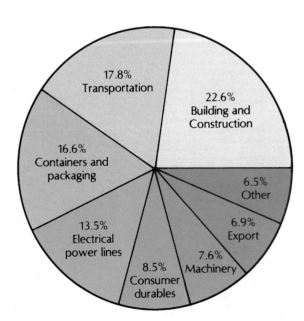

17.8% Transportation

22.6% Building and Construction

16.6% Containers and packaging

6.5% Other

6.9% Export

13.5% Electrical power lines

7.6% Machinery

8.5% Consumer durables

Figure 15 Uses of aluminum in the United States.

Refer to Table 8 (page 145) and Figures 14 and 15 (pages 144 and 145) in answering these questions. Later, you will use your answers in group and classroom discussions.

1. Do you think Plot I (Figure 14) is a good prediction for the future depletion of aluminum?
2. What might happen to cause aluminum ore reserves to be used as shown in Plot II?
3. What might happen to cause aluminum ore reserves to be used as shown in Plot III?

E.3 LOOKING BACK AND LOOKING AHEAD

In ending this *ChemCom* unit, you can stop and take stock of what you have learned thus far. To date, you have "uncovered" some of chemistry's working language (symbols, formulas, and equations), laboratory techniques, laws (law of conservation of matter and the periodic law) and theories (atomic-molecular). This knowledge can help you better understand a few important societal issues. Central among these issues is the use and abuse of the chemical resources of Spaceship Earth. Water, metals, petroleum, food, air, basic industries, and even personal health are all resources that need wise management to obtain maximum benefits for all people, while minimizing environmental costs.

We have also explored other factors that enter into policy decisions concerning "technological" problems. Although chemistry is often a crucial ingredient in recognizing and resolving such issues, many problems are too complex for a simple technological "fix." Tough decisions may be needed. Issues are not usually black or white, but many shades of gray. As voting citizens you will be concerned with a variety of issues that require some scientific understanding. The remaining units in *ChemCom* will continue to prepare you for this important role.

Next we will deal with petroleum, such an important nonrenewable chemical resource that it deserves a unit all to itself.

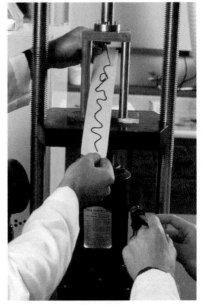

Pulling superconducting wire.

Beech Starship turboprop jet. Its structures are made up mainly of composites.

CHEMICAL ELEMENTS CROSSWORD PUZZLE

To be used with *YOUR TURN* (p. 105) Here are clues for the crossword puzzle your teacher will distribute.

Down

1. An unreactive, gaseous element that is a product of the nuclear reaction (fusion) of hydrogen atoms. This reaction occurred at the beginning of time and occurs today in stars such as our sun. The second most abundant element in the universe, it is quite rare on Earth. Small concentrations are found in some natural gas deposits. It is used in blimps because of its low density. (Only hydrogen, which is highly flammable, has a lower density). It is also used in cryogenic (low-temperature) work because it can be compressed to a liquid that has a temperature of $-269°$ C.

2. A reactive, metallic element. Its compounds are used as a medical "cocktail" to outline the stomach and intestines for X-ray examination. Its compounds also give green colors to fireworks.

4. A highly reactive metal. It is used in the manufacture of synthetic rubber and drugs. One of its compounds has been used to successfully treat a certain type of mental illness. It finds limited use in nuclear weapons.

6. A widely distributed nonmetal never found in its free, elemental state. It is an essential component in all cell protoplasm, DNA, and various animal tissues and bones. It is also one of the three main elements in fertilizers.

9. An unreactive gas. In the comic book world, a mineral containing this element could weaken Superman. In the real world, a radioactive form of this element is a by-product of most nuclear explosions; its presence in the atmosphere can indicate whether a nation is testing nuclear weapons.

10. A reactive metal with a high melting point. It is used in manufacturing rocket nose cones because this low-density substance is remarkably strong.

12. A reactive, silver-white metal that is second in abundance to sodium in ocean water. Due to its low density and high strength, its alloys are often used for structural purposes in the transportation industry, as in "mag" wheels. It is also used in fireworks and incendiary bombs because it ignites readily. Some of its compounds, such as Epsom salt and milk of magnesia, have medicinal uses.

14. A component of all living matter and fossil fuels; the black material on a charred candle wick.

18. Nicknamed quicksilver, it is the only metallic element that is a liquid at room temperature. It is used in thermometers because it expands significantly and regularly when heated. Its high density makes it a practical substance to use in barometers. (*Note:* A barometer is used to measure atmospheric air pressure.) It is a toxic "heavy" metal.

19. The lightest and most abundant element; the fuel of the universe. It is believed that all other elements were originally formed from a series of stellar nuclear reactions beginning with this element. It is found in numerous compounds such as water and in most carbon-containing compounds.

20. A highly reactive metal of low density. It is one of the three main elements found in fertilizer. Its compounds are quite similar to those of sodium, though typically more expensive.

22. A soft, dense metal used in bullets and car batteries. It was once used extensively both in plumbing and in paints. Concern over its biological effects caused a ban on its use for these purposes. It is being phased out as a gasoline additive for the same reason.

25. With the highest melting point of any pure element, it is the filament in ordinary (incandescent) lightbulbs. Its one-letter symbol comes from the name wolfram.

27. A metallic element. It is added to steel to increase its strength.

28. A metallic element that serves as the negative pole (electrode) in the common flashlight battery. It is used to plate a protective film on iron objects (as in galvanized buckets). Melted with copper, it becomes brass.

29. A metal that is used to make stainless steel. Combined with nickel, it forms nichrome wire which is used in toasters and other devices where high electrical resistance is desired to produce heat.

30. This metal has a relatively low melting point. It is used in fire detection and extinguishing devices as well as in electrical fuses.

31. The most chemically reactive metal. Though it is quite rare, it is used in some photoelectric cells and in atomic clocks, which have far greater accuracy than mechanical or electric clocks.

33. A reddish, lustrous, ductile, malleable metal that occurs in nature in both free and combined states. It forms the body of the Statue of Liberty. Other uses include electrical wiring, pennies, and decorative objects.

34. This magnetic, metallic element is used extensively for structural purposes. Outdoor stair railings may be made of this element.

38. A yellow, nonreactive, metallic element that has been highly valued since ancient times for its beauty and durability.

39. A metallic element that is used as a corrosion-resistant coating on the inside of cans used for packaging food, oil, and other substances.

Across

3. A highly reactive, gaseous nonmetal. Its compounds are added to some toothpastes and many urban water supplies to prevent tooth decay.

5. A reactive metal whose compounds make up limestone, chalk, cement, and the bones and teeth of animals. Milk is a good nutritional source of this element.

7. An expensive, silver-white metal used in jewelry. It is also used in some industrial processes to speed up chemical reactions.

8. A solid purple-black nonmetal which changes to a deep purple gas upon heating. An alcohol solution of this element

serves as an effective skin disinfectant. A compound of the element is added to sodium chloride (table salt) to prevent goiter.

10. Used in borosilicate (Pyrex) glass, Boraxo soap, drill bits, and control rods in nuclear power plants.

11. One of the three magnetic elements, this metal is used in 5-cent pieces and other coins, in electroplating, and in ni-chrome wire.

13. The most abundant metal in Earth's crust, this silver-white element is characterized by its low density, resistance to corrosion, and high strength. It is used for a variety of structural purposes, such as in airplanes, boats, and cars.

14. A hard, magnetic metal used in the production of steel. A radioactive form of this element is used in cancer treatment.

15. A silver-white, lustrous, radioactive metal. Used as fuel in nuclear power plants and in atomic warheads.

16. An unreactive, gaseous element used in advertising signs for the bright reddish-orange glow it produces when an electric current is passed through it.

17. A yellow nonmetal that occurs in both the free and combined states. It is used in making match tips, gunpowder, and vulcanized rubber. Its presence in coal leads to acid (sulfuric acid) rain if it is not removed before the coal is burned.

21. This metal is the best conductor of heat and electricity. Its scarcity prevents it from common use for such purposes. It was used extensively in the past in the manufacture of coins, but has become too expensive. It is used today for fine eating utensils and decorative objects. Some of its compounds are light-sensitive enough to be used in photographic film.

23. A gaseous nonmetal, the most abundant element on Earth. It makes up some 21% of Earth's atmosphere and is essential to most forms of life.

24. The second most abundant element in Earth's crust. It is the principal component of sand and quartz and finds use in solar cells, computer chips, caulking materials, and abrasives.

26. A metallic element used in nuclear power plant control rods and in Ni-Cad rechargeable batteries.

30. A red, highly reactive, fuming liquid with a foul smell. It finds limited use as a disinfectant.

32. An odorless, colorless, unreactive gas used in most incandescent light bulbs.

35. An element with a symbol based on its Latin name. It is used with lead in car batteries.

36. A soft, highly reactive metal. Its compounds include table salt, lye, and baking soda.

37. A gaseous nonmetal that makes up 78% of Earth's atmosphere. Its compounds are important components of proteins, fertilizers, and many explosives.

40. A highly reactive, greenish-yellow gas used as a bleach and water disinfectant. It is a component of table salt.

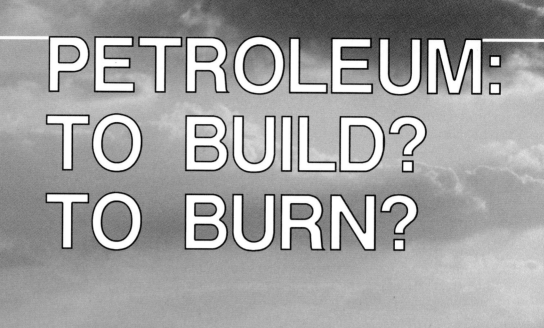

PETROLEUM: TO BUILD? TO BURN?

- What explains petroleum's dual importance as a fuel and as a building material?

- How can we make best use of the petroleum still remaining?

- What will happen to our way of life when global petroleum supplies become depleted?

- Can we find satisfactory alternatives to petroleum?

INTRODUCTION

The first *ChemCom* unit focused on an important renewable resource—water. The second explored some important *nonre-*newable resources. By now, you should see quite clearly how, as Spaceship Earth's passengers, we must rely on resources currently "on board."

Petroleum is a vitally important, nonrenewable resource. Our society runs on it. Nearly two-thirds of the nation's total energy needs are met by petroleum. In the form of gasoline, petroleum powers nearly every U.S. automobile some 10,000 miles (on average) each year. Petroleum-based fuel provides heat and electricity for many U.S. homes and industries.

Nearly 600,000 new compounds were registered by chemists in 1989 alone.

In a less visible role, petroleum provides the chemical starting materials needed to manufacture a remarkable array of familiar and useful products—items ranging from cassette tapes, credit cards, and carpeting to prescription drugs, artificial limbs, and electrical insulation. The title, "Petroleum: To Build? To Burn?" refers to these two roles of petroleum in modern society—as fuel and as chemical building material.

Important decisions about how to use and save petroleum lie ahead. In this unit we will consider our dependence on petroleum. As petroleum is nonrenewable and world use of it is high, how long will supplies last? An even more basic question is:

Gasoline lines in California. Will this scene be repeated?

What chemistry information can an informed consumer learn from this gasoline pump?

What in petroleum's chemical composition makes it such a valuable resource? The answer will help guide our options as supplies dwindle. Can we develop alternatives to serve as petroleum substitutes? Or should we reduce our use of this valuable material and even perhaps change the way we live?

Much depends on how seriously our society seeks answers to such questions. Unfortunately, national interest in these matters tends to vary with the price of petroleum—a price strongly influenced by economic and political conditions. Twice during the 1970s the flow of imported petroleum to the United States was interrupted. The cost of gasoline crept close to $2 per gallon; long lines appeared at gas stations; many persons reduced their use of heating oil by lowering thermostats and improving home insulation. For a few years these events led government and industry to intensify research on alternate energy sources.

However, by the mid-1980s petroleum prices had dropped somewhat, and so gasoline bills didn't leave as large a dent in the pocketbook. Oil sold in 1986 for as little as $14.50 a barrel; pump prices of 70 to 90 cents a gallon for gasoline were common. Interest in alternative energy sources declined.

Political tensions and military turmoil in the Middle East have highlighted the risks involved in relying on large quantities of imported petroleum. In 1990, about half of this nation's petroleum needs were met by imported supplies. Future strategic planning must take into account the fact that approximately 60% of the world's known petroleum reserves are located in just five Middle Eastern nations—Iran, Iraq, Kuwait, Saudi Arabia, and the United Arab Emirates.

By contrast, the combined petroleum reserves of the United States, Japan, and Europe equal only 12% of the world's known supply.

Forecasting the future price of petroleum is difficult. The price may remain stable for years. Or it may move to new heights or depths as political and economic conditions change. To predict the future of petroleum, we need to look hard at how we use it, how much is still available, and how fast it is being used.

A
PETROLEUM IN OUR LIVES

We burn petroleum for fuel, but we also make a remarkable variety of things from it. Let's look at some familiar products that are made directly from petroleum or from petroleum-based substances.

A.1 YOU DECIDE: IT'S A PETROLEUM WORLD

1. Study Figure 1. List the items in the figure that use petroleum or are made from it.
2. After you complete the list, your teacher will supply a version of Figure 1 in which all items that consume petroleum or are made from it are removed.
3. Compare the two figures. Add to your list those items you originally missed.
4. How many petroleum-based products did you overlook?

Figure 1 Life with petroleum.

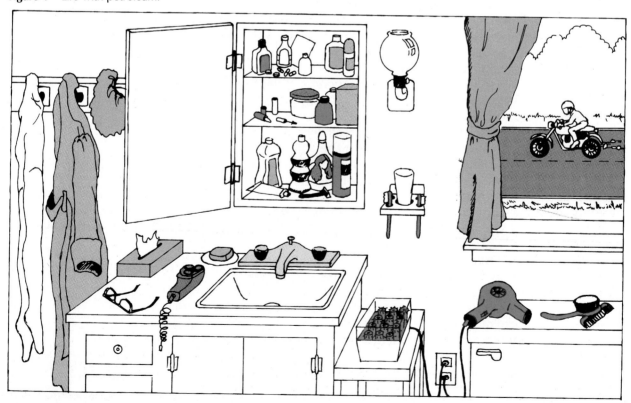

5. Suppose there were a severe petroleum shortage.
   a. Which five petroleum-based products shown in Figure 1 would you be most willing to do without?
   b. Which five would you be least willing to give up?

Were you surprised by all the items that use or are made from petroleum? Often we don't realize how important something is until we try to imagine life without it. Petroleum is such a large part of modern life that we tend to take it for granted. However, we must realize that the world is rapidly using up its limited supply of this nonrenewable resource. That leads to an important question.

A.2 PETROLEUM IN OUR FUTURE?

The United States consumes about 18 million barrels of petroleum each day. Much of this is used in manufacturing and shipping, not by individuals. However, if the 18 million barrels were distributed evenly among all U.S. residents, your daily "share" would be about three gallons.

One barrel contains 42 gallons of petroleum.

Petroleum literally powers our modern society. It fuels a large portion of personal, public, and commercial transportation; it heats homes and office buildings; it drives some turbines that generate our nation's electricity. As a rich source of chemical "building materials", petroleum also supplies reactants needed to produce plastics, fabrics, synthetic vitamins, and other items that greatly affect our lives. In short, petroleum is a significant— and, at least for now, irreplaceable—part of our standard of living.

Figure 2 shows how much of an "average" barrel of petroleum is used for burning (as an energy source) and for building (as a source of reactants to produce other useful materials). Only 13% is used for non-fuel purposes. The remaining 87% of a typical barrel of petroleum—over six times more—is burned as fuel.

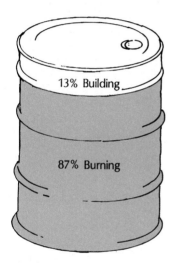

13% Building

87% Burning

Based on 1985 figures

Figure 2   Petroleum: burning and building.

Some petroleum experts predict that world oil production from known petroleum reserves will reach its peak around the turn of the century (see Figure 3 on page 156). After that, a steady decline in petroleum production may occur as reserves dwindle. In less than 100 years, petroleum production from presently-known reserves may be as low as it was in 1910. Back then, petroleum was used only for lighting. It served as a replacement for a limited supply of whale oil.

The price of petroleum is expected to increase steadily as it becomes increasingly scarce. Due to predictable supply-demand factors, petroleum will gradually become too costly for many of today's common uses. In a time of petroleum scarcity, how would you decide to use this resource? Would you burn it for its energy or build other substances from it?

How important do you expect petroleum to be in your life when you are about 40 years old?

Dimitri Mendeleev, the Russian chemist who arranged elements in a periodic table in 1869, recognized petroleum's value as a raw material for industry. He warned that burning petroleum as a fuel "would be akin to firing up a kitchen stove with bank notes." Petroleum's apparent abundance, ease of storage and handling, and relative low cost have led us to disregard Mendeleev's advice.

A time will come, however, when the choice to "build or burn" will confront all nations. Those decisions will depend

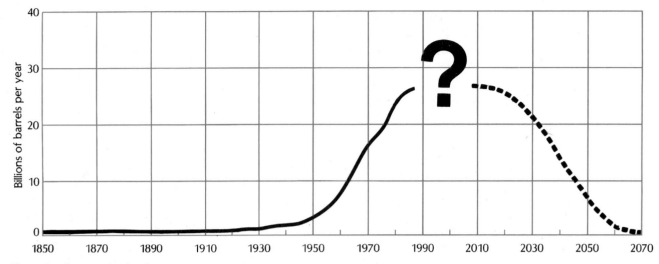

Figure 3 Past production from known petroleum reserves (shown by solid line). Expected future production from reserves (dashed line).

on knowing about petroleum's sources, uses, and possible alternatives.

We will start by finding out where we get our national supply of this important resource.

A.3 YOU DECIDE: WHO'S GOT THE OIL?

Like many other chemical resources, the earth's petroleum is unevenly distributed. Large amounts are concentrated in small areas. In addition, nations with large reserves do not necessarily consume large amounts of the resource. In other words, regions with a high demand for petroleum may be far away from regions with high petroleum reserves. As a result, nations often make exporting and importing arrangements, known as *trade agreements*.

Figure 4 indicates the regions where the world's known supplies of petroleum are located (in yellow). Such supplies, called *reserves*, can be tapped by available technology at costs consistent with current market prices. The regional distribution of the world's population is shown in green. Use the figure to answer these questions:

1. Which region has the most petroleum relative to its population?
2. Which region has the least petroleum relative to its population?

Figure 4 Distribution of world's petroleum reserves (yellow), population (green), and consumption of petroleum (rust).

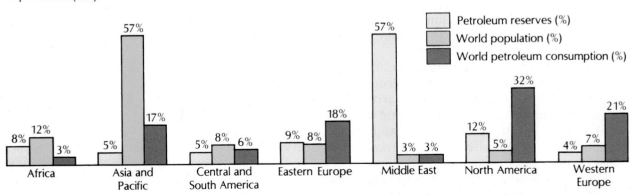

Figure 4 also shows (in rust) the regional distribution of the world's consumption of petroleum. Answer these questions.

3. Which regions consume a greater percent of the world's supply of petroleum than they possess?

4. Which regions consume a smaller percent of the world's supply of petroleum than they possess?

5. Which regions are likely to export petroleum?

6. Which regions are likely to import petroleum?

7. List several pairs of regions that might make petroleum trade agreements with each other. (A given region may be used more than once.)

8. Not all possible trade agreements are actually made. What factors might prevent trade relationships between regions?

9. a. What two regions are the largest petroleum consumers?

   b. Why do these two regions consume such large quantities of petroleum?

10. a. Compare North America and the Middle East in terms of (1) population, (2) petroleum reserves, and (3) petroleum consumption.

    b. What possible consequences are involved in these comparisons?

Thus far, we have recognized how greatly we depend on petroleum. Society's increasing reliance on this nonrenewable, limited resource must be analyzed carefully. However, before we can address such issues, we need a better understanding of petroleum itself. What features make petroleum so valuable for both building and burning? We will tackle this question next.

Offshore drilling rig.

PART A: SUMMARY QUESTIONS

1. About 87% of the petroleum used in the United States is burned as fuel. Yet the remaining 13% used for "building" has an immense impact on our lives.

   a. Support this claim by listing 10 household items made with petroleum.

   b. The United States uses 18 million barrels of petroleum each day. How many barrels of petroleum—on average—are burned as fuel daily in the U.S.?

   c. How many barrels of petroleum are used daily in the U.S. for building purposes?

2. Suppose petroleum's cost increased by 10%. Assume that the nation's supply of petroleum decreased at the same time—a one-time drop of 2 million barrels daily.

   a. Would you expect the prices of gasoline and petroleum-based products also to increase by 10%?

   b. If not, would you expect the increase to be greater or less than 10%? Why?

3. a. What kind of petroleum trade relationship is likely between North America and the Middle East?

   b. If other world regions become more industrialized and petroleum supplies decrease, how might the North American-Middle East trade relationship change?

4. The traditional unit of measure for petroleum, the barrel, equals 42 gallons. Assume that each barrel of petroleum provides 21 gallons of gasoline (after modification of some molecules). Your car can run 25 miles on a gallon of gasoline, and you travel 10,000 miles each year. How many barrels of petroleum must be processed to operate your car for a year?

PETROLEUM: WHAT IS IT? WHAT DO WE DO WITH IT?

Crude oil and related materials.

Petroleum has been called "black gold." Why is it so valuable? How does it differ from other resources such as the metallic ores that produce aluminum, iron, or copper?

Petroleum is chemically very different from metal ores. While a metallic ore usually contains only a single substance we want to use, petroleum is a mixture of hundreds of molecular compounds. These compounds share two desirable chemical properties: First, they are rich in energy that is released when the molecules are burned. Second, they can be chemically linked together or modified, producing a wide variety of useful "building" materials.

Chemists have learned how to combine small petroleum molecules into giant, chainlike molecules—the raw materials for films, fibers, artificial rubber, and plastics. They have also learned to convert petroleum into molecules found in perfumes, explosives, and medicines such as aspirin, acetaminophen, and codeine.

Petroleum is far more exciting and challenging to chemists than its black, sometimes gooey appearance might suggest. What kinds of molecules make petroleum such a chemical treasure? How can these molecules be separated from each other?

B.1 WORKING WITH BLACK GOLD

As pumped from underground, petroleum is known as **crude oil.** The greenish-brown to black liquid may be as thin as water or as thick as tar. Crude oil is transported by pipeline, train, tanker truck, barge, or ocean tanker to oil refineries. There it is separated into simpler mixtures—some ready for use and others requiring further chemical treatment.

First, salts (ionic compounds) and acids are removed from crude oil, leaving substances called **hydrocarbons.** These molecular compounds contain only two elements—hydrogen and carbon.

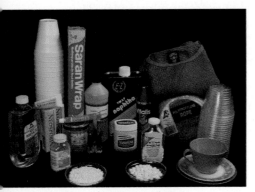

Petrochemical products.

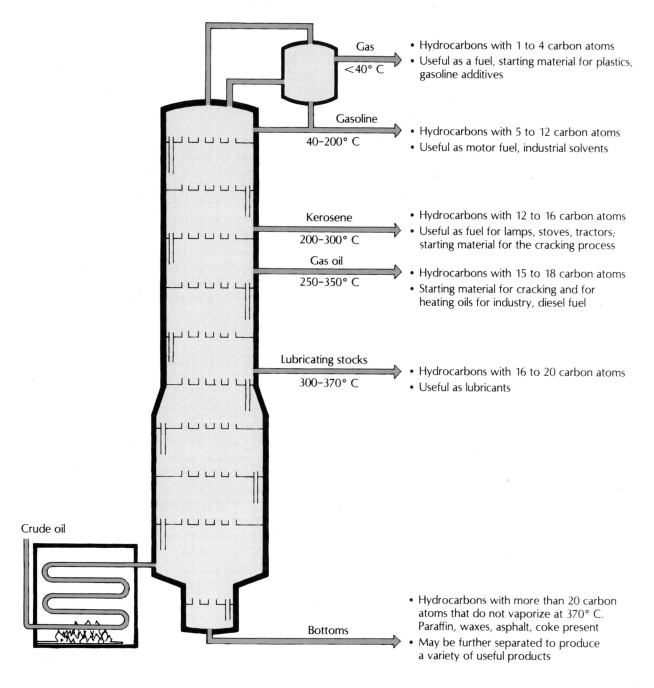

Gas
<40° C
- Hydrocarbons with 1 to 4 carbon atoms
- Useful as a fuel, starting material for plastics, gasoline additives

Gasoline
40–200° C
- Hydrocarbons with 5 to 12 carbon atoms
- Useful as motor fuel, industrial solvents

Kerosene
200–300° C
- Hydrocarbons with 12 to 16 carbon atoms
- Useful as fuel for lamps, stoves, tractors; starting material for the cracking process

Gas oil
250–350° C
- Hydrocarbons with 15 to 18 carbon atoms
- Starting material for cracking and for heating oils for industry, diesel fuel

Lubricating stocks
300–370° C
- Hydrocarbons with 16 to 20 carbon atoms
- Useful as lubricants

Crude oil

Bottoms
- Hydrocarbons with more than 20 carbon atoms that do not vaporize at 370° C. Paraffin, waxes, asphalt, coke present
- May be further separated to produce a variety of useful products

B.2 PETROLEUM REFINING

After the salts and acids are removed, the hydrocarbons are **refined**—separated by distillation into distinctive mixtures of substances with similar boiling points. Figure 5 illustrates the distillation, or fractionation, of crude oil. The crude oil is heated until many of its component substances boil away as vapors. During distillation, smaller molecules vaporize first and move toward the top of the distilling column. Each arrow pointing to the right indicates the fraction's name and its boiling point range. Higher-boiling fractions contain the largest molecules.

Crude oil is heated to about 400° C in the furnace. It is then pumped into the base of a distilling column (*fractionating tower*), which is usually more than 30 m (100 ft) tall. Collecting trays are arranged at different heights inside the column.

Figure 5 A fractionating tower. The cracking process converts larger hydrocarbon molecules into smaller ones more suitable for gasoline.

As hot crude oil enters the tower, molecules of substances with lower boiling points have gained enough thermal energy to break away from the liquid and rise into cooler portions of the distilling column. As they rise they cool. Substances with lowest boiling points remain as gases, rising to the top of the tower. There they are drawn off separately as petroleum's gaseous fraction.

Some substances condense to liquids again and fall into the trays located at different tower heights. These substances are drawn off as liquid fractions, each with a different boiling point range. Substances with the highest boiling points never become gases; they remain in the liquid state through the entire distillation process. These thick (viscous) liquids—called *bottoms*—drain from the column's base.

You already know the names of some petroleum distillation fractions, such as gasoline, kerosene, and lubricating oils. In the following activity you will have the chance to examine samples of some of petroleum's component fractions.

The names given to various fractions and their boiling ranges vary, but crude oil refining always has the general features illustrated.

B.3 LABORATORY ACTIVITY: VISCOSITY

Getting Ready

In this activity you will measure the densities and relative viscosities of several petroleum-based materials. For comparison, you will also measure the same properties for water.

To determine densities, you will measure the masses and volumes of liquid and solid samples.

Viscosity is the term for resistance to flow. A material with high viscosity flows slowly and with difficulty, like honey. A material with a low viscosity flows readily, like water. You will determine relative viscosities, which means ranking materials on a scale from the most viscous to the least.

In your laboratory notebook, prepare data tables like those on page 161, which you will use for reference.

Procedure

Sample Examination

1. Obtain the six materials listed in your sample examination table.
2. Record the state (solid or liquid) of each sample.
3. Based on Figure 5, which material would you expect to have
   a. the lowest boiling point?
   b. the highest boiling point?

Density Measurement

LIQUID SAMPLES

1. Your teacher will give you average values for the mass of an empty capped tube, the mass of a bead, and the volume of liquid in a sample tube. For convenience, record these values at the top of your data table.
2. Weigh each capped tube containing a petroleum product sample. Also weigh a capped tube containing water. Record the masses.

The viscosity of a fluid determines how fast it can flow.

Data Table   **SAMPLE EXAMINATION**

Material	Carbon Atoms Per Molecule	State at Room Temperature (Solid, Liquid)
Mineral oil	12–20	
Asphalt	More than 34	
Kerosene	12–16	
Paraffin wax	More than 19	
Motor oil	15–18	
Household lubricating oil	14–18	

Data Table   **DENSITY MEASUREMENTS**

Average mass of capped tube: _____
Average mass of bead: _____
Average volume: _____

Liquid	Mass of Capped Tube, Bead, and Liquid (g)	Calculated Mass of Liquid (g)	Calculated Density of Material (g/mL)
Water			
Mineral oil			
Kerosene			
Motor oil			
Household lubricating oil			

Solid	Mass of Sample (g)	Volume Increase (mL)	Calculated Density of Material (g/mL)
Paraffin wax			
Asphalt			

Data Table   **VISCOSITY MEASUREMENTS**

Material	Average Time for Bead to Fall (s)	Relative Viscosity
Water		
Mineral oil		
Kerosene		
Motor oil		
Household lubricating oil		

SOLID SAMPLES

3. Fill a 25-mL graduated cylinder to the 10-mL mark with water.
4. Weigh each solid sample carefully. Record the masses.
5. Carefully drop the first weighed solid sample into the water in the cylinder. Measure the *increase* in volume. Record this value.
6. Repeat Step 5 for the other solid sample.

Density Calculations

LIQUID SAMPLES

1. Calculate the mass (in grams) of each liquid sample, using masses obtained in Steps 1 and 2 for the total mass, the capped tube, and the bead:

Sample mass = total mass − (capped tube mass + bead mass)

Record the mass of each liquid sample.

2. Using your calculated sample mass and the volume of liquid in each capped tube, calculate the density of each sample (in grams per milliliter). Record these values.

For example, suppose the sample mass is 40.2 g and the volume is 36.7 mL:

$$\text{Sample density} = \frac{\text{sample mass}}{\text{average volume}} = \frac{40.2 \text{ g}}{36.7 \text{ mL}} = 1.10 \text{ g/mL}$$

SOLID SAMPLES

3. Using the sample masses and increases in water volume found in Step 5, calculate the solid sample densities (in grams per milliliter). The calculation is the same as the one illustrated for liquids, except the increase in water volume replaces the liquid volume.

Relative Viscosity

1. Determine the time needed for the bead to fall from top to bottom within the capped tube containing water. Follow this procedure:
   a. Hold the capped tube upright until the bead is at the bottom.
   b. Gently turn the tube horizontally. (The bead will stay at one end.)
   c. Quickly turn the tube upright so the bead is at the top.
   d. Record the number of seconds needed for the bead to fall to the bottom of the tube.
   e. Repeat this procedure three more times. Calculate the average time required for the bead to fall.
2. Repeat Step 1 for each liquid petroleum-based sample.
3. Rank your samples in order of relative viscosity, assigning number 1 to the least viscous material (the one through which the bead fell fastest).
4. Wash your hands thoroughly before leaving the laboratory.

Questions

1. In oil spills and fires, the oil's density plays a major role. Explain.
2. Propose a rule, based on your observations in this activity, about the connection between the number of carbon atoms in a molecule and its viscosity.
3. Suppose a classmate suggests that petroleum fractions can be separated at room temperature on the basis of their viscosities.
   a. Do you agree? Explain your answer.
   b. What would be some advantages of such a separation procedure?

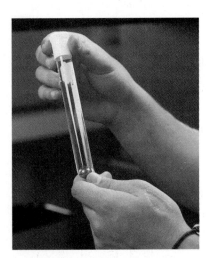

Apparatus for determining relative viscosity.

Rock Around the Clock

By Toni Rivers
Aurora News *Staff Writer*

As a child, Susan Landon spent a lot of time picking up and sorting rocks, never dreaming that this early interest would lead to a lifelong study of the earth's riches. This passion, combined with a a love of science and the outdoors plus some encouragement from her father, has led to a successful career as a consulting petroleum geologist. Susan explores for oil and natural gas in a world of limited known petroleum reserves.

Clients hire Susan to search for petroleum. Her searches for oil and natural gas begin in her Golden, Colorado office, where she spends many hours studying maps and reading articles to find likely areas in which to explore for oil. Susan looks for folded or faulted terrain that she can tentatively identify as a likely location for petroleum. Hydrocarbons may be trapped in these rough areas of the earth, either stored in organic material within the rock or as oil or gas in reservoirs. Susan also uses a personal computer and modeling programs to aid in her search. The programs use known data about the site and incorporate additional information (such as heat flow and geochemical guidelines) to predict the amount of oil or natural gas that could have been generated in that area. Armed with her geological knowledge and the computer simulations, Susan decides whether it would be economically feasible to investigate a promising site.

Susan examines satellite images, aerial photographs, and topographic maps prior to visiting the area to examine the geology in the field. She works with a team conducting chemical and structural analyses of the rocks. If the data indicate that a petroleum deposit may indeed be

Photo by Kate Lapides

present, the team recommends the drilling of a well. After drilling, Susan examines well logs and rock materials. Well logs represent measurements of electrical and physical properties of the rocks encountered during drilling. The rocks are tested with a variety of physical and chemical methods. These tests help Susan and her team determine whether to continue drilling or to complete the well.

Susan particularly enjoys the challenge of testing her educated guesses out in the field. For her, the most exciting aspect of her job is risk—intellectual and physical. Susan may spend months at a given site, and meets many of the local people. She and her team stay with a speculative well until oil is struck, or until continued exploration no longer indicates the presence of an economic store of hydrocarbons.

Most of the world has been mapped, but Susan enjoys looking for oil and natural gas in regions where there is little known geological information. For example, several years ago

Susan suggested locating a speculative well in west central Iowa. This was an unusual and risky approach since Iowa is generally considered an unlikely area for petroleum deposits. Two years and millions of dollars later, Susan was proved correct. Some oil was there, but it was not economically feasible to continue drilling. Susan continues to explore that geologic trend, looking for an economic deposit.

Susan spends a great deal of her time in exploration, but she also teaches effective techniques to others. She speaks at many professional meetings and conferences and has been an expert witness in legal actions involving petroleum exploration.

Susan finds a basic knowledge of chemistry is necessary to help her identify source rock and reservoirs in which hydrocarbons accumulate. A petroleum geologist also needs training in geology, biology, and mathematics. In Susan's opinion, a good liberal arts background as an undergraduate is good preparation for graduate work in geology.

Gasoline and Geography

When shipping gasoline and motor oils to different parts of the nation, petroleum distributors must consider both the ease of evaporation and viscosity of these products. Why must gasoline shipped to a northern state (such as Minnesota) in winter be different from that shipped to a southern state (such as Florida) in summer?

The petroleum fractions you just investigated represent a few of the great number of materials present in petroleum. The next activity will provide more detail about the substances obtained from each fraction, and what we do with them.

B.4 YOU DECIDE: CRUDE OIL TO PRODUCTS

The main hydrocarbon fractions in Figure 6 are listed in order of increasing boiling points. Low-boiling gas is shown near the top, and high-boiling residues near the bottom. Arrows point to typical refinery products from that fraction, which are sold to users or processors. Some of the ultimate uses of these products are also listed. The box at the bottom illustrates the variety of petroleum-based consumer products, and by-products are listed above the top fraction.

Your teacher will organize your class into small working groups. Your group will be assigned one of the petroleum fractions shown in Figure 6. Answer these questions regarding your fraction:

1. a. Do any uses of your fraction depend on petroleum's value as an energy source for burning?
   b. If so, name them.
2. a. Do any uses of your fraction depend on petroleum's value as a source of materials for building new substances?
   b. If so, name them.
3. Describe how life might change if your fraction and its resulting products were totally eliminated during a petroleum shortage.
4. Identify two uses of your fraction that are important enough to continue even during a severe petroleum shortage. Give reasons.
5. Based on your answers to the questions above, which do you believe is more important—burning petroleum to release energy or building new substances from it? Why?

The refined petroleum fractions you investigated earlier in this unit were originally separated from petroleum by distillation. Each fraction has different physical properties. How do chemists explain these differences?

In the following sections, we will examine the composition and structure of molecules found in petroleum. We will see again that properties of substances are related to their molecular structures.

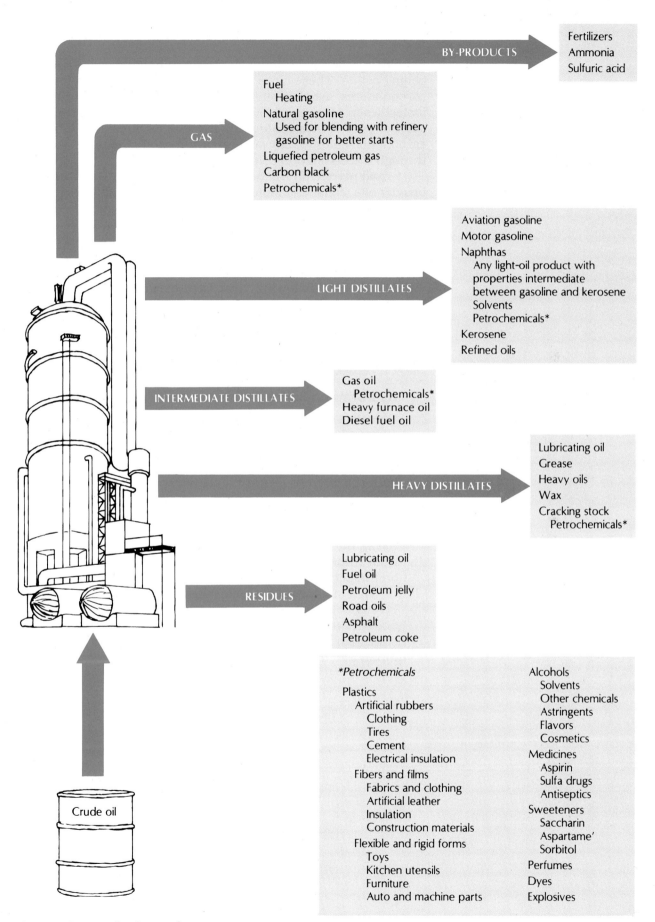

Figure 6 From crude oil to products.

B.5   A LOOK AT PETROLEUM MOLECULES

Petroleum's gaseous fraction contains compounds with low boiling points. These molecules, containing from one to four carbon atoms, are only slightly attracted to each other or to other molecules in petroleum. (Such forces of attraction between molecules are called **intermolecular forces**.) As a result, the hydrocarbon molecules readily separate from each other and rise through the distillation column as gases.

Liquid petroleum fractions, including gasoline, kerosene, and heavier oils, consist of molecules with five to about 20 carbon atoms. The greasy-solid fraction, which does not vaporize even at high distilling temperatures, contains molecules with even more carbon atoms. Among all petroleum-based substances, these solid-fraction compounds have the strongest intermolecular forces of attraction.

Complete the following *Your Turn* to learn more about physical properties of hydrocarbons.

Just as "interstate commerce" means trade between states, intermolecular forces means forces between molecules.

YOUR TURN

Hydrocarbon Boiling Points

Chemists often gather data regarding physical and chemical properties of substances. Although these data can be organized in many ways, the most useful ways uncover trends or patterns among the values. These patterns often trigger attempts to explain the regularities.

The development of the periodic table is a good example of this approach (Resources unit, page 107). Recall that you predicted a property of one element from values of that property for neighboring elements on the periodic table.

In a similar vein, we can seek patterns among boiling point data for some hydrocarbons. During evaporation and boiling, individual molecules in the liquid state gain enough energy to overcome intermolecular forces and enter the gaseous state.

Table 1

HYDROCARBON BOILING POINTS

Hydrocarbon	Boiling Point (° C)
Butane	−0.5
Decane	174.0
Ethane	−88.6
Heptane	98.4
Hexane	68.7
Methane	−161.7
Nonane	150.8
Octane	125.7
Pentane	36.1
Propane	−42.1

Answer the following questions about boiling point data given in Table 1.

1. a. In what pattern or order are Table 1 data organized?
    b. Is this a useful way to present the information? Why?
2. Assume we want to search for a trend or pattern among these boiling points.
    a. Propose a more useful way to arrange these data.
    b. Reorganize the data table based on your idea.
3. Use your new data table to answer these questions:
    a. Which substance(s) are gases (have already boiled) at room temperature (22° C)?
    b. Which substance(s) boil between 22° C (room temperature) and 37° C (body temperature)?
4. What can you infer about intermolecular attractions in decane compared with those in butane?
5. Intermolecular forces also help explain other liquid properties such as viscosity and freezing points.
    a. Based on their intermolecular attractions, try to rank pentane, octane, and decane in order of increasing viscosity. Assign "1" to the least viscous ("thinnest") of the three.
    b. Check with your teacher to see whether you are correct.

B.6   CHEMICAL BONDING

Hydrocarbons and their derivatives are the focus of a branch of chemistry known as *organic chemistry.* These substances are called "organic" compounds because early chemists thought plants or animals were needed to produce them. However, chemists now know how to make many organic compounds without any assistance from living systems.

Hydrocarbons are molecular compounds composed only of carbon and hydrogen atoms. In many hydrocarbon molecules, the carbon atoms are joined together, forming a backbone called a *carbon chain,* with hydrogen atoms attached to it. As you will soon see, carbon's ability to form chains helps explain why there are so many different hydrocarbons. In addition, hydrocarbons can be regarded as parents of an even larger number of compounds containing other kinds of atoms.

To learn how atoms are held together, we must first examine the arrangement of electrons in atoms. We have seen that atoms are made up of neutrons, protons, and electrons. Neutrons and protons are located in a dense, central region of the atom known as the *nucleus.* Studies have shown that electrons occupy different energy levels in the space surrounding an atomic nucleus. Each energy level (or *shell*) can hold only a certain number of electrons.

The first shell of electrons surrounding the nucleus has a capacity of two electrons. The second shell can hold a maximum of eight electrons.

Consider an atom of the noble gas helium (He). A helium atom has two protons in its nucleus and two electrons surrounding the nucleus. These two electrons occupy the first, innermost shell; this is as many electrons as this level can hold.

The next noble gas, neon (Ne), has atomic number 10; each of its atoms contains 10 protons and 10 electrons. Two of these electrons reside in the first shell. The remaining eight reside in the second shell. Note that both shells have reached their capacities, since the maximum number of electrons possible at the second level is eight.

Both helium and neon are chemically unreactive—their atoms do not combine with those of other atoms to form compounds. Sodium (Na) atoms, however, with atomic number 11, and therefore just one more electron than neon, are extremely reactive. Fluorine (F) atoms, having one less electron than neon, also are extremely reactive. The differences in the reactivities of elements are accounted for by their atoms' electron arrangements.

A useful guideline to understand the chemical behavior of many elements is to recognize that *atoms with filled electron shells are particularly stable*. The noble gases are essentially unreactive, since their atoms already have completely-filled shells of electrons. How does this guideline help explain the reactivity of elements sodium and fluorine?

When sodium metal reacts, sodium ions (Na^+) form. The $+1$ electrical charge indicates that each original sodium atom has lost one electron—Na^+ contains 11 protons but only 10 electrons. With 10 electrons, sodium ions possess completely-filled electron shells (two in first level, eight in second). Thus, sodium ions are highly stable; the world's entire natural supply of sodium is found in this form.

By losing an electron, each sodium atom has been oxidized—see the Resources unit, Section D.4.

By contrast, fluorine atoms react to form fluoride ions (F^-). The -1 electrical charge correctly suggests that each fluorine atom has gained one electron. The F^- ion contains 9 protons and 10 electrons. Once again, an element has reacted to attain the special stability associated with completely-filled electron shells.

By gaining an electron, each fluorine atom has been reduced—once again, Section D.4 of the Resources unit provides the background.

In molecular substances, atoms acquire filled electron shells by sharing electrons. Many molecular substances are composed of nonmetals whose atoms do not easily lose electrons. However, shared electrons can contribute to the shells of both atoms.

The hydrogen molecule (H_2) provides a simple example. Each hydrogen atom contains one electron. It is clear that one more electron is needed to fill hydrogen's first shell. Two hydrogen atoms can accomplish this by sharing their single electrons. If each electron is represented by a dot ($\cdot$), then a hydrogen molecule can be written in this way:

$$H\cdot + \cdot H \rightarrow H : H$$

The chemical bond formed between two atoms by sharing electrons is called a **covalent bond.** Through such sharing, both atoms achieve the stability associated with filled electron shells.

A carbon atom, atomic number 6, has six electrons—two in the first shell and four in the second shell. Note that four more electrons are needed to fill the second shell to its capacity of eight. This can be accomplished through covalent bonding.

Consider the simplest hydrocarbon molecule, methane (CH_4). In this molecule, each hydrogen atom shares its single electron with the carbon atom as the following representation suggests:

$$4 \, \text{H·} + \, \text{·} \overset{.}{\underset{.}{\text{C}}} \text{·} \rightarrow \text{H} \overset{\text{H}}{\underset{\text{H}}{\overset{..}{\underset{..}{:\text{C}:}}}} \text{H}$$

The dots represent only the outer-shell electrons for each atom. Such structures are called **electron-dot formulas.** The two electrons in each covalent bond "belong" to both bonded atoms. Count the dots surrounding each atom. Those dots placed between two atoms represent electrons shared by those atoms. Notice that each hydrogen atom in methane has a filled electron energy level (two electrons in the first shell). The carbon atom also has a filled outer shell (eight electrons).

For convenience, each pair of electrons in a covalent bond can be replaced by a dash, leading to another common way to draw covalently-bonded substances. This is called a **structural formula:**

$$\text{H} \overset{\text{H}}{\underset{\overset{..}{\text{H}}}{\overset{..}{:\text{C}:}}} \text{H}$$

Electron-dot formula
of methane, CH_4

$$\text{H} - \overset{\overset{\textstyle\text{H}}{\textstyle|}}{\underset{\underset{\textstyle\text{H}}{\textstyle|}}{\text{C}}} - \text{H}$$

Structural formula
of methane, CH_4

Atoms within molecules are arranged in distinctive three-dimensional shapes. These geometric structures help determine the physical and chemical properties of molecules. We can draw two-dimensional pictures of molecules on flat paper, but building models of them gives a more accurate picture. The following activity will give you a chance to do this.

B.7 LABORATORY ACTIVITY: MODELING ALKANES

In this activity you will make models of several simple hydrocarbons. The goal is to relate three-dimensional shapes of molecules to the names, formulas, and pictures used to represent molecules on paper.

Pictures of two types of molecular models are shown in Figure 7. Most likely, you will use ball-and-stick models. Each

Figure 7 Three-dimensional models:
(left) ball-and-stick, (right) space-filling.

ball represents an atom and each stick represents a covalent bond connecting two atoms. Real molecules are not composed of ball-like atoms located at the ends of stick-like bonds. Evidence shows that atoms contact each other, more like those in space-filling models. However, ball-and-stick models are useful, since they make it easy to see the structure and geometry of molecules.

Look again at the electron-dot structure and structural formula for methane (CH_4), the simplest hydrocarbon, on page 169. Methane is the first member of a series of hydrocarbons known as **alkanes,** which we explore in this activity. Each carbon atom in an alkane forms covalent bonds with four other atoms. Alkanes are considered **saturated hydrocarbons,** as each carbon atom is bonded to the maximum number of other atoms (four).

Procedure

1. Build a model of methane, CH_4. Compare your model with the electron-dot and structural formulas above. Note that the actual angles between atoms are *not* 90°, as you might think from the written formulas.

   Compare your model with the photographs of models in Figure 7. A close-fitting box built to surround a CH_4 molecule would have the shape of a triangular pyramid (a pyramid with a triangle as a base), as shown in Figure 8. This geometric figure is called a **tetrahedron.**

   Here's one way to think about this tetrahedral shape. Assume that the four pairs of electrons surrounding the carbon—all with negative charges—repel each other and stay as far away from each other as possible. This causes the four pairs of shared electrons to locate, so that the bonds point to the corners of a tetrahedron. The angles between the bonds are all 109.5°.

2. Build models of a two-carbon and a three-carbon alkane molecule. Recall that each carbon atom in an alkane is bonded to four other atoms.

   a. How many hydrogen atoms are present in the two-carbon alkane?

   b. How many are present in the three-carbon alkane?

   c. Draw a ball-and-stick model, similar to that in Figure 7, of the two-carbon alkane.

3. a. Draw electron-dot and structural formulas for the two- and three-carbon alkanes.

   b. The molecular formulas for the first two alkanes are CH_4 and C_2H_6. What is the molecular formula of the third?

   Examine your three-carbon alkane model and the structural formula you drew for it. Note that the middle carbon atom is attached to two hydrogen atoms, while the carbon atom at each end is attached to three hydrogen atoms. This molecule can be represented as $CH_3 — CH_2 — CH_3$, or $CH_3CH_2CH_3$. Such formulas provide information about how atoms are arranged in molecules. Thus for many purposes they are more useful than shortened molecular formulas such as C_3H_8.

   The general molecular formula for any alkane molecule can be written as C_nH_{2n+2}, where n is the number of carbon atoms in the molecule. Thus, even without building any models, we can predict the formula of a three-carbon alkane. (If $n = 3$, then $2n + 2 = 8$, and the formula is C_3H_8.)

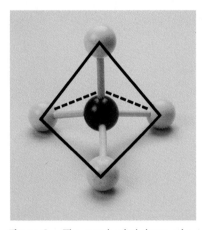

Figure 8 The tetrahedral shape of a methane molecule.

n = *any positive integer*

4. Use the general alkane formula to write molecular formulas for the first 10 alkanes. When you are done, compare your molecular formulas with the formulas given in Table 2 (page 172) to see whether your predictions are correct.

Names for the first 10 alkanes are also given in Table 2. These names are composed of a "root," followed by -*ane*. The root refers to the number of carbon atoms in the carbon chain or backbone. To a chemist, *meth*- means one carbon atom, *eth*- means two, *prop*- means three, and so on.

5. Write structural formulas for butane and pentane.

6. a. Name the alkanes with these formulas:
   (1) $CH_3CH_2CH_2CH_2CH_2CH_2CH_3$
   (2) $CH_3CH_2CH_2CH_2CH_2CH_2CH_2CH_2CH_3$

   b. Write shorter molecular formulas for the two alkanes listed in Question 6a.

7. a. Write a molecular formula for the alkane containing 25 carbon atoms.

   b. Did you decide to write a short-version or long-version formula for this compound? Why?

8. Name the alkane having a molar mass of
   a. 30 g/mol,
   b. 58 g/mol.

YOUR TURN

Alkane Boiling Points: Trends

Prepare a graph of boiling point data for the alkanes listed in Table 1 (page 166). The *x*-axis scale should range from 1 to 13 carbon atoms (even though you will initially plot data for 1 to 10 carbon atoms). The *y*-axis scale should extend from −200° C to +250° C.

1. From your graph, estimate the average *change* in boiling point (in degrees Celsius) when one carbon atom and two hydrogen atoms (— CH_2 —) are added to a given alkane chain.

2. The pattern of boiling points among the first 10 alkanes allows you to predict boiling points of other alkanes.

   a. From your graph, estimate the boiling points of undecane ($C_{11}H_{24}$), dodecane ($C_{12}H_{26}$), and tridecane ($C_{13}H_{28}$). To do this, continue the trend of your graph line with a dashed line (this is called **extrapolation**). Then read your predicted boiling points for C_{11}, C_{12}, and C_{13} alkanes on the *y* axis.

   b. Compare your predicted boiling points to actual values provided by your teacher.

3. We have already noted that a substance's boiling point depends (in part) on its intermolecular forces—that is, on attractions among its molecules. For alkanes you have studied, how are these attractions related to the number of carbon atoms in each molecule?

Table 2   **SOME MEMBERS OF THE ALKANE SERIES**

| | | Alkane Molecular Formulas | |
Name	Number of Carbons	Short Version	Long Version
Methane	1	CH_4	CH_4
Ethane	2	C_2H_6	CH_3CH_3
Propane	3	C_3H_8	$CH_3CH_2CH_3$
Butane	4	C_4H_{10}	$CH_3CH_2CH_2CH_3$
Pentane	5	C_5H_{12}	$CH_3CH_2CH_2CH_2CH_3$
Hexane	6	C_6H_{14}	$CH_3CH_2CH_2CH_2CH_2CH_3$
Heptane	7	C_7H_{16}	$CH_3CH_2CH_2CH_2CH_2CH_2CH_3$
Octane	8	C_8H_{18}	$CH_3CH_2CH_2CH_2CH_2CH_2CH_2CH_3$
Nonane	9	C_9H_{20}	$CH_3CH_2CH_2CH_2CH_2CH_2CH_2CH_2CH_3$
Decane	10	$C_{10}H_{22}$	$CH_3CH_2CH_2CH_2CH_2CH_2CH_2CH_2CH_2CH_3$

B.8   LABORATORY ACTIVITY: ALKANES REVISITED

Getting Ready

The alkane molecules we have considered so far are **straight-chain alkanes** in which each carbon atom is linked to only one or two other carbon atoms. Many other arrangements of carbon atoms in alkanes are possible. Alkanes in which one or more carbon atoms are linked to three or four other carbon atoms are called **branched-chain alkanes.** A branched-chain alkane may have the same number of carbon atoms as a straight-chain alkane.

In this activity you will use ball-and-stick molecular models to investigate some variations in alkane structures that lead to different properties.

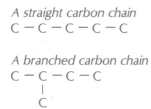

A straight carbon chain
C — C — C — C — C

A branched carbon chain
C — C — C — C
      |
      C

Procedure

1. Construct a ball-and-stick model of butane, C_4H_{10}. Compare your model with those built by others. How many different arrangements of atoms in the C_4H_{10} molecule can be constructed?

    Molecules having identical molecular formulas but different arrangements of atoms are called **isomers.** By comparing models, convince yourself that there are two isomers of butane. The formation of isomers helps explain the very large number of compounds that contain carbon chains or rings.

2. a. Draw an electron-dot formula for each butane isomer.

    b. Write a structural formula for each butane isomer.

3. As you might expect, alkanes containing larger numbers of carbon atoms have greater numbers of isotopes. For example, chemists have identified three pentane (C_5H_{12}) isomers. Structural formulas for the three pentane isomers are shown on page 173. Convince yourself that no other pentane isomer is possible. Build other possible isomer models, if you wish, to confirm this statement.

Table 3   **ALKANE ISOMERS**

Alkane	Structure	Boiling Point (° C)
C_5H_{12} isomers	$CH_3 - CH_2 - CH_2 - CH_2 - CH_3$	36.1
	$CH_3 - CH - CH_2 - CH_3$ $\qquad\quad \|$ $\qquad\quad CH_3$	27.8
	$\qquad\quad CH_3$ $\qquad\quad \|$ $CH_3 - C - CH_3$ $\qquad\quad \|$ $\qquad\quad CH_3$	9.5
Some C_8H_{18} isomers	$CH_3 - CH_2 - CH_2 - CH_2 - CH_2 - CH_2 - CH_2 - CH_3$	125.6
	$CH_3 - CH_2 - CH_2 - CH_2 - CH_2 - CH - CH_3$ $\qquad\qquad\qquad\qquad\qquad\qquad\quad \|$ $\qquad\qquad\qquad\qquad\qquad\qquad\quad CH_3$	117.7
	$\qquad\qquad\qquad\qquad CH_3$ $\qquad\qquad\qquad\qquad \|$ $CH_3 - CH - CH_2 - C - CH_3$ $\qquad\quad \|\qquad\qquad\quad \|$ $\qquad\quad CH_3\qquad\quad CH_3$	99.2

4. Now consider possible isomers for hexane, C_6H_{14}.
   a. Working with a partner, draw structural formulas as many *different* hexane isomers as possible. Compare your structures with those of other groups.
   b. How many possible hexane isomers were found by your class?
5. Build one or more of the possible hexane isomers, as assigned by your teacher.
   a. Compare the three-dimensional models built by the class with structures drawn on paper.
   b. Based on your study of the three-dimensional models, how many different hexane isomers are possible?

Alkane molecules having four or more carbon atoms have more than one possible structure. Your experience with hexane (six carbon atoms) should confirm that the number of different structures increases rapidly as the number of carbon atoms increases.

Since each isomer is a different substance, each must have characteristic properties. Let's examine boiling point data for some alkane isomers.

YOUR TURN

Alkane Boiling Points: Isomers

You have already observed that boiling points of straight-chain alkanes are related to the number of carbon atoms in their molecules. Increased intermolecular attractions are related to the greater molecule-molecule contact possible for larger alkanes.

For example, consider the boiling points of some isomers.

1. Boiling points for two sets of isomers are listed in Table 3 (page 173). Within a given series, how does the boiling point change as the number of carbon side-chains increases?

2. Match each boiling point to the appropriate C_7H_{16} isomer: 98.4° C, 92.0° C, 79.2° C.

   a. $CH_3 — CH_2 — CH — CH_2 — CH_2 — CH_3$
   $\qquad\qquad\qquad\quad |$
   $\qquad\qquad\qquad CH_3$

   b. $\qquad\qquad\qquad\qquad CH_3$
   $\qquad\qquad\qquad\qquad |$
   $CH_3 — CH_2 — CH_2 — C — CH_3$
   $\qquad\qquad\qquad\qquad |$
   $\qquad\qquad\qquad\qquad CH_3$

   c. $CH_3 — CH_2 — CH_2 — CH_2 — CH_2 — CH_2 — CH_3$

3. Below is the formula of a C_8H_{18} isomer.

   $\qquad\qquad\qquad\qquad CH_3$
   $\qquad\qquad\qquad\qquad |$
   $CH_3 — CH_2 — CH_2 — C — CH_2 — CH_3$
   $\qquad\qquad\qquad\qquad |$
   $\qquad\qquad\qquad\qquad CH_3$

   a. Compare it to each C_8H_{18} isomer listed in Table 3. Predict whether it would have a higher or lower boiling point than each of these other C_8H_{18} isomers.

   b. Would the C_8H_{18} isomer shown above have a higher or lower boiling point than each of the three C_5H_{12} isomers shown in Table 3?

Lucas well at Spindletop, Texas, 1901.

Chemists and chemical engineers are able to separate the complex mixture known as petroleum into a variety of useful substances. However, petroleum is a nonrenewable and limited resource. This fact poses important questions for our society. How can we best use various petroleum fractions? Should we use them for building or for burning? If for both, how much should be directed to each use? What future alternatives might help decrease our dependence on petroleum?

These questions will be explored in the following pages. Most petroleum currently used is burned as fuel; therefore, this use serves as our focus in Part C.

PART B: SUMMARY QUESTIONS

1. a. In what sense is petroleum similar to metallic resources such as copper ore?
   b. In what sense is it different from them?

2. A 50.0-mL sample of octane—a component of gasoline—has a mass of 35.1 g.

   a. What is the density of octane?
   b. What is the mass of a 100-mL sample of octane?

3. a. Describe two broad categories of uses for petroleum.

b. List two examples for each category.

4. Paraffin wax (candle wax) is a mixture of alkanes. A group of 25-carbon alkanes is one component of paraffin. Write the molecular formula for this group of alkanes.

5. a. List two features of molecular structure that determine the relative boiling points of hydrocarbons.

   b. How does each feature influence boiling points?

6. a. Explain what the term "isomer" means.

   b. Illustrate your explanation by drawing structural formulas for at least three isomers of C_7H_{16}.

EXTENDING YOUR KNOWLEDGE (OPTIONAL)

- Investigate the various compositions of gasoline sold in different parts of the nation. Does gasoline's composition relate to the time of year? If so, what factors help determine the optimum composition in various seasons?

- The hydrocarbon boiling points listed in Table 1 (page 166) were measured under normal atmospheric conditions. How would the boiling points change if atmospheric pressure were increased or decreased? (*Hint:* Butane is stored as a liquid in a butane lighter, yet escapes through the lighter nozzle as gas.)

- When 1,2-ethanediol (ethylene glycol—also known as antifreeze) is dissolved in an automobile's radiator water, it helps protect the water from freezing in winter. This is because the 1,2-ethanediol-water solution has a lower freezing point than that of pure water. Similarly, when an ionic substance such as table salt, NaCl, is dissolved in water, the solution also has a lower freezing point than pure water. However, while table salt is a highly undesirable additive for car radiators, 1,2-ethanediol (ethylene glycol) is a suitable additive. Why? (*Hint:* Compare the structures and properties of these two substances.)

1,2-Ethanediol (ethylene glycol).

$$\begin{array}{ccc} & H & H \\ & | & | \\ H - & C - & C - H \\ & | & | \\ & OH & OH \end{array}$$

PETROLEUM AS AN ENERGY SOURCE

No one knows the exact origin of petroleum. Most evidence indicates that it originated from plants and animals that lived in ancient seas some 500 million years ago. These organisms died and eventually became covered with sediments. Pressure, heat, and microbes converted what was once living matter into petroleum, which became trapped in porous rocks. It is likely that some petroleum is still being formed from sediments of dead organisms. However, its formation would occur far too slowly for us to consider petroleum a renewable resource.

Human use of petroleum can be traced back almost 5000 years. Ancient Middle Eastern civilizations used petroleum seeping out of the ground to waterproof ships and canals and to pave roads. By A.D. 1000, Arabs processed petroleum to obtain kerosene for lighting. Eleventh-century Chinese extracted oil

The John Benninghoff oil farm, Oil Creek, Pennsylvania, 1865.

from wells over a half-mile deep. Marco Polo observed and described oil fields in his travels through Persia in the thirteenth century.

The first U.S. oil well was drilled in Titusville, Pennsylvania in 1859. In the decades since then, our way of living has been greatly altered by petroleum's increasing use. The following activity will help you realize how much life has changed during our recent history of petroleum use.

C.1 YOU DECIDE: THE GOOD OLD DAYS?

Earlier in this century, petroleum was used far less than it is now. To investigate what life was like then, you will serve on a team to interview someone old enough to remember this period of our nation's past.

First, however, your class should decide what questions should be included in the interviews. Sample questions are given below. You may use these or develop your own set of 10 to 12 questions. All interview teams should use the same questions, so results can be compared later.

Sample Interview Questions

1. How would you describe the location where you lived as a child—urban, suburban, or rural?
2. What was the main source of heat in your childhood home?
3. How was this source of heat supplied? Did you obtain the fuel yourself or was it delivered to your home?
4. Considering cleanliness, convenience, and quantity of heat produced, how does that source of heat compare to what we use today?
5. What was the main source of lighting in your childhood home? What source of energy was used to provide the lighting?
6. What, if any, was the main means of public transportation? What provided the energy for this transportation?
7. What was the main source of private transportation? How common was this mode of transportation? What was its source of energy?
8. What fuel was used for cooking?
9. If you bought your food, rather than growing or raising it yourself, how was it packaged?
10. In what kind of container was milk obtained?
11. What kind of soap was used to wash clothes? How did its effectiveness compare to today's soaps and detergents?
12. What were the main fabrics used in clothes? From what were the fabrics made?
13. Were clothes easier or harder to care for than they are now? Please explain.

After deciding what questions to use in the interviews, your class will organize into separate interview teams. Each team should arrange to interview one team member's grandparent, a neighbor more than 70 years old, or a resident of a local retirement center.

A portable but inefficient light source from an earlier era.

Before conducting the interview, each team should practice by interviewing one of its own members. This practice interview will provide current information for comparison and will help you sharpen your interviewing skills. Summarize all questions and answers in a written outline or chart following each interview.

All interview-team results should be tabulated on a single class poster or bulletin board. The questions can be written in a vertical column; the most common answers can be written alongside each question. Each team can then place a check mark next to the answers they obtained. Interview information that cannot be added to the chart can be introduced during the class discussion.

Here are some suggested class discussion topics:

1. Summarize the main differences between earlier years and now regarding
   a. home heating.
   b. lighting.
   c. public transportation.
   d. private transportation.
   e. cooking.
   f. food packaging.
   g. clothes washing.
   h. clothing material.

2. Would a return to "the good old days" be a good thing? Why?

3. If current energy sources become depleted, will we have to return to a lifestyle similar to that of the past? Why?

Would *you* want to live in the "good old days"? Whatever your answer, of course, we still live in the here and now. That means we have to make the best possible use of our remaining energy sources—petroleum being a major one.

To help us understand our energy future, we will investigate energy sources that powered our society over the past century.

C.2 ENERGY: PAST, PRESENT, AND FUTURE

The sun is our planet's primary energy source. Through the process of **photosynthesis,** radiant energy from the sun is stored as chemical energy in plants. When animals eat these plants, they take in and store the energy in their own molecules. The organic molecules found in plants and animals are called **biomolecules.**

Solar energy and energy stored in biomolecules are the basic energy sources for life on our planet. Some of this energy is stored in wood, coal, and petroleum. Since the discovery of fire, human use of these fuels has been a major influence in civilization's development. As your interviews probably suggested, the forms, availability, and cost of energy greatly influence where and how people live.

In the past, our nation had abundant supplies of inexpensive energy. Until about 1850, wood, water, wind, and animal power satisfied all of our slowly-growing energy needs. Wood—the predominant energy source—was readily available due to the conversion of forests to farmland. Wood served as an energy source for heating, cooking, and lighting. Water, wind, and animal power provided transportation and "fueled" our machinery and industrial processes. In the next activity, you will see just how much all this has changed in the intervening years.

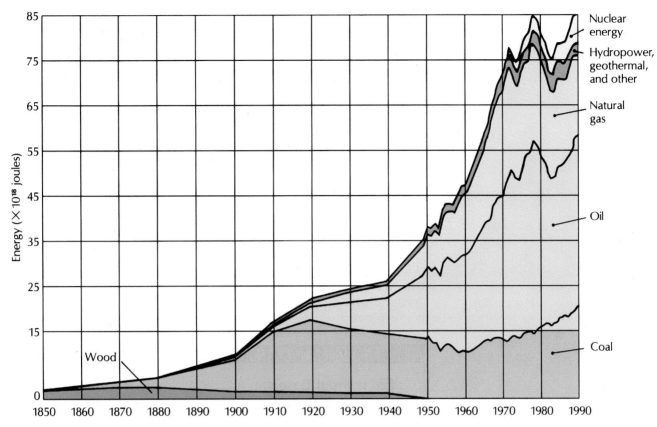

Figure 9 U.S. energy consumption by fuel type, 1850–1990.

Fuel Consumption Over the Years

Figure 9 shows how United States energy consumption has changed since 1850. It also shows the quantities of energy supplied by various fuel sources, such as coal, wood, and petroleum, for any year between 1850 and 1990. For example, the graph indicates that the nation used about 22×10^{18} joules (J) of energy in 1920. At that time coal was by far the major source of energy. The graph indicates that oil was second in importance. Lesser quantities of energy from wood, natural gas, hydropower/geothermal, and other sources were used to fuel the start of the Roaring Twenties.

Use Figure 9 to answer these questions:

1. a. Has U.S. energy consumption since 1850 remained constant, increased at a steady rate, or accelerated (grown at an increasing rate)?
   b. Describe at least two possible reasons for this general trend.
2. a. Over what time interval since 1850 did wood supply more than 50% of the nation's total energy?
   b. What was the chief mode of long-distance travel during that period?
3. a. What factors might explain the decline in wood use after that period?
   b. What energy source increased in importance next?

In 1920, the U.S. population was 106 million. Today it is more than 250 million.

The total energy used in the U.S. in 3.5 days is approximately 10^{18} J.

4. Compared to other energy sources, only a small quantity of petroleum was used before about 1910. What do you think petroleum's main use might have been at that time?

5. Oil became increasingly important about the same time that coal use reached its peak.
   a. When did that occur?
   b. What explains the growing use of petroleum after that date?

6. a. What is the most recent energy source to enter the picture?
   b. What is the major use of this energy source?

Changes in supplies and uses of energy are part of our nation's history. But what about the future—your future? How will the energy picture look as you enter the twenty-first century? Writers have tried to predict such events—one noteworthy effort is given below.

CHEMQUANDARY

Life without Gasoline

What would life be like without petroleum for fuel? In 1977, *Time* magazine asked science fiction writer Isaac Asimov to describe such a world. Asimov chose to set his prediction 20 years in the future—in 1997.

Here is an excerpt from Asimov's story about life in the "distant" year of 1997:

Anyone older than ten can remember automobiles. They dwindled. At first the price of gasoline climbed—way up. Finally only the well-to-do drove, and that was too clear an indication that they were filthy rich, so any automobile that dared show itself on a city street was overturned and burned. Rationing was introduced to "equalize sacrifice", but every three months the ration was reduced. The cars just vanished and became part of the metal resource.

There are many advantages, if you want to look for them. Our 1997 newspapers continually point them out. The air is cleaner and there seem to be fewer colds. Against most predictions, the crime rate has dropped. With the police car too expensive (and too easy a target), policemen are back on their beats. More important, the streets are full. Legs are king in the cities of 1997, and people walk everywhere far into the night. Even the parks are full, and there is mutual protection in crowds.

As for the winter—well, it is inconvenient to be cold, with most of what furnace fuel is allowed hoarded for the dawn; but sweaters are popular indoor wear and showers are not an everyday luxury. Lukewarm sponge baths will do, and if the air is not always very fragrant in the human vicinity, the automobile fumes are gone.

"The Nightmare of Life without Fuel." *Time*, 1977, April 25, p. 33. Reprinted with permission.

That's one writer's 1977 prediction regarding life in the late 1990s. In fairness to the author, remember that Asimov was attempting to "see" 20 years into the future.

Imagine that in 1997 *you* are invited to write your own predictions regarding "life without petroleum" in the year 2017—twenty years in your own future.

1. Write a story involving your predictions of "life without petroleum" set in the year 2017. Use these questions to guide your writing:

   a. How would your daily life change in such a world?

   b. What change would involve the hardest adjustment for you? Why?

   c. Which would be the easiest adjustment? Why?

2. It is clear from today's perspective that "actual life" in 1997 will not be as radically different as the 1977 story suggested. (If it were, it's unlikely the book you are now reading would be trucked from the publisher to your school!)

   a. Propose some actions we could take now as individuals to prevent this situation from becoming a reality by 2017.

   b. Propose some government actions that might help prevent such a scenario from occurring in the next 20 years.

Are we doomed to run short of energy? In considering this question, we must first understand how energy is stored in fuels and how we convert this chemical energy into other, more useful forms.

C.3 ENERGY AND FOSSIL FUELS

Petroleum, natural gas, and coal—the **fossil fuels**—can be regarded as forms of buried sunshine. Fossil fuels probably originated from biomolecules of prehistoric plants and animals. The stored energy released by burning fossil fuels is energy originally captured from sunlight during photosynthesis. Fossil fuel energy can be compared to the energy stored in a loaded mousetrap. Originally, energy was supplied to coil the spring and set the trap. Most of that energy is stored within the new arrangement of "loaded" mousetrap parts. When the trap is sprung, these parts rapidly rearrange and the trap returns to a lower-energy, more stable state. The energy that was stored in the loaded trap is quickly released during this process.

Likewise, chemical energy is stored in chemical compounds. When chemical reactions occur and atoms rearrange to form more stable structures, as during the burning of fuels, some of the stored energy is released in the form of thermal energy and light.

The formation and decomposition of water illustrate how chemists look at the energy involved in chemical reactions. The equation for producing water from hydrogen and oxygen gas is

A coal-burning power plant.

$$2 \text{ H}_2 \quad + \quad \text{O}_2 \quad \rightarrow \quad 2 \text{ H}_2\text{O} + \text{Energy}$$

Hydrogen   Oxygen   Water
gas   gas

This simple reaction releases a considerable amount of energy—either with explosive force if a mixture of hydrogen and oxygen gas is ignited, or in a more gradual, useful manner if the gases react in a fuel cell, producing electrical energy and heat.

In either case, it is useful to think about this reaction as taking place in separate (and imaginary) bond-breaking and bond-making steps. As a first step, imagine that all bonds in the reactant molecules are broken, producing separate atoms (Figure 10a, Step I). This bond-breaking step is an energy-requiring process—an **endothermic** change. The final imaginary step (Figure 10a, Step II) involves forming the new bonds needed to make two water molecules. The formation of bonds is an energy-releasing process—an **exothermic** change. Because the energy released in forming water molecule bonds is greater than the energy originally needed to break the bonds in hydrogen and oxygen gas, the entire chemical reaction (Step I + Step II) is exothermic. That is shown by placing energy on the product side of the equation.

By contrast, the reverse reaction, the decomposition of water (Figure 10b, Steps I and II), is an endothermic reaction. Notice that energy is on the reactant side of the equation.

$$\text{Energy} + 2 \text{ H}_2\text{O} \quad \rightarrow \quad 2 \text{ H}_2 \quad + \quad \text{O}_2$$

Water   Hydrogen   Oxygen
gas   gas

In this process, H — O bonds in water are broken (requiring energy) and H — H and O — O bonds are formed (releasing energy). More energy is needed to break the bonds in water molecules than is released in forming bonds in product molecules. Thus energy is required for this process—an endothermic change.

Fuel-burning releases thermal energy, or heat. Scientists and engineers have increased the usefulness of energy released by burning fuels. They have developed devices to convert thermal energy into other forms of energy. In fact, much of the energy we use goes through several conversions before reaching us.

Once an exothermic reaction begins, it continues to release energy until the reaction stops.

An endothermic reaction can proceed only if energy is continuously supplied.

Figure 10 (A) In Step I, bonds are broken, a process that requires energy. Since more energy is released in Step II than is required in Step I, the formation of water from H_2 and O_2 is exothermic. (B) The reverse process is endothermic.

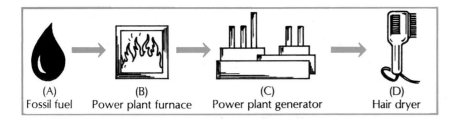

Figure 11 Tracing energy conversions between energy source and final use.

(A) Fossil fuel — (B) Power plant furnace — (C) Power plant generator — (D) Hair dryer

Figure 12 Some of the energy storage and conversion devices in an automobile.

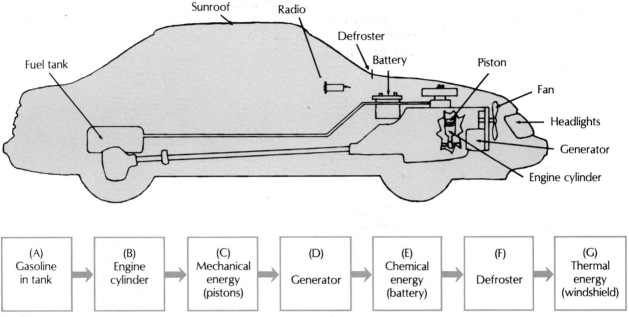

| (A)
Gasoline
in tank | (B)
Engine
cylinder | (C)
Mechanical
energy
(pistons) | (D)
Generator | (E)
Chemical
energy
(battery) | (F)
Defroster | (G)
Thermal
energy
(windshield) |

Figure 13 Tracing energy conversions in an automobile.

Assume the role of an "energy detective" in the following activity. We will follow some typical energy conversions, first in a hair dryer and then in an automobile.

YOUR TURN

Energy Conversion

Consider the energy-conversion steps needed to dry your hair with a hair dryer. Look at Figure 11. Starting at the left—with fossil fuel—examine the types of energy involved at each step:

A fossil fuel contains stored *chemical energy* (A). In an electric power plant, the fossil fuel burns to generate *thermal energy* (B). The power plant converts thermal energy to *electrical energy* (C). When the electricity reaches your hair dryer it is converted back to *thermal energy* (D) to dry your hair and also to *mechanical energy* as a small fan blade spins to blow the hot air—and even to *sound energy* (as any hair-dryer user knows!).

Now it's time to tackle an energy pathway in a more complex system. In one sense, an automobile—despite its appealing appearance—is just a collection of energy converters and energy-using devices. Some of these are shown in Figure 12.

Figure 13 summarizes an energy pathway that connects gasoline stored in the fuel tank to an operating windshield defroster. The types of energy used in two steps have already been named—the auto battery (E) involves *chemical energy*, and the windshield (G) receives *thermal energy*.

Name the type(s) of energy in each of the other steps involved in getting an automobile window defroster to operate.

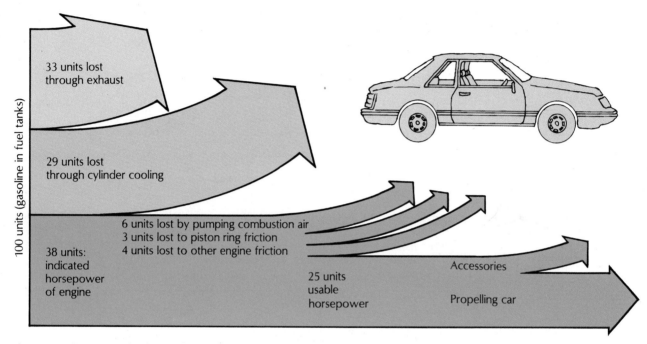

33 units lost through exhaust

29 units lost through cylinder cooling

6 units lost by pumping combustion air
3 units lost to piston ring friction
4 units lost to other engine friction

38 units: indicated horsepower of engine

100 units (gasoline in fuel tanks)

25 units usable horsepower

Accessories

Propelling car

Figure 14 Energy use in an automobile.

Although energy-converting devices have certainly increased the usefulness of petroleum and other fuels, some devices have produced new problems. Pollution sometimes accompanies energy-conversion steps. More fundamentally, some useful energy is *always* "lost" when energy is converted from one form to another. That is, no energy conversion is totally efficient; some energy always becomes unavailable to do useful work.

For example, consider an automobile that starts with 100 units of chemical energy in the form of gasoline (Figure 14).

Even a well-tuned automobile can convert only about 25% of the chemical energy in gasoline to useful mechanical energy (motion). The remaining 75% of gasoline's chemical energy is lost to the surroundings as heat. In the following *Your Turn*, you will see what this means in gallons of gasoline, and in terms of your pocketbook.

YOUR TURN

Energy Conversion Efficiency

Assume your family drives 225 miles each week. Also assume your car can travel 19.0 miles on a gallon of gasoline. How much gasoline does your car use in one year?

Questions such as this can be answered by using arithmetic. One approach is to add proper units to all values and multiply and divide them the same way numbers are processed.

The information given in the sample problem can be expressed this way:

$$\frac{225 \text{ miles}}{1 \text{ week}} \quad \text{and} \quad \frac{19.0 \text{ miles}}{1 \text{ gal}}$$

or, if needed, as inverted expressions:

$$\frac{1 \text{ week}}{225 \text{ miles}} \quad \text{and} \quad \frac{1 \text{ gal}}{19.0 \text{ miles}}$$

The desired answer must have the units:

$$\frac{\text{gal}}{\text{yr}}$$

Calculating the desired answer also involves using information you already know—there are 52 weeks in one year, $\frac{52 \text{ weeks}}{1 \text{ yr}}$. It also involves using the second unit above in an "upside down" version so units cancel to give the desired answer:

$$\frac{225 \, \cancel{\text{miles}}}{1 \, \cancel{\text{week}}} \times \frac{1 \text{ gal}}{19.0 \, \cancel{\text{miles}}} \times \frac{52 \, \cancel{\text{weeks}}}{1 \text{ yr}} = 616 \text{ gal/yr}$$

1. Assume your 19.0 miles-per-gallon automobile travels 200 miles each week.
   a. How far will the car travel in one year?
   b. How many gallons of gasoline will be used during the year's travels?

2. If gasoline costs $1.35 per gallon, how much would you spend on gasoline in one year?

3. Assume your automobile engine uses only 25% of the energy released by burning gasoline.
   a. How many gallons of gasoline are wasted each year due to your car's inefficiency?
   b. How much does this wasted gasoline cost at $1.35 per gallon?

4. Suppose you trade the car for one that travels 40.0 miles on a gallon of gasoline.
   a. How much gasoline would this new car use in one year?
   b. Compared to your first car, how many gallons of gasoline would you "save" by driving this more fuel-efficient automobile?
   c. How much money would you save on gasoline in one year?

5. If continued research leads to a car engine with 50% efficiency that can travel 50.0 miles on a gallon of gasoline,
   a. how much gasoline would be saved in one year over a car that was 25% efficient and averaged 19.0 miles per gallon?
   b. how much money would be saved?

Petroleum supplies are neither limitless nor inexpensive. Thus, increasing energy efficiency is important if we want maximum benefits from our remaining petroleum supplies. One way to increase overall energy efficiency is to reduce the number of energy conversions between the fuel and its final use. We can also try to increase the efficiency of our energy-conversion devices.

Unfortunately, devices that convert chemical energy to heat and then to mechanical energy are typically less than 50% efficient. Solar cells (solar energy → electrical energy) and fuel cells (chemical energy → electrical energy) hold promise either for replacing petroleum or for increasing the efficiency of its use.

But what is burning? What products form when petroleum-based fuels burn? How much energy is involved? We will investigate these questions next.

C.4 THE CHEMISTRY OF BURNING

You strike a match—a hot, yellow flame appears. You hold it to a candle wick. The candle lights and burns. These events are so commonplace you probably don't realize that complex chemical reactions are at work.

Candle-burning involves chemical reactions of the wax (composed of long-chain alkanes) with oxygen gas at elevated temperatures. Many chemical reactions are involved in such "burning," or **combustion.** For simplicity, chemists usually consider the overall changes involved. For example, the reaction involved in burning one wax component can be described by this way:

$$C_{25}H_{52}(g) + 38\ O_2(g)\ \rightarrow\ 25\ CO_2(g) + 26\ H_2O(g) + \text{Thermal}$$

Wax	Oxygen	Carbon	Water	energy
(alkane)	gas	dioxide gas	vapor	

This reaction is exothermic. The energy given off by the formation of the bonds in product molecules (carbon dioxide gas and water vapor) is greater than the energy needed to break the bonds in the wax and the oxygen gas reactant molecules.

Fuels provide energy as they burn. But how much energy can be obtained? How is the quantity of released energy measured? Find out for yourself in the following activity.

C.5 LABORATORY ACTIVITY: COMBUSTION

Getting Ready

As you know, the boiling points of hydrocarbons are related to the number of carbon atoms in each molecule. Is the quantity of thermal energy released in burning also related to the number of carbon atoms in each hydrocarbon molecule?

The quantity of thermal energy given off when a certain amount of a substance burns is its **heat of combustion.** When one mole of a substance burns, the thermal energy released is called its **molar heat of combustion.**

In this activity you will investigate relationships between the thermal energy released when a hydrocarbon burns, and the structure of the hydrocarbon. You will measure the heat of combustion of a candle (paraffin wax) and compare this quantity with known values for other hydrocarbons.

Prepare a data table similar to the one that follows.

Data Table

Initial mass of candle + index card	_____ g
Volume of water	_____ mL
Room temperature	_____ ° C
Initial temperature of water in can	_____ ° C
Final temperature of water in can	_____ ° C
Final mass of candle + index card	_____ g

Procedure

1. Prepare the candle for the experiment by holding a lighted match near its base, so that some melted wax falls onto a 3 × 5 index card. Immediately push the candle into the melted wax and hold it there for a moment to fasten it to the card.

2. Determine the combined mass of the candle and the index card. Record the value.

3. Carefully measure (to the nearest milliliter) 100 mL of chilled water. (The chilled water will be provided by your teacher. It should be 10 to 15° C colder than room temperature.) Pour the 100-mL sample of chilled water into an empty soft drink can.

4. Set up the apparatus shown in Figure 15. (Do not light the candle yet!) Adjust the soft drink can height so the candle wick is about 2 cm from the can bottom.

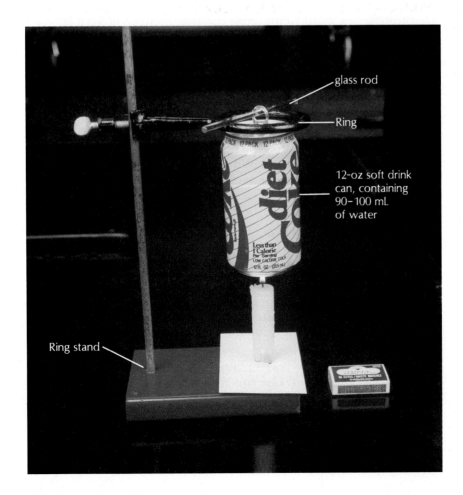

Figure 15   Apparatus for measuring heat of combustion.

5. Measure the room temperature and the water temperature to the nearest 0.2° C. Record these values.

6. Place the candle under the can of water. Light the candle. Stir the water gently with a stirring rod as it heats.

7. As the candle burns you may need to lower the soft drink can *cautiously* so the flame remains just below the can bottom.

8. Continue heating until the temperature rises as far above room temperature as it was below room temperature at the start. (*Example:* If the water was 15° C before heating and room temperature is 25° C, then you would heat the water 10° C *higher* than room temperature—to 35° C.)

9. When the desired temperature is reached, extinguish the flame.

10. Continue stirring the water until its temperature stops rising. Record the highest temperature reached by the water.

11. Determine the mass of the cooled candle and index card, including all wax drippings.

12. Wash your hands thoroughly before leaving the laboratory.

Calculations

One characteristic property of a material is the quantity of heat needed to raise the temperature of one gram of the material by 1° C. This value is the **specific heat** of the material. The specific heat of water, for example, is about 4.2 joules per gram. Therefore, for each degree Celsius that water is heated, we know that each gram of the water has absorbed 4.2 J of thermal energy.

Suppose we want to increase the temperature of 10 g of water by 5.0° C. How much thermal energy is needed?

The answer is reasoned this way: We know it takes 4.2 J to raise the temperature of 1 g of water by 1° C. However, compared to this standard, we have *10* times more water and *5* times greater rise in temperature. Thus we need 10 × 5, or *50* times more thermal energy to accomplish the task. So, 50 × 4.2 J = 210 J. In other words, we need 210 J to heat 10 g of water by 5.0° C.

The heat of combustion of a substance can be expressed either as the heat released when one *gram* of substance burns or when one *mole* of substance burns (the molar heat of combustion). Let's first find the heat of combustion per gram of paraffin wax.

Use data collected in the laboratory activity to complete the following calculations.

1. Calculate the mass of water heated. (*Hint:* The density of water is 1.0 g per mL—thus each milliliter of water has a mass of 1.0 g.)

2. Calculate the temperature change in the water. (This equals the final water temperature minus the initial water temperature.)

3. Find the quantity of thermal energy used to heat the water in the soft drink can. Use the values from Steps 1 and 2 to "reason out" the answer as was illustrated in the sample problem earlier.

4. Find the mass of paraffin burned.

5. Find paraffin's heat of combustion, in units of joules per gram of paraffin (J/g).

The exact value for the specific heat of water is 4.184 joules per gram. However, a rounded-off value of 4.2 J/g is quite useful for this laboratory activity.

Assume that the thermal energy absorbed by the water equals the thermal energy released by the burning paraffin. Thus, dividing the thermal energy (Step 3) by the mass of paraffin burned (Step 4), produces the answer:

$$\text{Heat of combustion} = \frac{\text{thermal energy released (Step 3)}}{\text{mass of paraffin burned (Step 4)}}$$

Questions

Your teacher will collect your heat of combustion data, expressed in units of kilojoules per gram of paraffin (kJ/g). Use combined class results for this value to answer the following questions.

1. How does your experimental heat of combustion (in kJ/g) for paraffin wax, $C_{25}H_{52}$, compare with the accepted value for butane, C_4H_{10} (see Table 4)?

Table 4   HEATS OF COMBUSTION

Hydrocarbon	Formula	Heat of Combustion (kJ/g)	Molar Heat of Combustion (kJ/mol)
Methane	CH_4	55.6	890
Ethane	C_2H_6	52.0	1560
Propane	C_3H_8	50.0	2200
Butane	C_4H_{10}	49.3	2859
Pentane	C_5H_{12}	48.8	3510
Hexane	C_6H_{14}	48.2	4141
Heptane	C_7H_{16}	48.2	4817
Octane	C_8H_{18}	47.8	5450

2. How do the molar heats of combustion (in kJ/mol) for paraffin and butane compare? (*Hint*: To make this comparison, first calculate the thermal energy released when one *mole* of paraffin burns. One mole of paraffin ($C_{25}H_{52}$) has a mass of 352 g. The quantity of thermal energy released will thus be 352 times greater than the thermal energy released by one gram of paraffin.)

3. Explain any differences noted in your answers to Questions 1 and 2.

4. Which hydrocarbon—paraffin or butane—is the better fuel? Explain your answer.

5. In calculating heats of combustion, you assumed that all thermal energy from the burning fuel went to heating the water.

   a. Is this a good assumption?

   b. What other laboratory conditions or assumptions might cause errors in your calculated values?

C.6 USING HEATS OF COMBUSTION

With abundant oxygen gas and complete combustion, the burning of a hydrocarbon can be described by the equation

Hydrocarbon + Oxygen → Carbon + Water + Thermal
                    gas   dioxide   energy

Note that energy is written as a product of the reaction, because energy is released when a hydrocarbon burns. As you found in the last laboratory activity, this energy can be expressed in terms of kilojoules for each gram (or mole) of fuel burned.

The equation for burning ethane is

$$2\ C_2H_6 + 7\ O_2 \rightarrow 4\ CO_2 + 6\ H_2O + \mathbf{?}\ kJ\ thermal\ energy$$

To complete this equation, we must add the quantity of thermal energy involved. A summary of data like that given in Table 4 (page 189) provides such information. Table 4 indicates that ethane's heat of combustion is 1560 kJ per mole—burning one mole of ethane released 1560 kilojoules of energy.

However, as a part of the chemical equation, thermal energy must be "balanced" just like other reactants and products. The balanced equation represents the burning of *two* moles of ethane ($2\ C_2H_6$). Thus total thermal energy released will be *twice* that released by when one mole of ethane burns:

$$2 \times 1560\ kJ = 3120\ kJ$$

The complete combustion equation is

$$2\ C_2H_6 + 7\ O_2 \rightarrow 4\ CO_2 + 6\ H_2O + 3120\ kJ\ thermal\ energy$$

Or, we could write a balanced equation for burning *one* mole of ethane:

$$C_2H_6 + 3.5\ O_2 \rightarrow 2\ CO_2 + 3\ H_2O + 1560\ kJ\ thermal\ energy$$

In other words, the amount of ethane specified affects all other amounts in the balanced equation, including the amount of energy.

CHEMQUANDARY

Splitting Molecules?

The equation appearing just above for burning one mole of C_2H_6 includes the expression "3.5 O_2." Does that mean that three "whole molecules" of O_2 and an added "half-molecule" of O_2 are needed in this reaction? Explain.

As you found in the previous laboratory activity (and as Table 4 suggests), heats of combustion can also be expressed as energy produced when one gram of hydrocarbon burns (kJ/g). Such values are useful in finding the thermal energy released in burning any mass of a fuel.

For example, how much thermal energy would be produced by burning 12 g of octane, C_8H_{18}? Table 4 indicates that when *one* gram of octane burns, 47.8 kJ of energy are released. Burning *12* times more octane will produce 12 times more thermal energy—or, $12 \times 47.8\ kJ = 574\ kJ$.

The calculation can also be written this way:

$$12.0\ \cancel{g\ octane} \times \frac{47.8\ kJ}{1\ \cancel{g\ octane}} = 574\ kJ$$

Heats of Combustion

To better understand the energy involved in burning hydrocarbon fuels, use Table 4 (page 189) to answer the following questions. The first one is already worked out as an example.

1. How much energy (in kilojoules) is released by completely burning 25 mol of hexane, C_6H_{14}?

    Table 4 indicates that the molar heat of combustion of hexane is 4141 kJ. Putting it another way, 4141 kJ of energy are released when *one* mole of hexane burns. Thus, burning *25 times more* fuel will produce 25 times more energy:

$$25.0 \ \text{mol } C_6H_{14} \times \frac{4141 \ \text{kJ}}{1 \ \text{mol } C_6H_{14}} = 104,000 \ \text{kJ}$$

    Burning of 25 mol of hexane would thus produce 104,000 kJ of thermal energy.

2. Write a chemical equation, including thermal energy, for the complete combustion of each alkane:

    a. Methane (main component of natural gas)

    b. Butane (variety of uses, including lighter fluid)

3. Examine the data summarized in Table 4.

    a. How does the trend in heats of combustion for hydrocarbons expressed in kJ/g compare with that expressed in kJ/mol?

    b. Assuming the trend continues to larger hydrocarbons, predict the heat of combustion for decane, $C_{10}H_{22}$, in units of kJ/g and kJ/mol.

    c. Which Question 3b prediction was easier? Why?

4. a. How much thermal energy is produced by burning two moles of octane?

    b. How much thermal energy is produced by burning one gallon of octane? (One gallon of octane has a mass of 2,660 g.)

    c. Suppose your car operates so inefficiently that only 16% of the thermal energy from burning fuel is converted to useful "wheel-turning" (mechanical) energy. How many kilojoules of useful energy would be stored in a 20-gallon tank of gasoline? (Assume that octane burning and gasoline burning produce the same results.)

5. The heat of combustion of carbon is 394 kJ per mole.

    a. Write a chemical equation for burning carbon. Include the quantity of thermal energy produced.

    b. Gram for gram, which is the better fuel—carbon or octane? Explain.

    c. In what applications might carbon (as coal) serve as a substitute for petroleum-based fuel?

    d. Describe one application where coal would be a poor substitute for a petroleum product.

Once automobiles became popular, demand for gasoline increased rapidly in the United States. The gasoline fraction normally represents only about 18% of a barrel of crude oil, and so researchers have sought ways to increase the quantity of gasoline obtained from crude oil. One key discovery is still in common use today: It is possible to alter the structures of some petroleum hydrocarbons. This important chemical technique deserves further attention.

C.7 ALTERING FUELS

As you might expect, not all fractions of hydrocarbons obtained from petroleum are necessarily—at any particular time—in equal demand or use. The market for one petroleum fraction may be much less profitable than another. For example, the invention of electric light bulbs caused the use of kerosene lanterns to decline rapidly in the early 1900s. Petroleum's kerosene fraction, composed of hydrocarbon molecules with 12 to 16 carbon atoms, then became a surplus commodity.

Chemists and chemical engineers are adept at modifying or altering chemical resources on hand to meet new market opportunities or problems. Such alterations might involve converting less-useful materials to more-useful products, or—as in the case of kerosene in the early 1900s—a low-demand material into high-demand materials.

Recall that the gasoline fraction obtained from refining includes hydrocarbons with 5 to 12 carbon atoms in each molecule.

By 1913, chemists had devised a process for cracking molecules in kerosene into smaller (gasoline-sized) molecules by heating the kerosene to 600–700° C. For example, a 16-carbon molecule might be cracked to produce two 8-carbon molecules:

$$C_{16}H_{34}(g) \xrightarrow{700°\ C} C_8H_{16}(g) + C_8H_{18}(g)$$

In practice, molecules containing from 1 to 14 or more carbon atoms can be produced through cracking. Product molecules containing 5 to 12 carbons are particularly useful components of gasoline. Some of the C_1 to C_4 molecules formed in cracking are immediately burned, keeping the temperature high enough for more cracking to occur.

More than a third of all crude oil currently undergoes cracking. The process has been improved by adding catalysts, such as aluminum oxide (Al_2O_3). A ***catalyst*** increases the speed of a chemical reaction (in this case the cracking process) but is not itself used up. Catalytic cracking is more energy efficient since it occurs at a lower temperature—500° C rather than 700° C.

Gasoline is sold in a variety of standards (and prices), as you probably know. Gasoline composed mainly of straight-chain alkanes, such as hexane (C_6H_{14}), heptane (C_7H_{16}), and octane (C_8H_{18}) burns very rapidly. Such rapid burning causes engine knocking and may contribute to engine problems.

Branched-chain alkanes burn more satisfactorily in automobile engines. The structural isomer of octane shown below has excellent combustion properties in automobile engines.

$$CH_3 - \underset{\underset{CH_3}{|}}{\overset{\overset{CH_3}{|}}{C}} - CH_2 - \underset{\underset{CH_3}{|}}{CH} - CH_3$$

This octane isomer is known chemically as 2,2,3-trimethyl pentane. Can you see how this name is related to the structure shown?

A commonly-used gasoline-quality scale assigns this hydrocarbon a rating (called an **octane number**) of 100. Straight-chain heptane (C_7H_{16}), a fuel with very poor performance, is assigned an octane number of zero. The higher the octane number, the better are the anti-knock characteristics of the gasoline. Octane ratings in the high 80s (85, 87, etc.) are quite common among gasolines today, as any survey of gas pumps will reveal.

The tall catalytic cracking units (``cats'') break crude oil down into valuable and useful products.

In earlier times, a relatively inexpensive way to increase the octane rating of gasoline was to add a substance such as tetra-ethyl lead, $(C_2H_5)_4Pb$, to the fuel. It slowed down the burning of straight-chain gasoline molecules, and added about three points to the "leaded" fuel's octane rating.

Unfortunately, lead from the treated gasoline was discharged into the atmosphere along with other exhaust products. Due to the harmful effects of lead in the environment, such lead-based gasoline additives are no longer in common use.

With this phase-out of lead-based additives in gasoline, alternative octane-boosting supplements have become increasingly important. A group of additives called **oxygenated fuels** are frequently blended with gasoline to enhance its octane rating. These substances are composed of molecules that include oxygen in addition to carbon and hydrogen. Although oxygenated fuels deliver less energy per gallon than do regular gasoline hydrocarbons, their economic appeal comes from their ability both to increase the performance rating (octane number) of gasoline and to reduce exhaust-gas pollutants. Two common oxygenated fuels are MTBE and methanol (methyl alcohol, CH_3OH).

United States production of methyl t-butyl ether (MTBE) started in 1979; in less than ten years annual production topped one billion gallons.

Flexible-fuel cars—designed to run on methanol, gasoline, or any mixture of the two—have been involved in demonstration programs in a number of major U.S. cities. A 10% alcohol-90% gasoline blend, sometimes called **gasohol,** can be used without engine adjustments or problems in nearly all automobiles currently in service. In addition to its octane-boosting properties, methanol's potential appeal also arises from the fact that it can be made from natural gas, corn, coal, or wood—a contribution toward conserving petroleum resources.

Leaded gasolines represented no more than about 5% of total U.S. gasoline sales in 1990. By contrast, as recently as 1983 over 45% of gasoline sold contained lead-based additives.

$$CH_3 - O - \overset{\displaystyle CH_3}{\underset{\displaystyle CH_3}{\overset{|}{\underset{|}{C}}}} - CH_3$$

Methyl-t-butyl ether (MTBE)

YOUR TURN

A Burning Issue

Methanol (CH_3OH) and ethanol (CH_3CH_2OH) are both used as gasoline additives or substitutes. Their heats of combustion are, respectively, 23 kJ/g and 30 kJ/g.

1. Consider their chemical formulas. Gram for gram, why are the heats of combustion of methanol and ethanol considerably less than those of any hydrocarbons we have considered? (See Table 4, page 189.) (*Hint*: What would happen if you tried to burn oxygen?)

2. Would you expect automobiles fueled by 10% ethanol and 90% gasoline to get higher or lower miles per gallon than comparable cars fueled by 100% gasoline? Why?

Other octane-boosting strategies involve altering the composition of petroleum molecules themselves. Since branched-chain hydrocarbons burn more satisfactorily than do straight-chain versions, a process called *isomerization* is commonly used. Hydrocarbon vapor is heated with a catalyst:

$$CH_3 - CH_2 - CH_2 - CH_2 - CH_2 - CH_3 \xrightarrow{\text{Catalyst}} CH_3 - \underset{\underset{CH_3}{|}}{CH} - \underset{\overset{CH_3}{|}}{CH} - CH_3$$

The branched-chain alkanes produced are blended with gasoline-sized molecules from cracking and distillation, producing good-quality nonleaded gasoline. Cracked and isomerized molecules can improve the burning properties of gasoline, but they also increase its cost. One reason is that extra fuel is used up in manufacturing such gasoline.

We have now examined petroleum's use as a fuel. We will next turn to petroleum's role as a source of chemicals from which an impressive array of useful substances and materials can be produced.

PART C: SUMMARY QUESTIONS

1. Even though petroleum has been used for thousands of years, it became a major energy source only in recent history. List three technological factors that might explain this fact.

2. Compare wood and petroleum as fuels. Identify some advantages and disadvantages of each.

3. From a chemical viewpoint, why is petroleum sometimes considered "buried sunshine"?

4. Complete an energy trace (like that on page 183) to show how energy is transferred from chemical energy stored in an automobile gas tank to the retraction of the sunroof.

5. Explain "energy efficiency."

6. One gallon of gasoline will produce about 132,000 kJ of energy when burned. Assuming that an automobile is 25% efficient in converting this energy into useful work,
   a. How much energy is "wasted" when a gallon of gasoline burns?
   b. Where does this "wasted" energy go?

7. Write a balanced equation for the combustion of propane (bottled gas).

8. Water gas (a 50–50 mixture of CO and H_2O) is made by the reaction of coal with steam. Since our nation has substantial coal reserves, water gas might serve as a substitute fuel for natural gas (composed mainly of methane, CH_4). Water gas burns according to this equation:
   $$CO + H_2 + O_2 \rightarrow CO_2 + H_2O + 525 \text{ kJ}$$
   a. How does water gas compare to methane in terms of thermal energy produced?
   b. If a water gas mixture containing 10 mol CO and 10 mol H_2 were completely burned, how much thermal energy would be produced?

9. The combustion of acetylene, C_2H_2 (used in a welder's torch), can be represented as:
   $$2 \, C_2H_2 + 5 \, O_2 \rightarrow 4 \, CO_2 + 2 \, H_2O + 2512 \text{ kJ}$$
   a. What is the heat of combustion of acetylene in kilojoules per mole?
   b. If 12 mol of acetylene burns, how much thermal energy is produced?

10. List two factors that would help you decide which hydrocarbon fuel to use in a particular application.

11. a. Explain the meaning of the "octane rating" of a fuel.
    b. List two ways to increase a fuel's octane rating.

EXTENDING YOUR KNOWLEDGE (OPTIONAL)

- Powdered aluminum and magnesium metal release considerable heat when burned (their heats of combustion are, respectively, 31 kJ/g and 25 kJ/g). Why would these highly energetic powdered metals be poor fuel substitutes for petroleum?

D

USEFUL MATERIALS FROM PETROLEUM

Just as an architect uses available construction materials to design a building, a chemist—in a sense a molecular architect—uses available molecules to design others to serve our purposes. Architects must know about the structures and properties of common construction materials. Likewise, chemists must understand the structures and properties of their raw materials, the "builder molecules." You will now explore the structures of some common hydrocarbon builder molecules and some products chemists make from them. In fact, you will have the chance to make one yourself.

D.1 BEYOND ALKANES

Carbon is a versatile building-block atom. It can form bonds to other atoms in several different ways.

Subscript and Spelling Alert! Every letter and number counts: Ethane's formula is C_2H_6. Ethene's formula is C_2H_4.

For example, in some hydrocarbon molecules, a carbon atom bonds to *three* other atoms—not to four. This series of hydrocarbons is called the **alkenes.** The first member of the alkene series is ethene, C_2H_4.

If each carbon atom must share eight electrons to fill its outer energy level completely, how is the carbon bonding in alkenes possible? In a **single covalent bond,** just two electrons are shared between two atoms. In a **double covalent bond,** however, four electrons are shared.

Single bond C:C or C — C

Double bond C::C or C = C

You will have an opportunity to work with models of such double-bonded compounds in the next laboratory activity.

Alkenes are more chemically reactive than the alkanes are. Many chemical reactions occur at their double bonds. Compounds containing double bonds are described as **unsaturated** since not all carbon atoms are bonded to their full capacity of four atoms.

Not all builder molecules are hydrocarbons. Some also contain one or more other elements, such as oxygen, nitrogen, chlorine, or sulfur. One way to think about many of these substances is to imagine that they are hydrocarbons with other elements substituted for one or more hydrogen atoms.

Adding other elements to hydrocarbon structures drastically changes the chemical reactivity of the molecules. Even molecules composed of the same elements can have quite different properties. The molecules that make up a permanent-press blouse and permanent antifreeze may each contain the same elements—carbon, hydrogen, and oxygen. The dramatic differences in the properties and uses of these substances are because of the arrangements of atoms in the two molecules.

We will do our own atom-arranging in the laboratory to learn more about this.

D.2 LABORATORY ACTIVITY: THE BUILDERS

Part 1 Alkenes

1. Examine the electron-dot and structural formulas for ethene, C_2H_4. Confirm that each atom has attained a filled outer shell of electrons:

H H
H:C::C:H
Electron-dot
formula

H—C=C—H (with H above each C)
Structural
formula

CH_2CH_2 or C_2H_4
Molecular
formulas

Organic compounds are systematically named by internationally agreed-upon rules devised by the International Union of Pure and Applied Chemistry —these rules are known as IUPAC nomenclature.

Alkene names follow a pattern much like that of the alkanes. The first three alkenes are ethene, propene, and butene. The same root as for alkanes is used to indicate the number of carbon atoms in the molecule's longest carbon chain; each name ends in -ene.

2. Examine the molecular formulas of ethene (C_2H_4) and butene (C_4H_8). Recall that the alkane general formula is C_nH_{n+2}. What general formula for alkenes is suggested by their molecular formulas?

3. Build a model of an ethene molecule and one of ethane (C_2H_6). Compare the arrangements of atoms in the two models. Note that although you can rotate the two carbon atoms in ethane about the single bond, the two carbon atoms in ethene resist rotation. This is characteristic of all double-bonded atoms.

For historical reasons, ethene is sometimes called ethylene.

H H H H
H—C=C—C—C—H
      H H

1-Butene, or simply butene

4. Build a model of butene (C_4H_8). Compare your model of butene to those made by other class members.

   a. How many different arrangements of atoms in C_4H_8 appear possible? Each arrangement represents a different substance—another example of isomers!

   b. Do the structural formulas in Figure 16 correspond to models built by you or your classmates?

   To distinguish isomers of straight-chain alkenes, the longest carbon chain is numbered, with double-bonded carbon atoms receiving the lowest numbers. The isomer name starts with the number assigned to the first double-bonded carbon atom; this explains the names 1-butene and 2-butene. Although the third structure above has a butene molecular formula, it is named as a methyl-substituted propene.

H H H H
H—C—C=C—C—H
   H   H

2-Butene

5. Do each of these pairs represent isomers, or are they the same substance?

   a. $CH_2{=}CH{-}CH_2{-}CH_3$, $CH_3{-}CH_2{-}CH{=}CH_2$

   b. $CH_2{=}C{-}CH_3$, $CH_3{-}C{-}CH_3$
         | ||
         CH_3 CH_2

6. How many isomers of propene (C_3H_6) are there?

H   H
H—C———C=C—H
   H |
         H—C—H
            H

Methylpropene

Figure 16 Some isomers of butene.

7. Are these two structures isomers or the same substance?

$$CH_2—CH_2 \quad \text{and} \quad CH_3—CH—CH_2$$
with structures shown as:

CH₂—CH₂ and CH₃—CH—CH₂ rings/chains:

$$\begin{array}{cc} CH_2—CH_2 & CH_3—CH—CH_2 \\ |\quad\quad| & \quad\quad|\quad\quad\quad| \\ CH_2\quad CH_2 & \quad\quad CH_2—CH_2 \\ \backslash\quad/ & \\ CH_2 & \end{array}$$

8. Based on your knowledge of molecules with single and double bonds between carbon atoms, build a model of a hydrocarbon molecule with a *triple* bond. Your completed model represents a member of the series known as **alkynes.** Write structural formulas for

   a. ethyne, commonly called acetylene.

   b. 2-butyne.

Part 2   Compounds of Carbon, Hydrogen, and Singly-Bonded Oxygen

1. Build as many different molecular models as possible using all nine of these atoms:

   2 carbon atoms (each forming four single bonds),
   6 hydrogen atoms (each forming a single bond), and
   1 oxygen atom (forming two single bonds).

   Diagram each completed structure on paper, indicating how the nine atoms are connected. Compare your structures with those made by other students. When you are satisfied that all possible structures have been produced, answer these questions:

   a. How many distinct structures did you identify?

   b. Write their structural formulas.

   c. Are these isomers? Explain.

2. The compounds you may have identified have distinctly different physical and chemical properties.

   a. Recalling that "like dissolves like," which compound should be more soluble in water?

   b. Which should have the higher boiling point?

D.3   MORE BUILDER MOLECULES

So far, we have examined just a small part of the inventory of builder molecules that "chemical architects" have available. Now we look at two important classes of compounds in which carbon atoms are joined in rings.

Picture what would happen if one hydrogen atom at each end of a hexane molecule is removed, and those two carbon atoms become bonded to each other.

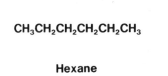

CH₃CH₂CH₂CH₂CH₂CH₃

Hexane

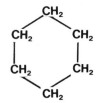

Cyclohexane

Cyclohexane is representative of the **cycloalkanes,** saturated hydrocarbons in which carbon atoms are joined in rings. Like

Space-filling models of hexane (upper) and cyclohexane (lower).

the alkanes, cycloalkanes are relatively unreactive chemically. Cyclohexane is the starting material for making nylon.

Benzene (C_6H_6) is the simplest member of an important class of cyclic builder molecules known as *aromatic compounds.* These compounds present a distinctly different chemical personality from those of cycloalkanes and their derivatives. A drawing of a cyclic benzene molecule, based on what you currently know about hydrocarbons, might look like this:

or

The pleasant odor of the first aromatic compounds discovered gave them their colorful name.

A space-filling model of benzene.

Chemists who originally investigated benzene proposed this and related structures. However, a puzzle remained. Carbon-carbon double bonds ($C=C$), such as those depicted above, are very reactive. Yet benzene did not behave as though it contained any carbon-carbon double bonds. A new understanding of chemical bonding was needed to explain benzene's puzzling structure.

Substantial evidence supports the notion that all carbon-carbon bonds in benzene are identical and are not usefully represented by alternating single and double bonds. To represent a benzene molecule on paper, chemists often use this formula:

Scanning tunneling micrograph of benzene.

The inner, dashed line represents the equal sharing of electrons among all six carbon atoms. The outer, unbroken line represents the bonding of carbon atoms to one another. Each "point" in the hexagon is the location of one carbon and one hydrogen atom— the six points thus account for benzene's formula, C_6H_6.

Small amounts of aromatic compounds are found in petroleum, but large quantities are produced by fractionation and cracking. Benzene and other aromatic compounds are present in gasoline, where they increase the fuel's octane rating. However, their primary use is as chemical builder molecules. Entire chemical industries (dye and drug manufacturing, in particular) have been based on the unique chemistry of aromatic compounds.

D.4   BUILDER MOLECULES CONTAINING OXYGEN

In constructing models, it is likely that you "discovered" two types of compounds containing oxygen. Here are two examples of one type:

$$CH_3 — OH \qquad CH_3CH_2 — OH$$

Methanol   Ethanol
(Methyl alcohol)   (Ethyl alcohol)

$CH_3CH_2CH_2OH$
1-Propanol

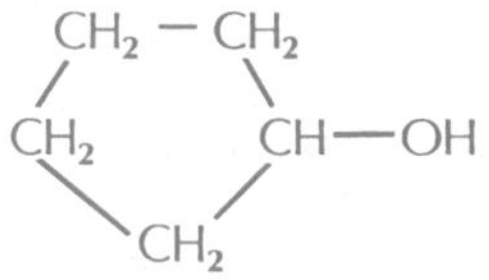
Cyclopentanol

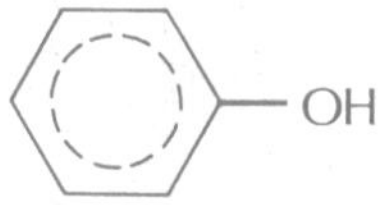
Phenol

Note that both molecules have an —OH group attached to a hydrocarbon chain. This general structure is characteristic of a class of compounds known as ***alcohols.***

If we use the letter R to represent *any* hydrocarbon chain, then the general formula for an alcohol can be written as

R — OH
Alcohol

The —OH is referred to as a ***functional group***—an atom or groups of atoms that impart characteristic properties to organic compounds. Alcohols, for instance, have certain properties in common. A functional group such as —OH can be incorporated into an alkane, an alkene, a cycloalkane, an aromatic compound (see examples in margin), or into other structures.

A second class of oxygen-containing compounds can be illustrated by these two substances:

CH_3 — O — CH_3	CH_3CH_2 — O — CH_2CH_3
Dimethyl ether	Diethyl ether

The substance ordinarily called "ether" is, chemically speaking, diethyl ether.

In this case, the structural feature that is common to both structures is —O—, the characteristic functional group for all ***ethers.*** Once again, if we use R to represent a hydrocarbon chain, the general structure for ether-type molecules becomes:

R — O — R
Ether

Re-examine the structural formula for the gasoline additive MTBE, found on page 194. Can you verify why this substance is classified as an ether?

Two other classes, ***carboxylic acids*** and ***esters,*** are versatile builder molecules. Their two other functional groups, each containing two oxygen atoms, are shown below.

O ‖ R — C — OH	O ‖ R — C — OR
Carboxylic acid	Ester

(also written RCOOH and RCOOR).

Note that both classes of compounds have one oxygen atom doubly-bonded to a carbon atom, and a second oxygen atom singly-bonded to the same carbon atom. Ethanoic acid (acetic acid) and methyl acetate are examples of each of these two types of compounds. Their structural formulas are given in the margin.

O
‖
CH_3 C — OH
Ethanoic acid (acetic acid)

O
‖
CH_3 C — OCH_3
Methyl acetate

Other functional groups may include nitrogen, sulfur, or chlorine atoms. When attached to hydrocarbons, these impart their own characteristic properties to the new molecules. The essential point is clear: Adding functional groups to builder hydrocarbons greatly expands the types of molecules that can be built.

D.5 CREATING NEW OPTIONS: PETROCHEMICALS

Less than 150 years ago, all objects and materials used by humans were created directly from "found" materials such as wood or stone, or were crafted from metals, glass, and clays. Fibers were cotton, wool, linen, and silk. All medicines and food additives came from natural sources. The only plastics were those made from wood (celluloid) and animal materials (shellac).

Today, many common objects and materials are ***synthetic***—created by the chemical industry from oil or natural gas. Such compounds are called ***petrochemicals.***

Some petrochemicals, such as detergents, pesticides, pharmaceuticals, and cosmetics, are used directly. Most petrochemicals, however, serve as raw materials (or intermediates) in production of other synthetic substances—particularly plastics.

Plastics include paints, fabrics, rubber, insulation materials, foams, glass-like substances, adhesives, molding, and structural materials. Total world production of petroleum-based plastics is five times that of aluminum products. Over a third of all the fiber, and 70% of the rubber, worldwide are created from petrochemicals.

What are suitable starting substances for building such petrochemicals? Apart from their ability to burn, alkanes have little chemical reactivity. Few substances can be built directly from them.

By contrast, alkenes and aromatics are important builder molecules. The two most industrially-important alkenes are ethene (ethylene) and propene. Aromatic builder molecules such as benzene and styrene can be obtained from petroleum by catalytic cracking and reforming.

Builder molecules are used to make thousands of chemicals; massive textbooks are needed just for the relevant equations. For simplicity, we will focus on just a few builder molecules—ethene, ethanol, and materials related to ethene.

Ethene (ethylene), because of the high reactivity of its double bond, is readily transformed into many useful products. For example, ethanol (ethyl alcohol) is formed when a water molecule reacts with the double-bond site of an ethene molecule:

SPECTRA fibers are the strongest fibers ever made.

$$
\underset{\text{Ethene}}{H-\overset{\overset{\displaystyle H}{|}}{C}=\overset{\overset{\displaystyle H}{|}}{C}-H} \quad + \quad \underset{\text{Water}}{H-OH} \quad \xrightarrow[\text{catalyst}]{\text{Acid}} \quad \underset{\text{Ethanol}}{H-\overset{\overset{\displaystyle H}{|}}{\underset{\underset{\displaystyle H}{|}}{C}}-\overset{\overset{\displaystyle H}{|}}{\underset{\underset{\displaystyle OH}{|}}{C}}-H}
$$

Note that the water molecule "adds" to the double-bonded carbon atoms by placing an H— on one carbon and an —OH group on the other. This type of chemical change is called an **addition reaction.**

Ethanol is used extensively as a solvent in varnishes and perfumes, in preparing many essences, flavors, pharmaceuticals, and in alcoholic beverages. It is also used as a fuel.

Polyethene (polyethylene), commonly used in bags and packaging, is an important **polymer.** A polymer is a large molecule typically composed of 500 to 20,000 or more repeating units (residues). In polyethene the repeating units are ethene (ethylene) residues. Polyethene is related to ethene in the same way that a lengthy paperclip chain is related to individual paperclips. The chemical reaction producing polyethene can be written this way:

$$n\,CH_2 = CH_2 \quad \longrightarrow \quad -CH_2CH_2CH_2CH_2CH_2CH_2-$$

Ethene   Polyethene

(ethylene)   (polyethylene)

This is also an addition reaction. Here ethene serves as a **monomer**—the small molecule from which the larger polymer molecule is made. Polymers formed in reactions such as this are—sensibly enough—called **addition polymers.**

A great variety of addition polymers can be made from monomers that closely resemble ethene. One or more of ethene's hydrogen atoms can be replaced by other atoms. These monomers form an array of useful polymers:

$$n\ CH_2 = CHCl \longrightarrow -CH_2\ CHCH_2\ CHCH_2\ CHCH_2\ CH-$$

with Cl, Cl, Cl, Cl substituents

Vinyl chloride
(Cl has replaced H)

Polyvinyl chloride (PVC) is used for shoes, leatherlike jackets, and plastic pipes.

$$n\ CH_2 = CHCN \longrightarrow -CH_2\ CHCH_2\ CHCH_2\ CHCH_2\ CH-$$

with CN, CN, CN, CN substituents

Acrylonitrile
(CN has replaced H)

Polyacrylonitrile is used in acrylic fiber for clothes and carpets

Styrene
(Aromatic ring has replaced H)

Polystyrene is used in insulation, coffee cups, coolers, toothbrush handles, and combs

The arrangement of covalent bonds in long, string-like polymer molecules causes them to coil loosely. A collection of polymer molecules (such as those in a piece of rubber or molten plastic) can intertwine, much like strands of cooked noodles or spaghetti. In this form the polymer is flexible and soft.

Engineers monitoring the production of Saran Wrap. Sarans are a type of plastic having vinylidine chloride ($CH_2 = CCl_2$) as their principal monomer.

Safety in Polymerization

By Daniel Jones
Richmond Daily *Staff Reporter*

Many remote communities in America that do not have the benefit of a local degreed physician rely on midwives and herbal healers to provide for their basic medical needs. Portia Bass' grandmother served as one of these special residents. As a child, Portia spent her days in her grandmother's home watching her prepare herbs and medicinal teas for those in need. It wasn't until she took a college class in organic chemistry that Portia realized how much chemistry her grandmother had used.

Today, inspired by her grandmother, Portia is a chemist in a process control and quality measurement laboratory. Portia is part of a technical operations team at E.I. DuPont de Nemours and Company's Waynesboro, Virginia, facility. Here three polymer products are manufactured. They include Lycra®, which is used in hosiery and clothing for active wear; nylon, used in household and automotive carpeting; and Permasep®, a fiber used in the process of sea water desalination. Portia and her team monitor quality-measurement systems that ensure the integrity of the products and assist in monitoring safety systems that protect the environment, the employees, and the community. They perform hundreds of analytical tests, identify and solve manufacturing problems, and perform routine instrument maintenance.

Each day, Portia begins her activities by making rounds. She visits the three polymer product departments to address their quality assurance needs. She then meets with her own research and development assistant and provides direction.

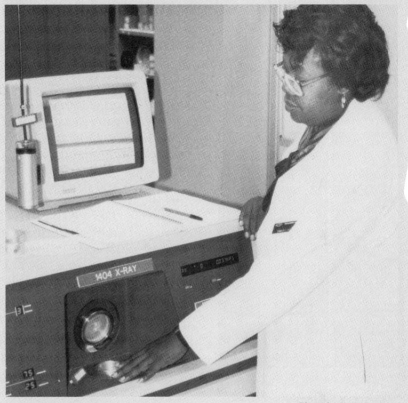

Photo by J. B. Swartz

When Portia leaves the building, her day may not be over. She is on call many nights of the week in order to keep the monitoring equipment of this 24-hour operation functional. If safety precautions go awry, the laboratory stops running analyses, which may lead to a loss of revenue. Portia must return to the plant to investigate malfunctioning monitoring instruments. When a power failure occurs, Portia ensures that all systems are working properly. Then Portia meets with the affected departments to determine how to prevent similar problems in the future.

As a responsible employee of DuPont, Portia identifies opportunities to strengthen and make the business more competitive. Part of her job is to comply with and continuously upgrade safety

systems. Therefore, as Portia develops new techniques and processing methods, she must keep in mind DuPont's policy and vision on protecting the local environment, citizens and employees. As she conducts research and development, she must produce timely memos and reports, keep accurate and thorough laboratory notebooks, and present two technical seminars a year.

Portia began her educational career at Miami University in Ohio where she received a B.A. She went to Purdue University to pursue an M.S. in analytical science. Portia took many chemistry and other science and computer courses. She also went through extensive on-the-job training in order to prepare for the varied responsibilities at DuPont.

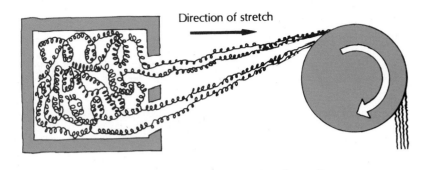

Figure 17 Orienting and uncoiling polymer chains can add strength and toughness to polymer material.

Direction of stretch

You have a convenient example already at hand! Human skin is composed of biological polymers. Gently press the palm of your hand and watch the skin stretch and then move back in place when you release the pressure. Imagine the large polymer molecules uncoiling and sliding a little so the skin can stretch under pressure—and then recoiling again when pressure is removed. Similar molecular events take place when a rubber band is stretched and released, or when a piece of soft plastic is squeezed.

Polymer *flexibility* can be increased by adding molecules that act as internal lubricants for the polymer chains. Untreated polyvinyl chloride (PVC) is used in rigid pipes and house siding. With added lubricant, polyvinyl chloride becomes flexible enough to be used in raincoats and shoes.

By contrast, polymer *rigidity* can be increased by cross-linking the polymer chains so they no longer readily move or slide. Compare the flexibility of a rubber band with that of a tire tread—polymer cross-linking is much greater in the relatively rigid auto tire.

Polymer *strength* and *toughness* can also be controlled. Here's one molecular recipe: First arrange the polymer chains so they lie generally in the same direction, as when you comb your hair. Then stretch the chains so they uncoil (see Figure 17). Polymers remaining uncoiled after this treatment make strong, tough films and fibers. Such materials range from the polyethene used in plastic bags to the polyacrylonitrile found in fabrics.

Not all polymer molecules are formed by addition reactions. Polymers such as proteins, starch, cellulose (in wood and paper), nylon, and polyester are also formed from monomers. However, unlike addition polymers, these polymers are formed with the loss of water molecules from adjacent monomer units. Such reactions are called **condensation reactions.** Polymers formed in this way are known as **condensation polymers.**

Condensation reactions can be used to make small molecules as well as polymers. In the next laboratory activity you will carry out a condensation reaction to make an ester. The reaction is a simple example of how organic compounds can be combined chemically to create new substances. Many synthetic flavorings and perfumes contain esters. And this type of reaction, repeated many times over, produces polyester polymers.

Everyday objects like skateboards are made of different polymers selected for their properties.

You probably know polyacrylonitrile better by another name—acrylic fiber.

D.6 LABORATORY ACTIVITY: PETROCHEMICALS

Getting Ready

In this activity you will produce a petrochemical by the reaction of an organic acid (an acid derived from a hydrocarbon) with an alcohol to produce an ester that has a pleasing fragrance. Many perfumes contain esters, and the characteristic aromas of many herbs and fruits come from esters in the plants.

For example, an ester called methyl acetate can be produced by the reaction of ethanoic acid (acetic acid) with methanol:

$$CH_3-\overset{\overset{\displaystyle O}{\|}}{C}-OH + H-O-CH_3 \xrightarrow{H_2SO_4} CH_3-\overset{\overset{\displaystyle O}{\|}}{C}-O-CH_3 + H-O-H$$

Ethanoic acid   Methanol   Methyl acetate   Water
(acetic acid)

To highlight the interplay of functional groups in the formation of an ester, we can write a general equation for this type of reaction, using the "R" symbols introduced earlier.

$$R-\overset{\overset{\displaystyle O}{\|}}{C}-OH + H-O-R \xrightarrow{H_2SO_4} R-\overset{\overset{\displaystyle O}{\|}}{C}-O-R + H-O-H$$

Carboxylic acid   Alcohol   Ester   Water

Note how the acid and alcohol functional groups combine to form an ester, with their remaining atoms joining to form a water molecule. The sulfuric acid (H_2SO_4) shown above the arrow does not become part of the product. It serves as a catalyst—it allows the reaction to proceed faster.

You will produce methyl salicylate in this laboratory activity, and will note the characteristic odor of this ester.

Procedure

1. Set up a ring stand, ring, wire screen, and Bunsen burner.

2. Prepare a water bath by adding about 70 mL of tap water to a 150-mL beaker. Add a boiling chip, then place the water bath on the wire screen above the burner.

3. Take a small, clean test tube to the dispensing area. Pour 2 mL of methanol into the tube. Next add 0.5 g of salicylic acid. Then *slowly and carefully add 10 drops of concentrated sulfuric acid to the tube.* As you dispense some of these reagents you may notice their odors. Do not smell any reagents directly, but record observations of any odors you notice.

Be careful not to splash the acid solution on yourself.

4. Return to your desk. Place the test tube in the water bath you prepared in Step 2. Light and adjust the burner. Start heating the beaker and contents.

5. When the water bath begins to boil, use test tube tongs to move the tube slowly in a small, horizontal circle. Keep the tube in the water, and be sure not to spill the contents. Notice any color changes. Continue heating until the water bath has boiled strongly for two minutes. Turn off the burner.

6. If you have not noticed an odor by now, hold the test tube with tongs and wave your hand across the top to waft any vapors toward your nose. Record your observations regarding the odor of the product. Compare your observations with those of other class members.

Carefully waft any vapor toward your nose.

7. Wash your hands thoroughly before leaving the laboratory.

Questions

1. a. From a handbook, find molecular formulas of the acid and alcohol from which you produced methyl salicylate.

b. Write a chemical equation for the formation of methyl salicylate.

2. Write the formula for amyl acetate, an ester formed from pentanol and ethanoic acid (acetic acid). (See molecular formulas in the margin.) Amyl acetate, with a pear-like odor and flavor, has many uses in products ranging from syrups to paints and shoe polish.)

$$C_5H_{11}OH$$
Pentanol

$$\overset{\displaystyle O}{\overset{\displaystyle \|}{CH_3\,C}} - OH$$
Ethanoic acid (acetic acid)

3. Classify each compound as a carboxylic acid, an alcohol, or an ester:

   a. $CH_3CH_2CH_2CH_2OH$

   b. $CH_3OCOCH_2CH_3$

   c. $CH_3\,\overset{\displaystyle |}{\underset{\displaystyle CH_2COOH}{CHCH_2CH_3}}$

   d. $CH_3\,\overset{\displaystyle O}{\overset{\displaystyle \|}{COH}}$

PART D: SUMMARY QUESTIONS

1. Give at least one specific example (name and formula) of
   a. an industrially-important alkene;
   b. an industrially-important aromatic compound.

2. Write an equation for the cracking of hexane into two smaller hydrocarbon molecules. (*Hint:* Remember the law of conservation of matter.)

3. a. Write the structural formula for a molecule containing at least two carbon atoms that represents (1) an organic acid, (2) an ether, (3) an ester, (4) an alcohol.
   b. Circle the functional group in each structural formula.
   c. Name each compound.

4. How does benzene differ from other cyclic hydrocarbons?

5. More than 90% of known chemical compounds are organic (hydrocarbons or substituted hydrocarbons). Identify two characteristics of carbon atoms that help explain such a large number of carbon-based substances.

6. In your own words describe the term "polymerization." Use an example of a "monomer → polymer" reaction as part of your answer.

7. Chemical synthesis is one of many branches of chemistry. Try your hand at planning some syntheses in the problems below. One molecule (identified by a question mark) is missing in each equation. Identify the molecule that will complete each equation. (*Hint:* If you are uncertain about the answer, start by completing an atom inventory. Remember that the final equation must be balanced.)

   a. A major type of alkane reaction (other than burning). The product, 1-chloroethane (ethyl chloride), was used to make the fuel additive tetraethyl lead.

   $$CH_3 - CH_3 + \textbf{?} \rightarrow CH_3 - CH_2 - Cl + HCl$$

   b. The major way to make 2-pentanol (isopropyl alcohol), used as rubbing alcohol.

   $$CH_3 - CH = CH_2 + \textbf{?} \rightarrow CH_3 - \overset{\displaystyle |}{\underset{\displaystyle OH}{CH}} - CH_3$$

   c. The conversion of a long-chain organic acid to soap.

   $$CH_2CH_2CH_2CH_2CH_2CH_2\,\overset{\displaystyle O}{\overset{\displaystyle \|}{C}} - OH + \textbf{?} \rightarrow$$

   $$CH_2CH_2CH_2CH_2CH_2CH_2\,\overset{\displaystyle O}{\overset{\displaystyle \|}{C}} - O^-\,Na^+ + H_2O$$

ALTERNATIVES TO PETROLEUM

Petroleum is a nonrenewable resource—the total inventory of available petroleum on Earth is decreasing. You know how dependent on petroleum we have become. Fortunately, chemists are already investigating substitutes for petroleum, both to burn and to build.

E.1 ALTERNATIVE ENERGY SOURCES

The way we live—including our homes, agriculture, and industries—requires considerable quantities of energy. Earlier (Section C.2) you discovered that the mix of energy sources used in the United States has changed over time. As energy needs have grown, the nation has relied increasingly on nonrenewable fossil fuels—coal, petroleum, and natural gas. What is the future for fossil fuels, and in particular, for petroleum?

Electricity is necessary for supporting our way of life.

YOUR TURN

Energy Dependency

To answer these concerns, we will start by getting a clearer picture of our energy dependency. Here again, examining the facts in an important societal issue involves interpreting numerical data. Consider the pie chart in Figure 18 (page 209).

1. Which fuel is the nation's most-used energy source?
2. What percent of our energy needs are met by fossil fuels?
3. What percent of our energy needs are met by renewable energy sources?

To interpret this pie chart more fully, we should also examine our total supplies of these fuels. Unfortunately, that information is not quite so easy to identify. We find conflicting estimates of the amounts of fossil fuels we have left. For purposes of discussion we will examine data presented in Table 5 (page 208). This represents a somewhat optimistic estimate of extractable supplies of fossil fuels.

Electricity is also generated from sources other than petroleum — such as hydroelectric (top), coal (left) and nuclear power (right).

Table 5   **ENERGY FROM RESERVES**

Source	Energy ($\times 10^{18}$ joules)
Oil and natural gas liquids	1,000
Natural gas	
Conventional sources	1,000
Unconventional sources	700
Coal	40,300

1.05 $\times$ 10^{18} J = 1 quad

4. Between 1980 and 2000 the United States will use an estimated 2000 quads of energy, or about 2×10^{21} joules of energy (an average of 100 quads yearly). If we continue to rely on petroleum for 42% of our total energy needs, and we use only U.S. petroleum (no imports), we will use 840 quads of petroleum by the year 2000 (0.42 $\times$ 2000 quads). How much of our extractable supply of petroleum would be left by the year 2000?

5. Complete the calculations described in Question 4 for natural gas (including both conventional and unconventional sources) and coal. Use data from Figure 18 and Table 5.

Estimates on a fuel's possible lifetime are subject to some serious uncertainties. As supplies of a fuel near exhaustion, our use of that fuel would decline and the fuel would likely become more expensive—thus extending the fuel's useful life-time. In addition, as costs increase, economic incentives prompt both searching for new reserves and extracting more fuel from what earlier were financially-prohibitive sites. Estimates of fuel supplies and future needs are just that—estimates. They are subject to change.

However, despite such limitations, your calculations still illustrate the broad picture: Future petroleum availability presents us with a real problem. Coal has a more promising future. Can coal serve as a substitute source of energy for dwindling petroleum supplies? Are the two fuels interchangeable?

Setting aside possible environmental issues for now, we need to explore ways in which petroleum is used as a fuel, and then judge coal's suitability for each major category. Consider Table 6.

Table 6   **PETROLEUM USE (1989)**

End-use Sector	Millions of Barrels/Day	Percent of Total Use
Transportation	10.9	63
Industrial	4.3	25
Residential/commercial	1.4	8
Electric utilities	0.7	4

Source: Energy Information Administration

6. What percent of petroleum is used at fixed-point (stationary) sites?

7. Could coal more readily substitute for petroleum in stationary or mobile uses? Why?

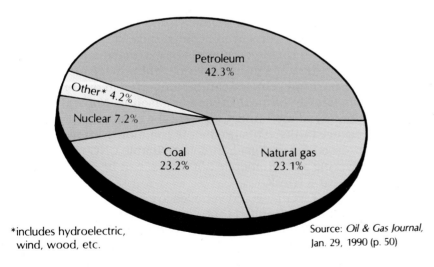

*includes hydroelectric, wind, wood, etc.

Source: *Oil & Gas Journal,* Jan. 29, 1990 (p. 50)

Figure 18   Percent of U.S. energy from various fuel sources.

The United States is a society "on the go." More than sixty percent of our petroleum use is for transportation, with personal automobiles being the main energy users. Even though efforts to revitalize and improve public transportation systems merit attention, most experts predict we will continue to rely on automobiles into the foreseeable future. (In addition, even mass transit

Over 40% of petroleum used in the U.S. goes to powering automobiles. Trucks and airplanes represent another 20% of U.S. petroleum use.

Oil shale rocks represent a reserve of "pre-oil" that is many times greater than the world's known reserves of conventional petroleum. A ton of this shale can typically contain the equivalent of 20–80 gallons of oil.

systems must have an energy source.) In that case, what options does chemistry offer us to extend, supplement, and perhaps even replace petroleum as an energy source?

The extraction of "solid petroleum" from *tar sands* and *oil shale rock* offers some promise. Unfortunately, these sources are very expensive, since needed technology is not adequately developed. Vast quantities of sand or rocks must be processed to recover this fuel. Major deposits of oil shale are located west of the Rocky Mountains. These rocks, formed originally from mud, contain kerogen—partially-formed oil. When the rocks are heated, kerogen decomposes to a material quite similar to crude oil.

Oil-shale processing confronts major problems. The biggest is high production costs. In terms of energy alone, current extraction methods "cost" the equivalent of a half barrel of petroleum to produce one barrel of shale oil. Others problems include gaining access to oil shale lands (80% are owned by the federal government), supplying the large amounts of water needed for processing, and dealing with air and water pollution generated by the processing. Given adequate funding, these problems might be solved. Meanwhile, research continues toward making shale oil processing a future commercial option. The price and availability of crude oil will play a large part in deciding shale oil production's future.

Another possible alternative to petroleum is producing a *liquid fuel from coal.* As you have already noted, our nation's coal supply is much larger than our supply of petroleum. The know-how to convert coal to liquid fuel (and also to builder molecules) has been available for decades. Germany used this technology as long ago as the 1940s. U.S. coal-to-liquid-fuel technology is well developed. At present, the cost of mining and converting coal to liquid fuel is considerably greater than the cost of producing the same quantity of fuel from petroleum. However, as petroleum prices increase, obtaining liquid fuel from coal may become a more attractive option.

Petroleum plantations have also been suggested. Some 2000 varieties of plants of the genus *Euphorbia* capture and store solar energy as hydrocarbon compounds, rather than as carbohydrates. Can these compounds be extracted and used as a petroleum substitute? Future research will provide answers.

About half of U.S. homes are heated by natural gas.

Gasoline-burning vehicles can be converted to dual-fuel vehicles which can run on *natural gas* or gasoline. Natural gas—composed mainly of methane, CH_4—can be compressed and held in high-pressure tanks. This product is commonly known as CNG (compressed natural gas). Such a refillable CNG tank, capable of powering an automobile 250 miles, can be comfortably installed in a car's trunk.

Over 30,000 CNG-powered vehicles are currently in operation in the U.S. It is estimated that the Soviet Union currently has about 0.5 million CNG-fueled trucks on the road. The use of natural gas, a clean-burning fuel, offers one strategy for extending the useful lifetime of the world's petroleum reserves.

Energy from nuclear fuels is discussed in the Nuclear unit later in this book.

Other alternative energy sources currently in use or under investigation include hydropower (water power), nuclear fission and fusion, solar energy, wind, and geothermal energies. Despite other problems and limitations, these particular options share one positive characteristic: unlike carbon-based fuels, they do not release carbon dioxide gas to the atmosphere. Carbon dioxide is one of a number of "greenhouse gases"—atmospheric gases that may be contributing to global warming.

We've identified several options for extending petroleum's useful life as an energy source without drastically altering our life-styles. More energy-efficient buildings and machines can be constructed, which will lessen our need for petroleum as fuel. We can also use alternative fuels, further reducing the need to "burn" petroleum. But what can replace petroleum as a source of chemical building materials?

We explore the issue of global warming later in the Air Unit.

E.2 BUILDER MOLECULE SOURCES

As petroleum supplies continue to decrease, it is likely that petroleum's use as a fuel will be severely restricted, but it will still be used as a source of petrochemicals. However, since petroleum supplies will someday be exhausted, alternatives to petroleum as a source of builder molecules must also be found eventually.

Coal's use as a chemical raw material—in addition to its continuing role as a fuel—is receiving increased attention. Coal is composed mainly of carbon. In principle, all the carbon compounds now manufactured from petroleum can also be obtained, through appropriate chemical reactions, from coal, water, and air. However, the expense and time involved in opening new coal mines and building conversion plants prevents any rapid conversion to coal. In addition, coal-processing is more costly (both financially and environmentally) than comparable processes for petroleum. Thus making coal products would be more expensive—at least until petroleum becomes much more costly than it is now.

Another future source of builder molecules will likely be plant matter—***biomass.*** A major component of biomass is cellulose, found in wood, leaves, and plant stems. Cellulose is a condensation polymer, composed of repeating sugar units built of carbon, hydrogen and oxygen.

Cellulose contains the basic carbon-chain structures needed to build petrochemicals. One possible scenario includes intensive

Cellulose, along with starch and sugar, are members of the family of compounds known as carbohydrates.

Like petroleum, coal can be used to produce energy or a range of organic chemicals.

forestry and cultivation of fast-growing plants, as well as use of organic wastes from homes and industries. Ethanol and other builder molecules are already being produced from sugar cane.

Using biotechnology, we can also convert biomass into raw materials from which petrochemicals can be synthesized. Bioengineering techniques are still in their infancy. However, the use of **enzymes** (biochemical catalysts for specific reactions) to help produce specific compounds is already under way. Biological production methods suitable for large-scale use can provide such key substances as ethanol and acetic acid. These products would be, of course, more costly than petrochemicals. However, they will become increasingly attractive as petroleum costs increase.

Significant advances are being made with **biopolymers**— biologically-grown polymers and plastics that resemble petroleum-based materials. For example, one British pilot plant produces about 50 tons annually of PHB-V, a polypropene-like plastic that can be used for films and bags. This polymer is produced by the bacterium *Alcaligenes eutrophus*. Part of the appeal of biopolymers is that—unlike petroleum-based polymers—they are fully biodegradable. They could some day serve as a renewable source of plastics—a source not dependent on petroleum supplies.

It is estimated that a 10,000-ton-per-year PHB-V plant could currently produce the polymer at $2 per pound.

It is likely that, at least for the forseeable future, petrochemicals will be manufactured from petroleum, coal, and biomass. The particular "mix" of these sources at a given time will be influenced by economics, politics, and available technology.

Even though we face difficult decisions concerning the use of petroleum for building and burning, chemistry is providing some options for meeting society's needs. However, most alternatives are expensive and not yet fully developed. Today, petroleum conservation is the key to "buying" enough time for the development of replacements to avoid drastic life-style changes. Conservation is also ecologically sound; it can help satisfy the basic needs of all global inhabitants, not just of those who are wealthy or have large reserves of oil. This unit will conclude by examining alternate viewpoints on how to promote petroleum conservation.

As usual, conservation involves making better use of what we have, using items longer, and recycling what we can (motor oil, for example).

PART E: SUMMARY QUESTIONS

1. Describe two major problems posed by our present use of energy sources.
2. Many experts feel that we should explore ways to use more renewable energy sources such as hydro-, solar, and wind power as replacements for nonrenewable fossil fuels.
   a. Why might this be a wise policy?
   b. For which major energy uses are these renewable sources *least* likely to replace fossil fuels? Why?
   c. Describe how your community might look if it decided to install wind and solar power devices on a large scale.
3. Consider coal, oil shale, and hydrocarbons from plants as possible petroleum substitutes. Which do you think holds the greatest promise for the future? Why?
4. Of the two broad uses of petroleum (as a fuel and as a raw material), which is likely to be curtailed first as petroleum supplies dwindle? Why?
5. What types of compounds do chemists seek as good petroleum substitutes? Why?

PUTTING IT ALL TOGETHER: CHOOSING PETROLEUM FUTURES

Petroleum is versatile. As a fuel, it can be used to produce heat and electricity. Unlike other fuels, it is also a convenient energy source for transportation. In addition to its use as fuel, petroleum is also an alchemist's dream come true. Although it cannot be converted into gold, this black liquid is routinely converted into more than 3000 products, including synthetic fibers, plastics, detergents, medicines, dyes, and pesticides.

The world is rapidly exhausting its known supplies of petroleum. However, as we can predict future shortages, we have a "time window" in which to develop new technologies and policies to supplement, extend, and replace petroleum.

Given its daily importance in our lives, decisions we make now about petroleum as consumers and citizens will help determine our future quality of life. As with all *ChemCom* issues, decisions about petroleum should be based on the best available information and should be reevaluated in light of new facts.

In the following activity you will work with classmates in developing a reasoned position on a petroleum policy question. You will shape your point of view by considering scientific facts as well as informed opinion.

F.1 CONFRONTING THE ISSUES

For two class days, you will serve on a team of experts dealing with an impending energy crisis. The following statement is the stage-setter for the activity:

> The technology needed to provide alternate sources of energy and builder molecules will not be adequately developed before the year 2100. By 2005—unless other actions are taken— U.S. petroleum supplies will decline enough, and imported oil costs will rise enough, to trigger an "energy crisis."
>
> Assume that in response to this situation, the government has identified several possible courses of action to conserve petroleum and delay the crisis—at least until large-scale alternatives to petroleum are available. Following further study and public discussion, one or more of three proposed policies will become law.

Policy Option I. The federal government will influence the use of petroleum as a fuel by imposing restraints (such as higher fuel taxes) and offering incentives (such as rebates on fuel-efficient cars and rewards for car-pooling). The goal is to decrease fuel applications of petroleum.

Policy Option II. The government will help support development of a national, interlinked system of mass transportation. Automobile use will be restricted to locations where the system is not yet completed.

Policy Option III. [Devise your own policy option. Form a new group with several other students and develop your own governmental policy.]

Separate teams of experts representing each policy option will participate in a special briefing session to be attended by government officials and influential citizens. Each team will support its own policy option.

Decide which policy option team you would like to join. Your team will select two members to speak on the panel. Your team's presentation, prepared during the first class period, should be based on individual reading assignments (or library research), this *ChemCom* unit, and personal opinion. Also include facts and arguments on why the action you support will lead to a more satisfactory future. Team members who will make up the audience should prepare some challenging questions to ask the teams supporting the other policy options.

In preparing for the presentation and question period, keep these points in mind:

- Agreement on certain scientific facts does not guarantee that individuals will reach the same conclusions regarding policies based on those facts. Personal and societal concerns and values also influence individual opinions.
- Scientists may disagree among themselves on future research and technological developments, based on their own beliefs and ideas.
- Given these realities, all citizens in a democracy should educate themselves on issues, form their own opinions, and attempt to influence public policy in light of their views.

Since these issues do not lead to "right" or "wrong" answers, you will be judged on your use of evidence and logic supporting your opinions and on the clarity of your presentations. Your group may decide to divide the work, separating into smaller subgroups to prepare material on different aspects of the proposal. For example, you might divide the issue so each panel member becomes expert on a different part of the problem. For example, one panelist might consider technical, scientific, and engineering aspects, while another considers economic and social concerns.

The briefing session will follow this schedule:

1. Each panelist has three minutes to present arguments in favor of their favored policy option.

2. Panel members then participate in a five-minute open question and answer session on the issues, directed by a moderator (or your teacher). The moderator prevents any panel member from dominating the discussion, and stops the session when time is completed.

3. Questions are received from the audience until five minutes remain in the class period.

4. The audience votes to show support for the best policy option. Because the government may enact more than one option, the audience then votes for their second-choice proposal.

For homework, each class member will prepare a letter to the editor of a newspaper, either supporting or criticizing some issue raised during the briefing session. The letter should be 100–300 words long.

F.2 Looking Back and Looking Ahead

This unit illustrates once again how chemical knowledge can help us deal with personal concerns and community issues involving resource use and abuse. Clearly, decisions that ignore or attempt to refute nature's laws are likely to produce higher "costs" than desired benefits. Chemistry does not provide single, correct answers to such major problems, but it does highlight key questions and gives us options to consider. Such knowledge can help us make better decisions on many difficult issues.

Another scientifically-complex issue arises in the next unit—one that involves both personal and societal dimensions. You will discover that the Petroleum Unit's theme—to build or to burn—applies equally well to food and nutrition. It's food for thought.

UNDERSTANDING FOOD

- Is there sufficient food to support the world's population?

- How can we become informed decision-makers about food choices and diets?

- What roles do various food substances play in supporting health and well-being?

- Why is the warning ''don't put chemicals in your mouth'' incorrect?

INTRODUCTION

Your body uses chemical reactions to capture, store, and release energy from foods and to build or rebuild itself with substances obtained from food.

In the previous unit, you learned that petroleum is not only burned as fuel, but is also the raw material for the manufacture of many products. Food, the focus of this unit, is also both a fuel and a building material. With molecules from food, human bodies build new cells, blood, and body tissues that are routinely replaced. Food molecules are also the fuel that is "burned" in the body to provide needed energy for all bodily activities from moving around to maintaining body temperature and even to thinking.

Almost any food can provide energy, although foods high in carbohydrates (sugars and starches) provide it more quickly than others. Food requirements for building are much more specific than those for providing energy. The major building-block molecules for body growth and development are proteins and fats. Vitamins and minerals are also absolutely necessary, although in very small quantities, somewhat like specialized parts needed in designing a custom car.

Traditional cultures have different diets, but almost all of them fulfill basic nutritional requirements. For example, a Mexican diet includes considerable protein from beans and rice; U.S. meals deliver substantial protein from beef; Italian menus include protein from pasta (processed grain) and cheese. Each tradition has its own recipes for selecting and preparing fruits and vegetables, which are sources of vitamins and minerals. Foods may appear quite different, but once digested, their role in human body chemistry is very similar.

For most cultures, diets that provide balanced nutrition developed historically without any pre-planned strategy. The great variety in diets arose from the differences in types of food crops that grew naturally in given areas.

For those who get enough to eat, most traditional diets provide good nutrition. But people in almost every part of the world are starving. Most world hunger is found in the **developing world,** composed of nations that have not become fully industrialized. In the **developed world,** where industry has matured, hunger is less common. In both developed and developing worlds, however, poverty is mainly responsible for hunger.

The developed world includes the United States, Canada, most of Europe, Australia, New Zealand, and parts of Asia and South America.

To understand hunger, one must first realize that there are two different ways to go hungry—ways based upon building and burning.

People who do not get enough to eat have too little to burn. This is called **undernourishment**—one type of hunger. However, it is possible to get enough fuel from the food without getting all the building-block substances the body needs to grow and maintain itself. This is called **malnourishment,** or malnutrition—a second type of hunger. Malnourishment is like trying to build a house with some essential supplies missing. You can have all the bricks you need, but if you run out of mortar, you can't finish the job. A person can be overweight and malnourished at the same time.

YOU DECIDE: KEEPING A FOOD DIARY

Keep a complete diary of everything you eat for three days. This information will be used later when we consider nutrition and food nutrients. Keep your diary either for a Thursday, Friday, and Saturday or for a Sunday, Monday, and Tuesday. Record each food item you eat and estimate its quantity. Include all beverages, except carbonated water, "no-calorie" flavored sodas, and tap water. Include snacks! Express your estimates of quantity as volume (such as milliliters, pints, tablespoons, and cups), mass (such as grams, ounces, or pounds), or count (slices or units such as number of eggs or bananas).

Your teacher will collect your completed diaries and redistribute them when it is time to analyze your diet.

You've probably been told (probably more often than you appreciated) to eat the right kinds of foods in the proper amounts. But what *are* the right kinds of foods? What does each actually do for us?

Traditional Vietnamese diets include many of the green vegetables available at this open market.

FOODS: TO BUILD OR TO BURN?

To "understand" food means to consider questions ranging from "What should we eat and why?" to "How can the world be properly fed?" However, the question "to build or to burn?"—a question of primary importance in "understanding" petroleum—will not be considered in this *ChemCom* unit. Our bodies, not our minds, control whether the various foods we eat will be used to build or to burn.

To begin our study of food, we will explore the types of molecules in food that are used for building and burning. This will also help us understand how diet influences health.

Breathing, talking, and even thinking require energy from food. Building muscles, growing hair, and wound-healing require building materials from food.

A.1 NUTRITIONAL IMBALANCES

Did it ever occur to you that even in the United States, people might be poorly fed? The first U.S. food consumption survey, completed in the 1930s, showed that about one-third of all Americans were poorly fed. Recent surveys by the U.S. Department of Agriculture reveal that only half of U.S. families have diets rated as "good," and that one-fifth eat "poorly."

Are you surprised that people in this "land of plenty" are not properly nourished? In many cases, people cannot afford enough proper food, or they make poor decisions about food. People who are severely malnourished—those who lack some molecular

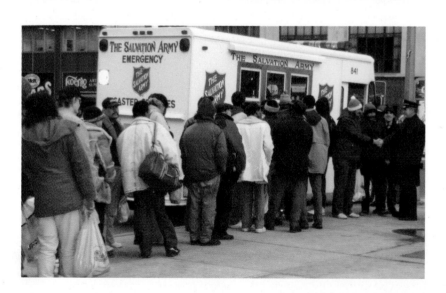

Food is a necessity for everyone.

building blocks needed by the body—may have physical symptoms such as fatigue, drying and yellowing of the skin, deterioration of hair texture, swollen joints, and increased susceptibility to illness. Eventually, they may die of malnourishment.

On the other hand, malnutrition does not necessarily mean that one is underfed. A person may not be getting sufficient amounts of all necessary nutrients, in spite of eating large amounts of nonnourishing foods.

Undernourishment occurs when the body does not get enough fuel to meet its needs. Since the body's energy needs always take priority over its building needs, too little energy available from foods in the diet can produce the same results as malnourishment. If the body does not receive enough energy, it eventually dies.

If a person does not eat enough, the body will try to meet its energy needs by using up stores of fat. If undernourishment continues after these are gone, the body begins to consume the protein in structural tissue as fuel. If undernourishment proceeds further, the body's organs, including the brain, begin to function poorly, and the person becomes weak and confused.

This is like trying to heat a wood house by burning parts of the building in the fireplace.

Small children are most severely damaged by eating poorly, because they are growing. Without proper nutrition they are susceptible to infectious diseases, stunted growth, and early death. Unless there is an extreme shortage of food, adults are affected less by poor nutrition, although their vitality, health, and ability to work may be greatly diminished.

A.2 YOU DECIDE: DIMENSIONS OF HUNGER

Many low-income people and large populations in certain parts of the world go without enough to eat. About one-half billion people—nearly 10% of the world's inhabitants—are undernourished. Of these, 10–14 million people die each year from hunger and hunger-related diseases, according to a World Health Organization (WHO) and United Nations (UN) report. Three-quarters of those who die are children. In the United States, 20 million people are malnourished or undernourished (8% of the population), even though we produce enough to sell food to other countries.

The United Nations Food and Agriculture Organization (FAO) surveyed world hunger in 1983–85. The FAO defines undernourishment by "dietary energy intake." Minimally-adequate energy intake is considered 1.4 times the rate of thermal energy given off by an inactive person. The 1.4 factor allows for body maintenance and minimum physical activity. Table 1 summarizes the FAO's regional findings.

Table 1   **UNDERNUTRITION IN DEVELOPING NATIONS**

	Africa	Far East	Latin America	Near East	Total
Total population (in millions)	440	1320	390	240	2390
Number undernourished (in millions)	140	291	55	26	512
Percent undernourished	32%	22%	14%	11%	21%

Questions

1. Why is the death rate from hunger higher for children than for adults?

2. What effect does undernourishment have on human activity?

3. Malnutrition is defined as inadequate intake of proteins, vitamins, and minerals. Malnutrition may occur even if the food energy intake is adequate. If Table 1 gave the number of malnourished people rather than undernourished people, would the totals be larger or smaller? Why?

4. Surveying nutrition levels for an entire nation is, at best, difficult. Agencies such as the World Health Organization and United Nations International Children's Emergency Fund (UNICEF) judge a country's nutritional status from its **infant mortality rate.**

   An infant mortality rate of 50 means that for every 1,000 live births, 50 infants less than a year old die. A country with an infant mortality rate of 50 or lower is considered to be adequately meeting nutritional and other basic needs of its people. Countries with infant mortality rates higher than 50 are judged to have unresolved hunger and malnutrition problems or poor medical care.

   Your teacher will provide you with a blank world map and data on infant mortality in various nations. Shade in (with a colored pencil or marker) all countries with infant mortality rates higher than 50. Next to the name of each country, write its infant mortality rate.

   a. Do any nations have unexpectedly high or low infant mortality rates?

   b. If so, which countries are they?

   c. Why did you find their values surprisingly low or high?

5. Does infant mortality seem to divide along any geographic lines? If so, describe them.

A.3 WHY HUNGER?

The average infant mortality value for the entire world is currently about 70. However, as your analysis of infant mortality

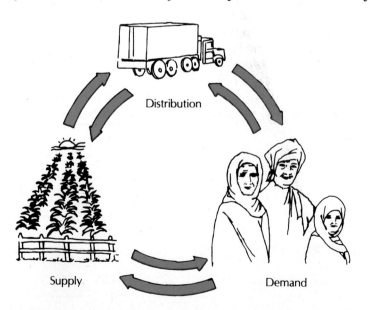

Figure 1 Food systems model.

data has revealed, there is actually a wide variation among countries. Why are there such great differences?

Infant mortality can result from several things, one of which is lack of food. The availability of food among countries also varies greatly.

Three factors determine the abundance or scarcity of any resource, whether it's gasoline, clean water, back-stage passes for a rock concert, or—most important of all—food. These basic factors, symbolized in Figure 1, are:

- Supply (How much is available?)
- Demand (How much is needed?)
- Distribution (Where is it and how can it be obtained?).

According to the best available data, the world has enough food for everyone. The World Hunger Project at Brown University estimates that sufficient food is produced globally to feed 20% more than the world's current population. In other words, the overall supply of food appears adequate to meet demands.

This estimate assumes an adequate vegetarian diet.

Why then is there world hunger? People cannot obtain suitable food in certain regions of the world. But that does not really answer the question, it just restates the problem. The *distribution* of food must certainly be one key to the puzzle (Figure 1).

PART A: SUMMARY QUESTIONS

1. a. In what way does this *ChemCom* unit follow the same "to build and to burn" theme as the Petroleum unit?

   b. If insufficient food is supplied to the body, which of those two uses has priority? Why?

2. a. In what sense does world hunger involve an "energy crisis"?

   b. In what sense is it a national resource crisis?

3. a. Distinguish between the terms *undernourished* and *malnourished*.

   b. Is it possible for a person to be malnourished but not undernourished?

   c. Can a person be undernourished without being malnourished?

4. a. Explain the wisdom of the old adage "Variety is the spice of life" concerning one's diet.

   b. Is simple "calorie counting" a wise way to approach dieting? Why or why not?

Variety is the essence of good eating.

B FOOD AS ENERGY

All human activity requires "burning" food for energy. In the following sections you will learn how much energy it takes to perform various activities and how to estimate the energy available from different kinds of food.

B.1 FOOD FOR THOUGHT—AND FOR ENERGY

Everyone who diets counts Calories. A Calorie is a measure of the energy present in food. For example, a standard serving of french fries (68 g) contains 220 Calories of food energy. The capital letter in Calories indicates that these are food Calories. Recall that a calorie (with a lower case "c") represents the thermal energy needed to raise the temperature of one gram of water one degree Celsius. The food Calorie (with an upper case "C") is a much larger unit. It equals 1000 calories, or one kilocalorie.

One food Calorie would increase the temperature of one kilogram (1,000 g, or one liter) of water by one degree Celsius.

To distinguish the two kinds of calories, remember the following relationships:

1000 calories (cal) = 1 Calorie (Cal)

Let's reconsider that serving of french fries. A 68-g serving delivers 220 kcal (220 Cal) to the hungry eater. Where did this food energy come from? The answer is simple: all food energy came from sunlight.

In photosynthesis, plants capture solar energy and use it to make large, energy-rich molecules from smaller, simpler ones. The sun's energy is converted to chemical energy that is stored within the structures of these molecules. We recover some of this stored energy when we eat the plants—or dine on meat and dairy products from animals that consumed green plants.

How do we know how much energy is stored in foods? Chemists determine this in just about the same way you found the heat of combustion of candle wax (Petroleum unit, page 186). The food is burned under controlled conditions, and the quantity of thermal energy it releases is carefully measured. This procedure is called **calorimetry**, and the instrument is called a **calorimeter**.

The energy content of a wide variety of foods have been determined and are available for diet planning. For example, the table in Appendix (page 522) includes energy values and nutrient values in common foods.

What is the energy contained in this serving of french fries?

For convenience, 1000 calories is also called one kilocalorie, 1 kcal.

All human activities are directly or indirectly powered by solar energy.

You constructed a simple calorimeter from a soft drink can in the Petroleum unit.

Calorie or Joule?

In earlier units we used the joule (rhymes with cool) as the standard unit of energy. Now we are using calories, but this is not an attempt to confuse you. The joule is the modernized metric system (SI) unit of energy and is roughly equivalent to the energy it takes to lift 100 g (about the weight of a large egg) one meter. Weight-conscious Americans may one day count joules instead of calories. This has not yet happened, so we will use the (uppercase) Calorie as the unit of food energy. You can translate (lowercase) calories into joules by using the following relationships:

$$1 \text{ calorie (cal)} = 4.184 \text{ joules (J)}$$
$$1 \text{ Calorie (Cal)} = 4.184 \text{ kJ}$$

Now for some pencil-and-paper practice with calorimetry.

YOUR TURN

Calorimetry

In a typical calorimeter, the thermal energy released by burning a sample of food heats a known mass of water. The temperature increase of the water is measured, and the thermal energy released by the reaction is then calculated. The procedures and calculations are similar to those you experienced in an earlier calorimetry experiment (Petroleum unit, pages 187 and 188).

It takes 1.0 calorie to raise the temperature of one gram of water by one degree Celsius. Thus water's specific heat, expressed in calorie units, is 1.0 calorie per gram per degree Celsius. Let's put this value to work in a sample problem, to review skills you learned in the Petroleum unit.

Suppose you want to warm 250 mL (250 g) of water from room temperature (22° C) to just under boiling (99° C). How much thermal energy will be needed?

Here's how the answer can be reasoned out: We know it takes 1.0 calorie to heat 1 g of water by 1° C. However, in this case, we have *250* times more water to heat, and rather than heating the sample by 1° C, we need to increase its temperature by 77° C (99° C − 22° C). The total thermal energy needed must be 250 times greater due to the larger mass, and 77 times greater due to the larger temperature change. To include *both* changes, the total energy needed must be 250 × 77, or about 19,000 times greater than the original 1.0 calorie. Thus, the final answer must be 1.0 cal × 19,000, or **19,000 cal.** Or, since it takes 1000 calories to equal a kilocalorie, the answer could also be expressed as **19 kcal.**

The problem solution can also be summarized this way, to show that all units involved combine to give the desired units of "calories" in the final answer:

$$\frac{1 \text{ cal}}{g^\circ C} \times 250\,g \times (99 - 22)^\circ C = 19,000 \text{ cal, or } \textbf{19 kcal}$$

Now let's try a food-based problem.

One ounce (28.4 g) of a popular frosted cereal contains three teaspoons (12 g) of sugar. When burned,

Although 250 × 77 produces 19,250 on a calculator, in this case this can be rounded off to 19,000.

this sugar is able to heat 860 g of water from 22° C to 85° C. How much energy was contained in the three teaspoons of sugar? Based on your answer, how many food Calories are contained in one teaspoon of sugar?

Once again we start with the fundamental water-heating relationship. We know it takes 1.0 cal of thermal energy to heat 1 g of water by 1° C. In this problem the burning sugar heated 860 g of water—860 times more. The temperature increase was 63° C—63 times more than our water-heating standard. Thus the total thermal energy involved must have been 860 × 63, or about 54,000 times more than the 1.0 cal standard. Thus, total energy in three teaspoons of sugar is 1.0 cal × 54,000 = **54,000 cal.** In food-energy units, this equals **54 Cal.**

Finally, if *three* teaspoons of sugar contain 54 Cal of food energy, then *one* teaspoon of sugar must contain 1/3 as much. Since 54/3 = 18, there are **18 Cal in one teaspoon of sugar.**

Now it's your turn.

1. The energy stored in one can of a certain diet drink is capable of heating 160 g of room-temperature (22° C) water to 60° C. How many Calories are contained in this diet drink?

2. Suppose you drink six glasses (250 g each) of ice water (0° C) on a hot summer day.

   a. Assume your body temperature is 37° C. How many calories of thermal energy does your body use in heating this water to body temperature?

   b. How many Calories is this?

   c. A serving of french fries contains 220 Cal. How many glasses of ice water would you have to drink to "burn off" the Calories in one serving of french fries?

   d. Based on your answer to Question 2c, is drinking ice water an efficient way to diet?

What happens to the energy stored in foods we eat? How much body mass is gained if excess food is consumed? The following activity will help you estimate this.

B.2 YOU DECIDE: ENERGY IN—ENERGY OUT

Table 2 provides estimates of the energy expended by a 150-lb person in various activities.

1. Use this table to estimate your own daily energy use:

   a. List your typical activities over a 24-hour period and estimate how long each activity takes.

   b. Calculate the total Calories used. Try to estimate energy uses for any activities not given in the table.

   c. An average 15- to 18-year-old female engaged in light activity consumes about 2300 Cal daily. The value for a 15- to 18-year-old male is about 3000 Cal. How does your own estimated energy use compare with these values?

Table 2   ENERGY EXPENDITURES

Activity	Energy Expended, Cal/hour*
Lying down or sleeping	80
Sitting	100
Driving automobile	120
Standing	140
Eating	150
Light housework	180
Walking, 2.5 mph	210
Bicycling, 5.5 mph	210
Lawn mowing	250
Golf, walking	250
Bowling	270
Walking, 3.75 mph	300
Volleyball, rollerskating	350
Tennis	420
Swimming, breaststroke	430
Swimming, crawl	520
Football, touch	530
Jogging, 11-min mile	550
Skiing, 10 mph	600
Bicycling, 13 mph	660
Football, tackle	720
Running, 8-min mile	850

*Based on a 150-pound person

Compare the total energy you use with the total food energy you consume.

2. Let's look at the consumption of an ice cream sundae. We will investigate how much exercise it would take to burn off the added Calories, and how much weight you would gain from eating it if you did not exercise.

   Two scoops of your favorite ice cream contain 250 Cal and the chocolate topping adds 125 Cal. Consult Table 2 to answer the following questions. (You must also know that 1 lb of body fat contains 4000 Cal of energy.)

   a. Assume that your regular diet (without the ice cream sundae) just maintains your current body weight. If you eat the ice cream sundae,
      (1) how many hours of playing tennis would burn it off?
      (2) how far would you have to walk (at 2.5 mph)?
      (3) how many hours must you swim (breaststroke)?

   b. If you choose not to exercise more than usual, how much weight will you gain from the sundae?

   c. Now assume that you consume a similar sundae three times each week for sixteen weeks. If you do not exercise to burn it off, how much weight will you gain?

   d. Of course, another alternative is available—you might decide not to eat the ice cream sundae. Would you decide to eat the sundae (involving either extra exercise or gaining weight) or not to eat the sundae (involving less pleasure)? Why?

It would take nearly four hours of just sitting to burn off the sundae's calories.

3. We have implied that eating an ice cream sundae will result in weight gain, unless you do additional exercise.

   a. Can you think of a plan that allows you to consume the sundae, do no additional exercise, and still not gain weight?

   b. Explain your plan and be prepared to discuss it in class.

This activity has been based on three possible scenarios:

I. If *total energy in* is equal to *total energy out*, a person will maintain current body weight.

II. If *total energy in* is greater than *total energy out*, a person will gain some body weight.

III. If *total energy in* is less than *total energy out*, a person will lose some body weight.

These runners are using energy at a rate of about 850 Cal/hr.

An individual wishing to lose weight must meet the third condition listed above—total energy consumed in food must be less than the total energy used. On the other hand, a person wishing to gain weight must take in more energy than is expended.

As wise dieters know, proper nutrition is not just a question of how much is eaten. *What* we eat also is critical. Some foods provide more energy than others, some are important for their nutrients, and some fill you up without providing much energy or nutrition. In the following section, we will examine major food groups, beginning with carbohydrates.

B.3 CARBOHYDRATES: THE ENERGIZERS

Sugars, starch, and cellulose are all carbohydrates.

Carbohydrates are compounds composed of only three elements—carbon, hydrogen, and oxygen. For example, glucose, the key energy-releasing carbohydrate in biological systems, has the formula $C_6H_{12}O_6$. When such formulas were first discovered, chemists were tempted to write the glucose formula as $C_6(H_2O)_6$—implying a chemical combination of carbon and water. So, they invented the term "carbo-hydrate," or water-containing carbon compound. We now know that water molecules are not actually present in carbohydrates, but the name has persisted.

Every moment of your life, carbohydrates are oxidized in your body to produce energy, CO_2, and H_2O.

Carbohydrates may be simple sugars such as glucose or composed of two or more simple sugar molecules combined in various ways (Table 3). Simple sugars are called **monosaccharides.** The most common monosaccharide molecules contain five or six carbon atoms bonded together. As shown in Figure 2, glucose (and most other monosaccharides) can exist either in a chain or a ring form. Do both forms have the same molecular formula? (Check by counting the atoms.)

Figure 2 Structural formulas for glucose. The chain and ring forms are interconvertible; the ring form predominates in the body.

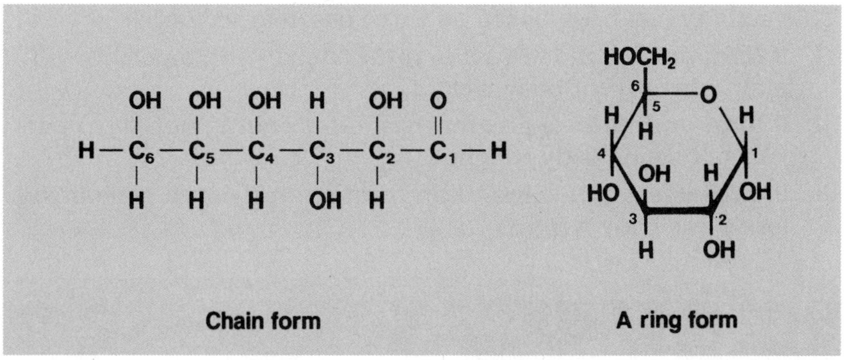

Chain form   **A ring form**

Figure 3 Formation of sucrose. The two shaded —OH groups react with the elimination of one H_2O molecule.

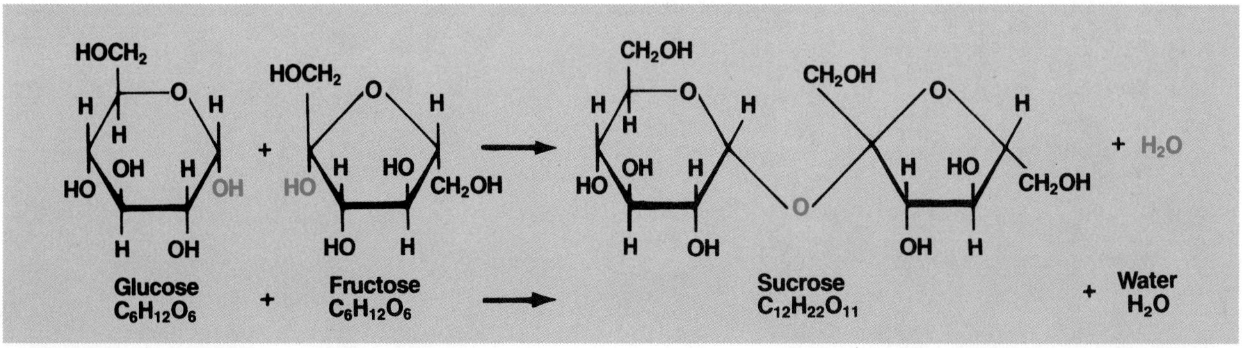

Glucose $C_6H_{12}O_6$ + Fructose $C_6H_{12}O_6$ → Sucrose $C_{12}H_{22}O_{11}$ + Water H_2O

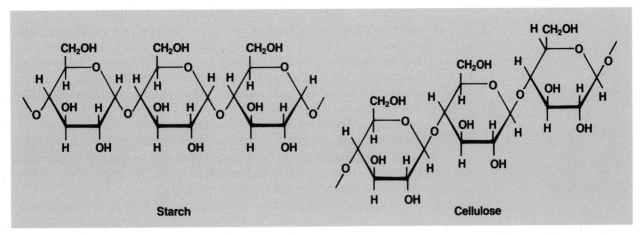

Starch

Cellulose

Sugar molecules composed of two simple sugar units are called **disaccharides.** Sucrose ($C_{12}H_{22}O_{11}$—ordinary table sugar) is a disaccharide in which the ring forms of glucose and fructose are joined (see Figure 3). As the molecular structures suggest, monosaccharides and disaccharides are composed of polar molecules. Thus they tend to be highly soluble in water, a polar solvent.

Polymers composed of units of simple sugar molecules are called **polysaccharides** (Figure 4). Starch, a major component of grains and many vegetables, is a polysaccharide composed of glucose units. Cellulose, the fibrous or woody material of plants and trees, is another polysaccharide formed from glucose. The types of carbohydrates are summarized in Table 3.

Figure 4 Polysaccharides. Starch and cellulose are both polymers of glucose. They differ in the arrangements of the bonds that join the glucose monomers.

Recall the "like dissolves like" rule.

Remember the discussion of polyethylene on page 201. A polymer is a large molecule composed of many smaller molecular units chemically bonded together.

Carbohydrates are all sugars or polymers of sugars.

Table 3   **CARBOHYDRATES**

Classification and Examples	Composition	Formula	Common Name or Source
Monosaccharides		$C_6H_{12}O_6$	
Glucose	—		Blood sugar
Fructose	—		Fruit sugar
Galactose	—		—
Disaccharides		$C_{12}H_{22}O_{11}$	
Sucrose	Fructose + glucose		Cane sugar
Lactose	Galactose + glucose		Milk sugar
Maltose	Glucose + glucose		Germinating seeds
Polysaccharides	Glucose polymers	—	
Starch			Plants
Glycogen			Animals
Cellulose			Fiber

During photosynthesis, green plants produce glucose. The overall reaction is as follows:

$$6\,CO_2 + 6\,H_2O + 686\ kcal \rightarrow C_6H_{12}O_6 + 6\,O_2$$

| Carbon dioxide | Water | Solar energy | Glucose | Oxygen gas |

Plants build these glucose molecules either into starch for energy storage, or into cellulose, becoming part of the plant's structure.

There are exceptions—cows and termites, for example, can digest cellulose.

Sugars and starch are rapidly digested in your body, making them convenient sources of energy. Cellulose is not digested. The glucose units in cellulose are bonded together differently than they are in starch (see Figure 4). The slight difference in bonding makes cellulose indigestible by most animals. However, cellulose, sometimes called fiber, is needed in the diet to keep the digestive system functioning properly.

Sugars and starch are the major energy-delivering substances in our diets. Even the smallest muscle twitch or thought requires energy. The body obtains most of this energy by burning the glucose molecules in sugars and starch. Each gram of carbohydrate delivers about 4 Calories of energy.

1 g carbohydrate = 4 Cal energy

Nutritionists recommend that about 60% of food energy come from carbohydrates. Most of the world's population obtains carbohydrates by eating grains. These grains are often consumed as rice, corn meal, wheat tortillas, bread, and pasta. In the United States we tend to eat more wheat breads and potatoes for carbohydrates than people do elsewhere. In all countries, fruits and vegetables also provide carbohydrates. Meats provide a small amount of carbohydrate in the form of glycogen, which is how animals store glucose. On average, each U.S. citizen consumes more than 90 lb (40 kg) of table sugar each year in beverages, breads, and cakes and as a sweetener. A 12-ounce non-diet cola drink contains nine teaspoons of sugar.

B.4 FATS: STORED ENERGY WITH A BAD NAME

Unlike carbohydrate and protein, the word "fat" has acquired its own general (and somewhat negative) meaning. To most people, "You're too fat" means that the person looks overweight. However, from a chemist's point of view, *fats* are a major category of biomolecules which have their own special characteristics and functions, just as carbohydrates and proteins do.

Fats are a significant part of our diet. They're present in meat, fish, and poultry; salad dressings and oils; dairy products; and grains. When our bodies take in more food than is needed for energy, much of the excess is converted to fat molecules and stored in the body. If food intake is not large enough to supply the body's energy needs, the body begins to burn stored fat.

Like carbohydrates, fats are composed of carbon, hydrogen, and oxygen. However, fats contain less oxygen than carbohydrates and contain more stored energy. Gram-for-gram, fat contains over twice the energy found in carbohydrates. Fats are generally nonpolar in nature and are only sparingly soluble in water. Because of their solubility and energy-storing properties, fat molecules are more like hydrocarbons than carbohydrates.

Fats are members of the class of biomolecules called **lipids.** Some lipids are builder molecules that form cell membranes. Others become hormones—chemical messengers that regulate processes in the body.

A typical fat molecule is a combination of a simple three-carbon alcohol called **glycerol** with three fatty acid molecules. (The formation of a typical fat is shown in Figure 5.) **Fatty acids** are a class of compounds made up of a long hydrocarbon chain with a carboxyl group (—COOH) at one end. The reaction producing a fat molecule is similar to one you already completed in the laboratory (page 204)—the production of an ester, methyl

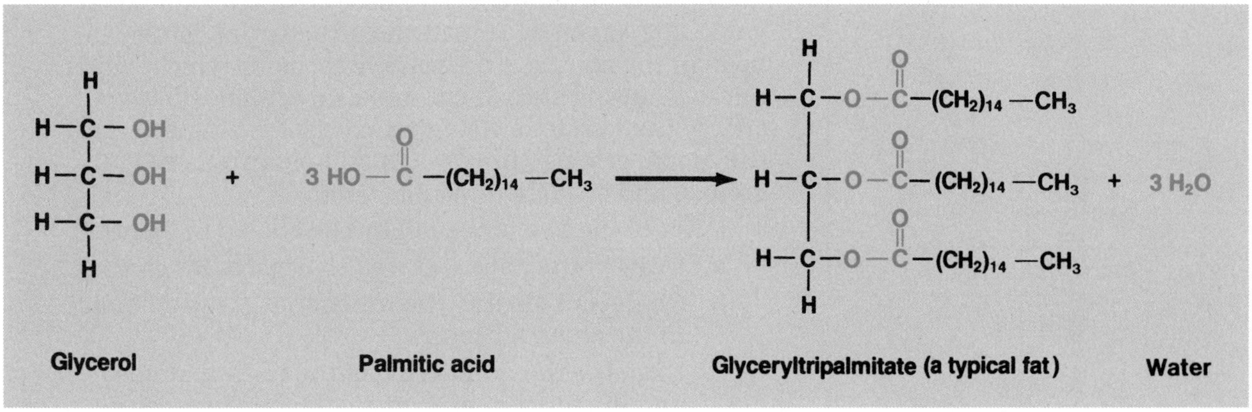

Glycerol   **Palmitic acid**   **Glyceryltripalmitate (a typical fat)**   **Water**

Figure 5 Formation of a typical fat, a triglyceride. Glycerol and three molecules of fatty acid combine in a condensation reaction to form a triester and eliminate three water molecules.

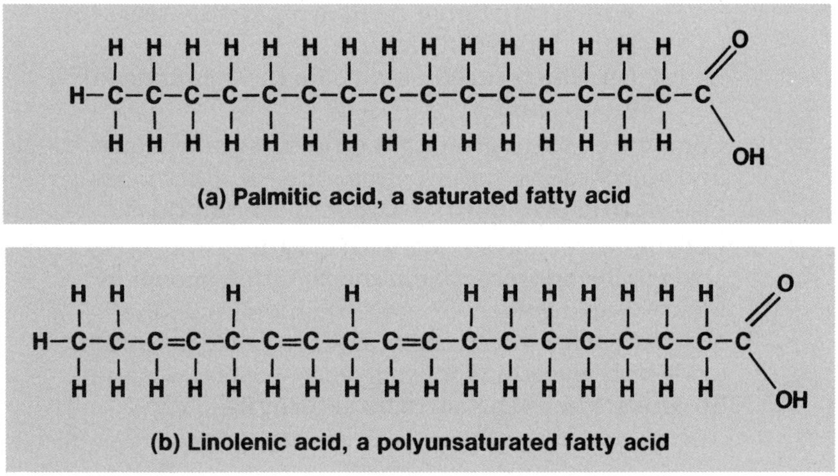

(a) Palmitic acid, a saturated fatty acid

(b) Linolenic acid, a polyunsaturated fatty acid

Figure 6 Typical fatty acids.

salicylate. However, here a molecule containing *three* —OH groups reacts with *three* molecules of acid. Three molecules of water are eliminated, producing a molecule containing three ester groups instead of one. Such a fat is known as a **triglyceride.**

Recall that hydrocarbons may be saturated (when containing only single carbon-carbon bonds) or unsaturated (when containing double or triple carbon-carbon bonds). Likewise, hydrocarbon chains in fatty acids are either saturated (Figure 6a) or unsaturated (Figure 6b). Fats containing saturated fatty acids are called **saturated fats;** fats containing unsaturated fatty acids are called **unsaturated fats.** Because of differences in their bonds, saturated and unsaturated fats participate differently in body chemistry.

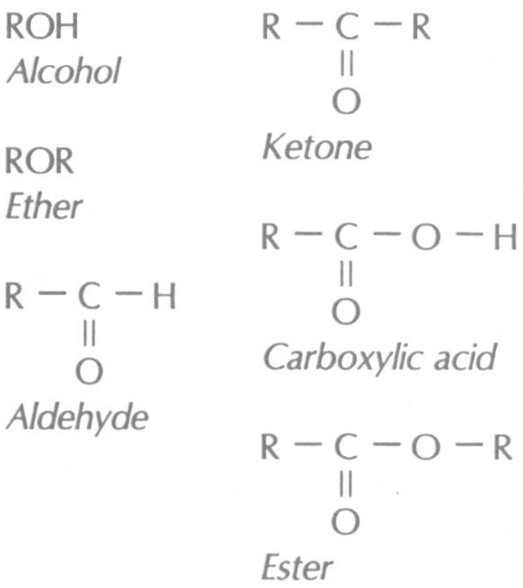

YOUR TURN

Functional Groups in Biomolecules

As you discovered in the Petroleum unit, functional groups strongly influence the properties of organic compounds.

Some classes of organic compounds in which particular functional groups appear are listed in the margin, with formulas written in their condensed forms (each R represents a hydrocarbon segment).

ROH
Alcohol

ROR
Ether

$R - C - H$
$\quad\;\; \| $
$\quad\;\; O$
Aldehyde

$R - C - R$
$\quad\;\; \| $
$\quad\;\; O$
Ketone

$R - C - O - H$
$\quad\;\; \| $
$\quad\;\; O$
Carboxylic acid

$R - C - O - R$
$\quad\;\; \| $
$\quad\;\; O$
Ester

Cortisol

Fructose

Glucose

A molecule may contain more than one functional group. For example, look at the structure of cortisol (a lipid) in the margin. Cortisol is a hormone which, when released during starvation, makes it possible to use energy from protein. Note that cortisol contains several functional groups: three —OH groups, two $C=O$ groups, and one $C=C$ double bond.

1. Refer to the two forms of glucose shown in Figure 2.
   a. Draw both chain and ring structures for glucose.
   b. Circle and identify the functional group(s) found in the chain structure.
   c. Examine the numbering of the carbon atoms and the functional groups attached to each carbon atom.
      (1) Which functional groups apparently react to form the ring structure?
      (2) On which carbon atoms do these functional groups appear?

2. Compare the straight-chain structures of fructose and glucose (See margin.) Describe the differences in the structures of these two monosaccharides.

3. In general, alcohols react with organic (carboxylic) acids to form esters. Using the equation shown in Figure 5 as a guide, write an equation (including structures) for the reaction of stearic acid (a fatty acid) with glycerol to form glyceryl tristearate (a fat). Stearic acid has this structural formula:

$$HO - \overset{\overset{\displaystyle O}{\displaystyle \|}}{C} - (CH_2)_{16}CH_3$$

4. Copy the following molecular structure on your own paper:

$$HO - \overset{\overset{\displaystyle O}{\displaystyle \|}}{C} - (CH_2)_7 - \overset{\overset{\displaystyle H}{\displaystyle |}}{C} = \overset{\overset{\displaystyle H}{\displaystyle |}}{C} - (CH_2)_7CH_3$$

   a. Circle and identify the functional group(s).
   b. Is this molecule a carbohydrate or a fatty acid? Why?
   c. Is it saturated or unsaturated? Why?
   d. Rewrite the molecular structure to show the carbon atoms in a continuous chain.

Saturated fats appear to contribute to coronary heart disease.

The term **polyunsaturated,** often used in food advertising, means that the food contains fats with two or more carbon-carbon double bonds in each fatty acid molecule. The term has become familiar because increasing evidence suggests that saturated fats may contribute to health problems, while some unsaturated fats may not. Saturated fats are associated with formation of plaque (fat-like or fibrous matter), which can block arteries. The result is a condition known as "hardening of the arteries," or atherosclerosis, a particular threat to coronary (heart) arteries and arteries leading to the brain. If coronary arteries are blocked, a heart attack can result, damaging the heart muscle. If arteries

Safety: As American as Apple Pie

By Jean Frances Henry
Watsonville Herald *Staff Reporter*

We take it for granted that the food we eat in local restaurants is safe to eat—if not always as good as Mom's. Thanks to the work of environmental health specialists such as Alicia Enriquez, the citizens of Santa Clara County can eat and drink with confidence. Alicia enforces California State and local health and safety ordinances that safeguard users of local restaurants and cafes. She also ensures the safety of public swimming pools, spas, and private septic systems. Another aspect of her job is running community awareness and education outreach programs. Other environmental health specialists enforce health and safety codes and develop educational programs in other areas, including toxic substances and waste control, disaster response, air and water quality protection, and occupational health.

Alicia begins her day early. She completes daily reports, returns telephone messages, and receives inquiries from the public and her clients. Then Alicia responds to consumer complaints and requests, and she conducts routine inspections. She visits a variety of establishments such as restaurants, liquor stores, bars, grocery stores, swimming pools, health spas, or even private residences. When Alicia inspects a pool or spa, she performs chemical tests to check for unhealthy conditions such as high chlorine levels or too acid or alkaline pH.

At food establishments, Alicia monitors food handling and preparation, verifies proper dish and utensil sanitation methods, investigates insect or rodent in-

Photo by Ernest Wong

festation, examines labeling techniques, and inspects hazardous materials storage. If Alicia finds certain food items are contaminated or mishandled, she is authorized to have the food destroyed. She presents her report immediately following the inspection. The establishment is given time to make adjustments to meet the minimum legal requirements. If the establishment does not comply, Alicia pursues legal action by issuing a citation or suspending the establishment's health permit.

The operator and the employees of a given establishment may not comply because they have difficulty in understanding proper food handling techniques and public health laws. In that case, Alicia reviews proper procedures, distributes educational manuals (some of which are translated into four different languages), and conducts food handling classes.

An Environmental Health Specialist should have a background in biology, especially microbiology; chemistry, especially in water and waste water chemistry; toxicology; ecology; physics; and environmental health. They use these skills to combine their observations in the field with science and law to determine whether there is a threat to the health and well-being of the public, and to take measures to eliminate any threats.

leading to the brain are blocked, a stroke may result, killing brain cells and harming various body functions.

Fat molecules in butter and other animal fats are nearly all saturated and form solids at room temperature. Fats from plant sources commonly contain molecules with several carbon-carbon double bonds. At room temperature these polyunsaturated fats are liquids (oils), such as safflower oil (91% unsaturated fat molecules), corn oil (87% unsaturated), and peanut oil (81% unsaturated).

A process called *partial hydrogenation* can add enough hydrogen atoms to the double bonds of a fat to convert it to a semisolid, while allowing some double bonds to remain. Such partially-hydrogenated molecules are used in margarines and shortening.

Fats are high-energy molecules. One gram of fat can release 9000 cal (9 Cal) of energy, which is more than double the energy released from an equal mass of carbohydrate or protein. It is not surprising that the body produces fat to store excess food energy efficiently and that it is difficult to "burn off" excess fat. Gram for gram, you must run more than twice as far or exercise twice as long to "burn up" fat as you do to burn off carbohydrates.

Currently, Americans get about 40% of their body energy from fats. The American Cancer Society and the American Heart Association both recommend that this be reduced to no more than 30%.

Fat consumption in the United States is decreasing, but is still high compared with recommended levels and with normal fat intake in most other countries. High consumption of fat is a factor in several "modern" diseases, including obesity and atherosclerosis. Most U.S. dietary fat comes from meat, poultry, fish, and dairy products. Deep-fried items, such as french fries, fried chicken, and potato chips, add even more fat to the diet. In addition, when your intake of food is higher than what you burn off with exercise, your body converts excess proteins and carbohydrates to fat for storage.

In the following questions, review what you have learned about energy in the body and energy-providing molecules. Then we will consider the nutrient family most directly involved in building—the proteins.

1 g fat = 9 Cal energy
1 g protein = 4 Cal energy
1 g carbohydrate = 4 Cal energy

The U.S. Department of Health and Human Services further recommends that less than 10% of total food energy come from saturated fats.

PART B: SUMMARY QUESTIONS

1. The energy stored in a one-half-ounce serving of raisins is capable of raising the temperature of 1000 g of room-temperature (22° C) water to 62° C. How many food Calories are contained in that serving of raisins?

2. People sometimes confuse the terms *hydrocarbon* and *carbohydrate*.

   a. Define and give an example of each.
   b. How are they similar?
   c. How are they different?

3. Use Table 2 to explain each of the following statements:

   a. *Breakfast is the most important meal of the day.* (*Hint:* Estimate how many Calories your body uses between dinner—at 6 p.m.—and breakfast—at 8 a.m.)

   b. *Until they are properly fed, starving individuals would have difficulty working for a living even if paying jobs were available.*

4. Assume that you require 3000 Cal of food energy each day to maintain your present body weight.

a. If you wished to obtain this energy by consuming the smallest mass of food, would fats or carbohydrates be your preferred food choice?

b. How many grams of this nutrient would be needed to supply this quantity of daily energy?

c. Would such a diet be healthy? Why?

5. It has been estimated that U.S. citizens carry around about 2.5 billion pounds of excess body fat.

a. How many Calories of food energy does this represent? (Note that a pound of fat contains about 4000 Cal of energy.)

b. If the excess energy calculated in Question 5a could somehow be diverted to feed the world's hungry, how many people could be fed for one year? (Assume an average human needs about 2600 Cal each day.)

6. a. Write the structural formulas for a typical (1) six-carbon carbohydrate and (2) six-carbon hydrocarbon.

b. Which compound should be more soluble in water? Why?

7. Is the following molecule a hydrocarbon, a carbohydrate, or a fat?

$$
\begin{array}{ccccc}
 & & H & & H \\
 & & | & & | \\
H-&C-&C-&C-&H \\
 & \| & | & | & \\
 & O & OH & OH & \\
\end{array}
$$

EXTENDING YOUR KNOWLEDGE (OPTIONAL)

It looks good but think of the Calories!

• Assume you currently consume 3000 Cal each day and want to lose 30 lb of body fat over the next two months (60 days).

a. If you decide to lose this weight only through dieting (no extra exercise), how many Calories would you need to omit from your diet each day?

b. How many food Calories would you still be allowed to consume daily?

c. Is this a sensible way to lose weight? Why?

|C

FOODS: THE BUILDER MOLECULES

Your body mass is roughly 60% water and 20% fat. The remaining 20% consists primarily of proteins, carbohydrates, and related compounds, and the major bone elements calcium and phosphorus.

In the United States, recent generations have, on average, grown taller than their parents. Better nutrition is largely responsible for this change. Our genes determine how tall we may grow, but nutrition determines—at least in part—actual height.

In the following sections you will explore food nutrients as builder molecules. You will soon discover the critical importance of protein as a body builder.

C.1 FOODS AS CHEMICAL REACTANTS

Biochemistry is the branch of chemistry that studies chemical reactions in living systems. Such processes are rarely simple. Consider the body's extraction of energy from disaccharides and polysaccharides. These carbohydrates are broken down by digestion into glucose, $C_6H_{12}O_6$, the primary substance used for energy in most living systems.

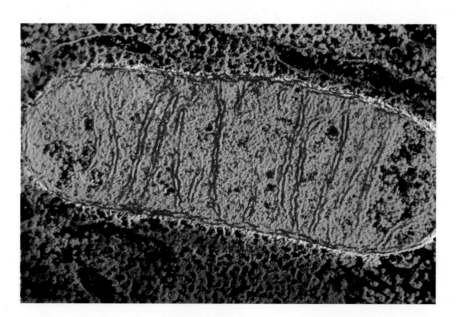

Much cellular respiration takes place in mitochondria. This photo shows details of a single mitochondrion under an electron microscope.

The *overall* reaction for extracting energy from glucose by burning is the same in the body as it is on a laboratory bench in the presence of air. Obviously, glucose is not burned with a flame inside the body. Not only would most of the energy escape uselessly as heat, but the resulting temperatures would kill cells. Yet in a sense that burning reaction does continuously occur within each human cell, in a series of at least twenty-two related chemical reactions or steps known as **cellular respiration.**

This process—and nearly every other biochemical reaction—can take place in the body only with assistance from a class of molecules called **enzymes.** Enzymes can be thought of as the body's "skilled worker" molecules. They help to make and break chemical bonds by interacting with certain molecules, just as selectively as the correct key interacts with its lock.

Enzymes are catalysts— compounds that help chemical reactions occur by increasing their rates of reaction.

C.2 LIMITING REACTANTS

The reactions that take place in the body, particularly those that build, require the presence of a complete set of ingredients, or reactants. In addition, there must be enough reactants to complete the reaction. The situation is like collecting ingredients to bake a cake. Consider this cake recipe:

2 cups flour	1½ tablespoons baking powder
2 eggs	1 cup water
1 cup sugar	⅓ cup oil

The combination of these ingredients will produce one cake. Now, suppose in the kitchen we find 14 cups flour, 4 eggs, 9 cups sugar, 15 tablespoons baking powder, 10 cups water, and 3⅓ cups oil. How many cakes can be baked?

Well, fourteen cups of flour is enough for seven cakes (two cups flour per cake). And there's enough sugar for nine cakes (one cup sugar per cake). The supplies of baking powder, water, and oil are sufficient for 10 cakes (confirm this with the recipe). Yet we cannot make either 7, 9, or 10 cakes with the available ingredients. Why?

We only have four eggs, or just enough for two cakes. The egg supply has limited the number of cakes we can bake. The excess quantities of the other reactants (flour, sugar, baking powder, water, oil) simply remain unused. If we want to bake more cakes, we have to find more eggs!

In chemical terms, the eggs in our cake-making example would be called the **limiting reactant** (or limiting reagent). The limiting reactant is the starting substance that becomes used up first when a chemical reaction occurs. It controls how much (or how little) product can be formed.

YOUR TURN

Limiting Reactants

1. Consider the same cake-making example discussed above, but this time assume that you have 26 eggs.
   a. How many cakes can be made now if the other ingredients are present in the same quantities?
   b. Which ingredient limits the number of cakes you can make this time? (In other words, what is the limiting reactant?)

2. A restaurant prepares carry-out lunches. Each completed carry-out lunch box requires: 1 sandwich, 3 pickles, 2 paper napkins, 1 carton of milk, and 1 container. Today's inventory: 60 sandwiches, 102 pickles, 38 napkins, 41 cartons of milk, and 66 containers.

   a. As carry-out lunches are prepared, which item will be used up first?

   b. Which item is the limiting reactant?

   c. How many complete carry-out lunches can be assembled?

3. A booklet is prepared from 2 covers, 3 staples, and 20 pages. Assume we have 60 covers, 120 staples, and 400 pages.

   a. What is the largest number of complete booklets that can be prepared with these supplies?

   b. Which is the "limiting reactant" in this system?

   c. How many of the other two "reactants" will be left over when the booklet preparation process stops?

In chemical reactions, just as in recipes, individual substances react in certain fixed quantities. These relative amounts are indicated in chemical equations.

Let's consider the equation for oxidation of glucose. First, the equation can be interpreted in terms of one glucose molecule:

$$C_6H_{12}O_6 \;+\; 6\,O_2 \;\rightarrow\; 6\,CO_2 \;+\; 6\,H_2O \;+\; \text{Energy}$$

| 1 Glucose molecule | 6 Oxygen molecules | 6 Carbon dioxide molecules | 6 Water molecules |

Suppose we had 10 glucose molecules and 100 oxygen molecules. Which substance would be the limiting reactant in this reaction? The equation tells us that each glucose molecule requires six oxygen molecules. Thus 10 glucose molecules would require 60 oxygen molecules for complete reaction. However, 100 oxygen molecules are available—which is more than we need! The 10 glucose molecules will react with 60 of these oxygen molecules, and 40 oxygen molecules will be left over.

Since the glucose is completely used up first, it is the limiting reactant. Once the 10 glucose molecules are consumed, the reaction stops. Additional glucose would be needed to continue it.

The notion of limiting reactants applies equally well to living systems. A shortage of a key nutrient or reactant can severely affect the growth or health of both plants and animals. In many biochemical processes, a product from one reaction becomes a reactant for other reactions. If a reaction stops due to the limiting reactant, all reactions following will also stop.

Fortunately, in some cases alternate reaction pathways are available. We have already said that if the body's glucose supply is depleted, glucose metabolism cannot occur. One backup system oxidizes fat from the body's reserves in place of glucose. Or, more drastic, structural protein can be broken down and used for energy until glucose is again available to the body.

Producing glucose from protein is much less energy-efficient than producing glucose from carbohydrates. But your body will use protein in this way if necessary.

Limiting Reactants: Chemical Reactions

A chemical equation can be interpreted not only in terms of molecules, but also in terms of moles and grams. (See page 126.) The reaction can be rewritten in terms of moles of all reactants and products:

$$C_6H_{12}O_6 \ + \ 6\,O_2 \ \rightarrow 6\,CO_2 \ + \ 6\,H_2O + \text{energy}$$

1 mol	6 mol	6 mol	6 mol
glucose	oxygen molecules	carbon dioxide	water

Finally, we can use molar masses to convert these mole values to grams. This interpretation then applies:

$$C_6H_{12}O_6 \ + \ 6\,O_2 \rightarrow 6\,CO_2 + 6\,H_2O + \text{energy}$$
$$180\ g \qquad 192\ g \quad 264\ g \quad 108\ g$$

If we needed to burn only 90 g of glucose—half the mass shown above—then only 96 g of oxygen would be needed—half the mass shown. If we had 90 mg glucose, 96 mg oxygen would be required to react with all of the glucose. Such relationships can be used to identify the limiting reactant.

Ammonia (NH_3) is an important fertilizer and is used to produce other fertilizers. It is made commercially by the following reaction:

$$N_2(g) + 3\,H_2(g) \xrightarrow[\text{Fe catalyst}]{\text{High temperature and pressure}} 2\,NH_3(g)$$

1. a. How many moles of each reactant and product are indicated by the equation?
   b. How many grams of each reactant and product are indicated by the equation?

2. Assume that a manufacturer has 28 kilograms of nitrogen gas and 9 kilograms of hydrogen gas. Also assume that the maximum amount of ammonia is produced from these reactants.
   a. Which reactant will be the limiting reactant?
   b. Which reactant will be left over (in excess)?
   c. How much of it will be left over?
   d. How much ammonia would be produced?

Here's an example of how these masses were obtained: One mole of water has a mass of 18.0 g. Six moles of water would have a mass six times larger than this: 6 × 18.0 g water = 108 g water.

Alternate reaction pathways are not a permanent solution to glucose depletion, however. If intake of a nutrient is consistently below that required by the body, that nutrient may become a limiting reactant in vital biochemical processes. The results can easily affect one's health.

Plants also must take in essential nutrients to support their growth and metabolism. For example, nutrients for algae must include carbon, nitrogen, and phosphorus. For every 41 g of carbon, algae require 7 g of nitrogen and 1 g of phosphorus. If any one of these elements is in short supply, it becomes a limiting reactant and affects algae growth.

In the following *Your Turn* you will compare limiting reactants in human and plant systems.

Algae often pollute lakes and streams that contain too much nitrogen and phosphorus.

Without water and essential nutrients, crops cannot live.

YOUR TURN

Limiting Reactants: Plants and Humans

Table 4 lists 22 elements currently known to be required in some quantity to support human life.

Table 4   ELEMENTS NEEDED FOR HUMAN NUTRITION

In major biomolecules	Carbon (C)
	Hydrogen (H)
	Oxygen (O)
	Nitrogen (N)
	Sulfur (S)
Major minerals	Calcium (Ca)
	Chlorine (Cl)
	Magnesium (Mg)
	Phosphorus (P)
	Potassium (K)
	Sodium (Na)
Trace minerals	Chromium (Cr)
	Cobalt (Co)
	Copper (Cu)
	Fluorine (F)
	Iodine (I)
	Iron (Fe)
	Manganese (Mn)
	Molybdenum (Mo)
	Nickel (Ni)
	Selenium (Se)
	Zinc (Zn)

Trace minerals are present at levels of 1 ppm or less. Higher concentrations may be toxic.

For comparison, a list of nutrients needed for the growth of common agricultural crops, such as corn and wheat, is given in Table 5. Crops cannot grow properly unless they have suitable nutrients, and in sufficient quantities. That means that farmers must consider limiting reactants in their crop production.

Table 5   PLANT NUTRIENTS NEEDED BY CROPS

Basic nutrients	Carbon (C) from CO_2 Oxygen (O) from CO_2 and H_2O Hydrogen (H) from H_2O
Primary nutrients	Nitrogen (N) Phosphorus (P) Potassium (K)
Secondary nutrients	Calcium (Ca) Magnesium (Mg) Sulfur (S)
Micronutrients	Boron (B) Chlorine (Cl) Copper (Cu) Iron (Fe) Manganese (Mn) Molybdenum (Mo) Zinc (Zn)

Most common fertilizers contain nitrogen, phosphorus, and potassium.

1. Which elements required for plant growth are not essential nutrients for humans?
2. Which elements required for human growth are not essential nutrients for plants?
3. Examine the label from a bottle of food supplement that provides 100% of a person's daily requirement of minerals. (See Figure 7.)
   a. Are all elements listed in Table 4 included among the ingredients?
   b. If not, which are missing?
4. a. Which plant nutrients are commonly added as fertilizer to increase soil productivity in developed nations?
   b. These nutrients can also serve as limiting reactants. If they are not available in a developing nation as added plant nutrients, how would this affect the nation's food production?

Figure 7 The label from a common food supplement.

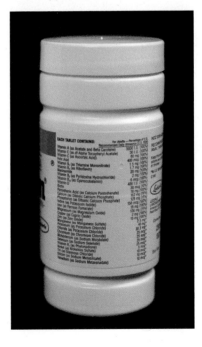

C.3   PROTEINS

Protein has been described as the primary material of all life. **Proteins** are the major structural components of living tissue. When you look at another person, everything you see is protein: skin, hair, eyeballs, nails. Inside the body, bones and cartilage, tendons, and ligaments all contain protein, as do birds' feathers and the fur, hooves, and horns of animals. In addition, most

The word "protein" comes from the Greek word proteios, *which means "of prime importance.*

	PROTEINS IN THE BODY	
Type	**Function**	**Examples**
Structural proteins		
Muscle	Contraction, movement	Myosin
Connective tissue	Support, protection	Collagen, keratin
Chromosomal proteins	Part of chromosome structure	Histones
Membranes	Control of influx and outflow, communication	Pore proteins, receptors
Transport proteins	Carriers of gases and other substances	Hemoglobin
Regulatory proteins		
Fluid balance	Maintenance of pH, water, and salt content of body fluids	Serum albumin
Enzymes	Control of metabolism	Proteases
Hormones	Regulation of body functions	Insulin
Protective proteins	Antibodies	Gamma globulin

Table 6

enzyme molecules that help control chemical reactions in the cell are proteins. Your body contains tens of thousands of different kinds of proteins. Table 6 lists just a few major roles of proteins in the human body.

Protein is constantly needed for new growth and for maintaining existing tissue. For example, red blood cells must be replaced every month. The cells that line the intestinal tract are replaced weekly. When we bathe we wash away dead skin cells.

Proteins are polymers built from small molecules called **amino acids.** Each amino acid contains carbon, hydrogen, oxygen, nitrogen; some also contain sulfur. Just as sugar molecules are building blocks for more complex carbohydrates, 20 different amino acids are the structural units of all proteins.

Proteins are composed of *very* long chains of amino acids; proteins have molecular weights from 5000 to several million. Just as the 26 letters of our alphabet combine in different ways to form hundreds of thousands of words, the 20 amino acids can combine in a virtually infinite number of ways to form different proteins.

All amino acids have similar structural features, as shown in Figure 8. Two functional groups, the amino group (— NH_2) and the carboxyl group (— COOH), are found in every amino acid molecule.

The combining of two amino acid molecules with loss of one water molecule, illustrated in Figure 9, is a typical condensation reaction. Like starch, nylon, and polyester (see page 204), proteins are condensation polymers.

Test your skill as a "molecular architect" in the following protein-building activity.

Building body protein.

Figure 8 Representative amino acids.

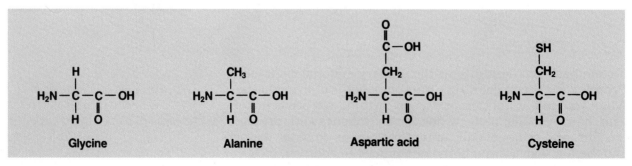

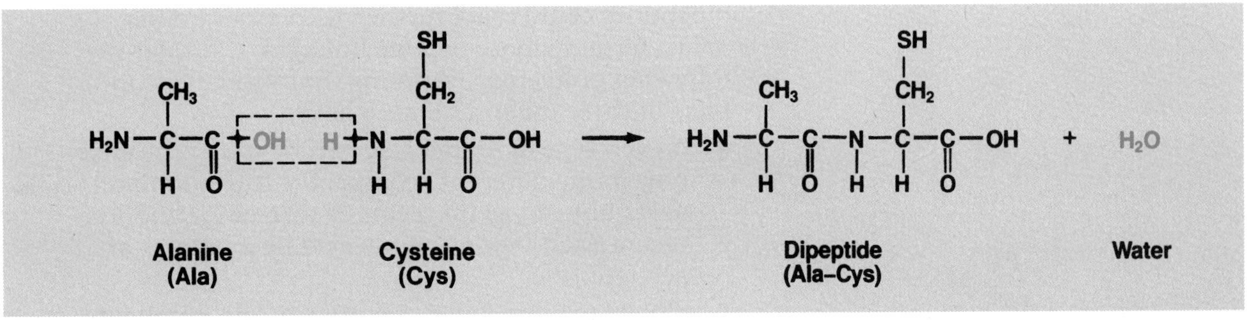

Alanine
(Ala)

Cysteine
(Cys)

Dipeptide
(Ala–Cys)

Water

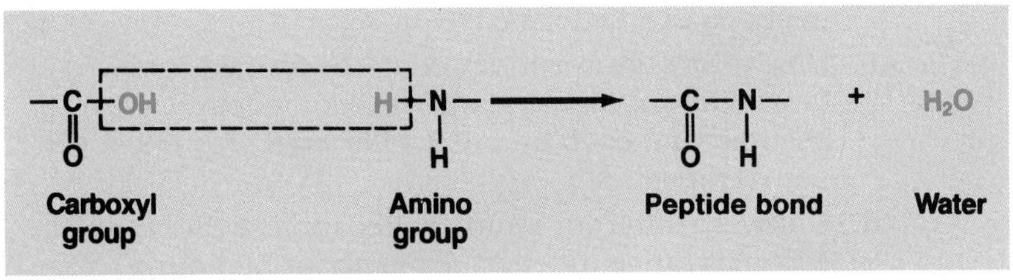

Carboxyl
group

Amino
group

Peptide bond

Water

Figure 9 Formation of a dipeptide from two amino acids. All proteins contain amino acids linked in this manner.

Figure 10 Formation of a peptide bond. Each amino acid can form peptide bonds with two other amino acids.

YOUR TURN

Molecular Structure of Proteins

1. a. Draw structures for glycine and alanine on your own paper (see Figure 8).
   b. Circle and identify the functional groups in each molecule.
   c. How do the two molecules differ?

2. Proteins are polymers of amino acids. Examine the sample equation in Figure 9 to see how a pair of amino acids link together. You will note that the amino acids link through the amine group on one amino acid and the carboxyl group on another. Each linkage is called a **peptide linkage,** or peptide bond, and is represented by

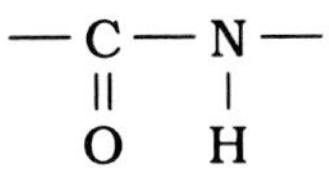

$$-\,\overset{\displaystyle}{\underset{\displaystyle O}{C}}\!-\!\overset{\displaystyle}{\underset{\displaystyle H}{N}}-$$

Peptide bond formation is shown in greater detail in Figure 10. Since each amino acid contains at least one amine group and one carboxyl group, it can form a peptide bond at either, or both, ends. With Figures 9 and 10 as models, complete the following:

   a. Using structural formulas, write the equation for the reaction between two glycine molecules. Circle the peptide bond in the dipeptide product.
   b. Using structural formulas, write equations for possible reactions between a glycine molecule and an alanine molecule. (*Hint:* Two dipeptide products are possible.)

3. Examine structural formulas of the two dipeptide products identified in Question 2. Note that each dipeptide still contains a reactive amino group and a reactive carboxyl group. That means that these

dipeptides could react further with other amino acids, forming more peptide linkages. Consider the following problems, assuming that you have supplies of three different amino acids:

a. If each type of amino acid can be used only once, how many different **tripeptides** (three amino acids linked together) can be formed? (*Hint:* Represent each type of amino acid by a letter—abc, acb, etc.)

b. If a given amino acid can appear any number of times in the tripeptide, how many different tripeptides can be formed?

c. How many tetrapeptides could be formed from four different amino acids? (For simplicity, assume that each amino acid is used only once per tetrapeptide.)

d. Given 20 different amino acids and the fact that proteins range in length from about 50 amino acid units to more than 10,000, would the theoretical number of distinct proteins be in the hundreds, thousands, or millions-plus?

e. How do these insights relate to the observed uniqueness of each living organism?

When foods containing protein reach your stomach and small intestine, peptide bonds between the amino acids are broken by enzymes known as **proteases.** The separate amino acids then travel through the intestinal walls to the bloodstream, to the liver, and then to the rest of the body. There they are building blocks for new proteins to meet the body's needs.

If you eat more protein than your body requires—or, alternatively, if your body needs to burn protein because carbohydrates are in short supply—amino acids react in the liver. There the nitrogen atoms are removed and converted into urea, which is excreted through the kidneys in urine. (This helps explain why a high-protein diet places an extra burden on one's liver and kidneys.) The remainder of the amino acid molecule is either converted to glucose and burned, or converted to storage fat.

The human body can synthesize 12 of the 20 amino acids. The other eight, called **essential amino acids,** must be obtained from protein in the diet. If an essential amino acid is in short supply in the diet, it can become a limiting reactant in building any protein containing that amino acid. When this happens, the only way the body can make that protein is by destroying one of its own proteins that contains the limiting amino acid.

Most animal proteins contain all eight essential amino acids in the needed quantities. Any protein that contains enough of all the essential amino acids is called a **complete protein.** Plant proteins and some animal proteins are incomplete; they do not contain adequate amounts of all eight essential amino acids.

Although no single plant protein can provide adequate amounts of all essential amino acids, certain combinations of plant proteins can. Such combinations of foods, which are said to contain **complementary proteins** (see Table 7), form a part of many diets in various parts of the world.

The essential amino acids

Isoleucine	*Phenylalanine*
Leucine	*Threonine*
Lysine	*Tryptophan*
Methionine	*Valine*
Histidine (for infants)	

Table 7   **COMPLEMENTARY PROTEINS**

Foods	Country
Corn tortillas and dried beans	Mexico
Rice and black-eyed peas	Southern United States
Peanut butter and bread	United States
Rice and bean curd	China and Japan
Rice and lentils	India
Wheat pasta and cheese	Italy

Because your body cannot store protein, a balanced protein diet is required daily. The recommended daily amount of protein is 15% of total daily Calories. Too much protein is as harmful as too little because excess protein causes stress on the liver and kidneys, organs that metabolize protein. Too much protein also increases the excretion of calcium ions (Ca^{2+}) which are important in nerve transmission and in bone and teeth structures. A protein-heavy diet can even cause dehydration, a problem particularly important to athletes.

Proteins are further discussed in the Risk unit.

Table 8   **RDAs FOR PROTEIN**

Age (yr) or Condition	Median Weight (lb)	Median Height (in)	RDA (g)
Infants			
0–0.5	13	24	13
0.5–1	20	28	14
Children			
1–3	29	35	16
4–6	44	44	24
7–10	62	52	28
Males			
11–14	99	62	45
15–18	145	69	59
19–24	160	70	58
25–50	174	70	63
51+	170	68	63
Females			
11–14	101	62	46
15–18	120	64	44
19–24	128	65	46
25–50	138	64	50
51+	143	63	50
Pregnant			60
Nursing			
First 6 mo.			65
Second 6 mo.			62

Specified RDAs are based on actual median heights and weights for U.S. population of designated age and sex, as in Table 8. The use of these figures does not imply that the height-to-weight ratios are ideal.

Source: Food and Nutrition Board, National Academy of Sciences—National Research Council, Recommended Dietary Allowances. Revised 1989.

How much protein is really needed? The Food and Nutrition Board of the National Academy of Sciences has established recommended dietary allowances (RDAs) for all required nutrients, including protein. (See Table 8.) Use information from the table for the following *Your Turn.*

Protein in the Diet

1. According to Table 8 (page 245), how many grams of protein should a 12-year-old boy of median weight and height consume each day?

2. How many grams of protein should a person of your age and gender eat each day, according to these RDA figures? (Assume median weight and height.)

3. Consider a 37-year-old female with 125-pound weight and median height.

   a. Would this individual's protein RDA be higher or lower than 50 g?

   b. Why?

4. Table 8 suggests that for each pound of body weight infants actually require more protein than adults. Why should RDA protein values per pound of body weight be highest for infants, and become progressively lower as a person ages?

5. a. What food do babies consume that provides most of their relatively high protein needs?

   b. Can you find any evidence in Table 8 to support your answer?

6. The average infant mortality rate in developing nations is higher than in developed nations and, as we have seen, is used as one indicator of a country's ability to feed its people.

   a. How do the RDA values for protein relate to this?

   b. Which groups are most likely to suffer if a nation has inadequate protein supplies? Why?

7. Some manufacturers of infant formula concentrates have been criticized for marketing their products in developing countries as substitutes for mother's milk. Why might these infant formula concentrates be acceptable substitutes in developed nations, but not in developing ones?

A 0–0.5 year infant requires 1.0 g protein for each pound of body weight (13 g protein/13 lbs weight = 1.0 g/lb). By contrast, a 30-year-old female requires only 0.36 g protein per pound (50 g/138 lb = 0.36 g/lb).

Mother's milk has been called a nearly perfect food. It contains carbohydrate, fat, and protein; contains adequate amounts of all essential amino acids; and is rich in vitamins. It is also a valuable source of calcium.

Cow's milk, alone or in the form of numerous dairy products, is also a common food for people of all ages. In the following laboratory activity you will analyze nonfat milk to find how much protein, carbohydrate, and energy value it actually contains.

C.4   LABORATORY ACTIVITY: MILK ANALYSIS

Getting Ready

In this laboratory activity, you will determine the percent of protein, carbohydrate, and water in nonfat milk. Once the composition of milk has been determined, you will calculate its food energy value. You will then compare your laboratory results with accepted values for nonfat milk.

The milk analysis will be carried out during two class sessions. You will first separate protein from nonfat milk by precipitating the protein and filtering off the solid. Then the quantity of water in nonfat milk will be found by evaporating the water and weighing the remaining milk residue. You will calculate the percent carbohydrate by difference—that is, once you know the percent of protein and water, you will assume the rest is carbohydrate.

Procedure, Day 1

Part 1: Removal of Milk Protein

1. Carefully weigh an empty 50-mL beaker. Record the mass.
2. Add 15 mL of nonfat milk to the beaker. Weigh the beaker and milk. Record the mass.
3. Using the results of Steps 1 and 2, calculate the mass of your milk sample.
4. Add 30 drops of concentrated acetic acid to the beaker containing the nonfat milk. (*Caution:* Keep your nose and face away from the concentrated acetic acid; wash skin immediately if any spills occur.) Swirl briefly, then allow the beaker to sit for five minutes. Observe the precipitate forming in the milk. Acid coagulates milk protein, forming the curd you are observing.
5. Weigh one fresh circle of filter paper. Record its mass. Support a short-stemmed funnel on a ring stand above a clean 150-mL beaker. Fold the filter paper and place it in the funnel.
6. Pour the coagulated milk into the funnel. Then add 2 mL of water to the empty beaker. With a spatula, attempt to remove as much of the white material clinging to the beaker walls as possible. Pour these loosened particles into the funnel. Repeat this beaker-cleaning step with a second 2-mL water sample.
7. The filtration will proceed slowly. Place your name on a paper towel next to your ring stand. In several hours, your teacher will remove the filter paper (with protein) from the funnel so the precipitate can air-dry overnight. The filtrate will also be saved for you to test tomorrow.
8. Wash your hands thoroughly before leaving the laboratory.

Removing protein from laboratory equipment.

Procedure, Day 2

Part 2: Determining Percent Milk Protein, Water, and Carbohydrate

Students at each laboratory table should divide into two groups. Group 1 will test and determine the percent protein in the milk. Group 2 will find the percent water in the milk. Each group's results will be shared with the other to provide complete information on the milk analysis. The total mass of nonfat milk is essentially made up of three parts—protein, water, and carbohydrate.

The mass of all mineral matter in milk is only about 1% of the total, and can be ignored.

Group 1: Determining and testing milk protein

1. Weigh the filtered, dried protein and filter paper from yesterday's laboratory activity. Record the total mass.

2. Calculate the mass of protein collected.

3. Finally, calculate the percent protein in your milk sample.

To verify that you actually extracted protein from your milk sample, complete these additional steps:

4. Label four test tubes 1, 2, 3, and 4. Add 1 mL of milk filtrate (collected in yesterday's filtration) to Tubes 1 and 2. Add two chips of dried milk protein to Tube 3 and to Tube 4.

5. Add 2 mL of Molisch reagent to Tubes 1 and 3. Gently shake to mix.

6. Holding Tube 1 on a 45-degree angle with a test tube holder, slowly add—without stirring or shaking—about 15 drops of concentrated sulfuric acid, allowing the drops to run down the inside surface of the tube. Do not point the open end of the tube toward yourself or anyone else. (*Caution:* Concentrated sulfuric acid is highly corrosive to skin, clothing, books, and other materials. Avoid spilling. Immediately flood skin with tap water if any acid is touched.) Allow the sulfuric acid to form an undisturbed layer on the bottom of the tube.

7. Repeat Step 6, using Tube 3.

8. Observe and record any differences between Tubes 1 and 3. Molisch reagent, in the presence of carbohydrate and concentrated sulfuric acid, will produce a purple layer near the bottom of the test tube. Based on your observations, which tube contains a high level of carbohydrate?

9. Add 5 mL of Biuret reagent to Tubes 2 and 4. If the solution changes to a purple or purplish blue color, protein is present. If no color develops at room temperature, place the two tubes in a hot-water bath, assembled from a 250-mL beaker containing 150 mL water, supported on a ring stand. Heat the water bath for two minutes, but do not allow the water to boil vigorously. Which tube gives a positive protein test?

10. Wash your hands thoroughly.

Share your calculated results with Group 2, and obtain Group 2's calculated results. Then move on to Part 3.

Group 2: Determining percent of water in milk.

1. Determine the combined mass of an empty evaporating dish and stirring rod. Record their combined mass.

2. Add 5 mL of fresh nonfat milk to the evaporating dish.

3. Weigh the evaporating dish, milk, and stirring rod together. Record their combined mass.

4. Calculate the mass of milk in the evaporating dish.

5. Set the evaporating dish and milk on top of a beaker half-full of water. (A 250-mL beaker probably will support the dish securely. Place a boiling chip in the beaker.)

6. Place the beaker-evaporating dish assembly on the wire gauze on a ring stand. Begin heating the water in the beaker to slowly evaporate the liquid from the dish. As a thin "skin" develops on the milk surface, break it with the stirring rod. Prevent the milk from burning by stirring it gently

and continuously. Do not allow any milk to transfer from the evaporating dish. (Do not set the stirring rod down on the laboratory bench top, for example.)

7. As the milk loses its moisture, it may resemble liquid paste. When there is no further change in consistency, stop heating. Allow the evaporating dish to cool. Wipe condensed water from the outside of the dish.

8. Determine the combined mass of the evaporating dish, solid milk residue, and stirring rod. Record this value.

9. Calculate the mass of milk solids that are left in the evaporating dish.

10. Now calculate the mass of water in your original 5-mL milk sample.

11. Finally, calculate the percent water in your milk sample.

12. Wash your hands thoroughly.

Use Group 1's value for the percent protein in the milk sample. Calculate the percent carbohydrate in the milk, and move on to Part 3 below.

Part 3: Calculating the Energy Value of a Serving of Nonfat Milk

Proteins and carbohydrates deliver the food energy found in nonfat milk. You now have laboratory values for the percents of protein and carbohydrate in a nonfat milk sample. From these data, calculate the food energy delivered by a typical serving of this milk.

Let's assume we have a one-cup serving of nonfat milk with a mass of 244 g. First, calculate the mass of each major nutrient category in this milk sample, then convert these masses to the quantity of food energy each contains. Organize your results in a chart similar to this one:

In whole milk, fat also contributes to the energy total. The quantity of food energy stored in these three major nutritional categories is as follows:

- *Fat: 9 Cal/g (9000 cal/g)*
- *Protein: 4 Cal/g (4000 cal/g)*
- *Carbohydrate: 4 Cal/g (4000 cal/g)*

Data Table

Mass of Milk	×	% Expressed as Decimal Fraction	=	Mass of Nutrient	Calories per Gram Nutrient	Calories from Each Major Nutrient
244 g	×	___ Protein	=	___ g Protein	4 Cal/g	___ Cal
244 g	×	___ Carbohydrate	=	___ g Carbohydrate	4 Cal/g	___ Cal
Total Calories per cup (244 g) of nonfat milk						___ Cal

Questions

1. Compare your results with the values given below for fresh nonfat milk:

Data Table

	Your Laboratory Values	Average Values for Nonfat Milk
Percent protein	_____ %	3.3%
Percent carbohydrate	_____ %	4.9%
Percent water	_____ %	91%
Total Calories/cup	_____ %	80 Cal

Milk contains mainly protein, fat, carbohydrates, and water.

2. If you add all the "average values" given in the Question 1 data table, you will find they do not total 100%. Can you think of any reasons why? (Not fair saying that it is due to poor laboratory results!)

3. Now add up your laboratory values shown in the Question 1 data table. They *should* total 100%. Why?

4. Young children sometimes discover at the breakfast table that they can make milk curdle if they pour orange juice into it. What is the composition of those milk curds? (*Hint:* Orange juice is rich in citric acid and vitamin C, ascorbic acid.)

5. A student analyzed the composition of whole milk, and found that one cup (244 g) contained 8.0 g fat, 8.0 g protein, and 11.0 g carbohydrate.

    a. How many Calories of food energy are contained in this one-cup sample?

    b. Compare your calculated Calories for whole milk with the comparable value for nonfat milk. What percent of total Calories are eliminated from whole milk when all the fat is removed?

PART C: SUMMARY QUESTIONS

1. Explain how the notion of a limiting reactant applies to
    a. human nutrition.
    b. soil nutrients in agriculture.

2. Valine is one of the essential amino acids.
    a. What does the word "essential" mean in reference to valine?
    b. How does the limiting reactant concept apply to essential amino acids?

3. Ammonia (NH_3) can be added directly to soil as a fertilizer or converted to other fertilizers. The following equation shows how ammonia can be converted to the fertilizer ammonium nitrate, NH_4NO_3.

$$NH_3(g) + HNO_3(l) \rightarrow NH_4NO_3(s)$$

If 34 g of NH_3 reacts with 63 g of nitric acid (HNO_3):

    a. which is the limiting reactant—NH_3 or HNO_3?
    b. what is the maximum mass of NH_4NO_3 that can be made?
    c. which reactant will be left over when the reaction stops?
    d. how much of that reactant will be left?

4. Proteins form part of all structures in a human body, yet a diet of protein alone would be unwise. Why?

5. Diagram the condensation reaction of two alanine molecules. Identify the functional groups in the reactants and in the product.

6. a. Calculate the total grams of protein a 150-pound, 17-year-old female should consume daily (refer to Table 8, page 245).
    b. Use the Appendix (see page 523) to determine how many ounces of chicken would be needed to supply this quantity of protein.
    c. How many cups of whole milk would supply this same amount?

7. a. What is the difference between a complete protein and an incomplete protein?
    b. Discuss their importance in planning a proper diet.

8. Copy the following structures on your own paper.
    a. Circle and identify the functional groups in each molecule.
    b. Which structure represents an amino acid?

(1) $CH_3 - CH_2 - C = O$
            $|$
            OH

(2) $HO - \overset{\displaystyle}{\underset{\displaystyle O}{C}} - \overset{\displaystyle H}{\underset{\displaystyle NH_2}{C}} - CH_3$

(3) $H_2N - CH_2 - C = O$
                    $|$
                    H

D

OTHER SUBSTANCES IN FOODS

Proteins, carbohydrates, and fats form the major building-block and fuel molecules of life. Other substances—vitamins and minerals—are just as important, even though your body requires them only in tiny amounts. Small but essential quantities of vitamins and minerals are supplied by the foods we eat, or by dietary supplements. What do they do in the body that is so important?

D.1 VITAMINS

Vitamins perform very specialized tasks. For example, vitamin D moves calcium ions from your intestines into the bloodstream. Without vitamin D, much of the calcium you ingest would be lost.

By definition, **vitamins** are biomolecules necessary in small amounts for growth, reproduction, health, and life. Despite their importance, the total quantity of all vitamins required by a human is about 0.2 g daily.

Although the term "vitamin" was coined in the early 20th century, earlier evidence had suggested that chemical substances other than fats, proteins, and carbohydrates are required by the body. For example, scurvy, with symptoms of swollen joints, bleeding gums, and tender skin, was once common among sailors. As early as the 1500s, scurvy was considered a symptom of food deficiency. After the mid-1700s, seafarers learned to carry citrus fruits on long voyages to prevent scurvy. We now know that the disorder is caused by lack of vitamin C. Other health problems are also caused by vitamin deficiencies.

About a dozen different vitamins have been identified. Their existence has been determined and proved by synthesizing them in the laboratory and then testing them in animal diets. Table 9 (page 252) illustrates how vitamins support human life.

Vitamins can be classified as fat-soluble or water-soluble (see Table 9). Your body absorbs fat-soluble vitamins into the blood from the intestine with the assistance of fats in the food you eat. These vitamins can be stored in body fat, and so it is not necessary to eat them daily. In fact, because they do accumulate within the body, they can become toxic if taken in large quantities.

As water-soluble vitamins are not stored in the body, they must be a part of your daily diet. Cooking can wash away or destroy some of them, such as the B vitamins and vitamin C.

Recall that "like dissolves like."

Water-soluble B vitamins in body cells help release energy from food. All are cofactors, small non-protein molecules that assist enzymes in performing their functions.

Table 9 — VITAMINS

Vitamin (Name)	Main Sources	Deficiency Condition
Water-soluble		
B₁ (Thiamine)	Liver, milk, pasta, bread, wheat germ, lima beans, nuts	Beriberi: nausea, severe exhaustion, paralysis
B₂ (Riboflavin)	Red meat, milk, eggs, pasta, bread, beans, dark green vegetables, peas, mushrooms	Severe skin problems
Niacin	Red meat, poultry, enriched or whole grains, beans, peas	Pellagra: weak muscles, no appetite, diarrhea, skin blotches
B₆ (Pyridoxine)	Muscle meats, liver, poultry, fish, whole grains	Depression, nausea, vomiting
B₁₂ (Cobalamin)	Red meat, liver, kidneys, fish, eggs, milk	Pernicious anemia, exhaustion
Folic acid	Kidneys, liver, leafy green vegetables, wheat germ, peas, beans	Anemia
Pantothenic acid	Plants, animals	Anemia
Biotin	Kidneys, liver, egg yolk, yeast, nuts	Dermatitis
C (Ascorbic acid)	Citrus fruits, melon, tomatoes, green pepper, strawberries	Scurvy: tender skin, weak, bleeding gums, swollen joints
Fat-soluble		
A (Retinol)	Liver, eggs, butter, cheese, dark green and deep orange vegetables	Inflamed eye membranes, night blindness, scaling of skin, faulty teeth and bones
D (Calciferol)	Fish-liver oils, fortified milk	Rickets: soft bones
E (Tocopherol)	Liver, wheat germ, whole-grain cereals, margarine, vegetable oil, leafy green vegetables	Breakage of red blood cells in premature infants, oxidation of membranes
K (Menaquinone)	Liver, cabbage, potatoes, peas, leafy green vegetables	Hemorrhage in newborns; anemia

How much is "enough" of each vitamin? It depends on your age and gender. Recommended Dietary Allowances (RDAs) for vitamins are summarized in Table 10.

μg = microgram = 10^{-6} g.

RE = retinol equivalents; 1 retinol equivalent = 1 μg of retinol

Table 10 — RDAs FOR SELECTED VITAMINS

Sex and Age	A (μg RE)	D (μg)	C (mg)	B₁ (mg)	B₂ (mg)	Niacin (mg)	B₁₂ (μg)	K (μg)
Males								
11–14	1000	10	50	1.3	1.5	17	2.0	45
15–18	1000	10	60	1.5	1.8	20	2.0	65
19–24	1000	10	60	1.5	1.7	19	2.0	70
25–50	1000	10	60	1.5	1.7	19	2.0	80
51+	1000	10	60	1.2	1.4	15	2.0	80
Females								
11–14	800	10	50	1.1	1.3	15	2.0	45
15–18	800	10	60	1.1	1.3	15	2.0	55
19–24	800	10	60	1.1	1.3	15	2.0	60
25–50	800	5	60	1.1	1.3	15	2.0	65
51+	800	5	60	1.0	1.2	13	2.0	65

Source: Food and Nutrition Board, National Academy of Sciences—National Research Council, Recommended Dietary Allowances, Revised 1989

Vitamins in the Diet

1. Carefully-planned vegetarian diets are nutritionally balanced. However, two vitamins pose a problem for people who are vegans (those who do not consume any animal products including eggs or milk).

   a. Use Table 9 to identify these vitamins and briefly describe the effect of their absence in the diet.

   b. How might vegans avoid this problem?

2. Complete the following data table, using data from Tables 10 and 11.

Data Table

Vegetable (one-cup serving)	Your RDA		No. Servings to Supply your RDA	
	B₁	C	B₁	C
Green peas	?	?	?	?
Broccoli	?	?	?	?

Table 11 VITAMINS B₁ AND C IN COMMON VEGETABLES

Vegetable (one-cup serving)	Vitamin (in mg)	
	B₁ (thiamine)	C (ascorbic acid)
Green peas	0.387	58.4
Lima beans	0.238	17
Broccoli	0.058	82
Potatoes	0.15	30

For comparison, one cup of orange juice contains 0.223 mg of vitamin B₁ and 124 mg of vitamin C.

   a. Would any of your table entries change if you were a member of the opposite sex? If so, which one(s)?

   b. Based on your completed table, why do you think variety in diet is essential?

   c. Why might malnutrition (because of vitamin deficiencies) be a problem even when people receive adequate supplies of food Calories?

3. Some people believe that to promote vitality and increase resistance to diseases, much larger amounts (megadoses) of certain vitamins should be taken. Of the two broad classes of vitamins, which is more likely to pose a health problem if consumed in large doses? Why?

4. Nutritionists recommend eating fresh fruit rather than canned fruit, and raw or steamed vegetables instead of canned or boiled vegetables.

   a. Which class of vitamins are they concerned about?

   b. Why is their advice sound?

To eat a nutritionally-balanced diet, one thing you must know is which foods deliver adequate amounts of the vitamins you need. Realizing that nutritionists may not yet know all the nutrients necessary for the best health, it is a good idea to build a diet around a *variety* of foods.

In the following laboratory activity you will find out how the vitamin content of common foods, in this case vitamin C, can be determined.

D.2 LABORATORY ACTIVITY: VITAMIN C

Getting Ready

Vitamin C, also known as ascorbic acid, is a water-soluble vitamin. It is among the least stable vitamins, meaning that it reacts readily with oxygen and so its potency can be lost through exposure to light and heat. In this laboratory activity you will investigate how much vitamin C is in a variety of popular beverages, including fruit juices, milk, and soft drinks.

This analysis for vitamin C is based on the chemical properties of ascorbic acid and iodine. Iodine (I_2) solution is capable of oxidizing ascorbic acid, forming the colorless products dehydroascorbic acid, hydrogen ions (H^+), and iodide ions (I^-):

$$I_2(aq) + C_6H_8O_6(aq) \rightarrow C_6H_6O_6(aq) + 2\,H^+(aq) + 2\,I^-(aq)$$

| Iodine | Ascorbic acid (vitamin C) | Dehydroascorbic acid | Hydrogen ion | Iodide ion |

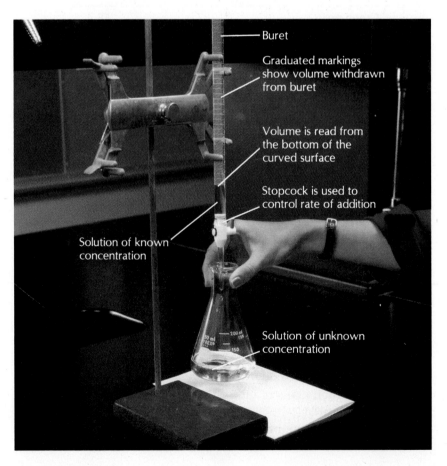

Figure 11 Titration apparatus.

You will perform a **titration,** a common procedure used for finding the concentrations or amounts of substances in solutions. You will add a known amount of one reactant slowly from a buret to another reactant until just enough for complete reaction has been added. You will recognize the complete reaction by a color change or other highly-visible change at the **endpoint** of the reaction. Knowing the reaction involved, you can calculate the unknown amount of the second reactant from the known amount of the first reactant.

The titration equipment is illustrated in Figure 11. Complete the procedure as demonstrated by your teacher.

In this analysis, the endpoint is signaled by the reaction of iodine with starch suspension, producing a blue-black product. Starch is added to the beverage to be tested, then an iodine solution is slowly added from the buret. As long as ascorbic acid is present, the iodine is quickly converted to iodide ion, and no blue-black iodine-starch product is observed.

However, when all the available ascorbic acid has been oxidized, the next drop of added iodine solution reacts with starch and you will see the blue-black color. The endpoint in the titration, then, is the *first sign of permanent blue-black color* in the beverage-containing flask.

The vitamin C in these bottles is the same compound found in oranges.

You will first complete a titration with a known vitamin C solution, which will allow you to find a useful conversion factor for finding the mass of ascorbic acid that reacts with each milliliter (mL) of iodine solution. You can then calculate the mass of vitamin C present in a 25-mL sample of each beverage.

Prepare a data table like the one below in your laboratory notebook.

Data Table

Beverage	mL Iodine Solution Used (from Part 2)	×	Conversion Factor (from Part 1)	=	mg Vitamin C per 25 mL Beverage	Rank (Highest to Lowest in Vitamin C)
1.		×		=		
2.		×		=		
3.		×		=		
4.		×		=		
5.		×		=		

Procedure

Part 1. Determining Conversion Factor

1. Measure 25 mL of vitamin C (ascorbic acid) solution into a 125-mL Erlenmeyer flask.
2. Add 10 drops of 1% starch suspension.
3. Fill a clean buret with iodine solution and record the starting volume.
4. Slowly add iodine solution to the flask as you gently swirl it. Continue until the endpoint is reached (when the first sign of blue color remains after at least 20 seconds of swirling). A piece of white paper placed under the flask will help you recognize the color.

5. Record the final buret volume. Calculate the volume of iodine solution used in the titration.

6. Calculate the number of milligrams of vitamin C that corresponds to 1 mL of iodine solution. This can be found by dividing 25 mg of vitamin C by the volume (in milliliters) of iodine solution used in the titration.

7. Record your calculated value in the "Conversion factor" column of your data table. (The factor has the units mg vitamin C per mL I_2 solution.)

Part 2. Analyzing Beverages for Vitamin C

Follow the procedure below for each beverage assigned for analysis by your teacher.

1. Measure 25 mL of beverage into a 125-mL Erlenmeyer flask.

2. Follow Steps 2 through 5 in Part 1. Note that the color of a beverage may affect the endpoint color. For example, red beverage + blue starch-iodine color → purple endpoint.

3. Write the calculated volume of iodine solution used in the titration in your data table. Also, enter the conversion factor value from Part 1.

4. Use the formula to find the mass (mg) of vitamin C in the sample.

5. Finally, rank by number (1–5) the five beverages, from highest vitamin C level (No. 1) to lowest vitamin C level (No. 5).

6. Wash your hands thoroughly before leaving the laboratory.

Questions

1. Among the beverages tested, were any vitamin C levels
   a. unexpectedly low, in your opinion? If so, explain.
   b. unexpectedly high, in your opinion? If so, explain.

2. What other common foods contain a high level of vitamin C?

Now we are ready to consider the trace nutrients known as minerals. What are they, and what do they do in the body?

D.3 MINERALS: PART OF OUR DIET

Minerals are important life-supporting materials in our diet. Some are quite common and others are likely to be found only on laboratory supply shelves. (Never taste *any* materials found in the chemistry laboratory.)

Some minerals become part of the body's structural molecules. Others help enzymes do their jobs. Still others help in maintaining the health of heart, bones, and teeth. The thyroid gland, for example, requires a miniscule quantity of iodine (only millionths of a gram) to produce the hormone thyroxine. The rapidly-growing field of bioinorganic chemistry explores how minerals function within living systems.

Of the more than 100 known elements, only 22 are believed essential to human life. Essential minerals are divided into two categories for convenience: **macrominerals**, or major minerals, and **trace minerals**. As the name suggests, your body contains rather large quantities, at least five grams, of each macromineral. Carbon, hydrogen, nitrogen, and oxygen are so widely present both in living systems and in the environment that they are not included in lists of essential minerals.

Table 12   **MINERALS**

Mineral	Source	Deficiency Condition
Macrominerals		
Calcium (Ca)	Canned fish, milk, dairy products	Rickets in children; osteomalacia and osteoporosis in adults
Chlorine (Cl)	Meats, salt-processed foods, table salt	—
Magnesium (Mg)	Seafoods, cereal grains, nuts, dark green vegetables, cocoa	Heart failure due to spasms
Phosphorus (P)	Animal proteins	—
Potassium (K)	Orange juice, bananas, dried fruits, potatoes	Poor nerve function; irregular heartbeat; sudden death during fasting
Sodium (Na)	Meats, salt-processed foods, table salt	Headache, weakness, thirst, poor memory, appetite loss
Sulfur (S)	Proteins	—
Trace minerals		
Chromium (Cr)	Liver, animal and plant tissue	Loss of insulin efficiency with age
Cobalt (Co)	Liver, animal proteins	Anemia
Copper (Cu)	Liver, kidney, egg yolk, whole grains	—
Fluorine (F)	Seafoods, fluoridated drinking water	Dental decay
Iodine (I)	Seafoods, iodized salts	Goiter
Iron (Fe)	Liver, meats, green leafy vegetables, whole grains	Anemia; tiredness and apathy
Manganese (Mn)	Liver, kidney, wheat germ, legumes, nuts, tea	Weight loss, dermatitis
Molybdenum (Mo)	Liver, kidney, whole grains, legumes, leafy vegetables	—
Nickel (Ni)	Seafoods, grains, seeds, beans, vegetables	Cirrhosis of liver, kidney failure, stress
Selenium (Se)	Liver, organ meats, grains, vegetables	Kashan disease (a heart disease found in China)
Zinc (Zn)	Liver, shellfish, meats, wheat germ, legumes	Anemia, stunted growth

Trace minerals are present in relatively small quantities, less than five grams in an average adult; however, they are as important as macrominerals are. Any essential mineral can become a limiting factor (limiting reactant), if it is not present in sufficient quantity.

The minerals, their sources, functions, and deficiency conditions are listed in Table 12. Several other minerals are known to be needed by other animals. These include, but are not limited to, arsenic (As), cadmium (Cd), and tin (Sn). These and perhaps other trace minerals may also be essential to human life.

The suggestion that arsenic—a widely-known poison— might be an essential mineral probably surprises you. In fact, it is not unusual for substances to be beneficial in low doses but toxic in higher doses.

In 1989, RDAs were reissued for various essential minerals. Table 13 summarizes these values for several macrominerals and trace elements. Use values given in Table 13 to answer the following questions.

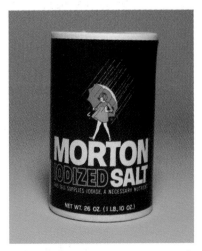

Iodized salt is an important source of the trace mineral iodine.

Table 13　　　　　　　　**RDAs FOR SELECTED MINERALS**

Sex and Age	Calcium (mg)	Phosphorus (mg)	Magnesium (mg)	Iron (mg)	Zinc (mg)	Iodine (μg)
Males						
11–14	1200	1200	270	12	15	150
15–18	1200	1200	400	12	15	150
19–24	1200	1200	350	10	15	150
25+	800	800	350	10	15	150
Females						
11–14	1200	1200	280	15	12	150
15–18	1200	1200	300	15	12	150
19–24	1200	1200	280	15	12	150
25–50	800	800	280	15	12	150
51+	800	800	280	10	12	150

Source: Food and Nutrition Board, National Academy of Sciences—National Research Council, Recommended Dietary Allowances. Revised 1989.

YOUR TURN

Minerals in the Diet

1. A slice of whole-wheat bread contains 0.8 mg iron. How many slices of whole-wheat bread would you need to eat to meet your daily iron allowance?

2. One cup of whole milk contains 288 mg calcium. How much milk would you have to drink each day to meet your daily allowance for this mineral?

3. One medium pancake contains about 27 mg calcium and 0.4 mg iron.
   a. Does a pancake provide a greater percent of your RDA for calcium or for iron?
   b. How did you decide?

4. a. How many grams of calcium or phosphorus do you need each year?
   b. Why is this figure so much higher than the RDAs for other essential minerals listed? (*Hint:* Consider their uses.)
   c. List several good sources for each of these two minerals.
   d. Do you think these sources would be readily available in developing countries?
   e. If not, predict the health consequences of their deficiency.
   f. Would any particular age group or sex be especially affected?

5. Most grocery-store table salt has a small amount of potassium iodide (KI) added to the main ingredient, sodium chloride (NaCl).
   a. Why do you think KI is added to the table salt?
   b. If you follow the advice of many heart specialists and do not add salt to your food, what other kinds of food could you use as sources of iodine?

"Iodized salt" refers to these products.

How is the mineral content of a particular food determined? We will explore one method in the following laboratory activity.

D.4 LABORATORY ACTIVITY: IRON IN FOODS

Getting Ready

In this laboratory activity, you will investigate the relative levels of iron found in foods such as broccoli, spinach, and raisins.

Iron in foods is in the form of iron(II) or iron(III) ions. Iron(II) is more readily absorbed from the intestine than is iron(III). Thus, supplements for treating iron-deficiency anemia are almost always iron(II) compounds. The most common ingredient is iron(II) sulfate, $FeSO_4$.

This laboratory activity is based on a very sensitive test for the presence of iron ions in solution. In this procedure, all iron in the sample is converted to iron(III) ions. The colorless thiocyanate ion, SCN^-, reacts with iron(III) to form an intensely red ion:

These ions are sometimes called ferrous (Fe^{2+}) and ferric (Fe^{3+}) ions.

$$Fe^{3+}(aq) \ + \ SCN^-(aq) \ \rightarrow \ Fe(SCN)^{2+}(aq)$$

| Iron(III) ion | Thiocyanate ion | Iron(III) thiocyanate ion (red color) |

The intense red color of the iron (III) thiocyanate ion is directly related to the concentration of iron(III) originally present in the solution. This test is so sensitive that iron concentrations so small they must be expressed as parts per million (ppm) produce a noticeable reddish color! Color standards with known concentrations of iron(III) will be available in the laboratory. You will estimate iron(III) concentrations by comparing the colors of test solutions with the color standards.

To remove the organic portions of foods, which would interfere with the tests, the samples will be heated to a high temperature. The organic compounds burn and are driven off as water vapor and carbon dioxide gas. Minerals present (such as iron) remain in the burned ash and are dissolved by an acid solution.

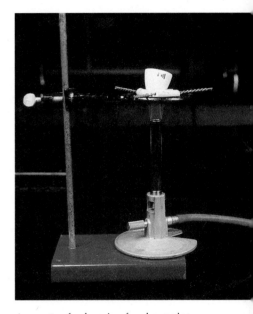

Apparatus for burning food sample.

Procedure

1. Record the names of the two food samples you have been assigned. Weigh a 2.5-g sample of each food into a separate porcelain crucible.
2. Place one food-containing crucible on a clay triangle supported by a ring stand. Heat the uncovered crucible with a hot burner flame.
3. Continue heating until the food sample has turned to ash (preferably grayish white). Do not allow the ash to be blown from the crucible.
4. Remove the burner and allow the crucible to remain on the clay triangle while it cools.
5. Begin heating the other food-containing crucible on a second clay triangle-ring stand set up. Continue heating until the sample has turned to ash.
6. Remove the burner and allow the second sample and crucible to cool on the clay triangle.
7. When the first sample has cooled, transfer the entire ash residue to a 50-mL (or larger) beaker. Add 10 mL of 2 M hydrochloric acid, HCl, to the beaker and stir vigorously for one minute. Then add 5 mL of distilled water.

The "2 M" (pronounced "two molar") HCl solution contains two moles of HCl in each liter of the solution. Molar concentration— also called molarity—is a convenient way to express the composition of solutions. Be careful not to splash the acid solution on yourself.

8. Prepare a filtration apparatus, including a ring stand, funnel support, and funnel. Place a piece of filter paper in the funnel and position a test tube under the funnel to collect the filtrate.

9. Pour the mixture from the beaker into the filtration apparatus and collect 5 mL of the filtrate in a test tube. Discard the residue on the filter paper, as well as the remaining solution.

"0.1 M potassium thiocyanate" means that each liter of this solution contains 0.1 mol of KSCN solute. A 5-mL sample of this solution thus contains 0.0005 mol of KSCN, or 5/1000 as much.

10. Add 5 mL of 0.1 M potassium thiocyanate solution, KSCN, to the test tube containing the filtrate. Seal with the stopper. Gently invert the tube once to mix the solution.

11. Compare the resulting red color to the color standards. It might be helpful to hold white paper behind the tubes while you make the comparison.

12. Record the approximate iron concentration present in your sample, based on your comparisons with the color standards.

13. Repeat Steps 7 through 12 with your other food sample.

14. Obtain iron results from other laboratory teams. Record the food product names and estimated iron levels in the resulting solutions.

If a light table is available, try looking down into the tubes while holding them over the light, which will intensify the color.

15. Wash your hands thoroughly before leaving the laboratory.

Questions

1. The color standards allowed you to estimate the percent of iron in the solutions prepared from your food samples. Do these percentages also apply to the original 2.5-g food samples? Why?

2. Name the foods that are (a) the best and (b) the poorest sources of iron among the food samples you tested.

3. What elements besides iron might be found in the ash?

D.5 FOOD ADDITIVES

Small amounts of vitamins and minerals occur naturally in food. Some foods, especially processed foods (e.g., packaged cookies or frozen entrees) also contain small amounts of **food additives**— substances added during processing to increase the nutritive value, storage life, visual appeal, or ease of production of foods.

A typical food label might give the following information:

Can you guess the identity of the food product with this label?

> Sugar, bleached flour (enriched with niacin, iron, thiamine, and riboflavin), semisweet chocolate, animal and/or vegetable shortening, dextrose, wheat starch, monocalcium phosphate, baking soda, egg white, modified corn starch, salt, nonfat milk, cellulose gum, soy lecithin, xanthan gum, mono- and diglycerides, BHA, BHT.

Quite a collection of ingredients! You probably recognize the major ingredients such as sugar, flour, shortening, and baking soda, and some additives such as vitamins (thiamine, riboflavin) and minerals (iron and monocalcium phosphate). But you probably do not recognize xanthan gum (an emulsifier) or BHT (butylated hydroxytoluene, a preservative).

Food additives are used for a variety of reasons. Some serve the purposes of preserving foods or increasing their nutritive value. Others are designed to produce a specific consistency, taste, or appearance. Intentional food additives have been used since ancient times. For example, salt has been used for centuries to preserve foods, and in hot weather spices helped disguise the flavor of food that was no longer fresh. As people have moved greater distances from farms, some manufacturers have relied more on food-preservation additives. Table 14 summarizes some of the major food additive categories. The structural formulas of a few common ones are shown in Figure 12.

A processed food may also contain contaminants that accidentally find their way into foods. Typical contaminants are pesticides, mold, antibiotics used to treat animals, insect parts, or food packaging materials or dirt from the processing plant.

Table 14   **FOOD ADDITIVES**

Additive Type	Purpose	Examples
Anticaking agents	Keep foods free-flowing	Sodium ferrocyanide
Antioxidants	Prevent fat rancidity	BHA and BHT
Bleaches	Whiten foods (flour, cheese); hasten cheese maturing	Sulfur dioxide, SO_2
Coloring agents	Increase visual appeal	Carotene (natural yellow color); synthetic dyes
Emulsifiers	Improve texture, smoothness; stabilize oil-water mixtures	Cellulose gums, dextrins
Flavoring agents	Add or enhance flavor	Salt, monosodium glutamate (MSG), spices
Humectants	Retain moisture	Glycerin
Leavening agents	Give foods light texture	Baking powder, baking soda
Nutrients	Improve nutritive value	Vitamins, minerals
Preservatives and antimycotic agents (growth inhibitors)	Prevent spoilage, microbial growth	Propionic acid, sorbic acid, benzoic acid, salt
Sweeteners	Impart sweet taste	Sugar (sucrose), dextrin, fructose, aspartame, sorbitol, mannitol

Figure 12 Common food additives.

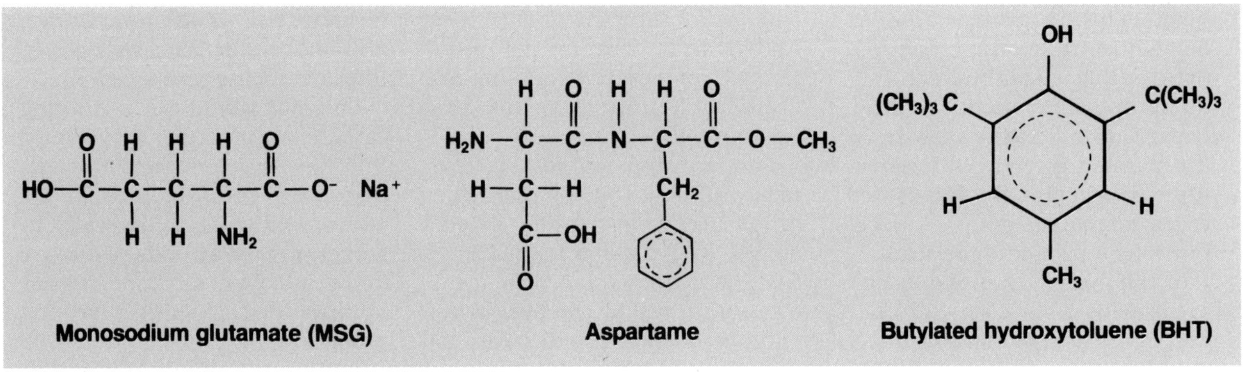

Monosodium glutamate (MSG)   Aspartame   Butylated hydroxytoluene (BHT)

Ms. Green Jeans

Photo courtesy of Illinois Farm Bureau

By Colin Mosley
Bloomington Blade *Staff Writer*

Movies and television shows often romanticize farm life. Sue Adams will tell you that working on a farm is a lot of hard work—even if she does find it rewarding. Sue and her husband, John, run a 1,000 acre farm in Atlanta, Illinois. Sue's daily chores depend on the time of year. The farming calendar begins before planting. Sue and John decide to continue environmentally sound no-tillage practices. This means that new crops are planted directly in the residue of previously harvested crops, so there is minimal loss of precious topsoil and moisture.

In the spring, Sue plants half of the fields in the corn, the other half in soy beans. Planting today is a highly mechanized process. As soon as the crops begin to grow, crop protection chemicals are applied. The chemicals Sue and John use decompose quickly when exposed to sunlight and have minimal soil contact. Using farm chemicals is not a hit and miss effort; Sue monitors these chemical applications. Her knowledge of chemistry is essential to ensure appropriate and safe use of farm chemicals. She understands how to use minimum amounts for maximum results and protection of the environment.

The autumn harvest is the most fulfilling time of year. The crops are harvested, dried, stored, and readied for market. Sue must keep track of market cycles and sell at the best price without losing profits due to spoilage. Each year, several fields are set aside for experimentation in the hope of safely enhancing yields. Sue keeps detailed records on all farm operations to help her determine which practices have been successful. During the winter months, Sue and her husband attend meetings to discuss their operation and keep current with the farming industry. Like other farmers, they share information and actively look for changes to improve their operations.

The majority of Sue's training came from practical farm work. She has supplemented this experience with agriculture classes offered by the local university. In addition, Sue attends seminars and reads farm journals to keep up with developments in farming practices.

Why is it not necessarily a good idea to eliminate all additives and preservatives?

When we buy food at grocery stores and restaurants, we assume it is completely safe to eat. For the most part, this is true. Nonetheless, in recent years many food additives or contaminants have been suspected of posing hazards to human health.

Food quality in the United States is protected by law. The basis of the law is the Federal Food, Drug and Cosmetic Act of 1938, through which Congress authorized the Food and Drug Administration (FDA) to monitor the safety, purity, and wholesomeness of food. This act has been amended in response to concerns over pesticide residues, artificial colors and food dyes, and potential **carcinogens** (cancer-causing agents) in foods. Manufacturers must complete tests and provide extensive information on the safety of any proposed food product or additive. A new product must be approved before it is put on the market.

According to the amended Act, ingredients that manufacturers had been using for a long time and that were known not to be hazardous were exempted from testing. These substances make up the "Generally Recognized as Safe" (GRAS) list instead of being legally defined as additives. This list, which is periodically reviewed in light of new findings, includes items such as salt, sugar, vinegar, vitamins, and some minerals.

The Delaney Clause (1958) requires that every proposed food additive be tested on laboratory animals (usually mice). Approval is denied if it causes cancer in the animals. Some people believe that the Delaney Clause was too strict: they argue that amounts comparable to those that cause cancer in animals would be vastly more than could ever be encountered in a human diet. As written, the law causes some genuine chemical quandaries.

Sodium nitrite ($NaNO_2$) is a color stabilizer and spoilage inhibitor in many cured meats, such as hot dogs and bologna. Nitrites are particularly effective in inhibiting the growth of the bacterium *Clostridium botulinum*, which produces botulin toxin, cause of the often-fatal disease known as botulism. Sodium nitrite may be a carcinogen. In the stomach, nitrites are converted to nitrous acid.

$$\text{NaNO}_2\text{(aq)} + \text{HCl(aq)} \rightarrow \text{HNO}_2\text{(aq)} + \text{NaCl(aq)}$$

Sodium   Hydrochloric   Nitrous   Sodium

nitrite   acid   acid   chloride

Nitrous acid can react with compounds formed during protein digestion, and some of the products formed are very potent carcinogens.

$$\text{HNO}_2 + \text{R}-\underset{\underset{\text{R}}{|}}{\text{N}}-\text{H} \rightarrow \text{R}-\underset{\underset{\text{R}}{|}}{\text{N}}-\text{N}{=}\text{O} + \text{H}_2\text{O}$$

CHEMQUANDARY

Nitrite Additives

To decide whether nitrites should be used to preserve meats, we can weigh the risks and benefits. These are summarized below.

	Use Nitrites	Eliminate Nitrites
Benefit	Minimize botulin toxin formation	Remove risk of possible carcinogens
Risk	Possibility of carcinogen formation in body	Increase risk of botulin toxin formation

More information and greater knowledge might help us arrive at the best decision. If the choice of "nitrites" or "no nitrites" were up to you, what questions would you want answered first?

Aspartame was approved by the Food and Drug Administration in 1981 and was introduced commercially in 1983.

Aspartame is an example of a dipeptide. See page 243.

We are a diet-conscious society, and sweeteners have attracted considerable attention. The sweetener aspartame (available under the trade names NutraSweet and Equal) is currently an ingredient in over 160 diet beverages and 3,000 other food products. Testing a compound like aspartame usually takes millions of dollars and years of research.

Aspartame is a chemical combination of two natural amino acids, aspartic acid and phenylalanine. Gram for gram, it contains roughly the same food energy as table sugar (sucrose), but it tastes much sweeter. Much smaller quantities of aspartame than sugar are needed to sweeten a product, and so it is used as a "low-Calorie" sweetener that is also safe for diabetics.

Aspartame may pose a health hazard to individuals who are unable to utilize this sweetener in their body chemistry. Scientific evidence continues to be collected, but no serious alarm regarding aspartame has yet been issued.

By law, most processed foods must be labeled with their ingredients listed in decreasing order of quantity. However, not all labels provide complete ingredient information, and some foods are exempt. The original 1938 legislation assigned approximately three hundred common foods, such as mayonnaise, standards of identity. The law listed the ingredients of these foods; any food containing them does not have to list them again. The standards of identity lists are readily available from the government.

Persons with specific conditions may have to avoid certain foods and food additives. Diabetics must restrict their intake of sugar. Persons with high blood pressure must avoid salt. Some persons are allergic to certain substances. If such restrictions apply to you, it is essential that you always read food labels. Sometimes a new ingredient will be used in a food you have used safely in the past.

Being aware of what we eat is a wise habit for everyone. In the following activity, you will investigate food labels and consider the additives.

D.6 YOU DECIDE: FOOD ADDITIVE SURVEY

1. As homework, collect the labels from ten packaged foods. Select no more than three of the same type of food—that is, no more than three breakfast cereals or three canned soups. Bring your set of labels to school.
2. Out of the ingredient listings on the packages, select ten additives that are not naturally found in foods.
3. Complete a summary table with the following format:
   a. List the ten additives in a vertical column along the left side of the page.
   b. Fill in vertical columns for each additive with the following headings: Food product in which found, purpose of additive (if known), other information regarding the additive.
4. Use Table 14 to review the purpose of specific food additives. Then answer this question: Which additives do you think should be included in that particular food? Provide reasons.

Decision-making in the grocery store.

5. a. Is it possible to purchase the same food product without some of the additives you found?

   b. If so, where?

   c. Is there a difference in price?

   d. If so, which is more expensive?

6. What alternatives can you propose for food additives that prevent spoilage?

PART D: SUMMARY QUESTIONS

1. Compare water-soluble and fat-soluble vitamins in terms of
   a. daily requirements,
   b. toxicity concerns regarding megadoses, and
   c. cooking precautions.

2. Defend or refute this statement: *Macrominerals are more important than trace minerals.* As part of your answer, give one example of each, including its function and dietary sources.

3. Based on serving sizes indicated in the Appendix (page 522), which food group—fruits and vegetables, dairy products, meats, grains—is the best source of
   a. calcium?
   b. iron?
   c. Vitamin C?
   d. Vitamin A?

4. a. How many cups of orange juice must a 17-year-old drink to meet the RDA for vitamin C? (Consult the Appendix.)
   b. How many cups of whole milk would be needed to meet this RDA?

5. Discuss this statement: *All food additives represent unnatural additions of chemicals to our food and should be prohibited.*

6. Consider the additives listed in Table 14.
   a. Which additive type do you think is the least essential? Why?
   b. Which are the most essential? Why?

7. Why is it wise to consider both risks and benefits when considering whether to ban certain food additives?

8. a. Describe the Delaney Clause.
   b. Give one argument in its favor.
   c. Give an argument against the Delaney Clause.

How many glasses of orange juice meet the RDA for vitamin C?

E PUTTING IT ALL TOGETHER: NUTRITION AROUND THE WORLD

What impression do you have of nutrition in the United States? Do you think we are the best-fed nation in the world? How does the diet of a typical U.S. resident compare with other diets around the world? You are now ready to analyze your own diet and representative diets from various parts of the world.

E.1 YOU DECIDE: DIET ANALYSIS

Your teacher will return the diet diary you completed in the opening days of this unit, and you will use the Appendix (page 523) and this unit to analyze the adequacy of your own diet. In the next section, you will compare the quality of your diet to other diets.

Judging the nutritional quality of a diet would be simple if we consumed neatly-packaged products labeled "carbohydrate," "protein," "fat," "vitamin C," and so on. Unfortunately for our analysis, most foods we eat are mixtures of nutrients. Some type of bookkeeping is useful for keeping track of the nutrients consumed.

The Appendix gives the nutrient content for some common foods. Suppose you ate a half-pound of sirloin steak and wanted to know how much iron you had consumed. The Appendix table gives an iron content of 10.2 mg for one pound of sirloin steak. You ate half this much, so you consumed 5.1 mg of iron. (Since serving sizes will necessarily be rough estimates, you could record the value as 5 mg iron.)

1. Using the Appendix and your three-day diet record, find your total three-day intake of each item listed below. You may estimate portion sizes. If something you ate isn't listed, estimate from values for similar foods.
   a. Food energy (in Calories)
   b. Iron (in milligrams)
   c. Vitamin B$_1$ (in milligrams)
   d. Protein (in grams)

Is this meal nutritionally balanced?

RDA values

Iron
  Female   *15*
  Male   *12*
Vitamin B₁
  Female   *1.1 mg*
  Male   *1.4 mg*
Protein
  Female   *44 g*
  Male   *59 g*

2. Divide each total by three to obtain a daily average for each.

3. Listed in the margin are approximate Recommended Dietary Allowances (RDAs) for daily intake of protein, iron, and vitamin B_1.

   a. Find the percent of the RDA that your diet furnished of (1) iron, (2) vitamin B_1, and (3) protein.

   b. According to the Food and Nutrition Board of the National Academy of Sciences, recommended daily energy intake for teenage females is 2,200 Calories and for males, 3,000 Calories. What percent of the recommended average food energy value did your diet furnish?

4. Considering your answers to Question 3, how does your diet rate in terms of nutritional balance?

5. What suggestions do you have to improve the overall quality of your diet?

6. Would you be willing to make such changes in your diet? Why?

7. a. Estimate your daily energy requirements over the time you kept your diet diary. (You can use the daily energy expenditure you calculated earlier, on page 226, if it still represents your general activities.)

   b. Compare your answer to Question 7a with your answer to Question 1a. Did you gain or lose weight over the three days?

E.2 YOU DECIDE: MEALS AROUND THE WORLD

Many factors influence food choices. Some are practical, such as cost and availability. Others result from cultural differences and habit. We have seen that protein needs can be met by different combinations of foods. In the United States we look primarily to meat, eggs, and dairy products for protein. To many Eskimos and Japanese, protein often means fish; to a Mexican it may be a rice-bean combination.

The food energy, protein, iron, and vitamin B_1 in meals from several cultures are listed in Table 15. The summary also includes, for comparison, a typical U.S. fast-food meal and a U.S. regular meal.

Table 15   **MEALS AROUND THE WORLD**

	Food Energy (Cal)	Protein (g)	Iron (mg)	Vitamin B_1 (mg)
Chinese	797	36	10.5	0.66
Eskimo	872	94	19.0	0.6
Japanese	766	47	8.8	0.56
Mexican	889	27	11.0	1.14
Ugandan	828	32	6.5	0.8
U.S. citizen				
Fast-food meal	886	23	4.8	0.08
Regular meal	1212	30	6.9	0.33

Source: Adapted from S. DeVore and T. White, *The Appetites of Man: An Invitation to Better Nutrition from Nine Healthier Societies.* Anchor Books, Anchor/Doubleday, Garden City, N.Y., 1978.

1. a. Which meal provides the best overall nutrition?
   b. How did you decide?
2. a. Multiply the nutrient values for your choice of "best meal" by three. (We will assume these new values are for a one-day, three-meal diet.)
   b. Compare your answers from Question 2a to the RDAs in the margin of Section E.1 and to a 2,600-Calorie daily energy allowance. Is your choice of "best" diet deficient in any of these four nutrient categories?
   c. If so, what type(s) of food(s) would you suggest to supplement that diet?
   d. Why?

This energy allowance is the average of male and female energy needs.

E.3 LOOKING BACK AND LOOKING AHEAD

As you conclude this *ChemCom* unit, we invite you to take stock of your progress in this chemistry course. You have considered many fundamental aspects of chemistry and chemical resources, as well as personal and social issues surrounding them. In remaining *ChemCom* units, you will extend your understanding of chemical principles by exploring other important resources and key issues associated with them.

Our general goal remains the same—to help you enter into enlightened public discussion of science-related societal issues. Chemistry and you can make a difference.

NUCLEAR CHEMISTRY IN OUR WORLD

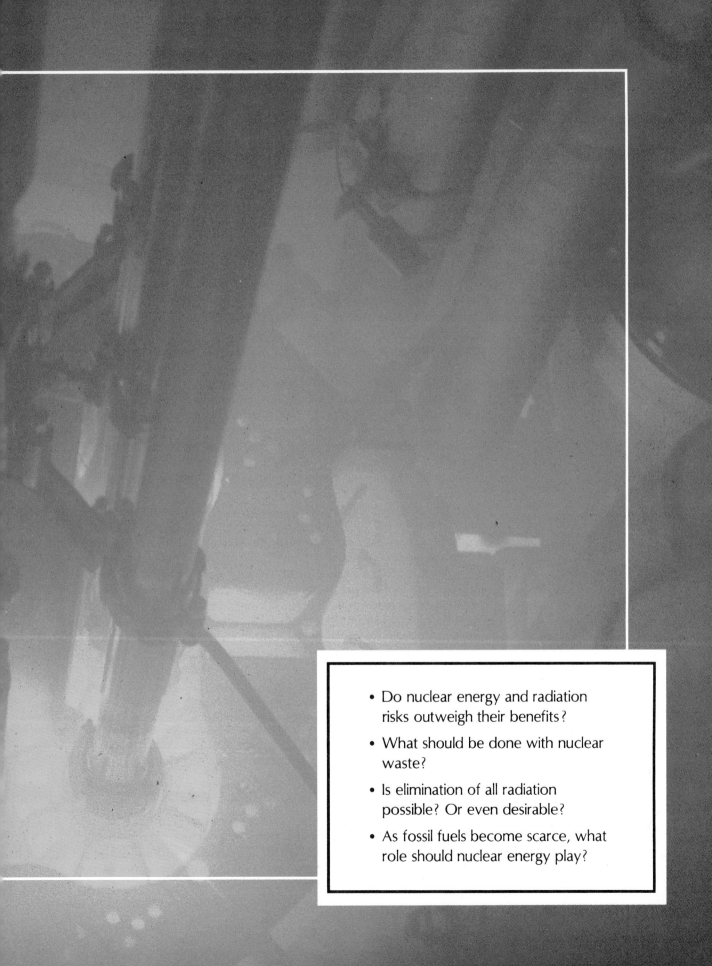

- Do nuclear energy and radiation risks outweigh their benefits?
- What should be done with nuclear waste?
- Is elimination of all radiation possible? Or even desirable?
- As fossil fuels become scarce, what role should nuclear energy play?

INTRODUCTION

This unit presents some of the most exciting discoveries of the past century—advances that have reshaped the world of science, as well as everyday life. You will learn much of what you will need for rationally considering some societal, political, economic, and ethical questions raised by nuclear technology.

Like all other stars, our sun runs on nuclear power. What is new is human use of nuclear energy. When scientists unlocked the secrets of the atom, they loosed the universe's strongest known force on our planet. The nuclear energy released from only a few grams of nuclear fuel is equal to that produced by burning thousands of gallons of gasoline. How can we best make use of this energy, while dealing wisely with its potential dangers, such as nuclear waste and nuclear weapons?

Almost every application of nuclear science can have either positive or negative aspects. Nuclear science has made important contributions to our energy needs, to industry, to biological research, and especially to medicine. Nuclear radiation, one cause of cancer, can also be used to treat cancer. But the production of nuclear energy and its use involve some risk of accidents or misuse. Any radioactive material must be handled with extreme care. Finally, all applications of nuclear technology contribute to a problem that has not yet been resolved: What should be done with radioactive waste?

Are the risks of nuclear technology worth its benefits? Some uses of nuclear technology create greater risks than others, and some offer greater benefits than others. Information in this unit will help you make better decisions on which uses of nuclear technology are worth their associated risks. As a voting citizen you will help influence nuclear technology's future.

How much of what you already know about nuclear science and technology is actually true? How much is false? And how much is a matter of controversy—even among experts? The following activity will allow you to assess your current knowledge of nuclear issues.

YOU DECIDE: PUBLIC UNDERSTANDING

Following is a survey consisting of a set of statements. First, complete the survey yourself. Then, during the next week, ask three others to respond: an adult born before 1950, an adult born after 1950, and either a high school junior or senior who is not presently taking chemistry.

All class survey results will be combined and analyzed in the final section of this unit.

Nuclear Phenomena Survey

These statements are designed to survey your understanding of nuclear-related phenomena. Indicate whether you agree (A), disagree (D), or are unable to answer because of insufficient knowledge (U).

For Item "0" Fill in your major source of knowledge of nuclear phenomena:

School = 1; Television = 2; Scientific magazines = 3; Magazines/newspapers = 4; Conversations with others = 5.

Yourself	Non-chem Student	Pre-1950 Adult	Post-1950 Adult	
				0. Major source of knowledge of nuclear phenomena. (See choices above)
				1. The atom is the smallest particle in nature.
				2. Home smoke detectors may contain radioactive materials.
				3. Radioactive materials and radiation are unnatural. They did not exist in the world until created by scientists.
				4. All radiation causes cancer.
				5. Most space occupied by an atom is "empty."
				6. Electromagnetic radiation should be avoided at all costs.
				7. Human senses can detect radioactivity.
				8. Nuclear wastes are initially "hot" both in temperature and in radioactivity.
				9. All atoms of a given element are identical.
				10. Radiation can be used to limit the spread of cancer.
				11. Individuals vary widely in their ability to absorb radiation "safely."
				12. Small amounts of matter change to immense quantities of energy in nuclear weapons.
				13. The human body naturally contains a small quantity of radioactive material.
				14. Physicians can distinguish cancer caused by radiation exposure from cancer having other causes.
				15. Television tubes emit radiation.
				16. Most nuclear waste generated to date has come from nuclear power plants.
				17. Radioactive and nonradioactive forms of an element have the same chemical properties.
				18. Cells that divide rapidly are more sensitive to radiation than are cells that divide slowly.
				19. Physicians use injections of radioactive elements to diagnose and treat certain disorders.
				20. Medical X rays involve potential risks as well as benefits.
				21. Nuclear reactors were originally designed to generate electricity.
				22. Nuclear plants are the only electric power plants that create serious hazards to public health and the environment.
				23. To date, no one has died from radiation released by nuclear power plants.
				24. Nuclear power plants do not emit air pollution during normal operation.
				25. Regardless of risks, nuclear power plants are needed to keep the nation functioning and less dependent on foreign oil.
				26. An improperly-managed nuclear power plant can explode like a nuclear weapon.

Yourself / Non-chem Student / Pre-1950 Adult / Post-1950 Adult

27. The main difference between a nuclear power plant and a coal-fired power plant is the fuel used to boil the water.
28. Some nuclear wastes must be stored for hundreds of years to prevent dangerous radioactivity from escaping into the environment.
29. Nuclear power presently supplies more than 10% of our country's total energy needs and is increasing in importance each year.
30. If the half-life of a radioactive substance is six hours, all of it will decay in 12 hours.
31. More federal funds have been spent on nuclear power development than on all other "alternative" energy sources (wind, solar, etc.) combined.
32. In the United States, the largest quantity of human-produced radiation comes from nuclear power plants.
33. Some states have banned construction of new nuclear power plants.
34. Nuclear wastes can be neutralized or made non-radioactive.
35. Nuclear power plants produce material that could be converted into nuclear weapons.
36. A nuclear power plant uses a much smaller mass of fuel than does a coal-fired plant.
37. A nuclear power plant is less expensive to build than is a coal-fired plant.
38. A national system for long-term storage of radioactive wastes is now operating.
39. The rate of radioactive decay can be slowed by extreme cooling.
40. The United States should increase its reliance on nuclear power to generate electricity.

Based on your survey results, consider these questions:

1. Do you think there is a need for better public education on nuclear issues? Why, or why not?
2. Do you think there is public fear of radiation? Give reasons for your answer.
3. Do you know what radiation is?

This is the only photograph made during construction of the first nuclear reactor. This November 1942 photograph shows the laying of a nineteenth layer of graphite. Layers of graphite containing uranium metal and uranium oxide were alternated with layers of "dead" graphite. There were 57 layers in all.

A

ENERGY AND ATOMS

A.1 LABORATORY ACTIVITY: RADIOACTIVITY

Getting Ready

The purpose of this activity is to see whether some common objects emit radiation. You will place objects on a piece of sensitive paper, which forms an image on its surface when exposed to radiation. Since sunlight itself is a form of radiation, the paper and items will be protected from it. Only radiation from radioactive materials will be able to expose the paper.

Procedure

1. Using forceps, place the five objects on a piece of the sunsensitive paper, one near each corner and one in the middle.
2. Place the paper and objects in a laboratory drawer and close it tightly. Your teacher will indicate the total storage time needed to insure adequate exposure.
3. Following storage, lift off each object and examine the paper as directed by your teacher. Note whether spots are left on the paper. In the absence of sunlight, the presence of a spot indicates that the paper was exposed to radiation and that the object responsible for the spot is radioactive.

Questions

1. Which objects are radioactive, based on this test?
2. Do you think radioactivity serves any useful purpose in the item(s) which produced a positive test?
3. Can you suggest a more effective method for detecting radioactivity?

   Although most common items are not radioactive, nuclear energy remains important in our daily lives, as you will soon see. First, however, we will clarify the meanings of two often-misunderstood terms—radioactivity and radiation.

Setup for placing objects in drawer.

A.2 DIFFERENT KINDS OF RADIATION

Atoms generally remain unchanged—an atom of aluminum always remains aluminum, an iron atom is always iron. However, some atoms may spontaneously change because of their unstable nuclei. Usually these atoms change to produce an atom

The plural of "nucleus" is "nuclei".

Recall that the atomic number represents the number of protons in an atom's nucleus.

of a different element (one with a different atomic number), an emitted particle, and released energy. Substances that can change spontaneously in this way are called **radioactive.**

Because the nucleus is broken down, the process is referred to as **radioactive decay.** The emitted particles and energy together make up **nuclear radiation.** Many benefits—and also hazards—of nuclear technology are due to nuclear radiation.

All objects (radioactive or not) give off the radiation called **electromagnetic radiation.** Some of the energy emitted during radioactive decay may be in the form of gamma rays, a high-energy type of electromagnetic radiation.

Figure 1 shows the major types of electromagnetic radiation and their sources. Arranging the different types of electromagnetic radiation in order from low to high energy, as in Figure 1, produces a **spectrum.** While cosmic and gamma rays are at the high-energy end of the spectrum, microwaves and radio waves are at the low end of the spectrum. Near the center is the familiar visible spectrum.

Each type of electromagnetic radiation has several common properties:

- It is a form of energy and has no mass.
- It travels at the speed of light.
- It can travel through a vacuum; unlike sound or ocean waves, its movement does not depend on a medium such as air or water to "carry" it.
- It is emitted by atoms as they decay, or after they are energized, such as heating the tungsten filament in a light bulb or lighting the fuse that explodes the compounds in fireworks.
- It moves through space as packets (bundles) of energy called **photons.** Each photon has a characteristic frequency, such as the frequencies of radio waves received by a radio.
- The energy of photons is related to their frequency—the higher the frequency of electromagnetic radiation, the higher its energy.

The quantity of energy that is carried by any type of radiation determines its effect on living things and other types of matter. **Ionizing radiation,** which includes all nuclear radiation

Frequency refers to the number of waves that pass by a given point in one second. For example, an AM radio frequency of 830 kHz (kilohertz) means that the radio signal involves 830,000 waves per second.

Figure 1 The electromagnetic spectrum.

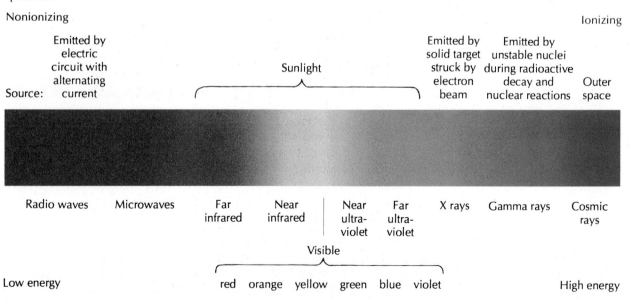

Nonionizing   Ionizing

				Emitted by solid target struck by electron beam	Emitted by unstable nuclei during radioactive decay and nuclear reactions	
Source:	Emitted by electric circuit with alternating current		Sunlight				Outer space

| Radio waves | Microwaves | Far infrared | Near infrared | Near ultra-violet | Far ultra-violet | X rays | Gamma rays | Cosmic rays |

Visible

red   orange   yellow   green   blue   violet

Low energy   High energy and the high-energy electromagnetic radiation (X rays, gamma rays), has the greatest energy and potential for harm. Energy from such radiation often causes electrons to be ejected from molecules, creating highly-reactive molecular fragments that can cause serious damage to living systems.

These fragments are often in the form of ions—hence the name "ionizing radiation."

Nonionizing radiation has lower energy. Electromagnetic radiation in ultraviolet, visible, and lower energy regions (see Figure 1) is nonionizing radiation. This form of radiation transfers its energy to matter, "exciting" the molecules, which vibrate or cause the electrons to move to higher energy levels. Chemical reactions sometimes occur as this energy is transferred to molecules. The reactions caused by a microwave oven in cooking food are one example.

Ultraviolet radiation from the sun can be harmful.

Excessive exposure to nonionizing radiation can be harmful. A sunburn, for example, results from overexposure to nonionizing radiation from the sun. Intense microwave and infrared radiation can be lethal. Ultraviolet radiation can cause skin cancer.

The difference in the effects of nonionizing and ionizing radiation is something like the difference between being hit by a speeding baseball and being hit by a speeding bullet. The body may absorb more energy from the baseball (or from nonionizing radiation), but with less damage, since the impact is spread over a large area. In the case of the bullet (or ionizing radiation), the smaller force is more focused and is often more damaging.

Scientists have long been interested in light and other types of radiation. However, nuclear radiation was hard to detect. When and how did scientists first identify it?

CHEMQUANDARY

Always Harmful?

How true is the statement "All radiation is harmful and should be avoided?"

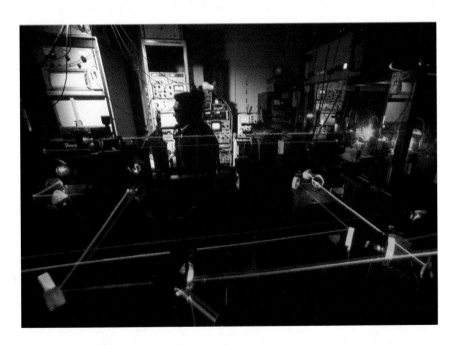

The laser (**l**ight **a**mplification by **s**timulated **e**mission of **r**adiation) amplifies electromagnetic radiation.

A.3 THE GREAT DISCOVERY

The history of our understanding of radiation began in 1895. In his studies of fluorescence, the German physicist W. K. Roentgen found that certain minerals glowed—or fluoresced—when hit by beams of electrons.

Beams of electrons are sometimes known as **cathode rays,** because they are emitted from the cathode when electricity passes through an evacuated glass tube. While Roentgen was working with a cathode ray tube shielded with black paper, he saw a glow of light coming from a piece of paper across the room. The paper, coated with a fluorescent material, would be expected to glow when exposed to radiation, but it was not in the path of the electrons from the tube. Roentgen concluded that there must be some unseen radiation from the tube that passed through the paper. He named the mysterious rays **X rays,** X representing the unknown.

Further experiments showed that although X rays penetrate many materials, they cannot pass through dense materials such as lead and bone. X rays are now known to be high-energy electromagnetic radiation.

Scientists soon realized how useful X rays could be in medicine, and the first X-ray photograph ever taken was of a human hand. Figures 2 and 3 show some modern X-ray pictures.

Roentgen's discovery excited other scientists. Soon hundreds of researchers, including the French physicist Henri Becquerel, were studying these new rays.

Fluorescent minerals glow in the dark when illuminated by ultraviolet radiation.

Modern X-ray devices are based on an electron beam striking a heavy-metal target such as silver.

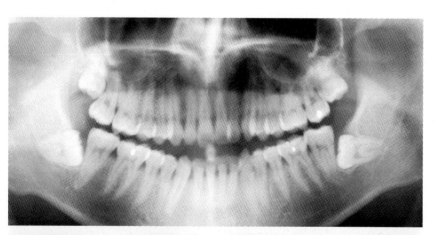

Figure 2 An X ray of a human jaw. Such X rays are useful for detecting cavities and other dental problems.

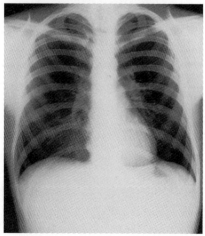
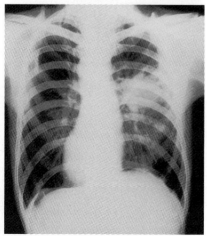

Figure 3 Chest X rays. Left, normal lungs; right, cancerous lungs.

Becquerel wondered if fluorescent minerals might emit X rays. In 1896, he placed a fluorescent mineral, which happened to contain uranium, in sunlight. He then wrapped a photographic plate in black paper, and placed it next to the mineral. If the mineral did emit X rays as it fluoresced, the film would become exposed even though it was shielded from sunlight. To Becquerel's delight, the developed plate darkened—the film had been exposed. He stored the covered photographic plates and mineral sample in a drawer.

Following that initial success, skies were cloudy for several days, preventing Becquerel from doing more experiments. He decided to develop the plates on the chance that the mineral fluorescence might have persisted, causing some fogging of the plates. But when he took the plates from the drawer, he was astounded. Instead of a faint fogging, the plates had been strongly exposed.

A fluorescent mineral in a darkened desk drawer could not cause such a high level of exposure. In fact, there was no satisfactory explanation for Becquerel's observations. He interrupted his work to study the mysterious rays apparently given off by the uranium mineral. These rays proved to be more energetic and possess much greater penetrating power than did X rays. Becquerel had discovered radioactivity.

CHEMQUANDARY

Scientific Discoveries

What do these events have in common with Becquerel's discovery of radioactivity?

- Louis Pasteur found that some chickens which had recovered from cholera sickness did not get sick again from another dose of cholera bacteria. He later became famous for inventing vaccinations.

- Charles Goodyear accidentally allowed a mixture of sulfur and natural rubber (a sticky material that melts when heated and cracks when cold) to touch a hot stove top; he noted that the mixture did not melt. Vulcanization, the process that makes rubber more widely useful by modifying its properties, resulted from this observation.

- Alexander Fleming noticed that in a dish of bacteria he was growing, a circle of bacteria had disappeared around some mold. He later discovered penicillin.

- Roy Plunkett withdrew gaseous tetrafluoroethene ($F_2C=CF_2$) from a storage cylinder, but the gas flow stopped long before the cylinder was empty. He cut the cylinder open with a hacksaw and discovered a white solid. Today we know this solid as Teflon (polytetrafluoroethene).

Further research revealed that all uranium compounds are radioactive. This led Pierre and Marie Curie to suggest that radioactivity might be a property of heavy elements. Finding that the radioactivity level of the uranium ore pitchblende was four to five times greater than expected from its known uranium content, the Curies suspected some other radioactive element was also present. After processing more than a ton of pitchblende, they isolated tiny amounts of two new radioactive elements—polonium (Po) and radium (Ra).

Interest in the new type of radiation continued to grow among scientists. Some realized that a better understanding of these rays could provide clues to the structure of atoms. One scientist who was particularly successful in penetrating the atom's mysteries was Ernest Rutherford.

A.4 NUCLEAR RADIATION

You will do some similar experimentation later in this unit.

Alpha (α), beta (β), and gamma (γ) are the first three letters of the Greek alphabet.

In 1899, Ernest Rutherford showed that radioactivity consisted of two different types of rays, which he named ***alpha rays*** and ***beta rays.*** He placed thin sheets of aluminum in the pathway of radiation from uranium. Beta rays penetrated more layers of aluminum sheet than alpha rays did. Shortly afterward, a third kind of radiation produced by radioactive elements was discovered. This radiation was called ***gamma rays.***

The three kinds of radiation were passed through magnetic fields, to learn about their electrical properties. It was known that when charged particles move through a magnetic field they are deflected by the magnetic force. The path of positively-charged particles is deflected in one direction, the path of negatively-charged particles in the opposite direction. Neutral particles and electromagnetic radiation are not deflected by magnetic fields.

An experiment in which all three types of radiation might be observed is shown in Figure 4.

Experiments with nuclear radiation in magnetic fields indicated that alpha rays are composed of positively-charged particles and beta rays are made up of negatively-charged particles. Gamma rays are not deflected by a magnetic field; these were later identified as high-energy electromagnetic radiation, similar to X rays.

The nature of radioactivity was thus established; and as often happens in science, a new discovery toppled an old theory. The established atomic theory held that atoms were the smallest, most fundamental unit of matter. After alpha, beta, and gamma rays were identified, scientists were convinced that atoms must be composed of still-smaller particles.

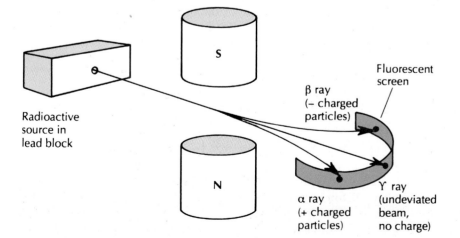

Figure 4 Lead block experiment, showing behavior of alpha (α) rays, beta (β) rays, and gamma (γ) rays in a magnetic field.

A.5 LABORATORY ACTIVITY: THE BLACK BOX

Getting Ready

Experiments like those of Roentgen, Becquerel, and Rutherford illustrate that indirect evidence may be essential for exploring properties of an object we cannot see or touch. In this activity you will try to identify objects in sealed boxes. In many ways this activity resembles the work of scientists in determining the nature of the atom—a more fundamental "sealed box."

Procedure

Two sealed boxes, numbered 1 and 2, are at your laboratory bench. Each box contains three objects, different from each other and from those in the other box.

1. Gently shake, rotate, or manipulate one of the boxes. From your observations, try to determine the size of each object, its general shape, and the material from which it is made. Record your observations, designating the three objects as A, B, and C.

2. Compare your observations and ideas about the three objects with those of other team members. What conclusions can you and your team reach? Can you identify the objects?

3. Repeat Steps 1 and 2 with the second box.

4. Make your final decisions about all the objects in Boxes 1 and 2. Identify each object by name and a sketch.

Questions

1. Which of your senses did you use to collect the data?

2. In what ways does this activity resemble efforts of scientists in exploring atomic and molecular structure?

3. Name some theories about the nature of the world that are based primarily on indirect evidence.

From another experiment, Rutherford proposed a fundamental atomic model that remains useful even today. In doing so he developed an ingenious, indirect way to look at atoms.

When you receive a present, you sometimes shake it to guess at the contents.

Rutherford conducted many important experiments on the nature of alpha rays. Here he is seen in his laboratory at McGill University in Montreal, Canada.

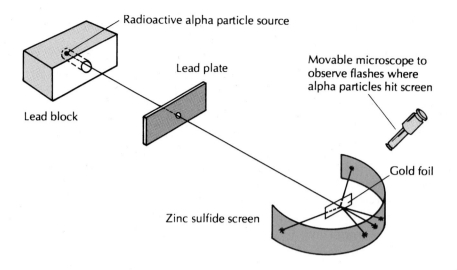

Figure 5 The alpha particle scattering experiment.

Radioactive alpha particle source

Lead plate

Movable microscope to observe flashes where alpha particles hit screen

Lead block

Gold foil

Zinc sulfide screen

A.6 GOLD FOIL EXPERIMENT

In the late 1800s this was known as the "plum pudding model", in reference to the distribution of raisins within this common English dish.

Prior to Rutherford's experiment several explanations had been proposed of how electrons and positively charged particles might be arranged in atoms. In the most accepted model, an atom was viewed as a solid mass of positively-charged materials, with the negatively-charged electrons embedded within, like raisins in a loaf of bread.

Hans Geiger and Ernest Marsden, working in Rutherford's laboratory in Manchester, focused a beam of alpha particles, the more massive of the two types of radioactive particles, at a sheet of gold foil 0.00004 cm (about 2000 atoms) thick. They surrounded the metal sheet with a specially-coated screen (Figure 5). The screen emitted a small flash of light where each alpha particle landed. This permitted the researchers to deduce the paths of the alpha particles interacting with the gold foil.

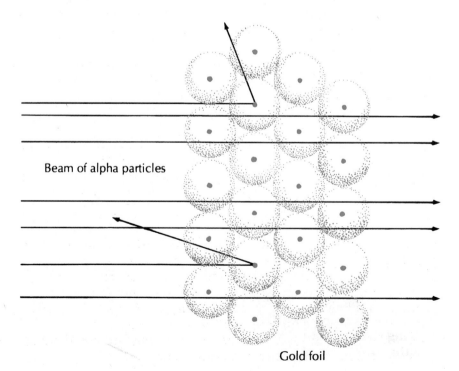

Beam of alpha particles

Gold foil

Figure 6 Result of the alpha particle scattering experiment. Most alpha particles passed through the foil; a few were deflected.

Rutherford expected that alpha particles would scatter as they were deflected by the gold atoms, producing a pattern similar to spray from a nozzle. He was in for quite a surprise.

First of all, most alpha particles passed straight through the gold foil as if nothing were there (Figure 6). This implied that most of the volume taken up by atoms is essentially empty space. But what surprised Rutherford even more was that a few alpha particles—about one in every 20,000—bounced back toward the source. Rutherford described his astonishment this way: "It was about as incredible as if you had fired a 15-inch shell at a piece of tissue paper and it came back and hit you."

What these few rebounding alpha particles encountered must have been relatively small, since most alpha particles missed it. But whatever they hit must also have been massive and electrically charged.

From these results, Rutherford developed the model of the nuclear atom. He named the tiny, massive, positively-charged region at the center of the atom the **nucleus.** He envisioned that electrons orbited around the nucleus, somewhat like planets orbit the sun.

Here, "massive" means heavy. A massive object may have a small volume.

A.7   ARCHITECTURE OF ATOMS

Since Rutherford's time, our understanding of atomic structure has expanded and, in some ways, changed. Rutherford's image of a central, massive nucleus surrounded mostly by empty space is still accepted. However, we now know from later research that, although useful, the idea of "orbiting electrons" is too simplified. Each electron is believed to occupy a specific region in which it spends most of its time. We can identify the region, but not the location of the electron at a given instant.

Further research revealed that the nucleus is composed of two types of particles—**neutrons,** which are electrically neutral, and **protons,** with a positive charge. A neutron and proton each have about the same mass, 1.7×10^{-24} g. While this mass is incredibly small, it is still much larger than the mass of an electron. As shown in Table 1, a mole of electrons has a mass of 0.0005 g, that amount of protons or neutrons has a mass of about 1 g. In other words, a proton or a neutron is about 2,000 times as massive as an electron. Protons and neutrons account for most of the mass of the universe.

Particles smaller than atoms are called "subatomic particles."

Protons—positive charge
Neutrons—no charge
Electrons—negative charge

Table 1   **THREE IMPORTANT SUBATOMIC PARTICLES**

Particle	Location	Charge	Molar Mass (g/mol)
Proton	Nucleus	1+	1
Neutron	Nucleus	0	1
Electron	Outside of nucleus	1−	0.0005

The diameter of a typical atom is about 10^{-8} cm, but an average nuclear diameter is only 10^{-12} cm, one ten-thousandth as big as the diameter of the entire atom. Looking at this another way, the nucleus occupies only about one trillionth (10^{-12}) of the volume of an atom. As a comparison, imagine that a billiard ball represents an atom's nucleus. On that scale, electrons surrounding this billiard-ball nucleus would occupy space extending more than a kilometer away in all directions.

As you learned in the Resources Unit, each atom of the same element has the same number of protons in its nucleus. This number of protons, called the **atomic number,** identifies the element. For example, because each carbon atom nucleus contains six protons, carbon has an atomic number of six.

However, all atoms of the same element do not necessarily have the same number of neutrons in their nuclei. Atoms of the same element having different numbers of neutrons are called **isotopes** of that element. Carbon atoms, each containing six protons, may have six, seven, or even eight neutrons. The composition of these three carbon isotopes is summarized in Table 2. The carbon isotope with eight neutrons has an unstable nucleus—it is radioactive and is called a **radioisotope.**

Table 2	THREE CARBON ISOTOPES			
Name	Total Protons (Atomic Number)	Total Neutrons	Mass Number	Total Electrons Outside Nucleus
Carbon-12	6	6	12	6
Carbon-13	6	7	13	6
Carbon-14	6	8	14	6

Isotopes are distinguished from each other by their different **mass numbers.** The mass number represents the total number of protons and neutrons in an atom of a given isotope. The three carbon isotopes in Table 2 have mass numbers of 12, 13, and 14. To specify a particular isotope, the atomic number and the mass number are added to the symbol for the element. For example, an isotope of strontium (Sr) with an atomic number of 38 and a mass number of 90 is written this way:

$$^{90}_{38}\text{Sr}$$

An ion of strontium-90 would be shown as $^{90}_{38}\text{Sr}^{2+}$. To name an isotope in words, just add the mass number to the element's name. The isotope depicted above is strontium-90.

The symbols, names, and nuclear composition of some isotopes are summarized in Table 3.

Table 3		SOME COMMON ISOTOPES			
Symbol	Name	Total Protons (Atomic Number)	Total Neutrons	Mass Number	Total Electrons
$^{1}_{1}\text{H}$	Hydrogen-1	1	0	1	1
$^{7}_{3}\text{Li}$	Lithium-7	3	4	7	3
$^{19}_{9}\text{F}$	Fluorine-19	9	10	19	9
$^{208}_{82}\text{Pb}$	Lead-208	82	126	208	82
$^{208}_{82}\text{Pb}^{2+}$	Lead-208, (II) ion	82	126	208	80

YOUR TURN

Isotope Notation

Suppose you know that one product of a certain nuclear reaction is an isotope containing 85 protons and 120 neutrons. It therefore has a mass number of

205 (85 protons + 120 neutrons). What is the name of this element?

$$^{205}_{85}?$$

Consulting the periodic table, we see that the element with atomic number 85 is astatine (At).

$$^{205}_{85}At$$

1. Prepare a summary chart similar to Table 3 for the following six isotopes. (Consult the periodic table for missing information.)

   a. $^{12}_{?}C$ c. $^{16}_{?}O$ e. $^{108}_{?}Hg$

   b. $^{14}_{7}?$ d. $^{24}_{12}?^{2+}$ f. $^{238}_{92}?$

2. What relationship do you note between total protons and total neutrons

   a. for atoms of lighter elements?

   b. for those of heavier elements?

A.8 LABORATORY ACTIVITY: ISOTOPIC PENNIES

Getting Ready

You found earlier (Resources unit, page 88) that pre-1982 and post-1982 pennies have different compositions. As you might suspect, they also have different masses. In this activity, a mixture of pre- and post-1982 pennies will represent the naturally-occurring mixture of two isotopes of the imaginary element "coinium." The pennies will allow you to learn one way that scientists can determine the relative amounts of different isotopes present in a sample of an element.

You will be given a sealed container which holds a mixture of ten pre-1982 and post-1982 pennies. Your container might hold any particular combination of the two "isotopes." Your task is to determine the isotopic composition of the element coinium *without* opening the container.

To illustrate how this can be done, let's consider a mixture of heavy billiard balls and light-weight ping pong balls rather than coins.

Say you are given a 10-ball mixture of billiard balls and ping pong balls in a sealed box. It is clear that ten billiard balls would weigh much more than 10 ping pong balls. Thus the more the mixture of 10 balls weighs, the more billiard balls you must have present.

An obvious—but important—notion is that the mass of the entire mixture equals the sum of the masses of all the billiard balls and the masses of all the ping pong balls. That idea can be expressed this way:

Total mass of balls = (Number of billiard balls × Mass of one billiard ball) + (Number of ping pong balls × Mass of one ping pong ball)

Now let's get back to the pennies. Following the billiard ball and ping pong ball example, this relationship applies:

Total mass of pennies = (Number of pre-1982 pennies × Mass of one pre-1982 penny) + (Number of post-1982 pennies × Mass of one post-1982 penny)

The total mass of pennies can be found by subtracting the mass of the empty container from the mass of the sealed container containing pennies.

Now we are ready to complete the penny calculations. For starters, we know there are 10 pennies in the container. So, if we let x = the total number of pre-1982 pennies, then $(10 - x)$ = number of post-1982 pennies.

Further, the mass of all pre-1982 pennies equals the number of pre-1982 pennies (x) multiplied by the mass of one pre-1982 penny. Likewise, the mass of all post-1982 pennies equals the number of post-1982 pennies $(10 - x)$ times the mass of one post-1982 penny.

To reduce the number of words, we can write that relationship this way:

Total mass of pennies = $(x \times$ mass of pre-1982 penny) + $[(10 - x) \times$ mass of post-1982 penny]

Our goal is to find the value of x—the number of pre-1982 pennies in the container. Once that value is known, we will have figured out the composition of the 10-penny mixture—without opening the container!

However, to solve for x, we first need to know the values of the three masses in the equation. That is what the following procedure is designed to do.

Procedure

1. Your teacher will give you a pre-1982 penny, a post-1982 penny, a sealed container with 10 mixed pre- and post-1982 pennies, and the mass of the empty container. Record the code number of your sealed container.
2. Find the mass of the pre-1982 penny and the post-1982 penny separately.
3. Find the mass of the sealed container of pennies.
4. Find the total mass of the 10 pennies. (*Hint:* Use data from Steps 1 and 3.)
5. Calculate the values of x—the number of pre-1982 pennies, and $(10 - x)$—the number of post-1982 pennies.
6. Calculate the percent composition of the element "coinium" from your data.

Questions

1. What property of the element "coinium" is different in its pre- and post-1982 forms?
2. a. In what ways is the penny mixture a good analogy or model for actual element isotopes?
   b. In what ways is the analogy misleading or incorrect?
3. Name at least one other familiar item that could serve as a model for isotopes.

Weighing sample on an electronic balance.

A.9 ISOTOPES IN NATURE

Most elements in nature are mixtures of isotopes. From a chemical viewpoint, this does not cause any real problems. All isotopes of an element behave virtually the same chemically—they only differ slightly in mass. Some isotopes of an element may be radioactive, while others are not.

The proportions of an element's naturally-occurring isotopes are usually the same everywhere on the earth. An element's accepted atomic and molar masses, as shown in the periodic table, represent averages based on the relative abundances of its isotopes. The following *Your Turn* illustrates this idea.

YOUR TURN

Molar Mass and Isotope Abundance

To calculate the molar mass of an element, you must use the concept of a weighted average. You can do this for the element "coinium" from your laboratory activity.

Suppose you found that $x = 4$, that is, your mixture contained four pre-1982 pennies and six post-1982 pennies. As decimal fractions, the composition of your mixture was 0.4 pre-1982 pennies and 0.6 post-1982 pennies. These fractions together with the mass of each type of penny (the two isotopes of "coinium") would be used in this equation to calculate the weighted average mass:

Avg. mass of a penny =
(fraction, pre-1982 pennies)(mass, pre-1982 penny) +
(fraction, post-1982 pennies)(mass, post-1982 penny)

1. Try that calculation for your actual coinium mixture.
2. Now calculate the average mass of a penny in your mixture another way: Divide the mass of your total penny sample by 10.
3. Compare your calculated average masses in Questions 1 and 2. (These results should convince you that *either* calculation leads to the same result. If not, consult your teacher.)

Now let's do an example for an actual isotopic mixture.

Naturally-occurring copper consists of 69.1% copper-63 and 30.9% copper-65. The molar masses of the pure isotopes are

copper-63	62.93 g/mol
copper-65	64.93 g/mol

Calculate the molar mass of naturally-occurring copper.

The equation for finding average molar masses is the same as the earlier equation you used for "coinium":

Molar mass =
(fraction of isotope 1)(molar mass of isotope 1) +
(fraction of isotope 2)(molar mass of isotope 2) + . . .

For copper, the average molar mass is found this way:

Molar mass of copper = (0.691)(62.93 g/mol) +
(0.309)(64.93 g/mol) = 63.5 g/mol

This is the value for copper given in the periodic table (rounded to the nearest 0.1 unit).

4. Naturally-occurring uranium (U) is a mixture of three isotopes:

Isotope	Molar Mass (g/mol)	% Natural Abundance
Uranium-238	238.1	99.28%
Uranium-235	235.0	0.71%
Uranium-234	234.0	0.0054%

a. Is the molar mass of naturally-occurring uranium closer to 238, 235, or 234? Why?

b. Calculate the molar mass of naturally-occurring uranium.

Marie Curie originally thought that only heavy elements were radioactive. It is true that naturally occurring *radioisotopes*—a convenient term for radioactive isotopes—are more common among the heavy elements. For example, isotopes of elements with atomic numbers greater than 83 (bismuth) are all radioactive. However, many natural radioactive isotopes are also found among lighter elements and it is even possible to create a radioactive isotope of any element. Table 4 lists some naturally occurring radioisotopes and their isotopic abundances.

TABLE 4   **SOME NATURAL RADIOISOTOPES**

Name	Symbol	Relative Isotopic Abundance (%)
Hydrogen-3	$^{3}_{1}H$	0.00013
Carbon-14	$^{14}_{6}C$	Trace
Potassium-40	$^{40}_{19}K$	0.0012
Rubidium-87	$^{87}_{37}Rb$	27.8
Indium-115	$^{115}_{49}In$	95.8
Lanthanum-138	$^{138}_{57}La$	0.089
Neodymium-144	$^{144}_{60}Nd$	23.9
Samarium-147	$^{147}_{62}Sm$	15.1
Lutetium-176	$^{176}_{71}Lu$	2.60
Rhenium-187	$^{187}_{75}Re$	62.9
Platinum-190	$^{190}_{78}Pt$	0.012
Thorium-232	$^{232}_{90}Th$	100
Uranium-235	$^{235}_{92}U$	0.72
Uranium-238	$^{238}_{92}U$	99.28

The history of science is full of discoveries that build upon earlier discoveries. The discovery of radioactivity was such an event itself. That discovery in turn led to new knowledge of atomic structure.

Who Are Radiation Therapists?

By Max Benbow
Brookline Dispatch *Staff Writer*

Photo by Beverly Buck

Beverly Buck has fulfilled her dream of a career that combines science and medicine by becoming a radiation therapist working in the field of radiation oncology. Radiation oncology is the field of medicine that treats tumors with radiation. Radiation therapists like Beverly deliver radiation treatments prescribed by physicians. Beverly is the Education and Development Coordinator at the Joint Center for Radiation Therapy in Boston, Massachusetts, and an instructor at Harvard Medical School. She is also in charge of the quality assurance program and makes sure equipment is functioning so that the radiation treatment is properly administered. Beverly also makes sure that patients are treated according to departmental policies. The Joint Center for Radiation Therapy facilities treat 200 cancer patients each day and provide services for 3,000 *new* cancer patients every year.

Typically, Beverly starts her day by attending new patient conferences, where she discusses treatment strategies. She then tours the center's facilities to deal with quality assurance issues. Next, Beverly teaches a radiation oncology class to radiation therapy students, medical students or hospital staff. After class, Beverly returns to her office to complete paperwork.

One of Beverly's new patients is a teenager who has been diagnosed with osteosarcoma, or bone cancer. The physicians recommend a combination of systemic (whole-body) treatment with chemotherapy, and localized treatment with radiation of the affected bone. The risk/benefit factors involved with both chemotherapy and radiation therapy for this patient are carefully considered. Radiation therapy is associated with risks; the radiation is powerful and can kill or genetically alter normal body cells. These risks must be balanced against the benefits of the particular treatment. Beverly works with the teenager and with the patient's family to determine whether the benefits outweigh the risks.

If all parties agree that radiation therapy is in the teenager's best interest, a planning session with Beverly's staff follows the initial consultation. During this session, data are collected indicating where the radiation beams will be delivered to the body to reach all the cancer cells, while sparing as much normal tissue as possible. A staff member enters this data into a computer that maps out beam delivery by taking into account absorption by tissues, multiple radiation fields, the distance from the radioactive source, and the half-life of the radioactive source.

Once the computerized dose distribution is complete, shielding blocks are made to protect all other areas of the body. These are custom-made for each patient in the Joint Center for Radiation Therapy machine shop. Radiation therapists in Beverly's department deliver the radiation treatments to the patient over several weeks, five days a week. There are no second chances in radiation therapy, for when tissue tolerance is down the risk of blood damage rises. Fortunately, radiation therapists are able to help a large percentage of their patients.

Radiation therapists go through an educational program lasting at least two years. They study nuclear chemistry, anatomy, physiology, radiation physics, radiobiology, radiation safety, pathology, oncology, and patient care methods. Many programs are college-based, awarding associate or baccalaureate degrees upon completion.

1. List two identifying characteristics and two examples of electromagnetic radiation.

2. The discovery of X rays led to investigations of the atomic nucleus. Describe historical events that connect these two research topics.

3. Describe how Becquerel was able to make distinctions among fluorescence, X rays, and natural radioactivity.

4. Describe experimental evidence supporting the idea that radioactive sources emit charged particles as well as electromagnetic radiation (gamma rays).

5. Describe experimental evidence supporting each statement:

   a. An atom is mainly empty space.

   b. An atom contains a tiny, yet relatively massive, positively-charged center.

6. Approximately how many electrons would it take to equal the mass of one proton?

7. Complete this table:

Data Table

Symbol	Name	Atomic Number	Total Protons	Mass Number	Total Neutrons
?	?	6	?	12	?
$^{60}_{27}$?	?	?	?	?	?
$^{207}_{?}$Pb	?	?	?	?	?

8. Potassium (K) occurs as a mixture of three isotopes:

Isotope	Molar Mass (g/mol)
Potassium-39	38.964
Potassium-40	39.964
Potassium-41	40.962

   a. If the molar mass of potassium is 39.098 g/mol, which isotope is the most abundant?

   b. Explain your answer.

9. Neon (Ne) is found in the earth's atmosphere at concentrations of about 1 part in 65,000. All three naturally-occurring neon isotopes are useful in neon signs and other applications. Vital statistics for neon's isotopes are in Table 5.

   a. Do you expect that neon's molar mass is closer to 20, 21, or 22? Why?

   b. Calculate the molar mass of neon.

Table 5	NEON ISOTOPES	
Isotope	**Molar Mass (g/mol)**	**% Natural Abundance**
Ne-20	19.992	90.51
Ne-21	20.994	0.27
Ne-22	21.991	9.22
		100.00

10. Almost all boron (B) atoms are found in two forms: boron-10 and boron-11. Both isotopes behave alike chemically and are useful in fireworks (green color), in the antiseptic boric acid, and in heat-resistant glass. However, only boron-10 is useful as a control material in nuclear reactors, as a radiation shield, and in instruments used to detect neutrons. If the molar mass of boron is 10.81 g/mol, which boron isotope must be more abundant in nature?

11. What is the minimum information needed to identify a particular isotope?

EXTENDING YOUR KNOWLEDGE (OPTIONAL)

Choose one of these subatomic particles and investigate how scientists determined its existence and properties: proton, neutron, electron, neutrino, quark, pi meson, positron, or gluon. What (if any) are the practical results of such scientific studies?

B

RADIOACTIVE DECAY

Some 350 isotopes of 90 elements are found in our solar system. About 70 of these isotopes are radioactive. Almost 1600 more isotopes have been made in the laboratory. For elements with atomic numbers of 83 or less, the natural abundance of radioactive isotopes is quite low compared to the abundance of stable isotopes.

Radioactive isotopes decay spontaneously, giving off alpha or beta particles and gamma radiation. The kind and intensity of radiation emitted helps determine the medical and industrial applications of radioisotopes. In addition, the three types of radiation present different hazards to human health.

Because nuclear radiation cannot be detected by human senses, various devices have been developed to detect it and measure its intensity. You will work with one type of radiation-detector in the following laboratory activity.

B.1   LABORATORY ACTIVITY: α, β, AND γ RAYS

Getting Ready

One early device for detecting radioactivity was the **Geiger counter** (see Figure 7, on page 292). It produces an electrical signal when particles coming from a radioactive source hit its detector. In this activity or teacher demonstration you will use a modern-day counter to compare the penetrating ability of alpha, beta, and gamma radiation through cardboard, glass, and lead.

When ionizing radiation enters the counter's detecting tube, or probe, ions are formed and enhance the electric current flowing in the tube. Most radiation counters register the current as both audible clicks and a meter reading. The unit of measure on the meter, counts per minute (cpm), indicates the **intensity** of the radiation.

A constant level of natural radioactivity, which is called **background radiation,** is always present in the environment. Because of that, before readings are taken from a known radioactive source, an initial background radiation reading must be taken. This background count is then subtracted from each reading taken from a radioactive source.

The radioactive materials in this activity pose no danger to you. Nuclear materials are strictly regulated by state and federal laws. The sources in this activity emit only very small quantities

A child being tested with a Geiger counter for radiation exposure.

A Geiger counter and its attachments.

Figure 7 Diagram of a Geiger counter, showing how radiation entering the probe causes ionization of gaseous atoms or molecules.

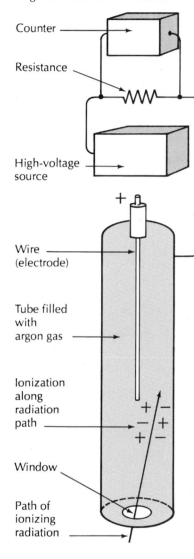

Counter

Resistance

High-voltage source

Wire (electrode)

Tube filled with argon gas

Ionization along radiation path

Window

Path of ionizing radiation

of radiation and their use requires no special license. Nevertheless, all radioactive samples will be treated with the same care that would be required for licensed materials. You will wear rubber or plastic gloves. Do not allow the radiation counter to come in direct contact with the radioactive material. Check your hands with a radiation monitor before you leave the laboratory.

Prepare a data table like the one below.

Data Table

Radiation	Counts per Minute (cpm)			
	No Shielding	Cardboard	Glass	Lead
Alpha				
Beta				
Gamma				

Procedure

Part 1: Penetrating Ability

1. Set up the apparatus shown in Figure 8.
2. Turn on the counter; allow it to warm for at least three minutes. Determine the intensity of the background radiation by counting clicks for one minute in the absence of any radioactive sources. Record this background radiation in counts per minute (cpm).
3. Put on your gloves. Using forceps, place an alpha source on the ruler at a point where it produces a nearly full-scale reading on the meter (Figure 8). Watch the meter for 30 seconds and estimate the average cpm detected during this period. Subtract the background reading from this value and record the result.
4. Without moving the radiation source, place a piece of cardboard (index card) between the probe and the source, as shown in Figure 9.

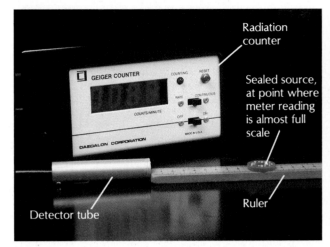

Figure 8 The apparatus setup for Part 1.

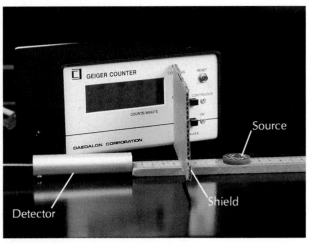

Figure 9 Place the shield between the probe and the radiation source.

5. Again watch the meter for 30 seconds. Correct the average reading for background radiation and record the result.
6. Repeat Steps 4 and 5 using a glass plate.
7. Repeat Steps 4 and 5 using a lead plate.
8. Repeat Steps 3 through 7 using a beta-particle source.
9. Repeat Steps 3 through 7 using a gamma-ray source.

Questions

1. Analyze your results from Steps 4 through 9. Which shielding materials were effective in reducing the intensity of each type of radiation?
2. How do the three types of radiation tested compare in penetrating power?
3. Of the shielding materials tested, which do you conclude
   a. is the most effective in blocking radiation?
   b. is the least effective?
4. What properties of a material do you think determine its radiation-shielding ability?

Part 2: Effect of Distance on Intensity

1. Prepare a data table containing two columns: one to record distance from the probe, the other to record radiation intensity (cpm) values.
2. Place a radioactive source designated by your teacher at the point on the ruler that produces nearly a full-scale reading (usually a distance of about 5 cm).
3. Record a corrected average reading over 30 seconds.
4. Move the source so the distance from the probe is doubled.
5. Record a corrected average reading over 30 seconds.
6. Move the source twice more, so the original distance is first tripled, then quadrupled, recording a corrected reading after each move. (For example, if you started at 5 cm, you would take readings at 5, 10, 15, and 20 cm.)
7. Prepare a graph, plotting the corrected cpm on the y axis, and the distance from source to probe (in cm) on the x axis.

Figure 10 The relationship between distance from source and intensity of radiation. Intensity is counts per minute in a given area. Note how the same amount of radiation spreads over a larger area as the distance from the source increases.

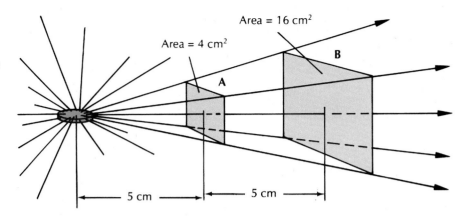

Questions

Analyze the graph you prepared in Step 7.

A factor is a number by which a number is multiplied or divided to become a new number.

1. By what whole-number factor did the intensity of radiation (measured in counts per minute) decrease when the initial distance was doubled?
2. Did this same whole-number factor apply when the distance was doubled again?
3. Try stating the mathematical relationship between distance and intensity using this factor and Figure 10.

Part 3: Shielding Effects

1. Use forceps to place a source, designated by your teacher, on the ruler at a distance that produces nearly a full-scale reading.
2. Take an average reading over 15 seconds, correcting for background.
3. Place one glass plate between the source and probe. Take an average reading over 15 seconds, correcting for background radiation.
4. Place a second glass plate between the source and probe. Take an average reading over 15 seconds, correcting for background radiation.
5. Repeat Steps 3 and 4, using lead sheets rather than glass plates.
6. Wash your hands thoroughly before leaving the laboratory.

Questions

1. How effective was doubling the shield thickness in blocking radiation intensity
   a. for glass?
   b. for lead?
2. When any part of the body is receiving medical or dental X rays, the rest of the body should be shielded with a special blanket. What material would be a good choice for this blanket? Why?
3. Which type of radiation (from a source outside the body) is likely to be most dangerous to living organisms? Why?

   You have found that the three kinds of radiation differ greatly in their penetrating abilities. Why is this so? What *are* alpha and beta particles? Where do they come from? We will address these questions in the next section.

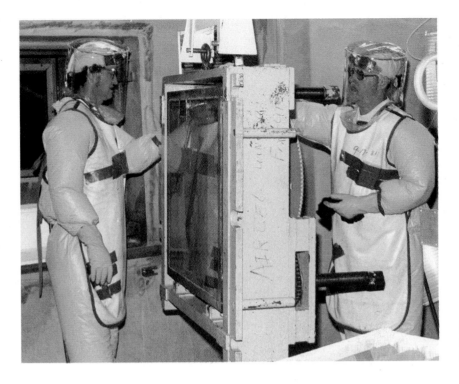

Radioactive materials are handled safely at Argonne National Laboratory—West in Idaho.

B.2 NATURAL RADIOACTIVE DECAY

An *alpha particle* is composed of two protons and two neutrons. It is the nucleus of a helium-4 atom: $^4_2\text{He}^{2+}$. Alpha radiation is emitted by radioactive isotopes of some elements with atomic numbers higher than 83. An alpha particle is nearly 8,000 times more massive than a beta particle, but has very poor penetrating power (as you noted in Laboratory Activity B.1). Alpha particles are stopped by a few centimeters of air. An alpha-emitter can be held safely for a short time in your hand, since alpha particles cannot penetrate skin.

The alpha particle's large mass can cause great damage, but only over very short distances. Because alpha particles are very powerful tissue-damaging agents once inside the body, alpha emitters in air or food are particularly dangerous to human life.

Figure 11 illustrates a radium-226 nucleus emitting an alpha particle. The radium nucleus loses two protons, so its atomic number drops from 88 to 86. It also loses two neutrons, so the mass number drops by four to 222, leaving an isotope of a different element, radon-222. The decay process can be represented by this equation:

$$^{226}_{88}\text{Ra} \longrightarrow \quad ^4_2\text{He} \quad + \quad ^{222}_{86}\text{Rn}$$

Radium-226   Alpha Particle   Radon-222

Atoms of two elements—helium and radon—have been formed from one atom of radon. Note that atoms are not necessarily conserved in nuclear reactions, as they are in chemical reactions. Atoms of different elements can appear on each side of a nuclear equation.

However, mass numbers and atomic numbers *are* conserved in nuclear reactions. In the equation above, the sum of mass numbers of the reactants equals that of the products (226 = 4 + 222). Also, the sum of atomic numbers of the reactants equals

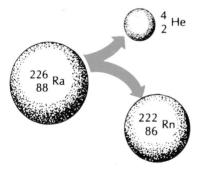

Figure 11 Alpha particle emission from radium-226. The mass number decreases by 4 (2p + 2n) and the atomic number decreases by 2 (2p).

Ionic charges, such as the 2+ charge on the alpha particle, are usually not included in nuclear symbols.

that of the products (88 = 2 + 86). Both of these relations hold true for all nuclear reactions.

Beta particles are fast-moving electrons emitted from the nucleus during radioactive decay. Since they are less massive than alpha particles and travel at very high velocities, beta particles have much greater penetrating power than do alpha particles. However, beta particles are not as damaging to living tissue.

During beta decay, a neutron changes into a proton and an electron. The proton remains in the nucleus, but the electron (a beta particle) is ejected at high speed. A third particle, an antineutrino, is also released. This equation describes the process:

$$\underset{\text{Neutron}}{{}^{1}_{0}\text{n}} \quad \rightarrow \quad \underset{\text{Proton}}{{}^{1}_{1}\text{p}} \quad + \quad \underset{\substack{\text{Beta particle}\\\text{(electron)}}}{{}^{0}_{-1}\text{e}} \quad + \quad \text{Antineutrino}$$

A beta particle is assigned a mass number of 0 and an "atomic number"—that is, a nuclear charge—of −1.

Figure 12 shows beta decay in the nucleus of lead-210, in which the nucleus loses one neutron, but gains one proton. Thus the mass number remains unchanged at 210, but the atomic number increases to 83. The new nucleus formed is that of bismuth-210.

$$\underset{\text{Lead-210}}{{}^{210}_{82}\text{Pb}} \quad \rightarrow \quad \underset{\text{Bismuth-210}}{{}^{210}_{83}\text{Bi}} \quad + \quad \underset{\substack{\text{Beta particle}\\\text{(electron)}}}{{}^{0}_{-1}\text{e}}$$

Once again, note that the sum of all mass numbers remains constant during this nuclear reaction. The sum of atomic numbers (the nuclear charge) remains constant, as well.

Alpha and beta decay often leave nuclei in an excited state. This type of excited state, described as metastable, is designated by the symbol m. For example, ⁹⁹ᵐTc represents a technetium isotope in a metastable excited state. Energy from isotopes in such excited states is released as *gamma rays*—high-energy electromagnetic radiation having as much (or more) energy per photon as X rays.

Of the three forms of radiation, gamma rays are the most penetrating, but under some circumstances—the least tissue-damaging over comparable distances. Tissue damage is related to the extent of ionization created by the radiation, expressed as the number of ionizations within each unit of tissue. *Alpha particles cause considerable damage over short range, but protecting against them is easy. Beta and gamma radiation do*

Beta decay is always accompanied by emission of an antineutrino.

Note in the equation that n, p, and e are used as the symbols, respectively, for a neutron, proton, and a beta particle—an electron. It is also acceptable to symbolize an electron (beta particle) by the Greek letter beta: ${}^{0}_{-1}\beta$.

Atomic number balance: 83 + (− 1) = 82

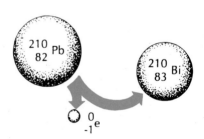

Figure 12 Beta decay of lead-210.

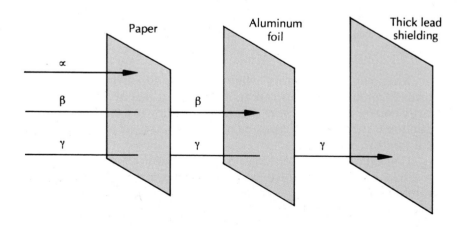

Figure 13 The relative penetrating powers of alpha (α), beta (β), and gamma (γ) radiation. Gamma rays are the most penetrating, alpha particles the least.

less damage over longer range, but it is more difficult to protect against them (see Figure 13).

Since gamma rays have neither mass nor charge, their emission does not change the mass or charge balance in a nuclear equation.

New isotopes produced by radioactive decay are also frequently radioactive and therefore decay further. Uranium (U) and thorium (Th) are the "parents" (reactants) in three natural decay series, which begin with U-238, U-235, and Th-232, respectively. Each series ends with formation of a stable isotope of lead (Pb).

The decay series starting with uranium-238 contains 13 steps, as shown in Figure 14. Table 6 summarizes general information regarding natural radioactive decay. Use the table to complete the following exercise.

Figure 14 The uranium-238 decay series. Diagonal lines show alpha decay, horizontal lines show beta decay. Here's how to "read" this chart: Locate radon-222 (Rn-222). The arrow to the left shows that this isotope decays to polonium-218 (Po-218) by alpha (α) emission. This nuclear equation applies:
$^{222}_{86}$Rn → $^{218}_{84}$Po + $^4_2$He.

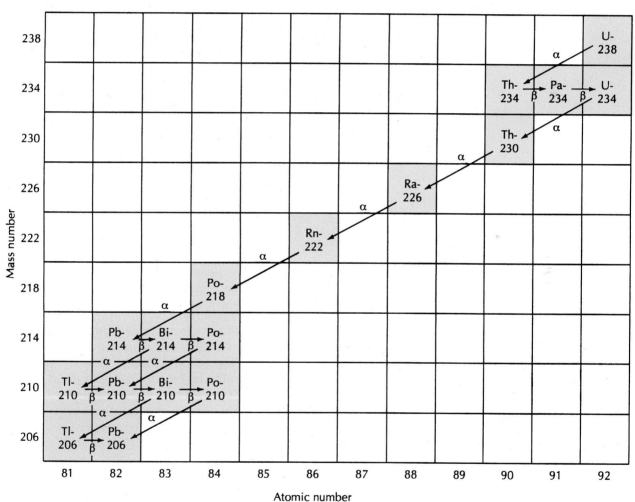

Table 6   CHANGES RESULTING FROM NUCLEAR DECAY

Type	Symbol	Change in Atomic Number	Change in Neutrons	Change in Mass Number
Alpha	$^4_2$He	Decreased by 2	Decreased by 2	Decreased by 4
Beta	$^0_{-1}$e	Increased by 1	Decreased by 1	No change
Gamma	$^0_0\gamma$	No change	No change	No change

Nuclear Balancing Act

The key to balancing nuclear equations is recognizing that both atomic and mass numbers are conserved.

Consider this question:

Cobalt-60 is a common source of ionizing radiation for medical therapy. Complete this equation for the beta decay of cobalt-60:

$$^{60}_{27}\text{Co} \rightarrow \ ^{0}_{-1}\text{e} + ?$$

Beta emission causes no change in mass number, as noted in Table 6. Therefore the new isotope will also have mass number 60. Thus we can write the unknown product as $^{60}?$. Because the atomic number increases by 1 during beta emission, the new isotope will have atomic number 28. The periodic table shows that nickel has this atomic number. The final equation is

$$^{60}_{27}\text{Co} \rightarrow \ ^{0}_{-1}\text{e} + ^{60}_{28}\text{Ni}$$

1. Write the appropriate symbol for the type of radiation given off in each reaction:

    a. The following decay process allows archaeologists to date the remains of ancient biological materials. Living organisms take in carbon-14 and maintain a relatively constant amount of it over their lifetime. After death no more carbon-14 is taken in, so the amount gradually decreases due to decay.

    $$^{14}_{6}\text{C} \rightarrow ^{14}_{7}\text{N} + ?$$

    b. This decay process takes place in some types of household smoke detectors.

    $$^{241}_{95}\text{Am} \rightarrow ^{237}_{93}\text{Np} + ?$$

2. Thorium (Th) occurs in nature as three isotopes: Th-232, Th-230, and Th-228. The first of these is the most abundant. Thorium's radiation intensity is quite low; its compounds can be used without great danger if kept outside the body. In fact, thorium oxide (ThO_2) was widely used in gas mantles in Europe and America during the gas-lighting era to speed combustion of the gas. This is the source of the radioactivity you detected in the lantern mantle you tested in Laboratory Activity A.1.

    Th-232 is the parent isotope of the third natural decay series. This series and the U-238 series are believed responsible for much of the heat generated inside the earth (The U-235 series contribution is negligible since the abundance of U-235 is quite low.)

    Complete these equations, representing the first steps in the Th-232 decay series, by identifying each of the missing items A, B, C, and D.

    a. $^{232}_{90}\text{Th} \rightarrow \text{A} + ^{228}_{88}\text{Ra}$

    b. $^{228}_{88}\text{Ra} \rightarrow \ ^{0}_{-1}\text{e} + \text{B}$

    c. $\text{B} \rightarrow \ ^{0}_{-1}\text{e} + \text{C}$

    d. $^{228}_{90}\text{Th} \rightarrow \ ^{4}_{2}\text{He} + \text{D}$

    e. $\text{D} \rightarrow \ ^{4}_{2}\text{He} + ^{220}_{86}\text{Rn}$

The Th-232 decay series finally ends, after several more steps, with formation of stable Pb-208.

Different radioactive isotopes have different lifetimes. Scientists have devised convenient ways to measure and report how fast various radioisotopes decay. In the next section, you will learn about these decay rates, which help determine how useful or hazardous a radioisotope may be.

B.3   HALF-LIFE: A RADIOACTIVE CLOCK

How long does it take for a sample of radioactive material to decay? Knowing the answer to this question allows scientists to predict the total time a radioisotope used in medical diagnosis will remain active within the body, to plan how long hazardous nuclear wastes must be stored, and to estimate the ages of ancient civilizations and of the world itself.

The rate of decay of radioisotopes is measured in half-lives. One **half-life** is the time it takes for one-half the atoms in a sample of radioactive material to decay. Consider carbon-14. This isotope has a half-life of 5730 years. If we start with 50 billion atoms of carbon-14, in 5730 years 25 billion atoms will have decayed to nitrogen-14, leaving 25 billion atoms of the original carbon-14. In another 5730 years, one-half of the remaining 25 billion atoms will decay, leaving 12.5 billion atoms of carbon-14. And so on.

Half-lives vary greatly for different radioisotopes. For example, the half-life of polonium-212 is 3×10^{-7} seconds, while that of uranium-238 is 4.5 billion years. Table 7 lists half-lives for some common radioisotopes.

After 10 half-lives—or 57,300 years—50 million carbon-14 atoms will still be present.

Table 7   **HALF-LIVES OF COMMON RADIOISOTOPES**

Isotope	Decay Process	Half-life
Radon-222	$^{222}_{86}Ra \rightarrow ^{218}_{84}Po + ^{4}_{2}He$	3.28 d
Hydrogen-3	$^{3}_{1}H \rightarrow ^{3}_{2}He + ^{0}_{-1}e$	12.3 y
Potassium-40	$^{40}_{19}K \rightarrow ^{40}_{20}Ca + ^{0}_{-1}e$	1.28×10^{9} y

After 10 half-lives, only about 1/1000th or 0.1% of the original radioisotope is still left to decay. (Can you verify this statement with your own calculations?) That means that the isotope's activity has dropped to 0.1% of its initial level of intensity. In many cases this is considered a safe level; in others it is not. Since there is no way to speed up the rate of radioactive decay, radioactive waste disposal is a very difficult problem. We will look into this in a later section.

The concept of half-life is explored further in the following activity.

B.4   LABORATORY ACTIVITY: HALF-LIFE

In this activity you will simulate radioactive decay with pennies. The pennies can be used to discover the relationship between the passage of time and the number of radioactive nuclei that decay.

Suppose that a heads-up penny represents an atom of a radioactive isotope of the element coinium—let's call it headsium.

The ages of excavated artifacts can be determined by measuring the extent of decay of radioactive isotopes in the organic artifacts.

The product of this isotope's decay is a tails-up penny—the isotope tailsium.

You will be given 80 pennies and a container. Placing all the pennies in the container heads up will represent the "starting" composition of our radioisotope. Each shake of the container will represent one half-life period. During this period a certain number of headsium nuclei will decay to give tailsium (some pennies will flip over).

Construct a data table like that below in your notebook. The first data entry has been made for you.

Data Table

Number of Half-lives	Number of Decayed "Atoms"	Number of Nondecayed "Atoms"
0	0	80

1. Place the 80 pennies heads up in the box.
2. Close the box and shake it vigorously.
3. Open the box. Remove from the box all atoms of decayed headsium (coins that have turned over). Record the number of decayed and undecayed atoms of headsium at the end of this first half-life.
4. Repeat Steps 2 and 3 three more times. At this point you will have simulated four half-lives. You should have five numbers in your final data summary, representing the number of atoms remaining after zero, one, two, three, and four half-lives.
5. Following your teacher's instructions, pool the class data by finding the total number of atoms decayed for the whole class after the first half-life, the second half-life, and so on.
6. Using your own data and class pooled data, prepare a graph by plotting the number of half-lives on the x axis and the number of undecayed atoms remaining for each half life on the y axis. Plot two graph lines—one for your own data, one for pooled class data. Label both graph lines.

Questions

1. a. Describe the appearance of your two graph lines. Are they straight or curved?
    b. Which set of data—your own or pooled class data—provided the more convincing demonstration of the notion of half-life? Why?
2. How many undecayed headsium nuclei would remain out of a sample of 600 headsium nuclei after three half-lives?
3. If 175 headsium nuclei remain out of an original sample of 2800 nuclei, how many half-lives must have passed?
4. Name one similarity and one difference between this simulation and actual radioactive decay. (*Hint:* Why was it advisable to pool class data?)
5. How could you modify this simulation to demonstrate that different isotopes have different half-lives?

6. a. How many half-lives would it take for a one mole of any radioactive atoms (6.02×10^{23} atoms) to decay to 6.25% (0.376×10^{23} atoms) of the original number of atoms?

   b. Would any of the original radioactive atoms still remain
      (1) after 10 half-lives?
      (2) after 100 half-lives?

7. a. In this simulation is there any way to predict when a particular penny will "decay"?

   b. If you could follow the fate of an individual atom in a sample of radioactive material, could you predict when it would decay? Why?

8. Can you think of another way to model the concept of half-life?

   The curves you constructed in this activity apply to the decay of every radioactive isotope. However, the important difference is that the half-life is unique for each isotope. One half-life may be measured in millions of years, or measured in only fractions of a second.

   The following exercise will give you practice applying the half-life concept.

YOUR TURN

Half-lives

1. Suppose you were given $1000 and told you could spend one-half of it in the first year, one-half of the balance in the second year, and so on. (One year thus corresponds to the half-life in this analogy.)

   a. If you spent the maximum allowed each year, at the end of what year would you have $31.25 left?

   b. How much would be left after 10 half-lives (that is, 10 years)?

2. Cobalt-60 is a radioisotope used as a source of ionizing radiation in cancer treatment; the radiation it emits is effective in killing rapidly-dividing cancer cells. Cobalt-60 has a half-life of five years.

   a. If a hospital starts with a 1000-mg supply, how many milligrams of Co-60 would it need to purchase after 10 years to replenish the original supply? Does the answer depend on how frequently cobalt isotope radiation was used to treat patients? Why?

   b. How many half-lives would it take for the supply of cobalt-60 to dwindle to
      (1) less than 10% of the original?
      (2) less than 1% of the original?
      (3) less than 0.1% of the original?

3. Even though the activity of a sample is only 0.1% of its original value after 10 half-lives, theoretically it would take virtually forever for a reasonably-sized sample of radioactive material to decay completely. To help you understand this concept, consider this analogy:

A person is attempting to reach a telephone booth, which is 512 m away. Assume that the person covers half this distance (256 m) in the first minute, half the remaining distance (128 m) during the second minute, half the remainder (64 m) in the third minute, and so on. In other words, the "half-life" for this moving process is one minute.

a. If the individual never covers more than half the remaining distance in each one-minute interval, how long—at least in theory—will it take the person to reach the phone booth?

b. How many half-lives will be needed to get within 25 cm of the booth?

4. Strontium-90 is one of many radioactive wastes of nuclear weapons. This isotope is especially dangerous if it enters the food supply. Strontium behaves chemically like calcium; the two elements belong to the same chemical family. Thus, rather than passing through the body, strontium-90 is incorporated into calcium-based material such as bone. The United States, the Soviet Union, and several other countries signed a nuclear test ban treaty in 1963, which ended most above-ground weapons testing. Some strontium-90 released in previous above-ground nuclear tests still remains in the environment, however.

a. Sr-90 has a half-life of nearly 28 years. Track the decay of Sr-90 originally present in the atmosphere in 1963 by following these instructions:

   (1) Using 1963 as year zero, when 100% of released Sr-90 was present, identify the year that represents one, two, three, etc., half-lives. Stop when you reach the year 2100.

   (2) Calculate the percent of original 1963 Sr-90 radioactivity present at the end of each half-life year.

   (3) Prepare a graph, plotting the percent of original 1963 Sr-90 radioactivity on the y axis, and the years 1963 to 2100 on the x axis.

   (4) Connect the data points with a smooth curve.

b. What percent of Sr-90 formed in 1963 still remains today?

c. What percent will remain in the year 2100?

Since we cannot see, hear, feel, taste, or smell radioactivity, we must use special detection devices to indicate its presence. You have already used a radiation counter. This and some other radiation detectors are explained in the next section.

B.5 RADIATION DETECTORS

One way to detect radioactive decay is to observe the results of the interaction of radiation with matter. In the radiation counter

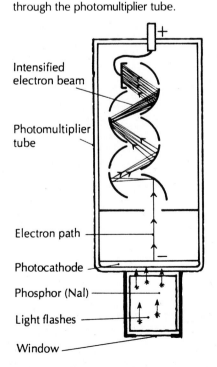

Figure 15 A scintillation counter probe. Ionizing radiation causes flashes of light (scintillations) in the phosphor. Each light flash is converted into an electron pulse that is increased many times as it moves through the photomultiplier tube.

Intensified electron beam

Photomultiplier tube

Electron path

Photocathode

Phosphor (NaI)

Light flashes

Window

you used earlier (Laboratory Activity B.1), for example, argon gas is ionized by entering radiation. The ionized gas conducts electric current, and an electric signal is generated as the ions and components of radiation pass through the probe.

Devices called **scintillation counters** detect entering radiation as light emitted by the excited atoms of a solid. The scintillation counter probe pictured in Figure 15 is lined with sodium iodide (NaI), which emits light when ionizing radiation strikes it.

Solid-state detectors, which monitor the movement of electrons through silicon and other semiconductors, are the primary detectors used today for detecting and measuring radioactivity.

You learned earlier in this unit that radioactivity will expose photographic film. Workers who handle radioisotopes wear film badges or other detection devices to measure their exposure. If they get a dose in excess of federal limits, they are temporarily reassigned to jobs that minimize exposure to radiation.

Ionizing radiation can also be detected in a cloud chamber. You will try out this detection method in the following activity.

B.6 LABORATORY ACTIVITY: CLOUD CHAMBERS

Getting Ready

A **cloud chamber** is a glass container filled with air which is saturated with water or other vapor, like the air on a humid day. If cooled, the air inside will become supersaturated. (Recall from the Water unit, page 40, that this is an unstable condition.) If a radioactive source is placed near a cloud chamber filled with supersaturated air, the radiation will ionize the air inside as it passes through the chamber. Vapor condenses on the ions formed, leaving a white trail behind each passing radioactive emission, revealing the path of the particle or ray. Figure 16 is a photograph taken of particle tracks under similar conditions.

The cloud chamber you will use consists of a small plastic container and a felt band moistened with 2-propanol (isopropyl alcohol). The alcohol evaporates faster than water and saturates

Cloud chamber trails resemble the "vapor trails" from high-flying aircraft.

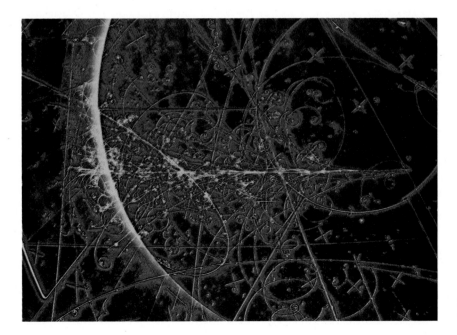

Figure 16 A photograph of particle tracks.

The temperature of the dry ice, solid carbon dioxide, will be −78° C.

air more readily. The cloud chamber will be chilled with dry ice to promote supersaturation and cloud formation.

Procedure

1. Fully moisten the felt band inside the cloud chamber with alcohol. Also place a small quantity of alcohol on the container bottom.
2. Using gloves and forceps, quickly place the radioactive source on the chamber bottom. Replace the lid.
3. To cool the chamber, embed it in crushed dry ice. Be sure the chamber remains level.
4. Leave the chamber on the dry ice for three to five minutes.
5. Dim or turn off the room lights. Focus the light source through the container at an oblique angle (not straight down) so it illuminates the chamber base. (If you do not observe any vapor trails, try shining the light through the container's side instead.)
6. Observe the air in the chamber near the radioactive source. Record your observations.

Questions

1. What differences—if any—did you observe among the tracks?
2. Which type of radiation do you think would make the most visible tracks? Why?
3. What is the purpose of the dry ice?

Recall that the radiation observed in a cloud chamber is emitted from an unstable, radioactive isotope which is eventually converted to a stable, nonradioactive isotope. Do you think it might be possible to reverse the process, converting a stable isotope into an unstable, radioactive isotope? You will find the answer to this question in the next section.

B.7 ARTIFICIAL RADIOACTIVITY

In 1919, to find out whether he could make radioactive elements in the laboratory, Ernest Rutherford enclosed nitrogen gas in a glass tube and bombarded it with alpha particles. After analyzing the gas remaining, he found that some nitrogen had been converted to an isotope of oxygen, according to this equation:

$$\underset{\text{Helium-4}}{^{4}_{2}\text{He}} \quad + \quad \underset{\text{Nitrogen-14}}{^{14}_{7}\text{N}} \quad \rightarrow \quad \underset{\text{Oxygen-17}}{^{17}_{8}\text{O}} \quad + \quad \underset{\text{Hydrogen-1}}{^{1}_{1}\text{H}}$$

Rutherford had produced the first synthetic or artificial nucleus, oxygen-17. He had successfully accomplished **transmutation** of the elements—the conversion of one element to another. However, the new element was not radioactive. Rutherford continued his work, but he was limited by the moderate energies of the alpha particles he had available. Other scientists, using improved tools, would reach Rutherford's goal.

By 1930, particle accelerators were developed that could produce the highly energetic particles needed for additional bombardment reactions. The first radioactive artificial isotope was produced in 1934 by the French physicists Frédéric and Irène Joliot-Curie (the son-in-law and daughter of Pierre and Marie

Curie). They bombarded aluminum with alpha particles, producing radioactive phosphorus-30:

$$^{27}_{13}\text{Al} + ^{4}_{2}\text{He} \rightarrow ^{30}_{15}\text{P} + ^{1}_{0}\text{n}$$

Since then, many transformations of one element to another element have been completed. In addition, a number of new elements have been synthesized in nuclear reactions.

YOUR TURN

Bombardment Reactions

Each of these reactions involves four particles:

- The **target nucleus** is the stable isotope that is bombarded.
- The **projectile** (bullet) is the particle fired at the target nucleus.
- The **product** is the heavy nucleus produced in the reaction.
- The **ejected particle** is the light nucleus or particle emitted from the reaction.

For example, consider the Joliot-Curies' production of the first synthetic radioactive isotope. The four types of particles involved are identified below:

Target nucleus		Projectile		Product nucleus		Ejected particle
$^{27}_{13}\text{Al}$	$+$	$^{4}_{2}\text{He}$	$\rightarrow$	$^{30}_{15}\text{P}$	$+$	$^{1}_{0}\text{n}$
Aluminum-27		Alpha particle		Phosphorus-30		Neutron

As you learned earlier, completing nuclear equations involves balancing atomic and mass numbers.

Nobelium (No) was produced by bombarding curium (Cm), a synthetic element, with nuclei of a light element. We can identify this element by completing this equation.

$$^{246}_{96}\text{Cm} + ? \rightarrow ^{254}_{102}\text{No} + 4\,^{1}_{0}\text{n}$$

As the sum of the product atomic numbers is 102, the projectile must have the atomic number 6 (96 + 6 = 102)—a carbon atom. The total mass number of products is 258, indicating that the projectile must have been carbon-12 (246 + 12 = 258). The completed equation is

$^{246}_{96}\text{Cm}$	$+$	$^{12}_{6}\text{C}$	$\rightarrow$	$^{254}_{102}\text{No}$	$+$	$4\,^{1}_{0}\text{n}$
Target nucleus		Projectile		Product nucleus		Ejected particles

For the following items, complete the equations by supplying missing numbers or symbols. Name each particle. Then identify the target nucleus, projectile, product nucleus, and ejected particle.

1. $^{59}_{27}? + ^{?}_{?}\text{n} \rightarrow ^{60}_{?}?$

   In this reaction, a naturally-occurring nonradioactive isotope is converted into a medically useful, radioactive form of the same element.

2. $^{96}_{42}? + ^{?}_{?}H \rightarrow ^{97}_{43}? + ^{1}_{0}?$

Until its synthesis in 1937, technetium (Tc) existed only as a "hole" in the periodic table; its isotopes are all radioactive. Any technetium originally on the earth has disintegrated. Technetium, the first new element produced artificially, is now used extensively in industry and medicine. Each year, for example, millions of bone scans are obtained through the use of technetium.

3. $^{209}_{83}? + ^{4}_{2}? \rightarrow ^{211}_{85}? + ? \, ^{1}_{0}n$

With the synthesis of astatine (At) in 1940, another gap in the periodic table was filled. Since its creation in the laboratory, naturally-occurring astatine has also been detected in very small quantities.

Not only does the ability to transform one element into another give us powerful technological capabilities, but it also has changed the way we view elements. Within the last 50 years, 17 **transuranium** elements (those with atomic numbers greater than uranium's atomic number of 92), have been added to the periodic table. For that reason the periodic table has expanded to include a new series of elements, the **actinide series.**

Sculptor Henry Moore created this work to commemorate the birth of the nuclear age.

CHEMQUANDARY

Transmutation of Elements

Ancient alchemists searched in vain for ways to transform lead or iron into gold (transmutation of the elements). Has transmutation now become a reality? From what you know about nuclear changes, do you think that lead or iron could be changed into gold? If you do, write equations for the reactions.

In the 1930s a bombardment reaction involving uranium-238 unlocked a new energy source to the world. It led to development of both nuclear power and nuclear weapons. This was the beginning of the nuclear age. Nuclear energy provides the focus of Part C.

PART B: SUMMARY QUESTIONS

1. Name the type of radioactive radiation released in each case:
   a. A radioactive iodine isotope decays to form a xenon isotope with a higher atomic number but the same mass number as the iodine.
   b. Technetium-99m decays, yet its atomic number and mass number both remain unchanged.

   c. A thorium isotope decays to form a radium isotope that has a lower atomic number and mass number than the original thorium.

2. Complete these equations:
   a. $^{60}_{27}Co \rightarrow ? + ^{0}_{-1}e$
   This reaction represents the decay mode of the medically important, synthetic radioisotope, Co-60.

b. $? \rightarrow {}^{40}_{20}\text{Ca} + {}^{0}_{-1}\text{e}$

About 0.01% of naturally-occurring atoms of this element are radioactive. It is one of the main radioisotopes in your body. It has a half-life of 1.28×10^9 years and decays as shown above.

c. ${}^{241}_{95}? \rightarrow {}^{?}_{?}? + {}^{4}_{2}\text{He}$

This synthetic radioisotope (half-life = 450 years) finds practical use in household ionization smoke detectors. Why would an alpha emitter such as this with a relatively long half-life be suitable for such an application?

3. Suppose you have a sample containing 800 nuclei of a radioactive isotope. After one hour, only 50 of the original nuclei remain. What is the half-life of this isotope?

4. You have 400 μg (micrograms) of a radioisotope with a half-life of five minutes. How much will be left after 30 minutes?

5. Gold (Au) exists primarily as one natural isotope, Au-197. A variety of synthetic radioisotopes of gold, with mass numbers from 177 to 203, have been produced. Suppose you have a 100-mg sample of pure Au-191, which has a half-life of 3.4 hours.

   a. Make a graph of its decay curve.

   b. Estimate how much Au-191 will remain after (1) 10 hours, (2) 24 hours, (3) 34 hours.

c. List two reasons why synthetic gold isotopes would not be a good substitute for natural gold in jewelry.

6. Describe three ways that ionizing radiation can be detected.

7. List the three types of radiation given off by radioactive sources in order of increasing penetrating power.

8. Starting in 1940, Glenn Seaborg and his associates at the University of California at Berkeley began a series of nuclear bombardment reactions that resulted in the discovery of new transuranium elements. The following two equations represent their synthesis of two transuranium radioisotopes. For each, name the projectile, the element formed, and the ejected particle(s).

   a. ${}^{239}_{?}\text{Pu} + ? \rightarrow {}^{242}_{?}\text{Cm} + {}^{1}_{0}\text{n}$

   Half-life = 24,400 years to form Cm-242, having a half-life of 163 days

   b. ${}^{239}_{92}\text{U} + ? \rightarrow {}^{238}_{93}? + 2\,{}^{1}_{0}\text{n}$

   Half-life = 2.1 days to form Pu-238, having a half-life of 89 years

9. Which radioisotope in Question 8 (Pu-239 or U-239) would be more useful to power a space probe? Why?

EXTENDING YOUR KNOWLEDGE (OPTIONAL)

- **Neutrinos** are fundamental particles with very little mass (much less than an electron), and no charge. Look into the discovery of the neutrino. It is a story of great scientific conviction and persistence. Would you expect an instrument such as a cloud chamber to show neutrino trails? Explain your answer.

- A variety of charged particles (such as alpha and beta particles), uncharged particles (neutrons), and gamma rays have been used as projectiles in nuclear bombardment research. What are advantages and disadvantages of each? How are the velocities of these nuclear projectiles controlled? How are they "aimed"? Topics you may wish to explore include electrostatic generators,

cyclotrons, and linear accelerators. Also of interest is the role played by nuclear reactors in synthesizing radioisotopes.

- U-235 is the parent isotope for the decay series ending with Pb-207. The entire series can be represented as:

${}^{235}_{92}\text{U} \rightarrow \text{[many steps]} \rightarrow {}^{207}_{82}\text{Pb} + ?\,{}^{4}_{2}\text{He} + ?\,{}^{0}_{-1}\text{e}$

Based on overall changes in atomic numbers and mass numbers from the parent isotope to the final stable product, how many total alpha and beta particles must be emitted during the decay of one atom of U-235?

- Look into the use of radioactive isotopes for dating artifacts and rocks, and for judging the authenticity of paintings.

C

NUCLEAR ENERGY: POWERING THE UNIVERSE

How did scientists first unleash the enormous energy of the atom, and how has atomic energy been used for generating electricity? These topics are our focus in the following sections.

C.1 SPLITTING THE ATOM

In the early years of World War II, the German scientists Otto Hahn and Fritz Strassman bombarded uranium with neutrons in the hope of creating a more massive nucleus. Much to their surprise, they found that one reaction product was barium—an atom only about half as massive as uranium.

The first to understand what had happened was an Austrian physicist, Lise Meitner, who had worked with Strassman and Hahn earlier. She suggested that neutron bombardment had split the uranium atom into two parts that were nearly equal in size. Other scientists immediately verified Meitner's explanation. The world had witnessed its first **nuclear fission reaction.**

Hahn and Strassman had actually triggered an array of related fission reactions. One reaction that might have produced the barium is this:

$$^{235}_{92}\text{U} + {}^{1}_{0}\text{n} \rightarrow {}^{140}_{56}\text{Ba} + {}^{93}_{36}\text{Kr} + 3\,{}^{1}_{0}\text{n}$$

Uranium-235   Neutron   Barium-140   Krypton-93   Neutrons

Scientists soon found that the uranium-235 nucleus can **fission** or split into numerous combinations of products, but usually into a heavier element (such as barium) and a less-massive element (such as krypton). Here is another example:

$$^{235}_{92}\text{U} + {}^{1}_{0}\text{n} \rightarrow {}^{143}_{54}\text{Xe} + {}^{90}_{38}\text{Sr} + 3\,{}^{1}_{0}\text{n}$$

Uranium-235   Neutron   Xenon-143   Strontium-90   Neutrons

Uranium-235 is the only naturally-occurring isotope that undergoes fission. Many synthetic nuclei—in particular uranium-233, plutonium-239, and californium-252—also split under neutron bombardment.

Austrian physicist Lise Meitner.

Over 200 different radioisotopes have been identified among the products of fission reactions — products with half-lives ranging from a fraction of a second to millions of years. Such a diverse mixture greatly increases the challenge and difficulty of waste disposal from nuclear reactors.

C.2 THE STRONG FORCE

The fission of uranium-235 and other fissionable isotopes releases at least a million times more energy than that produced in any chemical reaction. This is what makes nuclear explosions so devastating and nuclear energy so powerful.

The source of nuclear energy lies in the force that holds protons and neutrons together in the nucleus. This force, called the **strong force,** is fundamentally different from—and a thousand times stronger than—the electrical forces that hold atoms and ions together in chemical compounds. The range of the strong force extends only to the diameter of the atomic nucleus.

How is the strong force related to the energy released in nuclear reactions? Recall what you learned about the energy from petroleum and food. In chemical reactions, when chemical bonds are stronger in products than in reactants, energy is released—often as heat. In nuclear reactions the strong force can be stronger in product nuclei than in those of reactants, and this results in a release of energy. However, the energy from nuclear reactions is so much greater than that from chemical reactions that something more must be involved.

In chemical and physical changes, energy may be converted from one form to another, but we do not observe any overall energy loss or or gain. Mass is also observed not to increase or decrease in chemical reactions.

These observations are the basis of the law of conservation of energy and law of conservation of matter.

In nuclear reactions, it's not just mass, or just energy, that is conserved, but the two together. Mass and energy are related according to Einstein's famous equation, $E = mc^2$. The energy released (E) is equal to the mass lost (m) multiplied by the speed of light squared (c^2). The complete conversion of just one gram of matter to energy would release energy equal to that produced by burning 700,000 gallons of octane fuel!

When changes take place in atomic nuclei, energy and mass are interconverted in accord with the Einstein equation. In nuclear fission, the mass of the fission products is slightly less than the mass of the atom that originally split. The mass loss is so small that it does not affect the mass numbers of reactants or products. Even so, the conversion of these small quantities of mass into energy accounts for the vast power of nuclear energy.

Nuclear scientists refer to the small changes in mass in nuclear reactions as "mass defect."

C.3 CHAIN REACTIONS

Another important result of fission is the emission of two or three neutrons from the fragments of each nucleus. These neutrons can keep the reaction going by splitting more nuclei. The result is a **chain reaction.**

Recall, however, that most of an atom is empty space. The probability that a neutron formed in a fission reaction will split another nucleus depends on the amount of fissionable material available. Unless a certain **critical mass** (minimum volume) of fissionable material is present, the neutrons cannot encounter enough nuclei to sustain the chain reaction.

When a critical mass of fissionable material is present, a chain reaction results (Figure 17, page 310). Recognition that such reactions were possible and could be utilized in military weapons came shortly after the first fission reaction was

Uranium metal is refined and shipped in a "derby", or 167 kg.

Figure 17 A nuclear chain reaction. The reaction is initiated (*left*) by a neutron colliding with a uranium-235 atom. It continues, in chain-like fashion, as long as the emitted neutrons encounter other fissionable atoms. The products of each individual fission can vary.

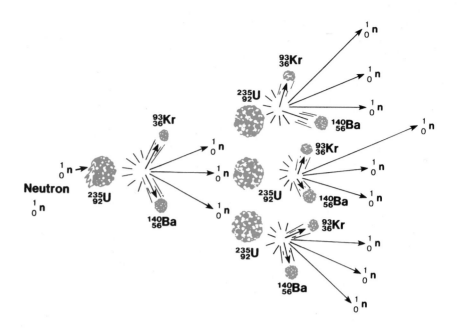

observed. Germany and the United States soon initiated projects to build "atomic bombs." U.S. aircraft dropped atomic bombs on Hiroshima and Nagasaki in Japan in 1945, near the end of World War II.

The following activity will give you a clearer picture of the dynamic nature of a chain reaction.

C.4 YOU DECIDE: THE DOMINO EFFECT

1. Obtain a set of dominoes or similarly-shaped objects. Set them up as shown in Figure 18. Arrange the dominoes so that when each one falls, it will knock over others. The more dominoes you use, the more dramatic the effect.
2. Knock over the lead domino.
   a. Observe the effect on the other dominoes.
   b. Would you call this an example of an expanding (out of control) or limited (controlled) chain reaction? Why?

Figure 18 The "domino effect." Dominoes arranged to simulate a chain reaction.

3. Set up the dominoes again. This time set up only a very few dominoes as in the first arrangement. Arrange the others so that when they fall, they will knock over only one other domino or none at all. Make a sketch of your design.

4. Knock over the lead domino. Observe the reaction. Is it an expanding or a limited chain reaction? Why?

5. a. Which of these two domino-tumbling cases is a better model of a nuclear bomb explosion? Why?

   b. Which better models a nuclear power plant reaction? Why?

6. Imagine that you had the dominoes arranged as in Step 3.

   a. What could you do to stop the reaction once it began?

   b. Do you think this method would be equally useful in stopping the reaction you observed in Step 2? Why?

7. a. In what way is this simulation like a nuclear chain reaction?

   b. How is it different?

   c. Can you think of another way to model a nuclear chain reaction?

By controlling the fission rate in a chain reaction, nuclear engineers make it possible to use the released heat to generate electricity. In the following section you will learn how this is done.

C.5 NUCLEAR POWER PLANTS

The first nuclear reactors were designed solely to produce plutonium-239 for use in World War II atomic weapons. Today, 110 commercial nuclear reactors (like that in Figure 19) produce electricity in the United States. In 1989, nuclear power met 5% of the

Figure 19 The Trojan nuclear power plant near Portland, Oregon. Such plants are characterized by tall, curved cooling towers.

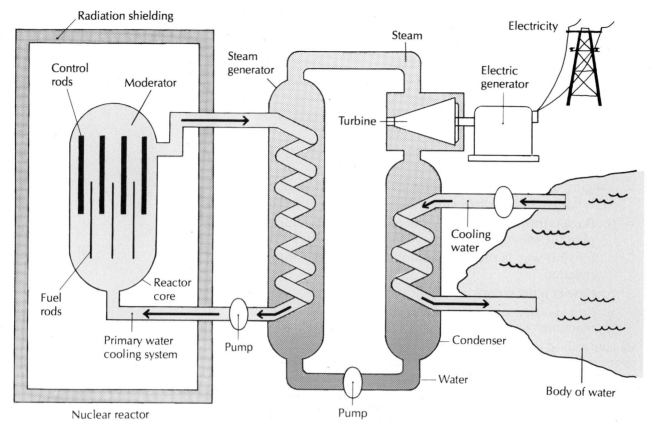

Figure 20 Diagram of a nuclear power plant.

nation's total energy needs, and generated nearly 20% of U.S. electrical power. On a global scale, an estimated 530 nuclear reactors in over 30 nations produce one-sixth of the world's electricity, and nearly 100 new nuclear power reactors were under construction in 1990.

Most power plants generate electricity by producing heat to boil water. The resulting steam spins the turbines of giant generators, producing electrical energy. A nuclear power plant is no exception. But, while coal-, oil-, and natural gas-powered generators use the heat of combustion of fossil fuels to boil water, nuclear power plants use the heat of nuclear fission reactions.

The essential parts of a nuclear power plant, diagrammed in Figure 20, are fuel rods, control rods, the moderator, the generator, and the cooling system.

Fuel Rods

Coal-fired power plants consume tons of coal daily. By contrast, the fuel for a nuclear reactor occupies a fraction of the volume needed for coal, and is loaded in only about once each year. Nuclear reactor fuel is in the form of pellets about the size and shape of short pieces of chalk. As many as 10 million fuel pellets may be used in one nuclear power plant. These pellets are arranged in long, narrow steel cylinders—the fuel rods. The fission chain reaction takes place inside these rods.

The fuel pellets contain uranium dioxide, UO_2. Most of this uranium is the nonfissionable uranium-238 isotope. Only a small fraction—about 3%—is fissionable uranium-235. That is enough to sustain a chain reaction but far from enough to permit a nuclear explosion.

Nuclear fuel pellets.

In contrast, weapons-grade uranium usually contains 90% or more of the fissionable uranium-235 isotope.

Close-up of fuel rod assembly.

Figure 21 Control rod drive shafts.

Control Rods

Certain materials, such as boron or cadmium, can absorb neutrons very efficiently. Such materials are placed in control rods. As neutrons are needed to trigger nuclear fission, their absorption by the nonfissionable control rods reduces the number available to cause fission. The rate of the chain reaction is controlled by moving the control rods up or down between the fuel rods (see Figure 21). Or, the reaction can be terminated altogether by dropping the control rods all the way down between the fuel rods.

Moderator

In addition to fuel rods and control rods, the core of a nuclear reactor also contains a moderator, which slows down high-speed neutrons so they can be more readily absorbed in other fuel rods to cause fissions. Heavy water (symbolized D_2O, where D is the hydrogen-2 isotope), regular water (termed "light water" by nuclear engineers), and graphite are the three most common moderator materials.

Generator

In all commercial nuclear reactors, the fuel and control rods are surrounded by a system of circulating water. In simpler reactors, the fuel rods boil this water, and the resulting steam spins the turbines of the electrical generator.

In another type of reactor, this water is superheated under pressure, and does not boil. Instead, it circulates through a heat exchanger, where it boils the water in a *second* cooling loop. This is the type of reactor shown in Figure 20.

Cooling System

The steam that has moved past the turbines is cooled by water taken from a nearby body of water. This water, now heated, flows back to the environment. The cooled steam condenses to liquid water and recirculates inside the generator. So much heat is generated that some also must be released into the air. The largest and most prominent feature of most nuclear power plants is a tall, gracefully tapered concrete cylinder—the cooling tower, where excess thermal energy is exhausted.

The core of a nuclear reactor is surrounded by concrete walls two to four meters thick. The reactor is designed to prevent the escape of radioactive material, should some malfunction cause radioactive material—including cooling water—to be released within the reactor itself. In addition, the reactor is housed in a building made with thick walls of steel-reinforced concrete, designed to withstand a chemical explosion or an earthquake.

Nuclear fission is not the only source of nuclear energy. In the next section you will learn about the nuclear reaction that fuels the stars (and, indirectly, all living matter).

The white fumes often seen rising from these cooling towers are not smoke, but rather condensed steam.

C.6 NUCLEAR FUSION

In addition to releasing energy by splitting massive nuclei, we can also generate large quantities of nuclear energy by *fusing*—or combining— lighter nuclei. **Nuclear fusion** involves the formation of a new, more massive atom by forcing two less-massive nuclei to combine. As with fission, the energy released by nuclear fusion can be enormous, due once again to the conversion of mass into energy.

Nuclear fusion powers the sun and other stars. Scientists believe that the sun formed when a huge quantity of interstellar gas, mostly hydrogen, condensed under the force of gravity. When gravitational pressure became great enough to heat the gas to about 15 million degrees Celsius, hydrogen atoms began fusing into helium. The sun began to shine, releasing the energy which drives our solar system. Scientists estimate that the sun, believed to be about 4.5 billion years old, is about halfway through its life cycle.

The following nuclear equation represents the sum of several important nuclear fusion reactions that occur in the sun. The ejected particles are **positrons,** particles with the mass of an electron, but carrying a positive charge.

$$4\,^1_1\text{H} \quad \rightarrow \quad ^4_2\text{He} \quad + \quad 2\,^0_{+1}\text{e}$$

Hydrogen-1   Helium-4   Positrons

How much energy does a nuclear fusion reaction produce? By adding the masses of products in the above equation and subtracting the masses of reactants, we find that 0.0069005 g of mass is lost when one mole of hydrogen atoms undergo fusion to produce helium. Using Einstein's equation, $E = mc^2$, we can calculate that the energy released through the fusion of one gram (one mole) of hydrogen atoms is 6.2×10^8 kJ. Here is one way to put that very large quantity of energy in perspective: The nuclear energy released from the fusion of one gram of hydrogen-1 equals the thermal energy released by burning nearly 5,000 gallons of gasoline.

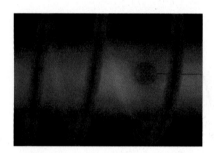

Figure 22 Pellet containing deuterium and tritium for laser fusion.

Nuclear fusion reactions have been used in the design of powerful weapons. The hydrogen bomb—also known as a thermonuclear device—is based on a fusion reaction that is ignited with a small atomic (fission) bomb.

Can we harness the energy of nuclear fusion to produce electricity? Scientists have spent more than several decades pursuing this possibility (Figure 22).

So far, the difficulties of maintaining the incredibly high temperatures (millions of degrees) needed to sustain controlled nuclear fusion have not been overcome. Even if scientists succeed in controlling nuclear fusion in the laboratory, there is still no guarantee that fusion reactions will become a practical source of energy. Low-mass isotopes to fuel such reactors are plentiful and inexpensive. However, confinement of the reaction would be very expensive. Furthermore, although the fusion reaction itself produces much less radioactive waste than nuclear fission, capturing the heat of the reaction and shielding it could generate just as great a volume of radioactive waste as is produced by fission power plants.

Bombardment of the containment walls by neutrons released in the fusion reaction would produce large quantities of radioactive materials.

In splitting and fusing atoms, we have unleashed the energy that fuels the universe. Much good has come of it. But we have also raised scientific, social, and ethical questions that have not been answered. Along with great benefits, there are also great risks. How much risk is worth how much benefit? We will explore that issue next.

PART C: SUMMARY QUESTIONS

1. a. Name three isotopes that can undergo neutron-induced fission.
    b. How is fission different from the radioactive decay that Ernest Rutherford explained?

2. Complete this equation for a nuclear fission reaction:

    $$^?_?n + ^{235}_{92}U \rightarrow ^{87}_?Br + ^{146}_{57}? + ?$$

3. a. What is a nuclear chain reaction?
    b. Under what conditions will a chain reaction occur?
    c. What is the difference between an expanding chain reaction and a controlled one?

4. Why is it impossible for a nuclear power plant to become a nuclear bomb?

5. a. In what ways is a nuclear power plant similar to a fossil-fuel-based power plant?
    b. In what ways is it different?
    c. Describe one advantage and one disadvantage of each type of power plant.

6. How does the system that controls the chain reaction in a nuclear power plant work?

7. Explain the difference between nuclear fission and nuclear fusion.

8. Explain how both of these statements can be true:
    a. Nuclear fusion has not been used for an energy source in the world.
    b. Nuclear fusion is the number one energy source in the world.

EXTENDING YOUR KNOWLEDGE (OPTIONAL)

• How and where did the elements that make up our bodies, the earth, and the universe originate? Investigate possible answers to this question.

• Investigate the breeder reactor—a nuclear reactor that produces more nuclear fuel than it uses.

LIVING WITH BENEFITS AND RISKS

Since the dawn of civilization, people have accepted the risks of new technologies to reap their benefits. Fire, one of civilization's earliest tools, gave people the ability to cook, keep warm, and forge tools from metals. When out of control, however, fire can destroy property and life. Every technology offers its benefits at a price.

Improvements in water systems, nutrition, and health care have given citizens of developed nations the longest average life span in history. Still, some people oppose new technologies, arguing that the benefits are not worth the risks. Many argued against the introduction of both trains and automobiles, for example. In more recent times, nuclear power has stirred a higher level of continuing opposition than most previous technologies.

In the following sections, you will examine how to balance for yourself the benefits and risks of any new technology. One must weigh the potential benefits of the technology against the harm or threats it poses to individuals, society, and the environment.

Every form of transportation has its risks!

One way to define an "acceptable" new technology is one having a low probability of harm—or having benefits that outweigh risks of danger. Unfortunately, risk-benefit analysis is far from an exact science. For instance, some technologies present immediate, high risks, while others may present chronic, low-level risks for years, or even decades. Some risks are impossible to measure with certainty. Some potential risks can be controlled by an individual, while others must be controlled by government. In short, it is very difficult to compare or "weigh" various risks. Still, decisions must be made.

Before considering the pros and cons of nuclear power, take a few minutes to weigh the benefits and risks of different modes of travel to complete a journey. This will help sharpen your ability to think in risk-benefit terms.

In many cases electing not to make any decision is, in fact, an actual decision—one with its own risks and benefits.

D.1 YOU DECIDE: THE SAFEST JOURNEY

Suppose you want to visit a friend who lives 500 miles (800 km) away, using the safest means of transportation. Insurance companies publish reliable statistics on the safety of different methods of travel. Using Table 8, answer these questions:

Table 8	RISK OF TRAVEL
Mode of Travel	**Distance at which one person in a million will suffer accidental death***
Bicycle	10 miles
Automobile	100 miles
Scheduled airline	1000 miles
Train	1200 miles
Bus	2800 miles

*On average, chance of death is increased by 0.000001.

1. Assume there is a direct relationship between distance traveled and chance of accidental death. (That is, assume that doubling distance doubles your risk of accidental death.)
   a. What is the risk factor value for traveling 500 miles by each mode of travel? For example, Table 8 shows that the risk factor (chance of accidental death) for biking increases by 0.000001 for each 10 miles. Therefore, the bike-riding risk factor in visiting your friend would be

$$500 \text{ mi.} \times \frac{0.000001 \text{ risk factor}}{10 \text{ mi.}} = 0.0005 \text{ risk factor}$$

   b. Which is the safest mode of travel (the one with the smallest risk factor)?
   c. Which is the least safe?
2. The results obtained in Question 1 might surprise many people. Why?
3. a. List the benefits of each mode of transportation.
   b. In your view, do the benefits of less-safe ways to travel outweigh their increased risks? Explain your reasoning.
4. Do you think these same statistics will be true 25 years from now? Why?

5. What factor(s) beyond the risk to personal safety would you include in your risk-benefit analysis before deciding how to travel?
6. a. Which mode of travel would you choose? Why?
   b. Would a similar risk-benefit analysis by other people always lead to the same decision? Why? (Or, putting it another way, is there *one* "best" way to travel?)

Some uses of nuclear energy and radioactivity are unquestionably worth their risks. These uses include compact power sources, radioisotopes for diagnosing and treating disease, smoke detectors, and many research and development applications. Other uses, such as stockpiling nuclear weapons, are far more controversial.

Our goal is to provide you with sufficient understanding to help you weigh the benefits and risks of new applications of nuclear technology now and in the future. We will begin by examining some benefits of radioisotopes.

D.2 BENEFITS OF RADIOISOTOPES

You have already learned how uranium's nuclear energy can be used to generate electrical power. Other nuclear technologies make use of the ionizing radiation given off as certain radioisotopes decay. Such applications include **tracer studies**, where the objective is to detect the presence of the isotope, as well as **irradiation**, where the radiation is used as an energy source.

Codiscoverers of Element 106, Lawrence Berkeley Laboratory, 1974. Left to right: Matti Nurmia, Jose R. Alonso, Albert Ghiorso, E. Kenneth Hulet, Carol T. Alonso, Ronald W. Lougheed, Glenn Seaborg, Joachim M. Nitschke.

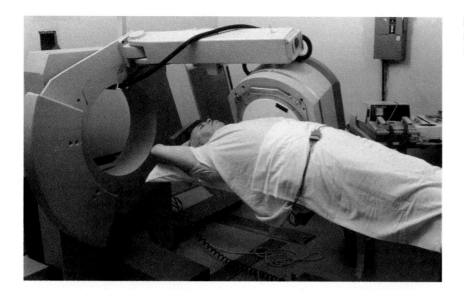

Figure 23 Injection of a radioisotope makes it possible to produce a non-invasive image of the abdomen.

Tracer studies are used in medicine to trace abnormalities in body function, to locate damaged areas, and in therapy. Doctors place radioisotopes with short half-lives into the body to find out what is happening. Such radioisotopes, known as **tracers,** have properties that make them ideally suited for this task. First, radioisotopes behave the same—both chemically and biologically—as stable isotopes of the element. Doctors know that certain elements collect in specific parts of the body. To investigate a given part of the body, they send the appropriate radioisotope. A solution of a tracer isotope is supplied to the body, or a biologically-active compound—synthesized to contain a radioactive atom—is fed to or injected into the patient (see Figure 23). A nuclear radiation detection system then allows the doctor to find out where the tracer distributed in the body.

For example, a radioisotope tracer is used to diagnose thyroid problems. The patient simply drinks a solution containing a radioactive iodine (I-131) tracer. The doctor then follows the tracer movement in the thyroid with a radiation detection system, and measures its rate of disappearance.

A healthy thyroid will incorporate a known amount of iodine. An overactive or underactive thyroid will take up more or less iodine. The doctor simply compares the measured rate of I-131 disappearance to the normal rate for someone of that age, gender, and weight, and takes appropriate action.

Technetium-99m, (Tc-99m) a synthetic radioisotope, has replaced exploratory surgery as a way to locate tumors in the brain, thyroid, and kidneys. Tumors are areas of runaway cell growth, and technetium concentrates where cell growth is fastest. A bank of radiation detectors around the patient's head can pinpoint a brain tumor's precise location. Phosphorus-32 can be used in a similar way to detect bone cancers.

In some cancer treatments, the diseased area is exposed to ionizing radiation to kill cancerous cells. For thyroid cancer, the patient receives a concentrated internal dose of radioiodine which concentrates in the thyroid. In other cancer treatments, an external beam of ionizing radiation (from cobalt-60) may be directed at the cancerous spot. Such treatments must be administered with great care—high radiation doses can also damage or kill normal cells.

Due to its versatility and convenience, technetium-99m has been called the "workhorse of nuclear medicine." The Food and Drug Administration approved two new Tc-99m-based imaging agents for the heart in 1991.

Recall that the "m" in Tc-99m indicates that the isotope is metastable — it readily changes to a more stable form of the same isotope, releasing a gamma ray (γ) in the process.

Raiders of the Temple of Doom

By Laverne Frey
Metairie Times Staff Reporter

The great Maya king, Yax Pac, and his family created a vast array of buildings at Copan, Honduras. Archeologist Will Andrews is investigating a small portion of the complex consisting of a large flat-topped temple used for rituals and public displays, a tomb, and living areas. He wants to determine which member of the royal family built this temple and was subsequently entombed there. Even though the tomb was thoroughly looted in antiquity, Will explores it, hoping the thieves left something behind. They may have left clues for the archeologist, such as small bones, pieces of pottery, or bits of jewelry. Will has found nothing inside the structures, but outside he has recently discovered an exciting clue: an inscribed altar, which had fallen from the temple top and was concealed in the jungle growth. Chac, brother of Yax Pac, is described as making offerings at the temple. For that reason, Will infers that Yax Pac was probably the builder.

Will is a professor of anthropology at Tulane University in New Orleans, Louisiana, where he teaches classes in anthropology and serves as a graduate student advisor. He arranges field work at Central American archeological sites for students, advises them on coursework, and helps them to locate employment after graduation. He is also Director of the Middle American Research Institute. As chief administrator, he is largely responsible for a collection of Middle American artifacts and serves as general editor of books published through the Institute. Finally, Will raises money to advance his own research at archeological sites in Central America like Copan.

Photo by E. Wyllys Andrews

Archeological research is physically demanding and the sites are usually uncomfortable, yet Will enjoys the dig. For him, this is the most exciting part of the job. He is challenged by getting the information from the ground, recording it, and then translating it into human lives. Archeological research is different from many other kinds of research because the major part of it is done in the field rather than in a library or a laboratory.

Will uses radiocarbon dating as a tool for determining the dates of objects from Maya culture. When he finds an object, Will looks for charcoal in the same stratigraphic layer. By making certain that the charcoal is contemporary with the object, he now knows that Chac's temple complex is from the time of the fall of the Maya civilization.

From the distribution of artifacts, archeologists believe that the Maya settled in Middle America in approximately 1000

BC. This commonly accepted date was apparently refuted when, at the site of Cuello, Belize, Maya artifacts were determined by radiocarbon dating to be from 2000 BC. Will was skeptical, but the data seemed excellent. Examinations of the colors and forms of the pottery vessels, however, indicated a much later time. Will knew something must be terribly wrong with the radiocarbon data. Charcoal had been collected from different levels. Will argued that the earliest level on which evidence of humans was found not only contained human-generated charcoal, but also much earlier environmental charcoal (left by forest fires). This environmental charcoal affected the radiocarbon-determined dates from early periods in history. As human history developed, the amounts of environmental charcoal became insignificant as compared to the human-generated charcoal.

Table 9   SELECTED MEDICAL APPLICATIONS OF RADIOISOTOPES

Radioisotope	Half-life	Use
Used as tracers		
Cobalt-48	71.3 d	Determine intake of vitamin B$_{12}$ (which contains nonradioactive cobalt)
Iron-59	45.6 d	Determine rate of red blood cell formation (these contain iron)
Chromium-51	27.8 d	Determine blood volume and lifespan of red blood cells
Hydrogen-3 (tritium)	12.3 y	Determine volume of water in person's body; determine use of (labeled) vitamin D in body; cellular chemistry research
Strontium-85	64.0 d	Bone scans
Gold-198	2.7 d	Liver scans
Used for irradiation therapy		
Cesium-137	30.0 y	Treat shallow tumors (external source)
Phosphorus-32	14.3 d	Treat skin cancers (external source)
Strontium-90	27.7 y	Treat eye disease (external source)
Iridium-192	74.2 d	Treat tumors with imbedded wire
Yttrium-90	64.0 h	Treat pituitary gland cancer internally with ceramic beads
Gold-198	2.7 d	Treat body cavity cancers with a radiocolloid that coats body cavity

Thallium heart scan.

The tracing and cell-killing properties of radioisotopes are used to diagnose and treat other forms of cancers. Other medical applications include the use of radiosodium (Na-24) to search for circulatory system abnormalities and the use of radioxenon (Xe-133) to help search for lung embolisms (blood clots) and abnormalities. Table 9 outlines other medical applications of radioisotopes.

Irradiation is used in industrial processes, including sterilizing medical disposables such as injection needles, surgical masks and gowns, and destroying microorganisms in food. Irradiation is also used to seal plastic containers.

Irradiation is a relatively simple procedure. An irradiation chamber contains pellets of a gamma-emitting radioisotope, usually cobalt-60. The material to be irradiated is placed on a conveyer belt that moves past the radioisotope at a specified rate.

Irradiation can be used to preserve food. It can destroy bacteria, molds, and yeasts that cause food to spoil (see Figure 24). High irradiation doses can sterilize vacuum-packed meat. Such meat can then be stored for years at room temperature without spoilage. Food irradiation has been approved for use in over 30 nations for over 40 different foods. Although the process is relatively common in European nations, Canada and Mexico, food processors in the United States have been slower to adopt this method.

One concern sometimes voiced regarding food irradiation is that the energetic radiation might break and rearrange chemical bonds in irradiated foods, creating potentially harmful products. At low radiation levels, this threat is regarded by many authorities as insignificant. Benefits of improving food storage life and

Figure 24 The strawberries on the right were preserved with gamma radiation; those on the left were not. Both were stored for 15 days; these photos were then taken. The irradiated strawberries are still firm, fresh-looking, and edible, and they have no mold.

Improvements in food storage lead to larger food supplies—a particular benefit for many developing nations.

reducing spoilage must—as usual—be weighed against such risks. Benefits must also be balanced with risks associated with alternative food-preservation methods.

Radioisotopes have been used in many fields for the past four decades. For a clearer sense of the value of this technology, complete the following activity.

D.3 YOU DECIDE: PUTTING ATOMS TO WORK

Each problem listed below has already been solved in real life through use of radioisotopes. Design your own solution to each, putting a radioisotope to work. You will work in teams.

Write a brief, description of each proposed solution. Each team member should also be prepared to describe one solution to the rest of the class.

Consider these points in working out your solutions:

- What type of radioisotope should be used? Consider half-life, type of radiation—alpha, beta, or gamma—and the physical or chemical state of the radioactive material.
- How should the system be designed? A sketch or diagram might help.
- What, if any, safety and health precautions are needed?
- Does the problem require use of a radioisotope over an extended time, or is a "one-shot" short-term approach needed?
- Could a non-nuclear technology solve the problem just as easily—or perhaps more easily?

In weighing advantages of each type of radiation, decide whether penetrating power and ionizing ability are important considerations in your application.

The answer to this question will help you specify the desired half-life of the radioisotope.

Problems

1. Many oil companies that pump oil and gas from Texas to midwestern states share the same pipelines. How could radio-isotopes help pipeline operators in Michigan decide which company's oil or gas is arriving at any particular time?
2. An automobile manufacturer is investigating ways to extend the life and efficiency of car engines. The manufacturer wants to compare how rapidly piston rings in several different engines will wear out.
3. Applying more fertilizer than crops are able to use can harm the environment. Excess fertilizer may contaminate water runoff, polluting nearby streams. An agricultural chemist wants to find out which fertilizer application method results in the highest crop uptake of fertilizer with the least water pollution.
4. A doctor is treating a patient who has inoperable lung cancer. She wants to kill the maximum number of cancer cells while minimizing damage to healthy tissues.

It is also a waste of money.

We have explored some of nuclear technology's potential for service and benefit. But what about the dangers of nuclear radiation? How are its biological effects measured and compared?

D.4 MEASURING IONIZING RADIATION

Radiation can be measured in several different ways. When you investigated the differences between alpha, beta, and gamma radiation (Laboratory Activity B.1) you measured radiation directly in counts per minute (cpm). It can also be measured as the quantity of radiation *absorbed* by the body, which determines how much tissue damage may be caused.

The **rem** measures the ability of radiation—regardless of source or cpm—to cause ionization in human tissue. Usually accidental exposures are so small that the dosage is stated in millirems (mrem). Part of the convenience of this unit is that one millirem of radiation produces essentially the same biological effects, whether the radiation is composed of alpha particles, beta particles, or gamma rays. In general, each mrem received increases our risk of dying from cancer by one chance in 4 million.

*The rem received its name as the abbreviation for **r**oentgen **e**quivalent **m**an.*

Each type of radiation can cause damage in different ways. X rays and gamma rays—ionizing forms of electromagnetic radiation—penetrate deeply into the body. However, they actually cause less damage than alpha or beta particles, if the amount of tissue traversed is taken into consideration. Alpha particles are easily stopped, but if they can reach the lungs or bloodstream, they can cause extensive damage over a very short distance (about 0.025 mm). This is due to their relatively large mass and slower velocities. The two main factors that determine tissue damage are the density (the number of ionizations within each unit area) and the dose (the quantity of radiation received).

Recall that an alpha particle is a helium nucleus, $^{4}_{2}He^{2+}$. This particle has a molar mass of 4.0 g/mol.

D.5 RADIATION DAMAGE: NOW AND LATER

Ionizing radiation breaks bonds and thus tears molecules apart. At low radiation levels, only comparatively few molecules are harmed. The body's systems can usually repair the damage.

However, the higher the dose (or quantity of radiation) received, the more molecules are affected. Damage to proteins and nucleic acids is of greatest concern because of their importance in body structures and functions, including those passed on to offspring. Proteins form much of the body's soft tissue structure and make up enzymes, the molecules that control bodily functions. When many protein molecules are torn apart within a small region, there may be too few functioning molecules left to permit the body to heal itself in a reasonable time.

See the Food Unit, Part C, for more background on proteins and enzymes.

Nucleic acids in DNA can be damaged in two different ways. Minor damage causes **mutations**—changes in the structure of DNA which may result in the synthesis of different proteins. Most mutations kill the cell. If the cell is a sperm or ovum, the change may appear as a birth defect. Some mutations may lead to cancer—a disease of cell growth and metabolism out of control. If, on the other hand, DNA in many body cells is severely damaged, the immediate effect is that proteins can no longer be synthesized to replace damaged ones. Death follows.

DNA molecules control cell reproduction and synthesis of bodily proteins.

Table 10 (page 324) lists the factors that determine the extent of biological damage from radiation. Table 11 (page 324) shows the biological effects of large dosages of radiation.

The effects of large radiation doses are drastic. Conclusive evidence that high radiation doses cause cancer has been gathered from uranium miners, accident victims, and nuclear bomb victims in World War II. Some of the best case studies were based on workers who painted numbers on radium watch dials. Unknowingly, they touched the paint brushes to their tongues to sharpen the tips, and thus swallowed radioactive radium.

The radium dial-markings glowed in the dark. Modern glow-in-the-dark watches are based on safe, nonradioactive materials.

Table 10 **BIOLOGICAL DAMAGE FROM RADIATION**

Factor	Effect
Dose	Most scientists assume that an increase in radiation dose produces a proportional increase in risk.
Exposure time	The more a given dose is spread out over time, the less harm it does.
Area exposed	The larger the body area exposed to a given radiation dose, the greater the damage.
Tissue type	Rapidly dividing cells, such as blood cells and sex cells, are more susceptible to radiation damage than are slowly dividing or non-dividing cells, such as nerve cells. Fetuses and children are more susceptible to radiation damage than are adults.

Table 11 **RADIATION EFFECTS**

Dose (rem)	Effect
0–25	No immediate observable effects.
25–50	Small decrease in white blood cell count, causing lowered resistance to infections.
50–100	Marked decrease in white blood cell count. Development of lesions.
100–200	Radiation sickness—nausea, vomiting, hair loss. Blood cells die.
200–300	Hemorrhaging, ulcers, deaths.
300–500	Acute radiation sickness. Fifty percent die within a few weeks.
>700	One hundred percent die.

Leukemia, cancer of the white blood cells, is the most rapidly-developing and common cancer associated with radiation. Other forms of cancer may also appear, as well as anemia, heart related problems, and cataracts (opaque spots on the lens inside the eye).

Considerable controversy continues regarding whether very low radiation doses can cause cancer. Most data concerning cancer have come from human exposure to high doses, with mathematical projection back to lower doses. Few studies have directly linked low radiation doses with cancer development. Although most scientists agree that natural levels of radiation are safe for most people, some authorities argue that *any* increase in radiation above natural levels increases the probability for cancer. This is similar to the reasoning that led to food additive regulations for carcinogens (Food Unit, page 260).

How much radiation do you experience each year? What are its sources? Do you have any control over the radiation? We will deal with these questions in the next section.

Natural levels of radiation at sea level are about 135 mrem (millirem) per year.

D.6 EXPOSURE TO RADIATION

Everyone receives background radiation at low levels from natural and human sources. Among natural sources are these:

- Cosmic rays—exceedingly high energy particles that bombard the earth from outer space
- Radioisotopes in rocks, soil, and groundwater—uranium (U-238, U-235), thorium (Th-232) and their decay products; other natural radioisotopes
- Radioisotopes in the atmosphere—radon (Rn-222) and its decay products, including polonium (Po-210)

Human sources of background radiation include:
- Fallout from nuclear weapons testing
- Increased exposure to cosmic radiation during air travel
- Radioisotopes released into the environment from nuclear power generation and other nuclear technologies

Some of the radiation we experience comes from sources within our bodies (see Figure 25). Total background exposure to radiation at sea level is estimated at 135 mrem each year. Figure 26 shows the relative quantity from each source.

What radiation level is considered safe? The government's present radiation standard allows the general public to receive an average dose of 170 mrem, and any particular individual to receive 500 mrem (or about three times that provided by natural background) annually. For those occupationally exposed, the annual limit is 5000 mrem.

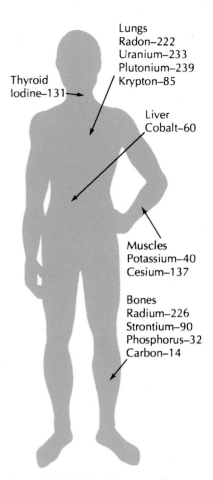

Figure 25 All living things contain some radioactive isotopes, including these, which are found in specific parts of the human body.

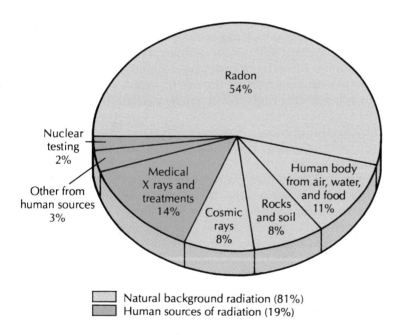

Natural background radiation (81%)
Human sources of radiation (19%)

Figure 26 Sources of background radiation. *From* Living in the Environment: An Introduction to Environmental Science, 6th ed., by G. Tyler Miller, Jr. Belmont, CA: Wadsworth Publishing Co., 1990, p. 452.

CHEMQUANDARY

Radiation Exposure Standards

Why are exposure-level standards different for some individuals than for the general public? Why are the standards different for those who are occupationally exposed?

Although we cannot avoid all radiation sources—particularly those from the earth and atmosphere—we can make choices about others.

- We can decide whether to have diagnostic X rays.
- We can decide whether to undergo medical tests that use radioactive isotopes.
- We can choose whether to fly and how often, thereby reducing exposure to cosmic radiation.
- We can choose where to live and can, if needed, adjust our home environment to reduce exposure to radon and other radiation sources.

D.7 RADON IN HOMES

You can locate this decay product as $^{222}_{86}Rn$ in the uranium decay series chart shown earlier on page 297.

The gaseous element radon (Rn)—the heaviest of the noble gases—has always appeared as a component of the earth's atmosphere. It is a decay product of uranium. In the 1980s the public first learned about high concentrations of radioactive radon gas in some U.S. homes.

Radon is produced as uranium-238 decays in the soil and in building materials. Some radon produced in the soil dissolves in groundwater. Many houses have foundation and basement floor cracks that permit radon from the soil and moisture below to seep in. There it stays—it has little chance to escape.

The threat of radon is that it decays to produce, in succession, radioactive isotopes of polonium (Po), bismuth (Bi), and lead (Pb). Thus radon gas that enters the body as part of inhaled air may become transformed, through radioactive decay, to toxic heavy-metal ions—ions that cannot be exhaled as gas. These radioactive metals emit potentially damaging alpha particles within the body. In homes with high radon gas levels, inhaled dust can also carry traces of polonium and other heavy-metal isotopes deposited by decaying radon. It is estimated that from 10,000 to 20,000 annual lung cancer deaths in the U.S. are due to the effects of radon gas.

Smoking itself is a significant risk factor for lung cancer. In addition, heavy smokers are considerably more susceptible to the effects of radon.

Radon has appeared as a problem because of changes in the way we build and use our homes. In older homes, outdoor air enters through doors, windows, and gaps around them. Air conditioning in new buildings decreases the need to open windows. To conserve energy, many new homes are built more air-tight than older homes used to be. The net result: Indoor air has little chance to mix freely with outdoor air.

Inexpensive radon test-kits are now available. Remedies for high radon levels in homes include increased ventilation, sealing cracks in floors, and removing radon from ground water.

Radon is one of many sources of background radiation to which each of us is exposed. Complete the following activity to estimate how much radiation you receive.

YOUR TURN

Your Annual Radiation Dose

On a separate sheet of paper list the numbers and letters found in the table on page 327. Then fill in the blanks with suitable values. When you finish, add the quantities to estimate your annual radiation dose.

Source of Radiation	Quantity per Year

1. Location of your community.

   a. Cosmic radiation at sea level (U.S. average). (Cosmic radiation is radiation emitted by stars across the universe. Much of this is deflected by the earth's atmosphere and ionosphere.) — **30 mrem**

   b. Add an additional radiation value based on your community's elevation above sea level:

   1000 m (3300 ft) above sea level = 10 mrem

   2000 m (6600 ft) above sea level = 30 mrem

   3000 m (9900 ft) above sea level = 90 mrem

   (Estimate mrem value for intermediate elevations.) — ____ mrem

2. House construction material. (Building materials contain a very small percent of radioisotopes.) Brick or concrete, 70 mrem; wood, 30 mrem. — ____ mrem

3. Ground. Radiation from rocks and soil (U.S. average). — **26 mrem**

4. Food, water, and air (U.S. average). — **28 mrem**

5. Fallout from prior nuclear weapons testing (U.S. average) — **4 mrem**

6. Medical and dental X rays.

   a. Chest X ray (number of visits times 10 mrem per visit). — ____ mrem

   b. Gastrointestinal tract X ray (number of visits times 200 mrem per visit). — ____ mrem

   c. Dental X ray (number of visits times 10 mrem per visit). — ____ mrem

7. Air travel (Increases exposure to cosmic radiation). Number of flights (1500 miles = 1 mrem) — ____ mrem

8. Power plants. If your home is within five miles of a nuclear or coal-fired power plant, add 0.3 mrem. — ____ mrem

Total — ____ **mrem**

This skier in Colorado is exposed to a higher radiation dosage than she would be at sea level.

Questions

1. a. How does your yearly radiation dose compare with the 170-mrem standard?

   b. How does it compare with average background radiation?

2. a. Could you reduce your radiation exposure by changes in your lifestyle? Explain.

   b. Would you want to make those changes? Why?

A major unanswered question faces everyone living in countries using nuclear technology: How should we dispose of nuclear waste?

D.8   NUCLEAR WASTE: PANDORA'S BOX

As we noted earlier, even if "cleaner" controlled-fusion reactors become a reality, they will also generate considerable radioactive waste due to neutron-bombardment of the walls of the confinement chamber.

Imagine this situation. You live in a home that was once clean and comfortable. But you have a major problem: you cannot throw away your garbage. The city forbids this because it has not decided what to do with the garbage. Your family has compacted and wrapped garbage as well as possible for about 40 years. You are running out of room. Some bundles leak and are creating a health hazard. What can be done?

The U.S. nuclear power industry and nuclear weapons industry share a similar problem. Spent (used) nuclear fuel and radioactive waste products have been accumulating for about 40 years. The material is still highly radioactive. It is uncertain where these materials will be permanently stored—or how soon. Let's take a closer look at the problem.

Up to a third of a nuclear reactor's fuel rods must be replaced each year. This is necessary since the uranium-235 fuel becomes depleted; accumulated fission products also interfere with the fission process.

The spent fuel rods are highly radioactive, with some isotopes remaining active for many thousands of years. Table 12 lists the half-lives of a few isotopes produced by nuclear fission. All of these—and hundreds more—are found in spent fuel rods.

Table 12   SOME ISOTOPES IN SPENT FUEL RODS

Isotope	Half-life
Plutonium-239	24,000 y
Strontium-90	27.7 y
Barium-140	12.8 y
Krypton-34	1.4 y

We will consider long-term waste disposal prospects in greater detail later in the unit.

By federal law, reactor waste must be stored on site, usually in nuclear waste storage tanks. Available storage space, however, is limited. Final disposal of radioactive waste is the responsibility of the federal government. The U.S. government has not yet opened any permanent disposal sites, although legal negotiations and development work currently point toward two such locations—one in New Mexico and one in Nevada.

The volume of military waste is much greater than the amount of commercial waste. This waste is in liquid form—a waste of extracting plutonium from spent fuel rods of military reactors. Nuclear weapons can be crafted from the plutonium.

Plutonium could also be extracted from the spent fuel rods of commercial reactors. However, such extraction is illegal in the United States, since such wastes of civilian reactors could be used in nuclear weapon production.

As radioisotopes in the liquid waste decay, they emit radiation and thermal energy. In fact, without cooling, such wastes can become hot enough to boil. This makes military waste containment extremely challenging.

The method of long-term radioactive waste disposal favored by the U.S. government (and by many other nations) is mined geologic disposal, shown in Figure 27. The radioactive waste would be buried at least 1000 m below the earth in vaults that would presumably remain undisturbed for thousands of years.

This cooling process for existing wastes is already under way at each nuclear reactor site.

To prepare the waste for burial, it would first be allowed to cool for 7–10 years. Spent fuel rods are placed in large pools of water. As time passes, the isotopes decay, lowering the level of radioactivity to a point where the materials can be safely handled. On-site nuclear waste storage is only a temporary measure; the tanks require too much maintenance to be safe for longer periods of time.

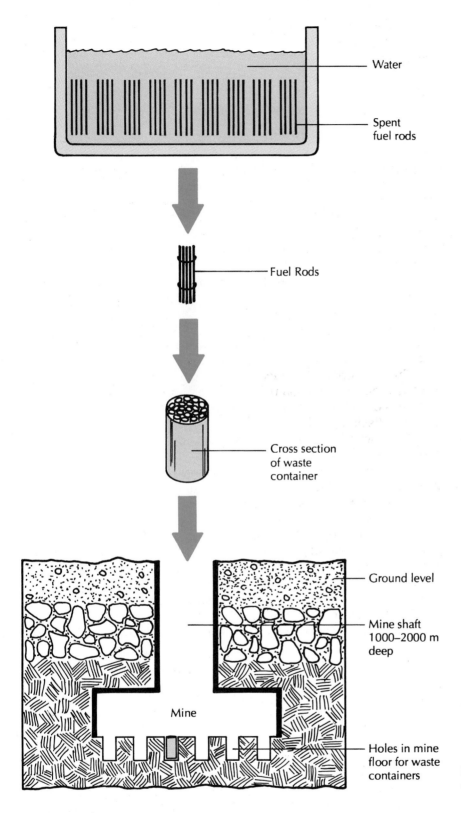

Water

Spent
fuel rods

Fuel Rods

Cross section
of waste
container

Ground level

Mine shaft
1000–2000 m
deep

Mine

Holes in mine
floor for waste
containers

Figure 27   The mined geologic
disposal plan.

Next, cooled radioactive wastes would be locked inside leak-proof packages. The currently-favored method is to transform the wastes into a type of glass or rock. This is *vitrification.* The glassy or rocky material would still be highly radioactive, but would be much less likely to leak or leach into the environment. The vitrified radioactive wastes would be sealed in special containers (made of glass, stainless steel, or concrete).

Nevada hazardous waste disposal
cell.

Two U.S. vitrification plants are now under construction—in New York and South Carolina. The Savannah River plant in South Carolina will be the world's largest vitrification facility. Vitrification has been used in France for over a decade, where 70% of the nation's electrical energy is produced by nuclear reactors.

Nowhere in the world, however, has nuclear waste yet been permanently buried. The problem in every country is to find politically and socially acceptable sites. In Japan, where land mass is at a premium, even deep ocean burial is being considered.

Some geologic sites formerly assumed to be stable enough for radioactive waste disposal were later discovered to be unsafe. For example, some plutonium was buried at Maxey Flats, Kentucky, in ground geologists believed would remain stable for thousands of years. Within 10 years, some buried plutonium had moved dozens of meters away.

How much high-level radioactive waste is there? A commercial nuclear reactor produces about 30 tons of spent fuel each year. This means that roughly 3000 tons of waste are generated each year by the 110 commercial reactors operating in the United States. The nuclear weapons program has contributed about 20 million liters of additional stored liquid waste.

In addition to these high-level radioactive wastes, millions of tons of lower-level radioactive waste have been produced, especially by mining and processing uranium for fuel. Hospitals and other users of radioactive substances also make small contributions to this total. Eventually, nuclear reactors themselves will become nuclear waste.

What are the current plans to resolve our long-term nuclear waste disposal problems? By U.S. law, the President has selected

A 22-ton spent nuclear fuel shipping cask rests virtually undamaged atop this demolished tractor-trailer rig bed after an 84-mph impact into a 10-foot thick concrete target.

two sites for permanent radioactive waste disposal from among options provided by the Department of Energy. The selected sites, located in regions of presumed geologic stability, are the Waste Isolation Pilot Plant (WIPP) near Carlsbad, New Mexico, and a volcanic ridge 100 miles northwest of Las Vegas, Nevada, known as Yucca Mountain. Both proposals have created considerable debate and controversy. Layers of legal, environmental, and development work still stand in the way of a final ''ok'' for either site. Even if all the barriers are overcome, full-scale storage efforts probably will not be possible in the near future.

The NIMBY syndrome is also at work —Not In My Back Yard.

Nuclear waste disposal is a pressing issue. However, another possible hazard of nuclear technology must be considered in any thorough risk-benefit analysis.

D.9 CATASTROPHIC RISK: A PLANT ACCIDENT

Although a nuclear power plant cannot become an atomic bomb, other accidents can occur—either through malfunction, earthquake, or human error—that could release large quantities of radioactive matter into the environment. Since the late 1970s we have seen nuclear power plant accidents at Three Mile Island in the United States and at Chernobyl in the Soviet Union.

Three Mile Island nuclear power plant.

Clean-up efforts at the damaged TMI power reactor, estimated to cost eventually over $1 billion, continued into the early 1990s.

The 1979 accident at the Three Mile Island (TMI) nuclear power plant at Middletown, Pennsylvania (near Harrisburg), was the most serious U.S. accident to date in a commercial nuclear power plant. The incident, resulting from an unanticipated and interrelated series of mechanical and operator failures, did not involve any known loss of human life. However, the accident—together with the evidence and testimony generated in later public hearings—contributed to an increased level of apprehension and "anti-nuclear" sentiment in much of the U.S. general public.

Nuclear reactor Unit 2 at TMI lost its flow of cooling water on the morning of March 28, 1979. Cooling water was lost due to a number of mechanical and human errors, triggered initially by an automatic shut-off of two water pump valves in the secondary cooling system. Even though the nuclear reactor automatically shut down, enough thermal energy was released to heat the core to over 5,000° C, causing about half of it (62 tons) to melt and fall to the reactor's bottom. About 32,000 gallons of radioactive cooling water surrounding the core eventually poured from an open safety relief valve. In addition, a still-unknown quantity of radioactive material escaped into the atmosphere. Alarmed by reports of radiation release and the possibility of a hydrogen gas bubble explosion (which did not occur), as many as 200,000 individuals within 50 miles of the plant evacuated the area.

Although the tragedy of complete plant meltdown was avoided at TMI, and although the main containment structure did remain intact, the TMI experience had a lasting impact on millions of U.S. citizens who remember the uncertainty and fear associated with the accident.

The Chernobyl disaster has remained the object of considerable study, debate, and concern. Reactor 4 at the Chernobyl Nuclear Power Station was a large, water-cooled, graphite-moderated nuclear power reactor. On April 26, 1986—some two years after startup—the reactor ran dangerously out of control, heating the cooling water to the boiling point. Pressure build-up from the resulting steam burst cooling pipes and, in a powerful explosion, blew the 1000-ton roof off the reactor. Radioactive debris flew nearly a mile skyward, fires were triggered (including the burning of graphite moderator material), and molten nuclear fuel spilled from control rods.

Chernobyl's radioactive cloud—including radioactive isotopes distilled from still-hot debris for days after—eventually covered the Northern Hemisphere. Although 97% of the radioactive material fell in Europe, lower levels of radioactive material were detected in nations ranging from China to Canada. Over 200 acute cases of radiation sickness were initially reported, including 31 deaths. Hundreds of thousands of people were evacuated from high-radiation areas within the Soviet Union. Officials estimate that cleanup costs will exceed $100 billion by the turn of the century.

Experts note that Chernobyl's reactor design included features known to be unnecessarily risky. Positive feedback—where increased water-boiling caused increased fission and heat, which, in turn, caused more water-boiling—was a consequence of the way the reactor was built. Initial reactor instability was caused by operating changes made for a special reactor experiment.

In addition, the Soviet reactor was not protected by a confinement vessel (a steel-reinforced concrete outer shell intended to isolate and confine accidentally-released radioactive materials). Such confinement vessels are a standard part of most nuclear reactors, including all those in the United States.

The Chernobyl disaster has contributed toward heightened public apprehension and concern regarding nuclear power. In the U.S.S.R. alone, over thirty nuclear power reactor orders have been cancelled or postponed since 1986.

Studies of such accidents will help us understand the potential risks of nuclear power. One study, made in the mid-1970s by Massachusetts Institute of Technology (MIT) scientists suggested that the chance of dying from a nuclear power plant accident—either from high radiation doses at the time of the accident, or

June 3, 1986, at the Chernobyl power station after the disaster.

from lower doses suffered from resulting fallout—would be a little greater than the chance of dying in a plane crash. (Keep in mind that airplane travel is very safe.)

However, although risk assessment calculations for airplane travel are quite certain, such calculations for nuclear accidents are so uncertain that the MIT study results could mean that nuclear plants are either much safer, or much more dangerous than air travel. The reason for such great uncertainty is that scientists must attempt a much more complicated calculation based on limited experience.

It is possible that all potential causes of nuclear power plant accidents have not been considered. To complicate matters, accident scenarios are different for each kind of nuclear power plant, and even for individual plants of the same general type.

Is nuclear power worth the risk? It is our responsibility to decide what we want for ourselves and our nation, and to make our wishes known to those who govern. What are your current impressions? Do you feel better prepared to approach these difficult issues? We hope so.

In the next part of this unit you will have an opportunity to review highlights of your study of nuclear phenomena, and to find out how other students respond to these questions.

PART D: SUMMARY QUESTIONS

1. a. Define the term "tracer" as it applies to medical uses of radioisotopes.

    b. Briefly describe one example of a medical tracer.

2. a. Discuss one industrial and one agricultural application of radioisotopes.

    b. Include a discussion of the relative risks and benefits of these applications.

3. From a human health standpoint, how does ionizing radiation differ from nonionizing radiation?

4. Name the common unit for measuring the biological effects of radiation.

5. Explain why alpha emitters are fairly harmless if outside the human body, but quite dangerous if inside it.

6. List four factors that determine the extent of biological damage caused by radiation.

7. Radiation is more destructive to rapidly-dividing cells than to those multiplying more slowly. How can this fact be regarded as a

    a. benefit? (That is, how can it be put to a positive use?)

    b. risk?

8. a. Briefly discuss three problems encountered in assessing the risks of radiation exposure at low dose levels.

    b. In the absence of better data, how do you think we should regulate allowable exposures at low dose levels?

9. Consider the following three radiation levels for humans. Explain why the values are different.

    a. the minimum radiation dose at which immediate, observable effects have been detected

    b. the maximum annual dose allowed for radiation workers

    c. the radiation standard set for an average person

10. Explain the nuclear waste disposal problem, using the concepts of radioactive decay, half-life, and radiation shielding.

11. Even if nuclear power plants were phased out, we would still need to deal with already-generated wastes, plus the much greater wastes associated with nuclear weapon production.

    a. Briefly describe one possible solution to this problem.

    b. Identify at least one technological and one practical (political) problem associated with your solution.

PUTTING IT ALL TOGETHER: SEPARATING FACT FROM FICTION

At the beginning of this unit you conducted a survey dealing with public understanding of nuclear phenomena. You probably found a range of responses. It is also likely that different people relied on different sources of information.

The survey results probably raised as many questions as they answered. This often happens in science, as attempts to answer one question create new questions. You have learned the answers to some survey items in working through this unit. Others may still be troublesome—particularly those involving opinion and judgement.

In this final activity you will reexamine your survey results to separate fact from fiction and to help clarify your own views on some important nuclear issues.

E.1 PROCESSING THE SURVEY INFORMATION

Part 1
Your teacher will hand out a copy of the survey you took at the start of this unit. As homework, retake the survey, answering the questions in light of what you have learned. This is *not* a test, and you will not be graded on your answers, so please do not use your text. Just answer the items based on your current knowledge and opinions.

Part 2
Your teacher will return your answers to the original survey. Compare your pre- and post-unit responses, noting the items for which your responses changed. Circle or otherwise mark these items for later discussion.

You will be assigned to work in a group of four to six students. By group consensus, assign each survey item to one or more of the categories listed on page 336. For convenience, use the symbols S, P, and V on the survey form.

Scientific reality (S). The item is either scientifically correct or incorrect as stated. It reflects a principle that can be supported or disproved in clean-cut scientific experiments.

Political reality (P). Data published in reputable journals, magazines, or newspapers would support the notion that the item reflects (either positively or negatively) the public opinion or current situation.

Value-laden statement (V). The item contains emotionally-charged words and reflects a distinctly pro- or anti-nuclear stance. Such an item may either be based on, or in contradiction to, scientific principles.

During the last part of class, you will report the results of your group analysis in a full-class discussion. The class will decide which items (approximately 10) deserve more discussion in tomorrow's class. Each item should fit one or more of these categories:

- Pre- and post-unit responses varied considerably.
- Post-unit responses are still highly debatable—some students strongly agree while others strongly disagree.
- Post-unit responses still reflect high uncertainty.

Each group will be assigned two items to discuss in greater detail in Part 3.

Part 3

In the first half of the period, return to your previous group and discuss your two assigned items. Use the following questions to guide your discussion. Some items might fit more than one category.

Scientific Reality (S)

1. Is the item correct or incorrect as stated?
2. If incorrect, how could the statement be corrected?
3. a. Within your group, was there much difference between the first and second survey answers to this statement?
   b. If so, what do you think caused the difference?
4. a. If the item was answered incorrectly, does the same misconception appear in other teenage and adult responses?
   b. How would that misconception affect opinions about nuclear phenomena? Would it tend to make people anti- or pro-nuclear?

Political Reality (P)

5. Do you agree or disagree with the majority opinion on the item? Why?
6. a. Is the political reality likely to change in the near future?
   b. Why?

Value-Laden Statement (V)

7. What word(s) suggest that the statement is value-laden?
8. Would the statement more likely be expressed by a pro- or anti-nuclear activist?
9. Does the statement reflect a scientific reality as well as a value position?

In the second half of the class period, two members of each group will give a brief (1–2 minute) oral report on the group discussion regarding their assigned items. Following these presentations, the full class will have an opportunity to raise any questions or issues of concern.

E.2 LOOKING BACK

As we stated earlier, the purpose of this unit is not to teach you everything known about nuclear chemistry or to provide the "right" answer on any particular nuclear issue. Our aim has been to provide you a foundation for further exploration of this important topic—an issue that involves scientific principles, technology, and societal concerns. With this foundation, you will be better prepared to influence our nation's future polices regarding nuclear power.

This wall of the power-plant building of the Atomic Energy Commission's National Reactor Testing Station in Idaho records the first known production of useful electric power from atomic energy. The future of the industry will depend on decisions made by an informed citizenry.

CHEMISTRY, AIR, AND CLIMATE

- Is global warming a growing threat? What can we do about it?

- How can chemistry help us establish and maintain good air quality?

- What are the possible implications of ozone-depletion in the atmosphere?

- What are the key benefits and burdens of fossil-fuel burning?

INTRODUCTION

We live *on* the earth's surface, but live *in* its atmosphere. Air surrounds us just as water surrounds aquatic life. And like the earth's crust and bodies of water, the atmosphere serves both as a mine for obtaining chemical resources and a sink for discarding waste products. We use some atmospheric gases when we breathe, burn fuels, and carry out various industrial processes. Humans, other living organisms, and natural events also add gases, liquid droplets, and solid particles to the atmosphere. These added materials may have no effect, or they may disrupt the local environment—or even global conditions.

Since human activities can sometimes lower air quality, important questions arise: Should air be regarded as a free resource? How clean should air be? What will it cost to maintain clean air? What financial and environmental costs are involved with polluted air? Who should be responsible for pollution control? Citizens will continue debating such questions at local, state, national, and international levels in the years ahead.

Acceptable answers to these difficult questions depend at least in part on understanding the chemistry of gases that make up the atmosphere. We need to know about the atmosphere's composition and structure, general properties of gases, processes influencing climate, and how the atmosphere becomes naturally renewed through recycling.

This unit explores basic chemistry related to these topics, and examines current pollution control efforts. It offers another opportunity to sharpen your chemical knowledge and decision-making skills.

Take a deep breath and exhale slowly. The air that moves so easily in and out of your lungs is our topic of study.

This photo shows the pollution-soiled Milwaukee Veterans Hospital partway through a chemical restoration.

LIVING IN A SEA OF AIR

It's said that we don't appreciate the value of things until we are forced to do without them or pay for them. This is certainly true of the earth's atmosphere. Except for astronauts, long-distance runners, patients with diseased lungs, and scuba divers, people seldom think about the sea of colorless, odorless gases surrounding them. You are probably no more aware of the approximately 14 kg of air you breathe daily than fish are aware of the water passing over their gills. As long as air is present and not too polluted, we tend to take it for granted. This is not wise, as we will soon see.

How much do you know about the atmosphere and current problems involving air quality? Test your knowledge by completing the following exercise.

A.1 YOU DECIDE: THE FLUID WE LIVE IN

On a separate sheet of paper indicate whether you think each numbered statement below is true (T) or false (F), or whether it's too unfamiliar to you to judge (U). Then, for each statement you believe is true, write a sentence describing a practical consequence or application of the fact. Reword each false statement to make it true.

Do not worry about your score. You will not be graded on this exercise; it's just intended to start you thinking about the mysterious fluid in which we live.

Fluids include liquids and gases.

1. You could live nearly a month without food, and a few days without water, but you would survive for only a few minutes without air.
2. The volume of a given sample of air (or any gas) depends on its pressure and temperature.
3. Air and other gases are weightless.
4. The atmosphere exerts nearly a 15-pound force on each square inch of your body.
5. The components of the atmosphere vary widely at different locations on Earth.
6. The atmosphere acts as a filter to prevent harmful radiation from reaching the earth's surface.
7. In the lower atmosphere, air temperature usually increases as altitude increases.

8. Minor air components such as water vapor and carbon dioxide play major roles in the atmosphere.

9. Two of the ten most-produced industrial chemicals are "mined" from the atmosphere.

10. Ozone is regarded as a pollutant in the lower atmosphere, but as an essential component of the upper atmosphere.

11. Clean, unpolluted air is a pure substance.

12. Air pollution first occurred during the Industrial Revolution.

13. No human deaths have ever been directly attributed to air pollution.

14. Natural events, such as volcanic eruptions and forest fires, can produce significant air pollution.

15. Destruction of materials and crops by air pollution involves a significant economic loss for our nation.

16. The main source of air pollution is industrial activity.

17. The "greenhouse effect" is a natural warming effect that may become harmful through excessive burning of fuels.

18. In recent years, rain in industrialized nations has become less acidic.

19. Most air pollution caused by humans originates with burning fuels.

20. Pollution control has not improved overall air quality.

When you are finished, your teacher will give you answers to these items, but will not elaborate on them. However, each item will be discussed at some point in this unit.

The next section includes some demonstrations and at-home activities that illustrate the nature of the air you breathe.

A.2 LAB DEMONSTRATION: GASES

Since atmospheric gases are colorless, odorless, and tasteless, you might incorrectly conclude that they are "nothing." However, gases, just like solids and liquids, have definite physical and chemical properties. Your teacher will perform demonstrations that illustrate some of these properties. The demonstrations will help you to answer four major questions about air.

- Demonstrations 1–3:   Is air really matter?
- Demonstrations 4–8:   What is air pressure all about?
- Demonstrations 9–10:   Why does air sometimes carry odors?
- Demonstrations 11–12:   Is air heavy? Will it burn?

For each demonstration, complete each of these four steps:

1. Before the demonstration, try to predict what will happen.

2. Carefully observe the demonstration. Explain any differences between your prediction and the actual outcome.

3. Try to identify the properties of gases that are being demonstrated. Try to decide why gases exhibit those properties.

4. Think of one practical application of each demonstrated gas property.

Complete these additional activities at home, recording your results and explanations in your notebook:

1. Place two straws in your mouth. Put the free end of one in a glass of water and the other outside the glass. Now try to drink the water through the straw. Explain what happens.

At-home activity.

2. Punch a hole, with the diameter of a straw, into the screw-on lid of a clean, empty jar. Insert a straw and seal the connection with clay, putty, or wax. Fill the jar to the brim with water, then screw the top on and try to drink the water through the straw. Explain your observations.
3. Based on your observations, what makes it possible to drink liquid through a straw?

The properties of the elusive stuff called air make it vitally important. Let's examine one aspect of air's importance.

A.3 AIR: THE BREATH OF LIFE

Seen from the moon, the earth's atmosphere blends with its waters and land masses, presenting a picture of considerable beauty. Other planets also possess exotic beauty, but their environments would be hostile to life as we know it. By contrast, our world supports millions of species of living organisms, from one-celled amoebas to redwood trees and elephants.

In the Water Unit you considered water's key role in supporting life on the earth. Although our present atmosphere was formed much later than the world's waters, air also helps sustain plants and animals.

A major role of the atmosphere is to provide oxygen gas needed for respiration. This activity will help you understand that role.

YOUR TURN

Breath Composition and Glucose Burning

1. Consider Figure 1 (page 344), which compares the composition of gases we inhale with that of gases we exhale.
   a. Summarize changes in air's composition that result from its entering and then leaving the lungs.
   b. How do you account for these changes?
   c. Assuming an average of 14 breaths each minute, how many breaths do you take in a 24-hour day?
   d. What factors could make your answer to Question 1c change? Why?
   e. Assume you inhale 500 mL of air in one breath.
      (1) How many liters of air do you inhale each minute?
      (2) Each day?
2. According to Figure 1, your lungs extract only a portion of the oxygen gas available in inhaled air. What do you think determines the amount of oxygen gas used?
3. Write the chemical equation for the "burning" (combustion) of 1 mol of glucose ($C_6H_{12}O_6$) with oxygen gas (O_2) to produce carbon dioxide (CO_2) and water (H_2O). This equation represents the overall changes involved in a series of gluose-burning reactions in the body.

Refer to page 237 to review limiting reactants.

a. If the same number of oxygen gas and glucose *molecules* were available, which would be the limiting reactant? Why?

b. If the same *masses* of oxygen gas and glucose were available, which would be the limiting reactant? Why?

c. Assume that your body extracts about 20 moles of oxygen gas from air daily. Given that information and the "glucose burning" equation you wrote, how many moles of glucose can your body burn each day?

d. A mole of glucose, $C_6H_{12}O_6$, has a mass of 180 g. Thus, how many grams of glucose could your body burn daily?

e. Burning a gram of glucose produces about 17 kJ of energy. Assuming that all of your body's energy comes from glucose, how much energy does your body generate daily?

4. a. What substance produced in your body's "burning" of glucose is not shown in Figure 1?

b. How could you verify that this substance is present in your exhaled breath?

In fact, fat-burning is also a source of body energy. One gram of fat produces about 38 kJ of energy.

Industrial and technological activity—including burning fossil fuels for energy—also help influence the atmosphere's inventory of CO_2 and O_2.

Plant life needs a continuous supply of carbon dioxide—a waste product of animal respiration. Through photosynthesis in green plants (discussed in the Food Unit), carbon dioxide combines with water, ultimately forming more glucose and oxygen gas. Photosynthesis and respiration are thus complementary processes—reactants for one become products for the other.

The earth's atmosphere cannot restore and cleanse itself if natural systems are burdened by excessive pollution. Important environmental problems can arise if human activities overwhelm natural recycling and cleansing systems. We will investigate some of these issues later in this unit. But first, more fundamental questions: What *is* the atmosphere? What are some of its key physical properties?

Figure 1 The composition of inhaled and exhaled air.

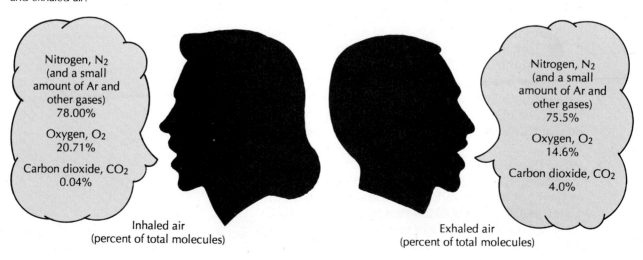

Nitrogen, N_2
(and a small amount of Ar and other gases)
78.00%

Oxygen, O_2
20.71%

Carbon dioxide, CO_2
0.04%

Inhaled air
(percent of total molecules)

Nitrogen, N_2
(and a small amount of Ar and other gases)
75.5%

Oxygen, O_2
14.6%

Carbon dioxide, CO_2
4.0%

Exhaled air
(percent of total molecules)

1. Compared to other resources you have studied—such as water, minerals, and petroleum—air has both similarities and differences. Describe
   a. two similarities, and
   b. two differences.

2. Defend or refute each of these statements about gas behavior. Base your position on gas properties you observed earlier in Part A.
   a. *An empty bottle is not really empty.*
   b. *Atmospheric pressure acts only in a downward direction.*
   c. *Gases naturally "mix" by moving from regions of lower concentration to regions of higher concentration.*
   d. *All colorless gases have similar physical and chemical properties.*

3. From a chemical point of view, why do people need to breathe faster when they hike at high altitudes than when they hike similar trails at lower altitudes?

4. A well-trained athlete takes about 30 breaths each minute during vigorous exercise (such as sprinting), inhaling about 4 L of air with each breath. Assume that at these conditions the athlete extracts about 0.15 mol O_2 from the air each minute.
   a. If all the extracted oxygen gas is used in glucose-burning, how many grams of glucose will be "burned" by the athlete each minute? (Hint: Refer to the *YOUR TURN* on page 343.)
   b. How much energy (in kilojoules, kJ) does this athlete expend each minute? (Refer to the same *YOUR TURN* for helpful information.)
   c. As you may recall from the Food unit, a Calorie (kilocalorie) equals about 4.2 kJ. How many Calories does this athlete expend each minute in vigorous exercise?

Hikers at high altitudes must breathe faster than those at low altitudes do.

INVESTIGATING THE ATMOSPHERE

Human-made air-quality problems began with the discovery and use of fire. Fires for heating, cooking, and metalworking created air pollution problems in ancient cities. In 61 A.D., the philosopher Seneca described Rome's "heavy air" and "the stink of the smoky chimneys thereof." The Industrial Revolution, beginning in the early 1700s, added more air pollution around large towns. Meanwhile, chemists and physicists were increasing their studies of the atmosphere's properties and behavior.

In the following sections you will extend your general understanding of atmospheric gases, based in part on demonstrations you have observed (page 342). This knowledge will help you predict specific gas behaviors. It will also clarify how solar energy interacts with atmospheric gases, creating weather and climate.

We will begin by preparing and investigating some atmospheric gases.

B.1 LABORATORY ACTIVITY: THE ATMOSPHERE

Getting Ready

Air, as noted earlier (Figure 1), is mostly composed of nitrogen gas (N_2) and oxygen gas (O_2), together with much smaller amounts of carbon dioxide and other gases. Each of air's components has distinct physical and chemical properties.

A high concentration of carbon dioxide helps to produce larger, healthier, and faster-growing plants in a greenhouse.

Oxygen gas extracted from air is used in a blowtorch.

Liquid nitrogen is used for freezing beef.

In this activity your class will generate two atmospheric gases—oxygen gas and carbon dioxide—and examine some of their chemical properties. In addition, your teacher may either provide samples of nitrogen gas for testing or demonstrate its properties.

Oxygen gas will be generated by this reaction:

$$2 \text{ H}_2\text{O}_2(\text{aq}) \xrightarrow{\text{MnO}_2} 2 \text{ H}_2\text{O(l)} + \text{O}_2(\text{g})$$

Hydrogen peroxide   Water   Oxygen gas

Manganese dioxide, MnO₂, serves as a catalyst in this reaction.

Carbon dioxide will be produced by adding antacid tablets to water. These tablets contain a mixture of sodium bicarbonate (NaHCO₃) and potassium bicarbonate (KHCO₃) together with citric acid (an organic acid present in lemons and oranges). When dissolved in water, bicarbonate ions (HCO₃⁻) react with hydrogen ions (H⁺) from the citric acid to produce carbon dioxide gas:

$$\text{H}^+(\text{aq}) + \text{HCO}_3^-\ (\text{aq}) \rightarrow \text{H}_2\text{O(l)} + \text{CO}_2(\text{g})$$

You will investigate the behavior of oxygen gas and carbon dioxide in the presence of burning magnesium, hot steel wool, and burning wood. The key question: do oxygen and carbon dioxide support the combustion of these materials?

Next, you will observe whether these gases react with lime-water—a solution of calcium hydroxide, Ca(OH)₂. Finally, the acid-base properties of oxygen gas and carbon dioxide will be investigated.

In some TV advertising, this release of carbon dioxide gas is simply called "fizz".

Acidic substances produce H⁺ ions when dissolved in water; basic substances produce OH⁻. In the Water Unit, page 52, you learned that the pH scale can be used to express the acidity or basicity of a solution. Most pH indicators change color quite sharply at one point on the scale. Universal indicator contains a mixture of pH-sensitive compounds; each changes color at a different pH.

On pages 398–401 of this unit, acids, bases, and pH are discussed further.

If a tank of compressed nitrogen gas is available, your class will also investigate similar properties for nitrogen gas.

If nitrogen gas is not available for testing, your teacher will provide the information needed to fill in those blanks.

Read the procedures below. Set up a data table in your notebook to record observations on the behavior of these gases.

Procedure

Part 1: Gas Preparation

ALL GROUPS

Label two 250-mL gas-collecting bottles "Sample 1" and "Sample 2." Label three 19 × 150 mm test tubes "Sample 3," "Sample 4," and "Sample 5."

NITROGEN GAS

Follow either Option A or B as directed by your teacher.

Option A: Your teacher will carry out a chemical reaction that produces nitrogen gas and will demonstrate the Part 2 nitrogen gas tests. Record all observations in your data table.

Option B: If this option is followed, the nitrogen gas will be dispensed (under your teacher's supervision) from a compressed nitrogen gas cylinder. Fill two 250-mL gas-collecting bottles and three 19 × 150 mm test tubes with nitrogen gas, as follows:

1. The gas-collecting trough should be filled with enough tap water to cover the bottom to a 3-cm depth.
2. Fill two gas-collecting bottles with water. Position them in the trough as your teacher directs.
3. Place the end of the tubing from the nitrogen gas cylinder under water in the trough, but not under either gas collection bottle.
4. Allow the nitrogen gas to bubble into the trough for several seconds. Then move the tube under the mouth of a collecting bottle.
5. Collect two bottles and three test tubes of nitrogen gas this way: When the first bottle is filled with nitrogen you will observe bubbles rising to the surface of the trough water. Hold a glass plate tightly over the mouth of the inverted jar and remove it from the trough. Set it upright on the table, with the glass plate covering the top. Move the tubing and fill the second bottle.
6. To collect a test tube of nitrogen gas, completely fill the test tube with water. Hold a finger tightly over the opening and invert the tube in the water tray. Direct the stream of nitrogen gas into the inverted test tube mouth. When gas fills the tube, stopper the tube mouth while it is still inverted and under water. Then remove the test tube from the tray.
7. Complete the gas tests outlined in Part 2.

CARBON DIOXIDE GAS

1. Omitting the burner, set up the apparatus illustrated in Figure 2.
2. Fill the gas-collecting trough with enough tap water to cover the bottom to a 3-cm depth. Fill two gas-collecting bottles with water. Position them in the trough as your teacher directs.
3. Add 250 mL of water to the 500-mL flask. Drop two antacid tablets into the water. (Break the tablets to fit through the flask neck, if necessary.)

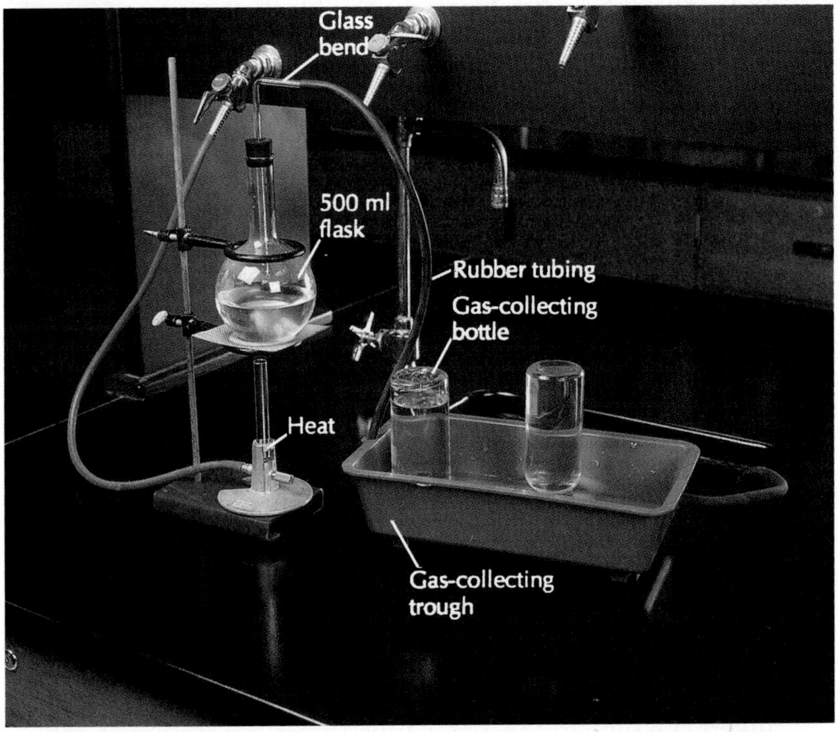

Figure 2   Gas-generating setup.

Labels on figure: Glass bend; 500 ml flask; Rubber tubing; Gas-collecting bottle; Heat; Gas-collecting trough

4. Quickly place the stopper with glass and rubber tubing into the flask. Place the other end of the tubing under water in the trough, but not under either gas collection bottle.

5. Allow the carbon dioxide gas to bubble into the trough for about ten seconds. Then move the tube under the mouth of a collecting bottle.

6. Collect two bottles and three test tubes of carbon dioxide gas this way: When the first jar is filled with carbon dioxide you will observe bubbles rising to the surface of the trough water. Hold a glass plate tightly over the mouth of the inverted jar and remove it from the trough. Set it upright on the table, with the glass plate covering the top. Move the tubing and fill the second bottle.

7. To collect a test tube of carbon dioxide gas, completely fill the test tube with water. Hold a finger tightly over the opening and invert the tube in the water tray. Direct the stream of gas into the inverted test tube mouth. When gas fills the tube, stopper the tube mouth while it is still inverted and under water. Then remove the test tube from the tray.

8. If carbon dioxide gas evolution slows down before you are finished, add another antacid tablet to the generating flask.

9. Complete the gas tests outlined in Part 2.

OXYGEN GAS

1. Set up the apparatus illustrated in Figure 2 for generating oxygen gas.

2. Fill the gas-collecting trough with enough tap water to cover the bottom to a 3-cm depth. Fill two gas-collecting bottles with water.

3. Weigh one gram of manganese dioxide (MnO_2) on a clean paper square. *Caution:* Avoid inhaling any MnO_2 dust.

4. Pour 200 mL of 3% hydrogen peroxide (H_2O_2) into a 500-mL flask. Then carefully pour the manganese dioxide sample into the flask.

5. Quickly place the stopper with attached glass and rubber tubing in the flask. Place the other end of the tubing under water in the trough, but not under either gas collection bottle. (Note: If the reaction is too slow to generate a steady stream of oxygen gas bubbles, heat the mixture *gently*—do not allow it to boil. Continue to heat gently as you move to Step 6.)

6. When the reaction is smoothly under way, allow gas to bubble into the water for one minute. Then move the tube under the mouth of a gas collecting bottle.

7. Collect two bottles and three test tubes of oxgyen gas this way: When the first jar is filled with oxygen you will observe bubbles rising to the surface of the trough water. Hold a glass plate tightly over the mouth of the inverted jar and remove it from the trough. Set it upright on the table, with the glass plate covering the top. Move the tubing to fill the second bottle.

8. To collect a test tube of oxygen gas, completely fill the test tube with water. Place a finger tightly over the opening and invert the tube in the water tray. Direct the stream of gas into the inverted test tube mouth. When gas fills the tube, stopper the tube mouth while it is still inverted under water. Then remove the test tube from the tray.

   If the reaction stops before you have collected enough gas, remove the stopper from the generating flask, turn off the burner, and allow the flask to cool for five minutes. Then add 20 mL of hydrogen peroxide solution to the reaction flask.

9. When enough gas has been collected, remove the stopper from the generating flask. Then turn off the burner.

10. Complete the gas tests outlined in Part 2.

Part 2: Gas Tests

Each group will perform the following tests on its assigned gas, and share results with the class. Record observations for all gases in your data table.

1. Light a Bunsen burner. Using tongs, hold the tip of a 8–10 cm-long piece of magnesium ribbon in the flame until it just ignites. *Caution:* Do not look directly at the intense light of burning magnesium. Quickly remove the cover plate from Sample 1 and plunge the burning magnesium into the jar. Hold the magnesium there until you and other team members have noted the result. Record your observations.

2. With the cover plate pushed slightly aside, quickly pour about 10 mL of water into Sample 2. Using tongs, hold a piece of steel wool (spread out; not in a tight ball) in the burner flame until it glows red hot. Quickly plunge the steel wool into Sample 2. Hold it there, noting the result. Examine the steel wool after it has been extinguished and cooled.

3. Using tongs, light a wood splint in the burner flame. Blow out the splint flame; then blow on the embers until they glow red. Remove the stopper from Sample 3; quickly plunge the

glowing splint into the jar. Record your observations. Turn off the burner.

4. Add about 2 mL of limewater to Sample 4. Stopper the tube and shake carefully. Note any changes in the liquid's appearance.

5. Add two drops of universal indicator solution to Sample 5. Stopper the tube and shake carefully. Match the resulting color with the indicator chart. Report the estimated pH to the class.

6. Wash your hands thoroughly before leaving the laboratory.

Questions

1. Why was it important to allow some gas to bubble through the water before you collected a sample?

2. Which gas appears to be
   a. most reactive?
   b. least reactive?

3. a. Which gas appears to support both rusting and burning?
   b. Roughly what percent of air molecules does this gas represent? (See Figure 1, page 344.)
   c. If the atmosphere contained a *higher* concentration of this gas, what might be some consequences?

4. Carbon dioxide is used in some types of fire extinguishers. Explain why.

5. Figure 1 suggests that human lungs expel carbon dioxide. Describe two ways you could verify that your exhaled breath contains carbon dioxide gas.

What gases—in addition to nitrogen, oxygen, and carbon dioxide—are present in the atmosphere? Using a variety of sampling and measuring techniques, scientists have pieced together a detailed picture of the atmosphere's chemical composition. This is the subject of the next section.

B.2   A CLOSER LOOK AT THE ATMOSPHERE

Most of the atmosphere's mass and all of its weather are located within 10 to 12 km of the earth's surface. This region, called the **troposphere** (after the Greek word meaning "to turn over"), is the part of the atmosphere in which we live. Let's examine the troposphere further.

Continuous gas mixing occurs in the troposphere, leading to a reasonably uniform chemical composition (Table 1, page 352). Analysis of trapped air in glacial ice core samples suggests that the troposphere's composition has remained relatively constant throughout human history.

In addition to gases listed in Table 1, actual air samples may contain up to 5% water vapor, although in most locations the range for water vapor is 1–3%. Some other gases are naturally present in concentrations below 0.0001% (1 ppm). These include hydrogen (H_2), xenon (Xe), ozone (O_3), nitrogen oxides (NO and NO_2), carbon monoxide (CO), and sulfur dioxide (SO_2). Human activity can alter the concentrations of carbon dioxide and some of air's trace components. Such activity can also add new substances that may lower air quality, as we will soon see.

The amount of water vapor in air determines the humidity.

The only component of the atmosphere visible from space is condensed water vapor in the form of clouds.

Table 1   **TROPOSPHERIC AIR**

Substance	Formula	Percent of Gas Molecules
Major components		
Nitrogen	N_2	78.08
Oxygen	O_2	20.95
Minor components		
Argon	Ar	0.93
Carbon dioxide	CO_2	0.032
Trace components		
Neon	Ne	0.0018
Ammonia	NH_3	0.0010
Helium	He	0.0005
Methane	CH_4	0.0002
Krypton	Kr	0.00011
Others	(see text)	>0.0001 each

The process of liquid air distillation is basically the same as petroleum distillation.

If air is cooled under pressure, it condenses to a liquid that boils at about −185° C. Distilling this liquid produces pure oxygen gas, nitrogen gas, and argon.

Imagine that we have one mole each of oxygen gas, nitrogen gas, and argon. Assume we seal these identical amounts within three very flexible balloons.

Here are four observations we could make regarding these samples:

I. All three balloons occupy the same volume, assuming external air pressure and temperature are the same for each.
II. All three balloons shrink to half this volume when outside air pressure is doubled and the temperature held constant.
III. All three balloons expand to the same extent when the temperature is increased by 10° C and the external air pressure held constant.
IV. All three balloons shrink to half their original volume when half the gas is removed and neither the external air pressure nor the temperature changed.

A balloon filled with one mole of *any* gas is observed to expand and contract in exactly these ways, provided temperature does not drop too low or external pressure rise too high. In other words, all gases share similar expansion and contraction properties.

Now it's your turn.

Avogadro's Law

The four observations described above suggest some important conclusions about gases. One of these is this: **Equal volumes of gases at the same temperature and pressure contain the same number of molecules.** This idea was first proposed by an Italian chemistry teacher, Amedeo Avogadro, in the early 1800s (it is commonly known as **Avogadro's law**).

If you look carefully, you can see the law at work in each of the four observations. First note that each balloon starts with the same number of molecules—a mole of them, or 6.02×10^{23} molecules.

In Observation I, all three balloons have the same volume at the same temperature and pressure—just as Avogadro suggested.

In Observation II, the external pressure is doubled and the gas volume becomes half of what it was. Despite these changes, all three balloons retain the same volume and contain the same number of molecules— just as Avogadro's Law specifies.

Explain how Avogadro's law is illustrated

a. in Observation III, and

b. in Observation IV.

An important consequence of Avogadro's law is that all gases have the same molar volume if they are at the same temperature and pressure. (The **molar volume** is the volume occupied by one mole of a substance.) Scientists refer to 0° C and one atmosphere (1 atm) pressure as **standard temperature and pressure,** or **STP.** *At STP, the molar volume of any gas is 22.4 L.*

The fact that all gases have the same molar volume under the same conditions simplifies our thinking about reactions involving gases. For example, consider these equations:

At STP, 22.4 L of gas contains one mole of molecules.

$$N_2(g) + O_2(g) \rightarrow 2\ NO(g)$$
$$2\ H_2(g) + O_2(g) \rightarrow 2\ H_2O(g)$$
$$3\ H_2(g) + N_2(g) \rightarrow 2\ NH_3(g)$$

You have learned that the coefficients in such equations indicate the relative numbers of molecules or moles of reactants and products. Using Avogadro's law (equal numbers of moles occupy equal volumes), you can also interpret the coefficients in terms of gas volumes:

1 volume $N_2(g)$ + 1 volume $O_2(g) \rightarrow$ 2 volumes $NO(g)$

2 volumes $H_2(g)$ + 1 volume $O_2(g) \rightarrow$ 2 volumes $H_2O(g)$

3 volumes $H_2(g)$ + 1 volume $N_2(g) \rightarrow$ 2 volumes $NH_3(g)$

The actual volumes could be any particular values, such as 1 L, 10 L, or 100 L. In the first equation, for example, we could combine 100 L of N_2 and 100 L of O_2, and expect to make 200 L of NO if the conversion is complete.

Rather than keeping track of the masses of reacting gases, chemists can monitor some reactions more easily by measuring the gas volumes involved. Unfortunately, these "short cuts" don't work for liquids and solids. There is no simple relation between moles of various solids or liquids and their volumes.

Complete the following activity to check your understanding of key concepts discussed in this section.

YOUR TURN

Molar Volume and Reactions of Gases

1. What volume would be occupied at STP by 3 mol of $CO_2(g)$?

2. In a certain reaction, 2 mol of NO(g) reacts with 1 mol of $O_2(g)$. How many liters of $O_2(g)$ would react with 4 L of NO gas?

3. The toxic gas carbon monoxide (CO) is produced when fossil fuels such as petroleum burn without enough oxygen gas. The CO eventually converts into CO_2 in the atmosphere. Automobile catalytic converters are designed to speed up this conversion:

   Carbon monoxide gas + Oxygen gas →
   Carbon dioxide gas

   a. Write the equation for this conversion.

   b. How many moles of oxygen gas would be needed to convert 50 mol of carbon monoxide to carbon dioxide?

   c. How many liters of oxygen gas would be needed to react with 1120 L of carbon monoxide? (Assume both gases are at the same temperature and pressure.)

Now that you have explored the composition and properties of gases at the bottom of the sea of air in which we live, let's continue our study of the atmosphere by "swimming" up to higher levels.

What limits the height to which these balloons can rise?

B.3 YOU DECIDE: ATMOSPHERIC ALTITUDE

If you were to dive beneath the ocean's surface, you would encounter increasing pressures and decreasing temperatures with increasing depth. Creatures deep in the ocean experience a much different environment than those living near the surface.

Likewise, the atmospheric environment at sea level is quite different than that at higher altitudes. From early explorations in hot-air and lighter-than-air balloons to current research about the atmosphere and beyond, scientists have gained a good understanding of conditions in all parts of the atmosphere.

Picture yourself in a craft designed to fly upward from the earth's surface to the farthest regions of our atmosphere. The instruments in your imaginary craft have been set to record altitude, air temperature, and air pressure. One-liter gas samples can be taken at any time. Automated instruments will give you a report on each sample's mass, number of molecules, and composition.

During your ascent, the composition of the air remains essentially constant—at 78% N_2, 21% O_2, 1% Ar, plus trace elements. At 12 km you notice you are above the clouds. Even the tallest mountains are far below. The sky is light blue; the sun shines brilliantly. The craft is now above the region where most commercial aircraft fly and above where weather develops.

A 12-km height equals about 7.5 miles or 39,000 feet.

Above 12 km, air composition is about the same as at lower altitudes, except your instruments detect more ozone (O_3). You also notice the air is quite calm, unlike the turbulence you encountered below 12 km.

Air samples taken at 50–85 km contain relatively few particles. Those present are ions such as O_2^+ and NO^+. Above 200 km, your radar detects various communication satellites in orbit.

Your aircraft now returns to the earth's surface. It's time to analyze the data you collected.

Plotting the Data

Table 2 summarizes the data recorded during the flight. The last two columns provide comparisons of equal-volume (1-L) samples of air at different altitudes.

Table 2   ATMOSPHERIC DATA

Altitude (km)	Temperature (° C)	Pressure (mmHg)	Mass (g) of 1-L Sample	Total Molecules in 1-L Sample
0	20	760	1.20	250×10^{20}
5	−12	407	0.73	150×10^{20}
10	−45	218	0.41	90×10^{20}
12	−60	170	0.37	77×10^{20}
20	−53	62	0.13	27×10^{20}
30	−38	18	0.035	7×10^{20}
40	−18	5.1	0.009	2×10^{20}
50	2	1.5	0.003	0.5×10^{20}
60	−26	0.42	0.0007	0.2×10^{20}
80	−87	0.03	0.00007	0.02×10^{20}

The unit mmHg—millimeters of mercury—is a common unit of pressure. See page 358.

Prepare two graphs. On one, plot temperature versus altitude; on the other, pressure versus altitude. Arrange your axes so that each graph nearly fills a sheet of graph paper. The x axis scale (altitude) for each graph should range from 0 to 100 km. The y axis scale (temperature) on the first graph should range from −100° C to +40° C. The y axis scale (pressure) in the second graph should extend from 0 to 780 mmHg.

Plot the data summarized in Table 2. Connect the points with a smooth line. (Note that a "line" may be straight or curved.) Use these graphs and knowledge gained from your flight to answer the questions on page 356.

Questions

1. Compare the ways air temperature and pressure change with increasing altitude.
   a. Which follows a more regular pattern?
   b. Try to explain this behavior.

2. Would you expect air pressure to rise or fall if you traveled from sea level to
   a. Pike's Peak (4270 m above sea level)?
   b. Death Valley (85 m below sea level)?
   c. Explain your answers.

3. Here's an observation you can make for yourself: When two rubber plungers (those that plumbers use) are pressed together, it becomes quite difficult to separate them.
   a. Why?
   b. Would it be easier or harder to separate them on top of a mountain?
   c. Why?

4. a. Suppose you take one-liter samples of air at several altitudes. How do the following change?
      (1) mass of the air sample
      (2) number of molecules in the air sample
   b. If you were to plot those two values (mass versus number of molecules) in a new graph, what would be the appearance of the plotted line?
   c. Why?

5. Scientists often divide the atmosphere into four layers: *troposphere* (nearest Earth), *stratosphere*, *mesosphere*, and *thermosphere* (outermost layer).
   a. Which flight data support the idea of such a "layered" atmosphere?
   b. Mark the graphs with vertical lines to indicate where you think various layer boundaries might occur.

In previous sections we have used the term "air pressure." In the next section we will clarify what scientists mean by pressure.

B.4 AIR PRESSURE

In everyday language, we speak of being pressured—meaning we feel too busy, or feel forced to behave in certain ways. The greater the pressure, the less "space" we feel we have. To scientists, pressure also refers to force and space, but in quite different ways.

Pressure represents the force applied to one unit of surface area:

$$\text{Pressure} = \frac{\text{Force}}{\text{Area}}$$

In the modernized metric system, force is expressed in a unit called the **newton** (N). Imagine holding a personal-sized bar of soap (with a mass slightly greater than 100 g) in your hand. The bar of soap would exert a force (or "push") downward on your hand of one newton (1 N). Expressed another way, at earth's surface, a 1-kg object exerts a force downward of about 9.8 N.

This force (or weight) is due to gravitational attraction. In space the object would be weightless.

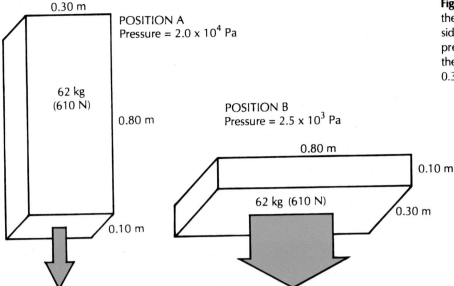

Figure 3 The pressure exerted by the granite slab depends upon which side is down. For the same block, the pressure is greatest for the side with the smallest area, in this case, the 0.30 m × 0.10 m side.

In the modernized metric system, if force is expressed in newtons (N) and area is expressed in units of square meters (m²), the resulting pressure unit is the pascal (Pa).

$$\frac{\text{Force in newtons (N)}}{\text{Area in square meters (m}^2)} = \text{Pressure in pascals (Pa)}$$

A pressure of one pascal is a relatively small value—it's roughly the pressure exerted on a slice of bread by a thin layer of butter.

To get a clearer idea of the notion of pressure, imagine a block of granite that is 0.80 m long, 0.30 m wide, and 0.10 m high. Its mass would be about 62 kg. At the earth's surface, this granite object would exert a force of 610 N.

Although the block's mass remains constant, the pressure it exerts—for example, on a floor—depends upon which side of the block faces downward (see Figure 3).

Here is the calculation of the block's pressure (in pascals) in each position:

Position A: $\dfrac{610 \text{ N}}{0.30 \text{ m} \times 0.10 \text{ m}} = \dfrac{2.0 \times 10^4 \text{ N}}{\text{m}^2} = 2.0 \times 10^4 \text{ Pa}$

Position B: $\dfrac{610 \text{ N}}{0.80 \text{ m} \times 0.30 \text{ m}} = \dfrac{2.5 \times 10^3 \text{ N}}{\text{m}^2} = 2.5 \times 10^3 \text{ Pa}$

Note that in Position A, the force of the rock is distributed over 0.030 m² (0.30 m × 0.10 m). In Position B, the same force is spread over a much larger area—0.24 m² (0.80 m × 0.30 m). Since the area is eight times greater in Position B, the pressure in Position B is only one-eighth as great as that in Position A.

Let's consider some practical applications of a scientific view of pressure.

CHEMQUANDARY

Pressure Puzzles

1. At various times in the history of fashion, spike-heeled shoes become popular. Unfortunately, during

these times floors become scarred with tiny dents. When tennis shoes or shoes with broader heels are worn, no such problem develops. Why? (See Figure 4.)

2. A person who accidentally walks onto thin ice on a lake can lower the risk of "falling through" by lying down on the ice or standing on a large piece of plywood. Why?

3. Beach or desert vehicles that need to move easily over loose sand are often equipped with special tires. Would you expect these tires to be wide or thin? Why?

Figure 4 The pressure a shoe exerts depends upon its area.

How do granite blocks and high-heeled shoes relate to the atmosphere? Well, as this unit's opening demonstrations showed, the atmosphere exerts a force on every object within it. On a typical day, at sea level, air exerts a force of about 100,000 N on each square meter of your body—a resulting pressure of about 100 kilopascals (kPa). This pressure is equal to one atmosphere (atm).

But there is yet another way to express pressure values. Pressure readings on the imaginary flight were given in **mmHg (millimeters of mercury).** A weather report may include "the barometric pressure is 30 inches of mercury." Apparently, air pressure can be expressed as the height of a mercury column. Why? A simple experiment will clarify matters.

Fill a graduated cylinder (or soft drink bottle) completely with water. Cover it with your hand and invert it in a container of water. Remove your hand. What happens to the water level inside the cylinder? What force supports the weight of the column of water in the cylinder?

Now imagine repeating the experiment with a taller cylinder, and again with an even taller cylinder. If the cylinder were made taller and taller, at a certain height water would no longer fill the cylinder entirely when it is inverted in a container of water. Why?

This experiment was first performed in the mid-1600s. Researchers discovered that one atmosphere of air pressure could only support a column of water as tall as 10.3 m (33.9 ft). If one tries the experiment with even taller cylinders, the water still drops to the 10.3-m level, leaving a partial vacuum above the liquid.

1 atm = 101 kPa

1 atm = 760 mmHg

One practical consequence is that, at one atmosphere pressure, well water cannot be lifted by a hand-pump any higher than 10.3 m.

Obviously, a barometer based on water would be extremely awkward to handle. Scientists replaced the water with mercury, a liquid that is 13.6 times more dense. The resulting mercury barometer (see Figure 5) is shorter than the water barometer by a factor of 13.6. Thus, at one atmosphere pressure, the mercury column has a height of 760 mm.

In the following sections we will study the effects of pressure and temperature changes on gas volume. This knowledge will help us understand how gases behave in our bodies, or trapped below ground, or in the atmosphere. We will consider the effect of changes in pressure first.

B.5   BOYLE'S LAW: PUTTING ON THE SQUEEZE

Unlike the volume of a solid or a liquid, the volume of a gas sample can easily be changed. Applying pressure to a sample of gas decreases its volume—it becomes "compressed." By compressing a gas, you can store a greater mass of the gas in a given container. Tanks of compressed gas are quite common. Propane tanks are used in campers, mobile homes, and houses in isolated areas; welders buy tanks of oxygen and acetylene gas; hospitals use tanks of oxygen gas for patients with breathing problems.

Tanks of gas are often used in chemistry laboratories. That observation leads to a puzzling *ChemQuandary.*

Figure 5   A mercury barometer. The atmosphere at sea level will support a column of mercury 760 mm high. The pressure unit "atmospheres" is thus related to pressure in millimeters of mercury. 1 atm = 760 mmHg.

CHEMQUANDARY

A Volume Discount?

A chemistry teacher notices a large difference in the price of hydrogen gas sold by two companies.

Company A offers a 1-L cylinder of hydrogen gas for $8. Company B offers a 1-L cylinder of the same gas for $15.

The teacher discovers that Company B offers a better bargain. How can that be?

How does the volume of a gas sample change when its pressure is increased? You already know the answer, from Observation II of the balloons on page 352. When the pressure on the balloons was doubled, their volumes decreased by one half.

This change in volume illustrates a relationship common to all gases. Suppose we work with 12 L of gas at a pressure of 2 atm. We observe that doubling the pressure to 4 atm cuts the volume to 6 L. If we double the presure once again, to 8 atm, the volume reduces to 3 L.

Let's summarize these data and complete a simple calculation:

Pressure (atm)	Volume (L)	Pressure × Volume (atm·L)
2	12	24
4	6	24
8	3	24

For a given sample of gas, the product of its pressure and volume always has the same value (assuming the temperature remains unchanged).

Such a relationship holds for any change in either the volume or pressure. If the volume of that gas sample is decreased to 4 L, the pressure will increase to 6 atm (4 × 6 = 24, as before).

This pressure-volume relationship is called **Boyle's law,** after the seventeenth-century English scientist who first proposed it. One way to state Boyle's law is this: *At a constant temperature, the product of the pressure and the volume of a gas sample is a constant value.*

The general mathematical statement of Boyle's law is

$$P_1V_1 = P_2V_2$$

where P_1 and V_1 are the original pressure and volume of a gas, and P_2 and V_2 are the new pressure and volume at the same temperature. Plotting a series of pressure and volume values for any gas sample gives a curve similar to that in Figure 6. Boyle's law allows us to make predictions about changes in the pressure or volume of a gas sample at constant temperature whenever any three of the values P_1, V_1, P_2, or V_2 are known.

Consider this example:

A certain steel gas tank in a chemistry laboratory has a volume of 1.0 L. It contains gas at a pressure of 56 atm. What volume would the gas from such a tank occupy at 1.0 atm at the same temperature?

We can use Boyle's law to solve the problem this way:

1. Identify the starting and final conditions:

$$P_1 = 56 \text{ atm} \qquad P_2 = 1.0 \text{ atm}$$
$$V_1 = 1.0 \text{ L} \qquad V_2 = \text{ ? L}$$

2. Rearrange the equation $P_1V_1 = P_2V_2$ to solve for the unknown, in this case, V_2 (the volume after the pressure decrease):

$$V_2 = \frac{P_1V_1}{P_2}$$

3. Substitute the values into the equation and solve for V_2:

$$V_2 = \frac{56 \text{ atm} \times 1.0 \text{ L}}{1.0 \text{ atm}} = 56 \text{ L}$$

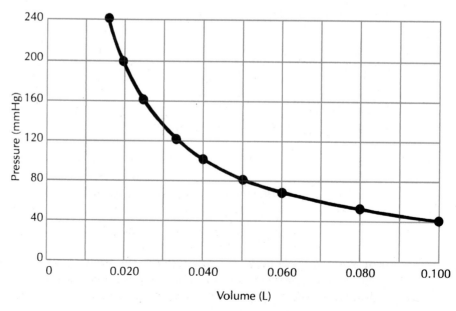

Figure 6 Boyle's law: The volume of a gas sample, maintained at constant temperature, is inversely proportional to its pressure. Hence the product of P × V is constant. A plot of pressure vs. volume for any gas sample at constant temperature will be similar to this one.

A reasoning method can be used to solve the same problem: If the pressure *decreases* from 56 to 1.0 atm, the volume will *increase* by a proportional amount. Therefore, to find the new, larger volume, the known volume must be multiplied by a pressure ratio larger than one:

$$1.0 \text{ L} \quad \times \quad \frac{56 \text{ atm}}{1.0 \text{ atm}} = 56 \text{ L}$$

If the gas pressure increases, then the volume must decrease. (This assumes the temperature remains constant.) In that case the pressure ratio used must be less than one. Similar reasoning applies to problems in which the initial and final volume are known and the final pressure is to be found.

Work these problems, which use Boyle's law.

YOUR TURN

P-V Relationships

1. Explain each statement:
   a. *Even when they have an ample supply of oxygen gas, airplane passengers become uncomfortable if the cabin loses its pressure.* (*Hint:* What will gases in the human body do if the body is exposed to a sudden drop in air pressure?)
   b. *Carbonated soft drinks "pop" when the bottle or can is opened.*
   c. *Tennis balls are sold in pressurized cans.* (*Hint:* Each tennis ball contains gases at elevated pressure to give it good bounce.)
   d. *When climbing a mountain or ascending a tall building in an elevator, your ears may "pop."*

2. You can buy helium gas in small aerosol cans to inflate party balloons. Assume that the container label indicates that the can contains about 7100 mL (0.25 cubic feet) of helium. This volume refers to the volume of helium at 1 atm pressure. If the can's volume is 492 mL, what is the pressure of the gas inside the can (at the same temperature)?

3. Suppose that on a hot, sticky spring afternoon, a tornado passes near your high school. The air pressure inside and outside your classroom (volume = 430 m³) is 760 mmHg before the storm. At the peak of the storm, pressure outside the classroom drops to 596 mmHg.
   a. To what volume would the air in the room try to change to equalize the pressure difference between the inside and the outside? (Assume no change in air temperature.)
   b. Why is it a good idea to open the windows slightly as such a storm approaches?

4. In the U.S., automobile tire pressure is usually measured in non-metric units of pounds per square inch (lb./in.²)—often (and incorrectly) expressed as

Dramatic changes in air pressure are associated with the passage of a tornado.

1 atm = 14.7 lb./in.²

"pounds" of air pressure. The tire gauge actually reports the *difference* in pressure between air inside the tire and the atmospheric pressure. Thus, if a tire gauge reads 30 lb./in.² on a day when atmospheric pressure is 14 lb./in.², the *total* tire pressure is 44 lb./in.².

   a. What volume of atmospheric air (at 14 lb./in.²) would be needed to fill a 40.0-L tire to a gauge reading of 30 lb./in.²?

   b. Why does pumping up an automobile tire by hand take such a long time?

In all these problems, we assumed that gas temperature remained constant. How does temperature affect gas volume? The answer to this question is important, since many reactions in laboratory work, in chemical processing, and all those in food preparation are done at roughly the same atmospheric pressure. Did you ever wonder why cakes and bread rise as they bake? Read on and find out why.

B.6 LABORATORY ACTIVITY: T-V RELATIONSHIPS

Getting Ready

Most forms of matter expand when heated and contract when cooled. As you know, gas samples expand and shrink to a much greater extent than do either solids or liquids.

In this activity you will investigate how the temperature of a gas sample influences its volume—assuming pressure remains unchanged. To do this, you will raise the temperature of a thin glass tube containing a trapped air sample, and then record volume changes as the air sample cools.

Procedure

1. Tie a capillary tube to the lower end of a thermometer, using two rubber bands (Figure 7). The open end of the tube should be placed closest to the thermometer bulb and 5–7 mm from the bulb's tip.

2. Immerse the tube and thermometer in a hot oil bath that has been prepared by your teacher. Be sure the entire capillary tube is immersed in oil. Wait for your tube and thermometer to reach the temperature of the oil (approximately 130° C). Record the temperature of the bath.

3. After your tube and thermometer have reached constant temperature, lift them so that about three-quarters of the capillary tube is elevated above the oil bath. Pause here for about three seconds to allow some oil to rise into the tube. Then quickly carry the tube and thermometer (on a paper towel to avoid dripping) back to your desk.

4. Lay the tube and thermometer on a paper towel on the desk. Make a reference line on the paper at the sealed end of the melting-point tube. Also mark the upper end of the oil plug

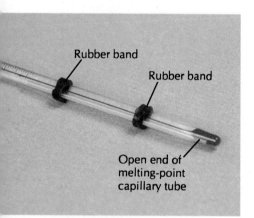

Figure 7 Apparatus for studying how gas volume changes with temperature.

Be careful not to touch the hot thermometer.

(Figure 8). Alongside this mark write the temperature at which the air column had this length.

5. As the temperature of the gas sample drops, make at least six marks representing the length of the air column trapped above the oil plug at various temperatures; write the corresponding temperature next to each mark. Allow enough time so that the temperature drops by 80 to 100 degrees. Since the tube has a uniform diameter, length serves as a relative measure of the gas volume.

6. When the thermometer shows a steady temperature (near room temperature), make a final length and temperature observation. Discard the tube and the rubber bands according to your teacher's instructions. Wipe the thermometer dry.

7. Measure and record (in centimeters) the marked lengths of the gas sample.

8. Wash your hands thoroughly before leaving the laboratory.

9. Prepare a sheet of graph paper for plotting your data. The vertical scale (length) should range from 0 to 10 cm; the horizontal scale (temperature) should include values from −350° C to 150° C. Label your axes and arrange the scales so the graph fills nearly the entire sheet. Plot the temperature-length data. Draw the best straight line through the plotted points. Using a dashed line, extend this straight graph line so that it intersects the x axis. Turn in one copy of your data; keep another copy to use in answering the following questions.

Questions

1. a. What was the total change in the length of your sample of gas from the first reading to the last?

   b. What was the corresponding overall change in temperature?

2. Use your Question 1 answers to find the change in length for each degree of temperature change. For instance, if the length decreased by 5.0 cm while the temperature dropped 100° C, the ratio would be

$$\frac{5.0 \text{ cm}}{100° \text{ C}} = 0.050 \text{ cm per } °C$$

3. Use the value calculated in Question 2 to find the gas temperature that would correspond to a sample length of 0 cm.

4. a. Compare the temperature found in Question 3 with the temperature noted at the point where your extended graph line intersected the horizontal axis. Both values represent estimates of the gas temperature required to shrink its volume to "zero." (This assumes, of course, that the temperature-volume trend continues to low temperatures.)

   b. Which is the better estimate of this "zero gas volume" temperature? Why?

5. If you were to continue cooling the trapped gas sample, do you think the gas would finally reach "zero volume"? Why?

   Experiments similar to the one you just performed were first completed in the late 1700s. They resulted in some important new ideas, including a more useful temperature scale.

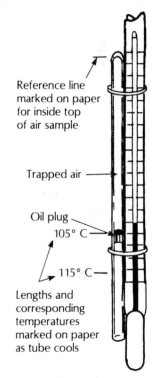

Reference line marked on paper for inside top of air sample

Trapped air

Oil plug
105° C

115° C

Lengths and corresponding temperatures marked on paper as tube cools

Figure 8 Marking the length and temperature of the air sample. The air trapped in this tube has cooled from 115° C to 105° C and shrunk as shown.

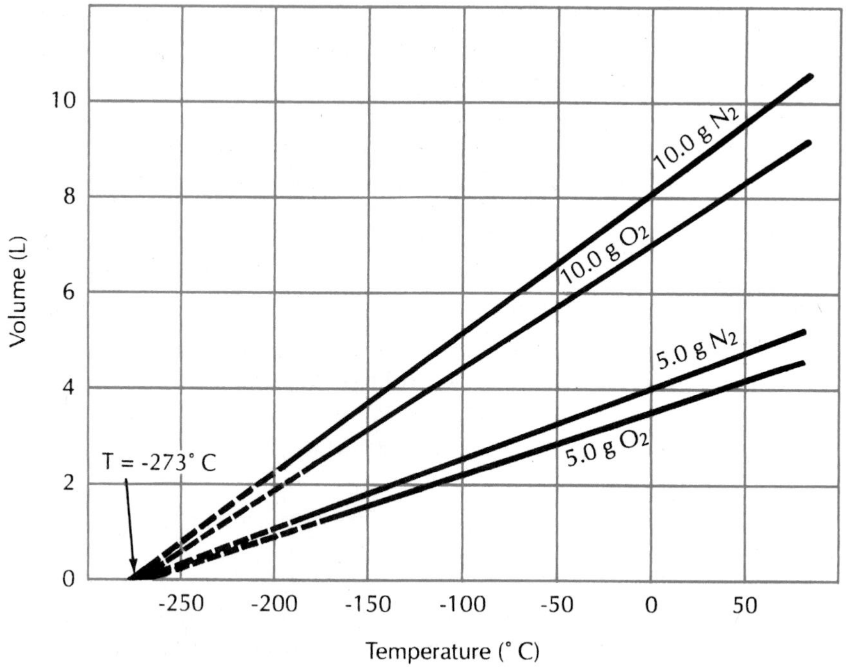

Figure 9 Temperature-volume measurements of various gas samples at 1 atm pressure. Extrapolation has been made for temperatures below liquefaction (O_2 is $-183°$ C, N_2 is $-196°$ C).

B.7 YOU DECIDE: A NEW TEMPERATURE SCALE

Studies of changes in gas volume caused by temperature changes at constant pressure were conducted in the 1780s by French chemists (and hot-air ballooning enthusiasts) Jacques Charles and Joseph Gay-Lussac. Data for oxygen and nitrogen gas are shown in Figure 9. The plots for different gases and different sample sizes end at different points. However, if extended to the x axis (an extrapolation), all graph lines meet at the same temperature.

Clearly, there is a simple relationship between gas volume and temperature (at constant pressure). However, expressing this mathematically proved difficult. Lord Kelvin (William Thomson, an English scientist), solved the problem by proposing a new temperature scale.

Let's see if pooled data found by your class in the just-completed lab activity can reveal what Kelvin discovered. Answer these questions:

1. At what temperature does your extended graph line intersect the x axis?

2. What would be the volume of your gas sample at this temperature?

3. Why is this volume only theoretical?

4. Now renumber the temperature scale on your graph, assigning the value zero to the temperature at which the graph intersects the x axis. The new scale expresses temperature in kelvins (K)—the kelvin temperature scale. One kelvin is the same size as one degree Celsius. However, unlike zero degrees Celsius, zero kelvins is the lowest temperature theoretically possible—absolute zero.

5. Based on your graph, what temperature in kelvins would correspond to 0° C, the freezing point of water? What temperature would correspond to 100° C, the boiling point of water at one atmosphere pressure?

6. Based on your answer to Question 5, how would you convert a given temperature in degrees Celsius units to its corresponding temperature in kelvins?

The new kelvin temperature scale allowed a simple statement of the temperature-volume relationship for gases. Doubling the kelvin temperature causes a given gas volume to double. Halving the kelvin temperature causes the gas volume to decrease by half, and so on. Such relationships are summarized in **Charles' law:** *At constant pressure, the kelvin temperature divided by the volume of a given gas sample is a constant value.* Or, expressing it another way,

$$\frac{T_1}{V_1} = \frac{T_2}{V_2}$$

CHEMQUANDARY

Behavior of Gases

Apply Charles' law in answering these questions:
1. Why does bread rise when baked? (*Hint:* $CO_2(g)$ is produced by yeast action.)
2. Is hot air more dense or less dense than cold air?
3. Why do hot air balloons rise?
4. If you can install only one thermostat in a two-story house, should it be placed on the first or second floor?

Try the following gas behavior problems using any approach you prefer. In each problem identify the variable (pressure or volume) that is assumed to be constant.

YOUR TURN

T-V-P Relationships

1. a. If the kelvin temperature of a gas sample in a steel tank increases to three times its original value, what will happen to the pressure of the gas? (*Hint:* "Steel tank" is a good indication that gas volume will remain constant.)
   b. Give an example of such a situation.
2. a. If a sample of gas is cooled at a constant pressure until it shrinks to one-fourth its initial volume, what change in its kelvin temperature must have occurred?
   b. Give an example of such a situation.
3. Explain why car owners in severe northern climates often add more air to their tires in winter and release air from them when summer arrives.
4. a. When the volume of a gas sample is reported, the pressure and the temperature must also be given. Why?
   b. This is not necessary for liquids and solids. Why?

5. Use gas laws to explain each situation:
   a. Thunderheads towering high into the sky form where warm, moist air and cold air masses meet.
   b. A weather balloon encounters both decreasing pressure and decreasing temperature as it rises. We observe that the balloon steadily expands.

Why do all common gases at normal atmospheric conditions behave in accord with Boyle's law and Charles' law? An explanation will be developed in the next section.

B.8 IDEALLY, GASES BEHAVE SIMPLY

By the early 1800s, scientists had discovered the gas laws you have just explored. Balloon flights also provided valuable information on the atmosphere's composition and structure. However, explanations for such consistent and similar behavior among gases were incomplete.

Bit by bit, however, scientists pieced together a comprehensive and satisfactory explanation of gas behavior—the kinetic molecular theory of gases.

To understand the theory, you must first understand the concept of kinetic energy. **Kinetic energy,** the energy possessed by a moving object, is sometimes called "energy of motion." Kinetic energy depends on the mass of the object and on its velocity.

At a given velocity, a more massive object has greater kinetic energy than does a less massive object. For example, even though they are traveling at the same speed, an 18-wheel truck has much greater kinetic energy than a small economy car.

If we consider two objects having equal masses, the one traveling faster has greater kinetic energy. This helps explain the difference, for example, between auto damage caused by an encounter with a tree at 5 mph and, say, at 10 mph.

Scientific laws describe the behavior (the "what") of nature, but do not provide explanations (the "why"). Scientific theories and models address "why" and "how" aspects of our natural world.

CHEMQUANDARY

Hammering Away at Kinetic Energy

Here are two questions that are less painful than they sound:

1. Which would you rather have dropped on your foot from shoulder height—a hammer or a nail? Why? (Note that both will reach your foot at roughly the same speed.)
2. Which would you rather have dropped on your foot—a hammer from shoulder height or a hammer from knee height? Why?

The **kinetic molecular theory** of gases is based on several postulates:

- Gases consist of tiny particles (atoms or molecules) that have negligible size compared with the great distances separating them.

A postulate is an accepted statement used as the basis of further reasoning and study.

- Gas molecules are in constant, random motion. They often collide with each other and with the walls of their container. Gas pressure is the result of molecular collisions with the container walls.
- Molecular collisions are elastic. This means that although individual molecules may gain or lose kinetic energy, there is no net (or overall) gain or loss of kinetic energy from these collisions.
- At a given temperature, molecules in a gas sample have a range of kinetic energies. However, the average kinetic energy of the molecules is constant and depends only on the kelvin temperature of the sample. In samples of different gases at the same temperature, the average kinetic energy of the molecules is the same. As temperature increases, so do the average velocities and kinetic energies of the molecules.

Analogies sometimes used to help picture gases at the molecular level include a room swarming with tiny gnats, or one full of bouncing superballs. Although helpful in giving us "mental pictures" of molecular behavior, such examples fail to represent these characteristics:

- The extremely small size of the gas molecules relative to the total volume of a gas sample. For example, at room temperature less than one thousandth of the volume of a carbon dioxide gas sample is actually occupied by molecules. The remaining space is empty.
- The extremely high velocities of gas molecules. At room temperature, for example, nitrogen gas molecules travel— on average—nearly 1700 km/h (1100 mph).
- The extremely high frequency of collisions.

Because of these differences, the actual behavior of gases can only be precisely represented through mathematical expressions.

Complete the following exercises to check your understanding of the kinetic molecular theory of gases.

YOUR TURN

Gas Molecules in Motion

You will use the kinetic molecular theory to explain five common observations regarding gas behavior. Where appropriate, you should consider such factors as the kinetic energies, spaces between molecules, and molecular collisions. A sketch of molecules in motion may also be useful for some items.

Here is a worked-out example of how the kinetic molecular theory can be applied in explaining a common observation:

Observation: Increasing the volume of a gas sample causes its pressure to decrease if the temperature remains constant.

Explanation: Increasing the volume of a sample of gas molecules gives the molecules more room to move around. Molecules must travel farther (on average) before they collide with (and bounce off) the container walls. Fewer molecular collisions with the walls in a given time interval means that the gas pressure will decrease.

Now it's your turn. Use the kinetic molecular theory to explain each of these observations:

1. Decreasing the volume of a gas sample causes the gas pressure to increase, if the temperature is held constant.
2. At constant volume, the pressure of a gas changes when the temperature changes.
3. The atmosphere exerts pressure on our bodies, yet this pressure does not crush us.
4. Filled balloons eventually leak even when they are tightly sealed.
5. Helium-filled balloons leak faster than those inflated by mouth.

Gases that behave as kinetic molecular theory predicts are called **ideal gases.** At very high pressures or very low temperatures, gases do not behave ideally. The gas laws we have considered do not accurately describe gas behavior under such conditions. At low temperatures, molecules move more slowly. The weak attractions between them may become so important that the gas will condense into a liquid. At high enough pressures—if the temperature is not too high—the gas molecules are forced so close together that these same forces of attraction may again cause a gas to condense. However, under the usual conditions encountered in our atmosphere, most gas behavior approximates that of an ideal gas. Such gas behavior is well explained by the kinetic molecular theory.

Now that you understand how chemists account for some properties of gases, you are ready to explore how the gases in our atmosphere interact with solar energy to create weather and climate.

PART B: SUMMARY QUESTIONS

1. Oxygen gas is essential to life as we know it. Our atmosphere is approximately 21% oxygen gas. Would a higher percent of atmospheric oxygen be desirable? Explain.

2. Explain the chemical change summarized below, using
   a. molecular pictures.
   b. a chemical equation.

   $1 L H_2$ + $1 L Cl_2$ → $2 L HCl$

   Hydrogen   Chlorine   Hydrogen
   gas   gas   chloride gas

3. Does Avogadro's law apply to liquids and solids? Explain your answer.

4. In terms of pressure exerted at various depths, how is our atmosphere similar to the oceans?

5. Explain why a suction-cup hook can support the weight of a small object.

6. Explain why living creatures are not normally found above the troposphere.

7. Solve these problems. As part of your answer, identify which gas variable is assumed constant :
   a. A small quantity of the inert gas argon (Ar) is added to light bulbs to reduce the vaporization of tungsten atoms from the filament. What volume of argon at

760-mmHg pressure is needed to fill a 0.210-L light bulb at 1.30-mmHg pressure?

b. A tank at 300 K contains 0.285 L of gas at 1.92 atm pressure. The maximum pressure the container is capable of withstanding is 5.76 atm. Assuming that doubling the kelvin temperature causes the pressure to double,

(1) at what temperature will the tank burst?
(2) would it explode in a fire at a temperature of 1275 K?

8. Convection, the process whereby warm air rises and cold air falls, is important to the natural circulation and cleansing of the troposphere. Explain from a molecular point of view why convection occurs.

EXTENDING YOUR KNOWLEDGE (OPTIONAL)

- In what ways is an "ocean of gases" analogy useful in thinking about the atmosphere? How does the atmosphere differ from the hydrosphere? (You may wish to compare a dive into the ocean with an ascent into the atmosphere.)

- Boyle's law is illustrated each time you breathe in or breathe out. Explain.

- The gas behavior described by Boyle's law is a matter of life and death to scuba divers. On the surface of the water, the diver's lungs, tank, and body are under 1 atm pressure. However, under water a diver's body is under the combined pressure of atmosphere and water.

  a. When divers are 10.3 m below the surface of the ocean, how much pressure do their bodies experience?

  b. Why are pressurized tanks needed when diving to great depths?

  c. What would happen to the volume of the tank if it were not made strong enough to withstand such pressure?

  d. Why is it necessary to exhale and rise slowly when ascending from the ocean depths?

  e. How do the problems of a diver compare with those of a pilot climbing to a high altitude in an unpressurized plane?

- If air at 25° C has a density of 1.28 g/L, and your classroom has a volume of 2×10^5 L,

  a. What is the mass of air in your classroom?

  b. If the temperature increased, how would this affect the mass of air in the room? Assume the room is not completely sealed.

- The kelvin temperature scale has played an important role in theoretical and applied chemistry.

  a. Find out whether zero kelvins (0 K) has been reached in the laboratory. If not, how close have scientists come to this temperature?

  b. Research from the field of **cryogenics** (low-temperature chemistry and physics) has many possible applications. Do research in the library to learn about activities in this field.

ATMOSPHERE AND CLIMATE

Imagine a place where mid-day sunshine makes a rock hot enough to fry an egg, where nights are cold enough to freeze carbon dioxide gas to dry ice, where the sun's ultraviolet rays can burn your exposed skin in minutes. That place is the moon. Its extreme conditions are due to the absence of an atmosphere.

The combination of the sun's radiant energy and the earth's atmosphere helps to maintain a hospitable climate for life on this planet. The atmosphere delivers the oxygen gas we breathe and makes exhaled carbon dioxide available to plants for photosynthesis. It also serves as a sink for airborne wastes from people, industry, and technology—a role which is causing increasing concern. And the atmosphere protects our skin from the sun's ultraviolet rays.

To understand the basis for our hospitable climate, it's important to know how solar energy interacts with our atmosphere. The sun warms the earth's surface. The earth's warm surface, in turn, warms the air above it. Since warm air expands, its density decreases, and so the warm air rises. Colder, more dense air

Mongolian sheepherders utilizing the sun's energy.

falls. These movements of warm and cold air masses help create continual air currents that drive the world's weather.

Let's look more closely at the sun's energy. What makes it so useful?

C.1 THE SUNSHINE STORY

The enormous quantity of energy produced by the sun is a result of the fusion of hydrogen nuclei into helium. Most of this energy escapes from the sun as electromagnetic radiation. About 9% of solar radiation is in the **ultraviolet (UV)** region of the electromagnetic spectrum, 46% is in the **visible** region, and 45% is in the **infrared (IR)** region. The complete solar spectrum is shown in Figure 10.

Electromagnetic radiation is composed of photons, each possessing a characteristic frequency and quantity of energy. The higher the frequency, the higher the energy of the photon. Photon energy determines the effect of radiation on matter.

Infrared radiation, with frequencies between about 10^{12} and 10^{14} Hz (hertz, or cycles per second), causes molecules to vibrate faster. As we noted in our study of the kinetic molecular theory (page 366), this raises the temperature.

Visible light is of higher energy than infrared (frequencies about 10^{14} Hz). Such radiation can energize electrons in some chemical bonds, with each photon delivering its energy to the electrons in just one chemical bond. Visible light also interacts with the electrons in chlorophyll molecules in green plants, providing the energy needed for the reactions involving photosynthesis.

The still-higher energy carried by photons of ultraviolet radiation, with frequencies ranging from about 10^{15} to 10^{16} Hz, can break single covalent bonds. As a result, chemical changes can take place in materials exposed to ultraviolet radiation—including damage to tissues of living organisms. This explains why you are cautioned to wear sun screen when exposed to sunlight for extended periods.

As solar radiation passes through the earth's atmosphere, it interacts with molecules and other particles in the atmosphere.

Nuclear fusion is discussed on page 314.

For further background on electromagnetic radiation, see the Nuclear unit, page 276.

Such photon-electron interactions are taking place right now in double bonds of molecules in your eyes, making it possible for you to see this printed page.

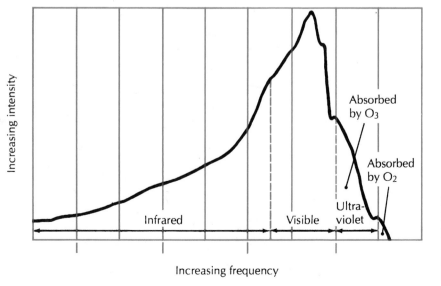

Figure 10 The solar spectrum. The higher the frequency, the higher the photon energy of the radiation. Intensity, plotted on the y axis, is a measure of the quantity of radiation at a given frequency.

Once it reaches earth's surface it is absorbed or used in other ways. To better appreciate the effects of solar radiation, let's briefly consider some factors that affect average global temperature.

C.2 EARTH'S ENERGY BALANCE

The mild 15° C (59° F) average temperature at the earth's surface is determined partly by the balance between the inward flow of energetic photons from the sun and the outward flow of energy into space. However, certain properties of the earth determine how much thermal energy our planet can hold near its surface—where we live—and how much energy it radiates back into space.

Figure 11 shows the fate of solar radiation as it enters our atmosphere. Some incoming solar radiation never reaches the earth's surface, but is reflected directly back into space by clouds and particles in the atmosphere. A small amount of solar radiation is also reflected when it strikes such materials as snow, sand, or concrete at the earth's surface.

About one-fourth of all incoming solar energy fuels the hydrologic cycle—the continuous cycling of water into and out of the atmosphere by evaporation and condensation.

Almost half of the solar energy is absorbed by the earth, warming the atmosphere, oceans, and continents. All objects above zero kelvins radiate energy, the quantity being directly related to the object's temperature. The earth's surface re-radiates most of the absorbed radiation, not at its original frequencies, but at lower frequencies—in the infrared region of the spectrum. This re-radiated energy plays an extremely important role in the world's energy balance. These lower-energy photons are absorbed by molecules in the air more easily than the original solar radiation, thus warming the atmosphere.

Carbon dioxide (CO_2) and water (H_2O) are good absorbers of infrared radiation. So are methane (CH_4) and halogenated hydrocarbons such as CF_3Cl. Clouds (concentrated droplets of water or

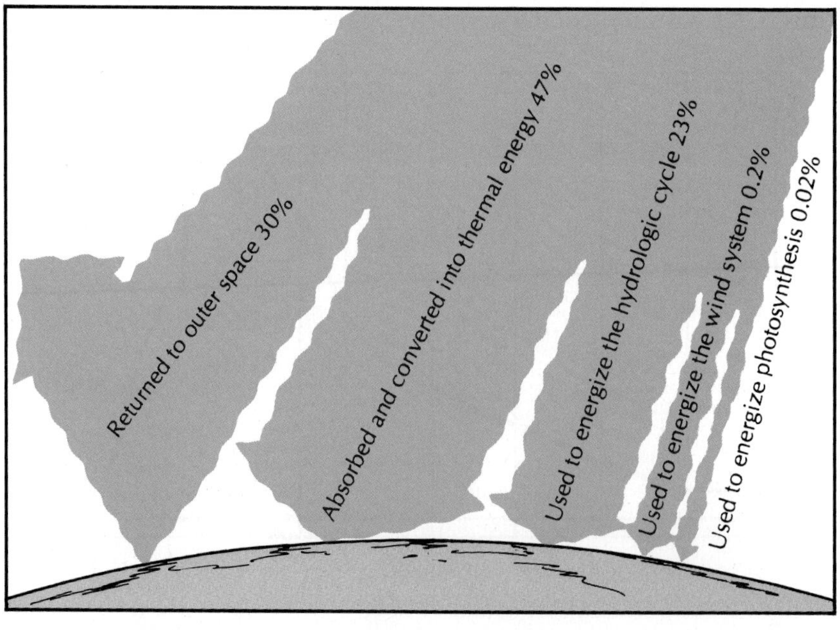

Visible light reflected in this way allows the earth's illuminated surface to be seen from space.

For more information, see the Water unit.

Figure 11 The fate of incoming solar radiation.

ice) also absorb infrared radiation. Energy absorbed by these molecules in the atmosphere is once again radiated toward the earth. Energy can pass back and forth between the earth's surface and molecules in the atmosphere many times before it finally escapes into outer space. This trapped energy keeps us warm.

Without water and carbon dioxide molecules in the atmosphere to absorb and re-radiate thermal energy to earth, our whole planet would reach thermal balance at a bone-chilling $-25°$ C $(-13°$ F), quite close to the average temperature on Mars.

CHEMQUANDARY

Grab Another Blanket!

Why does the outside temperature drop faster on a clear night than on a cloudy night?

The trapping and returning of radiation by carbon dioxide and other substances floating in the atmosphere is known as the *greenhouse effect,* because it resembles the way heat is held in a greenhouse on a sunny day. The planet Venus provides an example of a runaway greenhouse effect. The atmosphere of Venus, composed mainly of thick clouds of carbon dioxide, prevents the escape of most infrared radiation. Thermal balance on Venus is maintained at a much higher temperature than on the earth.

Check your understanding of the interaction of radiation with matter and the role of radiation in earth's energy balance by answering the following questions.

Gaseous substances that are good infrared absorbers —such as carbon dioxide, water vapor, methane, and halogenated hydrocarbons —are called greenhouse gases.

YOUR TURN

Earth's Energy Balance

1. Why is ultraviolet radiation potentially more harmful than infrared radiation?
2. Describe two essential roles played by visible radiation from the sun.
3. What will occur if human activities increase the concentration of carbon dioxide and other greenhouse gases in the troposphere?
4. Suppose our planet had a thinner atmosphere than it does now.
   a. How would average daytime temperatures be affected? Why?
   b. How would average nighttime temperatures be affected? Why?

Climate is influenced by other factors than the interaction of solar radiation with the atmosphere. These factors include the earth's rotation (causing day and night and influencing wind patterns), its revolution around the sun (causing seasons), its tilt on its axis (causing the uneven distribution of solar radiation and influencing wind patterns), and differing thermal properties of materials on its surface. In the next section we will examine the last of these factors.

C.3 AT THE EARTH'S SURFACE

If you have visited or lived in the South or Southwest, you may have noticed that many cars (and their seat cushions) are light colored. A property of materials called **reflectivity** helps keep the vehicles cool. When light photons strike a surface, some are absorbed—increasing the surface temperature—and some are reflected. The reflected radiation does not contribute to raising the object's temperature.

The color of an object is determined by the frequencies of the radiation it reflects. If all frequencies of the visible spectrum are reflected, the object appears white. If all visible frequencies are absorbed (and none are reflected), the object appears black. Because light-colored surfaces reflect more radiation, they remain cooler than do dark-colored surfaces.

Similarly, variations in the reflectivity of materials at the earth's surface help determine its surface temperature. On a hot day it is much more comfortable to walk barefoot across a plowed field than across an asphalt parking lot. The plowed field reflects almost 30% of the sun's rays, while the asphalt reflects very little. Clean snow reflects almost 95% of solar radiation, while forests are not very reflective.

CHEMQUANDARY

Some Reflections on Dust

1. What might happen if large quantities of dust were to settle out on snow fields at the North and South Poles?
2. What might happen if large quantities of dust of high reflectivity were to enter the atmosphere?

Heat capacity is often reported in units of joules per gram per degree Celsius, J/(g° C).

Each material at the earth's surface has a characteristic reflectivity and heat capacity, which together determine how fast the material warms up. **Heat capacity** is the quantity of thermal energy (heat) needed to raise the temperature of a given mass of material by 1° C. In effect, heat capacity is a measure of a material's storage capacity for thermal energy. The lower a material's heat capacity, the greater will be its temperature increase for a given quantity of added energy. The higher the heat capacity, the smaller the temperature increase for a given quantity of added energy. Thus, materials with higher heat capacity can store more thermal energy.

Water is uniquely suited by several attributes for its important role in the world's climate. One such attribute is its high heat capacity. Bodies of water are slow to heat up or cool down, and can store large quantities of thermal energy. By contrast, land surfaces cool off much more rapidly and reach lower temperatures at night.

Oceans, lakes, and rivers, therefore, have a moderating effect on temperature. For example, on a warm day breezes blow from the ocean toward the land, since the temperature over the land is higher. The warmer, less dense air rises, allowing cooler and more dense air from the ocean to move in. Then, in the evening, the land cools off more rapidly. The breezes shift direction, blowing from the now-cooler land toward the ocean. In general, temperatures fluctuate less near oceans or large lakes than they do in regions far from water.

YOUR TURN

Thermal Properties of Materials

1. Which would you expect to be cooler to the touch on a hot day in the sun:
   a. a concrete sidewalk or an asphalt sidewalk?
   b. a black plastic bicycle seat or a light-colored sheepskin bicycle seat?

2. Would you expect the average temperature to be lower during a winter with large quantities of snow or in one with very little snow?

3. Why is water—heat capacity 4.2 J/(g° C)—a better fluid for a hot-water bottle than alcohol—heat capacity 2.6 J/(g° C)?

4. Beach sand feels hotter than grass on a hot day. Which is more responsible for this observation— heat capacity or reflectivity?

5. Why does the temperature drop farther on a clear, cool night than on a cloudy, cool night?

6. Which of these two medium-sized cities, at the same latitude and longitude, would you expect to be hotter in the summer? Why?
   a. A city with many asphalt roads and concrete buildings.
   b. The same city, but located near a large body of water.

Can the thermal balance of our planet be upset? Is human activity affecting climate? We'll examine these questions in the next section.

C.4 CHANGES ON THE EARTH'S SURFACE

More than 100 years ago it was suggested that the rapidly-increasing use of fossil fuels might release enough carbon dioxide into the atmosphere to change the climate. You have learned (page 373) that water vapor and carbon dioxide (and other greenhouse gases) in the atmosphere act as one-way

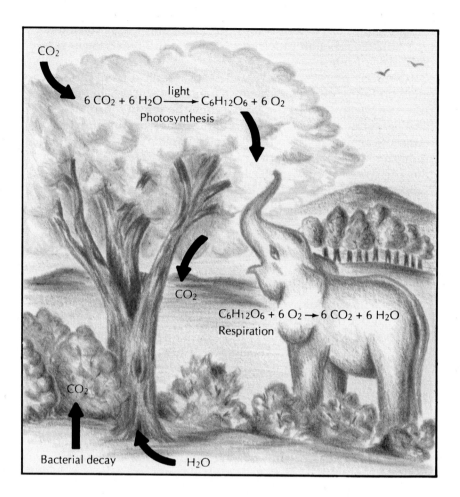

$$6\,CO_2 + 6\,H_2O \xrightarrow{\text{light}} C_6H_{12}O_6 + 6\,O_2$$

Photosynthesis

CO_2

$$C_6H_{12}O_6 + 6\,O_2 \rightarrow 6\,CO_2 + 6\,H_2O$$

Respiration

CO_2

CO_2

Bacterial decay H_2O

Figure 12 The carbon cycle. How does this figure illustrate the cycling of carbon throughout the biosphere?

screens. They let in sunlight, and then limit the escape of re-radiated infrared photons. This produces the greenhouse effect, which keeps our planet at a comfortable average temperature.

The greenhouse effect will remain stable as long as carbon dioxide and other greenhouse gases in the atmosphere remain at their normal levels and no significant amounts of new greenhouse gases are added. Both the hydrologic cycle (see page 16) and the carbon cycle (Figure 12) maintain constant concentrations of atmospheric water and carbon dioxide. However, human activity must be taken into consideration also.

The atmosphere contains about 12 trillion metric tons of water vapor, a quantity so large that it might seem impossible that human activity could significantly affect it. However, if global temperatures increase, more of the earth's slightly-warmer water will evaporate, increasing the atmospheric concentration of water vapor. As an important greenhouse gas, this increased water vapor would cause an even greater increase in global temperatures. A "spiralling-up" effect could occur—warmer temperatures producing more water vapor, producing warmer temperatures, and so on.

We do know that human activity has increased the level of carbon dioxide in the atmosphere by about 15% over the past century. We increase CO_2 levels in several ways: In clearing forests we remove vegetation, which consumes CO_2 through photosynthesis. We burn off clearings and scrap timber, releasing CO_2 to the atmosphere. When limestone—a form of calcium carbonate, $CaCO_3$—is converted to concrete, some CO_2 is released.

Planting Seeds in the City

By Trevor Turckes
Bothell Herald Staff Writer

Cities can be harsh and depressing places in which to live. As urban centers expand, concrete and glass structures replace the natural landscape. Air pollution and carbon dioxide levels may increase and foul the air. Overcrowding of human inhabitants may be stressful. However, careful cultivation of plant life within the city can help alleviate both environmental and psychological pollution.

An urban horticulturist like Brent Schmidt of Seattle, Washington, can help city dwellers become more comfortable with their environment. Brent is nature's advocate. He helps preserve existing plant life in Seattle and suggests different flowers, fruits, vegetables, and ornamental plants that could be cultivated to replace lost plant life.

Brent, an urban horticulturist, is his own boss. As a consultant, Brent provides information to private individuals, corporations, and public agencies about the best conditions for trees and other plants, the impact of construction on plant life, and appropriate plant selections for completing a building project. Brent also provides information on replacing current plantings with more aesthetically interesting plants and gives instructions on proper pruning techniques and general care. In fact, through public speaking engagements and demonstrations, he is involved in a plant "amnesty" program dedicated to improving urban plant conditions.

Each day for Brent is different. Typically, he will conduct business on two or three small projects in a day. For example, one recent day involved three on-site inspections. He first stopped at a city park where a large tree branch was threatening an adjacent home. Brent carefully

Photo by Shel Izen Photography

studied the tree to determine if the branch was likely to fall on the house.

Next, Brent visited a highway embankment where the plant life had died. Brent collected soil samples to help him discover what had killed the foliage and sent these samples to a laboratory for chemical analysis. He also cataloged the types of plant damage and identified possible causes.

Finally, Brent started a street survey for a small suburban community on the outskirts of Seattle. This job required a complete inventory of the trees located in the public rights-of-way. Brent determined species composition, management needs, tree condition rating, and whether the trees interfered with power lines or damaged sidewalks or streets. Brent particularly noted hazard trees. These are trees which are so damaged

that they are in danger of falling and destroying property or lives. Brent prepared a presentation for the City Council so that they were aware of the value of the city's trees and future management needs.

Urban horticulturists need to be prepared in many different areas. They are trained in entomology, tree and shrub diseases, plant physiology, general chemistry, and human resource management. Their skill is in using this knowledge to preserve nature at its best and develop pleasing urban environments for humans. To expand his career options, Brent is interested in becoming a zoological horticulturist. As such, he would be responsible for designing and helping maintain the exotic plant habitats now found in a zoo. The changes in modern zoos are opening up new career options for talented persons like Brent.

Deforestation contributes to increases in atmospheric CO_2.

Most significantly, of all, burning fossil fuels releases CO_2 into the air, as these equations clearly illustrate:

Burning coal: $C(s) + O_2(g) \rightarrow CO_2(g)$

Burning natural gas: $CH_4(g) + 2\,O_2(g) \rightarrow CO_2(g) + 2\,H_2O(g)$

Burning gasoline: $2\,C_8H_{18}(l) + 25\,O_2(g) \rightarrow 16\,CO_2(g) + 18\,H_2O(g)$

If more CO_2 is added to the atmosphere than can be removed by natural processes, its concentration will increase significantly. This could result in the atmosphere retaining enough additional infrared radiation to cause a rise in our world's surface temperature.

Has this effect already started? Evidence suggests that the global average surface temperature has increased by 0.3° C to 0.6° C over the past century (see Figure 13). The five warmest years (on average) in the last 100 years were all in the 1980s. Under a business-as-usual scenario (no steps taken to control release of greenhouse gases), an international panel of scientists has predicted an increase in global mean temperatures during the next century of about 0.3° C each decade—a greater increase than has been experienced since the last ice age ended 10,000 years ago.

Figure 13 Global warming. The average daily temperature in January, 1940, has been used as the zero point for comparison.

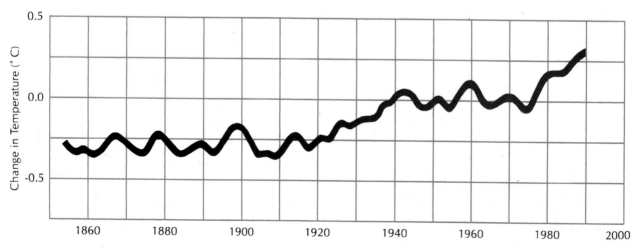

What are the projected effects of global warming? Based on a business-as-usual scenario, the oceans are predicted to rise about 6 cm each decade over the next century, leading to approximately a 20-cm increase by 2030. Regional climate changes would be expected, including reduced summer precipitation and soil moisture in North America. The greatest temperature increases are predicted above 40° latitude, where fossil fuel burning and seasonal changes in plant growth are greatest. This could have major impact on important food-growing areas. Some regions could lose arable land, while the best agricultural regions could shift locations.

The predicted ocean rise would be due to melting polar ice caps and the slight expansion of water at higher temperatures.

Although increasing carbon dioxide would have a warming influence on the globe, no one can yet predict exactly what the climate will do. Too many factors affect climate, and most of these affect each other, often in ways not well understood. Human settlements warm the earth by lowering its reflectivity—darkening it with cities and farms that replace forests and plains. Automobiles and air pollution affect local temperatures. Smog particles can both warm and cool the climate. On top of all this, the world's climate runs in cycles of alternating ice ages and warm periods. We may just be in the warm part of a cycle.

Indeed, some scientists predict that, far from approaching a period of global warming, we are nearing another ice age. In that case, an increase in CO_2 might be just what the world needs to counteract that trend. But don't count on it.

Table 3	CO$_2$ IN THE ATMOSPHERE
Year	Approximate CO$_2$ Level (ppm by volume)
1870	291
1900	287
1920	303
1930	310
1960	317
1965	320
1970	325
1972	328
1974	330
1976	332
1978	335
1980	338
1982	341
1984	344
1986	347
1988	351

C.5 YOU DECIDE: TRENDS IN CO$_2$ LEVELS

The CO_2 level data given in Table 3 show average measurements taken at the Mauna Loa Observatory in Hawaii.

Part 1

1. Plot the data in Table 3. Prepare your horizontal axis to include the years 1870 to 2050. The vertical axis will represent CO_2 levels from 280 ppm to 600 ppm. Plot the appropriate points, and draw a smooth curve representing the trend of the plotted points. (Do not draw a straight line or attempt to connect every point. A smooth curve shows general trends.)

2. Assuming the trend in your smooth curve continues from 1990 to 2050, extend your curve with a dashed line to the year 2050. This extrapolation is a prediction for the future, based on past trends.

A "curve" on a graph may appear either curved or straight.

Part 2

You will now make some predictions using the graph you have just completed. You will also evaluate these predictions.

1. What does your graph indicate about the general change in CO_2 levels since 1870?

2. Based on your extrapolation, predict CO_2 levels for
   a. the current year.
   b. the year 2000.
   c. the year 2050.

3. Does your graph predict a doubling of the 1870 CO_2 level?

4. Which predictions from Question 2 are the most likely to be accurate? Why?

Keep in mind that extrapolations of this type are always tentative. Completely unforeseen factors may arise in the future.

5. Describe factors that might cause your extrapolations to be incorrect.
6. What assumption is involved in making any extrapolation from known data?

C.6 LABORATORY ACTIVITY: CO$_2$ LEVELS

Getting Ready

The air we usually breathe has a very low CO$_2$ level. However, the CO$_2$ concentration in a small space can be substantially increased by burning coal or petroleum, decomposing organic matter, or accumulating a crowd of people or animals.

In this activity you will estimate and compare the amount of CO$_2$ in several air samples. To do this, the air will be bubbled through water that contains an indicator, bromthymol blue. Carbon dioxide reacts with water to form carbonic acid:

$$CO_2(g) + H_2O(l) \rightarrow H_2CO_3(aq)$$

As the concentration of carbonic acid in solution increases, bromthymol blue changes in color from blue to green to yellow.

Procedure

Part 1: CO$_2$ in Normal Air

1. Pour 125 mL of distilled or deionized water into a filter flask and add 10 drops of bromthymol blue. The solution should be blue. If not, add a drop of 0.5 M NaOH and gently swirl the flask.
2. Pour 10 mL of the solution prepared in Step 1 into a test tube. Put this aside; it is your control (to be used for comparison).
3. Assemble the apparatus illustrated in Figure 14 (without the candle).

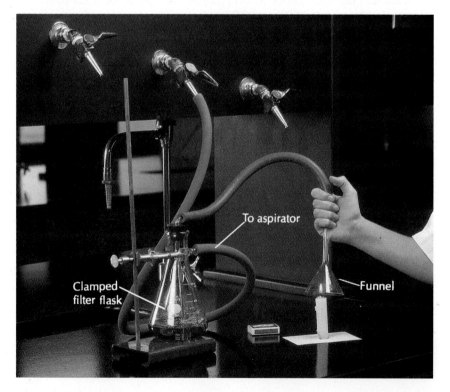

Figure 14 Apparatus for collecting air. Part 1 is done without candle.

4. Turn on the water tap so that the aspirator pulls air through the flask. Note the position of the faucet handle so you can run the aspirator at this same flow rate each time.

5. Let the aspirator run for five minutes. Turn off the water. Remove the stopper from the flask.

6. Pour 10 mL of the used indicator solution from the flask into a second test tube. Compare the color of this sample with the control. Save this test tube.

Part 2: CO_2 from Combustion

1. Empty the filter flask and rinse it thoroughly with distilled or deionized water.

2. Fill the flask with unused indicator solution according to Step 1 in Part 1. Reassemble the apparatus as in Step 3 in Part 1.

3. Light a candle and position it and the funnel so that the tip of the flame is level with the funnel base.

4. Turn on the water tap to the preset mark. Note the starting time. Run the aspirator until the indicator solution turns yellow. Record the time this takes in minutes.

5. Pour 10 mL of the indicator solution into a clean test tube. Compare the color with that of the other two solutions. Record your observations.

Part 3: CO_2 in Exhaled Air

1. Pour 125 mL of distilled or deionized water into an Erlenmeyer flask and add 10 drops of bromthymol blue. As before, add a drop of 0.5 M NaOH if the color is not blue.

2. Note the time, then exhale into the solution through a clean straw, until the indicator color changes to yellow. Record the time this takes.

Be careful not to suck the solution into your mouth.

3. Pour 10 mL of the indicator solution into a clean test tube. Compare the color with that of your other three solutions. Record your observations.

4. Wash your hands thoroughly before leaving the laboratory.

Questions

1. Compare the colors of the indicator solutions from each test. Which sample contained the most CO_2?

2. Compare the times and color changes with plain air and air from above the candle. Explain the differences.

3. Which contained more CO_2, air in the absence of the burning candle or exhaled air?

4. What effect would each of the following have on the time needed for the indicator solution to change color?
   a. Many plants were growing in the room.
   b. Fifty more people enter and remain in the room.
   c. The room has better ventilation.
   d. Half the people in the room begin smoking cigarettes.

C.7 YOU DECIDE: REVERSING THE TREND

Scientists believe they will have a clearer picture of the influence of CO_2 and other greenhouse gases on world climate within several years. This picture may confirm the already-emerging pattern of a global warming trend. Authorities in many nations have recognized, however, that the potential risks involved with global warming are sufficiently great to justify major action now.

Answer these questions. Be prepared to discuss your opinions in class.

1. Describe possible actions the world community and individuals might take to halt an increase in CO_2 in the atmosphere.

2. a. Do you think the public would seriously consider taking action to halt such a global warming trend?

   b. If so, which action in your answer to Question 1 do you believe would gain strongest support?

C.8 OFF IN THE OZONE

Although a small dose of ultraviolet radiation is necessary for health, too much is dangerous. In fact, if all ultraviolet radiation in sunlight were to reach the earth's surface, serious damage to living matter would occur. Ultraviolet photons, as we noted earlier, have enough energy to break covalent bonds. Resulting chemical changes can cause sunburn and cancer in humans and damage to many biological systems.

Fortunately, the earth has an ultraviolet shield high in the stratosphere. The shield consists of a layer of ozone, $O_3(g)$, which absorbs ultraviolet radiation. Here's how earth's vital ozone shield works:

As sunlight penetrates the stratosphere, the highest-energy ultraviolet photons react with oxygen gas molecules, splitting them into oxygen atoms.

$$O_2 + \text{Ultraviolet photon} \rightarrow O + O$$

Individual oxygen atoms are very reactive. They immediately react further, most combining with oxygen molecules to produce ozone. A third molecule (typically N_2 or O_2, represented by M in the equation below) carries away excess energy but is unchanged.

$$O_2 + O + M \rightarrow O_3 + M$$

Each ozone molecule formed can absorb a medium-energy ultraviolet photon in the stratosphere. Decomposition results, producing an oxygen molecule and an oxygen atom:

$$O_3 + \text{Ultraviolet photon} \rightarrow O_2 + O$$

These products can then carry on the cycle by undergoing the reaction already described, producing more ozone:

$$O_2 + O + M \rightarrow O_3 + M$$

The concentration of ozone in the stratosphere is remarkably small. If all the ozone molecules were located on the earth's surface at atmospheric pressure, they would form a layer only 3 mm thick (about the thickness of a hardback book cover). Our "ozone shield" is a fragile system.

The ozone layer is vitally important to supporting and protecting life on earth. One indication of its importance is to recognize what would happen if the layer were even modestly reduced. The Environmental Protection Agency estimates that a 5% ozone depletion—and resulting increase in ultraviolet radiation—would cause an annual increase of nearly a million U.S. cases of basal-cell and squamous-cell cancers (disfiguring but not fatal if treated), 30,000 additional cases of often-fatal melanoma skin cancer, decreased yields of some food crops, a sharp increase in sunburn and eye cataracts, and damage to some aquatic plant species.

Human activities may have already endangered this ozone layer. The major culprit appears to be chlorine atoms from chlorinated hydrocarbon molecules (also called chlorofluorocarbons, CFCs) such as the Freons (e.g., CCl_3F). These substances have been used as propellants in aerosol cans, fluids in the sealed cooling systems of air conditioners and refrigerators, and cleaning solvents.

Other gases that can deplete ozone are methane and other hydrocarbons, as well as nitrogen monoxide.

A satellite carrying instruments to monitor worldwide stratospheric ozone concentrations was launched in 1978. By 1986, data from the satellite indicated an "ozone hole" was growing over Antarctica. The "hole" is in an Antarctic region where some ozone depletion occurs normally on a yearly cycle. In recent years, annual ozone depletion has increased; nearly all the ozone in the lower stratosphere over Antarctica disappears for about six weeks in September and October each year.

Evidence indicates that similar ozone depletion has also started in the Arctic.

Several lines of converging evidence gathered since the mid-1980s have clearly linked the Antarctic ozone depletion with chlorine atoms found in CFCs. In fact, some atmospheric scientists had argued as early as the mid-1970s that chlorofluorocarbons posed a threat to the world's ozone layer.

Although CFCs are highly stable molecules, at an altitude of 30 km ultraviolet photons of suitable energy split chlorine atoms from them. The freed chlorine atoms can then participate in a series of reactions that destroy ozone:

$$Cl + O_3 \rightarrow ClO + O_2$$
$$ClO + O \rightarrow Cl + O_2$$

Notice that the chlorine atom consumed in the first reaction is regenerated in the second reaction. Thus, each chlorine atom can participate in a large number of these ozone-destroying reactions. The sum of these two reactions is

$$O + O_3 \rightarrow 2 O_2$$

This man is recovering Freons from refrigerator-cooling systems.

The net effect is conversion of ozone molecules into oxygen molecules, triggered by free chlorine atoms released from molecules such as the CFCs.

Due to growing concerns over threats to the earth's ozone layer, 56 nations—including the U.S.—signed a significant and historic agreement in 1990. The document established a timetable for banning all chlorofluorocarbon production in developed nations by the year 2000. This accord, a major amendment and strengthening of an earlier 1987 international agreement, also includes a $240 million environmental fund to assist developing nations to build industries that do not rely on ozone-depleting chemicals.

The 1987 agreement is known as the Montreal Protocol.

We have seen that human activity has the potential to activate effects that may modify the world's average temperature and our exposure to ultraviolet radiation. All that appears necessary is to trigger alterations in the normal concentrations of substances such as ozone and carbon dioxide in the atmosphere.

The chemistry of the atmosphere is quite complex and difficult to study. Even so, evidence of human alteration of the atmosphere is emerging. Additional evidence regarding human effects on the atmosphere will be explored in the following sections.

PART C: SUMMARY QUESTIONS

1. a. Compare infrared, visible, and ultraviolet radiation in terms of the relative energies of their photons.
   b. Cite one useful role each plays in a life process or a process important to life.
2. a. Explain why our atmosphere can be regarded as a one-way screen.
   b. How does this make the earth more hospitable to life?
3. List and briefly describe two functions of the stratosphere.
4. From a scientific viewpoint, why do tennis players and desert-dwellers wear white or light-colored clothing?
5. a. Compare ocean water and beach sand in terms of how quickly they heat up in the sun and how quickly they cool at night.
   b. What property of these two materials accounts for these differences?
6. Describe how atmospheric concentrations of CO_2 and water help to maintain moderate temperatures at the earth's surface.
7. List the two major ways humans increase the amount of CO_2 in the atmosphere.
8. What changes in atmospheric composition could result in
   a. an increase in the average surface temperature of the earth?
   b. a decrease in the average surface temperature of the earth?
9. Describe an important role of the world's ozone shield.

EXTENDING YOUR KNOWLEDGE (OPTIONAL)

- The presence of carbon dioxide in the atmosphere is only one part of the global carbon cycle. Investigate our current understanding of the carbon cycle, with particular attention to the role of oceans as a major "carbon sink."
- What effect might global warming have on ocean temperatures, and, indirectly, on the concentration of greenhouse gases in the atmosphere?
- Ice-core samples from the Antarctic have allowed scientists to estimate what the carbon dioxide concentrations in the atmosphere were many thousands of years ago. Prepare a report on how ice-core samples are able to reveal this information.

HUMAN IMPACT ON AIR WE BREATHE

Dirty air is so common in the United States that weather reports for some major cities now include indexes for certain air pollutants. Depending on where you live, cars, power plants, or industries may be the major polluters. However, air pollution is not only an outdoor problem. Indoor air can be polluted by cigarette smoke or by fumes that spontaneously evaporate from certain products, such as from polymeric materials in furniture.

Air pollution smells bad, looks ugly, and blocks the view of stars at night. But beyond being unpleasant, air pollution causes billions of dollars of damage every year. It corrodes buildings and machines. It stunts the growth of agricultural crops and weakens livestock. It causes or aggravates diseases such as bronchitis, asthma, emphysema, and lung cancer, adding to the world's hospital bills. Clean air has become a battle cry for an increasing number of individuals, municipalities, and nations.

D.1 TO EXIST IS TO POLLUTE

Many natural processes emit substances that could become pollutants, but in most cases their release occurs over such a wide area that we do not notice it. Furthermore, the environment may dilute or transform such substances before they can accumulate to harmful levels.

Automobile emissions are a principal cause of air-quality problems in Los Angeles.

By contrast, pollution from human activities is usually generated within small areas, such as localized effluent pipes, smoke stacks, or urban regions. When the quantity of a pollutant overwhelms the ability of nature to dispose of it or disperse it, air pollution becomes a serious problem. Many large cities are prone to high concentrations of pollutants. If air pollutants generated by large cities were evenly spread over the entire nation, they would be much less noticeable and would have substantially lowered concentrations.

Table 4 lists the major air pollutants and the quantities emitted worldwide from human and natural sources. These substances are all **primary air pollutants**—they enter the atmosphere in the chemical form listed. For example, methane (CH_4, the simplest hydrocarbon) is a by-product of fossil fuel use and a component of natural gas that leaks into the atmosphere. It is also produced by anaerobic bacteria and termites as they break down organic matter.

WORLDWIDE EMISSIONS OF AIR POLLUTANTS

Table 4 (10^{12} g/yr or 10^6 metric tons/yr)

Pollutant	Human Source	Quantity	Natural Source	Quantity
CO_2	Combustion of wood and fossil fuels	22,000	Decay; release from oceans, forest fires, and respiration	1,000,000
CO	Incomplete combustion	700	Forest fires and photochemical reactions	2,100
SO_2	Combustion of coal and oil; smelting of ores	212	Volcanoes and decay	20
CH_4	Combustion; natural gas leakage	160	Anaerobic decay and termites	1,050
NO_x	High-temperature combustion	75	Lightning; bacterial action in soil	180
NMHC	Incomplete combustion	40	Biological processes	20,000
NH_3	Sewage treatment	6	Anaerobic biological decay	260
H_2S	Petroleum refining and sewage treatment	3	Volcanoes and anaerobic decay	84

Source: Adapted from Stern et al. Fundamentals of Air Pollution, 2nd ed.: Academic Press, Inc.: Orlando, FL, 1984; pp. 30–31. Table adapted by permission of Elmer Robinson, Mauna Loa Observatory. Data based on conditions prior to 1980.

NO_x = nitrogen oxides

NMHC = nonmethane hydrocarbons

In addition to those listed in Table 4, there are several other important categories of air pollutants:

- *Secondary air pollutants.* These are substances formed in the atmosphere by chemical reactions between primary air pollutants and/or natural components of air. For example, sulfur dioxide (SO_2) reacts with oxygen gas in the air to form sulfur trioxide (SO_3)—the two oxides are always present together. Further reactions with water in the atmosphere can convert these sulfur oxides to sulfates (SO_4^{2-}) or sulfuric acid (H_2SO_4), a secondary pollutant partly responsible for acid rain (discussed in Section D.11).

- *Particulates.* This major category of pollutants includes all solid particles that enter the air, either from human activities (e.g., power plants, waste burning, road building, mining) or natural processes (e.g., forest fires, wind erosion, volcanic eruptions). Particulates include visible emissions from smoke stacks or automobile tail pipes.

- *Synthetic substances.* Some pollutants, such as the chlorofluorocarbons, are produced only by human activity; otherwise they would not be present at all.

D.2 YOU DECIDE: WHAT IS AIR POLLUTION?

Use Table 4 to answer these questions.

1. a. What pattern was used to organize the data?
   b. For what reason might this pattern have been chosen?
   c. Should the relative quantities of pollutants from human sources determine which pollutants should be reduced or controlled?
   d. If not, what other factors should be considered?

2. For all cases except one, natural contributions of these potentially polluting substances greatly exceed contributions from human activities.
   a. Does this imply that human contributions of these substances can be ignored? Why?
   b. For which substance does the contribution from human activity exceed that from natural sources?
   c. What does this suggest about modern society?

3. Refer to Table 1 (page 352). Which pollutants listed in Table 4 are also found naturally in the atmosphere at concentrations of 0.0001% or more?

4. What is the major source of human contributions to air pollutants listed in Table 4?

5. Considering the large quantities of potential air pollutants from natural sources, why might adding small quantities of substances that do not exist naturally in the atmosphere pose a problem?

D.3 YOU DECIDE: MAJOR POLLUTANTS

Air pollution is a by-product of manufacturing, transportation, and energy production. Table 5 (page 388) gives a detailed picture of the sources of some major air pollutants in the United States. Use this information to answer these questions.

TSP = Total suspended
particulates

SO$_x$ = Sulfur oxides
(SO$_2$ and SO$_3$)

NO$_x$ = Nitrogen oxides
(NO and NO$_2$)

HC = Volatile organic
compounds (methane
and other
hydrocarbons)

CO = Carbon monoxide

Table 5   **U.S. POLLUTION, 1987 (in 10^6 metric tons/yr)**

Source	TSP	SO$_x$	NO$_x$	HC	CO	Total
			Pollutant			
Transportation (petroleum burning)	1.4	0.9	8.4	6.0	40.7	57.4
Fuel burning for space heating and electricity	1.8	16.4	10.3	2.3	7.2	38.0
Industrial processes	2.5	3.1	0.6	8.3	4.7	19.2
Solid waste disposal and miscellaneous	1.3	0.0	0.2	3.0	8.8	13.3
Totals	7.0	20.4	19.5	19.6	61.4	127.9

1. a. Overall, is industry the main source of air pollution?
   b. If not, what is the main source?
2. For which pollutants is one-third or more contributed
   a. by industry?
   b. by transportation?
   c. by burning fuel for space heating and electricity (usually referred to as "stationary fuel burning")?

How much pollution do *you* produce? If you drive, you are a major polluter—automobiles contribute about half the total mass of air pollutants. When you spend time in heated buildings, use electricity, or buy food and other products, air has been polluted for your benefit. As a comic strip character once observed, "We have met the enemy, and he is us."

D.4   SMOG: HAZARDOUS TO YOUR HEALTH

When weather forecasters give the air quality index along with humidity and temperature, to what are they referring? The U.S. Environmental Protection Agency has devised an index based on concentrations of pollutants that are major contributors to smog over cities. You can see in Table 6 that the combined health effects of these pollutants can become quite serious. Smog can kill. During one of the deadliest smogs, in London in 1952, the usual death rate in the city more than doubled. Similar, although less severe, episodes have occurred in other cities.

The composition of smog depends on the type of industrial activity and power generation in an area, on climate, and on geography. Over large cities containing many coal- and oil-burning industries, power-generating stations, and homes, the principal components of smog are sulfur oxides and particulates.

Coal and petroleum both contain varying quantities of sulfur, from which sulfur oxides form during combustion. One successful approach to improving air quality sets limits on the quantity of sulfur allowed in the fuels burned.

Particulates from burning fossil fuels consist of unburned carbon or solid hydrocarbon fragments and trace minerals. Some particles contain toxic compounds of metals such as cadmium, chromium, lead, and mercury.

Table 6

| Air Quality Index Value | Air Quality Description | Air Pollutant Levels (micrograms per cubic meter) | | | | | Effects and Suggested Actions |
		Total Suspended Particulate Matter (24 Hours)	Sulfur Dioxide (24 Hours)	Carbon Monoxide (8 Hours)	Ozone (1 Hour)	Nitrogen Dioxide (1 Hour)	
500	Hazardous	1,000	2,620	57,000	1,200	3,750	Normal activity impossible. All should remain indoors with windows and doors closed. Fatal for some in high risk group.*
400	Hazardous	875	2,100	46,000	1,000	3,000	High risk group should stay quietly indoors. Others should avoid outdoor activity.
300	Very unhealthful	625	1,600	34,000	800	2,260	High risk group has more symptoms, and should stay indoors and reduce physical activity. All persons notice lung irritation.
200	Unhealthful	375	800	17,000	400	1,130	Those with lung or heart disease should reduce physical exertion. Healthy persons notice irritations.
100	Moderate	260	365	10,000	235	Not reported	Some damage to materials and plants. Human health not affected unless levels continue for many days.
50	Good	75	80	5,000	118	Not reported	No significant effects.

*High risk group includes elderly people and those with heart or lung diseases.

Fatality rates in severe smogs have been higher than predicted from known hazards of sulfur oxides or particulates alone. According to some researchers, this increase may be due to **synergistic interactions** (in which the combined effect of the two pollutants is greater than the sum of the separate effects alone).

Before discussing smog resulting from automobile emissions, we will survey what can be done to decrease pollution, and what industry is doing to clean up its smoke.

D.5   POLLUTION CONTROL

There are several basic ways to control air pollution:

- Energy technologies that cause air pollution can be *replaced* with technologies that don't require combustion, such as solar power, wind power, and nuclear power.
- Pollution from combustion can be *reduced* by energy conservation measures, such as getting more from what we burn and therefore burning less.
- Pollution-causing substances can be *removed* from fuel before burning. For example, most sulfur can be removed from coal.
- The combustion process can be *modified* so that fuel is more completely oxidized.
- Pollutants can be *trapped* after combustion.

All pollution control options cost money. When deciding upon a pollution control strategy, two key questions must be answered: What will the pollution control cost? What benefits will the pollution control offer?

CHEMQUANDARY

Airing Some Pollution Solutions

Consider this pollution-control option: "Clean the atmosphere after the pollution is emitted."

1. Is this a reasonable or practical strategy? Explain your answer.
2. Would cloud-seeding to cause rain, or issuing filtering devices such as gas masks to individuals be reasonable alternatives? Explain.

D.6   INDUSTRIAL EMISSION OF PARTICULATES

Power plants and smelters generate more than half of the particulate matter emitted in the United States. Several cost-effective methods for controlling particle emissions are used; great progress has been made in cleaning up this type of pollution.

Electrostatic precipitation. This is currently the most important technique for controlling pollution by particulates. Combustion waste products are passed through a strong electrical field, where they become charged. The charged particles collect on plates of opposite charge. This technique removes up to 99% of particulates, leaving only particles smaller than one-tenth of a micrometer (0.1 μm, where 1 μm $= 10^{-6}$ m in diameter). Dust and pollen collectors installed in home ventilation systems are often based on this technique.

Mechanical filtering. This works much like a vacuum cleaner. Combustion waste products pass through a cleaning room (bag house) where huge filters trap up to 99% of the particles.

Cyclone collection. Combustion waste products pass rapidly through a tight circular spiral chamber. Particles thrown outward to the walls drop to the base of the chamber where they are removed. This technique removes 50–90% of the larger, visible particles but relatively few of the more harmful particles (those smaller than 1 μm).

Scrubbing. This method controls particles and the sulfur oxides accompanying them. Substances that react with pollutants are added to the stream of combustion waste products.

In one kind of dry scrubbing (on the left in Figure 15), powdered limestone (calcium carbonate, $CaCO_3$) is blown into the combustion chamber where it decomposes:

$$CaCO_3(s) + Heat \rightarrow CaO(s) + CO_2(g)$$

The lime (CaO) then reacts with sulfur oxides to form calcium sulfite ($CaSO_3$) and calcium sulfate ($CaSO_4$):

$$CaO(s) + SO_2(g) \rightarrow CaSO_3(s)$$

$$CaO(s) + SO_3(g) \rightarrow CaSO_4(s)$$

These products are washed away as a slurry (a mixture of solids and water).

In an example of wet scrubbing (on the right in Figure 15), sulfur dioxide gas is removed by using an aqueous solution of calcium hydroxide, $Ca(OH)_2(aq)$. The sulfur dioxide reacts to form solid calcium sulfite, $CaSO_3$:

$$SO_2(g) + Ca(OH)_2(aq) \rightarrow CaSO_3(s) + H_2O(l)$$

Scrubbers, which can remove up to 95% of sulfur oxides, are required for all new U.S. coal-burning plants. Their use adds significantly to the cost of electrical power.

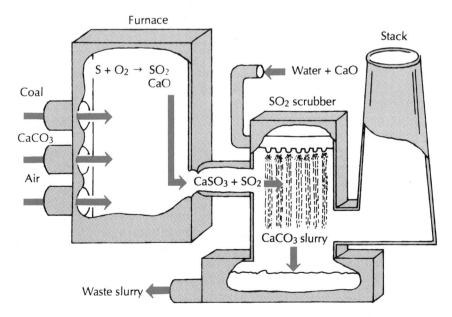

Figure 15 A scrubber for removing sulfur dioxide and particulate matter from products of industrial combustion processes. Dry scrubbing occurs in the furnace, and wet scrubbing in the SO_2 scrubber.

Wet scrubbing.

D.7 LAB DEMONSTRATION: CLEANSING AIR

Your teacher will demonstrate two pollution control methods.

Part 1: The Electrostatic Precipitator

1. Observe what happens to the smoke. Record your observations.
2. Observe the chemical reaction that occurs on the copper rod. Record your observations.

Part 2: Wet Scrubbing

1. Observe the color of the liquid and pH paper in each flask as the reaction proceeds. Record your observations.

Questions

1. Write an equation for the reaction that occured between HCl and NH_3 in Part 1.
2. What information did the universal indicator provide in each flask in Part 2?
3. What information did the pH paper at the neck of each flask provide?
4. What was the overall effect of the scrubbing, as shown by the indicators?
5. List the two ways the quality of the air in the reaction vessel was changed by wet scrubbing.
6. a. What advantages do precipitators have over wet scrubbers?
   b. What are their disadvantages?

CHEMQUANDARY

Steps Toward Clean Air

Explain why (1) treating smoke before it is released from power plants is an important goal, but why, at the same time, (2) it may mislead the general public concerning what is required to obtain clean air.

D.8 PHOTOCHEMICAL SMOG

The ill effects of pollution from automobiles were first noted in the Los Angeles area in the 1940s. A brownish haze that irritated the eyes, nose, and throat and damaged crops appeared in the air. Researchers were puzzled for some time because Los Angeles has no significant industrial or heating activities. The city has an abundance of automobiles and sunshine. Also, mountains rise on three sides of it. These geographic conditions produce temperature inversions about 320 days each year.

Normally, air at the earth's surface is warmed by solar radiation and by re-radiation from surface materials. This warmer, less dense air rises, carrying pollutants with it. Cooler, less polluted air then moves in. In a temperature inversion, a cool air mass is trapped beneath a less dense warm air mass, often in a valley or over a city. Pollutants cannot escape and their concentration may rise to dangerous levels. Los Angeles is smog-prone, primarily because of its location. But there is more to the story for Los Angeles smog was much worse than seemed reasonable.

As so often happens in science, a serendipitous discovery provided a piece of the puzzle of smog. In 1952, chemist Arie J. Haagen-Smit was attempting to isolate the ingredient in pineapples that is responsible for their odor. Working on a smoggy day, he detected a greater concentration of ozone (O_3) in his experiment than is normally found in clean, tropospheric air. He delayed his research to identify its source. Within a year, he published a ground-breaking paper, "The Chemistry and Physics of Los Angeles Smog," describing the importance of sunlight in smog chemistry, and coined the term **photochemical smog.**

For our purposes, this equation represents the key ingredients and products of photochemical smog:

Any reaction initiated by light is a photochemical reaction.

$$\text{Auto exhaust} + \text{Sunlight} + O_2(g) \rightarrow$$
$$(\text{Hydrocarbons} + CO + NO_x)$$

$$O_3(g) + NO_x(g) + \text{Organic compounds} + CO_2(g) + H_2O(g)$$
$$(\text{oxidants and irritants})$$

NO_x symbolizes any nitrogen oxides —particularly NO_2 and NO.

Nitrogen oxides are essential ingredients of such smog. At the high temperature and pressure of automotive combustion (2800° C and about 10 atm), nitrogen gas and oxygen gas react to produce the pollutant nitrogen monoxide (NO).

$$N_2(g) + O_2(g) + \text{Energy} \rightarrow 2\ NO(g)$$

In the atmosphere, nitrogen monoxide is oxidized to orange-brown nitrogen dioxide (NO_2).

$$2\ NO(g) + O_2(g) \rightarrow 2\ NO_2(g)$$

Carbon monoxide from automobile exhaust is also present.

The photochemical smog cycle begins as photons from sunlight initiate dissociation of NO_2 into NO and oxygen atoms (O). The atomic oxygen then reacts with oxygen molecules to produce ozone in the same way that it does in the stratosphere.

$$NO_2(g) + \text{Energy} \rightarrow NO(g) + O(g)$$

$$O_2(g) + O(g) \rightarrow O_3(g)$$

We have now accounted for two of the harmful and unpleasant ingredients of photochemical smog: Nitrogen dioxide has a pungent, irritating odor. Ozone is a very powerful oxidant. At concentrations as low as 0.1 ppm ozone can crack rubber, corrode metals, and damage plant and animal tissues.

The highly reactive ozone undergoes a complex series of reactions with the third essential ingredient of photochemical smog—hydrocarbons that escape from gasoline tanks or are emitted during incomplete combustion of gasoline. The products of these reactions cause burning eyes, are harmful to individuals with respiratory or heart disease, and can injure plants and damage materials such as rubber and paint.

Complete the following activity.

D.9 YOU DECIDE: AUTOS AND SMOG

Use data in Figure 16 (page 394) to answer these questions.
1. a. Between what hours do the concentrations of nitrogen oxides and hydrocarbons peak?
   b. Account for this fact in terms of traffic patterns.

Figure 16 Photochemical smog formation.

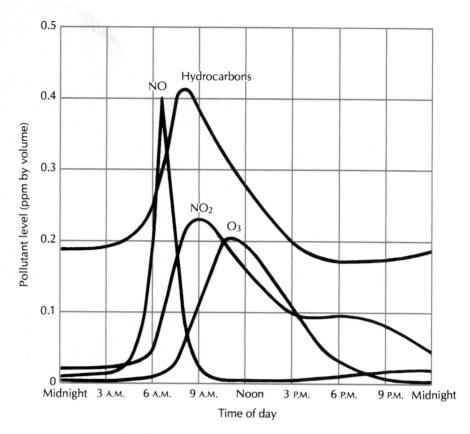

Figure 16 Photochemical smog formation.

2. Give two reasons why a given pollutant may be observed to decrease in concentration over several hours.

3. The concentration maximum for NO_2 occurs at the same time as the concentration minimum of NO. Explain this phenomenon.

4. Although ozone is necessary in the stratosphere to protect us from ultraviolet light, on the surface of the earth it is a major component of photochemical smog.

   a. Determine from Figure 16 which chemicals, or species, are at minimum concentrations when $O_3(g)$ is at maximum concentration.

   b. What does this suggest about the production of $O_3(g)$ in polluted tropospheric air?

   Smog is being produced faster than the atmosphere can dispose of it. However, the nation has made considerable progress in smog control. Many cities have cleaner air than they did 30 years ago. The following section will explore the control of pollution from automobiles.

D.10   CONTROLLING AUTOMOBILE EMISSIONS

In 1970 an amendment to the Federal Clean Air Act authorized the Environmental Protection Agency to set emissions standards for new automobiles. Maximum limits were set for hydrocarbon, nitrogen oxide, and carbon monoxide emissions.

These values were to be achieved in gradual steps by 1975. Improvements in automobile engines were made between 1970 and 1975 by modifying the air-fuel ratio, adjusting the spark timing, adding carbon canisters to absorb gasoline that would normally evaporate before combustion, and installing exhaust gas recirculation systems.

To decrease emissions enough to meet the standards completely, however, required further measures. The result was development of the **catalytic converter.** The converter is a reaction chamber attached to the exhaust pipe. The exhaust gases and outside air pass over several catalysts which help convert nitrogen oxides to nitrogen gas and hydrocarbons to carbon dioxide and water. The carburetor air-fuel ratio is set to produce exhaust gases with relatively high concentrations of carbon monoxide and hydrogen. These gases enter the first half of the catalytic converter where nitrogen oxides are reduced, for example,

$$2\ NO(g) + 2\ CO(g) \xrightarrow{\text{Catalyst}} N_2(g) + 2\ CO_2(g)$$

$$2\ NO(g) + 2\ H_2(g) \xrightarrow{\text{Catalyst}} N_2(g) + 2\ H_2O(g)$$

The second half of the converter then further oxidizes carbon monoxide and hydrocarbons to carbon dioxide and water.

What exactly is a catalyst? You have encountered catalysts several times now. Enzymes that aid in digesting food and in other body functions are organic catalysts. The manganese dioxide that you added in generating oxygen gas in the laboratory (page 349) was an inorganic catalyst. In every case, the catalyst increases the rate of a chemical reaction which, without the catalyst, would proceed too slowly to be useful. A catalyst is not considered a reactant, because it remains unchanged after the reaction is over.

How can a catalyst speed up a reaction and escape unchanged? Reactions can occur only if molecules collide with sufficient energy and at the correct orientation to disrupt bonds. The minimum energy required for such effective collisions is called the **activation energy.** You can think of the activation energy as an energy barrier that stands between the reactants and products. (See Figure 17.) Reactants must have enough energy to get over the barrier before reaction can occur. The higher the barrier, the fewer the molecules that have the energy to mount it, and the slower the reaction proceeds.

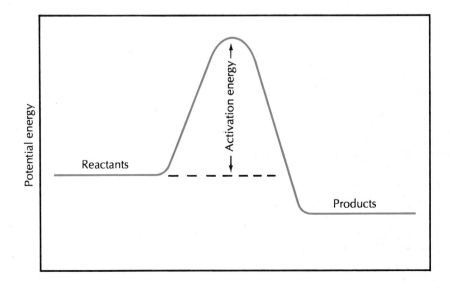

Figure 17 Activation energy diagram.

In San Diego, exhaust emissions from slow-moving traffic on crowded freeways are a major source of the photochemical smog shown here.

Emissions testing has become an essential component of tuning an automobile.

HC = hydrocarbons
CO = carbon monoxide
NO$_x$ = nitrogen oxides

A catalyst increases the rate of a chemical reaction by providing a different reaction pathway, one with a lower activation energy. In effect, the catalyst lowers the barrier. The result is that more molecules have sufficient energy to react and form the products within a given period of time. In automotive catalytic converters, a few grams of platinum, palladium, or rhodium act as catalysts. For this use, the metal samples are embedded in pellets of a solid carrier such as aluminum oxide, Al$_2$O$_3$.

Clean Air Act Amendments of 1990 have set new, more restrictive emission standards for U.S. automobiles manufactured in 1993 or later. Some of these newly-defined standards are summarized in Table 7, along with comparable values reported from earlier Clean Air Act standards. The 1990 Amendments specify that at least 40% of 1994 model year autos, 80% of 1995 model year autos, and 100% of 1996 and later model year autos must meet the new standards.

Table 7	EMISSION CONTROL REQUIREMENTS		
	Allowable Levels in Exhaust (g/mi)		
Auto Model Year	HC	CO	NO$_x$
Pre-1968 (uncontrolled)	8.6	87.5	3.5
1975–76	1.5	15	3.1
1980	0.41	7.0	2.0
1994–1996	0.25	3.4	0.4

Source: Taylor, K. C. "Automobile Catalytic Converters" in *Catalysis Science and Technology*; Anderson, J. R., Boudaert, M., Eds.; Springer-Verlag: New York, 1984; V. 5, Ch. 2, pp. 120–70.

CHEMQUANDARY

Controlling Air Pollution

From a practical viewpoint, why might controlling air pollution from over 180 million automobiles, buses, and trucks be more difficult than controlling air pollution from power plants and industries in the U.S.?

Environmental Enlightenment

By Mary Theresa Nalley
Annapolis Times Staff Reporter

Alexandra Allen is an attorney and engineer employed by the Greenpeace national office in Washington, DC. In her role as Atmosphere and Energy Policy Coordinator, Alexandra formulates policies and political strategies for Greenpeace on global warming and energy issues. Her efforts in the United States are undertaken in cooperation with Greenpeace counterparts in 23 other countries.

Alexandra depends on numerous information sources. These sources include federal and state governments, the United Nations, university research centers, industrial associations, and private research organizations. She also uses popular magazines and newspapers from around the world. These enable Alexandra to know the many dimensions—scientific, economic, and political—of environmental issues.

Alexandra uses this knowledge to evaluate proposals by governments and industries to address issues such as oil dependence and global warming. Public attention is focused on the potential consequences of global warming and the need to reduce reliance on fossil fuels. Improving the efficiency with which energy is used, and developing environmentally safe, renewable energy resources, is central to her work.

At Greenpeace, Alexandra works to make these issues widely understood—and acted upon—by citizens, governments, and industries. She has written critiques of federal energy legislation and has issued briefings for grassroots activists who

Photo by Shutter Priority

are seeking to encourage their political representatives to become leaders in energy issues. Alexandra gives many public presentations, frequently to school and religious groups concerned with environmental issues. She also gives interviews on energy and environmental issues to reporters from radio and television shows, newspapers, and magazines.

A knowledge of chemistry and other physical sciences gives Alexandra the background to understand the scientific components of many environmental issues. This knowledge also helps her to recognize when scientific knowledge is incomplete, and to appreciate the importance of precaution when evaluating potential consequences of new technologies. Alexandra prepared for her career by earning a B.S. in chemical engineering and public policy and a J.D. in law.

D.11 ACID RAIN

It started in Scandinavia. Then, it appeared in the northeastern United States. Now, the problem seems to exist in much of the industrialized world. Fish disappear from major lakes. The surfaces of limestone and concrete buildings and marble statues crumble. Crops grow more slowly and forests begin to die out. Although New England, Germany, and Scandinavia are among the regions hardest hit by acid rain, it is widespread in the industrialized world. Even the Grand Canyon suffers from acid rain due to air pollution from coal-fired power plants miles away.

Although the cause of German forest die-outs may still be subject to debate, the other problems have been definitely traced to acid rain. Naturally-occurring substances, chiefly carbon dioxide, have always caused rainwater to be slightly acidic. Normally, rainwater's pH is about 5.6. Carbon dioxide reacts with rainwater to form carbonic acid:

$$CO_2(g) + H_2O(l) \rightarrow H_2CO_3(aq)$$

Oxides of sulfur and nitrogen emitted from power plants, various industries, and automobiles also react with rainwater, to form acids that have lowered the pH of rainwater to 4–4.5 in the northeastern United States. The key reactions are

$$H_2O(l) + SO_2(g) \rightarrow H_2SO_3(aq)$$
Sulfurous acid

$$H_2O(l) + SO_3(g) \rightarrow H_2SO_4(aq)$$
Sulfuric acid

$$H_2O(l) + 2\,NO_2(g) \rightarrow HNO_3(aq) + HNO_2(aq)$$
Nitric acid   Nitrous acid

Occasionally the levels of these oxides in air produce enough acid to lower the pH to 3. (A pH of 4–4.5 is about the acidity of orange juice; a pH of 3 is about that of vinegar.)

Sulfuric acid contributes close to two-thirds of the acidity of rain in New England; acids of nitrogen contribute most of the other third.

This more acidic rain lowers the pH of lakes, killing fish eggs and other aquatic life; some species are more sensitive than others. Statues and monuments, such as the Parthenon in Greece, which have stood uneroded for centuries, suddenly began corroding because of acid rain and sulfates. The acid attacks calcium carbonate in limestone, marble, and concrete:

$$H_2SO_4(aq) + CaCO_3(s) \rightarrow CaSO_4(s) + H_2O(l) + CO_2(g)$$

Calcium sulfate is more water-soluble than calcium carbonate. Therefore, the stonework decays as the calcium sulfate is washed away to uncover fresh calcium carbonate that can react further with the acid rain.

Salts of sulfuric acid, which contain the sulfate ion (SO_4^{2-}), are also present in acid rain and atmospheric moisture. In the air they scatter light, causing haze. And they are potentially harmful to human health if they are deposited in large enough amounts in the lungs.

Many different and interrelated reactions are involved in producing acid rain. Studies aimed at a more complete understanding of the causes are under way. One puzzle is how sulfur dioxide is oxidized to sulfur trioxide. Oxygen gas dissolved in water oxidizes sulfur dioxide very slowly. The reaction may be

Air pollutants are responsible for the partial disintegration of this sculpture.

The lower the pH, the more acidic the solution.

accelerated in the atmosphere by sunlight or by catalysts such as iron, manganese, or vanadium in soot particles.

The control of acid rain is made difficult because air pollution knows no political boundaries. Acid rain often appears hundreds of kilometers from the sources of pollutants. For example, much of the acid that rains on Scandinavia is thought to come from Germany and the United Kingdom. The rain that falls on New England may come largely from the industrial Ohio Valley, in the Midwest.

One attempt to reduce acid rain is the legislation of the U.S. Clean Air Amendments of 1990. These state that the annual sulfur dioxide emissions in the lower forty-eight states and the District of Columbia must be lowered by 10 million tons from 1980 levels. In addition, nitrogen oxide emissions must be lowered by 2 million tons annually from 1980 levels. To achieve these reductions, the EPA issues permits to major electric utility plants specifying the maximum amount of sulfur dioxide they can release each year. However, plants with low emissions can auction or sell their excess permits to plants that produce more.

Have you made any personal observations of the effects of acid rain? In the following laboratory activity you will have the opportunity to observe first-hand the action of solutions with acidity approximately equal to that of acid rain.

D.12 LABORATORY ACTIVITY: ACID RAIN

Getting Ready

In this activity you will create a mixture similar to that in acid rain by burning sulfur in air and then adding water. You will observe the effects of acid rain chemistry on plant material (represented by an apple peel), living creatures (represented by a culture of microorganisms), an active metal, and marble.

Procedure

1. Cut a piece of skin from an apple, and place it in an empty 500-mL glass bottle. Cut a second piece of apple skin and set it aside for later comparison.

2. Fill a combustion spoon half full of powdered sulfur.

3. *In a fume hood:* Turn on a tap water spigot so that it drips slowly. (If there is no spigot in the hood, adjust one at a nearby laboratory bench, and return to the fume hood to perform the following procedures.) Light the Bunsen burner. Ignite the sulfur by holding the combustion spoon over the burner flame until you observe a blue flame. Quickly insert the spoon into the bottle and cover as much of the bottle opening as possible with a glass plate.

4. When smoke fills the bottle, remove the spoon. Quickly cover the bottle opening with the glass plate. Extinguish the sulfur fire by holding the spoon under the dripping tap water. Turn off the spigot.

5. Observe the contents of the bottle for approximately three minutes. Record your observations.

6. Add 10 mL of distilled water to the smoke-filled bottle. Quickly replace the lid. Take the bottle to your laboratory bench. Swirl its contents carefully for one minute.

The second piece of apple skin will serve as a control.

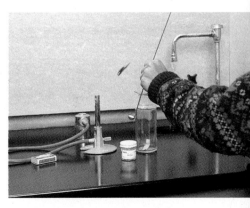

Collecting gas under a fume hood.

7. Place a drop of *Paramecium* (or mixed) culture on a microscope slide. (Pond water, if available, is a interesting alternative.) Examine the drop under the microscope. Look for living organisms. Record your observations.

8. Add three drops of solution from the bottle to the slide. Be sure that the drops fall evenly over the original drop of culture. Using a microscope, observe the events on the slide for three minutes. Record your observations.

9. Remove the apple skin from the bottle and note any changes in its appearance.

10. Using a stirring rod, place a drop of distilled water on pieces of red and blue litmus paper and on a piece of pH paper. Record your observations.

11. Pour about 2 mL of the liquid from the glass bottle into a test tube. Use a stirring rod to test the solution with each color of litmus paper and with pH paper. Record your observations. Acid rain has a pH of 4–4.5. Is your solution more or less acidic than this?

12. Drop a 1-cm length of magnesium ribbon into the test tube. Observe it for at least three minutes before recording your observations.

13. Add two marble chips to the solution in your bottle. Observe for at least three minutes. Record your observations.

14. Wash your hands thoroughly before leaving the laboratory.

Questions

1. Write an equation for the burning of sulfur in air.

2. When the gas produced by burning sulfur dissolved, what effect did it have on the acidity of the distilled water?

3. a. Describe what happened to the culture when the solution from the glass bottle was added.

   b. If this solution were steadily added to a small lake over a long period of time, might it affect organisms living there? Explain.

4. If liquid similar to the solution in the glass bottle were allowed to stand on a marble statue or on steel girders supporting a bridge, what effect might it have?

D.13 pH

Water and all its solutions contain both hydrogen and hydroxide ions.

- In *pure water* and *neutral solutions*, the concentrations of these ions are equal but very small.
- In *acidic solutions*, the hydrogen ion concentration is high and the hydroxide concentration is extremely low.
- In *basic solutions*, the hydroxide ion concentration is high and the hydrogen ion concentration is extremely low.

The pH concept is built on the relationship between hydrogen ions and hydroxide ions in water. The term pH stands for "power of hydrogen ion"—where "power" refers to a mathematical power (exponent) of 10. For example, a solution with 0.001 mol H^+ (10^{-3} mol H^+) per liter has a pH of 3.

The concept of pH was introduced in the Water unit, Section C.6.

A pH of 7 in a water solution at 25° C represents a neutral solution—one where H^+(aq) and OH^-(aq) both have a concentration of 10^{-7} mol per liter, or 10^{-7} M. The pH of pure water is 7.

Values of pH lower than 7 represent acidic solutions. The lower the pH value, the greater the solution's acidity. In an acidic solution, the concentration of H^+ ion is greater than that of OH^- ion. An acidic solution at pH 1 contains 10^{-1} mol (0.1 mol) H^+ in each liter of solution—its H^+ concentration is 0.1 M. This is more acidic than a solution at pH 2, where the hydrogen ion concentration is 10^{-2} mol per liter, or 0.01 M.

By contrast, values above pH 7 represent basic solutions. A solution with a pH of 14 contains 10^{-14} mol H^+ and 1 mol OH^- per liter—10^{-14} M for H^+ and 1 M for OH^-. That is considerably more basic than a solution at pH 8—with concentrations of 10^{-8} M for H^+ and 10^{-6} M for OH^-.

As you see, each step up or down the pH scale changes the acidity by a factor of 10. Thus, lemon juice, pH 2, is 10 times more acidic than a soft drink at pH 3—which, in turn, is 10,000 times more acidic than pure water at pH 7.

*A solution concentration expressed as moles solute per liter of solution is called its **molarity** or **molar concentration**, symbolized M.*

Figure 27, page 52, in the Water unit gives typical pH values for some common materials.

YOUR TURN

pH

1. Following are listed some common aqueous solutions with their typical pH values. Classify each as acidic, basic, or neutral. Arrange them in order of increasing hydrogen ion concentration.
   a. Stomach fluid, pH = 1
   b. A solution of baking soda, pH = 9
   c. A cola drink, pH = 3
   d. A solution of household lye, pH = 13
   e. Milk, drinking water, pH = 6
   f. Sugar dissolved in pure water, pH = 7
   g. Household ammonia, pH = 11
2. How many times more acidic is a cola drink than milk?

PART D: SUMMARY QUESTIONS

1. Identify the major types of air pollutants.
2. In what sense is "pollution free" combustion an impossibility?
3. Identify the major components of smog and their sources.
4. Define the term "synergism" and explain its relevance to air pollution.
5. In which region of the United States is acid rain most prevalent? Why?
6. a. Name the major substances responsible for acid rain.
   b. What are their sources?
7. How might efforts to control air pollution result in other kinds of pollution?
8. Pollution has sometimes been defined as "a resource out of place." Name a substance that is a resource in one part of the atmosphere, a pollutant in another part.

9. Write an ionic equation for the reaction of NO_2 with rainwater.
10. Which of these compounds do you recognize as acids? as bases?
    a. NaOH
    b. HNO_3
    c. CH_4
    d. $C_{12}H_{22}O_{11}$ (table sugar)
    e. H_2SO_3
11. Which of these solutions has the lowest pH? the highest pH?
    a. lemon juice
    b. stomach fluid
    c. drain cleaner (NaOH)
12. Technology to prevent acid rain is available. Why, then, is acid rain still a problem?

EXTENDING YOUR KNOWLEDGE (OPTIONAL)

- Carbon monoxide can interfere with the body's O_2 transport and exchange system. Investigate the health effects of CO and its relationship to traffic accidents.
- Investigate the advantages and disadvantages of various alternatives to the standard internal combustion engine. Options include the electric engine, gas turbine, Rankine engine, stratified charge engines, Wankel engine, Stirling engine, diesel engine, and expanded mass transportation systems.
- Make an acid-base indicator at home with red cabbage juice. (Consult your teacher for instructions.)

Scientists at the Department of Energy's Argonne National Laboratory are studying the effects of sulfur dioxide and ozone on crops.

PUTTING IT ALL TOGETHER: IS AIR A FREE RESOURCE?

Thus far we have investigated the general properties of gases, the structure and functions of the atmosphere, and how human activity may alter the atmosphere. We have also surveyed ways to control air pollution. However, we have not considered the overall success of such efforts. In fact, how clean should the air be? At what cost? These concerns will also be considered in this final activity.

E.1 AIR POLLUTION CONTROL: A SUCCESS?

You were introduced earlier to the main culprits of air pollution. You examined the relative amounts of total suspended particles (TSP), sulfur oxides (SO_x), nitrogen oxides (NO_x), hydrocarbons (HC), and carbon monoxide (CO) emitted by various sectors of our economy. Later several ways of controlling these emissions were described. Most of these control technologies were instituted since the early 1970s. How successful have they been?

Figure 18 (page 404) presents information summarizing changes in U.S. emissions of selected pollutants to the atmosphere from 1975 to 1987, as estimated by the U.S. Environmental Protection Agency. Refer to the figures to answer these questions.

1. a. Estimate the overall percent change in total emissions for each of the four pollutants, using the following formula:

$$\text{Percent change} = \frac{1987 \text{ value} - 1975 \text{ value}}{1975 \text{ value}} \times 100$$

   b. Do the overall trends represent an improvement or a worsening of air quality since 1970?

2. From 1975 to 1987, U.S. population increased 14% and the nation's economy grew by almost 50%. Why is it difficult to improve air quality under these conditions?

3. For each pollutant, which source contributed most significantly to the observed changes from 1975 to 1987?

4. a. In addition to emissions data, what other evidence would help you judge the impact of pollution-control technologies?

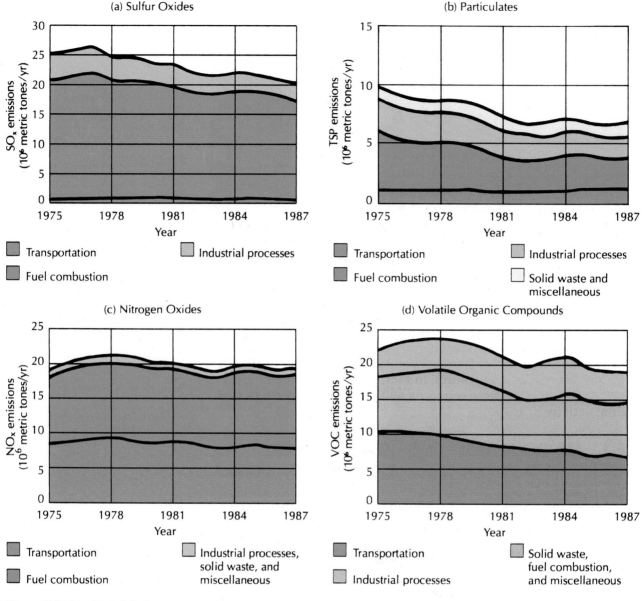

Figure 18 National trends in the emission of four air pollutants from 1975 to 1987: (a) sulfur oxides (SO$_x$); (b) particulates (TSP, total suspended particulates); (c) nitrogen oxides (NO$_x$); (d) volatile organic compounds (VOC; primarily hydrocarbons).

b. Do you agree or disagree with this statement? "Great strides have been made in improving the quality of the air we breathe." Explain your answer.

5. What information would help you decide whether to agree or disagree with this statement? "Stricter laws and better methods are needed to control air pollution."

E.2 YOU DECIDE: JUST ANOTHER RESOURCE?

Consider these two different viewpoints:

View A: Free use of air is a fundamental human right; therefore, taxing or fining individuals or industries that extract materials from or add pollutants to air is unjust.

View B: Free use of air is a fundamental human right; therefore air cleanliness should be guaranteed by government regulations that provide taxes or fines for individuals or industries that lessen air quality.

Complete the following assignment, working in a small group with classmates. Identify at least five scientific, practical, or social questions you would like answered before you decide which view to support. A review of the major topics considered in this unit may help you to identify some concerns or questions.

Given the potentially damaging effects of human activities on air quality, we must learn how to use the atmosphere wisely. As a first step, we must understand its chemical composition and some properties of gases. This is the focus of the next section.

E.3 PAYING THE PRICE

Earlier in this unit we noted that air pollution costs the United States an estimated $16 billion each year. This financial loss shows up in destroyed crops, weakened livestock, corrosion of buildings and machines, and higher workmen's compensation and hospital costs for those with air-pollution-related diseases. However, this does *not* include less visible, but potentially disastrous long-term costs associated with altering nature's cycles.

Of course, pollution control has its own costs. Whether one considers catalytic converters in automobiles or scrubbers in power plants, pollution control technologies increase the costs of material goods and energy. In other words, using the atmosphere as a "free" resource and repository actually involves real expense. With or without pollution control, citizens in industrialized nations pay a price for the quality of air they breathe.

Economists deal with pollution control policy issues (as they do many issues) in terms of cost-benefit analyses. Each consequence of a given policy is reduced to a common denominator: dollars. The total cost of any air pollution control policy is the sum of two elements. One is ***damage costs:*** tangible losses, such as those discussed above, and intangible costs, such as reduced visibility and respiratory irritation. The other element consists of ***control costs:*** the direct costs of pollution control methods along with any indirect costs, such as unemployment created by a plant shutdown or relocation.

The overall result of the costs and benefits of pollution control are combined in plots like those in Figure 19 (page 406). The plots start at the left with pollution levels reduced practically to zero (high air quality). As you might expect, at this point the cost of the control measures is the highest. Also, at the highest air quality on the left, the cost of pollution damage is very low. Note the changes as air quality is allowed to decrease, represented by moving from left to right on the figure. Control costs decrease as the level of pollution is allowed to increase. However, simultaneously, damage costs increase with increasing pollution levels.

The top curve represents the total financial cost to society of pollution controls and pollution damage. Look at the vertical line marked on the plot. At the pollution level indicated by point *a*, damage costs are given by distance *ab*, control costs are given by distance *ac*, and total costs to society are given by *ad*, the sum of *ab* and *ac*. Note that at point *a* the cost to society for control (*ac*) is greater than the cost due to damage (*ab*).

In economic theory, the best balance of control costs and damage costs is where the total cost curve reaches a minimum.

Figure 19 The cost of air pollution.

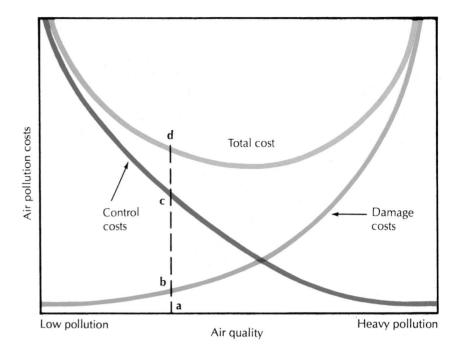

This point, will, of course, be different for different pollution and control combinations. Such a cost-benefit analysis is most easily completed for a single business that pays all control and damage costs. Pollution cost analyses are much more complicated in cases where control and damage costs apply to different groups.

Based on what you have learned in this unit and the relationships illustrated in Figure 19, answer these questions:

1. a. At low pollution levels (high air quality), which are more costly—control costs or damage costs?
   b. Explain your answer.
2. a. At high pollution levels (low air quality), which are more costly—control costs or damage costs?
   b. Explain your answer.
3. Is it possible—either technologically or economically—to eliminate
   a. all pollution costs?
   b. all damage costs?
   c. Explain your answers.
4. Assume that improved control technologies, such as efficient catalytic converters that use cheaper metals, appear. How would this affect the shape of the control costs curve?
5. a. In your opinion, which can be estimated with greater certainty—damage costs or control costs?
   b. Why?
   c. Describe some difficulties in estimating the other kind of cost.
6. For each point on the graph in Figure 19, total costs equal the sum of control costs and damage costs. Many economists believe the objective of pollution control is to minimize total costs.
   a. What assumptions are built into this cost-benefit analysis?
   b. Do you think these assumptions are valid? Why?

7. On a personal level, control costs often seem much higher than damage costs. Why?

8. a. Are benefits of cleaner air shared equally by all? Why?

   b. Are control costs of cleaner air shared equally by all? Why?

9. a. Expressed in dollars, how much is seeing a clear, blue sky worth to you?

   b. In dollars, how much is it worth to you to smell fresh, clean air?

   c. Are these questions fair?

   d. Are they important?

10. Counting only direct costs easily measured in dollars, total damage costs of U.S. air pollution have been estimated to be less than $100 yearly for each citizen.

    a. Do you think this is a fair way to express the total damage costs of air pollution?

    b. Why?

The crane is installing the top section of a desulfurization system.

E.4 LOOKING BACK

In this unit you have explored some interactions of matter and energy in our planet's atmosphere—interactions which include a variety of important chemical reactions. You also considered key social issues surrounding our use of the world's air—both as a source of reactants and as a depository for products of reactions.

The "sea of air" in which we are immersed remains our shared planetary home. Decisions you make in your personal life, as well as societal decisions at local, state, national, and international levels will help determine the future quality of the world's climates.

Air is often regarded as invisible. However, its effects remain not only highly visible, but also vitally important to every planetary inhabitant and community. We hope this unit has helped you become a more thoughtful consumer and custodian of this shared planetary resource.

HEALTH: YOUR RISKS AND CHOICES

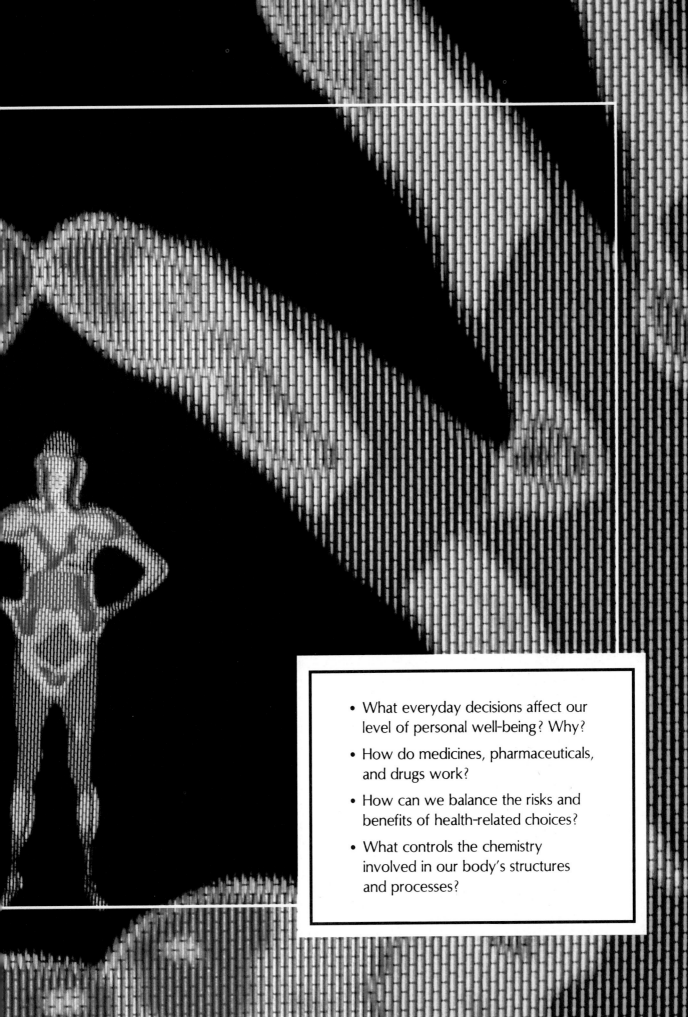

- What everyday decisions affect our level of personal well-being? Why?

- How do medicines, pharmaceuticals, and drugs work?

- How can we balance the risks and benefits of health-related choices?

- What controls the chemistry involved in our body's structures and processes?

INTRODUCTION

To a degree unparalleled in history, we have gained control over many illnesses. Diseases we rarely hear of today—tuberculosis, diphtheria, polio, and whooping cough—were once feared as much as we fear cancer. If people still perished from these diseases at the rate they did in 1900, over three-quarters of a million U.S. citizens would die from them yearly. Unfortunately, infectious diseases like tuberculosis are reappearing. However, their annual toll is fewer than 100,000 lives.

These diseases and others have been controlled by a combination of sanitation and mass immunization. That three-quarters of today's deaths result from degenerative diseases such as cancer, heart disease, and stroke—primarily diseases of aging—is evidence of our success.

However, many U.S. adults still die much earlier than necessary. Over half of these early deaths could be prevented by changes in personal behavior, according to the U.S. Centers for Disease Control. In fact, good health has become partly a matter of personal choice for most people in this country. Decisions you make every day help influence your level of current and future health.

Normally, we are born with important chemical systems already in operation within our bodies. These beneficial chemical interactions—involving such basic activities as energy production, body growth and maintenance, processing sensory data, and mental activity—are beyond our direct control. However, we may apply stress to these systems through a variety of personal and societal decisions. As a result, our health and well-being can be placed in jeopardy. Decisions regarding smoking, drugs, health care products, personal diet, and exercise, for example, all can influence the state of our "internal chemistry"—and thus the state of our well-being.

Our bodies are also affected by "external chemistry"—including factors under direct human control. Pollutants, sunlight, and other parts of the external environment can bring about chemical changes within us.

In this unit you will explore some chemical factors influencing your personal health and vitality. We will survey a range of key factors, extending from important internal body chemistry you cannot control, through factors you partially control, and on to some you fully control.

Decision-making related to our personal well-being remains a high priority for everyone. Such decisions, as usual, involve careful weighing of personal risks and benefits. Even if you elect to make no decision in a certain circumstance, that—in itself—could still be a decision involving your body's well-being. This unit is designed to help you anticipate some of those decisions.

The average life span in the United States is in the low seventies for men and in the high seventies for women.

Disks containing antibiotics kill any surrounding bacteria that are susceptible to them. The development of antibiotics made a tremendous contribution to our control over infectious diseases.

RISK AND PERSONAL DECISION-MAKING

A.1 MAKING JUDGMENTS ABOUT RISK

Scientists often identify and investigate events that routinely occur together, either at the same time or in a predictable sequence. Such research often involves factors or events related to personal and public health. Situations or incidents that regularly happen together are said to be **correlated.** When correlations are found, one scientific goal is to determine whether or how the two events are related.

Sometimes advocates of a given health-related position may imply that a high correlation means that one event necessarily caused the other. In fact, other events may have caused both. For example, when people start wearing overcoats, home heating bills generally increase. But overcoats do not cause heating bills to rise. The onset of cold weather directly causes both the appearance of overcoats and increased heating bills.

Correlation may also be pure coincidence. For many years skirt-hem heights and stock market prices increased and decreased together. Do you think there was an actual connection between these two trends?

Informed decision making is important in personal health care.

YOUR TURN

Events: Related or Not?

Examine the pairs of events listed on page 412 and express the relationship between them by choosing which phrase applies in each case: "correlates with," "directly causes," or "is not related to." (You may find that more than one phrase applies.)

For example, the events "spring" and "hay fever" are correlated for some people. After some allergy tests, a cause-effect relationship might be established. A given sufferer might find out that the renewed growth of ragweed in spring directly causes the hay fever symptoms. Thus even though spring and hay fever are correlated, the direct cause of the hay fever—at least in this example—would be ragweed.

1. Phase of the moon, tide height
2. Average temperature, season of the year
3. Number of ocean swimmers, tide height
4. Class attendance, grade in chemistry
5. Guns, homicides
6. Poverty, lack of food
7. Water temperature, amount of dissolved oxygen
8. Length of hydrocarbon chain, boiling point
9. Alcoholism, stress
10. Practice, solving chemistry problems
11. Pleasant personality, number of dates
12. Smoking, lung cancer
13. Glucose metabolism, energy production

CHEMQUANDARY

Cigarette Warnings

In 1966, the federal government ordered cigarette manufacturers to place this statement on each cigarette package and on each cigarette advertisement:

> CAUTION: The Surgeon General Has Determined That Cigarette Smoking May Be Dangerous To Your Health.

In 1970, the federal government changed the label:

> CAUTION: The Surgeon General Has Determined That Cigarette Smoking Is Dangerous To Your Health.

In 1985, officials decided that several stronger messages should be printed on smoking product packages and advertisements. One of them reads:

> SURGEON GENERAL'S WARNING: Smoking Causes Lung Cancer, Heart Disease, Emphysema, And May Complicate Pregnancy.

1. What do the changes in the warnings on cigarette packages indicate?
2. What did the Surgeon General imply by changing the words *caution* to *warning* and *may be* to *is* on the cigarette labels?

Medical Technologists: Part of the Diagnostic Team

By Lucy G. Ross
Selma Daily News *Staff Reporter*

Yolanda Villa knew while still in high school that she wanted to pursue a medical career, but she was uncertain as to which particular job suited her abilities and goals. On the day she attended a career fair at Fresno State University in California her uncertainty vanished. There, Yolanda learned about the job of a medical technologist—and her decision was made.

Yolanda learned that a medical technologist performs laboratory tests on urine and blood, cultures bacteria and viruses and identifies parasites. A medical technologist also types blood for transfusions. Yolanda helps physicians detect, diagnose, and treat patient illnesses.

Yolanda works the night shift at Valley Medical Center County Hospital in California. Yolanda must be adept at performing all types of laboratory work. She works in many departments within the hospital including hematology, blood banking, bacteriology, parasitology, and serology. She uses her knowledge of chemistry to help her perform meaningful tests involving human biochemistry. Her chemistry background helps her to interpret results produced by automated machines.

During her shift, Yolanda provides a variety of services to any department in need. She collects specimens, performs tests either by standard laboratory procedures or by using automated equipment, provides test results, and answers the questions of doctors and nurses. To minimize the risk of providing erroneous results, Yolanda must calibrate

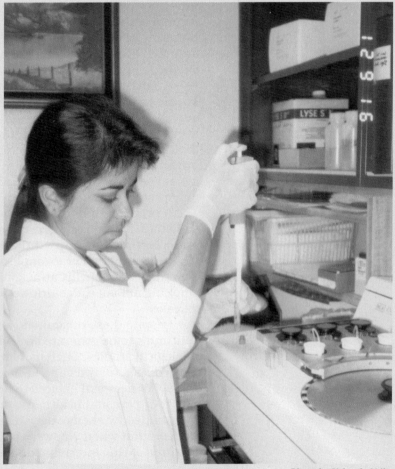

Photo by Yolanda Villa

automated equipment and periodically run controls. One of the most exciting aspects of Yolanda's job is working the blood bank in the trauma center. Patients in the trauma center use blood very quickly. Yolanda helps to save lives by providing typed blood for transfusions.

Yolanda must be conscientious and responsible. She is dealing with patients' lives, and doctors put their trust in her results. Yolands must also minimize risks to herself from being cut by glassware, burned by chemicals, or infected by diseased body

fluids. She does this by proper handling of specimens, materials, and equipment.

Physicians depend on laboratory procedures for assistance in diagnosing and treating diseases. The continued health and welfare of the patient is an important benefit of having qualified medical technologists on the health care team.

Yolanda has a B.S. in microbiology and a minor in chemistry from Fresno State University. Her course of study included classes in chemistry, microbiology, and biochemistry.

A.2 STUDYING HUMAN DISEASE

In chemical research, it is relatively easy to control most variables. In medical research, it is never easy to do so, partly because it is unacceptable to expose human subjects to potentially harmful treatments.

For that reason, scientists may begin by treating animals. Such experiments can produce useful results, but cannot definitely predict how humans will respond to the same treatments. Animal body chemistry is different in some ways from that of humans. In addition, some conditions can't be duplicated with animals. For example, it's not easy to coax laboratory animals to smoke.

Animal studies, are supplemented with **epidemiological studies.** Scientists study specific populations of people in a search for factors that cause or prevent disease. For example, they study victims of heart attacks, gathering information about their living habits to try to determine what makes some people prone to heart attacks. Or they study groups that have a much lower than average incidence of heart attacks to identify what may protect these individuals.

A problem that arises, however, is that a single epidemiological study may reveal correlations, but not evidence of a cause-and-effect relationship. At times, such findings may even mislead researchers. For example, one study concluded that coffee drinking causes heart attacks. But the study had ignored smoking among coffee-drinkers as a possible cause of heart disease.

Despite these difficulties, important and useful information continues to be generated by health-related research and epidemiological studies. Such data and findings can help guide informed risk analysis and decision-making, ranging from a variety of personal choices to health-related societal policies.

Your personal health and well-being are, in large measure, maintained by chemical systems that were already in place and in operation when you were born. We will next explore some key features of this interrelated system of "internal chemistry."

PART A: SUMMARY QUESTIONS

1. a. Describe a pair of events that are closely correlated *and* have a direct cause-effect relationship with each other. (Select an example not already discussed in this book.)

   b. Describe a pair of events that are closely correlated but do *not* have a direct cause-effect relationship with each other. (Again, select an example not already mentioned.)

2. a. Describe a health-related decision you recently made or are still considering.

   b. In your opinion, what advantages (benefits) and disadvantages (burdens or risks) are associated with your decision?

   c. What other options did you consider (or are you considering) before making a final decision?

   d. In your view, what advantages and disadvantages are connected with each of these other options?

3. Classify each of these traditional sayings as involving either correlation, cause-effect, both, or neither. In each case, explain your choice.

   a. *Haste makes waste.*

   b. *Too many cooks spoil the broth.*

   c. *An apple a day keeps the doctor away.*

   d. *Tall trees from little acorns grow.*

   e. *The early bird gets the worm.*

YOUR BODY'S INTERNAL CHEMISTRY

B.1 BALANCE AND ORDER: KEYS TO LIFE

Even when you dive into icy water or jog on a hot day, your body temperature rarely deviates more than two degrees from 37° C. If it does, you are probably ill. Likewise, your blood pH remains virtually constant, as do concentrations of many substances in your blood and cells. Your body would quickly fail if its chemistry became unbalanced.

Maintenance of balance in body systems is **homeostasis.** Failure of homeostasis leads to illness, and—if not corrected—eventually leads to death.

Body chemistry's most impressive and important feature is its controlled complexity. Every minute your cells make hundreds of different compounds, and do so more quickly and accurately than any chemical factory. These compounds take part in the multitude of reactions occurring simultaneously within each cell.

The best way to stay healthy? That is easy—help your body chemistry stay in balance. For example, eating a balanced diet provides your body with the building-block molecules and ions it needs to make new tissues. Exercise is also important. It keeps your cardiovascular system (heart, lungs, veins, and arteries) fit, so that blood circulates to all your cells.

See the Food unit.

The cardiovascular system supplies food and fuel to your tissues, and also the oxygen needed to burn that fuel.

To function effectively, cells must be supplied with needed chemical substances, their waste products must be removed promptly, and a proper temperature and pH must be maintained. Blood serves as the conduit for supplies and wastes. Also, blood protects cells from harmful changes in physical and chemical conditions, such as those caused by invading bacteria.

Under normal conditions, your body and its external environment both contain well-balanced bacterial ecosystems. Although harmful bacteria are always around us, they generally fail to cause disease. In large part that is because they must compete with harmless bacteria. Sickness often results if the harmless bacteria are suppressed and the disease-causing bacteria have a population explosion.

Harmful bacteria proliferate in a dirty environment. Before municipal sewage treatment started, drinking water supplies were continually threatened by armies of bacteria. Water supplies were often contaminated. We often overlook the fact that municipal sewage treatment has been a major contributor to public health.

Despite modern medicine and sanitation, occasionally we become sick. Fortunately, the body is very good at regaining its balance. Given a healthful environment, proper care, and a good diet, most people recover from most diseases by themselves. But in some cases the body needs assistance. Chemists have developed many drugs that promote recovery and relieve pain.

However, body chemistry is so delicately balanced that a medicine added to help one system regain equilibrium may throw other systems out of balance. This is what doctors mean by **side effects.** Sometimes we need to decide which creates greater problems—the disease or the cure.

In the following sections, we will explore the body's composition and chemistry, and investigate some built-in mechanisms that promote homeostasis.

B.2 ELEMENTS IN THE HUMAN BODY

Table 1 lists twenty-six elements making up your body, along with the quantities of each normally present in a healthy adult. These elements are found in biomolecules and as ions in body fluids.

Table 1   **ELEMENTAL COMPOSITION OF A 70-kg HUMAN ADULT**

Elements	Percent (%) of Body Mass
Hydrogen, oxygen, carbon, nitrogen, calcium	98
Phosphorus, chlorine, potassium, sulfur, magnesium	2
Iron, zinc	0.01
Copper, tin, manganese, iodine, bromine, fluorine, molybdenum, arsenic, cobalt, chromium, lithium, nickel, cadmium, selenium	Each less than 0.001

Oxygen, carbon, hydrogen, nitrogen, and calcium are the most abundant. Together, they make up about 98% of body mass. Sixty-three percent of all atoms in the body are hydrogen, 25% are oxygen, 10% are carbon, and 1.4% are nitrogen. Most of these atoms are present in organic compounds such as the carbohydrates, proteins, and fats described in the Food unit. Calcium—1.5% of the body's mass—is an important structural element in teeth and bones, and is involved in the passage of nerve impulses, muscle contraction, and blood clotting.

Elements such as iodine, selenium, copper, and fluorine are essential to health, even though they are normally present in less than 10 parts per million (ppm) of body mass. Table 2 describes functions of some trace elements in the body.

10 dollars out of 1,000,000 dollars also is 10 ppm.

Table 2   **MINERALS**

Mineral	Source	Deficiency Condition
Macrominerals		
Calcium (Ca)	Canned fish, milk, dairy products	Rickets in children; osteomalacia and osteoporosis in adults
Chlorine (Cl)	Meats, salt-processed foods, table salt	—
Magnesium (Mg)	Seafoods, cereal grains, nuts, dark green vegetables, cocoa	Heart failure due to spasms
Phosphorus (P)	Animal proteins	—
Potassium (K)	Orange juice, bananas, dried fruits, potatoes	Poor nerve function; irregular heartbeat; sudden death during fasting
Sodium (Na)	Meats, salt-processed foods, table salt	Headache, weakness, thirst, poor memory, appetite loss
Sulfur (S)	Proteins	—
Trace minerals		
Chromium (Cr)	Liver, animal and plant tissue	Loss of insulin efficiency with age
Cobalt (Co)	Liver, animal proteins	Anemia
Copper (Cu)	Liver, kidney, egg yolk, whole grains	—
Fluorine (F)	Seafoods, fluoridated drinking water	Dental decay
Iodine (I)	Seafoods, iodized salts	Goiter
Iron (Fe)	Liver, meats, green leafy vegetables, whole grains	Anemia; tiredness and apathy
Manganese (Mn)	Liver, kidney, wheat germ, legumes, nuts, tea	Weight loss, dermatitis
Molybdenum (Mo)	Liver, kidney, whole grains, legumes, leafy vegetables	—
Nickel (Ni)	Seafoods, grains, seeds, beans, vegetables	Cirrhosis of liver, kidney failure, stress
Selenium (Se)	Liver, organ meats, grains, vegetables	Kashan disease (a heart disease found in China)
Zinc (Zn)	Liver, shellfish, meats, wheat germ, legumes	Anemia, stunted growth

YOUR TURN

Elements in the Body

1. Select five elements found in the body. Using Tables 1 and 2, and what you know about these elements, answer these questions:
   a. Where in the body (or in what type of biomolecule) is each element found?
   b. What role does each element play in maintaining health?
2. Is it correct to say that elements highly abundant in the body—such as calcium and phosphorus—are more essential than trace elements such as iron and iodine? Why? (*Hint:* Consider the notion of a limiting reactant.)

3. a. Why might a change in diet be more likely to cause a deficiency of trace elements than of highly-abundant elements?

   b. Why are cases of overdose-poisoning more common among trace elements? (*Hint:* Consider percent change and chemical balance.)

To understand how cellular chemistry contributes to health and well-being, and what you can do to assist it, we will now investigate some of the basic principles involved.

B.3 CELLULAR CHEMISTRY

How quickly can you pull back your hand from a hot stove? How quickly can you move your foot from the accelerator to brake your car to a stop? Cellular chemical reactions must take place extremely rapidly to allow you to do these things.

A human cell makes hundreds of different substances— each at exactly the right moment and in precisely the amount required. In addition, it generates its own energy and chemical machinery to do so.

The cell is the scene of action in your body. Cellular chemistry is fast, efficient, and precise. You have learned that food is "burned" to supply the body's continuous energy needs. This occurs in the cell, where energy is released and used with great speed and efficiency. The body's building needs are also met with incredible efficiency within cells. Each healthy cell synthesizes exactly the molecules it needs—no more and no less—precisely when the need arises.

What's the secret behind this impressive performance? It lies with enzymes, which are present in all cells. **Enzymes** are biological catalysts. Like all catalysts, they speed up reactions without undergoing any lasting change themselves. The speed of an enzyme-catalyzed reaction is hard to comprehend. In one second, a single enzyme molecule in your blood can catalyze the decomposition of 600,000 H_2CO_3 molecules:

$$H_2CO_3(aq) \xrightarrow{\text{Enzyme}} H_2O(l) + CO_2(g)$$

In that single second, 600,000 molecules of carbon dioxide are liberated into your lungs as you exhale. Also in one second, an enzyme in saliva can free 18,000 glucose molecules from starch:

$$\text{-glucose-glucose-glucose} + H_2O(l) \xrightarrow{\text{Enzyme}} \text{-glucose-glucose} + \text{glucose}$$
$$\begin{array}{cc} \text{(portion of starch} & \text{(remaining portion} \\ \text{molecule)} & \text{of starch molecule)} \end{array}$$

Before exploring further how enzymes do their jobs, your teacher will conduct the following demonstration. Witness for yourself the speed of an enzyme catalyzed reaction!

B.4 LAB DEMONSTRATION: ENZYMES

Your teacher will demonstrate the decomposition of hydrogen peroxide to water and oxygen gas:

$$2\ H_2O_2(aq) \rightarrow 2\ H_2O(l) + O_2(g)$$

A teacher demonstration.

This reaction was used to generate oxygen gas in the Air unit, Laboratory Activity: The Atmosphere (page 349).

1. Manganese dioxide (MnO_2) was added to speed up the reaction—it served as an inorganic catalyst.

This demonstration will show how an enzyme can also speed up this reaction.

Following the demonstration, answer these questions:

Questions

1. What did the foam in the test with the fresh liver indicate?
2. Why was there little observable reaction when boiled liver was used?
3. Why does commercial hydrogen peroxide contain preservatives?
4. There is an old belief that when hydrogen peroxide is added to a cut, foaming shows that infection is present. What is the real reason?
5. a. What two features of hydrogen peroxide make it a useful treatment for wounds?
   b. Explain.

Let's find out why enzymes are so effective.

B.5 HOW ENZYMES WORK

Enzymes speed up reactions by making it easier for molecules to react. Both enzymes themselves and many of the molecules they help to react are very large. If the molecules are to react with each other at specific sites or functional groups, they must approach so these functional groups are close to each other.

In general, enzymes function in this manner:

- Reactant molecules—known as **substrates**—and enzymes are brought together. The substrate molecule fits into the enzyme at an **active site** where its key functional groups are properly positioned (Figure 1, page 420).

Figure 1 Model of the interactions of enzyme and substrate molecules.

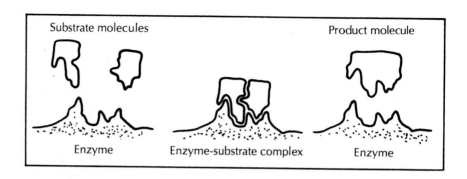

See Air unit, page 395.

See Food unit, page 252.

Figure 2 Diagram of a vitamin serving as a coenzyme.

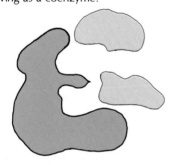

Without the coenzyme, substances A and B cannot be led to the active site of the enzyme and hence cannot react with each other.

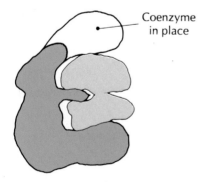

Coenzyme in place

With the coenzyme, substances A and B are oriented at the active site of the enzyme. Here they can react with each other.

- The enzyme then interacts with the substrate molecule(s), weakening key bonds and making the reaction more energetically favorable. Our discussion of automobile catalytic mufflers described how catalysts function—the reaction is speeded up because the activation energy barrier is lowered.
- The reaction occurs. Products depart from the enzyme surface, freeing the enzyme to interact with other substrate molecules.

Some enzymes require the presence of coenzymes. For example, B vitamins are coenzymes in the release of energy from food molecules. Figure 2 illustrates how some coenzymes function.

Enzymes are as selective as they are fast. How does the cell "know" it should complete only certain reactions, even though substrates for many other reactions are also available? Why do your cells *oxidize* glucose to CO_2 and water, instead of *reducing* it to CH_4 and water? Why do stomach cells digest protein rather than starch or fat? The answer to all these questions is the same: A given enzyme can catalyze only one specific type of reaction. Thus, a cell can only complete reactions for which it has enzymes. Thanks to the specificity of enzymes, cells have precise control over which reactions take place.

Every cell (except a blood cell) has an identical set of instruction molecules composed of chains of DNA (deoxyribonucleic acid) molecules. **Genes**—small segments of DNA molecules—store the instructions for specific traits such as hair color, height, and nose shape. Various chemical regulators "turn on" only those genes appropriate to the cell type. For example, genes that control stomach acid secretion would be turned on in stomach-lining cells, but not in cells of the eye. Exactly how these regulators choose the appropriate genes is still a mystery.

B.6 HOW ENERGY IS RELEASED AND STORED

Body chemistry is not only fast and selective, but also extremely energy-efficient. Here's why: Some cellular reactions release energy; others require energy. Just as money is often stored in a bank until needed, reserves of body energy are stored in carbohydrates and fats. Between its release from these energy-rich molecules and its use in the cell, energy is stored briefly in biomolecules called ATP (adenosine triphosphate). Think of it this way—between obtaining cash and spending it, you store the money in your pocket.

The body's primary energy-release reaction is the oxidation of glucose, which we can describe by this overall equation:

ATP provides the energy needed for human activity.

$$C_6H_{12}O_6(aq) + 6\ O_2(g) \rightarrow$$
$$6\ CO_2(g) + 6\ H_2O(l) + 2.87 \times 10^3\ kJ/mol\ glucose$$

See the Food unit, page 236.

This equation summarizes what happens during a sequence of more than 20 chemical reactions, involving more than 20 enzymes. Molecule by molecule, glucose passes through this sequence in cells throughout your body. Energy contained in glucose is set free bit by bit in individual reactions and immediately is placed in short-term ATP storage.

In this energy-storage reaction, ADP (adenosine diphosphate) adds a phosphate group to form ATP and water:

$$\text{Energy} + \text{ADP}(aq) + HPO_4{}^{2-}(aq) \rightarrow H_2O(l) + \text{ATP}(aq)$$

(31 kJ/mol ADP)   Hydrogen
                          phosphate ion

In addition to using glucose, your body can obtain energy from fatty acids stored in fats or from protein. To oxidize these substances, cells use many of the same enzymes used in glucose oxidation.

Oxidation of one mole of glucose produces enough energy to add 38 mol of ATP to the cell's short-term energy storage.

Thus, the quantity of energy stored in each ATP molecule is conveniently small. It can be used as needed to power individual steps in cellular reactions. Some steps in reactions require less energy than is stored in a single ATP molecule, while others must use the energy from several ATP molecules.

As energy is needed, it is released by the reverse of the energy-storage reaction shown above.

ATP

ADP

Your body stores and later releases energy from at least 100 mol (6.0×10^{25} molecules) of ATP daily. The structural formulas for ATP and ADP (page 421) depict ionic forms for the molecules—the forms of ATP and ADP found in body fluids.

The extraordinary efficiency of energy release, storage, and release is due to enzyme speed and specificity.

YOUR TURN

Enzymes and Energy in Action

Consider this sample problem: Table 2 on page 226 indicated that sitting burns 100 Calories per hour.

   a. If this energy were obtained from ATP and each mole of ATP yields 7.3 kcal (31 kJ), how many moles of ATP would provide the energy needed to sit for an hour?

   b. If each mole of glucose burned produces 38 mol of ATP, how many moles of glucose, $C_6H_{12}O_6$, would be needed to provide this energy? How many grams of glucose is that?

   First, we find the moles of ATP needed for one hour of sitting:

$$100 \text{ kcal} \times \frac{1 \text{ mol ATP}}{7.3 \text{ kcal}} = 14 \text{ mol ATP}$$

Since 38 mol ATP can be obtained from one mole of glucose, our "sitting" need for 14 mol ATP can be met with less than a mole of glucose:

$$14 \text{ mol ATP} \times \frac{1 \text{ mol glucose}}{38 \text{ mol ATP}} = 0.37 \text{ mol glucose}$$

How many grams is that? We first find that a mole of glucose has a mass of 180 g (its molar mass). Since we need less than one mole of glucose, its mass must be less than 180 g:

$$0.37 \text{ mol glucose} \times \frac{180 \text{ g glucose}}{1 \text{ mol glucose}} = 66 \text{ g glucose}$$

Now try these items:

1. a. Assume your body produces approximately 100 mol of ATP daily. How many moles of glucose must be consumed to produce this?

   b. How many grams of glucose is this?

2. One minute of muscle activity requires about 0.001 mol of ATP for each gram of muscle. How many moles of glucose must be oxidized for 454 g (one pound) of muscle to dribble a basketball for one minute?

Besides controlling the release and storage of energy, enzymes catalyze reactions that break down large food molecules into building blocks your cells can use. You will be invited to investigate this role of enzymes in the next activity.

Chew on This Problem!

Amylase, an enzyme present in saliva, catalyzes the release of glucose from starch. Under optimum conditions of temperature and pH, one molecule of amylase can generate as many as 18,000 molecules of glucose each second (as noted on page 418).

1. See if you can detect a change in the taste of a soda cracker (containing starch) as you chew one for a minute or more before swallowing it.
2. Describe any taste change you detect.
3. Explain what caused the change.

B.7 LABORATORY ACTIVITY: ENZYMES

Getting Ready

In this activity, the activity of two enzymes that aid in digestion will be detected by noting the products of the enzyme-catalyzed reaction.

The major protein in egg white—albumin—is digested in the small intestine by the enzyme **pepsin.** When albumin is decomposed in the laboratory, the extent of the reaction can be judged by the amount of cloudiness, or turbidity, that appears as time passes. The greater the turbidity, the larger the amount of protein decomposed. You will test the action of pepsin on albumin as you usually consume it—the white of a cooked egg.

The cloudiness is due to formation of an insoluble product.

An enzyme in saliva, amylase, breaks down starch molecules into individual glucose units. The glucose will be detected by Benedict's reagent as a yellow-to-orange precipitate. The amount of precipitate increases with the concentration of glucose.

See Lab Demonstration: Enzymes (page 418) and Your Turn: Enzymes and Energy in Action.

The activity of each enzyme will be observed and compared at two temperatures (room temperature and refrigerator temperature) and at several pH values.

You will be assigned to a group of four students. Each group member should carry out tests to check the activity of one of these:

1. Pepsin at room temperature.
2. Refrigerated pepsin.
3. Amylase at room temperature.
4. Refrigerated amylase.

Read the procedures below. Prepare a data table with appropriately labeled columns for data collected by each group member.

Day 1: Preparing the Systems

PEPSIN TESTS

1. Label four test tubes near the top with the temperature of your assigned test and a pH value of 2, 4, 7, or 8.
2. Using solutions provided by your teacher, place 5 mL of pH 2, 4, 7, and 8 solutions in the appropriately labeled tubes.

3. Place 1.5 g of egg white (the size of a large kidney bean) in each tube.

4. Add 5 mL of 0.5% pepsin solution to each tube. Continue with Steps 5–8 below.

AMYLASE TESTS

1. Label five test tubes near the top with the temperature of your assigned test and a pH value of 2, 4, 7, 8, or 10.

2. Using solutions provided by your teacher, place 5 mL of the pH 2, 4, 7, 8, and 10 solutions in the appropriate tubes.

3. Add 2.5 mL of starch suspension to each tube.

4. Add 2.5 mL of 0.5% amylase solution to each tube. Continue with Steps 5–8 below.

ALL TESTS

5. Insert a stopper in each tube and shake well.

6. Leave the tubes that are to remain at room temperature in the laboratory overnight as directed.

7. Give your teacher the tubes to be refrigerated.

8. Wash your hands thoroughly before leaving the laboratory.

Day 2: Evaluating the Results

PEPSIN TESTS

1. Observe the test tubes for cloudiness (turbidity).

2. Record your observations.

3. Share your data with other members of your group.

4. Wash your hands thoroughly before leaving the laboratory.

AMYLASE TESTS

1. Prepare a hot-water bath by adding about 100 mL of tap water to a 250-mL beaker. Add a boiling chip. Heat the beaker on a ring stand with a Bunsen burner.

2. Place 5 mL of Benedict's reagent in each tube. Replace the stoppers—being careful not to mix them up—and shake well.

3. Make sure the tubes are clearly labeled. Remove or loosen the stoppers and place the tubes in the water bath.

4. Heat the water bath until the solution of at least one tube has turned yellow or orange. Then heat for 2–3 minutes more.

5. Use a test tube holder to remove the tubes from the water bath. Place them in order of increasing pH.

6. Observe and record the color of the contents of each tube.

7. Share your data with other members of your group.

8. Wash your hands thoroughly before leaving the laboratory.

Questions

1. At which temperature was each enzyme most effective? At which pH?

2. Make a general statement about the effect of temperature on an enzyme-catalyzed reaction.

3. Bases that release relatively low concentrations of $OH^-(aq)$, such as aluminum hydroxide, $Al(OH)_3$, and magnesium hydroxide, $Mg(OH)_2$, are used in commercial antacid tablets.

Why must only *small* amounts of hydroxide ion be released in such preparations?

The body's proteins—especially enzymes—are very sensitive to changes in acidity or concentrations of foreign materials (such as heavy metal ions) in their environment. Yet acids and bases are continually added to and removed from cells and body fluids. How can the body handle these materials without adversely affecting vital body chemistry? Some background on acids and bases will provide the answer in the next part of this unit.

PART B: SUMMARY QUESTIONS

1. What is meant by homeostasis? How is it related to the normal functioning of your body?

2. Identify some factors that contribute to homeostasis in a healthy human body.

3. Name the five most common elements in the human body, in order of decreasing abundance.

4. a. List three characteristics of chemical reactions in cells.

   b. Show how each is important in everyday activities.

5. a. What class of cellular compounds is primarily responsible for the characteristics in question 4?

   b. Describe how these compounds work.

6. How is energy released from the oxidation of food materials stored in the body?

7. The production of one gram of protein requires about 17 kJ of energy. The molar mass of the protein albumin is 69,000 g/mol. How many ATP molecules must react to energize the formation of one mole (69,000 g) of albumin?

Eating right is one way to keep the body in balance.

ACIDS, BASES, AND BODY CHEMISTRY

C.1   STRUCTURE DETERMINES FUNCTION

In 1883 the Swedish chemist Svante Arrhenius defined an acid as any substance which, when dissolved in water, generates hydrogen ions (H^+). He defined a base as a substance that generates hydroxide ion (OH^-) in water solutions. For example, hydrogen chloride gas, HCl(g), when dissolved in water, produces hydrochloric acid—HCl, the primary acid in gastric juice. The hydrogen ion, H^+(aq), makes a solution acidic and reactive enough to behave like a typical acid.

Equations for making solutions of some common acids are shown below:

$$HCl(g) \xrightarrow{\text{Water}} H^+(aq) + Cl^-(aq)$$
$$\text{Hydrochloric acid}$$

$$HNO_3(l) \xrightarrow{\text{Water}} H^+(aq) + NO_3^-(aq)$$
$$\text{Nitric acid}$$

$$H_2SO_4(l) \xrightarrow{\text{Water}} H^+(aq) + HSO_4^-(aq)$$
$$\text{Sulfuric acid}$$

Most common acids are molecular compounds, containing covalently-bonded hydrogen atoms. At least one hydrogen atom in each molecule can be drawn off in water solution. The hydrogen atom leaves behind an electron and enters the solution as a hydrogen ion (H^+). As shown above, the remainder of the acid molecule—with hydrogen's electron attached—becomes an anion.

Many common bases, unlike acids, are ionic compounds—they already contain ions. When such a base dissolves in water, the ions separate from each other and disperse uniformly in the solution.

The hydroxide ion (OH^-) in solution imparts the properties we associate with basic solutions. Here are equations for the dissolving of some bases in water:

$$NaOH(s) \xrightarrow{\text{Water}} Na^+(aq) + OH^-(aq)$$

Sodium hydroxide

$$KOH(s) \xrightarrow{\text{Water}} K^+(aq) + OH^-(aq)$$

Potassium hydroxide

$$Ba(OH)_2(s) \xrightarrow{\text{Water}} Ba^{2+}(aq) + 2\ OH^-(aq)$$

Barium hydroxide

The reaction between equal amounts of $H^+(aq)$ and $OH^-(aq)$ to produce water results in disappearance of both the acidic and basic properties. This **neutralization** reaction can be represented by a total ionic equation. For the neutralization of hydrochloric acid, $HCl(aq)$, by sodium hydroxide, $NaOH(aq)$, the total ionic equation is:

$$H^+(aq) + Cl^-(aq) + Na^+(aq) + OH^-(aq) \rightarrow H_2O(l) + Cl^-(aq) + Na^+(aq)$$

Note that Na^+ and Cl^- ions appear on both sides of the equation. These are called **spectator ions** because they do not take part in the reaction. Omitting them from the equation leaves a **net ionic equation,** which shows only the reaction that takes place. The net ionic equation for this neutralization reaction is:

$$H^+(aq) + OH^-(aq) \rightarrow H_2O(l)$$

You can see why the acidic and basic properties of the reactants disappear. After neutralization, only water—a neutral substance—remains.

Why are some acids and bases harmful to skin, while others—including vinegar, sour milk, and citric acid—are safe for humans? In other words, what determines the strength of a given acid or base? We will explore this question in the next section.

Antacid tablets include bases that partially neutralize excess stomach acid. However, the highly reactive and toxic bases shown here are not used in antacid products.

C.2 STRENGTHS OF ACIDS AND BASES

Acids and bases are classified as strong or weak according to the extent they produce hydrogen ions, $H^+(aq)$, or hydroxide ions, $OH^-(aq)$, in water. When a "strong acid" dissolves in water, almost every molecule splits into a hydrogen ion and an anion. Nitric acid, for example, is a strong acid; formation of a nitric acid solution can be represented by this equation:

$$HNO_3 \xrightarrow{\text{Water}} H^+(aq) + NO_3^-(aq)$$

Virtually 100% of the original HNO_3 molecules form hydrogen and nitrate ions.

In a "weak acid" only a few acid molecules split into hydrogen ions and anions; most acid molecules remain as molecules in solution. Acetic acid, $HC_2H_3O_2$, is a weak acid. The equation for formation of an acetic acid solution is written:

$$HC_2H_3O_2(l) \underset{\text{Water}}{\rightleftharpoons} H^+(aq) + C_2H_3O_2^-(aq)$$

molecular form   ionized form

Vinegar is a dilute solution of acetic acid.

Some acids present in acid rain, such as sulfurous acid (H_2SO_3), nitrous acid (HNO_2), and carbonic acid (H_2CO_3), are weak. Others, such as sulfuric acid (H_2SO_4) and nitric acid (HNO_3), are strong.

See the Air unit, page 398.

A solution of acetic acid contains many more $HC_2H_3O_2$ molecules than H^+(aq) and $C_2H_3O_2^-$ (aq) ions. Note the double arrow written in the equation. One meaning of a double arrow is that the reactants are not completely consumed—the solution contains both reactants and products.

Ionic bases, such as sodium hydroxide, NaOH, and potassium hydroxide, KOH, are strong and highly caustic bases—their solutions contain only cations and OH^- ions. However, the concentration of OH^- ions in solution sometimes is limited by the low solubility of the base. Magnesium hydroxide, $Mg(OH)_2$, sometimes used as an antacid ingredient, is such a base.

A weak base common in the environment is ammonia, which forms OH^- ions in solution by this reaction:

$$NH_3(g) + H_2O(l) \rightleftharpoons NH_4^+(aq) + OH^-(aq)$$

Now it's your turn.

YOUR TURN

Acids and Bases

1. Hydrochloric acid, HCl, is a strong acid found in gastric juice.
    a. Write an equation for the formation of ions when this acid is dissolved in water.
    b. Name each ion.

2. Here are two acids are found in acid rain. For each, give the name and write an equation for formation of its ions in aqueous solution.
    a. H_2SO_4 (a strong acid): One of its ionization products is responsible for damaging buildings and monuments.
    b. H_2CO_3 (a weak acid): Decomposition of this acid gives the fizz to carbonated soft drinks.

3. Each of these strong bases has important commercial and industrial applications. Give the name of each and write an equation showing the ions formed in aqueous solution.
    a. $Mg(OH)_2$. This is the active ingredient in milk of magnesia, an antacid.
    b. $Al(OH)_3$. This compound is used to bind dyes to fabrics.

4. a. Write the total ionic equation for the reaction between HNO_3(aq) and $Mg(OH)_2$(s). This is one reaction that occurs when acid rain falls on the mineral magnesite.
    b. Write the net ionic equation for this reaction.

Under normal conditions, the pH of your blood rarely exceeds 7.45 or drops below 7.35. This fact appears quite remarkable, since large quantities of acid enter the blood daily. What chemical mechanisms does your body have to keep blood pH so constant? Read on.

C.3 ACIDS, BASES, AND BUFFERS IN THE BODY

Much of the acid that invades the human bloodstream comes from the carbon dioxide that cells give off as they oxidize glucose. Carbon dioxide reacts with water in the blood to produce carbonic acid, H_2CO_3.

$$CO_2(g) + H_2O(l) \rightarrow H_2CO_3(aq) \rightarrow H^+(aq) + HCO_3^-(aq)$$

The amount of carbon dioxide dissolved in the blood controls the concentration of carbonic acid.

Your body produces 10 to 20 moles of carbonic acid daily. Other acids, including phosphoric acid (H_3PO_4) and lactic acid ($CH_3CHOHCOOH$) are produced in the digestion of foods. Considering this continuous influx of acids, how does the body maintain a constant pH?

It uses chemical buffers. A **buffer solution** contains relatively high concentrations of a weak acid and a salt of that acid—or a weak base and a salt of that base. For example, citric acid (a weak acid) and sodium citrate (a salt of citric acid) form a buffer combination that is often found in commercial food products.

How does a buffer solution control pH? It contains an acid that can react with added base and also a base that can react with any added acid.

Earlier we saw that salts containing the OH^- ion are bases. The OH^- ion reacts as a base as follows:

$$H^+(aq) + OH^-(aq) \rightarrow H_2O(l)$$

Anions of weak acids act as bases in the same way, as shown below for bicarbonate ion (HCO_3^-).

A weak acid and its salt can buffer (protect) a solution against a large pH change caused by adding small amounts of acid or base. Here's how: If some base is added to a buffer solution, the buffer's weak acid neutralizes the base, preventing a large change in pH. If some acid is added to the solution, the buffer's weak base—the anion from the salt—neutralizes it, preventing a large change in pH.

The blood's primary buffer system is carbonic acid (H_2CO_3) and sodium bicarbonate ($NaHCO_3$). The addition of acid or base to this system results in these reactions:

$$H^+(aq) \quad + \quad HCO_3^-(aq) \quad \rightarrow \quad H_2CO_3(aq)$$

From added   Bicarbonate ion   Carbonic acid
   acid   acting as a base

$$OH^-(aq) \quad + \quad H_2CO_3(aq) \quad \rightarrow \quad HCO_3^-(aq) \quad + H_2O(l)$$

From added   Carbonic acid   Bicarbonate ion   Water
  base

The products become part of the buffer system that keeps the pH constant.

Other buffer systems also help maintain body pH balance. One involves the oxygen-carrying protein hemoglobin, a weak acid. Another is the phosphate buffer system composed of $H_2PO_4^-$ and HPO_4^{2-}.

Let's investigate buffer action in the laboratory. You will have the opportunity to witness the unique behavior of buffers, and build background to help explain your body's ability to maintain "friendly" pH levels in its systems.

The notion of a "buffer zone" between hostile nations is somewhat similar to a chemical buffer. Both involve the capacity to lessen the shock of any major change —either in strategic position or pH.

Which of these anions reacts as an acid with excess base and which reacts as a base with excess acid?

C.4 LABORATORY ACTIVITY: BUFFERS

Getting Ready

In this activity, you will prepare and test a carbonate buffer. Adding acid and base to water will be compared to adding acid and base to the buffered solution.

Your teacher will assign you to an "acid" group or a "base" group. Read the procedures below and prepare a data table. The table should contain five columns: original pH, pH after five drops of acid (base), initial volume of acid (base) in buret, final volume of acid (base) in buret, volume of acid (base) added.

Procedure

Acid Groups

WATER PLUS ACID

1. Fill a clean buret to above the zero mark with 0.50 M HCl. Briefly open the valve, letting solution run into a beaker until no air is left in the buret tip and the liquid surface is at or below the 0 mL mark. Record the volume.

2. Place 40 mL of deionized (or distilled) water in a clean 125-mL Erlenmeyer flask. Add 10 drops of universal indicator. Compare the color of the flask contents to the indicator scale. Record the pH.

3. Place the flask under the buret. Slowly open the buret valve and add five drops of acid to the flask. Swirl the flask. Record the pH of this unbuffered acidic solution. Retain this flask as a color standard for comparison with the buffered solution.

CARBONATE BUFFER PLUS ACID

4. Add 40 mL of 0.10 M NaHCO$_3$ solution to a clean 125-mL Erlenmeyer flask. Use a clean straw to blow your breath (containing carbon dioxide) into the flask for 3 min. You have now prepared the carbonate buffer. Discard the straw.

5. Add 5 drops of universal indicator. Swirl the flask. Record the solution color and pH.

6. Record the initial buret volume.

7. Add five drops of 0.50 M HCl from the buret to the flask and swirl. Record the color and pH.

8. Continue to add HCl solution until the color and pH are identical to those in the color standard flask from the water plus acid procedure above. Record the final buret volume.

9. Determine the volume of HCl solution added. Record this value.

10. Drain the HCl solution from the buret. Rinse the buret by pouring deionized or distilled water through it, allowing the water to drain into a beaker. Repeat this rinse step.

11. Wash your hands thoroughly before leaving the laboratory.

Base Groups

WATER PLUS BASE

1. Fill a clean buret to above the zero mark with 0.50 M NaOH. Briefly open the valve, letting solution run into a beaker until

no air is left in the buret tip and the liquid surface is at or below the 0 mL mark. Record the volume.

2. Place 40 mL of deionized (or distilled) water in a clean 125-mL Erlenmeyer flask. Add 10 drops of universal indicator. Compare the color of the flask contents to the indicator scale. Record the pH.

3. Place the flask under the buret. Slowly open the buret valve and add five drops of base to the flask. Swirl the flask. Record the pH of this unbuffered basic solution. Retain this flask as a color standard for comparison with the buffered solution.

CARBONATE BUFFER PLUS BASE

4. Add 40 mL of 0.10 M NaHCO₃ solution to a clean 125-mL Erlenmeyer flask. Use a clean straw to blow exhaled breath (containing carbon dioxide) into the flask for 3 min. You have now prepared the carbonate buffer. Discard the straw.

The 0.10 M designation means that each liter of solution contains 0.10 mol of NaHCO₃.

5. Add 5 drops of universal indicator. Swirl the flask. Record the solution color and pH.

6. Record the initial buret volume.

7. Add five drops of 0.50 M NaOH from the buret to the flask and swirl. Record the color and pH.

8. Continue to add NaOH solution until the color and pH are identical to those in the color standard flask from the water plus base procedure above. Record the final buret volume.

9. Determine the volume of NaOH solution added. Record this value.

10. Drain the NaOH solution from the buret. Rinse the buret by pouring deionized or distilled water through it, allowing the water to drain into a beaker. Repeat this rinse step.

11. Wash your hands thoroughly before leaving the laboratory.

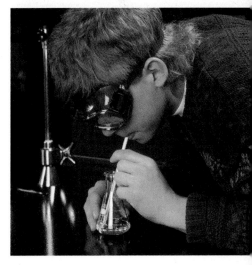

Preparing the carbonate buffer.

Questions

1. a. Did your carbonate buffer solution actually perform as a buffer?

   b. What observations support this answer?

2. a. Compare the volumes of acid needed to reach the same pH when added to water and to the carbonate buffer.

   b. Do the same for the base.

3. Write an equation showing how the carbonate buffer would prevent the pH of the blood from rising if a small quantity of base (OH⁻) were added.

4. A buffer is a solution of a weak acid and its salt, or a weak base and its salt.

   a. Classify each substance below as a strong or weak acid or base, or as the salt of a strong or weak acid or base.

      (1) KCl and HCl

      (2) NaOH and H₂O

      (3) NaNO₃ and HNO₃

      (4) NaC₂H₃O₂ and HC₂H₃O₂

   b. Now decide which one of these four pairs of substances would make the best buffer system.

C.5 pH IN BALANCE

Body pH balance is maintained even in many abnormal situations by the combined action of blood buffers, breathing rate, and the kidneys. Changes in breathing rate affect the concentration of dissolved carbon dioxide, which, we have seen, is a major source of acid in the blood.

Added in large enough concentrations, acid or base can overwhelm a buffer. In your body, the kidneys help prevent this, maintaining the body's pH balance on a day-to-day basis. They can excrete excess acidic or basic substances. They also provide a backup neutralization system for abnormal conditions. If the blood is too acidic, the kidneys produce the weak bases $HCO_3^-(aq)$ and $HPO_4^{2-}(aq)$ to neutralize it. If the blood is too basic, the kidneys neutralize it with the weak acids $H_2CO_3(aq)$ and $H_2PO_4^-(aq)$. The reaction products are eliminated in urine.

If blood pH drops and stays below 7.35, a condition known as **acidosis** develops. Mild acidosis can occur if the lungs temporarily fail to expel CO_2 efficiently, causing a build up of carbonic acid in the blood. The central nervous system is affected by acidosis, in mild cases causing mental confusion and disorientation. In extreme cases shock, coma, and even death can result.

When the pH of blood rises and stays above 7.4, **alkalosis** develops. Temporary alkalosis can occur after severe vomiting in which large amounts of hydrochloric acid (HCl) are lost from the stomach. Chronic alkalosis can produce weak, irregular breathing and muscle contractions. Severe alkalosis can lead to convulsions and death.

Apply what you have learned about pH balance in the body by completing this *Your Turn*:

Extreme physical exertion can cause body functions to become unbalanced temporarily.

YOUR TURN

Conditions that Affect pH Balance

1. Hyperventilation is a condition of forced, heavy breathing that typically occurs when an individual is frightened.
   a. How would this affect the concentration of CO_2 in the blood?
   b. How would this affect the blood's pH? (Fortunately, the body has an automatic response—fainting—that stops hyperventilation before serious damage is done.)
2. If you held your breath, how would this condition affect
   a. the concentration of CO_2 in the blood?
   b. the pH of the blood?
3. Strenuous muscle activity, such as long-distance running, can cause lactic acid to accumulate in the blood, resulting in a wobbly feeling in leg muscles. How would the accumulation of lactic acid affect blood pH?
4. Cardiac arrest occurs when the heart stops and blood circulation is halted, but cellular reactions

continue. When this occurs, doctors often inject sodium bicarbonate solution, $NaHCO_3$(aq), which contains the base HCO_3^-, directly into the heart muscle even before restarting the heart. (As depicted in television medical dramas, a doctor may order "sodium bicarb *STAT!*")

a. What effect would cardiac arrest have on blood pH? Why?

b. How would the injection counteract this effect?

5. What condition of acid-base imbalance might be caused by a large overdose of aspirin?

The Shell Game

Chicken eggshells are composed mainly of calcium carbonate, $CaCO_3$. The major source of carbon in the shells is carbon dioxide from the blood.

In summer, eggshells often become so thin that they easily break. Farmers solve this problem by feeding chickens carbonated (soda) water, water saturated with carbon dioxide. What causes the problem? How does soda water eliminate it? (*Hint:* Instead of perspiring, chickens pant to keep cool.)

We have explored the chemical composition of the human body and some mechanisms within it. It is time to explore some chemistry at the body's surface, where we have more control over what happens.

PART C: SUMMARY QUESTIONS

1. What is the difference chemically between
   a. an acid and a base?
   b. a strong acid and a weak acid?
   c. a strong base and a weak base?

2. You are given a sample of a mystery compound. You are told that the compound contains hydrogen. Can you conclude that the compound is an acid? Explain.

3. Describe the composition and function of a buffer system.

4. Name four conditions that can overload the body's buffer systems. In each case describe the chemistry of the overload and its effect on blood pH.

CHEMISTRY AT THE BODY'S SURFACE

Keeping clean may be important, but it is not always possible.

However, too much cleaning can damage the skin by removing too much natural oil and drying it out.

Keeping clean is important, not just for appearances, but for good health. Lack of cleanliness can even lead to infections, or to loss of teeth.

Considerable chemistry is involved in personal cleanliness, and it is—at least in large part—under your personal control. Understanding this important aspect of your body's "external chemistry" will help you make better decisions concerning your well-being.

First, let's consider the skin's surface and substances that can keep it clean—without damaging it.

D.1 KEEPING CLEAN WITH CHEMISTRY

Glands in human skin secrete important material, such as sweat and oil, onto the skin surface. These must be washed off fairly often, along with any dirt on the skin.

Have you ever wondered why a frog feels slimy? Glands in its skin secrete skin-moistening oils. Human beings also have glands to produce oils that keep skin flexible. Chapped lips show how uncomfortable a shortage of these oils can be.

The most obvious skin secretion is sweat. We sweat to keep our body temperatures at a constant level during hot or cold weather or during heavy exercise. Sweat—mostly water—is about 1% sodium chloride.

If sweat were just salty water, there would be little need to bathe with soap. However, areas of the body where sweat glands are concentrated also secrete the oils that produce body odors. These odors quickly become offensive as bacteria attack the oils.

So, keeping clean involves several tasks: removing dirt and grease we pick up from outside sources, and removing the sweat and excess oil from the skin before much bacterial action occurs. Mainly, though, skin cleaning involves removing oils and greases.

A variety of cleaning agents remove oil and dirt by dissolving them. For example, grease is highly soluble in a water solution of ammonia, NH_3(aq). That is why ammonia is an effective kitchen cleaner. Concentrated ammonia solutions are strong enough to damage human skin.

Water alone will not dissolve oil and grease. If you have mixed oil and vinegar (vinegar is a solution of acetic acid in water) to make salad dressing, you know why. Shake them all you want—when you stop, the oil and vinegar immediately start separating. Oil and water also fail to mix if you bathe or shower without soap. That is is why water—by itself—fails to clean your skin thoroughly.

To understand soap's cleaning ability, it is useful to review the molecular basis of solubility. The polarity of water molecules gives rise to hydrogen bonding between hydrogen atoms of one water molecule and oxygen atoms of nearby water molecules (Figure 3). Hydrogen bonds are much weaker than the covalent bonds that hold hydrogen and oxygen atoms together inside water molecules. But hydrogen bonds are strong enough to pull water molecules into clusters, causing water to "bead" on a flat surface. By contrast, nonpolar oil molecules are less attracted to each other. When water and nonpolar substances are mixed, hydrogen bonds hold the water molecules together so tightly that the nonpolar molecules are forced to form a separate layer.

Still, many substances do dissolve in water, because they are polar. Salt and rubbing alcohol are examples. Their ions or molecules are attracted to water molecules, so they fit comfortably among them.

Earlier you explored the meaning of "like dissolves like" and found that in general polar or ionic substances dissolve in water and nonpolar substances dissolve in nonpolar solvents. Compatible attractive forces are the key to solubility. As you will see, some large molecules can be soluble in polar solvents at one end and in nonpolar solvents at the other end.

Complete the following activity to review the connection between polarity and solubility.

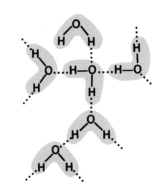

Figure 3 Hydrogen bonding in water.

See Water unit, pages 59–60.

Your Turn

Polarity and Solubility

1. Indicate whether each substance below is nonpolar, polar, or ionic. Then predict whether it is water-soluble or soluble in nonpolar solvents. Base your reasoning on bond polarity, charge, molecular shape, and the like-dissolves-like rule.
   a. NaOH, sodium hydroxide (a base used in making soaps)
   b. $(CH_3CH_2)_2O$, diethyl ether (an industrial solvent)
   c. CH_2OHCH_2OH, ethylene glycol (antifreeze)
   d. KNO_3, potassium nitrate (a fertilizer)
2. Ethanol (CH_3CH_2OH) is a water-soluble organic molecule. Its solubility in water is due to its small size and its polar —OH group, which allow for hydrogen bonding in water. Cholesterol ($C_{27}H_{46}O$), an animal fat associated with heart disease, is not water-soluble even though, like ethanol, it contains an —OH group.
   a. Why isn't cholesterol water soluble?
   b. Would you expect cholesterol to dissolve in nonpolar solvents? Why?

3. Consider the chemical structures of a fatty oil (a triglyceride) and glucose:

$$
\begin{array}{l}
\text{CH}_2\text{—O—}\overset{\displaystyle\overset{\text{O}}{\|}}{\text{C}}\text{—CH}_2\text{—CH}_2\text{—CH}_2\text{—CH}_2\text{—CH}_2\text{—CH}_2\text{—CH}_2\text{—CH}_3 \\
\text{CH —O—}\overset{\displaystyle\overset{\text{O}}{\|}}{\text{C}}\text{—CH}_2\text{—CH}_2\text{—CH}_2\text{—CH}_2\text{—CH}_2\text{—CH}_2\text{—CH}_2\text{—CH}_3 \\
\text{CH}_2\text{—O—}\overset{\displaystyle\overset{\text{O}}{\|}}{\text{C}}\text{—CH}_2\text{—CH}_2\text{—CH}_2\text{—CH}_2\text{—CH}_2\text{—CH}_2\text{—CH}_2\text{—CH}_3
\end{array}
$$

A triglyceride

$$
\begin{array}{c}
\text{CH}_2\text{OH} \\
\end{array}
$$

Glucose

a. Which will dissolve in water? Why?

b. Which will dissolve in gasoline? Why?

c. What is different about the two molecules?

4. Sodium lauryl sulfate, $CH_3(CH_2)_{11}OSO_3^- \ Na^+$, is a synthetic detergent. Do you think this compound is soluble in water? In oil? Explain your answer in terms of the rule "like dissolves like."

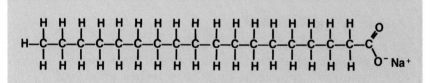

Figure 4 Sodium stearate, a soap. Commercial soaps are mixtures of structures such as these.

When it comes to solubility, skin cleaners, soaps, and detergents have split personalities. One end of each structure is polar and the other is nonpolar. For example, the long hydrocarbon chain in the soap sodium stearate (Figure 4) dissolves in oil but not in water. However, the oxygen atom at the other end of the structure has a negative charge, which is strongly attracted to polar water molecules.

Thus, sodium stearate and other soaps and detergents are strongly attracted to both water and oil. This enables wash water to remove oil and grease. The long, skinny molecules cluster around an oil droplet, with their water-insoluble ends pointing inward and their charged ends pointing out into the water (Figure 5). The oil-containing droplet enters the wash solution and is rinsed away.

Today, most people buy commercial soaps and detergents. In the nineteenth century, however, people often made their own

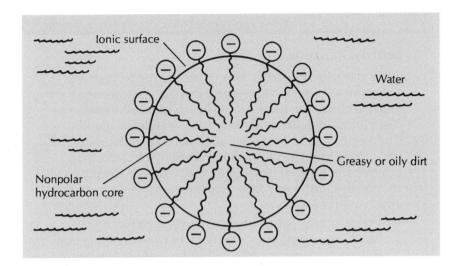

Figure 5 Spherical cluster of soap molecules in water. This is how soaps and detergents remove grease and oil from soiled surfaces.

Ionic surface

Water

Greasy or oily dirt

Nonpolar hydrocarbon core

soap from lye (sodium hydroxide, NaOH) and animal fat. Glyceryltripalmitate (a typical animal fat molecule) reacts with lye (a base) to form the soap sodium palmitate:

$$3\,NaOH + \begin{matrix} CH_3-(CH_2)_{14}-\overset{\overset{\displaystyle O}{\|}}{C}-O-\overset{\overset{\displaystyle H}{|}}{\underset{|}{C}}-H \\[2pt] CH_3-(CH_2)_{14}-\overset{\overset{\displaystyle O}{\|}}{C}-O-\overset{|}{\underset{|}{C}}-H \\[2pt] CH_3-(CH_2)_{14}-\overset{\overset{\displaystyle O}{\|}}{C}-O-\overset{|}{\underset{\overset{\displaystyle |}{H}}{C}}-H \end{matrix} \rightarrow 3\,Na^+\,{}^-O-\overset{\overset{\displaystyle O}{\|}}{C}-(CH_2)_{14}-CH_3 + \begin{matrix} H \\ | \\ H-C-OH \\ | \\ H-C-OH \\ | \\ H-C-OH \\ | \\ H \end{matrix}$$

Glyceryltripalmitate Sodium palmitate Glycerol

Because lye soap contains unreacted lye, it can damage skin.

Soap works because it is strongly attracted to both oil and water.

Benzoyl Peroxide and Acne

Acne pimples are small infections caused by bacteria that consume skin oil (sebum). During adolescence, many individuals produce too much skin oil. Dead cells can clump together and close the pores in oil glands. The key to controlling mild acne is to keep the skin very clean and the pores open. Abrasive lotions help remove the layer of dead cells, dirt, and oil. Keeping hands and hair away from the face also helps keep dirt and bacteria away.

1. Preparations containing benzoyl peroxide, a mild oxidizing agent, also are effective in controlling acne (Figure 6). How would this kind of substance help?

2. In severe acne cases, doctors sometimes prescribe antibiotics. Why are they effective?

Most acne remedies offer only temporary relief; the only real cure for acne is to outgrow it.

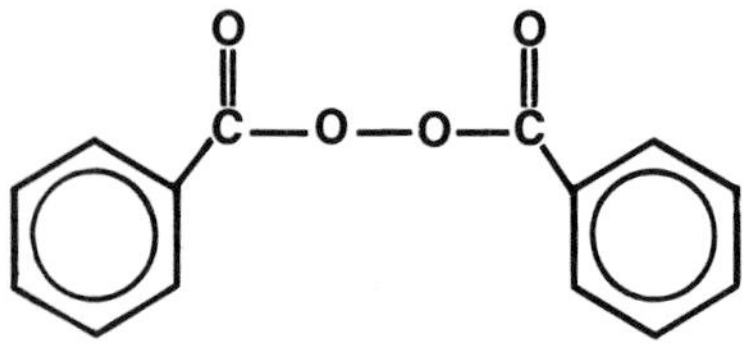

Figure 6 Benzoyl peroxide structure. This substance is used in controlling acne.

D.2 SKIN: IT'S GOT YOU COVERED

Skin represents both your body's contact with the outside world and your barrier against it. It protects you from mechanical damage and from bacteria. Skin helps keep your body temperature constant through sweating. Through the sense of touch, the skin offers an important source of information about the world. And it even plays a role in communicating human emotions.

Human skin, about 3 mm thick, has two major layers (Figure 7). The inner layer, the **dermis,** contains two kinds of protein fibers that give the skin strength and flexibility. Sweat and oil glands are located in the dermis, with tubes (ducts) leading to pores on the skin surface. Because all dermal cells are living, they must be supplied with blood.

Embarrassment is sometimes indicated, for example, by a facial blush.

If you bleed when your skin is scraped, the dermis has been reached.

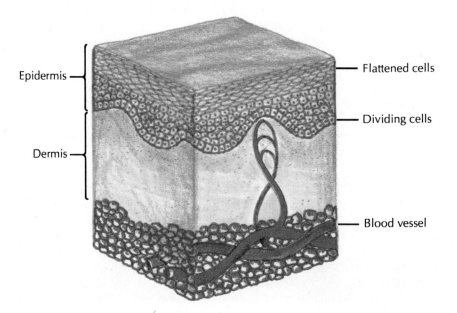

Figure 7 Human skin.

The cells of the dermal layer continually divide. This pushes some cells outward to form the **epidermis,** the skin's outer layer. As the cells are pushed outward, their nuclei die and their fluid is replaced by protein fiber. Oil secreted by glands in the dermis forms a protective film on the surface, keeping these dead cells soft, and preventing excessive water loss. This oily layer is slightly acidic, thereby protecting protein fibers that can be denatured by bases.

Older cells at the skin's surface continuously flake off in pieces which are usually too small to be visible. Dandruff is composed of dead epidermal cells that stick together, falling off in relatively large pieces. Some people waste considerable time and money trying to "cure" dandruff with germ-killing shampoos. Dandruff has nothing to do with germs. The best dandruff shampoos contain substances that prevent dead epidermal cells from clustering.

Maintaining healthy skin is a simple matter. Eat wisely. Keep clean, but don't overdo it. Too much bathing will remove all of your skin's oils, drying out and possibly damaging your skin. Most of all, avoid getting too much sun.

It may seem strange that skin cells should die and be replaced continuously. Can you think of a good reason why this should happen?

D.3 PROTECTING YOUR SKIN FROM THE SUN

The sun's radiation provides energy and light that we need and welcome, but its ultraviolet component can cause serious damage to exposed skin. The skin-darkening material that forms during a suntan is **melanin,** the same black pigment responsible for black hair and naturally dark skin. When an ultraviolet photon of suitable energy strikes a melanin-producing cell, it activates an enzyme that triggers the oxidation of the amino acid tyrosine. Less-energetic ultraviolet photons cause the modified tyrosine to form a polymer. The final melanin structure is a tree-like branching of chains of modified tyrosine.

The most immediate effect of excessive sun is sunburn. Even minimal sunburn injures cells and temporarily swells the dermal blood vessels. It may also increase the rate of cell division. A bad sunburn kills many cells. The skin blisters and the dermal cells divide more rapidly, thickening the epidermis.

Ultimately, tanning and particularly sunburning can lead to skin cancer. Scientists have conclusively linked nonmelanoma cancers to exposure to sunlight. About 300,000 U.S. citizens get nonmelanoma skin cancers yearly. Such cancers are rarely fatal. Melanoma skin cancers are also believed to be linked to excessive exposure to the sun. These cancers are much rarer, but are very often fatal.

Ultraviolet light and cancer are linked because of changes in cell molecules. Ultraviolet radiation is powerful enough to energize electrons in molecules, occasionally causing the molecules to break. These breaks are most threatening and destructive when they occur in DNA, the genetic-instruction molecules. Although cells have mechanisms to repair many of these breaks, if the breaks go unrepaired they can cause mutations in DNA. This kind of damage is greatest in rapidly-dividing tissue, since the mutations are quickly passed on to daughter cells. Skin cells, for

It is estimated that two of every three Australians will require treatment for at least one type of skin cancer in their lifetime. To urge greater protection from such skin damage, a "Slip! Slop! Slap!" campaign was launched in Australia—Slip on a shirt, Slop on sunscreen, and Slap on a hat.

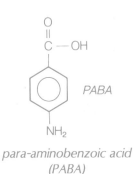

para-aminobenzoic acid
(PABA)

The Skin Cancer Foundation recommends the use of nothing lower than an SPF of 15, especially on the face.

Zinc oxide provides effective protection against solar radiation.

instance, are replaced monthly. Mutations caused by ultraviolet exposure are partly responsible for age spots, wrinkling, and general aging of skin. Eventually such mutations can lead to cancer.

Dark-skinned and tan individuals are more resistant than light-skinned people to the damaging effects of solar radiation. Melanin in the epidermis absorbs much of the sun's ultraviolet radiation, dispersing the energy and preventing it from damaging living, dividing cells below.

Good suntan lotions prevent both skin damage and tanning. The active ingredient that is used in many sunscreen lotions is **para-aminobenzoic acid (PABA).** The key to blocking ultraviolet radiation is the benzene ring in PABA. The benzene ring absorbs ultraviolet photons and spreads their energy among all six chemical bonds in the ring, converting it into harmless heat. In this way, ultraviolet photons are prevented from reaching the skin.

Sunscreens contain various concentrations of PABA. Table 3 describes the levels of protection provided.

Table 3   **SUN PROTECTION FACTORS (SPFs)**

Rating of Sun Protection Product	SPF Values	Protection
Minimal	2–4	Offers least protection; permits tanning. Recommended for people who rarely burn, but tan profusely.
Moderate	4–6	Offers moderate protection from sunburning; permits some suntanning. Recommended for people who burn minimally and tan well.
Extra	6–8	Offers extra protection from sunburn; permits limited suntanning. Recommended for people who burn moderately and tan gradually.
Maximal	8–15	Offers high protection from sunburn; permits little or no tanning. Recommended for people who burn easily and tan minimally.
Ultra	15 or more	Offers most protection from sunburn; permits no tanning. Recommended for people who burn easily and rarely tan.

You can explore the differences in sunscreen protection for yourself in the following activity.

D.4 LABORATORY ACTIVITY: SUNSCREENS

Getting Ready

In this activity you will observe the screening abilities of a series of oils or creams having different sun protection factors (SPFs, Table 3). The relative quantities of sunlight each allows to pass will be indicated by the effect on sun-sensitive paper. The papers exposed by these sunscreens will then be used to determine, by comparison, the sun protection factor of an unknown oil or cream.

The preparations to be tested will be spread on a transparent acrylic sheet that allows solar radiation to pass through.

The acrylic sheet by itself offers no SPF.

Read the Procedure below and prepare a data table in your notebook for recording your observations.

Procedure

1. Label four pieces of acrylic sheet with the SPF numbers of the four known samples. Label a fifth piece with the code number of your unknown.

2. Spread one drop of the appropriate oil or cream as evenly as possible over each acrylic sheet (but not on the labeled end).

3. Place the prepared acrylic sheets and two pieces of covered sun-sensitive paper in a carrying tray. Take the tray outside. (We assume the day is sunny!)

4. Lay the sun-sensitive paper on a flat surface, such as a sidewalk; place the pieces of acrylic on the paper. Write the numbers of the samples on the sun-sensitive paper next to each piece of acrylic.

5. Allow the samples to remain in the sunlight until the visible areas of the sun-sensitive paper fade to a very light blue color. This may take only a few seconds to as long as several minutes, depending on the sun's brightness.

Students performing laboratory activity.

6. Remove the acrylic sheets; quickly protect the print paper from the sun.
7. Return to the classroom, and record the relative shading provided by each preparation.
8. Wash your hands thoroughly before leaving class.

Questions

1. Compare the shading allowed by the unknown lotion with that allowed by the known lotions. Estimate the sun protection number for your unknown.
2. Suntanning is believed to be a major cause of skin cancer. However, most of us spend time in the sun anyway, trading off some probable future harm for the immediate pleasure of being outdoors, or of having a beautiful tan. Identify other trade-offs we make in everyday life that involve risks and benefits.
3. People with naturally dark skin have a lower incidence of skin cancer. Why?

Ultraviolet radiation has its dangers, but a little ultraviolet light is actually necessary for health.

D.5 GETTING A "D" IN PHOTOCHEMISTRY

Child labor laws subsequently ended this abuse.

During the Industrial Revolution in Europe, many children were forced to work indoors for as long as 12 hours daily. These children had little exposure to the sun. Many children developed **rickets,** a disease that caused their bones to become soft and easily deformed. Resting indoors only made the disease worse. Surviving victims frequently had bowed legs and other crippling disorders.

Doctors soon realized that children living outside cities rarely got rickets. City children with rickets were quickly cured if they were sent to the country. These clues eventually led to the discovery that sunlight prevented rickets. Scientists learned later that sunlight helps the body produce vitamin D from another compound, 7-dehydrocholesterol, which is present in all body cells (see Figure 8).

Figure 8 Sunlight produces vitamin D from a cholesterol relative. This is one example of how small differences in molecules may cause great differences in their behavior.

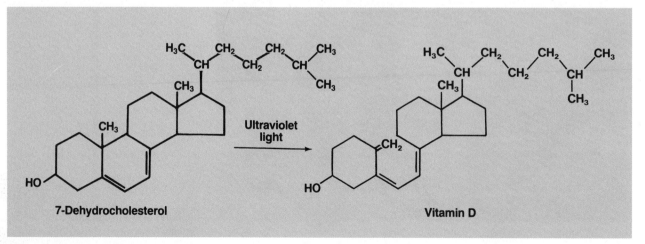

7-Dehydrocholesterol   Ultraviolet light   Vitamin D

Today hardly anyone gets rickets. The quantity of sunlight needed to prevent calcium deficiencies varies with the season and latitude. In Boston during the summer, for example, a daily 15-min exposure on the face alone is all that is needed to prevent rickets among Caucasians. In northern latitudes people of African descent suffer from vitamin D deficiency more often than Caucasians do. Can you explain this?

Additives in some foods also help prevent vitamin D deficiency. The body can convert these substances into vitamin D. For example, the ingredients listed on some milk cartons include the compound irradiated ergosterol, which has a chemical structure almost identical to that of 7-dehydrocholesterol. Today, doctors worry that the American diet may actually contain too much vitamin D. In excess it can cause unwanted calcium deposits, such as kidney and gall bladder stones.

D.6 OUR CROWNING GLORY

Among personal features in which people invest their time, money, and concern, hair ranks first for many individuals. It is—at various times—washed, waved, trimmed, bleached, curled or straightened, colored, cut, and combed.

Each hair grows out of a small, deep pocket in the scalp called a **follicle** (see Figure 9, page 444). Although hair is non-living fibrous protein, the growth of hair begins in living cells that are modified skin cells. These cells emerge from the bottom of the follicle, and move outward towards the surface of the scalp the way dermal cells move outward to become epidermal cells. But before they reach the surface, they die, leaving behind only the amino acid chains they have added to the bottom of the hair.

The structure of hair is quite complex, as shown in Figure 9 and Figure 10, page 444. A protein chain, **alpha keratin,** is the basic structural unit. Three coiled chains of alpha keratin form a supercoiled, three-strand rope; 11 three-stranded ropes make up

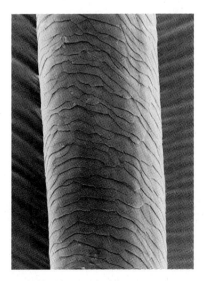

Magnified human hair (1,000✕).

Figure 9 Hair growing in a follicle.

Figure 10 The microscopic structure of a hair.

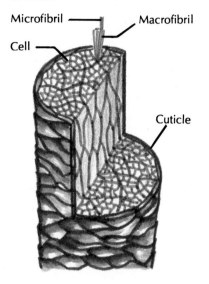

Microfibril — Macrofibril
Cell —
Cuticle

If hair lacks flexibility, it is regarded as brittle.

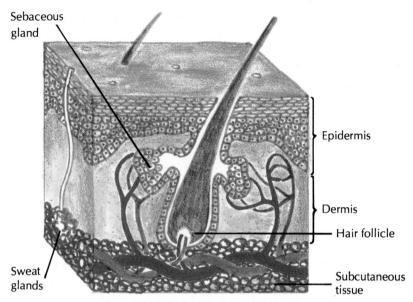

Sebaceous gland

Epidermis

Dermis

Hair follicle

Sweat glands

Subcutaneous tissue

a **microfibril.** Each hair is made of many bundles of microfibrils and is surrounded by a tough outer layer, the **cuticle.** The cuticle consists of several layers of flat cells that overlap like shingles on a roof.

Hair flexibility is due to the ability of protein chains in the cuticle layer to separate from one another, shifting position slightly without breaking. This flexibility makes it possible to style hair, but it can also lead to hair damage. You'll test the condition of your own hair as part of the following laboratory activity.

D.7 LABORATORY ACTIVITY: CHEMISTRY OF HAIR

Getting Ready

Healthy hair has a well-developed structure. Scalp oils and the hair's natural acid coating protect this structure. The same kinds of oil glands that lubricate skin keep the scalp and hair from drying out. In addition, oil helps protect the scalp from growth of bacteria and fungi. However, many agents can remove the oils, destroy the acid coating, and even damage the hair structure itself in extreme cases. Because hair is nonliving, it has no way to repair itself.

We use some damaging agents to satisfy our hair styling needs—that is, to change the structure of our hair and make it curly or straight. In Part 1 you will test the effectiveness of various solutions in altering hair's structure. In Part 2 you will test some observable characteristics of your own hair to determine its health.

Read Parts 1 and 2 and prepare two data tables, one for each part.

Procedure

Part 1: Effects of Various Solutions on Hair

For this part of the activity, you will be assigned to a four-student group. Each group member will be responsible for investigating the effect of one of these four treatments on a small hair sample:

Treatment A   pH 4, hydrochloric acid, HCl(aq)
Treatment B   pH 8, sodium hydroxide, NaOH(aq)
Treatment C   permanent wave solution
Treatment D   (1) permanent wave solution and
                 (2) permanent wave neutralizer

1. Obtain a hair bundle. Using a rubber band, securely fasten the hair to the end of a wooden splint as shown in Figure 11.

2. If you are completing Treatments A, B, or C, place 15 mL of your solution in a labeled test tube. If you are doing Treatment D, place 15 mL of permanent wave solution in one test tube and 15 mL of permanent wave neutralizer in a second tube. Label both tubes.

3. For Treatments A, B, or C, place a splint with hair in each solution for 15 min. For Treatment D, place a splint with hair in the permanent wave solution; allow it to remain for 10 min. Then rinse the hair under running water and place the splint in the test tube with the neutralizer for 5 min.

4. Begin work on Part 2 while the hair samples remain in the solutions as specified in Step 3.

5. After the specified times, remove the splints from the tubes and place them on paper toweling. Dab lightly with a folded paper towel to absorb excess moisture. Label the towel with the name of the solution in which the hair was immersed. Allow the hair to dry partially. (You can hasten drying with a light bulb or hair dryer.)

6. When the hair is fairly dry, remove the rubber band and carefully unwind the hair bundle from the stick. Do not disrupt the curl.

7. Compare the extent of curl in this hair sample with that observed in hair from the other three treatments. Rank the curliness of the four hair samples in 1–2–3–4 order, where "1" represents the curliest sample.)

8. Remove about six hairs from your hair bundle. Grasp each end of one hair and pull gently until the hair breaks. Repeat this test using a bundle of five hairs. Record your observations and share them with other members of your group.

9. Thoroughly moisten your bundle of hair under a gentle stream of tap water.

10. Squeeze out excess water from the hair by gently pressing as you pull the hair between two fingers. Do not squeeze or pull too hard.

11. Allow the hair to dry. (Again, you may hasten drying with a light bulb or hair dryer.)

12. Rank the extent of curl still present in each of the four hair samples.

13. Repeat the stretch test (Step 8) on one hair, and on a group of five hairs from your bundle. Record your observations and share with other members of the group.

Part 2: Testing Your Hair

1. Obtain a single 15-cm strand of hair from your head by clipping it with scissors. If you are courageous, you may elect instead to pull one hair from your head. If the hair is healthy, it will not break off, but will come out with its root, the little bulb at the end. If your hair has been colored, styled, permed,

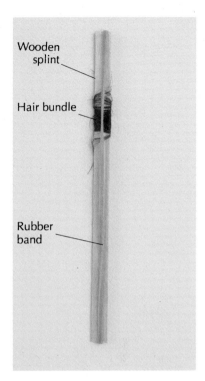

Figure 11 Hair bundle attached to wooden splint.

Wooden splint

Hair bundle

Rubber band

or otherwise treated, take your hair sample from just behind your ear. (This hair is least likely to have been affected by treatment.)

2. Hold one end of the hair sample between your thumb and index finger. Using your other hand, hold the hair between your thumbnail and index fingernail. Hold tightly as you slide your nails down the length of the hair—as though you were curling a gift ribbon.

3. Now hold the strand by both ends and gently pull. Stretch the strand for 15 seconds, then release and observe. If the curl is gone, your hair is structurally weak. The extent to which the curl returns indicates the relative strength of your hair structure. Record your observations.

STRETCH TEST

1. Obtain another single strand of hair from your head. Hold the strand ends between the thumb and index finger of each hand; stretch the hair gently. Do not jerk it. Healthy hair will stretch up to 30% (at average humidity), somewhat like a rubber band. Unhealthy hair has little or no stretch. A seriously damaged hair will break easily. Record the results.

2. Obtain another single strand of hair. Wet it with tap water. Repeat Step 1 with this wet strand.

3. If time permits, repeat Steps 1 and 2 with a single strand of hair donated by a classmate.

CUTICLE TEST

1. Hold a small bundle of your hair about 3 cm from your scalp with your thumb and finger.

2. Grasp the bundle near the outer end with the thumb and finger of the other hand, and pull your hand along the bundle toward your head. Record whether the hair strands pile up in front of your finger and thumb, or lie flat as your hand moves toward your head.

3. Wash your hands thoroughly before leaving the laboratory.

Questions

1. It takes more force to stretch coarse hair than fine hair. Why?
2. Explain the results of the cuticle test.
3. Is your hair healthy or damaged?
4. Which solutions were the best curling agents prior to rewetting?
5. Which solutions helped retain the curl after wetting?
6. Which solutions made the hair most brittle?
7. What combination of conditions cause the most damage to hair?
8. Propose a chemical explanation for the difference in the curl produced by water and that produced by permanent wave solutions.
9. Is an acidic or basic solution more damaging to hair? Why?
10. Permanent wave solutions are basic. Compare the results observed from treatment with sodium hydroxide solution and permanent wave solution.
11. How might you protect your hair after swimming and before sunbathing?

D.8 HAIR STYLING AND CHEMICAL BONDING

As we have seen (Figure 10), hair is made of intertwined protein chains. The individual chains are held in place by hydrogen bonding, ionic bonding, and disulfide bridges.

Hydrogen bonding is an unusually strong attraction between a polar (partially positive) hydrogen atom and a strongly electron-attracting atom like nitrogen or oxygen. Hydrogen bonding is depicted in Figure 12. In protein chains, the hydrogen atom in such a bond is usually covalently bonded to a nitrogen atom. The hydrogen atom is strongly attracted to an oxygen atom in a neighboring chain or in a folded-back portion of its own chain. All active proteins contain hundreds of hydrogen bonds closely spaced along their chains. The protein chains are held in their ball-like or sheet-like structures by these hydrogen bonds.

In many fibrous proteins, the chains do not remain fully extended, but are coiled, much like a "curly" telephone cord. Numerous hydrogen bonds keep the coils in place; others hold the chain to neighboring chains. Such protein coiling occurs in hair protein, as illustrated in Figure 13.

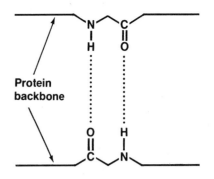

Hydrogen bonding

Figure 12 Hydrogen bonding between two chemical groups.

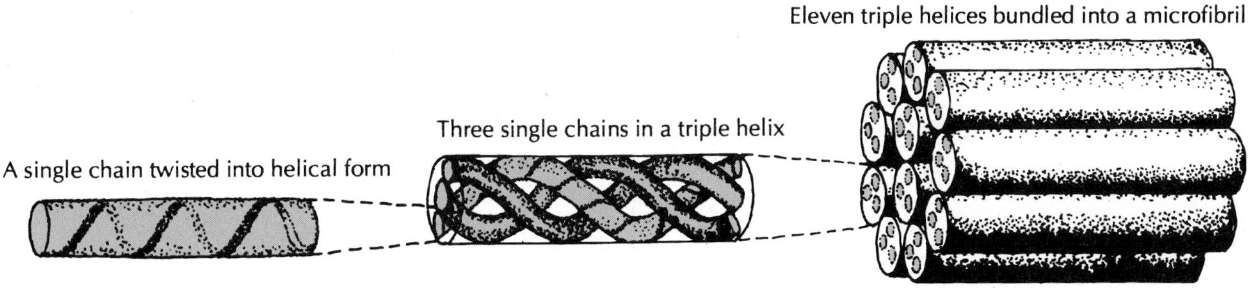

Eleven triple helices bundled into a microfibril

Three single chains in a triple helix

A single chain twisted into helical form

Figure 13 Hair keratin, a fibrous protein. The helical chains are twisted into a triple helix, and these helices are bundled into a microfibril. As shown in Figure 10, microfibrils form the core of each strand of hair.

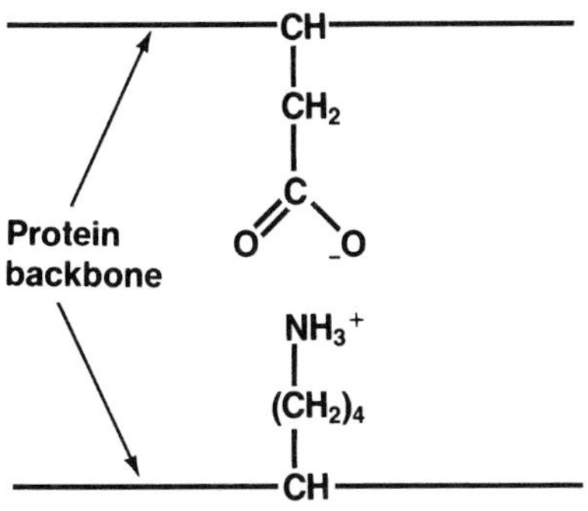

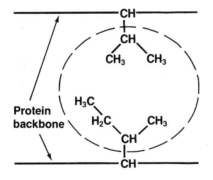

Ionic bonding

Figure 14 Ionic bonding, involving two chemical groups.

Nonpolar interactions

Figure 15 Interactions between two protein backbones involving nonpolar chemical groups, creating a region from which water molecules are excluded.

Ionic bonding (Figure 14) is an attraction between an ionic structure in one chain and an oppositely charged ionic structure in a neighboring chain or in a folded-back portion of the same chain. Such bonds are extremely important in hemoglobin, for example.

Nonpolar interaction (Figure 15) is a relatively weak attraction between nonpolar chemical groups. It often occurs in the

Hydrogen bonds, despite their importance, are considerably weaker than either covalent or ionic bonds. They can be more easily broken, as you will soon learn.

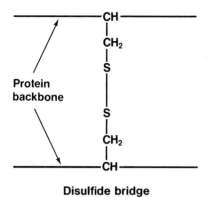

Disulfide bridge

Figure 16 Disulfide bond formed in cysteine (Cys) units.

interior of ball-like structures of globular proteins. Although weak, many such interactions help keep the structure intact, largely by preventing polar water molecules from entering.

Many proteins contain a few covalent bonds that link together neighboring chains or folded-back portions of the same chain. Most often these are disulfide bonds as illustrated in Figure 16.

Disulfide bonds between or within proteins can form between two sulfur-containing regions. The amino acid cysteine contains such an —S—H unit. Two cysteine residues can react at their —S—H units, losing hydrogen and forming a disulfide bond:

$$\sim\sim\sim S—H + H—S\sim\sim\sim \rightarrow \sim\sim\sim S—S\sim\sim\sim + H_2$$

Disulfide bonds provide the key to understanding the curling or straightening of hair. Hair styling is a matter of breaking bonds between protein chains and forming new ones. (If the protein chains do not form new bonds, the strands separate. This is one cause of split ends.)

Your laboratory work with hair confirmed what you already knew: If you wet your hair, it becomes easier to style. Here's why: Wetting your hair allows water molecules to break hydrogen and ionic bonds between hair strands. Water forms new hydrogen bonds with the side chains. Thus separated, the side chains no longer hold the strands tightly in their natural position. As you comb your hair, the strands are free to slide into new positions. When the water evaporates, these side branches form new hydrogen or ionic bonds in their new positions, locking the chains in whatever position they happen to be.

Solutions that are too acidic can permanently weaken hair. Even after the hair dries, some excess hydrogen ions may remain bonded to the side chains, preventing them from forming new ionic bonds.

Heat applied with blow-dryers and curling irons helps style hair quickly, because the higher temperatures speed up interactions between protein strands. But excessive heat can disperse hair oils, and even split protein chains.

The problem with the hair styling methods described so far is that once hair is wet again, their effects are quickly erased. To get a waterproof hairstyle—a permanent—it is necessary to rearrange bonds that are not affected by water. These are the covalent bonds of the disulfide bridges.

The curliness of your hair depends on how disulfide links between parallel protein chains are joined. When hair undergoes a

Figure 17 (a) Parallel protein chains before treatment, held in place by disulfide bonds. (b) A chemical reaction (reduction) breaks disulfide bonds and adds hydrogen atoms. Chains are now free to move relative to each other. (c) The hair is curled or straightened. (d) A chemical reaction (oxidation) reforms disulfide bonds between relocated chains.

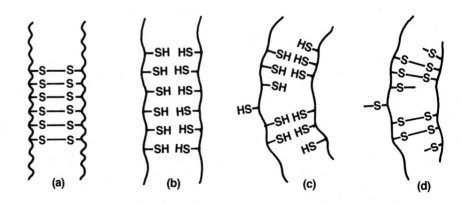

permanent, curls are created or removed in three steps. Here's the chemical recipe: First, break the disulfide links between protein chains. Next, use a form to curl or uncurl the hair. Third, rejoin the disulfide links between protein chains in their new orientation. Figure 17 illustrates the process.

A knowledge of protein chemistry helps explain the effects of hair treatments.

CHEMQUANDARY

A Permanent Permanent?

Could repeated chemical treatments either to curl or straighten your hair alter the hair permanently?

As you have learned, chemistry and chemical reactions are responsible for much of what happens inside and outside your body. In the next part of this unit, you will learn how body chemistry can be altered by drugs and how it responds to toxic substances.

PART D: SUMMARY QUESTIONS

1. a. What substances are removed during proper skin cleansing?
    b. Why must they be removed?
    c. What problems result from excessive skin cleansing?
2. Predict which of these materials would be soluble in water and which must be washed away with soap or detergent.
    a. Salt (NaCl), a component of sweat
    b. Non-diet soft drink (essentially sugar water) spilled on your hands
    c. Grease on your hands from eating french fries with your fingers
    d. Rubbing alcohol (70% 2-propanol, isopropyl alcohol, in water).
3. Explain the action of a soap or detergent in washing.

4. What are the functions of your skin?
5. Describe the chemical process of tanning.
6. Briefly describe the link between tanning and skin cancer.
7. Describe how a sunscreen protects the skin.
8. Describe the symptoms of rickets. How is this disease prevented?
9. Why does healthy hair stretch somewhat like a rubber band?
10. Explain the difference in stretch between dry and wet hair.
11. Explain the different effects water and permanent wave solution have on hair structure.

EXTENDING YOUR KNOWLEDGE (OPTIONAL)

•   Why is dark skin an advantage for people living in tropical countries? Why is light skin a disadvantage?

•   Investigate the causes and mechanism of formation for malignant melanoma, a serious form of cancer.

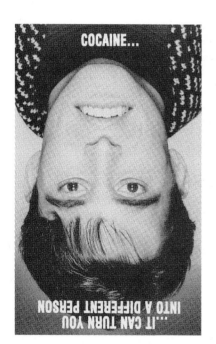

COCAINE...

"...IT CAN TURN YOU INTO A DIFFERENT PERSON

CHEMICAL CONTROL: DRUGS AND TOXINS IN THE HUMAN BODY

As the science of synthetic organic chemistry has advanced, many medicines have emerged. These substances have helped alleviate much illness and suffering. Life for many has become much more enjoyable than it might have been. But rather than relieving suffering, some substances have contributed to it. Drug addiction is present in every segment of society.

What are drugs? How do they work? Are they totally foreign to the human system? What does the body do to save itself from their negative effects?

E.1   A GLIMPSE OF DRUG FUNCTION

Drugs alter body or brain chemistry. In this sense, aspirin, amphetamines, crack, caffeine, nicotine from cigarettes, and the powerful painkiller morphine are all drugs. However, drugs differ

Most communities provide help and information regarding drug-related problems.

greatly in strength and effect. Some stimulate or depress the brain. Others relieve pain or stop infection. Still others make up for chemical deficiencies. All act at the molecular level, most often within a specific area of the body.

Toxins, by contrast, all harm the body. Sodium cyanide (NaCN), carbon monoxide (CO), dioxin, polychlorinated biphenyls (PCBs), and the potent nerve poison strychnine are all toxins. Chemical toxins, like drugs, function at the molecular level in the body. The difference between a drug and a toxin is often a matter of dose. Any substance, even water, can become toxic at too large a dose. An overdose of morphine can cause death by shutting down the respiratory system, but is a useful anaesthetic in very small doses.

Once transported to its action site in the body, how does a drug function? Drug specificity, like enzyme specificity, often depends upon molecular shape. Many drugs act on *receptors*— regions on proteins or cell membranes with just the shape and chemical properties needed to interact with the drug molecule and help it initiate the desired biological response.

As an example, consider adrenaline. which is produced naturally by the body. Adrenaline is used in many nasal drops and sprays used for relief of severe allergic symptoms. When you are suddenly frightened, the adrenal gland releases adrenaline. This hormone circulates in the bloodstream, activating the heart and other organs. Settled at its receptor sites, adrenaline initiates a cascade of reactions that prepare the body in various ways for the physical activity of "fight or flight." (It increases heart rate, for example.) A model of an adrenaline molecule at its receptor is shown in Figure 18.

To further illustrate drug action, let's look at some drugs that relieve intense pain. Classified as a *narcotic analgesics,* these include morphine, meperidine, and methadone. Analgesics relieve pain by blocking nerve signals from the pain source on their journey to the brain. Blocking occurs if drugs of the right shape and composition interact with receptors on proteins in the membranes of key brain cells. The drug molecule distorts the shape of the membrane protein enough to block the pain signal.

The receptor sites for narcotic analgesics appear to have these features:

- a negative ion site that can bind an ammonium ion (NH_4^+) or its equivalent
- a flat surface to which a flat cyclic group of atoms (an aromatic group) can bind
- between these, a cavity into which a chain of atoms connecting the aromatic group and the ammonium ion may fit

All potent analgesics studied thus far either have the shape needed to allow bonding to this receptor or can adopt it.

One might wonder why brain cells have receptors of just the right type for morphine-like drugs that are foreign to the body. It has been found that the brain's own natural painkillers, called *endorphins* and *enkephalins,* act at these same receptors.

Although the structural formulas of morphine and endorphins or enkephalins do not look much alike to the untrained eye (Figure 19, page 452), in fact several parts of the molecules are identical. These parts are believed to be a key to the action of these painkillers.

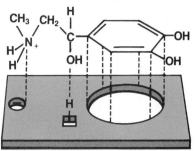

Figure 18 An adrenaline molecule at a receptor.

Ionic bonding   Hydrogen bonding   Nonpolar attractions between flat areas

The opium poppy is the source of morphine and other narcotic drugs. In medicine, these drugs are extremely valuable in helping control pain; on the street, they bring pain to addicts and their families.

Chemical Control: Drugs and Toxins in the Human Body / **451**

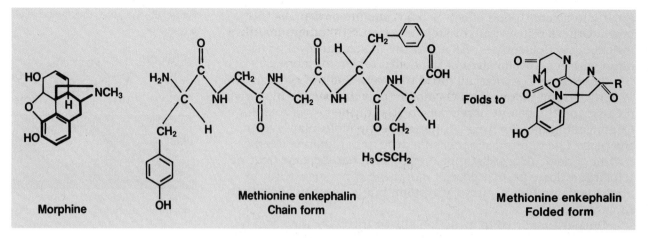

Morphine

Methionine enkephalin Chain form

Folds to

Methionine enkephalin Folded form

Figure 19 Morphine and an enkephalin, both painkillers. The protein chain of the methionine enkephalin (*Tyr-Gly-Gly-Phe-Met*) folds into a shape similar to that of morphine, a shape that fits the body's painkilling receptors.

Morphine and other narcotic analgesics are used in cases of severe or enduring pain, but for common aches and pains we use another kind of painkiller.

E.2 YOU DECIDE: PROS AND CONS OF ASPIRIN

The most widely-used pain killers belong to the family called the **salicylates.** Acetylsalicylic acid, commonly known as aspirin, is the most familiar. Aspirin is a versatile drug. It can reduce fever and swelling or inflammation, and it relieves pain.

Acetyl salicylic acid

Salicylic acid

Aspirin is an example of a drug made more useful by chemical modification. Originally it was made of salicylic acid, which produced severe irritation of the mouth and upper digestive tract. To reduce such irritation and help the molecule pass more rapidly into the blood and to appropriate target areas, chemists tried changing the molecular structure of salicylic acid. However, some changes rendered it useless as a drug. Others created unwanted side effects. When the H of the —OH group was replaced with an acetyl group, —CO—CH₃, chemists found what they wanted. This modification produced a drug that, although imperfect, has been a valued medication for nearly a century. Many other drugs have been tailored similarly to do specific jobs in the body.

Aspirin is a drug with highly beneficial uses. At low doses—usually one tablet daily—it can help prevent heart attacks. Normal doses of two or more tablets reduce pain and fever. In most cases it is regarded as completely safe. However, it has a few side effects.

It can induce bleeding ulcers and may promote fluid retention by the kidneys. And, since aspirin is an acidic compound, some people may get an upset stomach if they take it. High, prolonged doses of aspirin may cause loss of balance and slight hearing loss. Several studies have suggested an association—not a cause-effect link, but a possible connection—between aspirin and Reye's syndrome. This rare but sometimes fatal disorder sometimes affects children and teenagers recovering from influenza or chicken pox.

"Reye" is pronounced "rye."

Doctors may prescribe eight aspirin tablets or more daily for an arthritis sufferer. Imagine that *your* joints ached constantly, limiting your activity. Aspirin could relieve the pain.

1. Would you take the aspirin? In other words, would you prefer to live with the pain, or with the treatment's possible side effects?
2. If you decide to take aspirin, what might be done to counteract some of the long-term side effects?
3. Non-aspirin pain relievers such as ibuprofen (in Nuprin, Advil, Medipren, and others) and acetaminophen (in Datril, Tylenol, and others) are also available without prescription.
   a. What information would you obtain to decide whether any of these medications would be preferable to aspirin for arthritis?
   b. Where might you get this information?
4. Why should you take any medications only when they are really needed?

E.3 YOU DECIDE: EFFECTS OF ALCOHOL

Not all drugs act at specific receptors, as morphine and endorphins do. Alcohol appears to act on all or many neurons (nerve cells). It depresses transmission of nerve signals. This can slow down functioning of the entire brain.

The effect of alcohol on a person's behavior varies with the amount consumed, the individual's weight, and elapsed time since the alcohol was consumed. Table 4 (page 454) presents data for estimating the percent alcohol in the blood and lists the effects of various blood alcohol levels on behavior. For this table, it is assumed that the drinks are consumed within 15 minutes. One "drink" is defined as a bottle of beer, a glass of wine, or a shot (one ounce) of whiskey or other 86-proof liquor. To find the change in the blood alcohol percent over time, subtract 0.015% for each hour.

In most states, the legal alcohol limit for automobile driving is 0.10% (0.10 g of alcohol in 100 mL of blood). Driving with lower blood alcohol levels does not guarantee safe motoring. A study of 13,000 drivers revealed that the probability of causing a traffic crash doubled at a blood alcohol level of just 0.06%. The National Highway Traffic Safety Administration classifies a vehicle crash as alcohol-related when alcohol can be detected at any level in the driver.

1. If a 125-lb person consumes two bottles of beer, predict the individual's blood alcohol level if it is
   a. measured immediately.
   b. measured after two hours.
2. List two kinds of behavior you might observe in an individual having a blood alcohol level of 0.15%.
3. If a 175-lb person has six drinks in rapid succession and drives an automobile one hour later, will the individual be considered legally intoxicated in most states?

Table 4　　　　　　　　　**ALCOHOL IN THE BLOOD**

No. of Drinks	Blood Alcohol Level (Percent)* Body Weight (lbs)						
	100	125	150	175	200	225	250
1	0.03	0.03	0.02	0.02	0.01	0.01	0.01
2	0.06	0.05	0.04	0.04	0.03	0.03	0.03
3	0.10	0.08	0.06	0.06	0.05	0.04	0.04
4	0.13	0.10	0.09	0.07	0.06	0.06	0.05
5	0.16	0.13	0.11	0.09	0.08	0.07	0.06
6	0.19	0.16	0.13	0.11	0.10	0.09	0.08
7	0.22	0.18	0.15	0.13	0.11	0.10	0.09
8	0.26	0.21	0.17	0.15	0.13	0.11	0.10
9	0.29	0.24	0.19	0.17	0.14	0.13	0.12
10	0.33	0.26	0.22	0.18	0.16	0.14	0.13
11	0.36	0.29	0.24	0.20	0.18	0.16	0.14
12	0.39	0.31	0.26	0.22	0.19	0.17	0.16

Effect on Behavior	
Blood Alcohol Level (%)	Behavior
0.05	Lowered alertness; reduced coordination
0.10	Reaction time slowed 15–25%; visual sensitivity reduced up to 32%; headlight recovery 7–32 seconds longer
0.25	Severe disturbance to coordination; dizziness; staggering; senses impaired
0.35	Surgical anaesthesia; reduced body temperature
0.40	50% of people die of alcohol poisoning

*Data from MADD

4. If a 100-lb person consumes 10 drinks in rapid succession, will the individual be in any danger of death?

5. How long should a 200-lb person who has consumed three drinks wait before driving an automobile?

E.4　NOTES ON SOME OTHER DRUGS

Cocaine, like alcohol, acts on neurons, altering the transmission of nerve signals in several parts of the brain. It functions as an anesthetic by blocking the channels through which sodium ions move in and out of neurons. Without that movement, pain signals cannot be transmitted. It also interferes with the transmission of impulses between neurons. At the same time, it produces a "high", or euphoria. The biological basis for its euphoric effects are only partly understood. Cocaine can cause brain hemorrhages, dangerous increases in blood pressure, and even death.

Crack is a purified—and considerably more addictive—form of cocaine. Its addictiveness is due to the fact that crack is more potent than cocaine. Users often smoke crack in 10–15 minute "binges" over several hours, which can lead to addiction after the first use.

Ice is composed of rocklike crystals of methamphetamine, a central nervous system stimulant. This highly addictive and dangerous drug gives the user the same general effects as crack

Fatal doses of cocaine can range from as low as 20 mg to 1 g.

cocaine when smoked. However, unlike crack, ice produces a high that lasts for hours rather than minutes. Illegal methamphetamine manufacture is a $3 billion industry.

Designer drugs are the products of laboratory-based chemical reactions, involving the creation of new substances that, although structurally similar to legal drugs, produce the effects of drugs of abuse. Most designer drugs are narcotics or hallucinogens, going under such names as Ecstasy and China White. Although they are derived from legal substances, such designer drugs carry the same risks and dangers as illegal drugs.

Anabolic steroids have received public attention and notoriety due to their apparent ability to enhance athletic performance—mainly through stimulating growth of lean muscle mass. They are chemical variants of testosterone, the hormone that imparts masculine physical traits to individuals. Overuse of these drugs carries risks of kidney and liver damage, liver cancer, and heart disease. The use of anabolic steroids is formally outlawed for all athletes. Despite this, random checks of athletes continue to reveal some cases of steroid abuse in international competitions, college athletics, and professional sports.

Given all the damage that drugs and foreign substances can do within the body, you might wonder how we manage to survive. Fortunately, the body is not defenseless.

In the 1960s, intravenous injections of methamphetamine were known as "speed." Its use led to the street slogan "speed kills."

It is possible to detect traces of steroids at a concentration of one part per billion (ppb).

E.5 FOREIGN SUBSTANCES IN THE BODY

Your body has a number of defense mechanisms that help protect you from toxic substances and disease-causing organisms. For example, the membranes that cover body surfaces, including the lining of the digestive tract and the lungs, resist infection by most disease-causing organisms. These membranes also protect you against invasion by many chemicals in the environment. The acid in gastric juice (pH 1–2) also helps destroy many microorganisms in the stomach before they can enter the bloodstream.

These external defenses are backed by internal defenses. Let's look at two of them: how the liver detoxifies the blood, and how the body deals with the presence of foreign proteins.

Until actually absorbed, a substance is considered external, even if it is within the digestive or respiratory tract.

Detoxification in the Liver

Some digestion of foods and other swallowed substances takes place in the stomach, but most occurs in the small intestine. Digested food, other small molecules, and some ions pass through the lining of the small intestine into the blood, where they are carried directly to the liver. Undigested material and molecules or ions that do not pass through the intestinal wall proceed to the large intestine and are eliminated from the body. Some toxic substances that enter the stomach are removed from the body in this way.

The liver also separates useful from harmful or undesirable substances. Useful substances—including glucose and other simple carbohydrates, amino acids, and fatty acids—are released to the blood for general circulation to cells that need them. Some of these molecules are retained by the liver: glucose, which is stored as glycogen, the body's reserve carbohydrate; and amino acids, which are converted to proteins for use in the blood.

Some harmful or undesirable substances separated by the liver are eliminated from the body directly. Carried in bile from the liver to the intestines, they join other waste matter.

Other harmful substances undergo reactions in the liver that make them less toxic and more soluble in water. In this form they are more easily eliminated by the body. A typical chemical alteration in the liver is the conversion of benzene (not very water soluble) to catechol (water soluble):

$$O_2 + \text{⬡} \xrightarrow{\text{Enzyme}} \text{⬡—OH, OH}$$

Benzene   **Catechol**

Another typical reaction is the conversion of sulfite—a poison—to sulfate:

$$2\,SO_3{}^{2-}(aq) + O_2(aq) \xrightarrow{\text{Enzyme}} 2\,SO_4{}^{2-}(aq)$$

Sulfite ion   Sulfate ion

The enzyme catalyzing this reaction contains molybdenum ions. Without tiny amounts of these ions in the liver, many foods would poison us. The liver also chemically alters and eliminates many hormones and drugs that accumulate in the blood.

The liver's ability to detoxify materials is limited. Excessive ingestion of harmful substances can place a heavy burden on it. As a result, liver function may be diminished, which can cause problems in distribution of essential molecules—glucose and amino acids—and in synthesis of important proteins. Overburdening the liver also can result in the accumulation of harmful molecules in the body's fat reserves.

The liver is the body's largest internal organ; it is extremely important. In many ways it saves us from our bad eating, drinking, and perhaps even drug-taking habits. But it can take only so much abuse before damage occurs.

Defense Against Foreign Protein

In most cases, foreign proteins enter the body as part of disease-causing agents such as viruses, bacteria, fungi, and parasites. Body chemistry depends so strongly on having exactly the right protein at the right spot at the right time that any invader protein is a signal to marshal a defense against the potential harm it might do. The body's defense strategy, carried out by its immune system, involves building a protein that surrounds part of the invader molecule. Once surrounded, the invader cannot react to cause harm.

Any foreign protein that sets this defense mechanism in motion is called an **antigen;** the complementary substance created by the body to destroy the antigen's activity is an **antibody.** Figure 20 illustrates the action of antibodies. Formation of an antigen-antibody complex precipitates the invader from solution in the blood or other body fluids and allows it to be destroyed or otherwise removed by the body's waste disposal system.

Building antibodies with exactly the right complementary protein is no easy task. In your body, only certain kinds of white blood cells can do it. Once such cells learn to build a specific antibody, they can easily make more of the same. This is how you

Molybdenum is one of the trace minerals essential to human nutrition. See the Food unit, page 257.

Figure 20 Antibodies precipitate invading molecules.

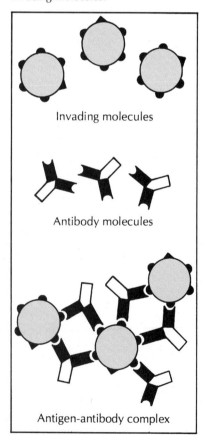

Invading molecules

Antibody molecules

Antigen-antibody complex

develop immunity to certain bacterial and viral infections. Once the blood has been exposed to a certain kind of bacteria, some of its white cells can henceforth rapidly synthesize the antibodies needed to destroy the bacteria. A person then has acquired an immunity to the disease caused by that bacterium.

Unfortunately, the body cannot protect itself against all disease-causing agents. The human immunodeficiency virus (HIV) is one of these agents. A person with HIV may develop acquired immunodeficiency syndrome, more commonly known as AIDS.

Once inside the body, HIV selectively enters cells that coordinate the work of the immune system, including those cells that manufacture antibodies. HIV can remain inactive within cells for an indeterminate period. During this time, an infected person may not be aware of the presence of the virus, but is capable of transmitting it to others. When the virus becomes active, the effectiveness of the immune system becomes compromised. Soon, the immune system is too depleted to defend the body against a host of opportunistic infections. Opportunistic infections are those infections that occur in a person whose immune system is already damaged.

The number of people exposed to HIV is growing. Research into vaccinations to prevent HIV infection before it occurs, and to find a cure for those already presenting symptoms of AIDS, is underway.

HIV exposure most frequently occurs through unprotected sexual intercourse, needles shared by intravenous drug users, and transfusions with improperly screened blood products. HIV can also be transmitted from infected mothers to babies before or during birth. People who engage in unprotected sex or who share unsterilized needles are at relatively high risk for contracting the virus. Some hemophiliacs and others receiving blood transfusions have contracted HIV because someone having the virus has donated blood.

In 1990, the World Health Organization estimated that about 10 million people worldwide were infected with the AIDS virus.

Certain conditions (such as Kaposi's sarcoma and Pneumocystis carnii infections) are found only rarely in persons with intact immune systems.

From June, 1981 to the end of 1990, over 160,000 AIDS cases had been reported in the United States alone. During the same period more than 100,000 AIDS-related deaths were reported.

Although every effort is made to screen blood products intended for medical use, the screening has not been 100% effective.

E.6 DRUGS IN COMBINATION

The effect of some combinations of drugs is simply a sum of the desirable actions of each (e.g., aspirin for a fever and an antibiotic for an infection). Other mixtures produce mainly undesirable effects. Some drugs interfere with each other. For example, the antibiotic tetracycline kills bacteria by binding free iron and other important ions in your system. This makes these ions unavailable to bacteria that need them. If you take iron tablets to compensate for anemia (iron-poor blood) and your doctor prescribes tetracycline at the same time, you could lose the benefits of both. The tetracycline may bind to the iron from the tablets, putting both tetracycline and iron out of commission.

Some combinations of drugs are deadly. When a medication is prescribed for you, it is essential to tell the doctor about any other drugs you are taking. Also, it is wise to understand the trouble you can get into by mixing drugs on your own.

One of the deadliest combinations is alcohol and sedatives, which include tranquilizers, sleeping pills, and the addictive street drugs known as "downers." Sedatives slow brain activity.

AIDS virus attacking a cell of the immune system.

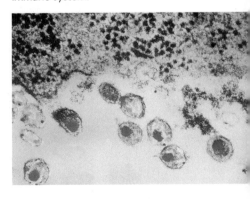

AIDS Aide

By Dennis Creech
Tacoma Tribune *Staff Reporter*

Today, patients and health care professionals work together as a team to make personal decisions important to the health of the patient. Physicians now view the body as a whole, not just as a particular disease, and recognize that understanding the patient contributes to healing.

Family practice physician Jeff Olliffe of Seattle, Washington, is a self-employed practitioner who specializes in treating patients who have the human immunodeficiency virus (HIV). People who are concerned about whether they have been exposed to HIV arrange an office visit to consult with Jeff. Risk factors for HIV exposure include unprotected sex, intravenous drug use, and transfusions with improperly screened blood products. Together, Jeff and the patient assess the patient's risk of infection. If a patient tests negative for HIV antibodies, Jeff advises them on how to stay that way. If a patient has HIV, then Jeff offers counseling on how to stay healthy and avoid transmitting the virus. Contracting the HIV virus does not mean that a patient has AIDS.

Eventually, a patient with HIV may develop acquired immune deficiency syndrome (AIDS). In this case, Jeff treats the symptoms, provides emotional support, and gives antibiotics to prevent opportunistic infections. Jeff gives his patients hope. He tells them that there is not yet a

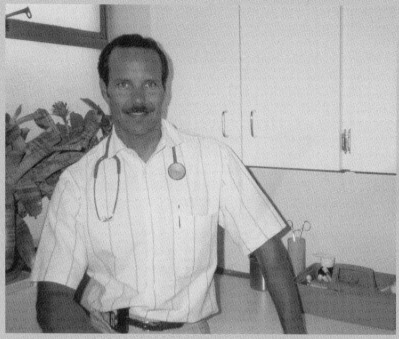

Photo by Brent Schmidt

cure for AIDS, but with life-prolonging treatments the quality of a patient's life can be improved, both psychologically and physically. Jeff is also responsible for claiming disability benefits for his patients. He assesses the patient's capabilities and needs so that the patient can get home health care and other social and health care services.

Jeff is a dedicated and compassionate health care professional. It is difficult for him to distance himself emotionally from his patients, especially when one of them dies. Jeff's own physical exercise routine is important in helping him cope with the depression brought about by

treating terminally ill patients. On the other hand, Jeff gets enormous satisfaction out of remedying patient illnesses, or solving psychosocial problems. Jeff knows that he is improving the quality of his patients' lives.

Jeff uses biochemistry and pharmacology in his work daily. For example, he needs to understand the physiological and chemical interactions of the body with medicines. He graduated with a B.A. in biology, with a minor in psychology, in preparation for medical school. After obtaining his medical degree, Jeff performed an internal medicine internship followed by a family practice residency.

They act by retarding communication between nerve cells. Like the interaction of air pollutants in smog, combining alcohol with sedatives or certain other drugs is **synergistic**—the total effect is greater than that of either drug alone. Together, sedatives and alcohol can so depress nerve activity that even involuntary functions, such as breathing, may stop. The lethal dose of a barbiturate (e.g., phenobarbital) is decreased by 50% when it is combined with alcohol.

See the Air unit, page 392.

The tranquilizer diazepam (the active ingredient in Valium) and alcohol is also a frequently toxic combination. Even antihistamines and alcohol can cause excessive drowsiness that can result in accidents, and the combination of narcotic analgesics and alcohol can upset control of body movements. In short, it is dangerous to combine alcohol and *any* drug.

E.7 CIGARETTE USE

To smoke or not to smoke is one of many decisions you must make that will influence your health. In 1964, about 40% of the U.S. population smoked. In 1990 that figure had dropped to less than 30%. Total sales of cigarettes peaked in 1982 and have declined gradually since then. However, smoking among U.S. adolescent females has increased by about 55% since 1968.

Some argue that there is still considerable uncertainty about the dangers of smoking. In many other decisions that affect health there is even more uncertainty. Later in this unit, you will learn more about how scientists evaluate risks, and about making risk-related decisions in the face of uncertainty.

Smoking is like puffing on a smokestack. Inside the glowing tip of a cigarette the temperature soars to 850° C, setting off chemical reactions that produce more than 3600 substances.

Carbon monoxide in the smoke severely reduces the blood's ability to carry oxygen to the cells. By reacting with hemoglobin 200 times faster than oxygen does, it forms bonds with hemoglobin's iron ions, preventing them from picking up and carrying oxygen. The body responds to this reduction in oxygen carriers by increasing the number of red blood cells. This thickens blood and puts stress on the heart.

Tars from smoke accumulate in the lungs. In an effort to clear the tars, the enzyme elastase is activated. While digesting tars, the enzyme also appears to digest lung membranes, scarring the lungs and reducing their ability to transfer oxygen gas to the blood. Emphysema often results.

Carbon monoxide in the blood of a pregnant woman seems to have a detrimental effect on the fetus. No one knows precisely how smoking damages the fetus, but there is no doubt that the fetus is deprived of necessary oxygen.

Numerous compounds in tobacco and smoke can cause cancer. Among these are nitrosamines and polycyclic aromatic hydrocarbons (PAHs), examples of which are given in Figure 21. The presence in smoke of carcinogenic compounds and other highly reactive materials means heavy smokers run a high risk of getting cancer.

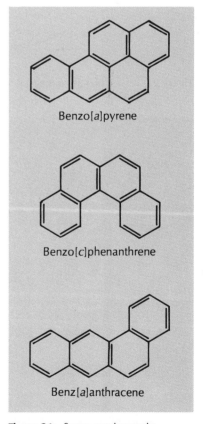

Benzo[a]pyrene

Benzo[c]phenanthrene

Benz[a]anthracene

Figure 21 Some carcinogenic compounds found in cigarette smoke. These are all polycyclic aromatic compounds.

E.8 LABORATORY ACTIVITY: CIGARETTE USE

Getting Ready

In this experiment you will observe the effects of cigarette smoke on a living organism. *Euglena* is a one-celled organism found in water; it "swims" by moving a thread-like projection (a flagellum).

Part 1 provides a procedure for creating a smoking apparatus and trapping particles from the smoke. Your teacher may, instead, choose to provide pre-smoked cigarette filters to use in the test with *Euglena*. In this case, you will do only Part 2.

Procedure

Part 1: "Smoking" the Cigarettes

In this part you will trap particles from the smoke of a nonfiltered, high-tar cigarette and a filtered, lower-tar cigarette and note any differences.

1. Set up the apparatus shown in Figure 22.
2. Turn on both aspirators.
3. Light the cigarette. Adjust the aspirator flow so that smoke is drawn through both chambers and none escapes into the room. Allow the cigarette (but not its filter) to burn completely.
4. Turn the aspirators off when no smoke is visible in either chamber.
5. Wearing disposable gloves, open each chamber and use forceps to remove the cotton. Place each piece of used cotton on

Figure 22 Apparatus that simulates cigarette smoking.

To aspirator

Upper chamber

To apparatus

To aspirator

Trap for water from aspirator

Rubber hose

Cotton for smoke drawn from lit end of cigarette

Plastic tube

Funnel

Cigarette

Rubber tubing

Glass tubing

Lower chamber

To aspirator

Cotton for smoke drawn from unlit end of cigarette

Rubber hose

a paper towel. Label the towel with the cigarette brand and whether the cotton is from the upper or lower chamber. Do not touch the material deposited on the cotton.

6. Repeat Steps 1–5 with a second cigarette.

7. Observe each cotton sample and record.

Part 2: Euglena Test

1. Wearing gloves, use forceps to pull off a wad (about the diameter of a quarter) of the cotton stained by the smoke coming from the upper chamber during smoking of one of the cigarettes.

2. Place the cotton wad in a 50-mL beaker and add 5 mL of water. With your forceps, press the cotton into the water and stir carefully until the water becomes stained brown with the smoke residue.

3. Place a drop of *Euglena* culture on each of two microscope slides and cover with a cover slip. Observe and record the natural swimming movements under the microscope.

4. Place two drops of the residue-containing solution on the *Euglena* culture on one of the slides and replace the cover slip. Observe and record the movements on this slide under the microscope.

5. Thoroughly rinse your dropper. Repeat Part 2 with a wad of cotton stained from the lower chamber of the cigarette.

6. Wash your hands thoroughly before leaving the laboratory.

Questions

1. Compare the appearance of each piece of cotton from one cigarette. Does it appear that less smoke residue comes from one end than the other?

2. Compare the cotton from the upper chamber during smoking of the two cigarettes. Do filtered, low-tar cigarettes appear to have less residue, as their makers claim?

3. Compare the movements of the *Euglena* on the treated and untreated slides.

Decision making is a part of everyone's life.

E.9 YOU DECIDE: SMOKING?

Smokers often say they derive pleasure from smoking. But evidence indicates that smoking is dangerous, too. U.S. Secretary of Health and Human Services Louis W. Sullivan has remarked, "Cigarettes are the only legal product that, when used as intended, cause death."

Some of that evidence is summarized below. How much risk would you be willing to endure, to gain whatever feeling of well-being smoking might offer?

• Smoking is the leading cause of preventable death in the U.S. In 1988 alone, more than 430,000 Americans died from smoking-related causes—more than a thousand deaths daily.

• According to the U.S. Centers for Disease Control, every year smoking causes more than 100,000 lung cancer deaths, 200,000 deaths due to cardiovascular disease, over 80,000 respiratory disease deaths (including emphysema), and 30,000 deaths due to other forms of cancer.

The second-largest cause of preventable deaths in the U.S. is alcohol.

- Smoking is estimated to shorten a person's life by an average of 18 years.
- Passive smoking—the day-to-day exposure of nonsmokers to cigarette smoke—is the third leading cause of preventable death in the U.S. Annually, it causes nearly 4,000 lung cancer deaths and about 32,000 heart disease deaths.
- Smoking during pregnancy exerts direct growth-retarding effects on fetuses. Babies born to women who smoke during pregnancy have (on average) 200 g less mass than do babies born to nonsmoking women.
- About 2,500 infant deaths yearly in the U.S. are due to mothers who smoke.
- The health of smokers can be greatly improved by quitting. After quitting, risks of health problems caused by smoking decline steadily for about 15 years, until the risk of death becomes nearly the same as those who never smoked.

Even in light of this evidence, some claim there is still no proof that cigarettes cause problems. All these statistics may be due to coincidence, they say.

It is up to you to decide who you will believe, and act accordingly. Scientists often need to make decisions in the face of uncertainty. In such cases, one strategy is to minimize the consequences of making a wrong decision. That is, scientists think through the consequences of each choice, *assuming the choice turns out to be incorrect.*

You can complete such a risk-benefit analysis for yourself. List the risks and benefits of these two decisions:

Option 1: You decide not to smoke.
Option 2: You decide to smoke.

Analyze all positive and negative factors that might influence either decision. Be prepared to discuss your choice with the class.

PART E: SUMMARY QUESTIONS

1. a. How are narcotic analgesics, such as morphine, believed to work in the brain?
    b. How are these like the brain's own painkillers?
2. a. Describe the effect of alcohol on nerve cells.
    b. Compare that with the effect of cocaine on nerve cells.
3. Give two reasons why you should be sure your doctor knows about all medications or drugs you are taking.
4. Should the fact that you are taking medication make any difference in your eating and drinking habits? Explain.
5. Describe at least four chemical processes that occur regularly in the liver.
6. a. List some ways the body deals with toxic substances.
    b. Why is it apparently unable to deal with the AIDS virus?
7. List the effects of cigarette smoke on lung tissues and on the circulatory system.

EXTENDING YOUR KNOWLEDGE (OPTIONAL)

- A few folk remedies for illnesses are effective. Chemical studies have shown that there is a molecular basis for their action. One example is the use of willow bark in treating pain. Look into the chemistry of folk remedies, and find why many are successful.
- Prepare a library report on some hazardous food-drug interactions.

PUTTING IT ALL TOGETHER: ASSESSING RISKS

F.1 RISKS FROM ALCOHOL AND OTHER DRUGS

Identifying key underlying causes of early death and assessing your own risk from these factors are important in improving your chances to live out your natural life span.

To assess your risk of having a heart attack, you can consider your family's medical history, your diet, your weight, and other personal habits such as smoking or exercise. With preventing heart attacks in mind, you might decide to modify your diet, lose weight, or exercise more. However, there is no guarantee that these changes can prevent a heart attack. This is one of many aspects of health that you cannot fully control.

You can't decide not to have a heart attack.

You can control some health risks to a greater degree. You *can* decide whether or not you will drink alcoholic beverages or take mind-altering drugs. As you know, the use and abuse of these substances is a grave concern for individuals, families, and society.

Below is a sampling of information obtained from reliable studies of alcohol and drug abuse. Use this information to assess risks you and your classmates may face as you contemplate your future. (In the next section you will use these facts in a risk-evaluation exercise.)

The Alcohol, Drug Abuse, and Mental Health Administration estimates that the total yearly cost to the nation of drug and alcohol abuse is as much as $175 billion.

Summaries of Studies

Alcohol

- Drivers who have been drinking are involved in over half of all highway deaths in the United States.
- Alcohol is directly or indirectly responsible for nearly 100,000 deaths yearly in the United States.
- Alcohol-related accidents are the number one cause of death among teenagers.
- Possible impairment due to alcohol abuse includes high blood pressure; diseases of the liver, pancreas, and intestines; blackout periods (long intervals during which there is no memory), severe vitamin deficiencies, cardiovascular damage, and neuroses.

- About 15 million Americans suffer from alcoholism or alcohol dependency. This is more than five times greater than total number of cocaine or crack users, and 30 times greater than all U.S. heroin addicts.
- Alcohol use extracts a cost in the U.S. of $15 billion in medical expenses and $117 billion in lost worker productivity annually.
- The life expectancy for heavy drinkers is an estimated 10–12 years shorter than that for the general public.
- Alcohol consumption during pregnancy can cause serious physical and mental deficiencies in children, known as Fetal Alcohol Syndrome (FAS). Drinking during pregnancy is a major cause of mental retardation in the U.S.
- Children of alcoholics are three to four times more likely to become alcoholics.

Mind-altering Drugs

- Possible impairment due to marijuana use includes decreased visual perception, loss of fine muscle control, headaches, dizziness, vomiting, and hallucinations. Evidence indicates genetic damage, lung damage, and lowered immune response, but cause-effect links have not been firmly established.
- Marijuana smoke may contain higher concentrations of cancer-causing substances than does tobacco smoke.
- Possible impairment due to cocaine use includes nasal ulcers; mental confusion, paranoia, and hallucinations; severe depression between doses (contributing to need for more); brain hemorrhaging and permanent changes in brain chemistry; lowered immune response; overdose death.
- The post-euphoric effects of cocaine appear to activate brain depression centers, thereby creating a desperate need to continue its use. This makes cocaine use addictive, like heroin.
- The suicide rate among users of heroin, barbiturates, and related drugs is five times higher than normal.

F.2 PERSONAL CONTROL OF RISK

How much can you reduce the risk of dying prematurely? How much can society help reduce your risk of premature death? To decide, it is necessary to know what causes human fatalities, and what, if anything, can be done to control those causes. You will evaluate risk factors in this activity.

1. Divide a piece of graph paper into four quadrants. Label the resulting chart as illustrated in the sketch in the margin.

2. Using common sense and current knowledge, select the quadrant in which to place each cause of death listed on page 465. For example, suppose "major earthquake" were on the list. It might be controllable (you could avoid living in earthquake-prone areas), but if work and family ties are sufficiently strong, you may be forced to stay in such an area. In this case, "major earthquake" would be located in the "no" column. And, the risks due to an earthquake are more known than unknown—if a major earthquake occurs there is some chance that you might be killed or injured. Therefore, the point should be in the "risk known" row. Thus "major earthquake" would be placed as shown in the diagram.

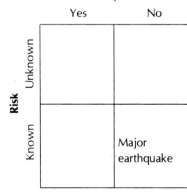

3. Form a group of students.
   a. Compare your chart with those of other group members. Try to reach agreement on where each cause of death should be located.
   b. Prepare a consensus chart, representing your group's combined ideas.
   c. Write reasons for your group's placement of each cause of death.
4. a. Review the information in Section F.1 on health risks involved with drinking alcoholic beverages and taking mind-altering drugs.
   b. Make a personal estimate of the risk of death or severely diminished quality of life that could be caused by alcoholic beverages and mind-altering drugs. Assign each a position on your chart.
   c. Compare your placements with those of other group members. If possible, reach agreement regarding the locations of these two new points. Add the data to the consensus chart prepared in Step 3.
   d. Write reasons for your group's placement of the two new points.
5. Are any of your four chart quadrants still empty? If so, think of five other causes of death in our society that belong in each empty quadrant. (It might help to recall causes of death discussed in previous units.)
6. If you were to work toward decreasing total fatalities in the United States during the coming year, in which quadrant(s) would you be able to help make the largest reductions? Why?
7. a. Examine the causes of death classified on the chart as "risk unknown." How can science help reduce fatalities from these causes of death?
   b. Examine the causes of death you have classified as uncontrollable. How might society help reduce fatalities from these causes?
8. What additional information would help you complete this exercise?

Selected Causes of Death in the United States

Stroke	Motor vehicle accidents
Cancer	Smallpox vaccination
Tornado	Appendicitis
Poison	Electrocution
Smallpox	Tuberculosis
Homicide	Emphysema
Lightning	Heart disease

F.3 LOOKING BACK

This unit has given you a variety of perspectives regarding your body's continuous encounters with chemistry—both internally and externally. Some observers have noted that we live in a chemical world. Since everything (that is, every *thing*) is composed of chemical substances, such a remark cannot be challenged. However, this unit has emphasised that we are *more* than just inhabitants of a chemical world. Our bodies are also active parts of that world.

In taking control of your personal health and well-being, you face both decisions that are clear-cut and decisions that involve considerable uncertainty. As this unit has illustrated, many of the health-related choices you encounter can be clarified and guided by a knowledge of the chemistry involved.

There is much you can do individually to control your health, life span, and well-being. Choose wisely!

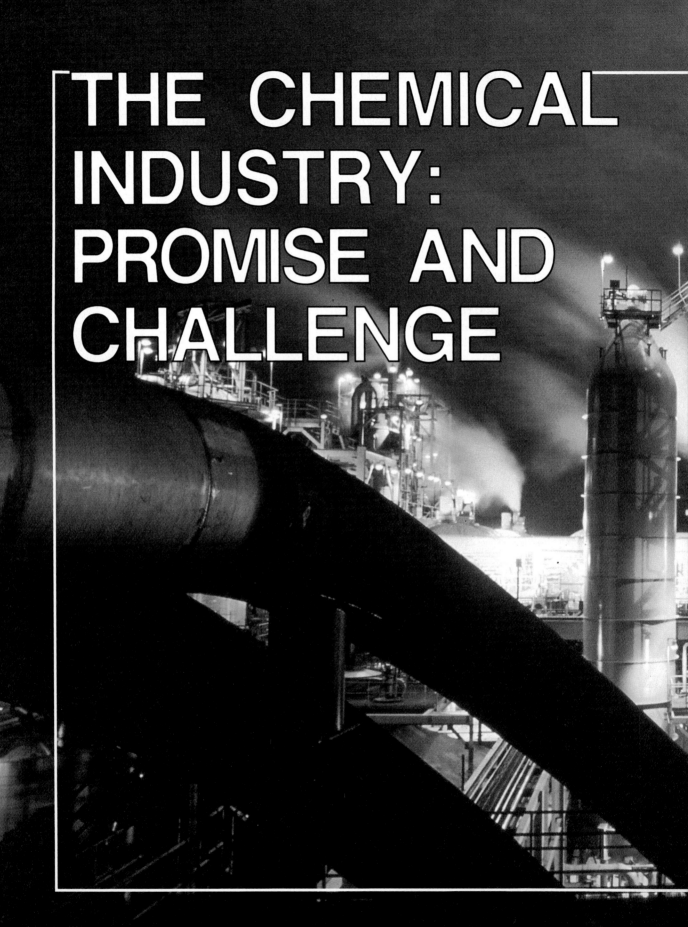

THE CHEMICAL INDUSTRY: PROMISE AND CHALLENGE

- What are the major activities, products, and services of the chemical industry?

- Do contributions by the chemical industry outweigh potential risks?

- What should be the role of chemical industry as a responsible social partner?

- What responsibilities does the public have in this partnership?

INTRODUCTION

An industrial firm is seeking permission from the Riverwood Town Council to build a chemical manufacturing plant on the edge of town. The plant would manufacture ammonia (NH_3) to sell as a fertilizer and to use in producing other substances. The prospect of jobs for Riverwood citizens has aroused favorable comment from some townspeople, but others are concerned that a chemical plant might reduce the quality of life in Riverwood.

The town's Industrial Development Authority has participated in meetings with EKS Nitrogen Products Company officials for several months. EKS is impressed with the advantages of locating a chemical manufacturing plant near Riverwood. The community has a stable, well-educated workforce, access to abundant electrical energy, a favorable tax base, excellent railroad and highway access, and an appealing lifestyle.

However, representatives of the Industrial Development Authority and EKS realize that community acceptance of the company would be important to the success of the project. EKS officials have arranged a series of public information meetings at Town Hall regarding the new plant and how it would affect the community.

Chemical Plant Proposed for Community

By Gary Franzen
Staff writer of Riverwood News

Riverwood officials and representatives of the EKS Nitrogen Products Company have met for several months to discuss the possibility of establishing a chemical plant in the city. This is the first major industry to propose locating in Riverwood. In six months, a Riverwood referendum will determine whether the company will be allowed to build the plant. Plans for the proposed plant were unveiled to townspeople last night at a special Town Hall meeting.

The Delaware-based company is the nation's third-largest producer of nitrogen-based chemicals. EKS's primary products are ammonia and nitric acid. EKS uses these as starting materials for a variety of other products, most notably nitrogen-based fertilizer and explosives. EKS also sells ammonia and nitric acid to other chemical companies. The proposed plant would produce ammonia and fertilizer.

Mayor Edward Cisko welcomed the plant as a boost to the town's economy. He noted that, following a town council recom-

Continued on page 2

Continued from page 1

mendation, he had formally invited the company to consider locating a plant in Riverwood. EKS Public Affairs Director Jill Mulligan said the plant would provide at least 200 new jobs. Recent layoffs at the sawmill have raised Riverwood's unemployment level to 7%.

Riverwood Environmental League members questioned the wisdom of locating a chemical plant nearby. Spokesperson Aaron Fosa expressed concerns regarding air quality, possible chemical spills, and waste disposal problems. He suggested that jobs could be created by other industries that might offer fewer potential problems.

Mulligan acknowledged that some chemical companies have previously contributed to such problems. But she said that many companies, including EKS, maintain well-controlled, clean operations. "EKS's Environmental Division continuously monitors processes and equipment to ensure the safest and most pollution-free operation possible. No industry is without risks. Knowing how to handle possible problems is an important part of any operation," Mulligan said.

Citizen reaction to the proposed plant was mixed. "I've got car payments and house payments to make," said Carson Cressey, an unemployed millworker. "Our savings won't last much longer. I hope I can get a job at that chemical plant."

"Unemployment has really cut into my business," said Cynthia Shapiro, owner of the sporting goods store. "I had to lay off my assistant. A new employer in town would help get things going again."

"If it's going to smell like the kitchen when my parents wash the floor, I don't want the plant," said ten-year-old Bobby Burns. "I hate the smell of ammonia!"

The schedule and location of public meetings with EKS representatives will be announced tomorrow.

A NEW INDUSTRY FOR RIVERWOOD?

Throughout the earlier *ChemCom* units you discovered that chemistry is concerned with the composition and properties of matter, changes in matter, and the energy involved in these changes. This unit will present examples of how chemical industries apply basic chemical principles to produce material goods and services.

The business of the chemical industry is to change natural materials in ways that make them more useful. Few people have observed such changes as they take place, or have even considered what is involved in making a useful product. This creates an aura of mystery about how chemical industries operate, how products are manufactured, and what to expect from a chemical plant. However, the industry is an important partner in modern society.

This unit will offer you the opportunity to plan, with the industry, for the future. You will begin by reviewing how the chemical industry helps address basic human needs and where the industry may be heading in coming years.

A.1 BASIC NEEDS MET BY CHEMISTRY

Since the early days of civilization, chemistry has been used to help meet a range of human needs. In colonial Massachusetts, as in other coastal colonies, seawater was evaporated to obtain salt used to preserve fish and cure hides. Fireplace ashes were washed to obtain potash (potassium hydroxide, KOH), used to make soap and candles from animal fats. In general, chemical technologies in earlier days were rather simple. They were on a small scale and were used to satisfy basic survival needs.

As chemical knowledge increased, better use was made of natural resources. New products and processes were created to satisfy basic survival requirements and to provide additional comfort and convenience. This is especially evident in chemical technologies developed over the past 50 years. During this period the chemical industry has grown from a few small companies producing a very limited range of basic products to hundreds of companies producing over 60,000 different products, forming the nation's third largest manufacturing industry. Only the machinery and electrical equipment industries are larger than the

The enormous pharmaceutical industry has been one result of applied chemistry.

chemical industry. Indeed, if food and petroleum industries are included, the chemical industry is the world's largest.

Products of Chemistry

All industries exist to supply needed products or services. Industries must do this in ways that enable them to pay employees and debts, support activities in research and development (R&D), marketing, plant maintenance and enhancement, and still deliver products to consumers at a net profit.

The chemical industry's range of products can be classified into three general categories of materials, based on their identities and intended uses:

- *Basic chemicals.* This category includes acids, bases (alkalies), salts, and common organic compounds. About one-fourth of the total value of U.S. chemical industry shipments are in this category.
- *Chemical products used in further manufacturing.* Included here are products such as pigments, plastic materials, and synthetic fibers. This category includes about one-fifth of total value of U.S. chemical industry production.
- *Finished chemical products.* These materials are either (a) for ultimate consumption (e.g., drugs, detergents, cosmetics), or (b) for materials and supplies in other industries (e.g., paints and building materials for the construction industry, and fertilizers for agriculture). Over half the total value of the nation's chemical industry production is for finished chemical products.

Firing porcelain toilets. Chemistry continually provides products that can contribute to making life easier and more pleasant.

Contributions of Chemistry

What areas of human activity and need are served by the chemical industry? The following summary highlights today's major contributions and some plans and expectations for the future.

New processes. In 1990, despite the nation's overall $76 billion trade deficit, the U.S. chemical industry generated a $16.5-billion positive trade balance—that is, significantly more product was exported than imported. Continued international competitiveness depends on constant improvements in existing processes and introduction of new ones. Advances in chemical catalysis and synthesis will give us, for example, tougher ceramics which will be able to withstand mechanical shock, high temperatures, and corrosive atmospheres. They will replace metals in many materials. Also emerging are composites—lightweight building materials to make aircraft, cars, homes, and appliances more energy-efficient and affordable.

More energy. Our country's energy needs are currently met primarily by fossil fuels—petroleum, coal, and natural gas. Ninety-two percent of the nation's energy production is based on chemical technology; this will remain true well into the twenty-first century. However, as fossil fuel supplies become less abundant and more costly, new chemistry-based energy sources will have to be tapped. Effective control of their use and reactivity will be needed to protect the environment and to provide energy at reasonable cost.

Availability of food. To provide adequate nutrition for the world's increasing population, improvements are needed in food production and preservation, in soil conservation, and the use of photosynthesis. Biotechnology holds promise for enhanced food

The nation's chemical industry has maintained a positive trade balance for over 50 years.

A Japanese supertrain.

Canning tomatoes. The food industry uses chemistry to improve the appearance and prolong the shelf life of many foods.

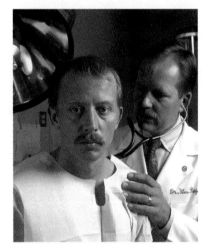

An AIDS patient with his physician. New drugs hold promise for those infected with the HIV virus.

The arthritic joint in this finger has been replaced by ceramic material, allowing normal movement.

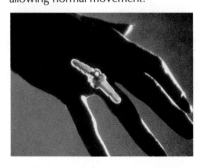

production through genetically-modified plants. In collaboration with workers in related scientific disciplines, chemists continue to play a central role in clarifying the chemistry of biological systems and life cycles. Such knowledge will enable the food industry to provide improved products and services, minimizing hunger and malnutrition.

Better health. Since the 1930s—but more dramatically since 1950—the pharmaceutical industry has applied the chemist's skill in manipulating molecules, the biochemist's understanding of cellular chemistry, and the chemical engineer's expertise in designing technologies to produce drugs that have contributed to healthier and more comfortable lives. However, new challenges posed by life-threatening diseases such as AIDS require fundamental and applied research by biochemists, organic chemists, and workers within the medical profession.

All life processes—birth, growth, reproduction, aging, and death, as well as mutation—involve chemical change. Chemistry and the chemical industry will continue to make important contributions to physiology and medicine through rational drug design and synthesis of new compounds that promote health and alleviate threats such as atherosclerosis, hypertension, cancer, and disorders of the central nervous and immune systems.

New materials. For 50 years, the industry has provided new materials for construction, clothing, and household uses. Synthetic fibers, for example, provide cheaper, easier to care for, and more versatile clothing, carpets, and wall coverings. The coming years will bring many changes in the materials we use, as new substances are tailored to replace and outperform traditional or scarce materials.

Better environment. Public concern has made the industry sensitive to the need for environmental protection. In the face of increasing world population, urbanization, and rising standards of living, the environment must be protected. Effective strategies for safeguarding our surroundings require that we know what chemicals are there, where they came from, and what we can do about them. Chemistry lies at the heart of the answers to each of these questions. The industry can provide services and methods, such as analytical techniques, that give early warning of

Strip-mining of coal in Pennsylvania. How can we remove huge quantities of raw materials without destroying the earth's beauty and natural balance?

emerging problems, help us determine their origins, and provide access to alternative products and processes to help avoid environmental damage.

Biotechnology. Remarkable progress in recent years by molecular biologists and biochemists has increased our understanding of basic chemical principles that determine the structure and function of macromolecules (such as proteins and DNA) within biological systems. The chemical industry is planning now for applications of new biotechnologies that result from the ability to control chemistry in living systems at the cellular level.

A.2 INDUSTRY AS A SOCIAL PARTNER

In recent years, U.S. industries and citizens have recognized their joint responsibility to insure that chemical products are manufactured with a net benefit and minimum hazard to society. The U.S. Environmental Protection Agency (EPA), as a representative of public interest, has contributed toward this cooperative arrangement.

The nearly-200 member companies of the Chemical Manufacturers Association (CMA) represent 90% of the nation's chemical-production capacity. As a requirement of membership, CMA member companies must commit to these principles:

- Be safe and environmentally responsible in the manufacture, transportation, storage, use and disposal of chemicals,
- Respond to community concerns about chemicals and operations,
- Help communities put emergency procedures in place to handle spills and other releases—procedures that also can be useful in responding to natural disasters,
- And keep the public and government officials informed about chemical-related health and environmental hazards.

The chemical industry has the responsibility to make products in ways that are as free from hazard as possible, in workplaces that are as safe as possible. Industry is obliged to deal honestly with the public to ensure that risks and benefits of chemical operations are clearly known.

DNA "fingerprinting" by examining autoradiographs. The pattern of DNA bands is unique for each individual.

These principles are part of Responsible Care®, a CMA initiative calling for continuous chemical industry improvements in health, safety, and environmental quality.

Responsible chemical companies are committed to reducing chronic risks—risks arising from long-term exposure to potentially hazardous substances. Industrial scientists—mostly chemists—have developed sensitive instruments and methods for testing the environment as well as human and animal tissues for chemical contamination.

Most data about the effects of chemical substances on health and the environment come from industrial laboratories. Toxicology research on the long-term effects of chemical compounds on human health has been accelerated in recent years.

No activity of the chemical industry or the government can completely eliminate the risks involved in manufacturing chemical substances, any more than the risks of riding in a car can be eliminated. Knowing the risks, continuing to explore them, and dealing with them prudently are essential.

These concerns are not the sole responsibility of the chemical industry. As users of the industry's products, we share this responsibility. We must learn some basic concepts about the manufacture of chemical products. These include how materials are processed, how energy needs are met, what raw materials are used and how they will be obtained, how unwanted materials are handled, what risks are inherent in the operation, and what potential for environmental harm exists. With such knowledge we can become active in decisions involving risks and benefits to us and to the environment.

To help prepare Riverwood citizens for meetings with EKS representatives, chemistry teacher Richard Knowland invited townspeople to his high school classroom to learn about the chemical industry and general processes it employs. Knowland asked some students to assist him in the presentation.

A.3 CLASS ACTIVITY: PERSPECTIVES

In this activity you will serve on a three-member team that will either present a demonstration of a typical chemical process carried out by industry or prepare a poster talk with information to help Riverwood citizens better understand the chemical industry. In your presentation, you will use knowledge gained from earlier *ChemCom* units or other resource materials.

Note that earlier *ChemCom* units included background on activities that represent typical industrial processes, such as

• distilling a liquid,
• testing sunscreen preparations, and
• preparing copper from copper ore.

Poster topics might cover information on the chemical industry such as

• The size and scope of the chemical industry
• Ways an industry can affect a community
• How industry views its responsibilities
• Problems with unwanted materials, safety, and various risks.

Teams making poster presentations should plan their talks and prepare one or two posters to illustrate or highlight major points. Your teacher can direct you to helpful background materials.

A.4 YOU DECIDE: PRODUCTS OF INDUSTRY

Some materials produced by the chemical industry are purified forms of natural resources or combinations of such materials. For example, sodium chloride not only serves as table salt, but is an important chemical raw material. It is mined as a solid from rock salt deposits or extracted from brine produced by forcing water into underground salt deposits.

Other products are totally new forms of matter that did not exist before synthesis by chemists. Many petrochemicals discussed in the Petroleum unit are examples of synthetic materials, which often replace natural materials. Synthetic detergents have replaced soap in many applications.

Working in small groups, answer these questions:

1. Consider a variety of products related to familiar categories such as food, clothing, sports, transportation, and health-care.
   a. List five examples of materials that are just purified forms of natural resources, such as carbonated water, butane fuel, or table sugar.
   b. List five examples of synthesized materials that involve new forms of matter, such as Teflon™, latex paint, or dishwashing liquid.

2. Now review your answers to Question 1:
   a. What are the sources for materials found in the five natural products?
   b. What are the sources for materials used in manufacturing the five synthesized materials?

3. a. Which synthesized materials on your list can serve as substitutes for natural products?
   b. For each of these materials, compare advantages and disadvantages of the substitute with those of the original material.

4. Which synthesized materials on your list involve a totally new product or process not previously available from natural products?

5. Do your answers to Questions 1–4 support or contradict slogans such as "Better things for better living through chemistry," or "Today, something we do will touch your life"? Explain.

YOUR TURN

Chemical Processing in Your Life

To sense how pervasive the products of chemical processing are in everyday affairs, try to list five items or materials around you that have *not* been produced or altered by the chemical industry. Start by considering everyday items—clothes, household items, means of transportation, books, writing instruments, sports and recreation equipment—whatever you routinely encounter.

Write answers to the following questions. Come to class prepared to discuss your answers.

1. a. Were any items on your list packaged in materials produced by the chemical industry?

   b. How important was the packaging material?

2. In what ways are items or materials on your list better or worse than manufactured or synthetic alternatives? Consider factors such as cost, availability, and quality.

3. If a product is "100% natural" does that mean it has not been processed by the chemical industry? Why? Support your answer with at least one example.

A.5 YOU DECIDE: ASSET OR LIABILITY?

Riverwood citizens will decide by referendum whether EKS will be allowed to build an ammonia production plant near their town. If you were a citizen of Riverwood, what would be your choice? How would you decide?

To help clarify these questions, you will have a class discussion regarding some benefits and risks of building such a chemical plant in Riverwood. Here are some factors you may wish to consider:

Positive Aspects

- *The local economy will be improved.* The plant will employ 200 local people, working in three shifts. This will add $4 million to Riverwood's economy each year. In addition, each plant employee will indirectly provide jobs for another four people in local businesses. This is quite desirable, since 7% of Riverwood's labor force of 21,000 is currently unemployed.

- *Farming costs will be lowered.* Fertilizer for farms near Riverwood is now trucked from a fertilizer plant 200 miles away. These transport costs increase farmers' expenses by $14 for each ton of ammonia-based fertilizer. Each year 700 tons of fertilizer is spread on farms in the Riverwood area. Local farmers thus stand to save about $9,800 each year in transportation costs.

- *Riverwood air quality will be enhanced.* A natural gas transmission company will build a line to deliver natural gas (methane, CH_4) to the Riverwood ammonia plant. Town residents, who have traditionally burned fuel oil in their home furnaces, could convert to natural gas. If all 11,000 Riverwood homes and businesses burned natural gas rather than oil, emissions of sulfur dioxide and particulate matter would decrease.

- *The tax base will be improved.* The ammonia plant will be taxed at the current commercial rate in Riverwood. This will provide a large increase in revenues for the community.

Negative Aspects

- *Injuries and accidents pose a threat.* Ammonia is manufactured at high pressure and high temperature. An accident at the plant could kill or injure nearby workers. For each 100 U.S. workers in ammonia-based fertilizer plants several reported cases of work-related injury or illness have been reported annually. Occasional worker-related deaths have also been reported in such plants.

- *Production involves chemical hazards.* Ammonia, a gas at ordinary temperature and pressure, is extremely toxic at high concentrations. It is often shipped in tanker trucks. An accident on the roadway or at the plant releasing large amounts of ammonia could create a health hazard. Although such accidents are rare, a tanker crash in Houston in the 1970s ruptured an ammonia tank. Five persons were killed and 178 were injured. Even though the overall accident rate has declined since the early 1980s, injuries and illnesses associated with storing and shipping ammonia are reported each year.

Since ammonia is less dense than air, it tends to rise away from the ground. Thus its toxicity is not as threatening as it would be if it were more dense than air.

- *Water quality could be threatened.* During production, small amounts of ammonia dissolve in water and enter waterways. The resulting water solution is basic—that is, it has a pH higher than 7. If the plant were to malfunction, excessive release of ammonia-laden wastewater could kill aquatic life in the Snake River.

- *The ammonia market might decline.* The fertilizer industry is among the largest consumers of ammonia. Current fertilizer-intensive agricultural methods have created controversy. In some cases crop yields have declined despite application of increased amounts of synthetic fertilizer. Some farmers have elected to use less synthetic fertilizer; ammonia demand may decline in coming years. This could hurt Riverwood's future economy, even though the plant would provide short-term economic assistance.

Riverwood citizens were given six months to weigh their decision prior to voting on the proposed plant. During this time, many tried to become acquainted with the chemical industry and the workings of an ammonia plant.

In the next part of this unit, you will find out what Riverwood citizens learned about the chemical industry and how the presence of a major chemical manufacturing operation might influence their lives.

PART A: SUMMARY QUESTIONS

1. a. Describe the nature of the partnership between industry and society.
   b. In what ways does each partner need the other?
   c. What benefits does each receive from the other?

2. Explain the statement, "The chemical industry plays a pervasive though often hidden role in our lives."

3. When making decisions on complex issues, it's sometimes possible to analyze some factors just like solving mathematics problems—by manipulating numbers. For example, when evaluating the use of the pesticide DDT in the tropics, one can compare the number of lives saved (because deaths from malaria spread by mosquitos declined) with the number of lives lost (because of toxic effects of DDT on human life). Or one can compare the money that is saved when new technology is implemented with the cost of that technology.

   a. What key factors or concerns related to Riverwood's ammonia plant decision would be overlooked if only "numerical data" were considered?
   b. How should each of these non-numerical factors be "counted" or "weighed"?

AN OVERVIEW OF THE CHEMICAL INDUSTRY

The Riverwood Rotary Club invited Susanna Sobinski, the proposed plant manager of the Riverwood ammonia facility, to speak at a luncheon meeting. She presented some slides of what the plant would look like and discussed how the plant's operations would fit into the entire chemical industry.

The chemical industry, loosely defined, is the nation's largest industry, said Sobinski. What John Winthrop, a *Mayflower* passenger, began in Massachusetts in 1635 with the production of alum—potassium aluminum sulfate, $KAl(SO_4)_2 \cdot 12H_2O$—and saltpeter—potassium nitrate, KNO_3—has become a colossus that includes many of today's leading industries. Petroleum, pharmaceuticals, tires, clothing, paint, and even processed foods are just a few products for which the chemical industry is wholly or partly responsible. Even if the large petroleum and food industries are excluded, the remaining chemical industries make roughly $1 of every $10 earned in manufacturing and employ more than one million U.S. citizens.

In the United States in 1990, 1.1 million workers were employed in producing chemicals and allied products.

One of EKS's most important products, ammonia, is among the nation's top 10 chemicals in terms of quantity produced, said Sobinski. Each year the chemical industry produces 64 kg of ammonia for every citizen in the United States. Other chemicals in the top 25 and their recent production levels are given in Table 1.

Despite the fact that about half of the "top 25" chemicals are organic substances, eight of the top ten are inorganic. Nitrogen gas, second in terms of total U.S. quantity produced, is a major raw material for EKS. Both nitrogen and oxygen gas—third-ranked in production—are separated by low-temperature distillation from liquified air.

Table 1 TOP 25 CHEMICALS PRODUCED IN THE UNITED STATES IN 1990

Rank	Name	Formula	Billions of Pounds
1	Sulfuric acid	H_2SO_4	88.6
2	Nitrogen	N_2	57.3
3	Oxygen	O_2	39.0
4	Ethene (ethylene)	C_2H_4	37.5
5	Calcium oxide (lime)	CaO	34.8
6	Ammonia	NH_3	33.9
7	Phosphoric acid	H_3PO_4	24.4
8	Sodium hydroxide	$NaOH$	23.4
9	Propene (propylene)	C_3H_6	22.1
10	Chlorine	Cl_2	21.9
11	Sodium carbonate	Na_2CO_3	19.8
12	Urea	$(NH_2)_2CO$	15.8
13	Nitric acid	HNO_3	15.5
14	Ammonium nitrate	NH_4NO_3	14.2
15	1,2-Dichloroethane (ethylene dichloride)	$C_2H_4Cl_2$	13.3
16	Benzene	C_6H_6	11.9
17	Carbon dioxide	$CO_2(l), CO_2(s)$	11.0
18	Vinyl chloride	C_2H_3Cl	10.6
19	Ethylbenzene	C_8H_{10}	9.0
20	Styrene	$C_6H_5CHCH_2$	8.0
21	Methanol	CH_3OH	8.0
22	Terephthalic acid	$C_6H_4(COOH)_2$	7.7
23	Formaldehyde (37%)	CH_2O	6.4
24	Methyl *tert*-butyl ether (MTBE)	$(CH_3)_3C(OCH_3)$	6.3
25	Toluene	$C_6H_5CH_3$	6.1
	Total organic		216.8
	Total inorganic		409.1
	Grand total		625.9

Source: *Chemical & Engineering News*, June 24, 1991, p. 31.

B.1 FROM RAW MATERIALS TO PRODUCTS

Petroleum—as you already know—is the source of many basic materials in the chemical industry, including a variety of substances listed in Table 1. You may also recall that the Petroleum unit featured a typical home scene (see page 154) which featured a large array of petroleum-based products. However, products based on petroleum are not the only contributions of the chemical industry. In fact, if we were to remove from the picture all materials that involved any type of chemical manufacturing or processing, the *entire* room (and surrounding house structure) would totally vanish.

Raw materials used by the chemical industry are extracted from the earth's crust, from oceans, and from the atmosphere. For example, Climax Mountain in Colorado (page 480) has furnished major quantities of the world's supply of molybdenum, an important metal in alloys for such diverse products as jet engines and bicycle frames.

Climax Mountain molybdenum mine.

1 metric ton = 1000 kg

YOUR TURN

Metals from Ores

A certain molybdenum ore contains 0.40% molybdenum (Mo). How many kilograms must be processed to produce 8 kg of molybdenum?

The percent value (0.40%—or 0.40 parts per 100) tells us that every 100 kg of ore contains 0.40 kg of Mo. Since we need 8 kg of Mo, the problem can be solved this way:

$$8 \text{ kg of Mo} \times \frac{100 \text{ kg of ore}}{0.4 \text{ kg of Mo}}$$
$$= 2000 \text{ kg of ore (2 metric tons)}$$

We can reason out the answer this way: If 100 kg of ore contain only 0.40 kg of molybdenum, then we clearly need *more* than 100 kg of ore to produce 8 kg of this metal. Well, 10 times more ore—1000 kg of ore—would produce 10 times more metal, or 4 kg of molybdenum. But we need 8 kg of the metal—twice that much. Thus we must use twice as much ore, or 2000 kilograms of ore.

Both approaches lead to the same answer—to obtain 8 kg of molybdenum, 2000 kg of ore must be processed.

1. How many kilograms of taconite, an ore containing about 25% iron, must be mined to produce one kilogram of iron?

2. What mass of rock would be left if you removed all the iron from 100 kg of taconite?

3. If the powdered rock from 10^9 kg of taconite were used to create a road foundation 40 m wide and 0.25 m thick, how long could the road be? Assume that the powdered rock has a density of 3.0×10^3 kg/m^3.

Not all the chemical industry's raw materials are dug from the earth. Chlorine gas, tenth in abundance of substances produced in the United States in 1990 (Table 1), is obtained by passing an electric current through a salt solution—NaCl(aq). Chlorine is used widely in chemical manufacturing processes, in solvents, and in plastics—notably polyvinyl chloride (PVC), used in automobile upholstery and plumbing. It also finds use in the production of swimming pool treatment supplies.

The process that produces chlorine at the same time produces sodium hydroxide, NaOH, the eighth most-produced chemical in the U.S. This strong base, also known as caustic soda, is commonly used in the neutralization of acids and the production of sodium salts.

Thus water and sodium chloride—both commonplace and non-hazardous substances—serve as starting materials for two industrially-important, hazardous substances. The large industry that has arisen around the production of chlorine and sodium hydroxide remains central to the well-being of the entire chemical industry.

The same "chlor/alkali process" also produces hydrogen gas and household bleach, sodium hypochlorite, NaOCl.

Once the desired raw materials are obtained and purified, some, such as sodium carbonate (Na_2CO_3), are used directly (for example, sodium carbonate is used for water softening). However, many raw materials are converted into **intermediates**—substances used to synthesize consumer products or other chemicals.

Sodium carbonate ranks eleventh in the most-produced list.

Sulfuric acid, the substance produced in the United States in largest quantity, is a very important intermediate. Figure 1 (page 482) provides a partial list of the many products and processes that depend on sulfuric acid.

Some raw materials are dug from the earth.

Plastics
Pharmaceuticals
Food processing
Agriculture
Textiles
Rubber
Paints, dyes, pigments
Petroleum
Pulp and paper manufacturing
Glass and ceramics
Ferrous metallurgy
Nonferrous metallurgy
Water and sewage treatment
Cleaning and refrigeration
Explosives

Figure 1 Uses of sulfuric acid.

Ammonia is another important intermediate. Although the EKS Company produces fertilizer from the ammonia it manufactures, it also sells ammonia to other chemical companies, where it is used in the manufacture of plastics, resins, fibers, and explosives. Similarly, EKS purchases chemicals from other chemical companies to use in its fertilizers.

Demand for the chemical industry's products steadily increases. As more and more natural resources are needed to produce such materials, problems arise. How do we remove huge quantities of raw materials from the earth's crust without destroying its beauty and natural balance? How do we dispose of massive amounts of unwanted materials, many of which contain toxic substances? How do we control pollution of air and water? How do we prevent and reduce the hazards of chemical spills, and safeguard plant workers and the general public from chemical hazards?

Many of these problems have proven harder to solve than problems of creating new and useful materials. For example, the goal of a totally accident-free, error-free industry is highly desirable, but almost impossible to achieve. Occasional errors in judgment and performance are, unfortunately, a part of all forms of human activity. However, industries can minimize them by anticipating, controlling, and—if possible—eliminating situations that could lead to difficulties. The National Safety Council ranked the U.S. chemical industry as the safest of all manufacturing industries four times during the decade of the 1980s. For example,

Loading a tank with sulfuric acid.

the chemical industry's rate of occupational injuries and illness in 1988 was over 40% lower than the comparable figure for U.S. industry as a whole.

B.2 FROM TEST TUBES TO TANK CARS

Many chemical reactions you have observed in *ChemCom* laboratory experiments are the same reactions used in industry to synthesize chemical products. Chemical reactions must be scaled up to produce large quantities of high-quality products at low cost. Four factors become crucial in the scale up: engineering, profitability, waste, and safe operation.

One way engineers reduce the cost of chemical manufacturing is to run reactions as continuous processes. Like tributaries entering a river and flowing to the ocean, the reactants flow steadily into reaction chambers and product flows out. Rate of flow, time, temperature, and catalyst composition must all be carefully controlled.

Chemical engineers face many challenges in designing manufacturing systems for industry. In your laboratory, the small quantity of heat generated by a reaction in a test tube may seem unimportant. But when thousands of liters react in huge tanks, that heat must be carefully anticipated and managed. Otherwise, the reaction temperature can rise, creating potentially dangerous and costly situations.

The need to make profits heightens the challenge for chemical engineers. For some products, one penny per liter in production costs can literally make the difference between profit and loss. Since few chemical reactions produce 100% of the material sought, profitability can often be enhanced by modifying reaction conditions to increase the yield of desired product.

Another problem industry faces is dealing with unwanted materials of the chemical processes. These chemicals can quickly accumulate when reactions occur on an industrial scale. A major problem for the EPA is managing the cleanup of hundreds of chemical waste dumps. These dumps are legacies of an earlier time when there were fewer people, and in proportion the United States seemed larger than it does now. In those days unwanted materials released into the air, rivers, and the ground seemed to disappear.

Pharmaceutical workers monitoring a continuous-flow process.

Waste minimization is another effective industrial strategy. Some chemical processes can be redesigned to decrease the quantity of solvents and excess reactants used.

When EPA put an end to such waste releases, many chemical industries discovered that some previously unwanted materials or products—sometimes with a little bit of additional processing—could become valuable commodities in their own right, often as intermediates in other chemical-manufacturing efforts. Thus instead of polluting the environment, these wastes-turned-resources provide a new source of income.

B.3   CLOSE-UP: THE EKS COMPANY

The EKS Company is a good example of how a modern chemical corporation is organized. The company is divided into product divisions and service departments. Each of the four product divisions concentrates on producing a different class of chemicals, as shown in Figure 2.

Within the service departments, Analytical Department chemists test the purity of the chemicals EKS produces and intermediates it purchases from other companies. This department also performs services related to quality control. The Environmental Department monitors the plant's wastes and their effects on the environment. The Research Department works to develop new products and improve old ones, to reduce operating costs and energy use, and to minimize by-products. The Public Relations Department deals with the news media, the government, and the general public. Riverwood citizens will contact this department when they have a concern about EKS's operations. Corporate Management oversees the work of all other divisions and handles personnel, company policy, and finances.

EKS invests 5% of its annual sales revenue in research and development (R&D) efforts—a figure comparable to the U.S. chemical industry average.

The company is owned by stockholders. Many EKS employees own shares in the company. Riverwood citizens can also buy EKS stock.

Figure 2   The EKS Company.

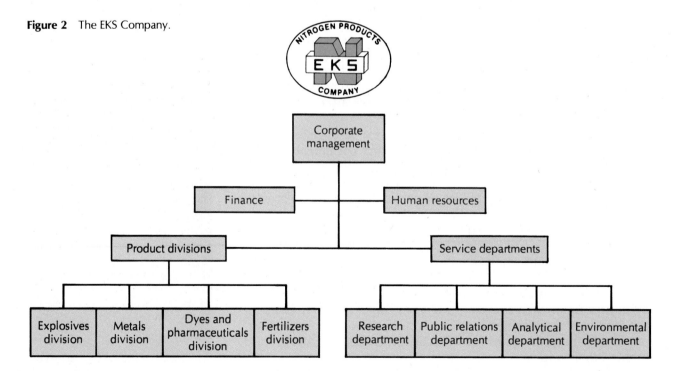

Researchers: Key to New Products

By Jessica Boese
Chapel Hill Chronicle *Staff Writer*

Many chemical industries have extensive research facilities in which they develop new products to sell. One such company is Burroughs Wellcome Co. in Research Triangle Park, North Carolina. Chemists such as Todd Blumenkopf design and synthesize molecules that after further testing may be used as medicines. Todd conceives of new compounds as likely candidates for treating specific conditions, keeping in mind the relationship between chemical structure and biological activity in the human body. Todd then devises a way to prepare the compound and performs this synthesis in the laboratory. The compound is tested in the laboratory by *in vitro* and *in vivo* methods to determine whether it has desirable results without dangerous side effects.

Todd synthesized a compound that may be used in the future to treat herpes virus infections. The particular compound has gone through the required laboratory testing and has been selected for "project status." The drug has been assigned to a project committee that will follow its course through the development process. Todd sits on this committee to provide information and discuss the properties of his compound. The objective of the committee is to collect data for an investigation of a new drug (IND) that will be filed with the U.S. Food and Drug Administration (FDA). An IND is usually a large set of documents containing laboratory and toxicology data. The drug goes through several trials before the FDA approves the drug for marketing. In Phase I, a clinical evaluation is performed to see how well the drug is tolerated in humans. In Phase II, a limited trial study is performed for efficacy. In Phase III, a clinical trial will be performed with thou-

Photo by Lisa Sedaris

sands of volunteer patients to collect data on efficacy and side effects. After data from all these trials are evaluated, the committee also prepares a new drug application (NDA) to file with the FDA for approval. Todd is made aware of the progress of these clinical trials only once every three months, when the committee meets. In the meantime, he has moved on to a new project in the laboratory.

As a youngster, Todd showed an interest in science. Todd's parents felt that with his disability he might be better accepted in science than in other fields, and so they encouraged him to pursue science. During his junior and senior years as an undergraduate at the University of California at Los Angeles, Todd worked for a young professor. Todd was motivated by research, enjoyed it, and decided to pursue research as a career. As Todd moved on in chemistry, he decided that he would like to work

for a pharmaceutical company. After receiving his Ph.D. from the University of California at Berkeley and a post-doctoral position and fellowship from the National Institutes of Health at the University of California at Irvine, he began a career as senior research scientist in the division of organic chemistry at Burroughs Wellcome Co. One reason Todd decided to pursue a Ph.D. in chemistry and a career as a research chemist is because each day is different. Research involves a variety of new tasks and challenges every day. Todd is able to control his own direction within the goals of the Burroughs Wellcome Co.

A good portion of Todd's free time is spent producing source material to help improve the accessibility of chemistry laboratories to those with disabilities. Todd is chairman of the American Chemical Society's Committee on Disabilities, which is sponsoring this project.

We will next examine two product areas of the EKS company: fertilizers and explosives. Although these are clearly different categories, both are based on at least one common raw material—nitrogen gas.

PART B: SUMMARY QUESTIONS

1. Provide evidence to support or refute the claim that the chemical industry plays a major role in our economy.

2. a. Identify the top three chemicals (in terms of quantity produced) in the United States.

   b. List two uses of each.

3. a. Identify three general categories of products made by the chemical industry.

   b. For each category, describe a typical product and suggest its usefulness.

4. Briefly describe several major factors that must be considered when a reaction is scaled up from a laboratory level to an industrial level.

5. What role is played by each of these within a chemical company?

   a. Analytical department

   b. Environmental department

   c. Public relations department

   d. Corporate management

   e. Research department

6. Unwanted materials from chemical processing plants can often be regarded as "resources out of place." Explain why.

Referendum Passes
EKS Riverwood Plant Approved by Voters

Riverwood citizens, voting in a special referendum yesterday, approved construction of the Riverwood chemical plant proposed earlier this year by EKS Nitrogen Products Company. The plant was endorsed by 61% of the voters, according to city officials.

EKS officials, expressing their gratitude at a press conference late last night, promised to begin construction within two months.

The plant, which will provide at least 200 new jobs for area workers, will produce ammonia and fertilizer.

THE CHEMISTRY OF SOME NITROGEN-BASED PRODUCTS

EKS Nitrogen Products Company is committed to producing high-quality fertilizer at a reasonable cost, using the best technology available. The company manufactures complete fertilizers, which provide the major nutrients needed by growing plants. The list of nutrients is slightly different for each fertilizer.

C.1 LABORATORY ACTIVITY: FERTILIZER

Getting Ready

In this laboratory activity you will play the role of a technician in the Analytical Department of the EKS company. You will be asked to identify some anions and cations in a fertilizer solution. First, you will perform tests on known solutions of three anions and three cations that are used in many fertilizers. By performing the same tests on the unknown fertilizer solution and comparing the results, you should be able to identify which ions are present.

Prepare the data table below in your notebook. The six "known" ions are listed across the top. Tests and reagents are listed in the left-hand column, keyed by procedure step numbers. The Xs indicate tests that are *not* needed.

Data Table   **ION TESTS**

		Anions		Cations			Unknown Fertilizer Solution
	PO_4^{3-}	NO_3^-	SO_4^{2-}	K^+	NH_4^+	Fe^{3+}	
1. Solution color							
2a. NaOH							
2b. $BaCl_2$							
2c. $BaCl_2$ + HCl							
3d. NaOH + litmus paper	X	X	X				
4e. Fe^{2+}/H_2SO_4	X		X	X	X	X	
6,7 Flame tests	X	X	X				

Procedure

Part 1:   Tests on Known Ions

Solutions of the six known ions are located in dropper bottles on your bench. Use them to perform the following tests.

COLOR

1. Note the solution colors and record them in your data table.

NaOH AND BaCl₂ TESTS

2. a. Place two or three drops of each known ion solution in a separate depression on a multiple-well spot plate. One by one, test each solution by adding one or two drops of 3 M sodium hydroxide (NaOH) solution. *Caution: Sodium hydroxide solutions can harm skin. Wash exposed area thoroughly if you contact any sodium hydroxide solution.* Record your observations. (If your plate has at least six clean, unused depressions, go on to the next step without washing it.)

    b. Place two or three drops of each known ion solution in a separate, unused depression on the spot plate. One by one, test each solution by adding one or two drops of 0.1 M barium chloride (BaCl₂) solution. *Caution: Barium-containing compounds are toxic. Wash your hands thoroughly if you contact this solution.* Record your observations. Do not clean the spot plate after these tests are completed.

    c. Add three drops of 6 M HCl to each of the six spot plate depressions containing BaCl₂ solution. *Caution: 6 M HCl is a strong, relatively concentrated acid solution. Wash exposed areas thoroughly if you contact this solution.* Record your observations. Clean and rinse the spot plate.

3. a. Place two drops of each known cation test solution into a separate clean, small test tube.

    b. Moisten three pieces of red litmus paper with distilled water; place them on a watch glass.

    c. Using a micropipet, add about 1 mL of 3 M NaOH to the solution in one test tube. Do not allow any NaOH to contact the test tube lip or inner wall. Immediately after adding the NaOH, stick a moistened red litmus paper strip onto the upper inside wall of the test tube. The strip must not contact the solution.

    d. Heat the test tube gently in a hot water bath for one minute, but do not boil the contents. Note your observations after waiting about 30 seconds.

    e. Repeat Steps 3c and 3d for each remaining test tube.

4. A mixture of Fe²⁺ and sulfuric acid produces a characteristic reaction in the presence of nitrate ion (NO₃⁻). This "brown ring test" (Fe²⁺/H₂SO₄) can be used to detect the presence of nitrate ions in a solution. Follow this procedure:

    a. Place eight drops of nitrate ion solution into a small, clean test tube.

    b. Add about 1 mL of FeSO₄ reagent and gently mix.

    c. Working carefully and slowly, pour 1 mL of concentrated sulfuric acid (H₂SO₄) along the inside of the tilted test tube so the acid flows along the wall into the tube's undisturbed solution. *Caution: Concentrated H_2SO_4 is a very corrosive, strong acid; if any contacts your skin, immediately wash affected areas with abundant running water and notify your teacher.*

d. Allow the test tube to stand without mixing for 1 to 2 minutes.

e. Observe any change that occurs at the interface between the two liquid layers. Record your observations.

FLAME TESTS

5. a. Obtain a platinum or nichrome wire inserted into glass tubing or into a cork stopper.

   The tubing or stopper will serve as a handle.

   b. Set up and light a Bunsen burner. Adjust the flame to produce a light blue, steady inner cone, and a more luminous, pale blue outer cone.

   c. Place about 2 mL of 12 M HCl in a test tube. Dip the wire into the HCl, and then insert the wire tip into the flame. Position the wire in the outer "luminous" part of the flame—*not* in the center cone. As the wire heats to a bright red, the flame may become colored. The color is due to metallic cations on the wire.

   d. Continue dipping the wire into the HCl and inserting the wire into the flame until there is little or no change in the flame's blue color when the wire is heated to redness. The wire is now clean.

6. a. Dip the clean wire into the Fe^{3+} solution. Then insert the wire into the flame as before. Note any change in flame color, the color's intensity, and the total time (in seconds) the color lasts.

   b. Clean the wire with HCl until there is no flame color produced.

   c. Repeat Steps 6a and 6b with the K^+ and NH_4^+ solutions.

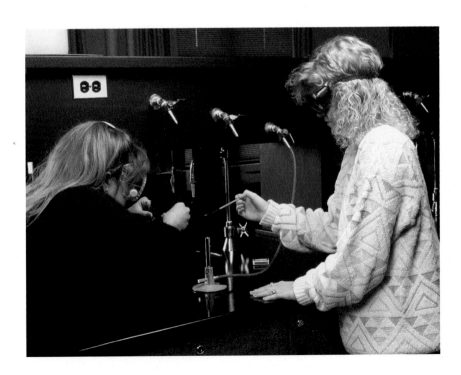

Performing flame tests.

7. After you have observed the flame colors for all three cations, observe the K⁺ flame a second time through a cobalt-blue glass (or a didimium glass). Again, note the color, intensity, and duration of the flame. Your partner can hold the wire in the flame while you observe. Then change places. Record all observations in your data table.

Part 2: Tests on Fertilizer Solution

1. Obtain about 5 mL of an unknown fertilizer solution from your teacher. The solution will contain one or more of the anions and cations tested in Part 1. Observe and record the unknown solution's color.
2. By following the earlier instructions in Part 1, conduct each data table test on the fertilizer solution. Use well-cleaned laboratory equipment, and record all observations. (Repeat a test if you want to confirm your observations.)
3. Compare your results with those obtained for the known solutions. Identify the anions and cations listed in the data table that are present in your fertilizer solution.
4. Wash your hands thoroughly before leaving the laboratory.

Questions

1. Name two compounds that could have supplied the ions present in your unknown fertilizer solution.
2. Describe a test you could perform to decide whether a fertilizer sample contains phosphate ions.
3. If litmus paper indicates that a certain fertilizer solution is basic, which ion(s) studied in this activity could be present in the solution?
4. Could a candle be used as a replacement for a Bunsen burner in doing flame tests? Explain.
5. Does information gathered in this activity allow you to judge whether a given fertilizer is suitable for a particular use? Explain.

Applying anhydrous ammonia fertilizer to the soil will help result in a healthy crop.

C.2 FERTILIZER'S CHEMICAL ROLES

Each year EKS manufactures more than 3 million tons of ammonia and more than 1.5 million tons of nitric acid. Most of these chemicals are used in producing fertilizers sold to farmers and gardeners.

Ammonia can also be directly applied to soil as a nitrogen-rich fertilizer.

The use of chemically-synthesized fertilizer in agriculture is a good example of materials substitution. Prior to its use, manure served as the primary soil-enriching material in crop-growing. Farmers add fertilizer to soil to increase the growth rate and yield of their crops. Recall the concept of a limiting reactant (Food unit, page 237). The purpose of all fertilizers is to add enough nutrients to soil so plants have all they need of each one.

The raw materials used by growing crops are mainly carbon dioxide from the atmosphere, water, and minerals from the soil. Mineral nutrients such as nitrate (NO_3^-), phosphate (PO_4^{3-}), magnesium (Mg^{2+}), and potassium (K^+) ions are absorbed by plant roots from the soil. Phosphate becomes part of the energy-storage molecule ATP (adenosine triphosphate; Risk unit, page 421), the nucleic acids RNA and DNA, and other phosphate-containing compounds. Magnesium ions are a key component of chlorophyll, essential for photosynthesis.

Potassium ions are present in the fluids and cells of most living things. Without adequate potassium ions, a plant's ability to convert carbohydrates from one form to another and to synthesize proteins would be hindered.

Nitrogen is critically important in plant growth. Plant cells are largely protein; nitrogen makes up about 16% of the mass of protein molecules. Abundant molecular nitrogen (N_2) is in the atmosphere, but it is so unreactive that plants cannot use it.

*Conversion of N_2 to nitrogen compounds usable by plants is called **nitrogen fixation.***

Ammonia (NH_3) or ammonium ion (NH_4^+) added to soil is oxidized to nitrate ions (NO_3^-) by soil bacteria. In building amino acids, plants first reduce the nitrate to nitrite ions (NO_2^-) and then to ammonia. They then use ammonia directly in amino acid synthesis. Unlike animals, higher plants can synthesize all the amino acids they need, starting with ammonia or nitrate ions.

Lightning and combustion can "fix" nitrogen from the atmosphere—they cause nitrogen gas to combine with other elements, forming compounds that plants can use. In addition, certain plants called **legumes** harbor nitrogen-fixing bacteria in their roots.

Clover and alfalfa are examples of legumes.

Lightning storms contribute to a series of reactions that "fix" atmospheric nitrogen as a dilute solution of nitric and nitrous acids, directly available for plant use.

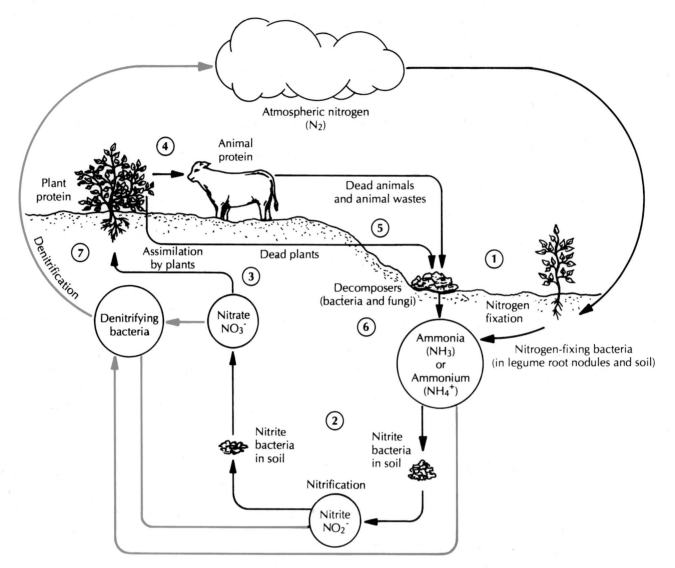

Figure 3 A simplified diagram of the nitrogen cycle.

Science and industry are exploring biological methods for making atmospheric nitrogen more available to plants. These include incorporating genes that produce nitrogen-fixing enzymes into microorganisms and even into higher plants. This would make it possible for plants or their bacteria to produce their own nitrogen fertilizer, just as the bacteria on legumes do.

When organic matter decays, much of the nitrogen released recycles among plants and animals, and some returns to the atmosphere. Thus some of the nitrogen gas removed from the atmosphere through nitrogen fixation eventually cycles back to its origin. Figure 3 shows the nitrogen cycle, which consists of the following steps:

1. Atmospheric nitrogen (N_2) is converted to ammonia (NH_3) or ammonium ion (NH_4^+) by nitrogen-fixing bacteria that live in legume root nodules or in soil.

2. Ammonia and ammonium ions, in turn, are oxidized by various soil bacteria—first into nitrite ions (NO_2^-) and then into nitrate ions (NO_3^-).

3. Most nitrogen taken up by the roots of higher plants is in the form of nitrate.

4. The nitrogen then passes along the food chain to animals that feed on plants, and to animals that feed on other animals.

5. When these organisms die, their proteins and other nitrogen containing molecules are broken down by decomposers (mostly bacteria and fungi).

6. Nitrogen not assimilated by the decomposers is released as ammonia or ammonium ion. Thus much nitrogen recycles through the living world without returning to the atmosphere.

7. Some nitrogen, however, is "lost" to the atmosphere after denitrifying bacteria convert ammonia, nitrite, and nitrate back to nitrogen gas.

A bag of lawn fertilizer. The 27–3–8 formula refers to the percents of nitrogen, phosphorus (as P_2O_5), and potassium (as K_2O) present.

YOUR TURN

Plant Nutrients

1. Some farmers alternate plantings of legumes with harvests of grain crops. Why?
2. Why is it beneficial to return non-harvested parts of crops to the soil?
3. Research on new ways to fix nitrogen might help lower farmers' operating costs. Why?
4. Briefly describe the effects on a plant having too few
    a. nitrate ions.
    b. phosphate ions.
    c. potassium ions.

In Laboratory Activity C.1 you identified some major ions present in fertilizer. In the next activity you will complete a quantitative study of one of these ions.

C.3 LABORATORY ACTIVITY: PHOSPHATES

Getting Ready

Most fertilizer packages list the percents (by mass) of the essential nutrients contained in the fertilizer. In this activity you will determine the mass and percent of phosphate ion in a fertilizer solution. The method you will use, called a **colorimetric method,** is based on the fact that the intensity of a solution's color indicates concentration of the colored substance. A chemical reaction will convert colorless phosphate ions (PO_4^{3-}) to colored ions. To determine the percent of phosphate ion present, you will compare the color of the unknown solution with colors of solutions with known concentrations.

To prepare the unknown fertilizer solution, dilute a solution of the fertilizer by a factor of 50. This dilutes it enough for comparison with the color standards.

Procedure

1. Label five test tubes as follows: 10 ppm, 7.5 ppm, 5 ppm, 2.5 ppm, and X.

ppm = parts per million

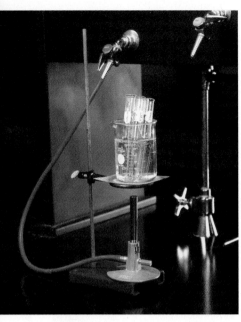

Water bath for heating samples.

2. Complete these steps to prepare the unknown fertilizer solution:

   a. Place 0.50 g of fertilizer in a 400-mL beaker. Label the beaker "original."

   b. Add 250 mL of distilled water. Stir until the fertilizer is completely dissolved.

   c. Pour 5.0 mL of this solution into a clean, dry 400-mL beaker labeled "dilute." Discard the remaining 245 mL of original solution.

   d. Add 245 mL of distilled water to the 5.0-mL solution in the "dilute" beaker. Stir to mix.

3. Pour 20 mL of the diluted solution into the test tube labeled X. Discard the remaining diluted solution.

4. In the tube labeled 10 ppm, place 20 mL of standard 10 ppm phosphate ion solution provided by your teacher. Add solutions and water to the other three test tubes as listed below:

Concentration (ppm)	Standard 10 ppm Phosphate Solution (mL)	Distilled Water (mL)
7.5	15	5
5	10	10
2.5	5	15

5. Add 2 mL of ammonium molybdate-sulfuric acid reagent to each of the four prepared standards and to the unknown.

6. Add a few crystals of ascorbic acid to each tube. Stir to dissolve.

7. Prepare a water bath by adding about 200 mL of tap water to a 400-mL beaker. Place the beaker on a ring stand above a Bunsen burner. Place the five test tubes in the water bath.

8. Heat the water bath containing the test tubes until a blue color develops in the 2.5-ppm solution. Turn off the burner.

9. Allow the test tubes to cool briefly. Then, using a test tube holder, remove the test tubes from the water bath and place them numerically in a test tube rack.

10. Compare the color of the unknown solution with those of the standard solutions. Place the unknown between standard solutions with the closest-matching colors.

11. Estimate the concentration (ppm) of the unknown solution from the known color standards. (For example, if the unknown solution color falls between the 7.5-ppm and 5-ppm color standards, you might decide to call it 6 ppm, or 6 g PO_4^{3-} per 10^6 g solution.) Record the estimated value.

12. Wash your hands thoroughly before leaving the laboratory.

Calculations

1. Calculate the mass of phosphate ion in the fertilizer using this equation. Place the numerical value of the unknown solution concentration (in ppm) in the blank.

$$\text{mass of } PO_4^{3-} \text{ (g)} = \frac{\underline{\quad} \text{ g } PO_4^{3-}}{10^6 \text{ g solution}} \times 250 \text{ g solution} \times 50$$

The factor 50 in the calculation takes into account the 50-fold dilution of the fertilizer solution. By multiplying the calculated mass of phosphate by 50, the mass is adjusted back to its "pre-diluted" value. Record the calculated mass of phosphate ion.

2. Calculate the percent phosphate ion (by mass) in the fertilizer sample:

$$\% \text{ PO}_4{}^{3-} = \frac{\text{Mass of phosphate ion (Step 11)}}{\text{Mass of fertilizer (0.50 g)}} \times 100$$

Record this value.

Questions

1. Name two household products or beverages for which you can estimate relative concentration just by observing color intensity.

2. Instruments called colorimeters are often used for determining solute concentration. They measure the quantity of light that passes through an unknown sample and compare it with the amount of light that passes through a known standard solution. What are the advantages of a colorimeter over the human eye?

3. Explain this statement: The accuracy of colorimetric analysis depends on the care taken in preparing the standards.

4. How could a reaction that produces a precipitate be used to determine the concentration of an ion?

5. a. Why is it important for farmers to know exactly the percent composition of fertilizers they use?

   b. What risks (or costs) are involved in applying more of a soil nutrient than is actually needed?

C.4 FIXING NITROGEN

In seeking ways to fix nitrogen artificially, scientists in 1780 first combined atmospheric nitrogen and oxygen by exposing them to an electric spark. However, the cost of electricity makes this process too expensive for any commercial use. A less expensive method, the **Haber process,** has replaced it. This is the process the EKS Riverwood plant will use to produce ammonia. Here is some of the chemistry behind it.

When atoms lose control of one or more of their electrons, forming ions, the process is called **oxidation.** The opposite process, of gaining electrons, is called **reduction.** Electrons can be transferred to or from atoms, molecules, or ions. As a result, all elements and compounds can be oxidized or reduced, and products of oxidation-reduction reactions can be atoms, molecules, or ions.

For review, see the Resources unit, page 136.

Consider the key Haber process reaction, depicted in the equation below with electron-dot formulas:

$$\begin{array}{c} \text{H} \\ :\text{N}:::\text{N}: + 3 \text{ H}:\text{H} \rightarrow 2 \text{ }:\overset{\textstyle \cdot\cdot}{\underset{\textstyle \cdot\cdot}{\text{N}}}:\text{H} \\ \text{H} \end{array}$$

Note that each nitrogen atom originally shares electrons with another nitrogen atom. Both nitrogen atoms have equal attraction

Figure 4 Nitrogen gas, shown in blue, and hydrogen gas, shown in yellow (left photo) react to form ammonia (right photo).

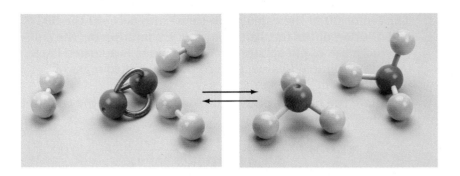

for their shared electrons. As the reaction progresses, each nitrogen atom becomes covalently bonded to three hydrogen atoms. The bonded atoms each share an electron pair—but they do not share equally. Nitrogen atoms have greater attraction for the shared electrons than do hydrogen atoms. Therefore, the nitrogen atom in each NH_3 molecule has acquired a part of hydrogen's original electrons. Each nitrogen atom has been *reduced* in its reaction with hydrogen.

Reduction is electron gain.

Similarly, each hydrogen atom has lost some control of its electron in the reaction. Each hydrogen atom has been *oxidized*.

Oxidation is electron loss.

Once nitrogen is chemically combined with another element, it can be easily converted to other nitrogen-containing compounds. The importance of the Haber process is that it converts difficult-to-use nitrogen molecules from air into easy-to-use ammonia molecules (Figure 4). For example, under proper conditions, ammonia will react readily with oxygen gas to form nitrogen dioxide:

$$4\ NH_3(g)\ +\ 7\ O_2(g) \rightarrow 4\ NO_2(g)\ +\ 6\ H_2O(g)$$

Oxidation-reduction reactions are sometimes called "redox" reactions.

This is also an oxidation-reduction reaction. In forming NO_2, each nitrogen atom has been oxidized—each has lost some control of electrons. Why? Because oxygen attracts electrons more strongly than does hydrogen. Each oxygen atom has been reduced—each has gained more control of electrons than it had in O_2.

Because the nitrogen atom in NH_3 has *more* control of its electrons than it had in N_2, the atom is said to have a **negative oxidation state**. In NO_2, the nitrogen atom has *less* control of its electrons than it had in N_2; it has a **positive oxidation state**. In N_2 and O_2 (and in all elements), each atom has a **zero oxidation state**.

All uncombined elements are assigned zero oxidation state. Oxidation state is a useful concept in understanding oxidation-reduction reactions.

The relative tendency of bonded atoms to attract electrons in compounds is called **electronegativity**. Numerical values have been assigned to this tendency. Electronegativity values for some common elements are shown in Table 2.

YOUR TURN

Electronegativity and Oxidation State

"Oxidation state" is sometimes referred to as "oxidation number."

Oxidation state is a convenient way to express the degree of oxidation or reduction of atoms in substances. Each atom in an element or compound can be assigned a numerical oxidation state. The higher (more positive) the oxidation state, the more the atom has been oxidized. The lower (less positive) the oxidation state, the more it has been reduced. In assigning oxidation states in binary compounds (compounds of two elements), atoms of more electronegative elements are given negative oxidation state values. These correspond to a gain of electrons (a reduced state). Similarly, atoms of lower electronegativity are assigned positive oxidation states—corresponding to loss of electrons (an oxidized state).

In aluminum oxide, Al_2O_3, which element has the positive oxidation state and which the negative oxidation state?

The values in Table 2 indicate that aluminum has an electronegativity of 1.5 and oxygen has 3.5. This means that oxygen has greater electron-attracting ability than does aluminum. Therefore, in aluminum oxide, aluminum is assigned a positive oxidation state and oxygen a negative oxidation state.

The combination of aluminum and oxygen

$$4 Al(s) + 3 O_2(g) \rightarrow 2 Al_2O_3(s)$$

is an oxidation-reduction reaction in which aluminum metal becomes oxidized. This is because its oxidation state changes from zero (in the free element) to a positive value. By contrast, oxygen gas becomes reduced—its oxidation state changes from zero to a negative value.

1. Consider these compounds. Using electronegativity values, decide which element in each compound is assigned a positive oxidation state and which is assigned a negative oxidation state.

   a. Sulfur trioxide, SO_3
   b. Hydrazine, N_2H_4
   c. Water, H_2O
   d. Hydrogen chloride, HCl
   e. Sodium chloride, NaCl
   f. Carbon monoxide, CO
   g. Iodine trifluoride, IF_3
   h. Manganese dioxide, MnO_2

2. a. Each of the following compounds is composed of a metallic and nonmetallic element. Decide which element in each compound has a negative oxidation state and which has a positive oxidation state.

   (1) Lead fluoride, PbF_2
   (2) Sodium iodide, NaI
   (3) Potassium oxide, K_2O
   (4) Nickel(II) oxide, NiO
   (5) Iron(III) chloride, $FeCl_3$
   (6) Lead(II) sulfide, PbS

   b. Consider your answers in Question 2a. What conclusion can you draw about the oxidation states of metals and nonmetals in binary compounds?

3. In this oxidation-reduction reaction, which element is oxidized and which is reduced?

$$Ni(s) + S(s) \rightarrow NiS(s)$$

Table 2 ELECTRONEGATIVITY

Element	Symbol	Value
Potassium	K	0.8
Sodium	Na	0.9
Magnesium	Mg	1.2
Manganese	Mn	1.5
Aluminum	Al	1.5
Zinc	Zn	1.6
Iron	Fe	1.8
Lead	Pb	1.8
Nickel	Ni	1.8
Tin	Sn	1.8
Copper	Cu	1.9
Silver	Ag	1.9
Hydrogen	H	2.1
Gold	Au	2.4
Carbon	C	2.5
Iodine	I	2.5
Sulfur	S	2.5
Bromine	Br	2.8
Chlorine	Cl	3.0
Nitrogen	N	3.0
Oxygen	O	3.5
Fluorine	F	4.0

Table 3   **INDUSTRIAL NITROGEN COMPOUNDS**

Compound	Structure	Use
Ammonia, NH_3	NH_3	Fertilizer, explosives, fibers, plastics
Nitric Acid, HNO_3	$HO-NO_2$	Fertilizer, explosives, manufacturing
Hydrazine, N_2H_4	H_2N-NH_2	Rocket fuel, plastics
Amines, $R-NH_2$ (e.g., propylamine)	$CH_3CH_2CH_2NH_2$	Intermediate
Nitrates, MNO_3 (e.g., sodium nitrate)	$Na^+NO_3^-$	Fertilizer, explosives, food preservation
Nitrites, MNO_2 (e.g., sodium nitrite)	$Na^+NO_2^-$	Textile bleach, manufacturing, food preservation

Hydroxylamine, NH_2OH	$H-\overset{\cdot\cdot}{N}-OH$
	       $\mid$
	       H
		Reducing agent

Phenylhydrazine, $C_6H_5N_2H_3$	⬡$-NHNH_2$	Dye intermediate
Urea, $(NH_2)_2CO$	$H_2N\underset{\underset{O}{\parallel}}{C}NH_2$	Fertilizer, plastics

R = Hydrocarbon group

M = Metal ion

The relative ease of conversion of one nitrogen compound to another is used in the chemical industry to make a large number of compounds from ammonia. Table 3 gives examples.

C.5 NITROGEN FIXATION AT RIVERWOOD

Modern ammonia plants give a 20%–30% conversion of reactants to ammonia, depending on the temperature and pressure used.

Producing ammonia from nitrogen gas and hydrogen gas is a chemical challenge. For example, the reaction does not use up all the available nitrogen and hydrogen to produce ammonia. As soon as ammonia molecules form in the reactor, they begin to decompose back to nitrogen and hydrogen molecules. This type of reaction—where products form reactants while reactants form products—is known as a **reversible reaction.** The ability of the reaction to proceed in both directions limits the amount of ammonia that can be obtained. Chemists represent reversible reactions with double arrows linking the products and reactants.

$$N_2(g) + 3\ H_2(g) \rightleftarrows 2\ NH_3(g)$$

A state of **dynamic equilibrium** is reached when the rate of product formation (in this case ammonia) equals the rate at which it decomposes. At dynamic equilibrium, the reaction appears to "stop," since forward and reverse changes exactly balance one another.

All reversible reactions in closed containers reach equilibrium if conditions such as temperature remain constant.

Although ammonia decomposes in the reactor due to the high temperature, it is stable once it cools to room temperature. One possible way to increase the yield of ammonia would be to remove the ammonia as soon as it forms, which would cause the reaction to shift forward. Even though such a scheme would be expensive, it would prevent the reaction from reaching equilibrium—ammonia would continue to form.

Since ammonia is stable at low temperatures, another yield-increasing plan might seem possible. Why not run the reactor at a low temperature, so the ammonia will not decompose? Unfortunately, this doesn't work. Simply mixing three volumes of hydrogen with one volume of nitrogen at ordinary temperatures does not produce any noticeable ammonia, regardless of how long the gases remain together.

Finding a suitable catalyst was the actual breakthrough that led to a workable, profitable ammonia process. The catalyst made it possible to produce ammonia at lower temperatures, where it is more stable.

Commercial ammonia production involves more than allowing nitrogen gas and hydrogen gas to react in the presence of a catalyst. First, of course, the reactants must be obtained. Nitrogen gas is taken from the air. Hydrogen is obtained from natural gas (mainly methane, CH_4). This is why Riverwood's ammonia plant requires construction of a natural gas pipeline.

Sulfur-containing compounds are removed from the natural gas by passing it through absorptive beds. Next, methane reacts with steam to produce hydrogen gas:

$$CH_4(g) + H_2O(g) \rightleftarrows 3\ H_2(g) + CO(g)$$

In modern ammonia plants, this endothermic reaction takes place at 200–600° C, at pressures of 200–900 atm. The ratio of methane (CH_4) to steam must be carefully controlled to prevent the formation of a variety of carbon compounds.

Carbon monoxide, a product of the hydrogen-generating reaction shown above, is converted to carbon dioxide, with the formation of additional hydrogen gas:

$$CO(g) + H_2O(g) \rightleftarrows H_2(g) + CO_2(g)$$

The hydrogen gas is then purified by removal of carbon dioxide and any unreacted methane.

Steam turbines compress the hydrogen and nitrogen to high pressures. Ammonia forms as the gases flow over a catalyst of reduced iron oxide (Fe_3O_4):

$$N_2(g) + 3\ H_2(g) \rightleftarrows 2\ NH_3(g)$$

The carbon dioxide can be removed in a variety of ways, including allowing it to react with calcium oxide (lime), forming solid calcium carbonate, or by dissolving it —at high pressure — in water.

Unreacted nitrogen and hydrogen gas are recycled, mixed with new supplies of reactants, and passed through the reaction chamber again.

C.6 NITROGEN'S OTHER FACE

Ammonia production has been important in developed nations for many years. As you have seen, one of its uses has been for agriculture. World ammonia production has increased dramatically since 1950, as farmers worldwide have increased their use of fertilizer. The chemical industry's ammonia-producing capacity has increased about 11 times in just the past decade.

Almost all chemical explosives contain nitrogen compounds, but before World War I, fixed nitrogen was available in large quantities only from nitrate deposits in Chilean deserts. During

Eighty percent of ammonia is used in fertilizer; 5% is used in explosives.

One use for explosives—the demolition of the Hotel Madison.

the war, home-based supplies of fixed nitrogen in the form of ammonia allowed Germany to continue fighting the war even after the British Navy cut off its shipping connections with Chile.

Explosives also have important non-hostile uses. Most road-cuts you see along interstate highways were carved by chemical forces unleashed by explosives. To cut through the stone faces of hills and mountains, road crews drill holes, drop in explosive cannisters, and detonate them. The explosion is generally caused by rapid formation of gaseous products from liquid or solid reactants. A gas takes up more than a thousand times the volume of the same molar quantity of solid or liquid.

To be useful, an explosive must react readily, but not too readily. Working with loud, dangerous explosives caused considerable trouble in the 1880s for a family named Nobel. It also made and lost fortunes for them several times. The father and his four sons were all interested in explosives, but Alfred, one of the sons, was the most persistent experimenter.

In 1846, the powerful explosive nitroglycerin (see page 503) was invented. It was too sensitive to be useful, though—one never knew when it was going to explode. The Nobels built a laboratory in Stockholm to explore ways to control this unstable substance. Carelessness, as well as ignorance of nitroglycerin's properties, led to many destructive explosions. Alfred's brother, Oscar, was killed in one of them. The city of Stockholm finally insisted that Alfred do his experimenting elsewhere. Grimly determined to make nitroglycerin less dangerous, Alfred rented a barge and continued his experiments in the middle of a lake. He finally discovered that if the oily nitroglycerin was adsorbed on finely divided sand (diatomaceous earth), it became stable enough to transport and store, but would still explode if activated by a blasting cap. This new form of the explosive was called dynamite.

A new era had begun. At first, dynamite served peaceful uses in mining and in road and tunnel construction. However, by the late 1800s it was also used in warfare.

This caused Alfred Nobel considerable anguish and motivated him to use his fortune to benefit humanity. His will provided support for annual prizes in physics, chemistry, physiology

A Nobel medallion.

Table 4   **NOBEL LAUREATES IN CHEMISTRY, 1980–91**

Year	Awardees	Contributions
1991	Richard R. Ernst, Switzerland, Federal Institute of Technology, Zurich	Improved technology for nuclear magnetic resonance, used in medical diagnosis and in revealing structure of complex molecules
1990	Elias Corey, United States, Harvard University	Established logical approaches to synthesizing complex organic molecules, including drugs
1989	Sidney Altman, United States, Yale University Thomas R. Cech, United States, University of Colorado at Boulder	Discovered RNA's role in catalyzing chemical reactions in cells
1988	Hartmut Michel, Robert Huber, Johann Deisenhofer, West Germany, Max Planck Institute	Mapped the structure of protein molecules essential in photosynthesis
1987	Donald J. Cram, United States, University of California at Los Angeles Charles J. Pedersen, United States, E. I. du Pont de Nemours Company, Inc. Jean-Marie Lehn, France, Louis Pasteur University	Clarified mechanisms of molecular recognition that are fundamental to enzymatic catalysis, regulation, and transport
1986	Dudley Herschbach, United States, Harvard University Yuan T. Lee, Taiwan, University of California at Berkeley John A. Polanyi, Canada, University of Toronto	Developed methods for tracking individual molecules in chemical reactions
1985	Herbert A. Hauptman, United States, Medical Foundation of Buffalo Jerome Karle, United States, Naval Research Laboratory	Developed direct mathematical methods to determine crystal structures of molecules from X-ray data
1984	R. Bruce Merrifield, United States, Rockefeller University	Developed method for solid-phase synthesis of peptides and other biopolymers
1983	Henry Taube, Canada, Stanford University	Determined mechanisms for electron-transfer reactions, especially in metal complex ions; the research has applications in industry and biology
1982	Aaron Klug, South Africa, Cambridge University	Developed technique to determine detailed structures of viruses and genetic components within cells
1981	Kenichi Fukui, Japan, Kyoto University Roald Hoffmann, United States, Cornell University	Applied mathematical description of atoms (quantum mechanics) to predict the outcomes of chemical reactions
1980	Paul Berg, United States, Stanford University	Completed fundamental studies of the biochemistry of nucleic acids, with particular regard to recombinant DNA
	Walter Gilbert, United States, Harvard University Frederick Sanger, United Kingdom, Cambridge University	Developed methods for determining the base sequences in nucleic acids

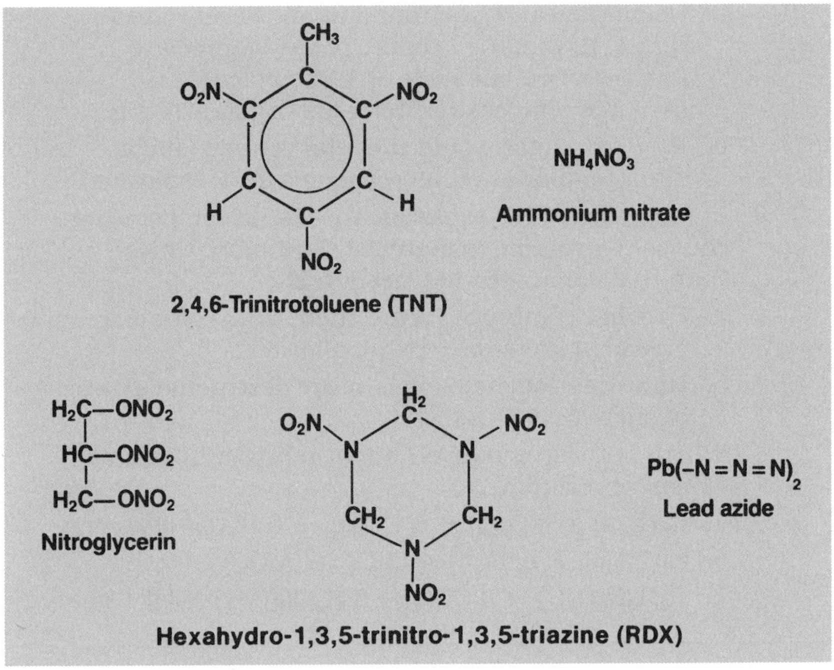

Figure 5 Some explosives EKS produces.

2,4,6-Trinitrotoluene (TNT)

NH_4NO_3

Ammonium nitrate

Nitroglycerin

Hexahydro-1,3,5-trinitro-1,3,5-triazine (RDX)

$Pb(-N = N = N)_2$

Lead azide

and medicine, literature, and peace. The Swedish parliament later added economics to the award categories. The Nobel prize, first awarded in 1901, is still regarded as the highest honor a scientist can receive. Recent Nobel laureates in chemistry are listed in Table 4, along with their contributions to chemical science.

EKS produces several chemicals in its Explosives Division. Names and formulas of some of these explosives are shown in Figure 5. The formulas are very different, but they all contain nitrogen atoms. Most have nitrogen in a positive oxidation state and carbon in a negative oxidation state within the same molecule. This creates conditions for a very rapid transfer of electrons from carbon to nitrogen, accompanied by release of vast quantities of energy.

Reactions of explosives are not reversible; they go to completion. Many different products are possible. Here are two examples of explosive reactions.

$$4\ C_3H_5(NO_3)_3(l) \rightarrow 12\ CO_2(g) + 6\ N_2(g) + 10\ H_2O(g) + O_2(g)$$
Nitroglycerin

$$4\ C_7H_5N_3O_6(s) + 21\ O_2(g) \rightarrow 28\ CO_2(g) + 10\ H_2O(g) + 6\ N_2(g)$$
TNT

Refer to these equations in answering the following *Your Turn*.

Explosive reactions are rapid exothermic oxidation-reduction reactions that release large amounts of gas.

YOUR TURN

Chemistry of Explosives

1. How many moles of gas are formed in the explosion of one mole of TNT?

2. Assume that a gas sample at a given temperature occupies 1000 times more space than the same number of moles of solid. Also assume that one mole of TNT occupies "one unit" of volume.

a. Using the value you found in answering Question 1, how many "units" of gas volume are formed when one mole of TNT explodes? (Assume temperature remains constant.)

b. By what factor would the total volume (at constant temperature) increase in a TNT explosion?

3. In fact, when TNT explodes, the rise in temperature causes the volume to increase eight *more* times than that calculated in Question 2b.

a. By what combined factor, then, does volume increase in an *actual* TNT explosion?

b. How does this help explain the destructive power of such an explosion?

4. Which of these equations might represent possible explosive reactions?

a. $C_5H_{12}(l) + 8 O_2(g) \rightarrow 5 CO_2(g) + 6 H_2O(g)$ + energy

b. $CaCO_3(s)$ + energy $\rightarrow CaO(s) + CO_2(g)$

c. $C_3H_6N_6O_6(s) \rightarrow 3 CO(g) + 3 H_2O(g) + 3 N_2(g)$ + energy

C.7 YOU DECIDE: FOOD OR ARMS

Chemicals useful in both war and peace are produced from ammonia. This nitrogen-containing compound is the starting material for explosives and for fertilizers. Thus, ammonia can be used either for destructive or constructive purposes.

1. Assume it is 1917, and World War I has started. A group seeks to ban the production of ammonia entirely, since it is used to produce destructive military explosives. The group asks you to join. What is your decision? Explain.

2. If the Haber process for ammonia production had been banned after World War I, what might have been some consequences? That is, how might the world be different?

3. Now compare the two faces of nitrogen with the two faces of nuclear energy. Answer Questions 1 and 2, substituting nuclear power for ammonia and nitrogen, and this year for 1917.

Like many other chemical companies, EKS has diversified chemical interests and activities. We'll next learn that EKS is also active in electrochemical processes—chemical changes that produce or are caused by electrical energy.

PART C: SUMMARY QUESTIONS

1. How does the concept of limiting reactants relate to the use of fertilizers?

2. Molecular nitrogen represents 78% of all the molecules in the atmosphere, yet nitrogen can be a limiting reactant for plants. Explain.

3. a. What is meant by oxidation state?

b. How is oxidation state related to oxidation and to reduction?

c. Illustrate how this concept applies to this equation:

$$4 NH_3(g) + 7 O_2(g) \rightarrow 4 NO_2(g) + 6 H_2O(g)$$

4. The following questions are based on this equation:

$$N_2(g) + 3 H_2(g) \rightleftharpoons 2 NH_3(g) + energy$$

a. What are the sources of the raw materials for this reaction?

b. Is the forward reaction endothermic or exothermic?

c. In light of your answer to Question 4b, would you expect the forward reaction to be favored at high or low temperatures?

d. What is the disadvantage of running the reaction at these temperatures?

e. What role does a catalyst play in this reaction?

EXTENDING YOUR KNOWLEDGE (OPTIONAL)

• Visit a garden store and read the labels on various fertilizer preparations. What chemical substances are commonly found in these fertilizers? How are the quantities of nitrogen, phosphorus, and potassium in various fertilizers reported? How do the compositions of various fertilizers vary for different uses? Can you find any fertilizers made up of only one chemical compound? If so, what is the name and formula of the compound? For what uses is the fertilizer recommended? Why?

• Scientists have long debated whether they are responsible for societal consequences of their discoveries. Do think scientists have more responsibility than other citizens in these decisions? Should scientists try to control society's uses of their discoveries, helping to insure that the discoveries are not used for destructive or evil purposes? Or, is this a matter for all members of society to decide? If so, how do they become well enough informed to make wise decisions?

CHEMICAL ENERGY ↔ ELECTRICAL ENERGY

Riverwood residents have found that EKS Nitrogen Products Company is a positive contributor to life in the town. The company is now considering diversifying into the production of aluminum.

Aluminum is obtained from its ore, bauxite, by electrolysis. This process requires so much electricity that electrical costs are an important factor in plant location. The hydroelectric plant at the Snake River Dam produces considerably more electrical power than is needed to serve Riverwood and surrounding communities. Power company officials have offered EKS large quantities of electrical power at very competitive rates.

The following laboratory activities and discussions provide background on electrochemistry. This information will help you understand how the proposed new plant will operate.

D.1 LABORATORY ACTIVITY: VOLTAIC CELLS

Getting Ready

In the Resources Unit (page 136) you learned that some metals release electrons (become oxidized) more readily than others—they are more active. The relative tendencies for metals in contact with water to release electrons can be summarized in an activity series of the metals (see Table 5). A metal higher in the activity series will give up electrons more readily than one that is lower.

The differing tendencies of metals to lose electrons can be harnessed to obtain electrical energy from a chemical reaction. We do this by constructing a **voltaic cell** in which electrons flow spontaneously through a wire connecting the two metals. The flow of electrons is called **current.** In this laboratory activity you will study several voltaic cells.

When two metals of differing electron-releasing tendencies are connected in a voltaic cell, an **electrical potential** is created

Voltaic cells are also called electrochemical cells.

Table 5　　　**ACTIVITY SERIES OF COMMON METALS**

Metal		Products of Metal Reactivity		
Li(s)	→	Li$^+$(aq)	+	e$^-$
Na(s)	→	Na$^+$(aq)	+	e$^-$
Mg(s)	→	Mg^{2+}(aq)	+	2 e$^-$
Al(s)	→	Al^{3+}(aq)	+	3 e$^-$
Mn(s)	→	Mn^{2+}(aq)	+	2 e$^-$
Zn(s)	→	Zn^{2+}(aq)	+	2 e$^-$
Cr(s)	→	Cr^{3+}(aq)	+	3 e$^-$
Fe(s)	→	Fe^{2+}(aq)	+	2 e$^-$
Ni(s)	→	Ni^{2+}(aq)	+	2 e$^-$
Sn(s)	→	Sn^{2+}(aq)	+	2 e$^-$
Pb(s)	→	Pb^{2+}(aq)	+	2 e$^-$
Cu(s)	→	Cu^{2+}(aq)	+	2 e$^-$
Ag(s)	→	Ag$^+$(aq)	+	e$^-$
Au(s)	→	Au^{3+}(aq)	+	3 e$^-$

between the metals. This electrical potential, which is measured in volts (V), is somewhat like water pressure in a pipe. It represents the "push" that drives electrons through the wire connecting the two metals. The greater the difference in activity of the metals, the greater the "electron pressure," or electrical potential, of the cell.

To provide both electrical conduction inside the cell and receptors for electrons leaving the wire or external circuit, a voltaic cell is prepared by immersing each metal in a solution of its ions. A porous cup allows the two solutions maintain electric contact. The cup must contain channels that are large enough to permit the flow of dissolved ions, but small enough to prevent gross mixing of the solutions.

An unglazed flower pot makes a good porous cup.

Procedure

Prepare an appropriate data table for the following procedures.

Zinc-copper Electrochemical Cell

1. Pour 75 mL of Zn^{2+} solution into a clean 250-mL beaker.
2. Fill a porous cup about 3/4 full of Cu^{2+} solution.
3. Using steel wool, shine strips of copper and zinc.
4. Avoiding spilling, carefully place the porous cup in the beaker. Be sure the top of the cup remains above the liquid level in the beaker. (See Figure 6, page 508.)
5. Attach wire leads to the metal strips. Then attach one wire lead to the voltmeter. (If your voltmeter has selectable scales, select a scale with an approximate range of 0 to 2 V.) Very quickly and lightly touch the second wire lead to the other terminal of the voltmeter. If the needle moves in the positive direction, secure the wire to the terminal. If the needle moves in the negative direction, detach the first wire lead, reverse the positions of the leads, and attach them to the terminals.
6. Record the reading on the voltmeter dial.
7. Disconnect the wire leads, remove the metal strips, and dispose of the liquids as your teacher directs.

Figure 6 A zinc-copper electrochemical cell.

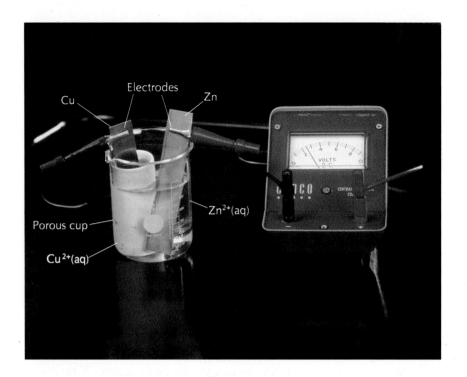

Magnesium-copper Electrochemical Cell

1. Refer to the activity series of metals and predict the change in your results with a magnesium-copper cell.
2. Repeat Steps 1–7 above, using a piece of magnesium ribbon and 75 mL of Mg^{2+} in place of zinc and its solution.

Iron-copper Electrochemical Cell

1. Refer to the activity series of metals and predict the change in your results with an iron-copper cell.
2. Repeat Steps 1–7 in the procedure for the zinc-copper electrochemical cell, using an iron strip and 75 mL of Fe^{3+} solution in place of zinc and its solution.

Studying Electrode Size

1. Obtain zinc and copper strips half as wide as the original electrodes used earlier.
2. Repeat Steps 1–7 in the zinc-copper electrochemical cell procedure.
3. Disconnect the wire leads. Remove the zinc and copper electrodes from the system. Replace them with a new zinc and copper strip half again as wide.
4. Repeat Steps 1–7 in the zinc-copper procedure.
5. Wash your hands thoroughly before leaving the laboratory.

Questions

1. a. Rank the three voltaic cells you prepared in order of decreasing electrical potential.

   b. Explain the observed order in terms of the activity series.

2. Predict whether the electrical potential of cells composed of these metal pairings would be higher or lower than that of the Zn-Cu cell:

   a. Zn and Cr   b. Zn and Ag   c. Sn and Cu

3. How did decreasing the size (surface area) of the electrodes affect the measured electrical potential?

4. Would a Ag-Au cell be a practical device? Why?

D.2 ELECTROCHEMISTRY

In the voltaic cells you made in the laboratory activity, each metal and the solution of its ions was a **half-cell.** In the zinc-copper cell, oxidation (electron loss) occurred in the half-cell with zinc metal immersed in zinc nitrate solution. Reduction (electron gain) took place in the half-cell composed of copper metal in copper(II) chloride solution. The activity series helps us predict that zinc is more likely to be oxidized (lose electrons) than copper. The **half-reactions** (individual electron-transfer steps) for this cell are:

Oxidation: $Zn(s) \rightarrow Zn^{2+}(aq) + 2\ e^-$

Reduction: $Cu^{2+}(aq) + 2\ e^- \rightarrow Cu(s)$

The electrode at which oxidation takes place is the **anode.** Reduction occurs at the **cathode.**

The overall reaction in the zinc-copper voltaic cell is simply the sum of the two half-reactions, added so electrons cancel:

$$Zn(s) \rightarrow Zn^{2+}(aq) + \cancel{2\ e^-}$$
$$\underline{Cu^{2+}(aq) + \cancel{2\ e^-} \rightarrow Cu(s)}$$
$$Zn(s) + Cu^{2+}(aq) \rightarrow Zn^{2+}(aq) + Cu(s)$$

Because a barrier separates the reactants (Zn and Cu^{2+}), electrons released by zinc in the zinc-copper voltaic cell must go through the wire to reach copper ions. The greater the difference in reactivity of the two metals, the greater the tendency to transfer electrons and the greater the cell potential. For example, a cell containing zinc and gold and their ions generates a larger potential than does a zinc-copper cell.

Voltaic cells represent a simple way to convert chemical energy to electrical energy in small portable containers. Chemists have packaged various combinations of metals and ions to make useful commercial cells. In ordinary dry cells (Figure 7)—often called batteries—zinc is the anode and manganese dioxide (MnO_2) is the cathode. The solution of ions contains ammonium and zinc chlorides in the most common dry cells. In alkaline batteries, the solution contains potassium hydroxide (KOH).

Nickel-cadmium (NiCad) batteries are rechargable—when this battery discharges, the reactants Cd and NiO_2 are converted, respectively, to $Cd(OH)_2(s)$ and $Ni(OH)_2(s)$. These solid products cling to the electrodes, allowing them to be converted back to reactants when the battery is placed in a recharging circuit.

An automobile battery, known as a lead storage battery, is composed of a series of electrochemical cells. As illustrated in Figure 8 (page 510), each cell consists of lead plates that serve as one electrode and lead dioxide plates (PbO_2) that serve as the other electrode. All plates are immersed in sulfuric acid. When you turn the key in the ignition, an electrical circuit is completed. Chemical energy in the lead storage battery is converted to electrical energy that runs the starter motor, and the lead electrode is oxidized (it loses electrons). These electrons travel through the circuitry to the lead dioxide electrode, reducing it

These words can be easily kept straight. Anode and its process (oxidation) both start with vowels. Cathode and its process (reduction) both start with consonants.

Figure 7 Despite the differences in size, each of these dry cells generates 1.5 V, since they are based on the same chemistry.

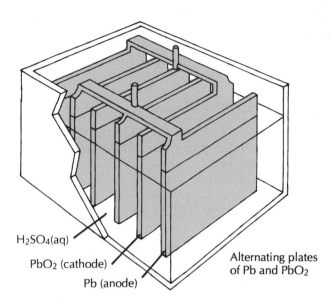

Figure 8 One cell of a lead storage battery.

H₂SO₄(aq)

PbO₂ (cathode)

Pb (anode)

Alternating plates of Pb and PbO₂

(the electrode gains electrons). As the electrons travel between the electrodes, they energize the car's electrical systems.

The oxidation and reduction half-reactions in a discharging car battery are

Oxidation: $Pb(s) + SO_4{}^{2-}(aq) \rightarrow PbSO_4(s) + 2\ e^-$

Reduction: $PbO_2(s) + SO_4{}^{2-}(aq) + 4\ H^+(aq) + 2\ e^- \rightarrow$

$PbSO_4(s) + 2\ H_2O(l)$

The overall reaction is the sum of the two half-reactions:

$$Pb(s) + SO_4{}^{2-}(aq) \rightarrow PbSO_4(s) + \cancel{2\ e^-}$$
$$\underline{PbO_2(s) + SO_4{}^{2-}(aq) + 4\ H^+(aq) + \cancel{2\ e^-} \rightarrow PbSO_4(s) + 2\ H_2O(l)}$$
$$PbO_2(s) + Pb(s) + 4\ H^+(aq) + 2\ SO_4{}^{2-}(aq) \rightarrow 2\ PbSO_4(s) + 2\ H_2O(l)$$

If an automobile battery is used too long without recharging, it runs down because the lead sulfate formed eventually coats both electrodes and reduces their ability to produce current. To

Accidentally leaving headlights on for extended times with the ignition off is one way a car battery can become run down or dead.

Jump-starting a car battery.

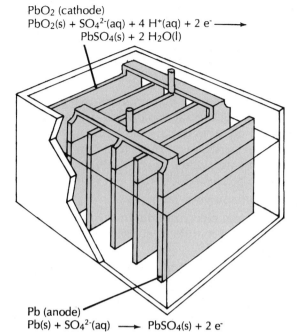

DISCHARGING

PbO$_2$ (cathode)
PbO$_2$(s) + SO$_4$$^{2-}$(aq) + 4 H$^+$(aq) + 2 e$^-$ $\longrightarrow$
PbSO$_4$(s) + 2 H$_2$O(l)

Pb (anode)
Pb(s) + SO$_4$$^{2-}$(aq) $\longrightarrow$ PbSO$_4$(s) + 2 e$^-$

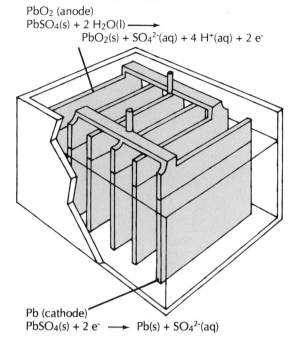

CHARGING

PbO$_2$ (anode)
PbSO$_4$(s) + 2 H$_2$O(l) $\longrightarrow$
PbO$_2$(s) + SO$_4$$^{2-}$(aq) + 4 H$^+$(aq) + 2 e$^-$

Pb (cathode)
PbSO$_4$(s) + 2 e$^-$ $\longrightarrow$ Pb(s) + SO$_4$$^{2-}$(aq)

Figure 9 Charging and discharging a car battery.

maintain the battery's charge, a generator or alternator converts some mechanical energy from the car's running engine to electrical energy, which recharges the battery. Recharging causes electrons to move in the opposite direction through the battery. This reverses the direction of the battery's chemical reaction. Reversing the reaction charges the battery (Figure 9).

Lead storage batteries can be quite dangerous when they are being rapidly charged from an outside source of electric energy. Hydrogen gas released at the lead electrode can be ignited by a spark or flame, causing an explosion.

It's estimated that about 70% of used car batteries are currently recycled in this country, leading to the recovery of substantial quantities of lead metal, sulfuric acid, and battery casing polymer.

This is one example of how a potentially hazardous disposal problem has been transformed into support for a profitable recycling industry.

YOUR TURN

Getting a Charge from Electrochemistry

Consider the following sample questions about a voltaic cell in which lead (Pb), silver (Ag), and solutions of lead nitrate, Pb(NO$_3$)$_2$ and silver nitrate, AgNO$_3$, are appropriately arranged:

    a. Predict the direction of electron flow in the wire connecting the two metals.

    b. Write equations for the two half-reactions.

    c. Which metal is the anode and which the cathode?

Here's how answers to these questions can be expressed:

    a. Table 5 (page 507) shows that lead is the more active metal. Therefore, electrons should flow from lead to silver.

b. One half-reaction involves forming Pb^{2+} from Pb, as shown in Table 5. The other half-reaction produces Ag from Ag^+, which can be written by reversing the Table 5 equation.

$$Pb \rightarrow Pb^{2+} + 2\ e^-$$

$$Ag^+ + e^- \rightarrow Ag$$

c. In the cell reaction, each Pb atom loses two electrons. Lead metal is therefore oxidized. By definition, then, lead metal is the anode. Each Ag^+ ion gains one electron. This is a reduction reaction. Since reduction takes place at the cathode, silver metal must be the cathode.

Now try these questions on your own:

1. Predict the direction of electron flow in a voltaic cell made from each pair of metals in solutions of their ions.

   a. Al and Sn   b. Pb and Mg   c. Cu and Fe

2. We design a voltaic cell using the metals tin and cadmium. The overall equation for the reaction is:

$$Sn^{2+}(aq) + Cd(s) \rightarrow Cd^{2+}(aq) + Sn(s)$$

   a. Write the half-reactions.

   b. Which metal, Sn or Cd, loses electrons more easily?

3. Sketch a voltaic cell composed of a $Ni-Ni(NO_3)_2$ half-cell and a $Cu-Cu(NO_3)_2$ half-cell.

4. In each of these cells, identify the anode and the cathode. (Assume that appropriate ionic solutions are used with each.)

   a. Cu-Zn cell   c. Mg-Mn cell

   b. Al-Zn cell   d. Au-Ni cell

D.3 LABORATORY ACTIVITY: ELECTROPLATING

Getting Ready

All reactions you observed on pages 507–508 were spontaneous. Materials were arranged so electrons would spontaneously move through wires. Voltaic cells involving such reactions generate electrical energy to run motors and perform other useful work.

By contrast, electrical energy can be used to "force" nonspontaneous or difficult oxidation-reduction reactions to occur. Charging a lead storage battery in an automobile is one example. Electroplating is another.

In electroplating, electrical energy from a battery or other source provides electrons to convert metal ions to atoms. Electroplating produces a thin layer of metal deposited on another surface to protect the surface or to make it more beautiful. Coating inexpensive jewelry with a very thin layer of gold makes it more attractive.

An electroplating cell used to accomplish these chemical changes consists of two electrodes (anode and cathode), a solution of ions, and a source of electricity. In this laboratory activity

The change from metal ions to atoms is a reduction process.

Electroplating is one particular form of electrolysis, a technique you used in the Resources unit, page 138.

you will electroplate an object of your choice. The object will become one of the electrodes; a piece of copper will serve as the other electrode.

Procedure

Part 1: Preliminary Electroplating Test

1. Place 250 mL of 0.5 M $CuSO_4$ in a 400-mL beaker.
2. Attach the alligator clips of two wire leads to the terminals of a 6-V battery.
3. Attach the other ends of the leads to two carbon (graphite) sticks, which will serve as electrodes.
4. Dip the carbon electrodes into the solution in the beaker. Do not allow the electrodes to touch each other. See Figure 10.
5. Allow the current to flow until you observe a change in one of the electrodes. Record your observations.
6. Disconnect the leads from the battery. Remove the carbon electrodes and rinse them with running tap water.

Part 2: Electroplating an Object

1. Place 250 mL of 0.5 M $CuSO_4$ in a 400-mL beaker.
2. Clean the object to be plated with the steel wool pad. Decide which wire lead should be attached to the copper strip and which to the object, based on Part 1 observations. Connect the wires to the copper and to the object.
3. Immerse the object and the copper strip in the plating solution. Do not let the electrodes touch each other. Attach wire-lead alligator clips to appropriate battery terminals.
4. Allow current to flow until copper plating is observed. See Figure 11.
5. Record your observations.
6. Disconnect the leads from the battery. Remove the object from the plating solution with tongs. Rinse the object under running tap water. Dry it with a paper towel.
7. Examine the object and record your observations.
8. Wash your hands thoroughly before leaving the laboratory.

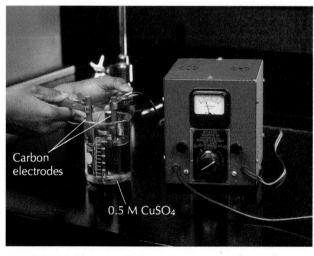

Figure 10 Electrolysis cell setup.

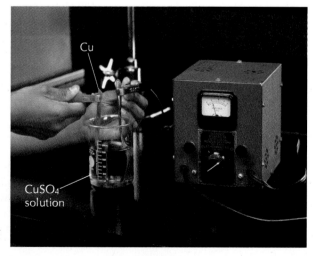

Figure 11 Electroplating cell setup.

Metals in the Marketplace

By Bruno Corsini
Pawtucket Dispatch *Staff Writer*

Why do many metallic objects stay so shiny over years of use? Electrochemistry and electroplating are the reasons. Electroplating is the process by which a metal (such as chromium, silver, or gold) is attached to the surface of an article to give it a more attractive, and in many cases a more protective, finish. Gene Kropp is a Technical Field Engineer and Salesman for Technic Inc. of Rhode Island. Gene provides equipment, supplies, or information to electroplaters.

Unlike some other salespeople who only need a "silver tongue", Gene has a real knowledge of silver, and other metals. To do his job well and with efficiency, Gene uses his extensive experience with and knowledge of electrochemistry. Gene's customers rely on his knowledge of the craft, the products, and the business. Gene represents a company that not only sells chemical systems and equipment, but maintains the equipment after the sale. This service includes training employees to use the systems; helping to recover precious metals; determining engineering changes to meet a specific customer's needs in processing or equipment; and purchasing chemicals on a periodic basis.

On a typical day, Gene visits four or five of his previously established accounts. These are usually routine sales calls—supplying chemicals and equipment and ordering replacements for delivery on his next visit. Gene also visits potential customers, supplying price quotations and literature for electroplating chemicals and equipment. This helps him develop new business for the future. Sometimes Gene has a "code call"—an emergency telephone call placed by

Photo by Jody Kropp

one of his customers who is experiencing trouble with an electroplating system. Gene helps them solve the problem over the telephone or in person. This is when Gene's knowledge of electrochemistry and electroplating is most valuable for Technic Inc. Through the process of elimination and by using "tricks-of-the-trade", Gene is able to solve many technical problems and reduce waste—concerns that chemists and engineers have tackled since technology began.

Gene has always been interested in chemistry, yet he was unable to find adequate funds for a four-year chemistry degree. In-

stead he chose to attend Essex Community College in Baltimore and get a degree in general studies with a concentration in chemistry. While he was a student, Gene held a part-time job in chemistry. Through a job posting in a community college, he found a position as a laboratory technician in a plating shop. He enjoyed the combination of chemistry and mechanics, and decided to pursue a career in the field. In preparation for his current position, Gene obtained a certificate from a one-week intensive course in his field and plenty of on-the-job training.

Questions

1. a. Which electrode was the anode?
   b. Which was the cathode?
2. In which direction did electrons flow during the reaction?
3. Write the half-reaction for
   a. the oxidation   b. the reduction.
4. Diagram and label the parts of an electroplating cell for
   a. plating a ring with gold.
   b. plating silver onto spoons.
   c. purifying copper metal.

D.4 INDUSTRIAL ELECTROCHEMISTRY

When a solution of sodium chloride in water (brine) is electrolyzed, chlorine gas, Cl_2, is produced at the anode and hydrogen gas, H_2, at the cathode (Figure 12). Sodium ions remain in solution, but electrolysis leaves hydroxide as the negative ion in solution replacing the chloride ion:

Electrolysis is the use of electrical energy to cause chemical change.

$$2\ Na^+(aq) + 2\ Cl^-(aq) + 2\ H_2O(l) \rightarrow 2\ Na^+(aq) + 2\ OH^-(aq) + H_2(g) + Cl_2(g)$$

This one electrolysis reaction produces three important, high-volume industrial chemicals: hydrogen gas, chlorine gas, and sodium hydroxide. The hydrogen and chlorine gases can be used without additional purification, because no other gases are released at the anode and cathode. The sodium hydroxide, on the other hand, must be purified, since it remains in solution with unreacted sodium chloride.

Chlorine and sodium hydroxide rank among the top ten chemicals in terms of U.S. production (by mass).

The industrial production of aluminum is another major process that uses electrical energy to produce chemical change.

In the nineteenth century, aluminum was a semiprecious metal, despite the fact that it is the most plentiful metal ion in the earth's crust. The 3-kg (6-lb.) aluminum pyramidal cap on the Washington Monument in Washington, D.C., cost considerably more than the same mass of silver would have cost when the cap was installed in 1884. Aluminum was expensive because it was very difficult to reduce to the metallic state.

The aluminum cap on the Washington Monument. The cap is about four inches high.

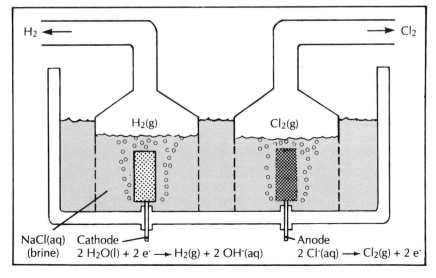

H_2 Cl_2

$H_2(g)$ $Cl_2(g)$

NaCl(aq)   Cathode   Anode
(brine) $2\ H_2O(l) + 2\ e^- \rightarrow H_2(g) + 2\ OH^-(aq)$ $2\ Cl^-(aq) \rightarrow Cl_2(g) + 2\ e^-$

Figure 12   Electrolysis of NaCl(aq).

Aluminum ion, Al³⁺, is very stable. No common substances give up electrons easily enough to reduce aluminum ions to aluminum metal. For example, carbon, which is an excellent reducing agent for metal compounds such as iron oxide or copper sulfide, simply doesn't work with aluminum compounds.

In 1886, one year after his graduation from Oberlin College in Ohio, Charles Martin Hall devised a method for reducing aluminum using electricity (see Figure 13). Hall's discovery became the basis of a rapidly-growing and important aluminum industry. He founded the Aluminum Corporation of America (ALCOA) and was a multimillionaire at the time of his death in 1914.

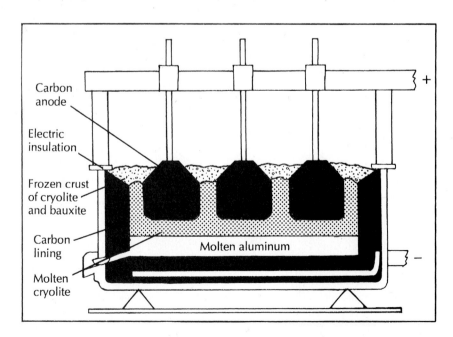

Figure 13 The Hall process for aluminum manufacture.

Hall's aluminum-production method—still known as the Hall process—is used worldwide. Aluminum oxide (bauxite) is dissolved in molten cryolite (Na_3AlF_6) at a temperature of 950° C in a large steel tank lined with carbon. The carbon tank lining is made the negative electrode by a source of direct current. This carbon cathode transfers electrons to aluminum ions, reducing them to molten metal. Molten aluminum sinks to the bottom, where it is drawn off periodically. The aluminum is then formed into various shapes and used to manufacture everything from stepladders to airplane parts.

The positive electrode (anode), which is also made of carbon, is oxidized during the reaction. As the carbon-rod anodes slowly burn away, they are lowered farther into the molten cryolite bath. The half-reactions for making aluminum are:

$$4\ Al^{3+}(melt) + 12\ e^- \rightarrow 4\ Al(l)$$

$$3\ C(s) + 6\ O^{2-}(melt) \rightarrow 3\ CO_2(g) + 12\ e^-$$

Ions from cryolite carry the electric current in the molten mixture.

Because they use large quantities of electricity, aluminum plants are often located near sources of hydroelectric power; many are in the Pacific Northwest. Electricity from hydropower generally costs less than electricity from thermal power plants (those that produce steam to spin the generator turbines).

Molten aluminum.

Removing aluminum bars from their molds.

D.5 YOU DECIDE: PLANNING FOR AN INDUSTRY

Your class will divide into working teams of three students each. Your teacher will either assign each group one of the "top 25" chemicals produced in the U.S., as reported in Table 1, page 479, or will give each group a choice from a number of materials listed in the table.

A proposal has been made to locate a new chemical plant near your community. Your assigned substance is being considered as a major product of the plant. Your group has been asked

Transporting bauxite ore by barge.

by the community to make a brief report regarding what citizens should know about such a plant's activity and possible implications for the community.

Here are the topics on which you should report:

1. Sources of starting materials, and their transportation to the plant.
2. Energy needs and their possible effects on individual citizens and the town.
3. Procedures for producing, storing, and distributing the product.
4. Waste-disposal concerns and other possible environmental impact of the plant.
5. Typical uses for the product.

Your teacher will provide suggested sources of material for this research activity.

PART D: SUMMARY QUESTIONS

1. Does the electrical potential produced in a voltaic cell depend on
   a. the size of the cell (the mass of metal forming each electrode)?
   b. the specific metals used?
2. For highest electrical potential, should a voltaic cell's two metals be close together or far apart on the activity series? Explain.
3. The following questions refer to this equation:

   $$PbO_2(s) + Pb(s) + 4 H^+(aq) + 2 SO_4^{2-}(aq) \rightarrow$$
   $$2 PbSO_4(s) + 2 H_2O(l)$$

   a. Does this equation represent the charging or discharging of a lead storage battery?
   b. Electrical energy or work can be extracted from this reaction. What does that imply about the reverse reaction?
   c. Would the reverse reaction be endothermic or exothermic?
   d. Would the reverse reaction represent battery charging or discharging?
   e. Why can the condition of a lead storage battery be tested with a hygrometer, a device that measures liquid density?
   f. In a fully charged condition, will the liquid density be greater or less than in a discharged state? Why? (*Hint:* Sulfuric acid solutions have a greater density than that of liquid water.)
   g. Identify the species being oxidized and the species being reduced.

   h. Under what conditions will a lead storage battery produce hydrogen gas?
   i. Why does this pose a hazard?
4. Magnesium and aluminum are both active metals. Would a voltaic cell using these two metals produce a large electrical potential? Why?
5. Predict the direction of electron flow in a voltaic cell composed of each pair of metals and their ions:
   a. Al and Cr
   b. Mn and Cu
   c. Fe and Ni
6. Compare chemical reactions in voltaic cells with those in electroplating cells. Consider
   a. energy released or absorbed.
   b. spontaneity vs. nonspontaneity.
   c. direction of electron flow.
7. Iron and copper were available to humans as free metals long before aluminum was— even though aluminum is much more abundant in earth's crust.
   a. Why were iron and copper available first?
   b. Why is aluminum oxide reduction more difficult than iron oxide reduction?
   c. How is the aluminum oxide reduction carried out?
8. a. Write the overall equation for making aluminum by the Hall process.
   b. How many moles of electrons are needed to reduce enough Al^{3+} ions to produce twenty moles (5400 g, or 5.4 kg) of Al?

E

PUTTING IT ALL TOGETHER: CHEMICAL INDUSTRY PAST, PRESENT, AND FUTURE

E.1 FUTURE DEVELOPMENTS

Figure 14 summarizes some of the major factors that drive advances in chemical technology. At its most general level, this model suggests that new problems or concerns stimulate new solutions—which, in turn, eventually stimulate newer problems and concerns.

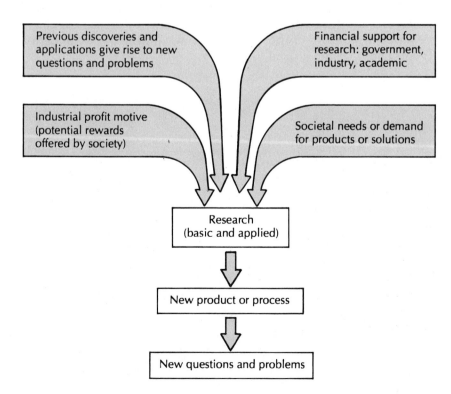

Previous discoveries and applications give rise to new questions and problems

Financial support for research: government, industry, academic

Industrial profit motive (potential rewards offered by society)

Societal needs or demand for products or solutions

Research (basic and applied)

New product or process

New questions and problems

Figure 14 The evolution of chemical technology.

The figure indicates that four major influences usually activate and guide industrial research efforts:

- Questions or problems regarding previous discoveries and applications.
- Availability of financial support for the research.
- Societial demands for new products or solutions.
- The search for new or improved sources of profit.

In many cases the products of industrial research are improvements in well-established products. The automobile tire industry provides a good example. At a distance, with the possible exceptions of the whitewall stripe and the general dimensions, contemporary tires look much the same as those manufactured a half-century or more ago. However, the durability, safety, and performance characteristics of present-day tires are far superior to those of earlier eras. This is due directly to changes in the composition of the tires—changes made possible by research efforts.

In other cases, the results of industrial research lead to new high-performance items that either replace older products or open up entirely new—and sometimes unexpected—applications. Artificial valves for hearts, new moisture-retaining soil conditioners, "instant" color cameras, tear-resistant "paper", and artificial sweeteners are all examples of such products.

Regardless of the technological advance, the Figure 14 model suggests that the appearance of a new product or process eventually leads to new questions and problems. These concerns bring the industry back to the top of the figure. A new cycle of research and development activity is thus initiated.

Using the model given in Figure 14 as a starting point, work in a group to develop an idea for a new chemical product or process. It might be something as general as synthetic rubber, or something highly specific, such as a new kind of pencil eraser.

As part of your initial brainstorming for a suitable idea, consider whether there's a need for your product or process. If so, describe the nature of the need. If not, what kind of public campaign might create a need?

Malaysian workers processing raw rubber.

To focus your group's attention on a single product or process, outline your idea by using the questions below as a guide.

Prepare a presentation to the class explaining your idea and the factors that might influence its development. The entire class will be given the chance to vote on the best idea.

1. a. Assuming a need exists, how will your product or process fill the need?
   b. If your product or process will serve as an alternative to a current product or process, what are the advantages of the new development over the old?
2. a. What financial and human resources will be needed?
   b. Will multidisciplinary teams be needed?
   c. Describe the nature of the development task.
3. a. What matter and energy resources will be needed?
   b. Are adequate supplies of these resources available in the United States or must they be imported?
   c. If the latter is the case, where might we obtain them?
   d. Are any political issues involved?
4. a. What safety tests must be run?
   b. What are some potential negative environmental effects of widespread use of your product or process?
   c. Will people have reason to object to the location of the facilities that produce the product or use the process? Why?
   d. Will people be motivated to argue in favor of your facility?
5. What, if any, ethical considerations are involved in the development and use of your product or process?
6. How long might it take to develop your idea into a marketable product or process?

E.2 LOOKING BACK AND LOOKING AHEAD

In using the *ChemCom* program, you have discovered that chemical concepts are involved in all changes in matter and energy that occur on our planet. Beyond this, you have explored contributions of chemistry and chemical technology to the growth and well-being of human communities, as well as to problems this activity has created.

To maximize benefits and minimize chemical technology's costs (and risks), individuals must combine an understanding of chemistry, other sciences, and technology with their own values in making informed personal and societal decisions. Chemistry will help improve modern life as long as citizens continue asking questions, weighing options in light of the best available information, and making intelligent decisions.

We hope this course has encouraged you to continue a life-long exploration of science-related issues. Whether you decide to study more chemistry or not, many opportunities are available to further your "chemical common sense".

Your real opportunity is to look ahead to your future to decide what kind of world you want—and how you, science, technology, and other components of society can contribute toward attaining it. As we have suggested, the challenge is great. But so are the potential rewards.

APPENDIX: COMPOSITION OF FOODS

	Measure	Mass	Energy	Protein	Carbohydrate	Fat	VITAMINS Vitamin A	Vitamin B₁	Vitamin B₂	Vitamin B₆	Vitamin B₁₂	Niacin	Vitamin C	MINERALS Calcium	Iron	Potassium	Sodium
		g	Cal	g	g	g	IU	mg	mg	mg	μg	mg	mg	mg	mg	mg	mg
BEVERAGES																	
Club soda	12 oz	355	0	0	0	0	0	0	0	0	—	0	0	18	—	1	78
Coffee	6 oz	180	3	—	.54	.01	0	0	.02	—	—	1.26	0	13	.02	117	2
Cola drink	12 oz	369	159	0	40	0	0	0	0	0	—	0	0	11	.18	7	20
Fruit-flavored drink	12 oz	372	179	0	45.8	0	0	0	0	0	—	0	0	15	.26	37	52
Diet drink	12 oz	355	0	0	.43	0	0	0	0	0	—	0	0	14	.46	6	76
Tea	8 oz	240	0	—	.06	.01	—	0	—	—	—	—	—	5	.1	58	19
BAKERY AND GRAINS																	
Breads																	
Bagel	1	100	296	11	56	2.57	—	.38	.29	.044	—	3.53	0	42	2.65	74	360
Biscuit, enr*	2″	28	103	2.1	12.8	4.8	t†	.06	.06	—	—	.5	t	34	.4	33	175
Cornbread, whl grd	2″	45	93	3.3	13.1	3.2	68	.06	.09	—	—	.3	t	54	.5	71	283
English muffin, enr	1	27	130		4	1	t	.23	.136	—	—	2	t	20	1.08	—	—
French or Vienna, enr	1 slice	20	58	1.8	11.1	.64	t	.06	.04	.01	0	.5	t	9	.4	18	116
Mixed grain		100	257	9.96	46.6	3.72	t	.39	.38	.103	0	4.16	t	104	3.26	218	412
Pita, whole wheat	1	42	140	6	24	2	t	.2	.068	—	—	2.4	t	40	1.8	—	—
Pumpernickel	1 slice	32	79	2.9	17	.4	—	.07	.04	.05	0	.4	—	27	.8	145	182
Roll, dinner, enr	1	38	113	3.1	20.1	2.2	t	.11	.07	—	—	.8	t	28	.7	36	192
Roll, hamburger/hot dog, enr	1	40	119	3.3	21.2	2.2	t	.11	.07	—	—	.9	t	30	.8	38	202
Roll, whole wheat	1	35	90	3.5	18.3	1	t	.12	.05	—	—	1.1	t	37	.8	102	197
Rye	1 slice	23	56	2.1	12	.3	—	.04	.02	.02	0	.3	—	17	.4	33	128
Wheat	1 slice	100	255	9.55	47	4.1	t	.46	.32	.109	0	4.52	t	126	3.49	138	539
White, enr	1 slice	23	62	2	11.6	.79	t	.06	.05	.009	t	.6	t	20	.6	24	117
Whole wheat	1 slice	23	56	2.4	11	.7	t	.06	.02	.04	0	.6	t	23	.5	63	121
Cracker, graham	1	14.2	55	1.1	10.4	1.3	0	.01	.03	—	—	.2	0	6	.2	55	95
Cracker, soda	1	2.8	12.5	.26	2	.37	0	t	.001	—	0	.03	0	.6	.04	3.4	31
Muffin, bran, enr	1	40	104	3.1	17.2	3.9	90	.06	.1	—	—	1.6	t	57	1.5	172	179
Muffin, whole wheat	1	40	103	4	20.9	1.1	t	.14	.05	—	—	1.2	t	42	1	117	226
Pancake, plain, enr	4″	27	62	1.9	9.2	1.9	30	.05	.06	—	—	.4	t	27	.4	33	115
Pancake, whole wheat	4″	45	74	3.4	8.8	3.2	80	.09	.07	—	—	.4	t	50	.54	—	—
Pizza, cheese, 14″	1/8	65	153	7.8	18.4	5.4	410	.04	.13	—	—	.7	5	144	.7	85	456

*enr = enriched
†t = trace
Source: United States Department of Agriculture

BAKERY AND GRAINS Breads (cont.)	Measure	Mass	Energy	Protein	Carbohydrate	Fat	VITAMINS Vitamin A	Vitamin B$_1$	Vitamin B$_2$	Vitamin B$_6$	Vitamin B$_{12}$	Niacin	Vitamin C	MINERALS Calcium	Iron	Potassium	Sodium
		g	Cal	g	g	g	IU	mg	mg	mg	µg	mg	mg	mg	mg	mg	mg
Pretzel, twisted	1	16	62	1.6	12.1	.7	0	.003	.008	.003	t	.1	0	4	.2	21	269
Taco shell		100	453	8.79	65.7	19.5	—	.29	.15	—	0	1.72	—	142	2.6	—	—
Tortilla, corn	6″	30	63	1.5	13.5	.6	6	.04	.015	.022	0	.3	0	60	.9	—	—
Waffle, enr	5½″	75	209	7	28	7.4	248	.13	.19	—	—	1	t	85	1.3	109	356
Cereals																	
Bran flakes, 40%, Post	1 C.	47	152	5.3	37.3	.8	2072	.6	.7	.8	2.5	8.3	—	21	7.5	251	431
Corn flakes, Kellogg's	1¼ C.	28	110	2.3	24.4	.1	1250	.4	.4	.5	—	5	15	1	1.8	26	351
Corn, puffed, Kix	1½ C.	28.4	110	2.5	23.4	.7	1250	.4	.4	.5	1.5	5	15	35	8.1	44	339
Granola, Nature Valley	1 C.	113	503	11.5	75.5	19.6	—	.39	.19	—	—	.83	—	71	3.78	389	232
Oat flakes, fortified	1 C.	48	177	5.3	20.5	.4	2116	.6	.7	.9	2.5	8.4	—	68	13.7	343	429
Oats, puffed, Cheerios	1¼ C.	28.4	111	4.3	19.6	1.8	1250	.4	.4	.5	1.5	5	15	48	4.5	101	307
Oatmeal, ckd	1 C.	234	145	6	25.2	2.4	38	.26	.05	.047	—	.3	—	20	1.59	132	1
Rice, puffed	1 C.	14	56	.9	12.6	.1	—	.02	.01	.011	—	.42	—	1	.15	16	0
Wheat, Cream of, ckd	1 C.	251	134	3.8	27.7	.5	—	.2	.1	—	—	1.5	—	51	10.3	43	2
Wheat, flakes, Total	1 C.	33	116	3.3	26	.7	5820	1.7	2	2.3	7	23.3	70	56	21	123	409
Wheat germ, toasted	1 C.	113	431	32.9	56.1	12.1	—	1.89	.93	1.1	—	6.31	7	50	10.2	1070	4
Wheat, granules, Grapenuts	1/4 C.	28.4	101	3.3	23.2	.1	1250	.4	.4	.5	1.5	5	—	11	1.23	95	197
Wheat, puffed	1 C.	12	44	1.8	9.5	.1	—	.02	.03	.02	—	1.3	—	3	.57	42	0
Wheat, shredded	1 large	23.6	83	2.6	18.8	.3	—	.07	.06	.06	—	1.08	—	10	.74	77	0
Desserts and Sweets																	
Apple or brown betty	1 C.	215	325	3.4	64	7.5	220	.13	.09	—	—	.9	2	39	1.3	215	329
Cake, angel food	1/10	45	121	3.2	27	.1	0	.004	.06	—	—	.1	0	4	.1	40	127
Cake, cheese	1/10	100	302	5.42	28.5	19.2	254	.03	.13	.064	.495	.46	5	56	.48	98	222
Cake, devil's food	2 × 3 × 2″	45	165	2.2	23.4	7.7	68	.009	.045	—	—	.1	t	33	.4	63	132
Cake, gingerbread	3 × 3 × 2″	117	371	4.4	60.8	12.5	110	.14	.13	—	—	1.1	0	80	2.7	531	277
Cake, pound	3 × 3 × ½″	30	142	1.7	14.1	8.8	84	.009	.03	—	—	.1	0	6	.2	18	33
Cake, sponge	1/10	50	149	3.8	27	2.85	225	.03	.07	—	—	.1	t	15	.6	44	84
Cake, white	1/10	50	188	2.3	27	8	15	.005	.04	.025	—	.1	t	32	.1	38	162
Candy, caramel	1	5	20	.2	3.88	.536	t	.002	.009	—	—	.018	t	7.5	.071	9.64	11.4

BAKERY AND GRAINS Desserts and Sweets (cont.)	Measure	Mass	Energy	Protein	Carbohydrate	Fat	VITAMINS Vitamin A	Vitamin B$_1$	Vitamin B$_2$	Vitamin B$_6$	Vitamin B$_{12}$	Niacin	Vitamin C	MINERALS Calcium	Iron	Potassium	Sodium
		g	Cal	g	g	g	IU	mg	mg	mg	μg	mg	mg	mg	mg	mg	mg
Candy, chocolate bar	1 oz	28	147	2.2	16	9.2	80	.02	.1	—	—	.1	t	65	.3	109	27
Candy, chocolate fudge	1″ cube	21	84	.6	15.8	.3	t	t	.02	—	—	t	t	16	.2	31	40
Candy, peanut brittle	1 oz	25	119	1.6	23	2.6	0	.05	.01	—	—	1	0	10	.7	43	9
Chocolate, baking	1 oz	28	143	3	8.2	15	20	.01	.07	—	—	.4	0	22	1.9	235	1
Chocolate, semisweet	1 oz	28	144	1.2	16.2	10.1	10	t	.02	—	—	.1	t	9	.7	92	1
Chocolate syrup	1 T.	18.7	46	.45	11.7	.49	t	.005	.015	—	—	.1	0	3	.3	53	10
Cooky, brownies	2 × 2 × ¾″	30	146	2	15.3	9.4	60	.05	.03	—	—	.2	t	12	.6	57	75
Cooky, chocolate chip, 2⅓″	1	10	51	.55	6	3	10	.01	.01	—	—	.1	t	3.5	.2	11.8	34.8
Cooky, fig bar	1	14	50	.55	10.5	.775	15	.005	.01	—	—	.05	t	11	.15	27.8	35.3
Cooky, gingersnap	1	7	29.4	.39	5.59	.62	5	.003	.004	—	—	.03	t	5.1	.16	32.3	40
Cooky, macaroon	1	14	67	.7	9.3	3.2	0	.006	.02	—	—	.1	0	4	.1	65	5
Cooky, oatmeal and raisin, 3″	1	14	63	.9	10.3	2.2	7	.015	.011	—	—	.1	t	3	.4	52	23
Custard, baked	1 C.	265	305	14.3	29.4	14.6	930	.11	.5	—	—	.3	1	297	1.1	387	209
Danish pastry	1	42	179	3.1	19.4	10	130	.03	.06	—	—	.3	t	21	.4	48	156
Doughnut, cake	1	32	125	1.5	16.4	6	26	.05	.05	—	—	.4	t	13	.4	29	160
Doughnut, raised	1	30	124	1.9	11.3	8	18	.05	.05	—	—	.4	0	11	.5	24	70
Eclair, custard	1	100	239	6.2	23.2	13.6	340	.04	.16	—	—	.1	t	80	.7	122	82
Honey	1 T.	21	64	.1	17.8	0	0	.002	.014	.004	0	.1	t	1	.1	11	1
Jams	1 T.	20	54	.1	14	t	t	t	.01	.005	0	t	0	4	.2	18	2
Jellies	1 T.	18	49	t	12.7	t	t	t	.01	—	—	t	1	4	.3	14	3
Molasses, blackstrap	1 T.	20	43	0	11	—	—	.02	.04	.054	—	.4	—	137	3.2	585	19
Molasses, light	1 T.	20	50	0	13	—	—	.01	.01	—	—	t	—	33	.9	183	3
Pie, apple, 9″	1/6	160	410	3.4	61	17.8	48	.03	.03	—	0	.6	2	1	.5	128	482
Pie, chocolate cream	1/6	100	264	4.58	29.4	15.1	264	.1	.17	.047	.366	.72	t	84	1.08	142	273
Pie, lemon meringue	1/6	140	357	5.2	52.8	14.3	238	.05	.11	—	—	.3	4	20	.7	70	395
Pie, pecan	1/6	160	668	8.2	82	36.6	256	.25	.11	—	—	.5	t	75	4.5	197	354
Pie, pumpkin	1/6	150	317	6	36.7	16.8	3700	.04	.15	—	—	.8	t	76	.8	240	321

BAKERY AND GRAINS Desserts and Sweets (cont.)	Measure	Mass	Energy	Protein	Carbohydrate	Fat	VITAMINS Vitamin A	Vitamin B₁	Vitamin B₂	Vitamin B₆	Vitamin B₁₂	Niacin	Vitamin C	MINERALS Calcium	Iron	Potassium	Sodium
		g	Cal	g	g	g	IU	mg	mg	mg	μg	mg	mg	mg	mg	mg	mg
Pie crust, enr	9"	135	675	8.2	59.1	45.2	0	.27	.19	—	—	2.4	0	19	2.3	67	825
Pudding, bread, w/raisins	1 C.	265	496	14.8	75.3	16.2	800	.16	.5	—	—	1.3	3	289	2.9	570	533
Pudding, chocolate	1 C.	260	385	8.1	66.8	12.2	390	.05	.36	—	—	.3	1	250	1.3	445	146
Pudding, rice, w/raisins	1 C.	265	387	9.5	70.8	8.2	290	.08	.37	—	—	.5	t	260	1.1	469	188
Pudding, tapioca cream	1 C.	165	221	8.3	28.2	8.4	480	.07	.3	—	—	.2	2	173	.7	223	257
Sugar, cane	1 T.	12	46	0	11.9	0	0	0	0	—	—	0	0	0	t	t	t
Sugar, brown, packed	1 C.	220	821	0	212	0	0	.02	.07	—	—	.4	0	187	7.5	757	66
Sugar, confection-er's	1 C.	120	462	0	119	0	0	0	0	—	—	0	0	0	.1	4	1
Sugar, raw	1 T.	14	14	.06	12.7	.07	t	.003	.016	—	—	.04	.3	7	.6	—	—
Syrup, corn	1 T.	20	57	0	14.8	0	0	0	.002	—	—	t	.1	9	.8	—	—
Syrup, maple	1 T.	20	50	0	12.8	0	0	—	—	—	—	—	0	33	.2	26	3
Flours																	
Buckwheat	1 C.	100	333	11.7	72	2.5	0	.58	.15	.578	0	2.9	0	33	5	656	1
Corn	1 C.	117	431	—	89.9	3	400	.23	.07	—	—	1.6	0	7	2.1	—	1
Pastry, wheat	1 C.	100	364	7.5	79.4	.8	0	.03	.03	.045	0	.7	0	17	.5	95	2
Potato	1 C.	110	386	8.8	87.9	.88	t	.46	.15	.008	0	3.74	19	36.3	18.9	1747	37.4
Rice	1 C.	125	479	7.5	107	.4	0	.52	.14	.2	0	7.2	0	11	6.8	—	—
Rye, dark	1 C.	128	419	20.9	87.2	3.3	—	.78	.28	.384	0	3.5	0	69	5.8	1101	1
Rye, light	1 C.	80	286	7.5	62.3	.8	—	.12	.05	.07	0	.5	0	18	.9	125	1
Wheat, enr	1 C.	110	400	11.6	83.7	1.1	0	.48	.28	.066	0	3.9	0	18	3.2	105	2
Whole wheat	1 C.	120	400	16	85.2	2.4	0	.66	.14	.41	0	5.2	0	49	4	444	4
Grains																	
Bran, wheat	1 C.	57	121	9	35.4	2.6	0	.41	.2	.468	0	12	0	67.8	8.49	639	5.13
Bran, rice	1 C.	105	278	12.7	60.6	12.8	0	1.93	.19	—	—	29.6	0	72	16.9	750	t
Cornmeal, whl grd	1 C.	118	427	10.6	88	4	566	.35	.09	.29	0	2.2	—	20	2.1	293	1
Cornstarch	1 T.	8	29	t	7	.05	0	0	.006	t	—	.002	0	0	.04	.32	.32
Macaroni, enr, ckd	1 C.	140	151	4.8	32.2	1	0	.2	.11	.029	0	1.5	0	11	1.2	85	1
Noodles, egg, enr, ckd	1 C.	160	200	6.6	37.3	2.4	112	.22	.13	.04	t	1.9	0	16	1.4	70	3
Pasta, whole wheat	4 oz	113	400	20	78	1	200	.6	.85	—	—	8	10.8	20	5.4	—	—
Popcorn	1 C.	14	54	1.8	10.7	.7	—	.055	.02	.03	0	.3	0	2	.4	33.6	t
Rice, brown	1 C.	196	704	14.8	152	3.6	0	.68	.08	1	0	9.2	0	64	3.2	420	16
Rice, white enr	1 C.	195	708	13.1	157	1.5	0	.86	.06	.3	0	6.8	0	47	5.7	179	10
Rice, wild	1 C.	160	565	22.6	121	1.1	0	.72	1.01	—	0	9.9	0	30	6.7	352	11
Spaghetti, enr, ckd	1 C.	140	155	4.8	32.2	.6	0	.2	.11	—	0	1.5	0	11	1.3	85	1
Tapioca	1 C.	152	535	.9	131	.3	0	0	.15	—	—	0	0	15	.6	27	5

	Measure	Mass	Energy	Protein	Carbohydrate	Fat	VITAMINS Vitamin A	Vitamin B₁	Vitamin B₂	Vitamin B₆	Vitamin B₁₂	Niacin	Vitamin C	MINERALS Calcium	Iron	Potassium	Sodium
		g	Cal	g	g	g	IU	mg	mg	mg	μg	mg	mg	mg	mg	mg	mg

DAIRY AND EGGS

Cheese

	Measure	Mass	Energy	Protein	Carbohydrate	Fat	Vit A	Vit B₁	Vit B₂	Vit B₆	Vit B₁₂	Niacin	Vit C	Calcium	Iron	Potassium	Sodium
Bleu	1 oz	28	100	6.07	.66	8.15	204	.008	.108	.047	.345	.288	0	150	.09	73	396
Brick	1 oz	28	105	6.59	.79	8.41	307	.004	.1	.018	.356	.033	0	191	.12	38	159
Brie	1 oz	28	95	5.88	.13	7.85	189	.02	.147	.067	.468	.108	0	52	.14	43	178
Camembert	1 oz	28	85	5.61	.13	6.88	262	.008	.138	.064	.367	.179	0	110	.09	53	239
Cheddar	1 oz	28	114	7.06	.36	9.4	300	.008	.106	.021	.234	.023	0	204	.19	28	176
Colby	1 oz	28	112	6.74	.73	9.1	293	.004	.106	.022	.234	.026	0	194	.22	36	171
Cottage, creamed	1 C.	210	217	26.2	5.63	9.45	342	.044	.342	.141	1.3	.265	t	126	.29	177	850
Cottage, dry	1 C.	145	123	25	2.68	.61	44	.036	.206	.119	1.19	.225	0	46	.33	47	19‡
Cottage, lowfat, 2%	1 C.	226	203	31	8.2	4.36	158	.054	.418	.172	1.6	.325	t	155	.36	217	918
Cream	1 oz	28	99	2.14	.75	9.89	405	.005	.056	.013	.12	.029	0	23	.34	34	84
Edam	1 oz	28	101	7.08	.4	7.88	260	.01	.11	.022	.435	.023	0	207	.12	53	274
Feta	1 oz	28	75	4	1.16	6	—	—	—	—	—	—	0	140	.18	18	316
Gouda	1 oz	28	101	7.07	.63	7.78	183	.009	.095	.023	—	.018	0	198	.07	34	232
Gruyère	1 oz	28	117	8.45	.1	9.17	346	.017	.079	.023	.454	.03	0	287	—	23	95
Limburger	1 oz	28	93	5.68	.14	7.72	363	.023	.143	.024	.295	.045	0	141	.04	36	227
Monterey jack	1 oz	28	106	6.94	.19	8.58	269	8.58	.111	—	—	—	0	212	.2	23	152
Mozzarella	1 oz	28	80	5.5	.63	6.12	225	.004	.069	.016	.185	.024	0	147	.05	19	106
Mozzarella, part skim	1 oz	28	72	6.88	.78	4.51	166	.005	.086	.02	.232	.03	0	183	.06	24	132
Muenster	1 oz	28	104	6.64	.32	8.52	318	.004	.091	.016	.418	.029	0	203	.12	38	178
Parmesan	1 oz	28	111	10	.91	7.32	171	.011	.094	.026	—	.077	0	336	.23	26	454
Parmesan, grated	1 T.	5	23	2	.19	1.5	35	.002	.019	.005	—	.016	0	69	.05	5	93
Provolone	1 oz	28	100	7.25	.61	7.55	231	.005	.091	.021	.415	.044	0	214	.15	39	248
Ricotta	1 C.	246	428	27.7	7.48	31.9	1205	.032	.48	.106	.831	.256	0	509	.94	257	207
Ricotta, part skim	1 C.	246	340	28	12.6	19.4	1063	.052	.455	.049	.716	.192	0	669	1.08	308	307
Romano	1 oz	28	110	9	1	7.64	162	—	.105	—	—	.022	0	302	—	—	340
Roquefort	1 oz	28	105	6.11	.57	8.69	297	.011	.166	.035	.182	.208	0	188	.16	26	513
Swiss	1 oz	28	107	8.06	.96	7.78	240	.006	.103	.024	.475	.026	0	272	.05	31	74
Processed, American	1 oz	28	106	6.28	.45	8.86	343	.008	.1	.02	.197	.02	0	174	.11	46	406
Processed, Swiss	1 oz	28	95	7	.6	7.09	229	.004	.078	.01	.348	.011	0	219	.17	61	388
Cheese food, American	1 oz	28	94	5.57	2.36	6.93	200	.009	.126	.04	.363	.021	0	141	.24	103	274
Cheese food, Swiss	1 oz	28	92	6.2	1.28	6.84	243	.004	.113	—	.652	.029	0	205	.17	81	440
Cheese spread, American	1 oz	28	82	4.65	2.48	6.02	223	.014	.122	.033	.113	.037	0	159	.09	69	381

Cream

	Measure	Mass	Energy	Protein	Carbohydrate	Fat	Vit A	Vit B₁	Vit B₂	Vit B₆	Vit B₁₂	Niacin	Vit C	Calcium	Iron	Potassium	Sodium
Half and Half	1 C.	242	315	7.16	10.4	27.8	1050	.085	.361	.094	.796	.189	2.08	254	.17	314	98

‡unsalted

DAIRY AND EGGS
Cream (cont.)

	Measure	Mass	Energy	Protein	Carbohydrate	Fat	VITAMINS Vitamin A	Vitamin B$_1$	Vitamin B$_2$	Vitamin B$_6$	Vitamin B$_{12}$	Niacin	Vitamin C	MINERALS Calcium	Iron	Potassium	Sodium
		g	Cal	g	g	g	IU	mg	mg	mg	µg	mg	mg	mg	mg	mg	mg
Whipping, light	1 C.	239	699	5.19	7.07	73.8	2694	.057	.299	.067	.466	.1	1.46	166	.07	231	82
Whipping, heavy	1 C.	238	821	4.88	6.64	88	3499	.052	.262	.062	.428	.093	1.38	154	.07	179	89
Whipped, pressurized	1 C.	60	154	1.92	7.49	13.3	548	.022	.039	.025	.175	.042	0	61	.03	88	78
Sour cream	1 C.	230	493	7.27	9.82	48.2	1817	.081	.343	.037	.69	.154	1.98	268	.14	331	123
Frozen Desserts																	
Ice cream	1 C.	133	269	4.8	31.7	14.3	543	.052	.329	.061	.625	.134	.7	176	.12	257	116
Ice cream, rich	1 C.	148	349	4.13	31.9	23.6	897	.044	.283	.053	.537	.115	.61	151	.1	221	108
Ice milk	1 C.	131	184	5.16	28.9	5.63	214	.076	.347	.085	.875	.118	.76	176	.18	265	105
Sherbet	1 C.	193	270	2.16	58.7	3.82	185	.033	.089	.025	.158	.131	3.86	103	.31	198	88
Milk																	
Whole	1 C.	244	150	8.03	11.37	8.15	307	.093	.395	.102	.871	.205	2.29	291	.12	370	120
Lowfat, 2%	1 C.	244	121	8.12	11.7	4.68	500	.095	.403	.105	.888	.21	2.32	297	.12	377	122
Skim	1 C.	245	86	8.35	11.8	.44	500	.088	.343	.098	.926	.216	2.4	302	.1	406	126
Buttermilk	1 C.	245	99	8.11	11.7	2.16	81	.083	.377	.083	.537	.142	2.4	285	.12	371	257
Whole, dry	1 C.	128	635	33.6	49	34.2	1180	.362	1.54	.387	4.16	.827	11	1168	.6	1702	475
Nonfat, dry	1 C.	120	435	43.4	62.3	.92	43	.498	1.86	.433	4.84	1.14	8.11	1508	.38	2153	642
Nonfat, dry, instant	1 C.	68	244	23.8	35.5	.49	18.3	.281	1.18	.235	2.71	.606	3.79	837	.21	1160	373
Condensed, sweetened	1 C.	306	982	24.2	166	26.6	1004	.275	1.27	.156	1.36	.643	7.96	868	.58	1136	389
Evaporated	1/2 C.	126	169	8.58	12.6	9.53	306	.059	.398	.063	.205	.244	2.37	329	.24	382	133
Evaporated, skim	1/2 C.	128	99	9.63	14.4	.26	500	.057	.394	.07	.305	.222	1.58	369	.37	423	147
Chocolate	1 C.	250	208	7.92	25.8	8.48	302	.092	.405	.1	.835	.313	2.28	280	.6	417	149
Malted, powder	1 T.	21	86	2.74	15.2	1.78	68	.111	.142	.078	.164	1.07	0	56	.16	159	96
Whey, dry, sweet	1 T.	7.5	26	.96	5.56	.08	3	.039	.165	.044	.177	.094	.11	59	.07	155	80
Yogurt																	
Plain	1 C.	227	139	7.88	10.5	7.38	279	.066	.322	.073	.844	.17	1.2	274	.11	351	105
Plain, skim	1 C.	227	127	13	17.4	.41	16	.109	.531	.120	1.39	.281	1.98	452	.2	579	174
Fruit, lowfat	1 C.	227	225	9.04	42.3	2.61	111	.077	.368	.084	.967	.195	1.36	314	.14	402	121
Eggs																	
Whole	1 lge	50	79	6.07	.6	5.58	260	.044	.15	.06	.773	.031	0	28	1.04	65	69
White	1 lge	33	16	3.35	.41	t	0	.002	.094	.001	.021	.029	0	4	.01	45	50
Yolk	1 lge	17	63	2.79	.04	5.6	313	.043	.074	.053	.647	.012	0	26	.95	15	8
Whole, dried	1 T.	5	30	2.29	.24	2.09	98	.015	.059	.02	.5	.012	0	11	.39	24	26
FATS AND OILS																	
Fats																	
Butter	1 T.	14.1	101	.12	.008	11.5	433	t	.004	t	—	.006	0	3.37	.022	3.62	117
Margarine	1 T.	14.1	101	0	0	11.4	465	0	.006	0	.012	.003	.024	4.23	—	5.97	133
Vegetable shortening	1 T.	12.8	115	0	0	12.8	—	—	—	—	—	—	—	—	—	—	—

FATS AND OILS (cont.)	Measure	Mass	Energy	Protein	Carbohydrate	Fat	VITAMINS Vitamin A	Vitamin B$_1$	Vitamin B$_2$	Vitamin B$_6$	Vitamin B$_{12}$	Niacin	Vitamin C	MINERALS Calcium	Iron	Potassium	Sodium
		g	Cal	g	g	g	IU	mg	mg	mg	μg	mg	mg	mg	mg	mg	mg
Oils																	
Corn	1 T.	13.6	120	0	0	13.6	—	—	—	—	—	—	—	—	—	—	—
Olive	1 T.	13.5	119	0	0	13.5	—	—	—	—	—	—	—	.02	.05	—	0
Peanut	1 T.	13.5	119	0	0	13.5	—	—	—	—	—	—	—	.01	0	0	.01
Safflower	1 T.	13.6	120	0	0	13.6	—	—	—	—	—	—	—	—	—	—	—
Sesame	1 T.	13.6	120	0	0	13.6	—	—	—	—	—	—	—	—	—	—	—
Soybean	1 T.	13.6	120	0	0	13.6	—	—	—	—	—	—	—	.01	0	—	0
Sunflower	1 T.	13.6	120	0	0	13.6	—	—	—	—	—	—	—	.03	0	—	.01
FRUITS AND FRUIT JUICES																	
Apple	1	150	81	.27	21	.49	74	.023	.019	.066	0	.106	7.8	10	.25	159	1
Apple, dried	10 rings	64	155	.59	42	.2	0	0	.102	.08	0	.593	2.5	9	.9	288	56
Apple juice	1 C.	248	116	.15	29	.28	2	.052	.042	.074	0	.248	2.3	16	.92	296	7
Applesauce, unsw	1 C.	244	106	.4	27.5	.12	70	.032	.061	.063	0	.459	2.9	7	.29	183	5
Apricot	3	114	51	1.48	11.7	.41	2769	.032	.042	.057	0	.636	10.6	15	.58	313	1
Apricot, dried	10 halves	35	83	1.28	21.6	.16	2534	.003	.053	.055	0	1.05	.8	16	1.65	482	3
Apricot nectar	1 C.	251	141	.92	36	.22	3304	.023	.035	—	0	.653	1.4	17	.96	286	9
Avocado	1	272	324	3.99	14.8	30.8	1230	.217	.245	.563	0	3.86	15.9	22	2.05	1204	21
Banana	1	175	105	1.18	26.7	.55	92	.051	.114	.659	0	.616	10.3	7	.35	451	1
Blackberries	1 C.	144	74	1.04	18.3	.56	237	.043	.058	.084	0	.576	30.2	46	.83	282	0
Blueberries	1 C.	145	82	.97	20.5	.55	145	.07	.073	.052	0	.521	18.9	9	.24	129	9
Cherries	1 C.	145	104	1.74	24	1.39	310	.073	.087	.052	0	.58	10.2	21	.56	325	1
Crabapple (slices)	1 C.	110	.83	.44	21.9	.33	44	.033	.022	—	0	.11	8.8	20	.39	213	1
Cranberries	1 C.	95	46	.37	12	.19	44	.029	.019	.062	0	.095	12.8	7	.19	67	1
Currants, black	1 C.	112	71	1.57	17.2	.45	258	.056	.056	.074	0	.336	202	61	1.72	361	2
Dates	10	83	228	1.63	61	.37	42	.075	.083	.159	0	1.82	0	27	.96	541	2
Fig	1	65	47	.48	12.2	.19	91	.038	.032	.072	0	.256	1.3	22	.23	148	1
Fig, dried	10	189	477	5.7	122	2.18	248	.133	.165	.419	0	1.3	1.6	269	4.18	1332	20
Grapefruit	1/2	241	38	.75	9.7	.12	149	.043	.024	.05	0	.3	41.3	14	.1	167	0
Grapefruit juice	1 C.	247	96	1.24	22.7	.25	—	.099	.049	—	0	.494	93.9	22	.49	400	2
Grapes, slip skin	1 C.	153	58	.58	15.7	.32	92	.085	.052	.1	0	.276	3.7	13	.27	176	2
Grapes, adherent skin	1 C.	160	114	1.06	28.4	.92	117	.147	.091	.176	0	.48	17.3	17	.41	296	3
Grape juice	1 C.	253	155	1.41	37.8	.19	20	.066	.094	.164	0	.663	.2	22	.6	334	7
Guava	1	112	45	.74	10.7	.54	713	.045	.045	.129	0	1.08	165	18	.28	256	2
Kiwi fruit	1	88	46	.75	11.3	.34	133	.015	.038	—	0	.38	74.5	20	.31	252	4
Kumquat	1	20	12	.17	3.12	.02	57	.015	.019	—	0	—	7.1	8	.07	37	1
Lemon juice	1 T.	15.2	3	.06	.99	.04	2	.006	.001	.007	0	.03	3.8	2	.02	15	3
Lime juice	1 T.	15.4	4	.07	1.39	.02	2	.003	.002	.007	0	.015	4.5	1	0	17	0

FRUITS AND FRUIT JUICES (cont.)	Measure	Mass	Energy	Protein	Carbohydrate	Fat	VITAMINS Vitamin A	Vitamin B₁	Vitamin B₂	Vitamin B₆	Vitamin B₁₂	Niacin	Vitamin C	MINERALS Calcium	Iron	Potassium	Sodium
		g	Cal	g	g	g	IU	mg	mg	mg	μg	mg	mg	mg	mg	mg	mg
Lychee	1	16	6	.08	1.59	.04	—	.001	.006	—	0	.058	6.9	0	.03	16	0
Mango	1	300	135	1.06	35	.57	8060	.12	.118	.277	0	1.21	57.3	21	.26	322	4
Melon, cantaloupe	1/2	477	94	2.34	22.3	.74	8608	.096	.056	.307	0	1.53	112	28	.57	825	23
Melon, casaba	1/10	245	43	1.48	10	.16	49	.098	.033	—	0	.656	26.2	8	.66	344	20
Melon, honeydew	1/10	226	46	.59	11.8	.13	52	.099	.023	.076	0	.774	32	8	.09	350	13
Mulberries	1 C.	140	61	2.02	13.7	.55	35	.041	.141	—	0	.868	51	55	2.59	271	14
Nectarine	1	150	67	1.28	16	.62	1001	.023	.056	.034	0	1.34	7.3	6	.21	288	0
Orange	1	180	62	1.23	15.4	.16	269	.114	.052	.079	0	.369	69.7	52	.13	237	0
Orange juice	1 C.	248	111	1.74	25.8	.5	496	.223	.074	.099	0	.992	124	27	.5	496	2
Papaya	1	454	117	1.86	30	.43	6122	.082	.097	.058	0	1.02	187	72	.3	780	8
Passion fruit	1	35	18	.4	4.21	.13	126	—	.023	—	0	.27	5.4	2	.29	63	5
Peach	1	115	37	.61	9.65	.08	465	.015	.036	.016	0	.861	5.7	5	.1	171	0
Peach, dried	10 halves	130	311	4.69	79.7	.99	2812	.003	.276	.087	0	5.68	6.3	37	5.28	1295	9
Peach nectar	1 C.	249	134	.67	34.6	.05	643	.007	.035	—	0	.717	13.1	13	.47	101	17
Pear	1	180	98	.65	25	.66	33	.033	.066	.03	0	.166	6.6	19	.41	208	1
Pear, dried	10 halves	175	459	3.28	122	1.1	6	.014	.254	—	0	2.4	12.3	59	3.68	932	10
Pear nectar	1 C.	250	149	.27	39.4	.03	1	.005	.033	—	0	.32	2.7	11	.65	33	9
Persimmon	1	200	118	.98	31.2	.31	3640	.05	.034	—	0	.168	12.6	13	.26	270	3
Pineapple	1 C.	155	77	.6	19.2	.66	35	.143	.056	.135	0	.651	23.9	11	.57	175	1
Pineapple juice	1 C.	250	139	.8	34.4	.2	12	.138	.055	.24	0	.643	26.7	42	.65	334	2
Plum	1	70	36	.52	8.59	.41	213	.028	.063	.053	0	.330	6.3	2	.07	113	0
Pomegranate	1	275	104	1.47	26.4	.46	—	.046	.046	.162	0	.462	9.4	5	.46	399	5
Prickly pear	1	137	42	.75	9.86	.53	53	.014	.062	—	0	.474	14.4	58	.31	226	6
Prune	10	97	201	2.19	52.7	.43	1669	.068	.136	.222	0	1.64	2.8	43	2.08	626	3
Prune juice	1 C.	256	181	1.55	44.6	.08	9	.041	.179	—	0	2.01	10.6	30	3.03	706	11
Quince	1	151	53	.37	14	.09	37	.018	.028	.037	0	.184	13.8	10	.64	181	4
Raisins, packed	1 C.	165	488	4.16	12.9	.9	0	.185	.3	.31	0	1.83	9	46	4.27	1362	47
Raspberries	1 C.	123	61	1.11	14.2	.68	160	.037	.111	.07	0	1.1	30.8	27	.7	187	0
Rhubarb	1 C.	122	26	1.09	5.53	.24	122	.024	.037	.029	0	.366	9.8	105	.27	351	5
Strawberries	1 C.	149	45	.91	10.4	.55	41	.03	.098	.088	0	.343	84.5	21	.57	247	2
Tangerine	1	116	37	.53	9.4	.16	773	.088	.018	.056	0	.134	26	12	.09	132	1
Tangerine juice	1 C.	247	106	1.24	25	.49	1037	.148	.049	—	0	.247	76.6	44	.49	440	2
Watermelon	1 C.	160	50	.99	11.5	.68	585	.128	.032	.23	0	.32	15.4	13	.28	186	3
MEATS **Beef** Chuck roast	1 lb	454	1164	83	0	90	130	.485	.794	1.7	13.7	14.6	0	32	9.44	1374	266
Corned, brisket	1 lb	454	896	66.58	.63	67.6	—	.195	.712	1.32	8.07	16.6	0	30	7.66	1348	5519
Dried	1 oz	28	47	8.25	.44	1.11	—	.02	.09	—	.52	1.06	—	2	1.28	126	984
Flank steak	1 lb	454	888	87.4	0	57	50	.499	.680	1.87	13.4	20.6	0	22	8.9	1585	321
Ground beef, lean	4 oz	113	298	20	0	23.4	22.5	.057	.237	.28	2.64	5.1	0	9	1.99	295	78

MEATS Beef (cont.)	Measure	Mass	Energy	Protein	Carbohydrate	Fat	VITAMINS Vitamin A	Vitamin B₁	Vitamin B₂	Vitamin B₆	Vitamin B₁₂	Niacin	Vitamin C	MINERALS Calcium	Iron	Potassium	Sodium
		g	Cal	g	g	g	IU	mg	mg	mg	µg	mg	mg	mg	mg	mg	mg
Ground beef, regular	4 oz	113	351	18.8	0	30	40	.043	.171	.27	2.99	5.06	0	10	1.96	258	77
Liver	4 oz	113	161	22.6	6.58	4.34	39941	.292	3.14	1.06	78.2	14.4	25.3	6	7.71	365	82
Pastrami	1 oz	28	99	4.9	.86	8.27	—	.027	.048	.05	.5	1.44	.9	2	.54	65	348
Porterhouse steak	1 lb	454	1289	78.8	0	105.6	300	.44	.739	1.62	11.85	15.3	0	29	7.83	1305	222
Rib roast	1 lb	454	1503	72.8	0	132	310	.349	.576	1.39	12.45	12.4	0	39	7.63	1180	241
Round steak	1 lb	454	1093	88	0	79.5	110	.435	.748	2.02	12.21	15.97	0	23	8.5	1434	232
Short ribs	1 lb	454	1761	65.3	0	164	—	.322	.535	1.34	11.6	11.6	0	41	7.03	1053	224
Sirloin steak	1 lb	454	1179	82.7	0	91.5	220	.503	.88	1.71	12.58	13.9	0	34	10.2	1331	234
Smoked, chopped	1 oz	28	38	5.7	.53	1.25	—	.024	.05	.1	.49	1.3	0	—	.81	107	357
T-bone steak	1 lb	454	1394	76	0	118.5	300	.422	.712	1.58	11.6	14.8	0	30	7.58	1248	217
Tenderloin	1 lb	454	1095	84.1	0	81.6	—	.54	.97	1.74	12	13.9	0	30	10.9	1422	223
Lamb																	
Leg	1 lb	454	845	67.7	0	61.7	—	.59	.82	1.05	8.2	19	—	.39	5.1	1083	237
Chops	1 lb	454	1146	63.7	0	97	—	.57	.79	1.05	8.2	18.5	—	35	4.7	1019	223
Liver	1 lb	454	617	95.3	13.2	19.6	229070	1.81	14.9	1.36	472	76.5	152	45	49.4	916	236
Shoulder	1 lb	454	1082	59	0	92	—	.53	.73	1.05	8.2	17.1	—	35	3.9	942	206
Pork																	
Bacon	1 lb	454	2523	39	.42	261	0	1.67	.472	.64	4.2	12.6	0	34	2.7	631	3107
Bacon, Canadian style	1 lb	454	714	93.6	7.61	31.6	0	3.4	.78	1.77	3.02	28.2	0	36	3.07	1560	6391
Ham, boneless	1 lb	454	827	79.6	14.1	47.9	0	3.9	1.14	1.52	3.75	23.8	—	.32	4.5	1508	5974
Leg	1 lb	454	1182	77.4	0	94.4	.30	3.24	.889	1.81	2.79	20.5	3.2	25	3.87	1405	214
Loin, chop	1 chop	151	345	20	0	28.7	9	.948	.294	.45	.86	5.33	.8	7	.85	346	63
Shoulder	1 lb	454	1249	73	0	103	30	3.08	1.19	1.26	3.25	16.8	3	24	4.59	1325	286
Spareribs	1 lb	454	804	48	0	66.3	30	1.74	.768	1.18	2.45	13.6	—	19	2.78	728	212
Veal																	
Breast	1 lb	454	828	65.6	0	61	—	.48	.87	1.22	5.7	22	—	39	9.7	1050	230
Chuck	1 lb	454	628	70.4	0	36	—	.52	.94	1.22	5.7	23.6	—	40	10.5	1126	246
Cutlet	1 lb	454	681	72.3	0	41	—	.53	.96	1.22	5.7	24.2	—	41	10.9	1157	253
Liver	1 lb	454	635	87.1	18.6	21.3	102060	.9	12.3	3.04	272	51.8	161	36	39.9	1275	331
Rib roast	1 lb	454	723	65.7	0	49	—	.48	.87	1.22	5.7	22	0	38	9.8	1051	230
Rump roast	1 lb	454	573	68	0	31	—	.5	.9	1.22	5.7	22.8	—	38	10	1090	238
Luncheon and Sausage																	
Bologna, beef	1 oz	28	89	3.31	.55	8.04	—	.016	.036	.05	.4	.746	t	3	.4	44	284
Bologna, beef and pork	1 oz	28	89	3.31	.79	8.01	—	.049	.039	.05	.38	.731	t	3	.43	51	289
Bologna, pork	1 oz	28	70	4.34	.21	5.63	—	.148	.045	.08	.26	1.1	t	3	.22	80	336
Bratwurst, ckd	1 link	85	256	12	1.76	22	—	.429	.156	.18	.81	2.72	1	38	1.09	180	473
Braunschweiger	1 oz	28	102	3.83	.89	9.1	3984	.071	.432	.09	5.69	2.37	t	2	2.65	57	324
Brotwurst	1 oz	28	92	4.04	.84	7.88	—	.071	.064	.04	.58	.936	t	14	.29	80	315

MEATS Luncheon and Sausage (cont.)	Measure	Mass	Energy	Protein	Carbohydrate	Fat	VITAMINS Vitamin A	Vitamin B$_1$	Vitamin B$_2$	Vitamin B$_6$	Vitamin B$_{12}$	Niacin	Vitamin C	MINERALS Calcium	Iron	Potassium	Sodium
		g	Cal	g	g	g	IU	mg	mg	mg	µg	mg	mg	mg	mg	mg	mg
Frankfurter, beef	1	45	145	5.08	1.08	13.2	—	.023	.046	.05	.74	1.13	t	6	.6	71	461
Frankfurter, beef and pork	1	45	144	5.08	1.15	13.1	—	.09	.054	.06	.58	1.18	t	5	.52	75	504
Italian sausage, ckd	1 link	67	216	13.4	1	17.2	—	.417	.156	.22	.87	2.79	1	16	1	204	618
Kielbasa	1 oz	28	88	3.76	.61	7.7	—	.065	.061	.05	.46	.816	t	12	.41	77	305
Knockwurst	1 link	68	209	8.08	1.2	18.8	—	.233	.095	.11	.8	1.86	t	7	.62	136	687
Liver cheese	1 oz	28	86	4.3	.59	7.25	4958	.06	.631	.13	6.96	3.33	1	2	3.07	64	347
Liverwurst	1 oz	28	93	4.01	.63	8.09	—	.077	.292	—	24.2	—	—	7	1.81	—	—
Mortadella	1 oz	28	88	4.64	.87	7.2	—	.034	.043	.035	.42	.758	t	5	.4	46	353
Pepperoni	1 slice	5.5	27	1.15	.16	2.42	—	.018	.014	.01	.14	.273	.018	1	.08	19	112
Polish sausage	1 oz	28	92	4	.46	8.14	—	.142	.042	.05	.28	.976	0	3	.41	67	248
Pork and beef sausage	1 link	13	52	1.79	.35	4.71	—	.096	.019	.01	.06	.438	—	—	.15	—	105
Pork sausage	1 link	28	118	3.31	.29	11.4	—	.155	.046	.07	.32	.804	0	5	.26	58	228
Salami, hard	1 slice	10	42	2.29	.26	3.44	—	.06	.029	.05	.19	.487	t	1	.15	38	186
Summer sausage	1 slice	23	80	3.69	.53	6.88	—	.039	.069	.07	1.06	.94	t	2	.47	53	334
Vienna sausage	1	16	45	1.65	.33	4.03	—	.014	.017	.02	.16	.258	0	2	.14	16	152
NUTS AND SEEDS																	
Almonds	1 C.	142	849	26.4	27.7	77	0	.34	1.31	.142	0	5	t	332	6.7	1098	6
Brazil nuts	1 C.	140	916	20	15.3	93.7	t	1.34	.17	.238	0	2.2	14	260	4.8	1001	1
Cashews	1 C.	140	785	24.1	41	64	140	.6	.35	.325	0	2.5	0	53	5.3	650	21
Chestnuts, fresh	1 C.	160	310	4.6	67.4	2.7	0	.35	.35	.527	0	1	9.6	43	2.7	726	10
Coconut, shredded	1 C.	80	277	2.8	7.5	28.2	0	.04	.02	.035	0	.4	2	10	1.4	205	18
Coconut, liquid	1 C.	240	53	.7	11.3	.5	0	t	t	.045	0	.2	5	48	.7	353	60
Hazelnuts	1 C.	135	856	17	22.5	84.2	144	.62	.738	.735	0	1.2	t	282	4.6	950	3
Hickory nuts	15 small	15	101	2.1	2	10.1	—	.08	—	—	—	—	0	9	.4	64	0
Macadamia nuts	1 C.	134	940	11	18.4	98.8	0	.469	.147	—	0	2.87	—	94	3.23	493	6
Peanuts	1 C.	144	838	37.7	29.7	70.1	t	.46	.19	.576	0	24.6	0	104	3.2	1009	7
Peanut butter	1 T.	15	86	3.9	3.2	8.1	0	.018	.02	.05	0	2.4	0	11	.3	123	18
Pecans	1 C.	108	742	9.9	15.8	76.9	140	.93	.14	.183	0	1	2	79	2.6	651	t
Pine nuts	1 oz	28	180	3.7	5.8	14.3	10	.36	.07	—	0	1.3	t	3	1.5	170	1
Pistachios, shelled	1 C.	128	739	26	31.7	61.9	299	1.05	.223	—	0	1.38	—	173	8.67	1399	7
Pumpkin seeds & squash	1 C.	140	774	40.6	21	65.4	100	.34	.442	—	0	3.4	—	71	15.7	—	24
Sesame seeds	1 C.	150	873	27.3	26.4	80	99	.27	.2	.126	0	8.1	0	165	3.6	610	59
Sunflower seeds	1 C.	145	812	34.8	28.9	68.6	70	2.84	.33	1.8	0	7.8	—	174	10.3	1334	4
Tahini	1 T.	15	89	2.55	3.18	8.06	—	.183	.071	—	0	.818	0	64	1.34	62	17
Walnuts	1 C.	100	651	14.8	15.8	64	30	.33	.13	.73	0	.9	2	99	3.1	450	2

	Measure	Mass	Energy	Protein	Carbohydrate	Fat	VITAMINS Vitamin A	Vitamin B$_1$	Vitamin B$_2$	Vitamin B$_6$	Vitamin B$_{12}$	Niacin	Vitamin C	MINERALS Calcium	Iron	Potassium	Sodium
		g	Cal	g	g	g	IU	mg	mg	mg	μg	mg	mg	mg	mg	mg	mg
POULTRY																	
Chicken																	
Light meat	1 lb	454	216	23.5	0	12.8	115	.068	.1	.56	.39	10.3	1.1	13	.92	237	76
Dark meat	1 lb	454	379	26.7	0	29.3	273	.098	.234	.39	.47	8.33	3.4	18	1.57	285	117
Light meat, no skin	1 lb	454	100	20.4	0	1.45	25	.06	.081	.48	.34	9.33	1.1	10	.64	210	60
Dark meat, no skin	1 lb	454	136	21.9	0	4.7	78	.084	.201	.36	.39	6.8	3.4	13	1.12	241	93
Breast	1/2	181	250	30.2	0	13.4	121	.091	.123	.77	.5	14.3	1.5	16	1.07	319	91
Drumstick	1	110	117	14	0	6.34	69	.054	.13	.22	.25	3.97	2	8	.75	151	61
Thigh	1	120	199	16.2	0	14.3	136	.058	.144	.24	.28	5.1	2.1	9	.93	181	71
Wing	1	90	109	8.98	0	7.82	72	.024	.043	.17	.15	2.9	.3	6	.47	76	36
Liver	1	32	40	5.75	1.09	1.23	6576	.044	.628	.24	7.35	2.96	10.8	3	2.74	73	25
Canned, boned	5 oz	142	234	30.9	0	11.3	—	.021	.183	.5	.42	8.98	2.8	20	2.25	196	714
Liver pâté	1 T.	13	26	1.75	.85	1.7	94	.007	.182	—	—	.977	1.3	1	1.19	—	—
Duck																	
Domesticated	1 lb	454	1159	33	0	113	483	.565	.603	.55	.73	11.3	8	30	6.89	600	181
Liver	1	44	60	8.24	1.55	2.04	17559	—	—	—	23.7	—	—	5	13.4	—	—
Goose																	
Domesticated	1 lb	454	1187	50.7	0	107	176	.272	.784	1.24	—	11.5	—	38	8	985	234
Liver	1	94	125	15.3	5.94	4.03	29138	.528	.838	.72	—	6.11	—	40	—	216	132
Turkey																	
Light meat	1 lb	454	286	39	0	13.2	12	.101	.207	.86	.75	9.24	0	23	2.18	489	106
Dark meat	1 lb	454	243	28.7	0	13.3	8	.111	.307	.49	.58	4.34	0	26	2.57	396	108
Liver	1	102	140	20.4	4.21	4.05	18403	.062	2.21	.78	64.6	10.35	4.6	7	11	303	98
Canned, boned	5 oz	142	231	33.6	0	9.74	0	.02	.243	—	—	9.4	2.8	17	2.64	—	663
SALAD DRESSINGS AND SAUCES																	
Salad Dressings																	
Bleu cheese	1 T.	15.3	77	.7	1.1	8	32	0	0	—	—	0	.3	12.4	0	—	—
French	1 T.	15.6	67	.1	2.7	6.4	—	—	—	—	—	—	—	1.7	.1	12.3	213
Italian	1 T.	14.7	68.7	.1	1.5	7.1	—	—	—	—	—	—	—	1	0	2	116
Mayonnaise	1 T.	13.8	99	.2	.4	11	39	0	—	—	—	—	0	2	.1	5	78.4
Russian	1 T.	15.3	76	.2	1.6	7.8	106	.01	.01	—	—	.1	1	3	.1	24	133
Thousand Island	1 T.	15.6	58.9	.1	2.4	5.6	50	—	—	—	—	—	—	2	.1	18	109
Sauces																	
Barbecue	1 C.	250	188	4.5	32	4.5	2170	.075	.05	.188	0	2.25	17.5	48	2.25	435	2038
Catsup	1 T.	15	16	.3	3.8	.1	210	.01	.01	.016	0	.2	2	3	.1	54	156
Horseradish, prepared	1 T.	15	6	.2	1.4	t	—	—	—	.022	0	—	—	9	.1	44	14
Mustard	1 T.	15	15	.9	.9	.9	—	—	—	—	—	—	—	18	.3	21	195
Soy	1 T.	18	11	1.56	1.5	0	0	.009	.023	.031	0	.605	0	3	.49	64	1029
Tartar	1 T.	14	31	.1	.9	3.1	30	t	t	—	—	t	t	3	.1	11	99
Vinegar	1 T.	15	2	t	.9	0	—	—	—	t	0	—	—	1	.1	15	t

	Measure	Mass	Energy	Protein	Carbohydrate	Fat	VITAMINS Vitamin A	Vitamin B₁	Vitamin B₂	Vitamin B₆	Vitamin B₁₂	Niacin	Vitamin C	MINERALS Calcium	Iron	Potassium	Sodium
		g	Cal	g	g	g	IU	mg	mg	mg	µg	mg	mg	mg	mg	mg	mg
SEAFOOD AND SEAWEED																	
Abalone	3 oz	85	89	14.5	5	.64	—	.16	.12	—	—	—	—	27	2.7	—	255
Anchovy, in oil, drained	5	20	42	5.78	0	1.94	—	.016	.073	.041	.176	3.98	—	46	.93	109	734
Bass	3 oz	85	82	15	0	1.98	—	.09	.03	—	3.25	1.9	—	—	.71	232	59
Bluefish	3 oz	85	105	17	0	3.6	338	.049	.068	.342	4.58	5.06	—	6	.41	316	51
Carp	3 oz	85	108	15	0	4.76	25	.008	.036	.162	1.3	1.34	1.4	35	1.05	283	42
Catfish	3 oz	85	99	15.5	0	3.62	—	.038	.09	—	.002	1.82	—	34	.83	296	54
Caviar, black and red	1 T.	16	40	3.9	.64	2.86	—	—	—	—	—	—	—	42	1.7	27	240
Clams	9 large	180	133	23	4.62	1.75	540	.18	.38	.14	89	3.17	—	83	25	564	100
Cod	3 oz	85	70	15	0	.57	34	.065	.055	.208	.772	1.75	.9	13	.32	351	46
Crab	3 oz	85	71	15.6	0	.51	20	.037	.037	.272	9.08	.934	1.8	39	.5	173	711
Eel	3 oz	85	156	15.7	0	9.9	2954	.128	.034	.057	2.55	2.98	1.3	17	.43	232	43
Flat fish, flounder and sole species	3 oz	85	78	16	0	1	28	.076	.065	.177	1.29	2.46	—	15	.3	307	69
Haddock	3 oz	85	74	16	0	.61	47	.03	.031	.255	1.02	3.23	—	28	.89	264	58
Halibut	3 oz	85	93	17.7	0	1.95	132	.051	.064	.292	1	11.97	—	40	.71	382	46
Herring	3 oz	85	134	15	0	7.68	80	.078	.198	.257	11.6	2.74	.6	49	.94	278	76
Kelp	1 T.	14.2	—	—	5.53	.157	—	—	.046	—	—	.784	—	156	.014	753	429
Lobster	3 oz	85	77	16	.43	.76	—	.368	.041	—	.786	1.23	—	26	.54	236	272
Mackerel	3 oz	85	174	15.8	0	11.8	140	.15	.265	.339	7.4	7.72	.3	10	1.38	267	76
Oysters	6 medium	84	58	5.9	3.29	2.08	282	.128	.139	.042	16	1.1	—	38	5.63	192	94
Perch	3 oz	85	80	15.8	0	1.39	34	.08	.094	.2	.85	1.7	2.72	91	.78	232	64
Pike	3 oz	85	75	16.4	0	.58	60	.049	.054	.099	—	2.16	3.2	48	.47	220	33
Salmon	3 oz	85	121	16.9	0	5.39	34	.19	.32	.695	2.7	6.68	8.2	10	.68	417	37
Sardines, in oil, drained	2	24	50	5.9	0	2.75	54	.019	.054	.04	2.15	1.26	—	92	.7	95	121
Scallops	3 oz	85	75	14.3	2	.64	—	.01	.055	—	1.3	.978	—	21	.25	274	137
Shark	3 oz	85	111	17.8	0	3.83	198	.036	.053	—	1.27	2.5	—	29	.71	136	67
Shrimp	3 oz	85	90	17.3	.77	1.47	8.26	.024	.029	.088	.987	2.17	—	44	2.05	157	126
Smelt	3 oz	85	83	15	0	2.06	—	—	.102	—	2.92	1.23	—	51	.77	247	51
Snails	3 oz	85	117	20	6.6	.34	72	.022	.091	.291	7.7	.893	—	48	4.28	295	175
Snapper	3 oz	85	85	17.4	0	1.14	—	.039	.003	—	—	.241	—	27	.15	355	54
Swordfish	3 oz	85	103	16.8	0	3.41	101	.031	.081	.281	1.49	8.23	.9	4	.69	245	76
Trout	3 oz	85	126	17.7	0	5.62	49	.277	.261	1.43	6.6	7.6	.4	36	1.27	307	44
Tuna, in water	1 can	165	216	48.8	0	.83	130	.08	.19	.39	1.6	19	—	20	5.28	518	588
Whitefish	3 oz	85	114	16	0	4.98	2050	.128	.108	—	—	2.72	—	—	.31	269	43
SOUPS																	
Asparagus, cream of	1 C.	244	87	2.28	10.7	4.09	445	.054	.078	.012	—	.778	2.8	29	.8	173	981
Bean, black	1 C.	247	116	5.64	19.8	1.51	506	.077	.054	.094	.02	.534	.8	45	2.16	273	1198

SOUPS (cont.)	Measure	Mass	Energy	Protein	Carbohydrate	Fat	VITAMINS Vitamin A	Vitamin B₁	Vitamin B₂	Vitamin B₆	Vitamin B₁₂	Niacin	Vitamin C	MINERALS Calcium	Iron	Potassium	Sodium
		g	Cal	g	g	g	IU	mg	mg	mg	μg	mg	mg	mg	mg	mg	mg
Bean, with frankfurters	1 C.	250	187	9.99	22	6.98	869	.11	.065	.133	—	1.02	.9	86	2.34	477	1092
Beef bouillon	1 C.	240	16	2.74	.1	.53	0	.005	.05	—	—	1.87	0	15	.41	130	782
Beef noodle	1 C.	244	84	4.83	8.98	3.08	629	.068	.059	.037	.2	1.06	.3	15	1.1	99	952
Celery, cream of	1 C.	244	90	1.66	8.82	5.59	306	.029	.049	.012	—	.332	.2	40	.62	123	949
Chicken broth	1 C.	244	39	4.93	.93	1.39	0	.01	.071	.024	.24	3.34	0	9	.51	210	776
Chicken, cream of	1 C.	244	116	3.43	9.26	7.36	560	.029	.061	.017	—	.82	.2	34	.61	87	986
Chicken gumbo	1 C.	244	56	2.64	8.37	1.43	136	.02	.05	.063	—	.664	4.9	24	.89	75	955
Chicken noodle	1 C.	241	75	4.04	9.35	2.45	711	.053	.06	.027	—	1.38	.2	17	.78	55	1107
Chicken rice	1 C.	241	60	3.53	7.15	1.91	660	.017	.024	.024	—	1.12	.1	17	.75	100	814
Clam chowder, New England	1 C.	244	95	4.81	12.4	2.88	8	.02	.044	.083	8.01	.961	2	43	1.48	146	914
Minestrone	1 C.	241	83	4.26	11.2	2.51	2337	.053	.043	.099	0	.942	1.1	34	.92	312	911
Mushroom, cream of	1 C.	244	129	2.32	9.3	8.97	0	.046	.09	.015	.05	.725	1	46	.51	101	1031
Onion	1 C.	241	57	3.75	8.18	1.74	0	.034	.024	.048	0	.6	1.2	26	.67	69	1053
Oyster stew	1 C.	241	59	2.11	4.07	3.83	71	.022	.036	.012	2.19	.234	3.1	22	.98	49	980
Pea, split, with ham	1 C.	253	189	10.3	28	4.4	444	.147	.076	.068	—	1.47	1.4	22	2.28	399	1008
Potato, cream of	1 C.	244	73	1.74	11.4	2.36	288	.034	.037	.037	—	.539	0	20	.48	137	1000
Tomato	1 C.	244	86	2.06	16.6	1.92	688	.088	.051	.112	0	1.41	66.5	13	1.76	263	872
Turkey noodle	1 C.	244	69	3.9	8.63	1.99	292	.073	.063	.037	—	1.4	.2	12	.94	75	815
Vegetable, beef	1 C.	244	79	5.58	10.1	1.9	1891	.037	.049	.076	.31	1.03	2.4	17	1.11	173	957
Vegetable, vegetarian	1 C.	241	72	2.1	12	1.93	3005	.053	.046	.055	0	.916	1.4	21	1.08	209	823
VEGETABLES AND VEGETABLE JUICES																	
Alfalfa, sprouts	1 C.	33	10	1.32	1.25	.23	51	.025	.042	.011	0	.159	2.7	10	.32	26	2
Artichoke, globe	1 medium	128	65	3.4	15.3	.26	237	.1	.077	.143	0	.973	13.8	61	2.1	434	102
Artichoke, Jerusalem	1 C.	150	114	3	26	.02	30	.3	.09	—	—	1.95	6	21	5.1	—	—
Asparagus	1 C.	134	30	4.1	4.94	.3	1202	.15	.166	.2	0	1.5	44	28	.9	404	2
Black beans, dry	1 C.	200	678	44.6	122	3	60	1.1	.4	—	0	4.4	—	270	15.8	2076	50
Black eye peas, ckd	1 C.	165	178	13.4	29.9	1.3	580	.5	.18	.18	0	2.3	28	40	3.5	625	2
Beets	1 C.	136	60	2	13.6	.2	28	.068	.028	.06	0	.54	15	22	1.24	440	98
Beet greens	1 C.	38	8	.7	1.5	.02	2308	.038	.08	.04	0	.152	—	46	1.2	208	76

VEGETABLES AND VEGETABLE JUICES (cont.)	Measure	Mass	Energy	Protein	Carbohydrate	Fat	VITAMINS Vitamin A	Vitamin B_1	Vitamin B_2	Vitamin B_6	Vitamin B_{12}	Niacin	Vitamin C	MINERALS Calcium	Iron	Potassium	Sodium
		g	Cal	g	g	g	IU	mg	mg	mg	μg	mg	mg	mg	mg	mg	mg
Broccoli	1 C.	88	24	2.6	4.6	.3	1356	.058	.1	.14	0	.56	82	42	.78	286	24
Brussels sprouts	1 C.	88	38	3.3	7.88	.26	778	.12	.08	.19	0	.65	74	36	1.2	.342	22
Cabbage, common	1 C.	70	16	.84	2.76	.12	88	.03	.02	.066	0	.2	33	32	.4	172	12
Cabbage, Chinese	1 C.	70	9	1.05	1.53	.14	2100	.028	.049	—	0	.35	31.5	74	.56	176	45
Carrots	1 C.	110	48	1	11	.2	30942	.1	.064	.16	0	1	10	30	.54	356	38
Carrot juice	1 C.	227	96	2.47	22	—	24750	.13	.12	.534	0	1.35	20	8.3	1.5	767	105
Cauliflower	1 C.	100	24	1.98	4.9	.18	16	.076	.058	.23	0	.634	71	28	.58	356	14
Celery	1 C.	120	18	.8	4.36	.14	152	.036	.036	.036	0	.36	7.6	44	.58	340	106
Chard, Swiss	1 C.	36	6	.64	1.34	.08	1188	.014	.032	—	0	.144	10.8	18	.64	136	76
Chives	1 T.	3	1	.08	.11	.02	192	.003	.005	.005	0	.021	2.4	2	.05	8	0
Collards	1 C.	186	35	2.9	7	.4	6194	.054	.119	.125	0	.696	43	218	1.16	275	52
Corn	1 C.	154	132	4.96	29	1.8	432	.208	.09	.084	0	2.6	10.6	4	.8	416	23
Cucumber	1 C.	104	14	.56	3	.14	46	.032	.02	.054	0	.321	4.8	14	.28	156	2
Eggplant	1 C.	82	22	.9	5	.08	58	.074	.016	.078	0	.492	.14	30	.44	180	2
Endive	1 C.	50	8	.62	1.68	.1	1026	.04	.038	.1	0	.2	3.2	26	.42	158	12
Garbanzos, dry	1 C.	200	720	41	122	9.6	100	.62	.3	—	0	4	t	300	13.8	1594	52
Garlic	1 clove	3	4	.2	.9	.02	t	.01	t	—	0	t	t	1	t	16	1
Green beans	1 C.	110	34	2	7.85	.013	735	.092	.116	.081	0	.827	17.9	41	1.14	230	6
Kale	1 C.	67	33	2.21	6.7	.47	5963	.074	.087	.182	0	.67	80.4	90	1.14	299	29
Kidney beans, ckd	1 C.	185	218	14.4	39.6	.9	10	.2	.11	—	0	1.3	—	70	4.4	629	6
Kohlrabi	1 C.	140	38	2.38	8.68	.14	50	.07	.028	.21	0	.56	86.8	34	.56	490	28
Leeks	1	124	76	1.86	17.5	.37	118	.074	.037	.2	0	.496	14.9	73	2.6	223	25
Lentils, ckd	1 C.	200	212	15.6	38.6	t	40	.14	.12	—	0	1.2	0	50	4.2	498	—
Lentil sprouts	1 C.	77	81	6.9	17	.43	35	.176	.099	.146	0	.869	12.7	19	2.47	248	8
Lettuce, Iceberg	1 C.	75	10	.7	2.2	.12	250	.05	.05	.028	0	.148	5	15	.4	131	7
Lettuce, romaine	1 C.	56	8	.9	1.3	.12	1456	.056	.056	—	0	.28	13.4	20	.62	162	4
Lima beans, ckd	1 C.	170	208	11.6	40	.54	630	.238	.163	.328	0	1.77	17	54	4.2	969	29
Mung bean sprouts	1 C.	104	32	3	6	.2	22	.088	.128	.092	0	.778	13.6	14	.94	154	6
Mushrooms	1 C.	70	18	1.46	3	.3	0	.072	.3	.068	0	2.88	2.4	4	.86	260	2
Navy beans, ckd	1 C.	190	224	14.8	40.3	1.1	0	.27	.13	—	0	1.3	0	95	5.1	790	13
Okra	1 C.	100	38	2	7.6	.1	660	.2	.06	.2	0	1	21	82	.8	302	8
Onions, green	1 C.	100	26	1.7	5.5	.14	5000	.07	.14	—	0	.2	45	60	1.88	256	4
Onions, mature	1 C.	160	54	1.88	11.7	.42	0	.096	.016	.25	0	.16	13.4	40	.58	248	4
Parsley	1 C.	60	26	2.2	5.1	.4	5100	.07	.16	.098	0	.7	103	122	3.7	436	27
Parsnips	1 C.	155	102	2.3	23	.8	50	.11	.12	.13	0	.2	16	70	.9	587	12
Peas, green	1 C.	146	118	7.9	21	.58	934	.387	.193	.247	0	3.05	58.4	36	2.14	357	7

VEGETABLES AND VEGETABLE JUICES (cont.)	Measure	Mass	Energy	Protein	Carbohydrate	Fat	VITAMINS Vitamin A	Vitamin B₁	Vitamin B₂	Vitamin B₆	Vitamin B₁₂	Niacin	Vitamin C	MINERALS Calcium	Iron	Potassium	Sodium
		g	Cal	g	g	g	IU	mg	mg	mg	μg	mg	mg	mg	mg	mg	mg
Peas, split, ckd	1 C.	200	230	16	41.6	.3	80	.3	.18	—	0	1.8	—	22	3.4	592	26
Peppers, sweet	1 C.	100	24	.86	5.3	.46	530	.086	.05	.164	0	.54	128	6	1.2	196	4
Peppers, hot chili	½ C.	75	30	1.5	7	.15	578	.068	.068	.21	0	.713	182	13	.9	255	5
Pickles, dill	1 large	100	11	.7	2.2	.4	100	t	.02	.007	0	t	6	26	1	200	1428
Pimentos	3 med.	100	27	.9	5.8	.5	2300	.02	.06	—	0	.4	95	7	1.5	—	—
Pinto beans, ckd	1 C.	190	663	43.5	121	2.3	0	1.6	.4	1	0	4.2	t	257	12.2	1870	19
Potato	1 C.	150	114	3.2	25.7	.2	t	.15	.06	—	0	2.3	30	11	.9	611	5
Potato, baking, flesh & skin	1 large	202	220	4	32.8	.2	t	.15	.07	.7	0	2.7	31	14	1.1	782	6
Pumpkin	1 C.	245	49	1.76	12	.17	2651	.076	.19	.139	0	1	11.5	37	1.4	564	3
Radish	10	45	7	.27	1.6	.24	3	.002	.02	.032	0	.135	10.3	9	.13	104	11
Rutabaga	1 C.	140	64	1.5	15.4	.28	810	.1	.1	.14	0	1.5	60	92	.6	335	7
Sauerkraut	1 C.	235	42	2.4	9.4	.33	120	.07	.09	.31	0	.5	33	85	1.2	329	1755
Soybeans, ckd	1 C.	180	234	19.8	19.4	10.3	50	.38	.16	—	0	1.1	30.6	131	4.9	972	4
Soybean curd (tofu)	3.5 oz	100	72	7.8	2.4	4.2	0	.06	.03	—	0	—	—	100	5.2	—	354
Soybean milk	1 C.	226	75	7.7	5	3.4	90	.18	.065	—	0	.5	—	47.5	1.8	—	—
Soybean sprouts	1 C.	70	90	9	7.8	4.68	8	.238	.082	.124	0	.804	10.6	48	1.48	338	10
Spinach	1 C.	55	14	1.8	2.4	.2	4460	.06	.11	.14	0	.3	28	51	1.7	259	39
Squash, summer	1 C.	130	25	1.4	5.5	.28	530	.07	.12	.186	0	1.3	29	36	.5	263	1
Squash, winter	1 C.	205	129	3.7	31.6	.4	8610	.1	.27	.18	0	1.4	27	57	1.6	945	2
Sweet potato	1	130	136	2	32	.38	26082	.086	.191	.334	0	.876	30	29	.76	265	17
Tomato	1	123	24	1.1	5.3	.26	1394	.074	.062	.059	0	.738	21.6	8	.59	254	10
Tomato juice	1 C.	243	46	2.2	10.4	.2	1940	.12	.07	.366	0	1.9	39	17	2.2	552	486
Tomato paste	1 C.	262	215	8.9	48.7	2	8650	.52	.31	.996	0	8.1	128	71	9.2	2237	100
Turnips	1 C.	130	39	1.3	8.6	.13	t	.05	.09	.117	0	.8	47	51	.7	348	64
Turnip greens	1 C.	55	15	.83	3	.17	4180	.039	.055	.145	0	.33	33	105	.61	163	22
Vegetable juice cocktail	1 C.	242	41	2.2	8.7	.2	1690	.12	.07	.338	0	1.9	22	29	1.2	535	484
Water chestnuts	4 avg	25	20	.4	4.8	.1	0	.04	.05	—	0	.2	1	1	.2	125	5
Watercress	1 C.	35	7	.8	1.1	.04	1720	.03	.06	.045	0	.3	28	53	.6	99	18
Yams	1 C.	200	210	4.8	48.2	.4	t	.18	.8	.51	0	1.2	18	8	1.2	1508	17
Yellow wax beans	1 C.	125	28	1.8	5.8	.3	290	.09	.11	.098	0	.6	16	63	.8	189	4

OBJECTIVES

Supplying Our Water Needs

Upon completion of this unit, you will be able to:

1. List and use the units of the modernized metric system (SI) in measurements of length, volume, mass, and density. (A.1)
2. Discuss direct and indirect water uses and their importance for water conservation. (A.5, A.8, A.9)
3. Describe the function and operation of the hydrological cycle and indicate the primary storage reservoirs of the earth's water supply. (A.6, A.7)
4. Discuss some effects of water's unusual physical properties on plants and animals. (B.1)
5. Define the terms solution, solvent, and solute, and apply them in an example.
6. Classify matter in terms of elements, compounds, and mixtures; and distinguish between different types of mixtures (solutions, colloids, and suspensions) in a laboratory setting. (B.2-B.4)
7. Interpret the symbols and formulas in a balanced chemical equation in terms of atoms and molecules. (B.5)
8. Describe the three basic subatomic particules (proton, neutron, and electron) and their connection to the polarity and solubility of a compound. (B.6, C.1)
9. Define the terms insoluble, unsaturated, saturated, and supersaturated, and calculate solution concentration as a percentage. (C.1, C.2)
10. Use solubility curves to describe the effect of temperature on solubility, and calculate percent saturation. (C.1, C.2, C.4)
11. Demonstrate the ability to organize and interpret environmental or other data in graphs or tables. (C.1, C.5, C.10)
12. Given the pH of a substance, classify it as acidic, basic, or neutral. (C.6)
13. Determine the formula and name of a simple ionic compound when provided with the anion's and cation's names and charges. (C.7)
14. Evaluate the risks of contaminants in our water supply, with particular attention to heavy-metal ions of lead, mercury and cadmium. (C.10)
15. Compare and contrast natural and artificial water purification sytems, and assess the risks and benefits of water softening and chlorination. (D.1, D.3–D.5)

Conserving Chemical Resources

Upon completion of this unit, you will be able to:

1. Compare and contrast science and technology. (Introduction)
2. State the law of conservation of matter, and apply the law by determining whether a given chemical equation is balanced. (A.2, A.3)

3. Describe the Spaceship Earth analogy, and apply it to the terms "throw away" and "using up." (A.4, A.5, A.7)

4. List common types and sources of municipal waste, and describe attempts to reuse and recycle waste. (A.5, A.6)

5. Define and give examples of renewable and nonrenewable resources. (A.5, A.7)

6. Distinguish between chemical and physical changes and/or properties when given specific examples of each. (B.1)

7. Classify selected elements as metals, nonmetals, or metalloids based on observations of their chemical and physical properties. (B.2, B.3)

8. Use the periodic table to (a) predict physical and chemical properties of an element; (b) write formulas for various compounds; (c) identify elements by their atomic masses and atomic numbers; and (d) locate periods and groups (families) of elements. (B.4, B.6)

9. Construct a workable periodic table and explain its organization, given chemical and physical properties of a set of elements. (B.5)

10. Compare the reactivities of selected elements, and explain the results in terms of the structure of their atoms. (B.7-B.9)

11. Discuss the development of new materials as substitutes for dwindling resources. (B.10)

12. Explain from a chemical viewpoint the problems and solutions involved in restoring the Statue of Liberty. (B.11)

13. List the three primary layers of our planet and some resources that are "mined" from each region. (C.1)

14. Write balanced chemical equations and relate them to the law of conservation of matter. (C.2)

15. Define the term mole, and calculate the molar mass of a compound when provided with its formula and the atomic masses of its elements. (C.3)

16. Outline the production of a metal from its ore (using copper as an example) and list four factors which determine the profitability of mining. (D.1)

17. Calculate the percent composition by mass of a specified element in a given compound. (D.2)

18. Define oxidation and reduction, and compare the three most common redox-reaction methods for separating metals from their ores. (D.4)

19. Use supply and demand data to estimate the lifetime of a given resource, and discuss options such as reusing, recycling, and substitution. (E.1-E.3)

Petroleum: To Build? To Burn?

Upon completion of this unit, you will be able to:

1. Compare the usage of petroleum for "building" and "burning", and the benefits and burdens of each usage. (A.2)

2. Identify regions of high petroleum usage and regions of petroleum reserves, and discuss the economic and political implications of petroleum supply and demand. (A.3)

3. Describe the chemical makeup of petroleum and its differences from other resources. (B.1)

4. Identify differences in density and viscosity among common petroleum products, and explain the relationship between the differences and the number of carbon atoms in their molecules. (B.2, B.3)

5. Describe the process of fractional distillation, and list the five major fractions of petroleum distillation and typical products manufactured from each fraction. (B.2, B.4)

6. Name the first ten alkanes and draw structural and electron-dot formulas for each. (B.5, B.7)

7. Describe the processes involved in ionic and covalent bonding. (B.6)

8. State and explain the effect of carbon length and side groups on the boiling point of a hydrocarbon. (B.7, B.8)

9. Define the term isomer and draw structural formulas for at least three isomers of a given hydrocarbon. (B.8)

10. Trace the history of energy sources and consumption patterns in the United States, and account for major changes. (C.2)

11. Explain endothermic and exothermic reactions in terms of bond breaking and bond forming, and give examples of each type of reaction. (C.3)

12. Identify energy conversions in an automobile, and calculate savings resulting from increased automobile efficiency. (C.3)

13. Define the terms heat of combustion and specific heat, and calculate energies of various combustion reactions. (C.4-C.6)

14. Write balanced equations for the combustion of hydrocarbon fuels, including energy changes. (C.6)

15. Define the term octane number, state its relationship to grades of gasoline, and identify two ways of increasing octane number. (C.7)

16. Compare saturated and unsaturated hydrocarbons in terms of molecular models, formulas, structures, and physical and chemical properties. (D.2, D.3)

17. Identify the functional groups for common alcohols, ethers, carboxylic acids, and esters. (D.4, D.6)

18. Describe polymerization and give one example of addition and condensation reactions. (D.5)

19. Describe major sources of energy for the United States of today, and alternative sources of fuels for the future. (E.1, E.2)

Understanding Foods

Upon completion of this unit, you will be able to:

1. Compare the uses of food in terms of "building" and "burning." (Introduction, B.1)

2. Distinguish malnutrition from undernutrition, and identify parts of the world where these problems are most acute. (Introduction-A.3)

3. Define calorie and joule, and calculate energy changes from calorimetry data. (B.1)

4. Correlate weight gain or loss with caloric intake and human activity. (B.2)

5. Compare and contrast mono-, di-, and polysaccharides in terms of structural formulas and properties. (B.3)

6. Identify key functional groups in carbohydrates and fats, and write an equation for the formation of a typical fat. (B.3, B.4)

7. Distinguish between saturated and unsaturated fats, and relate the consumption of each to health. (B.4)

8. Define and illustrate the concept of limiting reactant in biochemical examples and in calculations. (C.2)

9. Describe how functional groups in amino acids interact in protein formation. (C.3)

10. Describe five functions of proteins in the body. (C.3)

11. Discuss the concepts of essential amino acids, complete protein, and complementary protein, with respect to a balanced diet. (C.3)

12. Separate and measure protein and carbohydrates in nonfat milk, and calculate a sample's caloric value. (C.4)

13. Distinguish water-soluble from fat-soluble vitamins (with specific examples of each) and discuss the implications of these differences in terms of dietary needs. (D.1)

14. Analyze the vitamin C content of foods by performing titrations. (D.2)

15. Identify minerals used in the body, and distinguish between macrominerals and trace minerals. (D.3)

16. Determine the iron content of foods by colorimetry. (D.4)

17. Discuss the relative risks and benefits of various types of food additives in terms of their purposes, and provide specific examples. (D.5)

18. Discuss the role of the Food and Drug Administration (FDA) and federal regulations in ensuring food safety. (D.5)

19. Compare and contrast menus from several cultures in terms of calories and nutritional balance, and analyze the nutritional quality of food recorded in a personal food diary. (E.2)

Nuclear Chemistry in Our World

Upon completion of this unit, you will be able to:

1. List at least three examples of nuclear technology and/or natural radioactivity that affect daily life. (A.1)

2. Distinguish between ionizing and nonionizing radiation and their biological effects. (A.2)

3. Discuss general properties of electromagnetic radiation, and specific properties of various regions of the electromagnetic spectrum. (A.2)

4. Describe the experiments of Roentgen, Becquerel, the Curies, and Rutherford, and explain how they led to modifications in the atomic model. (A.3, A.4, A.6)

5. Describe the properties and locations of the three major subatomic particles. (A.7)

6. Define the term isotope, and interpret isotope notation. (A.7, A.8)

7. Use molar masses and isotopic abundance data to calculate average mass and relative abundance of elements. (A.9)

8. Compare and contrast the general properties of alpha, beta, and gamma radiation, including penetrating power, and discuss safety considerations in terms of shielding abilities of cardboard, glass, and lead. (B.2)

9. Balance nuclear equations and use them to describe natural radioactive decay. (B.2)

10. Explain the concept of half-life and discuss the implications of half-life for natural radioactivity and nuclear waste disposal. (B.3, B.4, D.8)

11. Describe radiation detectors and their operating principles. (B.5, B.6)

12. Define nuclear transmutation and write a nuclear equation to illustrate the process. (B.7)

13. Distinguish nuclear fission from nuclear fusion. (C.1, C.6)

14. Use the equation $E = mc^2$ to compare the energies produced by nuclear fission and by typical exothermic chemical reactions. (C.2)

15. Explain the energy effects of a chain reaction and compare a controlled and an uncontrolled reaction. (C.3-C.5)

16. Identify the main components of a nuclear power plant and describe their functions. (C.5)

17. Assess relative risks and benefits of various nuclear technologies (such as power generation, medical applications, and industrial tracing techniques). (D.2, D.5-D.7)

18. List and briefly explain some factors that determine the amount of biological radiation damage. (D.5)

19. Compare the ionizing radiation produced by various sources, including radon, that are encountered by a typical United States citizen. (D.6, D.7)

20. Discuss the problems and possible solutions associated with nuclear waste generation and disposal. (D.8)

Chemistry, Air and Climate

Upon completion of this unit, you will be able to:

1. Describe common physical and chemical properties of air. (A.1, A.2)

2. Compare the chemical properties of nitrogen, oxygen, and carbon dioxide. (B.1)

3. Identify the major components of the troposphere and indicate their relative concentrations. (B.2)

4. Show how Avogadro's Law and the concept of molar volume clarify the interpretation of chemical equations involving gases. (B.2)

5. Describe with words and mathematical equations the inter-relationships among amount, temperature, volume, and pressure of a gas (Avogadro's, Charles' and Boyle's Laws), and list one practical appliation of each law. (B.2, B.4-B.8)

6. Define and apply in appropriate situations the terms molar volume, standard temperature and pressure (STP), Kelvin temperature scale, and absolute zero. (B.2, B.5-B.8)

7. Sketch or graph the relationship between altitude and air pressure. (B.3)

8. Discuss air pressure and explain how to measure it. (B.4)

9. Account for the gas laws in terms of the kinetic molecular theory of gases. (B.8)

10. Compare the various components of solar radiation. (C.1)

11. Describe how reflection, absorption and re-radiation of solar radiation account for the earth's energy balance. (C.2)

12. Explain how differing heat capacities and reflectivities of various land covers and water can influence local climates. (C.3)

13. Describe the greenhouse effect, its natural incidence and causes, and the significance of industrial contributions. (C.4, C.5)

14. Use graphical extrapolation to predict future CO_2 concentrations, and outline assumptions and problems associated with such predictions. (C.5)

15. Compare the production of CO_2 from combustion with that from respiration. (C.6)

16. Describe the function of the ozone layer and how human activities may be affecting it. (C.8)

17. List the major categories of air pollutants and discuss the relative contributions of various human and natural factors to each category. (D.1-D.3)

18. Describe major general strategies for controlling pollution, and specific strategies for particulates. (D.5-D.7)

19. Describe chemical reactions and geographic and meteorological factors which contribute to photochemical smog. (D.8)

20. Interpret graphs and tables related to automotive-induced air pollution. (D.8-D.10)

21. Explain the role of activation energy in a chemical reaction, and give an example of how a catalyst affects it. (D.9)

22. Describe the role of catalytic converters in reducing automotive emissions of unburned hydrocarbons, carbon monoxide, and nitrogen oxides. (D.10)

23. Describe sources and consequences of acid rain. (D.11-D.13)

24. Define the terms acid and base, give examples of each, describe their formation with balanced ionic equations, and relate hydrogen ion concentration to the pH scale. (D.11-D.13)

25. Interpret historical emissions data to assess the success of various pollution control efforts. (E.1)

26. Discuss air pollution in terms of the trade-offs between control costs and damage costs. (E.2-E.3)

Health: Your Risks and Choices

Upon completion of this unit, you will be able to:

1. Provide examples of correlation, and determine the causal relationship between the members of a given pair of events. (A.1)

2. Define epidemiology, and describe some benefits and limitations of epidemiological studies. (A.2)

3. Define homeostasis and give examples of how it is related to maintaining good health. (B.1)
4. Describe the major elements of the human body and their function in maintaining health. (B.2)
5. Explain how enzymes work and list several factors that may alter their effectiveness. (B.3-B.7)
6. Describe cellular energy production and storage, including the role of ATP. (B.6)
7. Define and give examples of acids and bases, and use net ionic equations to describe the neutralization reaction. (C.1-C.5)
8. Describe the components of a buffer and explain how it prevents acidosis and alkalosis. (C.3-C.5)
9. Apply the concept of "like dissolves like" to skin cleansing and the function of soap. (D.1, D.2)
10. Sketch the parts of human skin and describe their functions. (D.2)
11. Describe the effect of sunlight on skin and the effectiveness of PABA in sunscreens. (D.3, D.4)
12. Describe hair structure, the types of bonding in hair protein, and the effects of various hair treatment chemicals on hair. (D.6-D.8)
13. Distinguish between drugs and toxins, and describe circumstances where a substance's usual effect on homeostasis may be reversed. (E.1, E.6)
14. Use the concept of receptors to account for drug specificity and for the action of narcotic analgesics. (E.1)
15. Contrast the benefits and burdens associated with aspirin use. (E.2)
16. Outline the effects of common drugs on the human body, and the body's chemical defenses against these drugs. (E.3-E.5)
17. Discuss the role of antigen-antibody complexes in protecting the body against infectious organisms, and contrast the AIDS virus to other viruses. (E.5)
18. Use the concept of synergism to explain the hazards of combining drugs and medicines. (E.6)
19. Evaluate the products of cigarette smoking. (E.7-E.9)
20. Assess personal control of risks in terms of the maintenance of good health and well-being. (F.1, F.2)

The Chemical Industry: Promise and Challenge

Upon completion of this unit, you will be able to:
1. List the functions of the chemical industry and the general categories of industrial products, including present contributions and future expectations. (A.1)
2. Contrast responsibilities of the public and of industry in preserving the quality of life in a community. (A.2, A.3)
3. Outline the types of products produced by the chemical industry, and explain the importance of intermediates in production. (A.4, B.1)

4. Evaluate the potentially positive and negative impacts of a chemical industry on a community. (A.5)

5. Compare natural and synthetic products, providing examples of each. (B.1)

6. Describe the role of chemical engineers in industry, and the factors that must be considered in changing from laboratory-scale reaction levels to industrial levels. (B.2)

7. Outline the major divisions and departments of a typical chemical industry, and explain their interrelationships. (B.3)

8. Analyze a fertilizer sample for its major components, and describe their importance (particularly nitrogen compounds) in agriculture. (C.1, C.2)

9. Use colorimetry to quantify phosphate content in fertilizer samples. (C.3)

10. Apply oxidation-reduction concepts to nitrogen fixation in the Haber process. (C.4)

11. Use electronegativity values to determine oxidation states. (C.4)

12. Describe factors that must be controlled in the equilibrium synthesis of ammonia. (C.5)

13. Trace the history and development of explosives, including the contributions of Alfred Nobel. (C.6)

14. Develop and evaluate voltaic cells, using the activity series of common metals. (D.1, D.2)

15. Use the concept of half-reactions to describe commercial electrochemical cells, including their charging and discharging reactions. (D.2, D.4)

16. Demonstrate the technique of electroplating. (D.3)

17. Describe the industrial applications of electrolysis for brine decomposition and for aluminum production. (D.4)

18. Identify key considerations involved in the development of a new chemical process or product. (E.1)

GLOSSARY

acid
molecular substance or other chemical that releases $H^+(aq)$ ions in aqueous solution

acidosis
harmful condition in which blood pH stays below 7.35

activation energy
minimum energy required for successful collision of reactant particles in a chemical reaction

active site
in biochemistry, the site on an enzyme where the substrate molecule is made ready for reaction

activity series
ranking of elements in order of chemical reactivity

addition polymer
polymer (such as polyethene) formed by addition reactions at double bonds

addition reaction
a reaction at the double (or triple) bond in an organic molecule that results in adding or bonding atoms to each atom of the double (or triple) bond; one type of polymerization

adsorption
the process of attracting and holding something on the surface (of charcoal, for example)

aeration
mixing of air (particularly, oxygen gas) into a liquid, as in water flowing over a dam

aerobic bacteria
oxygen-consuming bacteria

alcohol
nonaromatic organic compound whose molecules contain one or more —OH groups

alkalosis
harmful condition in which blood pH stays above 7.4

alkane
hydrocarbon having a general formula CnH_{2n+2} whose molecules contain only single covalent bonds

alkene
hydrocarbon whose molecules contain a double covalent bond

alkyne
hydrocarbon whose molecules contain a triple covalent bond

alloy
solid mixture consisting of atoms of different metals

alpha keratin
key structural protein unit of hair

alpha particle (ray)
helium nucleus emitted during radioactive decay

amino acid
organic compound whose molecules contain an amino (—NH_2) and a carboxyl (—COOH) group; proteins are polymers of amino acids

amylase
enzyme in saliva that catalyzes breakdown of starch to glucose

anaerobic bacteria
bacteria that do not require oxygen to live

anaerobic glycolysis
cellular process for quick release of energy from glucose by non-oxygen-consuming reactions; lactic acid is produced

anion
ion possessing a negative charge

anode
electrode at which oxidation occurs in electrochemical cell

antibody
complementary protein created by body to inactivate specific foreign protein molecules (antigens)

antigen
foreign protein that triggers body's defense mechanisms to produce antibodies

aquifer
porous rock structure that holds water beneath the earth's surface

aromatic compound
compound such as benzene, whose molecules are cyclic and can be represented as having alternating double and single bonds between carbon atoms

atmosphere
all the air surrounding the earth

atmosphere (atm)
a unit of pressure, represented by a column of mercury 760 mm high

atomic mass
mass of an atom

atomic number
number of protons in an atom; distinguishes atoms of different elements

atoms
smallest particles possessing the properties of an element; all matter is composed of atoms

Avogadro's law
equal volumes of gases at the same temperature and pressure contain the same number of molecules

background radiation
radiation from naturally radioactive sources in the environment

base
chemical that yields $OH^-(aq)$ ions in aqueous solution

beta particle (ray)
electron emitted during radioactive decay

biodegradable
able to be broken down into simpler substances by bacteria

biomass
matter in plant materials

biomolecules
large molecules found only in living systems

biopolymers
polymers made by organisms

biosphere
a combination of portions of the earth's waters, land, and atmosphere that supports living things

boiling point
the temperature at which a substance changes from the liquid to the gaseous state

Boyle's law
at constant temperature, the product of the pressure and volume of a given gas sample is a constant

branched-chain alkane
alkane that consists of molecules in which one or more carbon atoms are bonded to three or four other carbon atoms; for example,
$$CH_3—CH—CH—CH_3$$
$$\quad\quad | \quad\quad |$$
$$\quad CH_3 \quad CH_3$$

buffer solution
solution that resists changes in pH; contains a weak acid and a salt of that acid, or a weak base and its salt

C

Calorie (Cal)
an energy unit used to express food energy;
1 Cal = 1000 cal, or 1 kcal

calorimetry
technique for determining heat of reaction or other thermal properties, and for finding caloric value of foods

carbohydrate
energy-rich compound composed of carbon, hydrogen and oxygen; examples are starch and sugar

carbon chain
carbon atoms linked to one another, forming a string-like sequence in a molecule

carboxylic acids
organic compounds whose molecules contain the —COOH group

carcinogen
substance that causes cancer

catalyst
substance that speeds up a chemical reaction but is itself unchanged

catalytic converter
reaction chamber in auto exhaust system designed to reduce harmful emissions

cathode
in an electrochemical cell, the electrode at which reduction occurs

cathode ray
beam of electrons emitted from cathode when electricity passes through evacuated tube

cation
ion possessing a positive charge

cellular respiration
oxidation of glucose or other energy-rich substances in living cells to produce CO_2, H_2O, and energy

cellulose
polysaccharide composed of chains of glucose molecules; makes up fibrous and woody parts of plants

Celsius degree (° C)
a degree on the Celsius temperature scale, 1.8 as large as a Fahrenheit degree

ceramics
materials made by heating or "firing" clay or components of certain rocks; include bricks, glass, and porcelain

chain reaction
in nuclear fission, reaction that produces enough neutrons to allow the reaction to continue

Charles' law
at constant pressure, the volume of a given gas sample is directly proportional to the kelvin temperature

chemical bond
force that holds atoms or ions together in chemical compounds

chemical change
change in matter resulting in a change in the identity of one or more substances

chemical compound
substance composed of two or more elements that cannot be separated by physical means

chemical equation
combination of chemical formulas that represent what occurs in a chemical reaction, such as
$2 H_2(g) + O_2(g) \rightarrow 2 H_2O(g)$

chemical equilibrium
condition when forward and reverse reactions occur at same rate, and concentrations of all reactants and products remain unchanged

chemical formula
combination of symbols that represents the elements present in a substance with subscripts showing the number of atoms of each element, for example, the formula for ammonia is NH_3

chemical property
property of a substance related to a chemical change undergone by the substance

chemical reaction
change in matter in which one or more chemicals
are transformed into new or different chemicals

coefficient
number preceding a formula in a chemical equation;
specifies the relative number of units participating
in the reaction

coenzyme
molecule or ion that assists an enzyme in
performing its function

colloid
mixture containing macro-size particles that are
small enough to remain suspended

colorimetric method
method for determining concentration of a solution
by observing color intensity

combustion
burning

complementary proteins
two or more proteins that, in combination only,
include all essential amino acids

complete protein
a single protein containing adequate amounts of all
the essential amino acids

compound
substance composed of two or more elements that
cannot be separated by physical means

concentration
quantity of solute dissolved in a specific quantity of
solvent or solution

condensation
conversion of a substance from a gaseous to the
liquid or solid state

condensation polymer
polymer formed by condensation reactions; for
example, polyester

condensation reaction
chemical combination of two molecules,
accompanied by loss of water or another small
molecule, such as,
$$CH_3OH + HO\,C\,CH_3 \rightarrow CH_3O\,C\,CH_3 + H_2O$$
$$\qquad\quad \| \qquad\qquad\quad \|$$
$$\qquad\quad O \qquad\qquad\quad O$$

condensed formula
formula such as $CH_3CH_2CH_3$, in which symbols are
written on same line and subscripts are used; in
contrast to structural formula

conductor
material that allows electricity to flow through it

conservation of matter, law of
matter is neither created nor destroyed in chemical
reactions

control
in an experiment, a setup duplicating all conditions
except the variable being tested

control cost
in cost-benefit analysis, total cost of controlling a
potentially damaging effect (for example, air
pollution)

correlated
happening together; scientists often identify and
seek explanation for correlated events

corrosion
deterioration or ''eating away'' of a material

covalent bond
a force that holds two atoms tightly to each other,
found when the two atoms share one or more
electron pairs

cracking
process in which hydrocarbon molecules from
petroleum are converted to smaller molecules

critical mass
mass of fissionable material needed to sustain a
nuclear chain reaction

crude oil
petroleum as it is pumped from underground

cryogenics
studies of the chemistry and physics of materials
and systems at very low temperatures

current
flow of electrons

cuticle
tough outer layer in, for example, hair

cycloalkane
saturated hydrocarbon whose molecules contain
carbon atoms joined in a ring

D

damage cost
in cost-benefit analysis, total cost of tangible and
intangible damage

data
objective pieces of information, often the
information gathered in experiments

denaturation
alteration of protein shape and function by
disruption of folding and coiling in molecules

density
the mass per unit volume of a given material

dermis
inner layer of the skin

developed world
fully industrialized nations

developing world
nations not fully industrialized

dipeptide
compound made from two amino acids

disaccharide
compound made from two simple sugars; for
instance, maltose (made from two glucose units)

distillate
condensed products of distillation

distillation
method of separating substance, using differences
in their boiling points

double covalent bond
bond in which four electrons are shared by two bonded atoms

dynamic equilibrium
in a reversible reaction, the state of product formation occurring at the same rate as product decomposition

E

electrical conductivity
the ability to conduct an electric current

electrical potential
potential for moving or pumping electric charge in an electrical circuit or by an electrochemical cell; measured in volts

electrochemical cell
device for carrying out electrolysis or producing electricity from a chemical reaction

electrodes
two strips of metal or other conductors serving as contacts between the solution or molten salt and the external circuit in an electrochemical cell; reaction occurs at each electrode

electrolysis
use of electrical energy to bring about a non-spontaneous oxidation-reduction reaction

electromagnetic radiation
radiation moving at the speed of light, ranging from low-energy radio waves to high-energy cosmic and gamma rays; includes visible light

electrometallurgy
use of electrical energy to process metals or their ores

electron
negatively-charged particle present in all atoms

electron dot formula
formula for a substance, in which dots representing the outer electrons in each atom show the sharing of electron pairs between atoms

electronegativity
tendency of bonded atoms to attract electrons in compounds

electroplating
deposition of a thin layer of metal on a surface by electrolysis

elements
fundamental chemical substances from which all other substances are made

endorphins
natural painkillers produced in the brain

endothermic
a process requiring energy

endpoint
point during a titration at which the reaction is complete

enkephalins
natural painkillers produced in the brain

enzyme
catalyst for a biochemical reaction

epidermis
outer layer of the skin

essential amino acid
one of eight amino acids that the human body cannot synthesize; must be included in the diet

esters
organic compounds containing the —COOR group, where R represents any stable arrangement of carbon and hydrogen atoms

ether
organic compound containing the functional group —O—

evaporation
conversion of a substance from the liquid to the gaseous state

exothermic
an energy-releasing process

extrapolation
estimate of a value beyond the known range (the continuation of a curve on a graph past the measured points, for example)

F

family (periodic table)
vertical column of elements in the periodic table; also called a group; members of a family share similar properties

fat
lipid resulting from reaction of glycerol and fatty acids; storage form for food energy in animals

fatty acid
organic compound whose molecules consist of a long hydrocarbon chain and a —COOH group; combined with glycerol in fats

fibrous protein
protein whose molecules form rope-like or sheet-like structures; found in hair, muscles, skin

filtrate
liquid collected after filtration

filtration
separation of solid particles from a liquid by passing the mixture through a material that retains the solid particles

fluorescence
emission of visible light from a material, following its exposure to ultraviolet radiation

force
the cause of a body's motion or weight, brought about by its mass and by gravity

formula unit
group of atoms or ions represented by chemical formula of a compound; simplest unit of an ionic compound

fossil fuel
petroleum, natural gas, or coal

fraction (petroleum)
mixture of petroleum-derived substances of similar boiling points and other properties

freezing point
the temperature at which a substance changes from the liquid to the solid state

frequency
number of vibrations or cycles per unit of time

functional group
atom or group of atoms that imparts characteristic properties to an organic compound; —Cl, —OH, or —COOH, for example

G

gamma ray
high-energy electromagnetic radiation emitted during radioactive decay

gaseous state
state of matter having no fixed volume or shape

Geiger counter (radiation counter)
device that produces an electrical signal in the presence of ionizing radiation

gene
segment of DNA molecule that stores instructions for a specific trait, such as hair color

globular protein
protein whose molecules assume ball shapes and are water soluble because of polar and ionic groups on surface; may function as hormone, enzyme, or carrier protein

glycogen
polymer made of repeating glucose units; synthesized in liver and muscles as reserve source of glucose

gram (g)
SI unit of mass commonly used in chemistry (kilogram is SI base unit for mass)

greenhouse effect
retention of energy at or near the earth's surface, as carbon dioxide and other atmospheric gases capture escaping radiation and return it to the earth's surface; result is surface warming

groundwater
water that collects underground

group (periodic table)
See family

H

Haber process
industrial process for catalyzed synthesis of ammonia from nitrogen and hydrogen

half-cell
metal (or other electrode material) and its surrounding solution of ions in a voltaic cell

half-life
time needed for decay of one-half the atoms in a sample of radioactive material

half-reaction
half of oxidation-reduction reaction in which electrons are either lost or gained; for example, the process that occurs in one half-cell of a voltaic cell

hard water
water containing relatively high concentrations of calcium (Ca^{2+}), magnesium (Mg^{2+}), or iron(III) (Fe^{3+}) ions

heat capacity
quantity of heat required to raise the temperature of a given sample of matter by $1°$ C

heat of combustion
quantity of thermal energy released when a specific amount of a substance burns

heat of fusion
quantity of heat required to convert a specific amount of a solid to a liquid at its melting point

heavy metals
metals of high atomic mass, generally from fifth or sixth row of the periodic table

heterogeneous
not uniform throughout; as, in a heterogeneous mixture

homeostasis
maintenance of balance in all body systems

homogeneous
uniform throughout; as, in a homogeneous mixture

hormone
biomolecule that serves as a specific messenger to stimulate biochemical activity at specific sites in the body

hydrocarbons
molecular compounds composed solely of carbon and hydrogen

hydrogen bonding
attraction between molecules, or between parts of the same molecule, involving hydrogen atoms and strongly electron-attracting atoms such as nitrogen or oxygen

hydrologic cycle
circulation of water between the earth's atmosphere and crust

hydrometallurgy
water-using methods for processing metals or their ores

I

ideal gas
gas that behaves as predicted by kinetic molecular theory

infant mortality rate
for every 1000 live births, the number of infants that die within their first year

infrared radiation
electromagnetic radiation of slightly lower energy than visible light; raises temperature of objects that absorb it

intensity (radiation)
measure of quantity of radiation per unit time

intermediate (chemical)
product of chemical industry used to synthesize consumer products or other chemicals, sulfuric acid is an intermediate in the manufacture of certain detergents

intermolecular forces
forces holding molecules together

interpolation
inserting a value between the known values in a series (such as reading a part of a curve between two measured points)

ion
an atom or group of atoms that has become electrically charged by gaining or losing electrons

ionic bond
attraction between oppositely charged ions in an ionic compound

ionic compound
substance composed of ions

ionizing radiation
electromagnetic radiation or high-speed particles possessing enough energy to ionize atoms and molecules; emitted during radioactive decay

irradiation
treatment (of food, for instance) with radiation

isomer
compound having the same molecular formula, but a different structural formula, than another compound

isotopes
atoms of the same element having different numbers of neutrons

K

kinetic energy
energy associated with the motion of an object

kinetic molecular theory of gases
theory that accounts for properties of gases based on kinetic energy and constant random motion of molecules.

L

legumes
plants that harbor nitrogen-fixing bacteria in their roots

length
linear distance; the SI base unit of length is the meter (m)

limiting reactant
the starting substance used up first as a chemical reaction occurs

lipid
a fat or other member of a class of biomolecules not soluble in water

liquid state
state of matter with fixed volume but no fixed shape

liter (L)
unit of volume; equal to 1 dm^3, 1000 cm^3, or 1000 mL

M

macromineral
essential mineral present in amount of 5 g or more in adult human body

malleable
a property related to a material's ability to be flattened without shattering

malnourishment
receiving inadequate amounts of essential nutrients such as protein, vitamins, minerals

mass
amount of matter in something

mass number
sum of the number of protons and neutrons in an atom of a given isotope

melanin
body pigment responsible for dark skin and dark hair

mesosphere
region of atmosphere outside stratosphere

metal
element having certain properties, owing to its position in the left part of the periodic table

metalloid
element with properties intermediate between those of metals and nonmetals

meter (m)
SI base unit of length

microfibril
bundle of coiled protein chains; a component of hair, for instance

milliliter (mL)
unit of volume; equal to 1 cm^3

millimeters of mercury (mmHg)
a pressure unit; 1 atm = 760 mmHg

mixture
combination of substances in which each substance retains its separate identity

molar concentration
concentration of a solution expressed in moles of solute per liter of solution

molar heat of combustion
the thermal energy released by burning one mole of a substance

molar mass
mass (usually in grams) of one mole of a substance

molar volume
volume occupied by one mole of a substance; at STP, molar volume of a gas is 22.4 L

molarity
concentration of a solution expressed as moles of solute per liter of solution; also called molar concentration

mole (mol)
an amount of substance or chemical species equal to 6.02 X 10²³ units, where the units may be atoms, molecules, formula units, electrons or other specified entities; chemist's "counting" unit

molecular structure
arrangement and bonding of atoms in a molecule

molecule
smallest particle of a substance retaining the properties of the substance; a particle composed of two or more atoms joined by covalent bonds

monomer
compound whose molecules react to form a polymer

monosaccharide
simple sugar, such as glucose

N

narcotic analgesic
drug that relieves intense pain

negative oxidation state
negative number assigned to atom in a compound when that atom has greater control of its electrons than as free element

net ionic equation
equation showing only those chemicals that participate in a reaction involving ions in aqueous solution

neuron
nerve cell

neutralization
reaction of an acid with a base, in which the characteristic properties of both are destroyed

neutron
neutral particle present in nuclei of most atoms

newton (N)
a unit of force in the metric system; roughly equal to the force exerted on your hand by a 100-g bar of soap

nitrogen fixation
conversion of nitrogen gas (N_2) to nitrogen compounds usable by plants

nonconductor
material that does not allow electricity to flow through it

nonionizing radiation
electromagnetic radiation possessing insufficient energy to ionize atoms or molecules; for example, visible light

nonmetal
element having certain properties, owing to its position in the right part of the periodic table

nonpolar
having no electrical asymmetry or polarity, as in a nonpolar molecule

nonpolar interaction
weak attraction between nonpolar chemical groups

nonrenewable resource
resource that will not be replenished by natural processes during the time frame of human experience

nuclear fission
splitting of one atom into two smaller atoms; undergone by uranium-235 when bombarded with neutrons

nuclear fusion
combining of two atomic nuclei to form a single more massive nucleus

nuclear radiation
the particles and energy emitted from radioactive atoms

nucleus, atomic
dense central region in an atom; contains all protons and neutrons

nutrients
components of food needed in the diet

O

octane number
rating indicating combustion quality of gasoline

ore
rock or mineral from which it is profitable to recover a metal or other useful substance

organic compound
compound composed mainly of carbon and hydrogen atoms; a hydrocarbon or a compound derived from a hydrocarbon

oxidation
any process in which electrons are lost or the extent of electron control decreases

oxidation-reduction (redox) reaction
reaction in which oxidation and reduction occur

oxygenated fuels
oxygen-containing fuel additives, such as methanol, that increase octane rating and reduce pollutants

P

para-aminobenzoic acid (PABA)
active ingredient in many sunscreen lotions

patina
a surface film or coating, such as the stable green coating on copper exposed to the atmosphere

pepsin
enzyme that aids in digesting protein

peptide
a chain of amino acids; part of a protein

peptide linkage
—CONH— linkage formed by reaction of the —NH₂ group of one amino acid and the —COOH group of another amino acid; linkage between amino acid residues in proteins

periodic law
when elements are arranged in order of increasing atomic number, elements with similar properties occur at regular intervals

periodic table
table in which elements, arranged in order of increasing atomic number, are placed so that those with similar properties are near each other

periods (periodic table)
horizontal rows of elements in the periodic table

petrochemical
substance produced from petroleum or natural gas

petroleum
liquid fossil fuel composed mainly of hydrocarbons, but also containing compounds of nitrogen, sulfur and oxygen, along with small amounts of metal-containing compounds

pH
number representing acidity of an aqueous solution; at 25° C, solution with pH 7 is neutral, pH < 7 is acidic, pH > 7 is basic

photochemical smog
smog produced when sunlight interacts with nitrogen oxides and hydrocarbons in atmosphere

photon
packet of energy present in electromagnetic radiation

photosynthesis
process by which green plants make sugars from carbon dioxide and water in the presence of sunlight

physical change
change in matter in which the identity of the substance involved is not changed, such as the melting of ice

physical property
property that can be observed or measured without changing the identity of a sample of matter; for example, color, boiling point

polar
having electrical poles, or regions of positive and negative charge, as in a polar molecule

polyatomic ion
ion containing two or more atoms, such as SO_4^{2-}

polymer
substance whose large molecules are composed of many identical repeating units

polysaccharide
polymer made from simple sugar molecules; starch, for example

positive oxidation state
positive number assigned to atom in a compound when that atom has less control of its electrons than as free element

positron
particle with mass of electron but possessing a positive charge

precipitate
insoluble solid substance that has separated from a solution

pressure
force applied to one unit of surface area

primary air pollutant
pollutant in the form originally emitted to the atmosphere

product
substance formed in a chemical reaction

protease
enzyme that aids digestion of proteins

proteins
polymers made from amino acids; important compounds in body such as hair, nails, muscle, enzymes, hormones

proton
positively charged particle present in nuclei of all atoms

pyrometallurgy
use of thermal energy (heat) to process metals or their ores

R

radioactive decay
emission of alpha, beta, or gamma rays by unstable isotopes

radioactivity
spontaneous decay of unstable atomic nuclei accompanied by emission of ionizing radiation

radioisotope
a radioactive isotope

reactant
starting substance in a chemical reaction

receptors
proteins in membranes of key body cells, shaped to receive the molecule of a hormone, drug or other activator and, having done so, to activate chemical processes within the cell

recycling
reprocessing materials in manufactured items so they can be reused as raw materials for manufacturing new items

reduction
any process in which electrons are gained or the extent of electron control increases

reflectivity
a surface's property of returning radiation that strikes it

rem
unit indicating power of ionizing radiation to cause damage to human tissue (roentgen equivalent man)

renewable resource
resource that is replenished by natural processes in the time frame of human experience

reversible reaction
chemical reaction in which reverse reaction can occur simultaneously with forward reaction

rickets
disease caused by lack of vitamin D; occurs in absence of exposure to sunlight, which helps body to produce vitamin D

salicylates
family of painkillers that includes aspirin (acetylsalicylic acid)

saturated fat
fat whose molecules contain no carbon-carbon double bonds

saturated hydrocarbon
hydrocarbon consisting of molecules in which each carbon atom is bonded to four other atoms

saturated solution
solution in which the solvent has dissolved as much solute as it can stably retain at a given temperature

science
a group of disciplines that gather, analyze and organize knowledge about natural phenomena and natural objects

scintillation counter
sensitive radiation-measuring device; produces flashes of light in the presence of ionizing radiation

sewage treatment plant
installation built for post-use cleaning of municipal water

shell
an energy level surrounding the nucleus of an atom

single covalent bond
bond in which two electrons are shared by the two bonded atoms

solid
state of matter having a fixed volume and fixed shape

solubility
quantity of a substance that will dissolve in a given quantity of solvent to form a saturated solution

solute
the dissolved substance in a solution, usually the component present in the smaller amount

solution
homogeneous mixture of two or more substances

solution concentration
quantity of solute dissolved in a specific quantity of solvent or solution

solvent
component of a solution present in the largest amount

specific heat
quantity of heat needed to raise the temperature of 1 g of a material by $1°$ C

spectator ions
ions that are present but do not participate in a reaction in solution

spectrum
range of radiation waves, from low to high energy

STP
standard temperature and pressure; $0°$ C and 1 atm

starch
polysaccharide made by plants to store glucose

state
the form—gas, liquid, or solid—in which matter is found

straight-chain alkane
alkane consisting of molecules in which each carbon atom is linked to no more than two other carbon atoms, such as $CH_3CH_2CH_2CH_3$

stratosphere
region of atmosphere outside troposphere

strong force
force of attraction between particles in atomic nucleus

structural formula
chemical formula showing the arrangement of atoms and covalent bonds in a molecule

subscript
character printed below a line of type; in H_2O, for example, the subscript 2 indicates the number of H atoms

substrate
reactant molecule or ion in an enzyme-catalyzed biochemical reaction

supersaturated solution
solution containing a higher concentration of solute than a saturated solution at the given temperature

superscript
character printed above a line of type; in Cl^-, the superscript $-$ indicates the charge of the chloride ion

surface water
water on the surface of the ground

suspension
mixture containing such large, dispersed particles that it appears cloudy; muddy water, for instance

symbol
a one- or two-letter expression that represents an element; the symbol Na represents sodium

synergistic interaction
combination of interactions that produces a total effect greater than the sum of the individual interactions; for example, combined effect of air pollutants

synthetic
created industrially from petroleum

technology
application of science to create useful goods and services

temperature
degree of hotness or coldness of a substance, as measured on a thermometer

tetrahedron
a regular triangular pyramid; the four bonds of each carbon atom in molecules of alkanes point to the corners of a tetrahedron

thermosphere
outermost region of the earth's atmosphere

titration
laboratory technique used to determine the concentration of a solution, or the amount of a substance in a sample

toxin
substance harmful to the body

trace mineral
essential mineral present in quantities of less than 5 g in adult human body

tracer, radioactive
radioactive isotope used to follow movement of material; used in medicine to detect abnormal functioning in body, for example

transmutation
conversion of one element to another; unknown before discovery of radioactivity

transuranium element
element having an atomic number higher than that of uranium

triglyceride
an ester whose molecules were formed by combination of glycerol with three fatty acid molecules; a fat

tripeptide
compound made from three amino acids

troposphere
region of atmosphere from the earth's surface to 10 km outside it

turbidity
cloudiness

Tyndall effect
pattern caused by reflection of light from suspended particles in a colloid

U

ultraviolet radiation
electromagnetic radiation of slightly higher energy than visible light; can cause tissue damage

undernourishment
receiving less food than needed to supply bodily energy needs

unsaturated fat
fat whose molecules contain carbon-carbon double bonds

unsaturated hydrocarbon
hydrocarbon whose molecules contain double or triple bonds; for example, alkenes, alkynes

unsaturated solution
solution containing a lower concentration of solute than a saturated solution at the given temperature

V

viscosity
measure of a fluid's resistance to flow

visible radiation
electromagnetic radiation visible by human eye

vitamins
biomolecules needed in small amounts for body function; must be provided in food or as food supplement

vitrification
formation of a glasslike substance

voltaic cell
electrochemical cell in which a spontaneous chemical reaction is used to produce electricity

W

water softening
removal from water of ions that cause its hardness (see hard water)

X

X rays
high-energy electromagnetic radiation; normally unable to penetrate bone or lead, but can penetrate less-dense materials

Z

zero oxidation state
neither oxidized nor reduced; the state of an uncombined element

INDEX

Numbers in **boldface** type refer to pages on which illustrations may be found.

A

Accidents, motor vehicle, 453, 465
Acetic acid. *See* Ethanoic acid
Acetylsalicylic acid, 452–453
Acid-base neutralization, 52, 427
Acid-base scale, **51**
Acidosis, 432
Acid rain, 398–401
Acids, 51–52, 471
   and body, 429–433
   carboxylic, **200**
   fatty, 230–**231**
   strength, 427
   structure and function, 426–427
Acne, 438
Acquired immune deficiency syndrome (AIDS), 457
Acrylonitrile, **202**
Actinide series, 306
Activation energy, **395**
Active sites, 419–**420**
Addition polymers, 201–204
Addition reaction, 201
Additives, food, 260–266, **261**
Adenosine diphosphate (ADP), 420–422
Adenosine triphosphate (ATP), 420–422
ADP. *See* Adenosine diphosphate (ADP)
Adrenaline, **451**
Adsorption, 501
AEC. *See* Atomic Energy Commission (AEC)
Aeration, 45, **70–72**
Aerobic bacteria, 46
Aerogel, 116
AIDS. *See* Acquired immune deficiency syndrome (AIDS)
Air,
   chemistry, and climate, 338–407
   cleansing, 392
   inhaled and exhaled, **344**
   national trends, **404–407**
   pollution, 96, **340**, **385–400**, **394**, **396**, **398**, 403–407
Air pressure, 354–359
Alanine, **242**, **243**
Alcaligenes, 212
Alcohol, 199–200, **231**, 453–454, 462–464
   and blood, 453–454
   and drugs, 457–459
   and toxins, 457–459
Aldehydes, **231**
Alkalinity, 51
Alkalosis, 432

Alkanes, 166, 169–174
   boiling points, 173–174
   branched-chain, **172**
   isomers, 173
   straight chain, **172**
Alkenes, 196–198, 201
Alkynes, 198
Alloys, 116
Alpha decay, 295–297
Alpha keratin, 443, **447**
Alpha particle emission, **205**–297
Alpha particle scattering experiment, **282**
Alpha rays, **280**–283
Altitude, and atmosphere, 354–356
Alum, 478
Aluminum, **100**
   and electrochemistry, 515–517
   oxide, 192, 517
   properties of, 145
   recycling, **97**, 129
   supply and demand, 145–146
   uses, **145**
   and Washington Monument, **515**
Amines, 498
Amino acids, **242**–244, **243**
   essential, 244
Amino group, 242
Ammonia, 29, 386, 479, 482, 491–**492**, **496**, 498
   household, 29, 52
Ammonia production, 495–500
Ammonium chloride, 60
Ammonium nitrate, 479, **503**
Ammonium sulfate, 54
Amylase, 423–425
Anabolic steroids, 455
Anaerobic bacteria, 57
Analgesics, 451–453
-ane, 166, 171
Anions, 32, 52
Anode, 139, 509–**511**, **510**
Antacid, 427
Antibiotics, **410**
Antibodies, **456**–457
Anticaking agents, 261
Antigens, 456–457
Antimycotic agents, 261
Antineutrino, 296
Antioxidants, 261
Appendicitis, 465
Aquifer, 15–16
Aromatic compounds, 199–202
Arrhenius, Svante, 426
Ascorbic acid. *See* Vitamins, C
Asimov, Isaac, 180
Aspartame, **261**, 264
Aspartic acid, **242**
Asphalt, 161

Aspirin, **452–453**
Atherosclerosis, 232
Atmosphere, 17, 96
   and altitude, 351, 354–356
   chemical composition, **120**, 351
   and climate, 370–384
   investigating, 342–343, 346–369
   pressure unit, 356–357
Atomic bomb, 310
Atomic Energy Commission (AEC), **337**
Atomic mass, 108
Atomic number, 109–111, 295–298
Atoms, 24, **28**
   architecture of, 283–284
   counting, 91–92
   counting and weighing, 124–126
   and energy, 275–290
   inventory, 92
ATP. *See* Adenosine triphosphate (ATP)
Automobiles
   accidents and, 453, 465
   batteries in, **511**
   energy and, 183–184
   pollutants from, 393–396
   and smog, 393–396
Avogadro, Amedeo, 353
Avogadro's law, 353–354
Azurite, 134

B

Background radiation, 291
Bacteria
   aerobic, 46
   anaerobic, 57
   and water purification, 64
Baking soda. *See* Sodium bicarbonate
Balanced equations, 91–93
Balancing equations, 122–124
Ball-and-stick model, **169**
Barium,
   -140, 328
Barium hydroxide, 427
Barometer, **359**
Bases, 51–52
   and body, 429–453
   strength, 427
   structure and function, 426–427
Battery, **510–511**
Bauxite, 517
Becquerel, Henri, 278–279
Benedict's reagent, 424

Benzene, **199–200**, **456**, 479
Benzo(a)anthracene, **459**
Benzo(c)phenanthrene, **459**
Benzo(c)pyrene, **459**
Benzoyl peroxide, **438**
Beta decay, **296–297**
Beta particles, 296
Beta rays, 280
BHT. *See* Butylated
        hydroxytoluene (BHT)
Biodegradable substances, 46
Biomass, 211
Biomolecules, 178
Biopolymers, 212
Biosphere, **376**
Biotechnology, **472**
Biotin, 252
Black box experiment, 281–283
Black gold, 158
Bleach, laundry, 74
Bleaches, 261
Blood, and alcohol, 453–454
Body
    and acids, bases, and buffers,
        429–433
    and chemistry, 415–425
    elements in, 416–418
    and pH, 432–433
    weight, and energy, 226–228
Boiling, 23
Boiling point
    of alkanes, 173–174
    of hydrocarbons, 166
    of water, 22
Bombardment reactions,
        305–306
Bonding, chemical, 30, 167
Bonds, chemical, 27
    covalent, 168
        single and double, 196
    disulfide, **448**
    and energy, 182
    and hair, **447–448**
    and hydrocarbons, 168
    hydrogen, **435**, **447**
    ionic, **447**
    peptide, **243**
Boron, 313
Bottoms, **159**
Botulism, 263
Boyle's law, 359–362, **360**
Branched-chain alkanes, **172**,
        193
Breath, composition, **344**
Brine, 515
Brittleness, 106
Bronze, 135
Brown ring test, 488
Buffers, and body, 429–33
Buffer solution, 429–433
Bunsen burner, **89**
Burning
    chemistry of, 186
    glucose, 343–344
Butane, 166
Butene, **197**
Butylated hydroxytoluene (BHT),
        261

C
Cadmium, 57,
Calciferol, 252
Calcium, 257
    in body, 416
    ion test, 34–35
    in water, 65–68
Calcium carbonate, 65, 67–68
Calcium chloride, 48
Calcium hydroxide, 51
Calcium hypochlorite, 74
Calcium stearate, **68**
Calcium sulfate, 67
Calgon (sodium hexameta-
        phosphate), 65–67
Calories, 224
    and food composition,
        523–537
Calorimeter, 224
Calorimetry, 224
Cancer, 439–440, 459, 461–462,
        465
Candle wax. *See* Paraffin
Carbohydrates, 228–230
    classification of, 228–229
    energy value, 230
    milk, 249
Carbon
    in body, 416
    burning of, 91–92
    chains, 167
    compounds of, 196–199
    isotopes of, 284
Carbon cycle, **376**
Carbon dioxide, 72, 92, 210–211,
        344, **346**, 479
    atmospheric, 372–382
    measuring levels, 380–381
    properties, 348–351
Carbon monoxide, 386, 388, 389,
        459
Carbonic acid, 51, 429–433
Carboxyl group, 242
Carboxylic acids, **200**, **231**
Carcinogens, 263, 459, 461–462
Cardiovascular system, 415
Careers in Chemistry,
    AIDS Aide, **458**
    Beautiful Chemistry, **142**
    Environmental
        Enlightenment, **397**
    Keeping Florida Fresh, **14**
    Medical Technologists: Part of
        the Diagnostic Team, **413**
    Metals in the Marketplace, 514
    Ms. Green Jeans, **262**
    Planting Seeds in the City, **377**
    Preserving the Past, **118**
    Raiders of the Temple of
        Doom, **320**
    Researchers: Key to New
        Products, **485**
    Rock Around the Clock, **163**
    Safety: As American as Apple
        Pie, **233**
    Safety in Polymerization, **203**
    Taking the Risk Out of
        Swimming, **73**

Who Are Radiation
        Therapists? **289**
Catalysts, 192–193
Catalytic converter, 395–396
Catalytic cracking, 192
Catechol, 456
Cathode, 139, 509–**511**, **510**,
Cathode rays, 278
Cathode ray tubes, 278
Cations, 32, 52
Cause-effect vs. correlation,
        411–412
Cellular chemistry, 418
Cellular respiration, 237–239
Cellulose, 211–212, **229–230**
Celsius temperature scale, **23**
Centi-, 5
Centimeter, 5–6
Ceramics, 140–**141**
Cesium
    -137, 321
Chain reactions, 309–311, **310**
Chains, carbon, 167
Chalcocite, **132–134**, **133**
Chalcopyrite, 134
Chalk, 67
Change, and physical properties,
        102
Charcoal absorption/filtration,
        9–10
Charles, Jacques, 364
Charles' law, 365
Chemical bonds. *See* Bonds,
        chemical
Chemical changes, **102–103**
Chemical compounds.
        See Compounds
Chemical elements.
        See Elements
Chemical engineers, 192–195
Chemical equations. *See*
        Equations, chemical
Chemical formulas. *See*
        Formulas, chemical
Chemical industry, 466–521
    overview of, 478–486
    products of, 475
Chemical properties, 28,
        102–103, 106–107, 109
    See also Physical properties
        and Properties
Chemical reactions. *See*
        Reactions, chemical
Chemical reactivity, 112–115
Chemical resources, and
        conservation, 94–148
Chemical symbols. *See* Symbols,
        chemical
Chemicals
    organic and inorganic, 471
    produced in United States,
        471, 479
Chemistry
    air, 338–407
    basic needs met by, 471
    and biotechnology, **472**
    and body, 415–425
    of burning, 186

cellular, 418
contributions of, 471
and drugs and toxins,
    450–462
electro-. *See* Electrochemistry
and energy, 471, 506–518
and the environment,
    472–**473**
and explosives, **500**-504
and food, 471
and hair, 443–449
and health, **472**
and industry. *See* Chemical
    industry
internal, 415–425
and new materials and
    processes, 471
and nitrogen products,
    487–505
and Nobel prize, **501**–503
nuclear, 270–337
organic, 167, 471
photo-, 395, 442–443
products of, 471
ChemQuandaries
    Airing Some Pollution
        Solutions, 390
    Always Harmful?, 277
    Behavior of Gases, 365
    Benzoyl Peroxide and Acne,
        438
    Chew on This Problem! 423
    Cigarette Warnings, 412
    Controlling Air Pollution, 396
    Discovery of Metals, 135
    Frozen Smoke? 116
    Gasoline and Geography, 164
    Grab Another Blanket! 373
    Hammering Away at Kinetic
        Energy, 366
    Life without Gasoline, 180
    Nitrite Additives, 264
    Nuclear Power Worldwide, 331
    A Penny for Your Thoughts, 88
    A Permanent Permanent? 449
    Pressure Puzzles, 357
    Radiation Exposure
        Standards, 325
    Recycling Limits, 129
    Risk-Free Travel? 318
    Scientific Discoveries, 279
    The Shell Game, 433
    Some Reflections on Dust, 374
    Splitting Molecules? 190
    Steps Toward Clean Air, 392
    Transmutation of Elements,
        306
    Vitamin D Deficiency, 443
    Vitamin D Solubility, 443
    A Volume Discount? 359
    Water, Water Everywhere, 7
    What Price Survival?, 483
    Wondering about Resources
        and Waste, 99
Chernobyl, 331–**333**
Chloride ion test, 35
Chlorination, 69, **74**–75
Chlorine, 107, 257, 479

atoms, 383
gas, 74
in water treatment, 69, 74–75
Chlorofluorocarbons (CFCs), 383
Chromium, 121, 257
    -51, 321
Cigarettes
    and health, 459, 461–462
    and smoke, **459**–461
Clay, 140–**141**
Cleaning, skin, 434–438
Climate,
    and atmosphere, 370–384
    chemistry, and air, 338–407
Clostridium botulinum, 263
Cloud chamber, **303**–304
Clouds, and water, 16, **352**
Coal, 181, **208**, 210–**211**, 212
    and sulfur, 96, 388
Cobalamin, 252
Cobalt, 257
    -48, 321
    -60, 301
Cocaine, 450, 454–455
Coefficients, 92
Coenzyme, **420**
Cofactors, 251
Colloid, 24
Color Additives Amendment, 263
Colorimetric methods, 493
Coloring agents, 261
Combustion, 186–190
    and carbon dioxide, 381
    heats of, 186–190
Complementary proteins,
    244–245
Complete protein, 244
Composites, 140–**142**, **145**–**146**
Compounds, 27
    aromatic, 199–202
    organic, 57, 471
    unsaturated, 196
Concentration, solution, 42–43
Condensation, 64
Condensation polymers, 204
Condensation reaction, 204
Conductivity, electrical, 10, 106
Conductors, 106
Confirming tests, 32
Conservation
    of chemical resources, 84–148
    of matter, law of, 91, 94
    in nature and community,
        120–130
Continuous-flow process, **483**
Control, 32, 90
Control costs, 405–407
Control rods, **312**–**313**
Conversion, of energy, **183**–186
Cooling system, **313**–314
Copper, 116–117, 136–139, 257
    density, 104
    electrolysis of, **139**
    and penny, **88**–89
    properties, 103, 113, 132
    recycling, **132**
    sources and uses, 131–139
Copper(I) sulfide, 133

Copper(II) nitrate, 95
Copper(II) sulfate, 60
Core, of Earth, **20**
Correlation vs cause-effect,
    411–412
Corrosion, 116–**117**
Cortisol, **232**
Costs, control and damage,
    405–407
Counters
    Geiger, **291**–**292**
    radiation, 302
    scintillation, **302**
Counts per minute (cpm), 291
Covalent bonds, 168
    single and double, 196
cpm. *See* Counts per minute
    (cpm)
Crack, 454
Cracking, catalytic, **159**–160,
    192–**193**
Critical mass, 309
Crude oil. *See* Oil, crude
Crust, of Earth, **120**
Cryogenics, 369
Cryolite, 517
Crystals, **52**–**53**
Cubic centimeter, 7
Cubic decimeter, 7
Cultures, and diets, 218, 267–269
Curie, Marie, 279–280, 288,
    304–305
Curie, Pierre, 279–280, 304–305
Current, 506
Curves, solubility, 40–41
Cuticle, **444**
Cycloalkanes, 198
Cyclohexane, **198**
Cyclone collection, 391
Cyclopentanol, **200**
Cysteine, **242**–**243**

D

Damage costs, of pollution,
    405–407
Dandruff, 439
Data, 36
DDT, 62
Death, causes of, 465
Decane, 166
Decay
    beta, **296**–297
    particle, 295–297
    radioactive, 291–307
Deci-, 5
Deforestation, **378**
Delaney Clause, 263
Denaturation, 439
Density, 21–22, 104–105
    of water, 22
Deoxyribonucleic acid (DNA),
    323, 439–440, **473**
Dermis, **438**–439
Desulfurization, **407**
Detector,
    radiation, 302–303
    solid-state, 303

Detergents, 68–69, 436–437
Detoxification, 455–456
Developed world, 218
Developing world, 218
Diatomic molecules, 92
1,2-Dichloroethane, 479
Diet, 218–223
    analysis, 267–269
    and minerals, 256–259, 417
    and protein, 244–246
    and vitamins, 443
Dipeptides, **243**
Disaccharides, 229
Discards, 96–**98**
Diseases,
    infectious, 410
    studying, 414
    and vitamins, 442–443
Disinfection, 71–**72**
Dissolved oxygen (DO), 45–51
    needed by fish, **46**
Distillates, **159**
Distillation
    of crude oil, **159**–160
Disulfide bonds, **448**
DNA. *See* Deoxyribonucleic acid
    (DNA)
DO. *See* Dissolved oxygen (DO)
Dolomite, 67
Domino chain reaction, 310–311
Double covalent bond, 196
Drugs
    and alcohol, 457–459
    combined, 457–459
    defined, 450
    designer, 455
    functions, 450–452
    mind-altering, 464
    and toxins, 450–462
Ductility, 132
Dynamic equilibrium, 498
Dynamite, 501

E

Earth
    atmospheric changes,
        375–384
    carbon dioxide levels, 372–382
    composition of, **120**
    energy balance of, 372–374
    surface of, 374–379
    and water, **17**
Ecosystems, 415
Eggshells, 433
Einstein, Albert, 309
EKS Company, 484–486
    divisions of, **484**
Electrical nature of matter,
        29–31
Electrical potential, 506–509
Electricity, **207**–208
    and nuclear energy, 312
Electrochemical cells, 506–509
Electrochemistry, 509–512
    aluminum, 515–517
    industrial, 515–517
    principles of, 509–512

Electrocution, 465
Electrodes, 138
Electrolysis, 135, 138–**139**
Electromagnetic radiation, 276
Electromagnetic spectrum, 276,
        371
Electrometallurgy, 138
Electron-dot formulas, 169
Electronegativity, 496
Electrons, 30, 167, 283
Electroplating, 512–514, **513**
Electrostatic precipitation,
        390–391
Elements, 27, 104–105
    and body, 416–418
    common, 105
    and electronegativity,
        496–497
    grouping, 108, 110
    and limiting reactants, 240
    needed by humans, 240
    needed by plants, 241
    periodic table, 107–**111**
    properties of, 105
    symbols, 28, 105
    transuranium, 306
Emissions, 386, 393–**396**,
        403–407, **404**
Emphysema, 465
Emulsifiers, 261
Endorphins, 451
Endothermic change, **182**
Endpoint, 255
-ene, 197
Energy
    activation, **395**
    and activities, 226
    and atoms, 275–290
    chemical and electrical,
        506–518
    conversions, **183**–186
    dependency, 207–209
    earth's balance, 372–374
    and Einstein equation, 309,
        314
    and enzymes, 422
    and exercise, 226–228
    from food, 224–235, 522
    and fossil fuels, 181–185, **209**
    and fusion, **314**–315
    kinetic, 366–368
    and milk, 249–250
    nuclear, 275–290, 308–315
        benefits and risks, 316–334
        and electricity, **208**
    past, 87, 178–180
    petroleum as source of,
        176–195
    policy options, 214
    release and storage, 420–422
    solar, 210, **370**–374
    sources, 178–181, 207–212
    thermal, 93
    units, 224–225
Engineers, 483
    See also Chemical engineers
Engines, 402
Enkephalins, 451–**452**

Environmental Protection
        Agency (EPA), 388, 394
    and chemical industry, 483
Enzymes, 418–425, **420**
    and detoxification, 455–456
    and energy, 212, 422
EPA. *See* Environmental
        Protection Agency (EPA)
Epidemiology, 414
Epidermis, **438**–439
Equations, chemical, 28
    balanced, 91–93
    balancing, 122–124
    net ionic, 427
    and substance state, 92
    symbols, and formulas, 28
Equations, nuclear, 295–296
    balancing, 298
Equilibrium, dynamic, 498
Essential amino acids, 244
Essential minerals, 257–258
Esters, **200**, 231
Ethane, 166
Ethanoic acid, **205**–206
Ethanol, 60, **199**
Ethene, **196**–197, 201, 479
Ethene dichloride, 479
Ethers, **200**, 231
Ethylbenzene, 479
Ethylene. *See* Ethene
Ethylene dichloride. *See* Ethene
        dichloride
Ethylene glycol, **175**
Ethylene oxide. *See* Ethene oxide
Euglena, 460–461
Euphorbia, 210
Evaporation, **16**, 64
Exercise, and energy, 226–228
Exothermic change, **182**
Explosives, **500**–504
Extrapolation, 171

F

Facts, 33
Fahrenheit temperature scale,
        23, 35
Families of elements, 110
FAO. *See* United Nations Food
        and Agriculture
        Organization (FAO)
Fats, 230–**231**, 232–234
    consumption of, 234
    energy value, 230
    partial hydrogenation of, 234
    polyunsaturated, 232
    saturated and unsaturated,
        231–232
Fatty acids, 230–**231**
FDA. *See* Food and Drug
        Administration (FDA)
Federal Clean Air Act, 394
    Amendments of 1990, 396
Federal Food, Drug, and Cosmetic
        Act, 263
Fertilizer, 487
    chemical roles of, 491–493
    composition of, 487–490, **493**

phosphates in, 493–495
Fiber. *See* cellulose
Fibers
    acrylic, 204
    optical, **140**
    synthetic, **201**
Fibrous proteins, 447
Filtrate, 8
Filtration, 8–10, 64–67, **66**
    activated charcoal, 74
    sand, **70**
Fish
    and dissolved oxygen, **46**
    and temperature, 47
Fish kill
    and heavy metal ions, 54–58
    and Riverwood, 2–4, 20,
        36–37, 63, 76
Fission, nuclear, 308–311
Fixation, nitrogen, 491–**492**,
        495–496, 498–500
Flavoring agents, 261
Fleming, Alexander, 279
Flocculation, **70**
Fluids, 341
Fluorescence, 278–279
Fluorescent minerals, 279
Fluoridation, 71
Fluorine, 107, 257
Folic acid, 252
Follicle, hair, 443–**444**
Food
    additives in, 260–266
    or arms, 504
    and body weight, 226–228
    to build or to burn, 220–223
    as builder molecules, 236–250
    as chemical reactants,
        236–237
    composition of common,
        236–241, 523–537
    diary, 219
    as energy, 224–235
    irradiation of, **321**
    and RDA, 245
    supplements, **241**
    systems model, **222**
    understanding, 216–269
    vitamins and minerals in,
        251–266
Food and Agriculture Organ-
        ization. *See* United
        Nations Food and
        Agriculture Organization
        (FAO)
Food and Drug Administration
        (FDA), 263
Forces,
    intermolecular, 166
    strong, 309
Foreign substances, in body,
        455–457
Formaldehyde, 479
Formula unit, 92
Formulas, chemical, 28
    electron-dot, 169
    ionic, 54
    structural, 169

and symbols, 29
    and equations, 29
    writing, 54
Fossil fuels, 181–185
Fractionating tower, **159**
Fractions, and petroleum
        refining, **159**–160
Freezing, of water, 22
Freezing point, 22
Freons, 383
Frequency, 276
Fructose, **228**, 229, **232**
Fruit, and composition, 529–530
Fuel rods, **312–313**
Fuels
    altering, 192–195
    consumption, 208
    fossil, 181–185
    liquid, 210
    oxygenated, 194
    and petroleum, 155
    and sources, 208
Functional groups, 200, **231**
Funnel, 8
Fusion
    heat of, 19
    nuclear, **314–315**

G

Galactose, 229
Galvanized steel, 57–58
Gamma decay, 296–297
Gamma radiation, 280
Gamma rays, **280**, 291–297, **296**
Gas bubble disease, 79, 82
Gas oil, **159**
Gaseous state (g), 92
    of water, 17
Gases, **159**, 342–343
    and Avogadro's law, 353
    and Boyle's law, 359–362
    carbon dioxide, **344**, 372–382
    and Charles' Law, 365
    and density, 22
    and equations, 92
    hydrogen, 495–496
    ideal, 368
    kinetic molecular theory of,
        366
    molar volume, 353–354
    molecules in motion, 366
    natural, 210
    nitrogen, **344**
    noble, 168
    oxygen, 40, **344**
    solubility of, 40–41
    temperature and solubility,
        40–41
    and waste, 96
Gasohol, 194
Gasoline, **153**, **159**, 193, 210
Gay-Lussac, Joseph, 364
Geiger counter, **291–292**,
Geiger, Hans, 282
Gemstones, 121

Generally Recognized As Safe
        (GRAS) list, 263
Generator, **312–313**
Genes, 420
Geothermal energy, 210
Glaciers, and Earth's water, 17
Glass, recycling, 129
Glass shielding, 292–294
Global warming, 211, **378–384**
Globular proteins, 448
Glucose, **228**, 229, **232**, 418
    burning, 343–344, 420–421
    formation of, 45, 229, 344
Glycerol, 230–**231**, **437**
Glyceryltripalmitate, **231**, **437**
Glycine, **242**
Glycogen, 229
Gold, 113, 121, 135
    -198, 321
Gold, black. *See* Black gold
Gold foil experiment, 282
Goodyear, Charles, 279
Grains, and composition,
        523–524
Gram, 21
Graphite, 116
Graphs, 47–49
    and solubility, 40–41
GRAS. *See* Generally Recognized
        As Safe (GRAS) list.
Greenhouse gases, 211, 373
Groundwater, 15–**16**, 17, 67
Groups, and periodic table of
        elements, 110–111
Groups, functional, 200, **231**
Gypsum, 67

H

Haagen-Smit, Arie J., 393
Haber process, 495
Hahn, Otto, 308
Hail, 17
Hair,
    chemistry, 443–449
    styling and chemical bonding,
        447–449
Hair keratin, 443, **447**
Half-cell, 509
Half-life, 299–302
Half-reactions, 509–511
Hall, Charles Martin, 516
Hall process, **516–517**
Hardness of water, 64, 67–69
Health
    and chemistry, **472**
    risks and choices, 408–465
    and smog, 388–390
    and water, 11
Heart disease, 410, 465
Heat
    and Earth, 372–379
    specific, 188
Heat capacity, 19, 374–375
Heat of combustion, 186–190
Heat of fusion, 19
Heat of vaporization, 19

Heavy metals,
  contamination of water by,
    56–58
Helium, 361
Hemoglobin, 429
Heptane, 166
Heterogeneous mixture, 23
Hexane, 60, 166, **198**
Hiroshima, 310
Histidine, 244
HIV. *See* Human immuno-
    deficiency virus (HIV)
Homeostasis, 415–416
Homicide, 465
Homogeneous mixture, 24
Homogenized milk, **24**
Hormones, 242
Human immunodeficiency virus
    (HIV), **457**
Humectants, 261
Humidity, 351
Hunger
  dimensions of, 221–223
  world, 222–223
Hydrazine, 498
Hydrocarbons, 158-**159**, 160,
    164, 386, 388
  boiling points, 166
  halogenated, 372
  heats of combustion, 189–190
  polycyclic aromatic (PAHs),
    459
Hydrochloric acid, 51
Hydroelectric power, **208**
Hydrogen, 107
  -3 (tritium), 321
  in body, 416
  bomb, 315
  bonding, **435**, **447**
  compounds of, 197–198
  fusion, 314
  gas, 495–496
  molecule of, **30**
  and pH, 52
Hydrogenation, 234
Hydrogen peroxide, 122
Hydrogen sulfide, 386
Hydrologic cycle, **16**
Hydrometallurgy, 138
Hydropower, 210
Hydrosphere, **120**
Hydroxides
  and pH, 52
Hydroxylamine, 498
Hypochlorous acid, 74

I

Ice, 454–455
Ice caps, and Earth's water, 17
-ide, 53
Ideal gases, 368
Industrial Revolution, 342, 346,
    442
Industry, chemical. *See* Chemical
    industry
Infant mortality rate, 222
Infrared (IR), 276

Infrared radiation, **276**, **371**
Inorganic substances, 481
Intensity, of radiation, **294**, **296**
Interactions
  nonpolar, **447**–448
  synergistic, 459
Intermediates, 481–483
Intermolecular forces, 166
Internal chemistry, 415–425
International System of Units
    (SI). *See* SI units
International Union of Pure and
    Applied Chemistry
    (IUPAC), 197
Iodine, 60, **257**
Ion exchange method, 65–67
Ionic bonds, **447**
Ionic compounds, 31
  dissolving, 55–56
  naming, 54
  writing formulas for, 54
Ionizing radiation, 276, 322–326
Ions, 31
  common, 53
  counting and weighing,
    124–126
  heavy metal, 56–58
  and ionic compounds, 52–54
  net equation, 427
  polyatomic, 54
  spectator, 427
  tests for, 32–35
IR. *See* Infrared (IR)
Iridium,
  -192, 321
Iron, 112–113, 117, 135, 257
  -59, 321
  -copper electrochemical cell,
    508
  in foods, 259–260
Iron(III) ion test, 34
Iron(III) oxide, **113**
Irradiation, 318–322, **321**
Isoleucine, 244
Isomerization, 194
Isomers, 172–174, 197–198
Isotopes
  of carbon, 284
  common, 284
  and fuel rods, 328
  of hydrogen, 287–288
  and molar mass, 287
  in nature, 286–288
  notation, 284–285
  and pennies, 285–286
  radioactive, 284–288
  of uranium, 288
  See also Radioisotopes
IUPAC. *See* International Union
    of Pure and Applied
    Chemistry (IUPAC)

J

Joliot-Curie, Frédéric, 304–305
Joliot-Curie, Irène, 304–305
Joule, 179
  and calorie, 225

K

Kelvin, Lord. *See* Thomson,
    William
Kelvin temperature unit, 364–365
Keratin
  hair, 443, **447**,
Kerosene, **159**
Ketone, 161
Kilo-, 21
Kinetic energy, 366–368
Kinetic molecular theory, 366
Krypton
  -34, 328

L

Laboratory, safety in, xvi–xvii
Lactic acid, 432
Lactose, 229
Lakes, and Earth's water, 17
Landfills, 97, 98
Laser, 277
Law
  Avogadro's, 353–354
  Boyle's, 359–362
  Charles', 365
  of conservation, 91, 94
  periodic, 110
Lead, 56, 194
  block experiment, 282
  red, 56
  shielding, 292–294
  storage battery, **510**
Lead azide, **503**
Leavening agents, 261
Legumes, 491
Length, 5
Leucine, 244
Life span, 410
Lightning, 465
Limestone, 67
Limiting reactants, 237–241
Limiting reagents, 237–241
Linkage, peptide, **243**
Linolenic acid, **231**
Lipids, 230
Liquids
  and density, 22
  and equations, 92
Liquid state (l), 92
  of water, 17
Liter, 6–7
Lithosphere, **120**
Liver, 455
  and detoxification, 455–456
Lysine, 244

M

Macrominerals, 256–257
Magnesite, 67
Magnesium, 112, 113, 115, 257
  in water, 67–69
Magnesium carbonate, 67
Magnesium-copper
    electrochemical cell, 508
Magnesium hydroxide, 51

Magnesium oxide, 112
Malachite, 134
Malleability, 106, 132
Malnourishment, 218
Maltose, 229
Manganese, 257
Mantle, of Earth, **120**
Manufacturing, chemicals for, 471
Marsden, Ernest, 282
Mass, 21
    atomic. *See* Atomic mass
    critical. *See* Critical mass
    defect, 309
    molar. *See* Molar mass
    number, 295–298
Matter
    at atomic level, 27
    creation and destruction, 91
    electrical nature of, 29–31
    law of conservation of, 91, 94
    states of 17
Maxey Flats, Kentucky, 330
Measurement, and metric
    system, 4–7
Meats, and composition, 530–532
Mechanical filtering, 391
Medicine, and radioisotopes, 319
Megadose, of vitamins, 253
Meitner, Lise, **308**
Melanin, 439
Meltdown, 332
Melting point, 105
Menaquinone, 252
Mendeleev, Dimitri, **108**–110, 155
Meperidine, 451
Mercury, 57
    barometer, **359**
Mercury(II) nitrate, 57
Mesosphere, 356
Metalloids, 105–107
Metals, 105–107
    activity series, 507
    alternatives to, 143
    densities of, 105
    heavy, 56–58
    melting points of, 105
    and ores, 135–139
    reactivities of, 105, 113–115, 135–136, 506–509
    reserves, **144**–146
    sources and replacements, 131–143
Meter, 5–6
Methadone, 451
Methamphetamine, 455
Methane, 72, 166, **169**–**170**, 372, 386, 388
Methanol, **199**, 479
Methionine, 244
Methyl acetate, **200**, **205**
Methylmercury ion, 57
Methyl *tert*-butyl ether (MTBE), 479
Metric system, and measure-
    ment, 4–7. *See also* SI
    units

Metric ton, 480
Microfibril, **444**
Microgram (μg), 252
Microwave radiation, 276
Milk
    analysis of, 246
    and composition, 249
    homogenized, **24**
Milli-, 5
Milliliter, 6
Millimeters of mercury (mmHg), 358
Millirem (mrem), 324
Minamata Bay, Japan, 57
Mined geologic disposal plan, 328–331, **329**
Mineral oil, 161
Minerals, 134
    in body, 417
    in diet, 256–259, 417
    essential, 257–258
    fluorescent, 279
    and hard water, **67**
    macro- and trace, 256–257, 417
    RDAs of, 258
Mitochondria, **236**
Mixtures
    classification of, 23–26
    heterogeneous, 23
    homogeneous, **24**
    and solutions, 23–25
mmHg. *See* Millimeters of
    mercury (mmHg)
Models,
    food systems, **222**
    molecular, **169**–171
Moderator, **312**–313
Molar heat of combustion, 186
Molarity, 124
Molar mass, 124, 126,
Molar volume, 353–354
Molecular structure, 29
Molecules, 27
    builder, 196–206, 236–250
    counting and weighing, 124–126
    diatomic, 92
    gas, 353–354
    and hydrocarbons, 196–199
    nonpolar, 60
    and substrates, 419–**420**
    See also Biomolecules
Moles, 124–127, **125**
Molybdenum, 257, 456, 480–481
Monomer, 201
Monosaccharides, 228
Monosodium glutamate (MSG), **261**
Moore, Henry, **306**
Morphine, 451–452
Mortality rate, infant, 222
Motor oil, 161
Mrem. *See* Millirem (mrem)
MSG. *See* Monosodium
    glutamate (MSG)
Mutations, 323

N

Nagasaki, 310
Naphthalene, 60
Narcotic analgesics, 451–452
Natural gas, 210
Negative oxidation state, 496
Nerve cells, 453
Net ionic equation, 427
Neurons, 453
Neutralization, acid-base, 52, 427
Neutral substances, 52
Neutrinos, 307
Neutrons, 30, 283–288, 296–297
Newton, 356–357
Niacin, 252
Nickel, 257
Nickel-cadmium (NiCad)
    batteries, 55
Nitrates, **492**, 498
Nitric acid, 51, 94, 479, 498
Nitrites, 498
Nitrogen, 107, **344**, **347**, 479
    in body, 416
    compounds, industrial, 498
    cycle, **492**
    fixation, 491–492, 495–496, 498–500
    gas, **344**
    oxides, 386, 388, 389, 393–400, **404**
    products, 487–504
    properties, 348–351
Nitroglycerin, **503**
Nitrosamines, 459
Nitrous acid, 264
Nobel, Alfred, **501**
Nobel, Oscar, 501
Nobel prize, **501**–503
Nonane, 166
Nonconductors, 106
Nonionizing radiation, **276**–277
Nonmetals, 105–107
    densities of, 105
    melting points of, 105
    reactivities of, 105
Nonpolar interaction, **447**–448
Nonpolar molecules, 60
Nonpolar solvents, 60
Nonrenewable resources, 95–97, 152
Notation, and isotopes, 284–285
Nourishment, under- and mal-, 218
Nuclear age, birth of, **306**
Nuclear chain reaction, 309–311, **310**
Nuclear chemistry, in our world, 270–337
Nuclear decay, 295–297
Nuclear energy, 275–290, 308–315
    benefits and risks, 272, 316–334
Nuclear equations, 295–296
    balancing, 298

Nuclear fission reaction, 308–311
Nuclear fusion, **314–315**
Nuclear phenomena, survey on, 272–274, 335–337
Nuclear power, 272, 331
Nuclear power plants, **311–314, 312,** 331–334, **332, 333**
Nuclear radiation, 322–328, **325**
    background, **325**
    from human sources, **325**
Nuclear reactors, **274, 312**
Nuclear waste, 328–331, **329**
Nucleus, 167, 283–284
Number
    atomic. *See* Atomic number
    octane. *See* Octane number
    oxidation. *See* Oxidation state
NutraSweet, 264
Nutrients,
    in foods, 261, 522
    and plants, 241
Nutrition
    and food composition, 523–537
    imbalances in, 220–221
    and limiting reactants, 240
    world, 218–224, 267–269

O

Oceans,
    and Earth's water, 17
    and resources, 121
Octane, 166, **193**
Octane number, 193
Oil. *See also* Petroleum
    crude, **158,** 164–167, **165**
    lubricating, household, 161
    motor, 161
    shale, 210
    -water separation, 8–9
Opium, 451
Ores, 121, 127, 134
    evaluating, 133–135
    and metals, 127, 131–132, 135–139
Organic chemistry, 167
Organic compounds, 57, 167, 471
Oxidation
    number. *See* Oxidation state
    -reduction reactions, 137–138, 495–496
    state, negative, positive, and zero, 496
Oxides, 96, 386, 388–389, 393–400, **404**
Oxygen, 107, **344,** 479
    -17, 304
    atoms, 92
    in body, 416
    compounds of, 197–198
    gas, **347**
        dissolved in water, 41, 45–46, 79
    molecule of, **30**
    properties of, 103, 349–351
    supply and demand, 44–46
Oxygenated fuels, 194
Ozone, 74, 382–384, 393

P

PABA. *See* Para-aminobenzoic acid (PABA)
PAHs. *See* Polycyclic aromatic hydrocarbons (PAHs)
Pain, 451–452
Palmitic acid, **231**
Pantothenic acid, 252
Paper, 128
Para-aminobenzoic acid (PABA), **440**
Paraffin, 161
Paramecium, 400
Parthenon, 398
Particles, ejected, 305
Particulates, 387–389, **391, 404**
Parts per million (ppm), 416
Pasteur, Louis, 279
Patina, 117
Penicillin, 116
Pennies, 88–91
    and isotopes, 285–286
Pentane, 166
Pentanol, **206**
Pepsin, 423–425
Peptide linkage (bond), **243**
Percent composition of ores, 134
Periodic law, 110
Periodic table, **107–111**
Periods, and periodic table, 110
Petrochemicals, **158,** 200–206
Petroleum
    alternatives to, 207–212
    to build or to burn, 150–215
    as an energy source, 176–195
    in our future, 155–156, 200–206
    molecules, 166
    origin of, 176
    in our lives, 154–157
    refining, **159–160**
    reserves and consumption, 153, 154, **156**
    usage, 154, 209, 213–215
    useful materials from, 196–206
pH, 401
    adjustment of, **70**
    in body, 432–433
    of common materials, 52
    scale, **52**
Pharmaceutical industry, **470–472**
Phenol, **200**
Phenylalanine, 244
Phenylhydrazine, 498
Phosphate, and fertilizers, 493–495
Phosphoric acid, 51, 479
Phosphorus, 257
    -32, 321
Photochemical reaction, 393
Photochemical smog, 392–396
Photochemistry, 395, 442–443
Photons, 276, 371
Photosynthesis, 45, 178, 229, 344
Physical changes, **102**

Physical properties, 21, 102, 106–107, 109–110
    and chemical properties, 102
    and petroleum, 160–162
    of water, 21–23
    See also Chemical properties and Properties
Pigments, 471
Plants
    as fuel source, 210
    and limiting reactants, 240
    and nutrients, 241
Plaque, 232
Plastics, 140, 201, 471
    See also Polymers
Plating, electro-, 512–514, **513**
Platinum, 121
Plunkett, Roy, 279
Plutonium,
    -239, 328
Poison, 451, 465
Polarity, 30–**31**
    and solubility, 60
Polar solvents, 60–61
Pollutant Standards Index, 389
Pollutants
    worldwide emissions of, 386
Pollution
    and air, 385–400
    and automobiles, 393–396
    control, 390, 403–407
Polo, Marco, 177
Polonium, 280
Polyacrylonitrile, **202,** 204
Polyatomic compounds, 54
Polycyclic aromatic hydrocarbons (PAHs), **459**
Polyester, 204
Polyethene, 116
Polyethylene. *See* Polyethene
Polymerization, 204
Polymers, 201–**204,** 229
    addition, 201
    condensation, 204
Polysaccharides, **229**
Polystyrene, **202**
Polyunsaturated fats, 232
Polyvinyl chloride, **202**
Poppy, opium, 451
Porcelain, **471**
Positive oxidation state, 496
Positrons, 314
Post-chlorination, **70**
Postulate, 366
Potash, 470
Potassium, 257
Potassium hydroxide, 51, 470
Potassium nitrate, 40
Potential, electrical, 506–509
Power
    nuclear, 311–314
    and petroleum, 176–195
Pre-chlorination, 69–**70**
Precipitation, 32
    electrostatic, 390–391
    of water, **16**
Preservatives, 261
Pressure, 356–359, **357, 358**

air, 354–359
and temperature and volume relationships, 365
-volume relationships, 361–362
See also Boyle's law
Primary air pollutants, 386
Products
of chemical industry, 475
and crude oil, 164–167, **165**
of nuclear bombardment, 305
of reactions, 28, 92
Projectile particles, 305
Propane, 93, 166
Propanol, **200**
Propene, 197, 479
Properties 102–105, 115–116
of aluminum, 145
of copper, 89–91, 132
determination of, 115
of metalloids, 105–107
of metals, 105–107
of nonmetals, 105–107
and periodic variation, of water, 21–23
See also Chemical properties and Physical properties
Propylene. *See* propene
Proteases, 244
Proteins, 241–250
in the body, 242
chains, 242
complementary, 244–245
complete, 244
and food composition, 523–537
and denaturation, 439
fibrous, 447
globular, 448
and hair, 447–449
in milk, 246–250
protective, 242
RDAs of, 245
regulatory, 242
structural, 242
transport, 242
Protons, 30, 283–288
PSI. *See* Pollutant Standards Index (PSI)
Pyridoxine, 252
Pyrometallurgy, 138

R

"4 Rs", 127
Radiation
background, 291, 324–**325**
cosmic, **276**
counters, **302**
damage, 323–324
detector, **302–303**
dosage per year, 326–327
electromagnetic, **276**, **371**
exposure to, 324–327
gamma, **276**
infrared, **276**, **371**
intensity of, **294**, **296**
ionizing, **276**, 322–326

kinds of, 275–277
microwave, **276**
nonionizing, **276**–277
nuclear, 276
and solar spectrum, **276**, **371**
ultraviolet, **277**, **371**, 439–440
Radioactive decay, 276, 298–302
Radioactivity, 275–276
artificial, 304–306
discovery of, 279
Radioisotopes, 284–288
benefits of, 318–322
and half-lives, 298–302
and medicine, 319
See also Isotopes
Radiosodium, 321
Radioxenon, 321
Radium, 280, 323
-226, 295
Radon, in houses, 326
Rain
acid. *See* Acid rain
and Earth's water, 17
Raw materials, for industry, 479–483
RDA. *See* Recommended dietary allowance (RDA)
RDX, **503**
RE. *See* Retinol Equivalents (RE)
Reactants, 28, 92
chemical, 236–237
limiting, 237–241
Reactions, chemical, 28
addition, 201
condensation, 204
of gases, 354
oxidation-reduction, 495–496
reversible, 498
Reactions, nuclear, 308–309
bombardment, 305–306
chain, 309–311, **310**
fusion, **314**
Reactivity,
chemical, 112–115
metal, 113–115, 135–136, 506–509
Reactors, nuclear, **311–312**
Reagents, limiting, 237–241
Receptors, **451**
Recommended dietary allowance (RDA), 245, 258, 268
Recycling, 97, **127–130**, **128**
Redox reactions, 137–138
Reducing agents, 138
Reduction, 135–139, 495–496
Reference solution, 32
Refining, 159
Reflectivity, 374
Rem. *See* Roentgen equivalent man (rem)
Renewable resources, 95–97
Reserves, **144–146**
Residues, **165**
Resins
ion-exchange, 65–69
regeneration of, 69
Resources, 95

chemical, and conservation, 84–148
nonrenewable, 95–97, 152
recycling, **127–130**
renewable, 95–97
replacing, 127
sources of, 120, 121
of South Africa, 121
substitution of, 89
usage of, **86**, 88–101, **144–146**
and waste, 95–97
Respiration, 344
cellular, 237–239
Retinol, 252
Retinol Equivalents (RE), 252
Reversible reactions, 498
Riboflavin, 252
Rickets, 442–443
Risk
and decision-making, 411–414
control of, 464–465
Risk-benefit analysis, 316–318, 334
Risk factor
for ions, 59
Rivers, and Earth's water, 17
Riverwood, **3**
and chemical industry, 468–477, 486, 506
and fish kill, 2–4, 20, 36–37, 63, 76
water emergency, 2–4, 18
Roentgen equivalent man (rem), 323
Roentgen, W. K., 278
Rubber
discovery of, 279
Rust, 112–113
Rutherford, Ernest, 280–283, **281**, 304

S

Safety, in laboratory, xvi–xvii
Salicylates, 452
Salicylic acid, 452
Salt
iodized, 257
Saltpeter, 478
Saturated
fats, 231–232
hydrocarbons, 170, 196
solutions, 39
Science and technology, 86–87
Scintillation counter, 302
Screening, 69–**70**, 71–**72**
Scrubbing, **391**
Seaborg, Glenn T., **318**
Secondary air pollutants, 387
Sedatives, 457–459
and alcohol, 457–459
Selenium, 81, 257
Seneca, 346
Settling, **70–72**
Sewage treatment, 71–**72**
plant, 71–**72**
Shale oil, 210

Shampoos, 439
Shell, of atom, 167
Shielding, lead and glass,
    292–294
Side effects, 416
Silver, 113, 135
Single covalent bond, 196
SI units, 5–6, 225
Skin, 434–443
    and the sun, 439–443
Sludge, 71–72
    gas, 72
Smallpox, 465
    vaccination, 465
Smog, 388–390
    and automobiles, 392–396
    and cities, 388
    components of, 388, 393–394
    photochemical, 393–394
Smoke, and cigarettes, **459–461**
Snow, and Earth's water, 17
Soap, 68, 433–439, **436, 437**
Sodium, 257
Sodium bicarbonate, 52,
    429–433
Sodium carbonate, 65, 479, 481
Sodium chloride, 52–53, **55**, 60
    brine, 515
    crystals, **52, 53**
Sodium hexametaphosphate,
    65–67
Sodium hydroxide, 51, 91
Sodium hypochlorite, 74
Sodium iodide, 303
Sodium lauryl sulfate, 436
Sodium nitrate, 498
Sodium nitrite, 263, 498
Sodium palmitate, **437**
Sodium stearate, 436
Softening of water, 64–69
Solar energy, 210, **370–373, 372**
Solar radiation, **372**
Solar spectrum, **371**
Solid state (s), 92
    of water, 17
Solids
    and density, 22
    and equations, 92
    solubility of, 39–40
Solid-state detectors, 303
Solubility, 39–42, 229
    curves, 40–42
    of gases, 40–41
    and polarity, 60
    and temperature, 40–41,
        46–47
Solute, 24
Solution, 24
    buffer, 429–433
    concentration, 42–43
    and mixtures, 23–25
    percent by mass, 42–43
    saturated, 39
    supersaturated, 40
    unsaturated, 39
Solvent, 24
South Africa, resources of, 121
Space-filling model, **169**

Specific heat, 188–190
Spectator ions, 427
Spectrum
    electromagnetic, 276
    infrared, **371**
    solar, 276, **371**
    visible, 276, **371**
SPFs. *See* Sun protection factors
        (SPFs)
Spillway, **80**
Standard temperature and
        pressure (STP), 353–354
Starch, 229, 418
States
    of matter, 92
    of water, 17
Statue of Liberty, **102, 116–117**
Steel, galvanized, 57–58
Steroids, anabolic, 455
Storage battery, **510–511**
STP. *See* Standard temperature
        and pressure (STP)
Straight-chain alkanes, **172**
Strassman, Fritz, 308
Stratosphere, 356
Stroke, 465
Strong force, 309
Strontium
    -85, 321
    -90, 302, 321, 328
Structural formulas, 169
Structure, molecular, 29, 426–427
Styrene, **202**, 479
Subatomic particles, 283
Subscripts, 28, 92
Substrates, 419–**420**
Sucrose, **228**, 229
Sugars, 228–230
Sulfate, ion test, 35
Sulfur, 257
    and coal, 96, 388
    dioxide and trioxide, 96, 386,
        388–389, **404**
Sulfuric acid, 51, 479, **482**
    uses of, 51, **482**
Sulfurous acid, 398, 427
Sun, 370–375
    and nuclear power, 272
    and skin, 439–443
Sun protection factors (SPFs), 440
Sunscreens, 441
Superconductors, **146**
Supersaturated solutions, 40
Supertrain, **471**
Surface tension, 23
Surface water, 15–16
Suspensions, 24
Sweeteners, 261
Symbols, chemical, 28
    of elements, 28, 105
    formulas, and equations, 29
Synergistic interactions, 459
Synthetics, 200–204, 387, 471

T

Table sugar. *See* Sucrose
Taconite, 480–481

Target nuclei, 305
Tar sands, 210
Technetium
    -99m, 319
Technology, chemical, 519–520
Technology and science, 86–87
Teflon, 279
Temperature
    and Earth, 372–384
    fish, 47
    kelvin, 364–365
    scales, 23
    and solubility, 40–41, 46–47
    and volume and pressure
        relationships, 365
    -volume relationship, 362–365
        See also Charles' law
Tension, surface, **23**
Terephthalic acid, 479
Testing, water, 32–35
Tetracycline, 457
Tetraethyl lead, 57, 194
Tetrahedron, **170**
Thallium, **321**
Thermal energy, 93–94
Thermosphere, 356
Thiamine, 252
THMs. *See* Trihalomethanes
Thomson, William, 364
Three Mile Island, 331–**332**
Threonine, 244
Tin, 121
Titanium, 121
Titration, 255
TNT. *See* Trinitrotoluene (TNT)
Tocopherol, 252
Toluene, 479
Ton, metric, 480
Tornado, 361, 465
Total suspended particles (TSP),
        404
Town council meeting, and
        consensus, 77–82
Toxins
    defined, 451
    and drugs, 450–462
Trace minerals, 256–257
Tracers, 318–322, **319, 321**
Transmutation, 304–306
Transuranium elements, 306
Trash, 96–99
Travel, and risk, **317–318**
Triglyceride, **231**
Trihalomethanes (THMs), 74–75
Trinitrotoluene (TNT), **503**
Tripeptides, 244
Troposphere, 351–352, 356
Tryptophan, 244
TSP. *See* Total suspended
        particles (TSP)
Tuberculosis, 465
Turbidity, 66
Tyndall effect, 24–**25**

U

Ultraviolet (UV), **276**, 372
    radiation, 74, **277**, 439–440

Undernourishment, 218, 221
UNICEF. *See* United Nations
    International Children's
    Emergency Fund
    (UNICEF)
United Nations Food and
    Agriculture Organization
    (FAO), 221
United Nations International
    Children's Emergency
    Fund (UNICEF), 222
United States,
    consumption of resources, 86
    energy consumption, **179**
    food quality in, 263
    fuel sources, **209**
    groundwater hardness in, **67**
    nutrition in, 220–221,
        267–269
    petroleum reserves, 153
    resources, 121
    water use in, **13**
Unsaturated compounds, 196
Unsaturated fats, 231–232
Unsaturated solutions, 39
Uranium, 279–280, 308–312,
    309, **310**
    -238, **297**
Uranium dioxide, 312
Urea, 60, 479, 498
UV. *See* Ultraviolet (UV)

V

Valine, 244
Vaporization, heat of, 19
Vapor trails, **303**
Vegetables
    and composition, 535–537
    and vitamins, 253
Vinyl chloride, **202**, 479
Vinylidine chloride, **202**
Viscosity, **160–162**
Visible spectrum, 276, **371**
Vitamins, 251–256, **420**
    B, 251–253
    C, 253–256, **256**
    D, 442–443
    in the diet, 253
    fat-soluble, 251–252
    and photochemistry, **442**
    RDAs of, 252
    water-soluble, 251–252
Vitrification, 329–331
Volatile organic compounds
    (VOC), **404**
Voltaic cells, 506–509
Volume, 21
    and pressure relationships,
        356–362
    See also Boyle's law
    and temperature and pressure
        relationships, 365
    and temperature relation-
        ships, 362–366
    See also Charles' law
Voyager, 143

W

Washing soda, 68
    See also Sodium carbonate
Washington Monument, **515**
Waste
    and energy, 97, 99
    of industrial processes,
        483–484
    municipal, 96–**98**, 99
    nuclear, 328–331
    and resources, 95–97
Water
    and activities, 18
    in aquifers, 15
    in atmosphere, 372–373
    and chlorine, 69, 74–75
    contaminants in, 20–38
    cycle, **16**
    decomposition of, 181–182
    formation of, 28, 122,
        181–182
    foul, 8–10
    ground, 15
    hard, 64, 67–69
    and health, 11
    and milk, 249
    molecular view, 26–27
    molecule of, **30**
    municipal purification of,
        69–75
    natural purification of, 64
    oxygen in, 41, 45–46, 79
    physical properties of, 21–23,
        374–375
    and polarity, 59–60
    pollution of, 31–32
    pure and impure, 31–32
    purification and treatment,
        8–10, 63–75
    quality of, 2–19
    softening, 64–**69**
    states of, 17, **21**
    supplying our needs, 2–83
    surface, **15–16**
    tap, 32
    testing, 32–35
    treatment plants, **15**, **71**, 74
    usage, 11–**13**, 17–19
    use diary, 10–11
    vapor, **352**
Weight, body, 226–228
WHO. *See* World Health
        Organization (WHO)
Winthrop, John, 478
World
    developing and developed, 218
    hunger, 222–223
    nutrition, 218–224, 267–269
World Health Organization
        (WHO), 222

X

X rays, **278–279**
X-ray tube, 278

Y

Your Turn
    Alkane Boiling Points:
        Isomers, 173–174
    Alkane Boiling Points: Trends,
        171
    Alternatives to Metals, 143
    Avogadro's Law, 353
    Balanced Equations, 93–94
    Balancing Equations, 123
    Bombardment Reactions,
        305–306
    Breath Composition and
        Glucose Burning,
        343–344
    Burning Issue, A, 194
    Calorimetry, 225
    Chemical Elements Crossword
        Puzzle, 105, 147–148
    Chemical Processing in Your
        Life, 475–476
    Chemistry of Explosives,
        503–504
    Conditions that Affect pH
        Balance, 432–433
    Describing Solution
        Concentrations, 43–44
    Earth's Energy Balance, 373
    Electronegativity and
        Oxidation State, 496–497
    Elements in the Body,
        417–418
    Energy Conversion, 183–184
    Energy Conversion Efficiency,
        184–185
    Energy Dependency, 207–209
    Enzymes and Energy in
        Action, 422
    Events: Related or Not?
        411–412
    Fuel Consumption Over the
        Years, 179–180
    Functional Groups in
        Biomolecules, 231–232
    Gas Molecules in Motion,
        367–368
    Getting a Charge from
        Electrochemistry,
        511–512
    Half-lives, 301–302
    Heats of Combustion, 191
    Hydrocarbon Boiling Points,
        166–167
    Ionic Compounds, 54
    Isotope Notation, 284–285
    Limiting Reactants, 237–238
    Limiting Reactants: Chemical
        Reactions, 239
    Limiting Reactants: Plants
        and Humans, 240–241
    Matter at the Microlevel, 27
    Metal Reactivity, 136
    Metals from Ores, 480–481
    Meters and Liters, 6–7
    Minerals in the Diet, 258
    Molar Mass and Isotope
        Abundance, 287–288

Molar Masses, 126
Molar Volume and Reactions of Gases, 354
Molecular Structure of Proteins, 243–244
Nuclear Balancing Act, 298
Percent Composition, 134
Periodic Table, 110–112
Periodic Variation in Properties, 109–110
pH, 401
Plant Nutrients, 493
Polarity and Solubility, 435
Properties: Physical or Chemical? 103–104

Protein in the Diet, 246
P-V Relationships, 361–362
Solubility and Solubility Curves, 41–42
Symbols, Formulas, and Equations, 29
Thermal Properties of Materials, 375
T-V-P Relationships, 365
U.S. Water Use, 12
Uses of Copper, 132–133
Vitamins in the Diet, 253
Your Annual Radiation Dose, 326–327
Yttrium, -90, 321

Z
Zero oxidation state, 496
Zinc, 115, 257
-copper electrochemical cell, 507
density, 104
and penny, 88
properties of, 113
Zinc oxide, **440**

VISUAL CREDITS

PHOTOGRAPHS

WATER

Opener: © Tim Haske/Profiles West; **page 2:** © Bryan Stephens; **page 5, figs. 6, 8:** © American Chemical Society, Greg Nauman Photographer; **page 14:** photo by Patrick Karney; **page 15:** California Dept. of Water Resources; **page 21:** © Tom Bean/The Stock Market; **page 22:** State of Maine, Dept. of Transportation; **fig. 10:** © Oscar Palmquist/Lightwave; **fig. 11 all:** Dr. Peter Cooke, Electron Microscope Unit, Eastern Regional Research Center, Agricultural Research Service, USDA; **page 25:** © Kip Peticolas/Fundamental Photographs; **fig. 13:** © American Chemical Society, Greg Nauman Photographer; **page 27:** Courtesy of the IBM Corp.; **page 28, figs. 16, 17, 18, 19, page 36:** © American Chemical Society, Greg Nauman Photographer; **page 38:** Tom Bean/The Stock Market; **page 44:** © Pedro Coll/The Stock Market; **page 45:** © Dean Hulse/Rainbow; **page 52:** © Dr. Jeremy Burgess/Photo Researchers, Inc.; **fig. 28:** Molecular Simulations, Inc.; **page 58:** © Linda Moore/Rainbow; **page 61:** © American Chemical Society, Greg Nauman Photographer; **page 62:** U.S. EPA; **page 64:** © Oscar Palmquist/Lightwave; **fig. 30:** © American Chemical Society, Greg Nauman Photographer; **page 68:** Courtesy of Diedrich Chemicals; **page 71:** Courtesy Metropolitan Water District of Southern CA. **page 72:** City of Jacksonville, FL; **page 73:** Photo by Shutter Priority; **page 74:** PPG Industries, Inc.; **page 77:** © Bob Daemmrich Photography; **page 80:** © Grant Heilman Photography, Inc.; **page 82:** © Roy Orsch/The Stock Market.

RESOURCES

Opener: Courtesy of Kennecott Corp., Kennecott; **page 86 left:** © Dan McCoy/Rainbow; **right:** © Oscar Palmquist/Lightwave; **page 87 top:** © Alain Nogues/Sygma; **bottom:** © Kelly R. Foster/The Stock Market; **figs. 1, 2, 3:** © American Chemical Society, Greg Nauman Photographer; **page 95:** © Jose Fuste Raga/The Stock Market; **page 96:** © Trut Goriez; **page 100:** The World Bank/IFC/MIGA; **page 101:** The City of New York Dept. of Sanitation; **page 102 top:** © Dan Cornish; **bottom:** © Tom Kelly; **page 104:** © Ann Hawthorne; **fig. 7:** © American Chemical Society, Greg Nauman Photographer; **page 108:** courtesy of John Schultz/PAR-NYC; **page 113:** © Linda Moore/Rainbow; **fig. 9:** © American Chemical Society, Greg Nauman Photographer; **page 118:** Photo by David Scott, The Getty Conservation Institute; **page 119:** © George Disario/The Stock Market; **page 123:** Courtesy of Inland Steel Co.; **page 124:** © American Chemical Society, Greg Nauman Photographer; **page 127:** © Comstock Photos; **page 128:** © Steve Elmore/Tom Stack & Associates; **page 130:** The City of New York Dept. of Sanitation; **page 133 top:** © Joel E. Arem; **bottom:** Copper Development Association, Inc; **page 137:** Aluminum Association; **fig. 12:** © American Chemical Society, Greg Nauman Photographer; **page 140:** Sprint/United Administration Services Group, Visual Communications Center; **fig. 13 varistors, plasma spray:** PAR/NYC, Inc. **potter's wheel:** © Bill Stanton/Rainbow; **electric kiln:** © S. E. Byrne/Lightwave; **ceramic turbine blades:** courtesy of General Electric; **making turbine blades:** courtesy Doug Wilson; **pottery bowls:** © Dan McCoy/Rainbow; **fired brick, micrograph of graphite fibers:** PAR/NYC, Inc.; **micrograph of kaolin: page 142:** Courtesy of the Don Drees Collection; **page 143:** © Mark Greenberg/Visions; **page 145:** PAR/NYC, Inc.; **page 146 top:** N.Y. State College of Ceramics, Alfred University; **bottom:** Beech Aircraft Corp.

PETROLEUM

Opener: Courtesy of Consolidated Natural Gas Co.; **page 152:** State of CA Energy Commission; **page 153:** © Aldo Matrocola/Lightwave; **page 157:** Courtesy of American Petroleum Inst.; **page 158 top:** Courtesy of ARCO Library; **bottom:** © Bryan Stephens/John Schultz/PAR-NYC Inc.; **page 160:** © Oscar Palmquist/Lightwave; **page 162:** © American Chemical Society, Greg Nauman Photographer; **page 163:** Courtesy of Kate Lapides; **figs. 7, 8:** © American Chemical Society, Greg Nauman Photographer; **page 174:** Texas Mid-Continent Oil and Gas. Courtesy of the American Petroleum Inst.; **page 175:** © American Chemical Society, Greg Nauman Photographer; **page 176:** Courtesy Drake Museum. American Petroleum Inst.; **page 177:** Courtesy Standard Oil Company N.J. American Petroleum Inst.; **page 181:** © Grant Heilman Photography; **page 188:** © American Chemical Society, Greg Nauman Photographer; **page 192:** Courtesy of U.S. Airforce; **page 193:** © Wes Thompson/The Stock Market; **page 198 both, 199 top:** © American Chemical Society, Greg Nauman Photographer; **bottom:** Courtesy IBM Almaden Research Center; **page 201:** Allied Signal, Inc.; **page 202:** Courtesy Dow Chemical Co.; **page 203:** Photo by J. B. Swartz; **page 204:** © Brent Jones; **page 205:** © American Chemical Society, Greg Nauman Photographer; **page 207:** © Dan McCoy/Rainbow; **page 208 Glen Canyon:** U.S. Dept. of Interior, Bureau of Reclamation, Photo by Tom Fredmann; **generating plant, cooling towers:** American Mining Congress; **page 211:** American Mining Congress; **page 215:** © American Chemical Society, Greg Nauman Photographer.

FOOD

Opener: © Dan McCoy/Rainbow; **page 219:** Courtesy of United Nations; **page 220:** The Salvation Army; **page 223:** Produce Marketing Association; **page 224:** © Greg Davis/The Stock Market; **page 227:** © Joel Dexter/Lightwave; **page 233:** Photo by Ernest Wong; **page**

235: © Bryan Stephens; **page 236:** © CNRI; **page 240:** © Rob Nelson/Picture Group; **fig. 7:** © Bryan Stephens; **page 242:** © Charles Gupton/The Stock Market; **page 247:** © American Chemical Society, Greg Nauman Photographer; **page 249:** © American Chemical Society, Greg Nauman Photographer. Muller Milk Carton used by permission of Muller Pinehurst Dairy, Inc.; **fig. 11:** © American Chemical Society, Greg Nauman Photographer; **page 255:** Natrol; **page 257:** PAR/NYC, Inc.; Morton © Salt package used by permission of Morton International, Inc., Morton Salt; **page 259:** © American Chemical Society, Greg Nauman Photographer; **page 262:** Courtesy of Illinois Farm Bureau; **page 263:** © Richard Gross; **page 265:** National Down Syndrome Society; **page 266:** PAR/NYC, Inc.; **page 268:** © American Chemical Society, Greg Nauman Photographer.

NUCLEAR

Opener: United States Dept. of Energy; **page 274:** Argonne National Laboratory; **page 275:** © American Chemical Society, Greg Nauman Photographer; **page 277 top:** Courtesy of Atlantic City Convention and Visitors Bureau; **bottom:** © Dan McCoy/Rainbow; **fig. 2:** Courtesy of Dr. Sidney L. Horowitz/School of Dentistry and Oral Surgery/Columbia U.; **fig. 3:** American Cancer Society, Photographed by James Morehead, Source: Dr. Cooney; **page 281 top:** © Bryan Stephens; **bottom:** Courtesy Rutherford Museum, McGill University, Montreal, Canada; **page 286:** © American Chemical Society, Greg Nauman Photographer; **page 289:** Photo by Beverly Buck; **page 291:** © Vienna Report/Sygma; **page 292:** U.S. Dept. of Energy, Photo by Frank Hoffman; **figs. 8, 9:** © American Chemical Society, Greg Nauman Photographer; **page 295:** Courtesy Argonne National Laboratory; **page 299:** © Diego Goldberg/Sygma; **page 303:** © Patrice Lorez/CERNI; **page 306:** U. of Chicago; **page 308:** U.S. Information Service; **page 309:** U.S. Department of Energy, Photo by Frank Hoffman; **fig. 18:** © American Chemical Society, Greg Nauman Photographer; **fig. 19:** © Oscar Palmquist/ Lightwave; Energy Technology Visuals Collection/Dept. of Energy; **page 313:** © Antony S. Draper; **fig. 21:** U.S. Department of Energy. Energy Technology Visuals Collection; **fig. 22:** © Dan McCoy/Rainbow; **page 316:** © Jon Jacobson; **page 318:** Courtesy of Lawrence Berkeley Laboratory; **fig. 23:** National Institute of Health, Bethesda, MD; **page 319:** Courtesy of H. A. Ziessman, M.D.; **page 320:** Photo by E. Wyllys Andrews; **page 321:** General Electric Company; **fig. 24:** Courtesy Nuclear Energy Association, Washington, D.C.; **page 327:** © T. R. Youngstrom; **page 330:** U.S. Ecology, Inc.; **page 331:** Sandia National Laboratories; **page 332:** U.S. Nuclear Regulatory Commission; **page 333:** © Sygma; **page 337:** Argonne National Laboratory.

AIR

Opener: © Dan McCoy/Rainbow; **page 340:** Courtesy of Diedrich Chemicals; **page 342:** © American Chemical Society, Greg Nauman Photographer; **page 343:** Linde Union Carbide Industrial Gases, Inc.; **page 346:** Courtesy Liquid Carbonic; **page 347:** Courtesy Union Carbide; **page 347:** PAR/NYC, Inc.; **fig. 2:** © American Chemical Society, Greg Nauman Photographer; **page 352:** NASA; **page 354:** © Joan Baron/The Stock Market; **figs. 6.4 both, 5:** © American Chemical Society, Greg Nauman Photographer; **page 361:** National Severe Storms Lab.; **figs. 7, 8:** © American Chemical Society, Greg Nauman Photographer; **page 370:** Courtesy United Nations; **page 377:** Photo by Shel Izan Photography; **page 378:** Courtesy William Albert Allard; **fig. 14:** © American Chemical Society, Greg Nauman Photographer; **page 383:** © Giry/REA/Picture Group; **page 385 both:** South Coast Air Quality Management District; **page 392:** © American Chemical Society, Greg Nauman Photographer; **page 396:** © Alan Pitcairn/Grant Heilman Photography; **page 396:** © Thomas Braise/The Stock Market; **page 397:** Photo by Shutter Priority; **page 398:** © Field Museum of Natural History; **page 399:** © American Chemical Society, Greg Nauman Photographer; **page 402:** Argonne National Laboratory; **page 407:** Northern Indiana Public Service Co.

RISKS

Opener: © Dan McCoy/Rainbow; **page 410:** Pfizer, Inc.; **page 411:** © Henley & Savage/The Stock Market; **page 413:** Photo by Yolanda Villa; **page 419:** © American Chemical Society, Greg Nauman Photographer; **page 421:** © Joe Sohm/The Stock Market; **page 425:** © Patti & Milt Putnam/The Stock Market; **page 431:** © American Chemical Society, Greg Nauman Photographer; **page 432:** © Guy Gillette/Photo Researchers, Inc.; **page 434:** © Joe Barabam/ The Stock Market; **page 437:** Oscar Palmquist/Lightwave; **page 440:** © Paul Barton/The Stock Market; **page 441:** © American Chemical Society, Greg Nauman Photographer; **page 443:** E. Kairinen, Gillette Research Institute; **page 445:** © American Chemical Society, Greg Nauman Photographer; **page 449:** Zubas/Courtesy of Modern Salon Magazine; **page 450 top:** Partnership for a Drug Free America. Fortis Fortis and Associates, Inc.; **bottom:** Courtesy of Odyssey House; **page 451:** U.S. Dept. of Justice/Drug Enforcement; **page 457:** © CDC/Science Source/Photo Researchers, Inc.; **page 458:** Photo by Brent Schmidt; **fig. 22:** © American Chemical Society, Greg Nauman Photographer; **page 461:** © Oscar Palmquist/Lightwave.

INDUSTRY

Opener: © Gabe Palmer/The Stock Market; **page 470:** © Tom Hollyman; **page 471 top:** Swindell Dressler International Co.; **bottom:** Japan Railways Group; **page 472 top:** © Tom Myers/Photo Researchers, Inc.; **middle:** © Lawrence Migdale/Photo Researchers, Inc.; **bottom:** The American Ceramic Society; **page 473 top:** © Francois Gohier/Photo Researchers, Inc.; **right:** © David Parker/Science Photo Library/Photo Researchers, Inc.; **page 480:** AMAX, Inc.; **page 481:** PAR/NYC, Inc.; **page 482:** Courtesy Stauffer Chemical Company; **page 483:** © Will & Deni McIntyre/Photo Researchers, Inc.; **page 485:** Photo by Lisa Sedaris; **page 489:** © American Chemical Society, Greg Nauman Photographer; **page 490:** ConAgra Fertilizer Co.; **page 491:** National Severe Storms Laboratory; **page 493:** BP America; **page 494, fig. 4:** © American Chemical Society, Greg Nauman Photographer; **page 499:** © Randall Hyman; **page 500 all:** Ira Wyman/Sygma; **page 501 top:** Courtesy of Public Affairs/State Highway

LINE ART

RESOURCES

Fig. 5: Adapted from *Characterization of Municipal Solid Waste in the United States, 1960–2000.* Franklin Associates, LTD.; Prairie Village, Kansas, 1986. Prepared for U.S. EPA; **fig. 10:** Adapted from Nielson, N. "Keeping the Torch Lit", *Materials Performance,* 1984, 24 (4): 80. Reprinted with permission from the National Association of Corrosion Engineers, © NACE; **fig. 15:** Reprinted with permission from N. N. Greenwood and A. Eainshaw, *Chemistry of the Elements,* © 1984, Pergamon Press LTD.

PETROLEUM

Page 179: U.S. Dept. of Energy; **fig. 18:** *Oil and Gas Journal,* Jan. 29, 1990, p. 50.

NUCLEAR

Figs. 5, 6: Ebbing, Darrell D. *General Chemistry* (3rd ed.). **Figs. 7.8–7.9, pgs. 235–236:** Copyright © 1990 by Houghton Mifflin Co. Used with permission.

RISKS

Fig. 13: Reprinted with permission by Dickerson and Geis from *The Structure and Action of Proteins.* Benjamin-Cummings, Menlo Park, CA 1969. Illustration © R. E. Dickerson and I. Geis; **fig. 20:** From *Biochemistry* (2nd ed.) by Lubet Stryer. Copyright © 1975, 1981. Reprinted with the permission of W. H. Freeman and Co.

INDUSTRY

Figs. 8, 9, 12: *Rigal's Handbook of Industrial Chemistry* (7th ed.), James A. Kent (ed.). Copyright © 1974 by Van Nostrand Reinhold Co., Inc. All rights reserved.

TEXT/TABLES

FOOD

Page 269 Table 15: Adapted from S. DeVore and T. White, *The Appetites of Man: An Invitation to Better Nutrition from Nine Healthier Societies.* Anchor/Doubleday, Garden City, N.Y.; 1978.

AIR

Page 386 Table 4: Adapted from Stern et al. *Fundamentals of Air Pollution* (2nd ed.); Academic Press, Inc.; Orlando, FL, 1984; pp. 30–31. Table dated by permission of Elmer Robinson, Mauna Loa Observatory. Data based on conditions prior to 1980.

CHEMICAL MATRIX

Concept	Wat.	Res.	Petro.	*ChemCom* Unit Food	Nuc.	Air	Risk	Ind.
Metric (SI) measurement	I	U	E	U	U	U	U	U
Scale and order of magnitude	I	U	U	U	U	U	U	U
Physical & chemical properties	I	E	E	U	E	E	E	E
Solids, liquids and gases	I	U	E		U	E	U	U
Solutions and solubility	I	E	U	U	U	U	E	U
Elements and compounds	I	E	E	E	E	U	U	U
Nomenclature	I	E	E	E	E	U	U	U
Formula and equation writing	I	E	E	E	U	U	U	U
Atomic structure	I	E	E		E			
Chemical bonding	I	U	E	E		U	E	U
Shape of molecules	I		E	U			E	U
Ionization	I	U	E		E	E	E	E
Periodicity		I/E/U						
Mole concept		I	E	U	E	E	U	U
Stoichiometry		I	E	E		U	U	U
Energy relationships		I	E	E	E	E	E	E
Acids, bases, & pH	I			E	·	E	E	U
Oxidation-reduction		I		U		U	U	E
Reaction rate/kinetics				I	E	U	E	U
Gas laws					I/E/U			
Equilibrium								I/U
Chemical analysis	I	E	E	E		U	U	U
Synthesis			I			U		E
Biochemistry				I	U		E	
Industrial chemistry	I	E	E	E	E	E	E	E
Organic chemistry			I	E			E	
Nuclear chemistry					I/E/U			

CODE: I = Introduced   E = Elaborated   U = Used